ACCA

Strategic Business Reporting

Practice & Revision Kit

BPP Learning Media is an **ACCA Approved Content Provider** for the ACCA qualification. This means we work closely with ACCA to ensure our products fully prepare you for your ACCA exams.

In this Practice & Revision Kit, which has been reviewed by the **ACCA examining team**, we:

- Discuss the **best strategies** for revising and taking your ACCA exams
- Ensure you are well **prepared** for your exam
- Provide you with **lots of great guidance** on tackling questions
- Provide you with **four** mock exams

For exams in September 2020, December 2020, March 2021 and June 2021

Third edition 2020

ISBN 9781 5097 8395 3
Previous ISBN 9781 5097 2454 3
e-ISBN 9781 5097 2932 6

British Library Cataloguing-in-Publication Data
A catalogue record for this book is available
from the British Library

Published by

BPP Learning Media Ltd
BPP House, Aldine Place
142–144 Uxbridge Road
London W12 8AA

www.bpp.com/learningmedia

Printed in the United Kingdom

Your learning materials, published by BPP Learning Media Ltd, are printed on paper obtained from traceable, sustainable sources.

We are grateful to the Association of Chartered Certified Accountants for permission to reproduce past examination questions. The suggested solutions in the practice answer bank have been prepared by BPP Learning Media Ltd, unless otherwise stated.

BPP Learning Media is grateful to the IASB for permission to reproduce extracts from the International Financial Reporting Standards including all International Accounting Standards, SIC and IFRIC Interpretations (the Standards). The Standards together with their accompanying documents are issued by:

The International Accounting Standards Board (IASB) 30 Cannon Street, London, EC4M 6XH, United Kingdom.

Email: info@ifrs.org Web: www.ifrs.org

A note about copyright

Dear Customer

What does the little © mean and why does it matter?

Your market-leading BPP books, course materials and e-learning materials do not write and update themselves. People write them on their own behalf or as employees of an organisation that invests in this activity. Copyright law protects their livelihoods. It does so by creating rights over the use of the content.

Breach of copyright is a form of theft – as well as being a criminal offence in some jurisdictions, it is potentially a serious breach of professional ethics.

With current technology, things might seem a bit hazy but, basically, without the express permission of BPP Learning Media:

- Photocopying our materials is a breach of copyright
- Scanning, ripcasting or conversion of our digital materials into different file formats, uploading them to Facebook or e-mailing them to your friends is a breach of copyright

You can, of course, sell your books, in the form in which you have bought them – once you have finished with them. (Is this fair to your fellow students? We update for a reason.) Please note the e-products are sold on a single user licence basis: we do not supply 'unlock' codes to people who have bought them secondhand.

And what about outside the UK? BPP Learning Media strives to make our materials available at prices students can afford by local printing arrangements, pricing policies and partnerships which are clearly listed on our website. A tiny minority ignore this and indulge in criminal activity by illegally photocopying our material or supporting organisations that do. If they act illegally and unethically in one area, can you really trust them?

IFRS

Contents

Finding questions

Question index

The questions in section 1 are preparation questions to help consolidate your knowledge before you move onto the exam-standard questions in section 2. The questions in section 2 are grouped according to the structure of the exam. Section A of the exam will contain two questions, the first on groups and the second on ethical and reporting issues. Section B of the exam will contain two 25-mark questions which could cover any area of the syllabus. Here we have generally categorised questions containing analysis/appraisal of information and current issues under 'Section B-type questions' however, these areas could be examined in either section of the exam.

Questions which require consideration of an issue from the perspective of an investor or other stakeholder are marked below with an asterisk *.

The IASB's *Conceptual Framework for Financial Reporting* was substantially revised and reissued in March 2018. References to the *Conceptual Framework* or the revised *Conceptual Framework* throughout this Kit refer to the March 2018 version unless otherwise stated.

Mock exam 3

Mock exam 4 (September/December 2019 exam)

Topic index

Listed below are the key SBR syllabus topics and the numbers of the questions in this Kit covering those topics. We have also included a reference to the relevant Chapter of the BPP SBR Workbook, the companion to the BPP SBR Practice and Revision Kit, in case you wish to revise the information on the topic you have covered.

If you need to concentrate your practice and revision on certain topics or if you want to attempt all available questions that refer to a particular subject, you will find this index useful.

Syllabus topic	Question numbers	Workbook chapter
Accounting policies (IAS 8)	31, 32, 34, 45, Mock exam 1: Q4	2
Agriculture (IAS 41)	64, 69	4
Alternative performance measures (APMs)	26, 37, 38, 40, 48, Mock exam 2: Q3, Mock exam 3: Q3	18
Business combinations (IFRS 3)	11 – 16, 27, 29, 45, Mock exam 1: Q1, Mock exam 2: Q1, Mock exam 3: Q1, Mock exam 4: Q1	11 – 13
Conceptual Framework	11, 16, 25, 26, 28, 32, 39, 42, 45, 46, 47, Mock exam 1: Q4, Mock exam 2: Q4	1
Consolidated statement of cash flows	15, 16, 23, 37	17
Deferred tax (IAS 12)	14, 24, 35, 41, 49, 58, 67, Mock exam 3: Q2	7
Disposals of investments	12, 13, 14, Mock exam 2: Q1, Mock exam 3: Q1	13
DP 2018/1 *Financial Instruments with Characteristics of Equity*	32	8
ED 2018/1 *Accounting Policy Changes (Amendments to IAS 8)*	31	2
ED 2019/5 *Deferred Tax Related to Assets and Liabilities Arising from a Single Transaction*	35	7
ED 2019/6 *Disclosure of Accounting Policies*	Mock exam 3: Q4	20
Ethics	19–25, 30, 40, Mock exam 1: Q2, Mock exam 2: Q2, Mock exam 3: Q2, Mock exam 4: Q2	2

Syllabus topic	Question numbers	Workbook chapter
Fair value (IFRS 13)	26, 27, 29, 55, 62, 64, 65, 67, Mock exam 1: Q4, Mock exam 2: Q3	4
Financial instruments (IFRS 9)	12, 13, 14, 32, 36, 42, 46, 54, 56, 58, 59, 60, 65, 67, Mock exam 1: Q3, Mock exam 2: Q1, Mock exam 3: Q3	8
Foreign currency (IAS 21)	18, Mock exam 3: Q1	16
IFRS Practice Statement 1 *Management Commentary*	38, 49	18
IFRS Practice Statement 2 *Making Materiality Judgments*	26, 27, 28, 30, 34, Mock exam 1: Q3, Mock exam 1: Q4, Mock exam 2: Q4, Mock exam 3: Q4	20
IFRS 1 *First-time Adoption of IFRS*	29	20
Integrated reporting	39, 45, 46	18
Interim reporting (IAS 34)	Mock exam 4: Q4	18
Joint arrangements (IFRS 11)	11, 59, Mock exam 3: Q3	15
Leasing (IFRS 16)	12, 20, 22, 25, 34, 35, 43, 61, 62, Mock exam 3: Q3, Mock exam 4: Q3	9
Measurement	26, Mock exam 1: Q4, Mock exam 2: Q3	1
Non-current assets held for sale and discontinued operations (IFRS 5)	16, 21, 39, 40, 41, 43, 55, 58, Mock exam 4: Q4	14
Pensions (IAS 19 *Employee Benefits*) Amendments to IAS 19 (Plan Amendment, Curtailment or Settlement 2018)	12, 13, 33, Mock exam 2: Q1, Mock exam 3: Q2 33	5
Related party transactions (IAS 24)	27, 28, 30, 55, Mock exam 2: Q2	2
Revenue recognition (IFRS 15)	16, 30, 31, 34, 43, 47, 48, 52, 62	3
Segment reporting (IFRS 8)	38, 44, Mock exam 1: Q3, Mock exam 2: Q2	18
Share-based payment (IFRS 2)	35, 42, 63, 64, Mock exam 1: Q1	10
Step acquisitions (IFRS 10)	11, Mock exam 1: Q1, Mock exam 2: Q1	12

The Exam

Computer-based exams

With effect from the March 2020 sitting, ACCA have commenced the launch of computer-based exams (CBEs) for this exam with the aim of rolling out into all markets internationally over a short period. BPP materials have been designed to support you, whichever exam format you are studying towards. For more information on these changes, when they will be implemented and to access Specimen Exams in the Strategic Professional CBE software, please visit the ACCA website. Please note that the Strategic Professional CBE software has more functionality than you will have seen in the Applied Skills exams.

www.accaglobal.com/gb/en/student/exam-support-resources/strategic-professional-specimen-exams-cbe.html

Important note for UK students who are sitting the UK variant of Strategic Business Reporting

If you are sitting the UK variant of the Strategic Business Reporting exam you will be studying under International standards, but between 15 and 20 marks will be available for comparisons between International and UK GAAP.

This Practice & Revision Kit is based on IFRS Standards **only**. An online supplement covering the additional UK issues and providing additional illustrations and examples is available on the Exam Success Site; for details of how to access this, see the inside cover of this Kit.

Approach to examining the syllabus

The Strategic Business Reporting syllabus is assessed by a 3 hour and 15 minute exam. The pass mark is **50%**. All questions in the exam are **compulsory**.

At the revision stage, we advise students to revisit the following main syllabus requirements so that you have a good understanding of the overall objectives of this exam. Remember, ACCA's examining team expect you to be able to:

- Demonstrate **professional competences** within the business reporting environment. You will be examined on concepts, theories, and principles, and on your ability to question and comment on proposed accounting treatments.
- Relate professional issues to relevant concepts and practical situations. The **evaluation of alternative accounting practices** and the **identification and prioritisation** of issues will be a key element of the exam.
- Exercise **professional** and **ethical judgement**, and **integrate technical knowledge** when addressing business reporting issues in a business context.
- Adopt **either a stakeholder or an external focus** in answering questions and demonstrate personal skills such as **problem solving**, **dealing with information** and **decision making**. You will also have to demonstrate **communication skills** appropriate to the scenario.
- Demonstrate specific professional knowledge appropriate to the **preparation and presentation of consolidated and other financial statements** from accounting data, to conform with relevant accounting standards. Here, you may be required to interpret financial statements for different stakeholders and/or communicate the impact of changes in accounting regulation on financial reporting.

The ACCA website contains a useful explanation of the verbs used in exam questions. See: 'What is the examiner asking?' available at www.accaglobal.com/uk/en/student/sa/study-skills/questions.html

Format of the exam

<table>
<tr><th colspan="2">100 marks, two sections, each section 50 marks</th><th>Marks</th></tr>
<tr><td>Section A</td><td>Two compulsory scenario-based questions, totalling 50 marks
Question 1:<ul><li>Based on the financial statements of group entities, or extracts thereof (syllabus area D)</li><li>Also likely to require consideration of some financial reporting issues (syllabus area C)</li><li>Numerical aspects of group accounting will be a maximum of 25 marks</li><li>Discussion and explanation of numerical aspects will be required</li></ul>Question 2:<ul><li>Consideration of the reporting implications and the ethical implications of specific events in a given scenario</li></ul>Two professional marks will be awarded to the ethical issues question.</td><td>50
(incl. 2 professional marks)</td></tr>
<tr><td>Section B</td><td>Two compulsory 25-mark questions
Questions:<ul><li>May be scenario, case-study, or essay based</li><li>Will contain both discursive and computational elements</li><li>Could deal with any aspect of the syllabus</li><li>Will always include either a full or part question that requires the appraisal of financial and/or non-financial information from either the preparer's or another stakeholder's perspective</li></ul>Two professional marks will be awarded to the question that requires analysis.</td><td>50
(incl. 2 professional marks)</td></tr>
<tr><td colspan="3">Current issues
The current issues element of the syllabus (Syllabus area F) may be examined in Section A or B but will not be a full question. It is more likely to form part of another question.</td></tr>
</table>

Analysis of past exams

The table below shows when each element of the syllabus has been examined and the section in which the element was examined.

Workbook chapter		Specimen exam 1	Specimen exam 2	Sept 2018	Dec 2018	Mar/ Jun 2019	Sept/ Dec 2019
	Fundamental ethical and professional principles						
2	Professional behaviour and compliance with accounting standards	A	A	A	A	A	A
2	Ethical requirements of corporate reporting and the consequences of unethical behaviour	A	A	A	A	A	A
	The financial reporting framework						
1	The applications, strengths and weaknesses of an accounting framework	A, B	A	B	A, B	B	A, B
	Reporting the financial performance of a range of entities						
3	Revenue		B	B	A	B	B
4	Non-current assets		A, B	A, B	A, B		
8	Financial instruments		A	A		B	A, B
9	Leases		B		A	B	
5	Employee benefits	A				A	B
7	Income taxes		A		B	A	A
6	Provisions, contingencies and events after the reporting period		A	B		A	
10	Share-based payment						A
4, 8	Fair value measurement	B					A
19	Reporting requirements of small and medium-sized entities (SMEs)						
4, 9, 18	Other reporting issues		B				B
	Financial statements of groups of entities						
11, 14–17	Group accounting including statements of cash flows	A	A	A	A	A	A, B
11, 15	Associates and joint arrangements		A	A		B	B
12, 13	Changes in group structures	A	A	A	A	A	
16	Foreign transactions and entities					A	

Workbook chapter		Specimen exam 1	Specimen exam 2	Sept 2018	Dec 2018	Mar/ Jun 2019	Sept/ Dec 2019
	Interpreting financial statements for different stakeholders						
18	Analysis and interpretation of financial information and measurement of performance	A, B	B	B	B	B	B
	The impact of changes and potential changes in accounting regulation						
20	Discussion of solutions to current issues in financial reporting	A, B	B	A, B	A, B	B	B

IMPORTANT!

The table above gives a broad idea of how frequently major topics in the syllabus are examined. It should **not be used to question spot** and predict, for example, that a certain topic will not be examined because it has been examined in the last two sittings. The examining team's reports indicate that they are well aware that some students try to question spot. The examining team avoid predictable patterns and may, for example, examine the same topic two sittings in a row. Equally, just because a topic has not been examined for a long time, this does not necessarily mean it will be examined in the next exam!

Syllabus and Study Guide

The complete SBR syllabus and study guide can be found by visiting the exam resource finder on the ACCA website.

Examinable documents

The following documents are examinable for sittings up from September 2019 to June 2020. Knowledge of new examinable regulations issued by 31 August will be required in examination sessions being held in the following exam year. Documents may be examinable even if the effective date is in the future.

The syllabus and study guide offers more detailed guidance on the depth and level at which the examinable documents will be examined.

	International Accounting Standards (IASs)/International Financial Reporting Standards (IFRSs)
IAS 1	Presentation of Financial Statements
IAS 2	Inventories
IAS 7	Statement of Cash Flows
IAS 8	Accounting Policies, Changes in Accounting Estimates and Errors
IAS 10	Events After the Reporting Period
IAS 12	Income Taxes
IAS 16	Property, Plant and Equipment
IAS 19	Employee Benefits

	International Accounting Standards (IASs)/International Financial Reporting Standards (IFRSs)
IAS 20	Accounting for Government Grants and Disclosure of Government Assistance
IAS 21	The Effects of Changes in Foreign Exchange Rates
IAS 23	Borrowing Costs
IAS 24	Related Party Disclosures
IAS 27	Separate Financial Statements
IAS 28	Investments in Associates and Joint Ventures
IAS 32	Financial Instruments: Presentation
IAS 33	Earnings per Share
IAS 34	Interim Financial Reporting
IAS 36	Impairment of Assets
IAS 37	Provisions, Contingent Liabilities and Contingent Assets
IAS 38	Intangible Assets
IAS 40	Investment Property
IAS 41	Agriculture
IFRS 1	First-time Adoption of International Financial Reporting Standards
IFRS 2	Share-based Payment
IFRS 3	Business Combinations
IFRS 5	Non-current Assets Held for Sale and Discontinued Operations
IFRS 7	Financial Instruments: Disclosures
IFRS 8	Operating Segments
IFRS 9	Financial Instruments
IFRS 10	Consolidated Financial Statements
IFRS 11	Joint Arrangements
IFRS 12	Disclosure of Interests in other Entities
IFRS 13	Fair Value Measurement
IFRS 15	Revenue from Contracts with Customers
IFRS 16	Leases
IFRS for SMEs	IFRS for Small and Medium-sized Entities

	Other Statements
	Conceptual Framework for Financial Reporting (March 2018)
	The International <IR> Framework
IFRS Practice Statement 1	Management Commentary
IFRS Practice Statement 2	Making Materiality Judgements
	EDs, Discussion Papers and Other Documents
ED 2019/6	Disclosure of Accounting Policies (Proposed amendments to IAS 1 and IFRS Practice Statement 2)
ED 2019/5	Deferred Tax related to Assets and Liabilities arising from a single transaction (Proposed amendments to IAS12)
ED 2018/1	Accounting Policy Changes (Amendments to IAS 8)
DP 2018/1	Financial Instruments with Characteristics of Equity

Important note

Many of these IFRS standards are also tested in Financial Reporting (FR). The technical knowledge required for SBR is **an extension** of that required for FR. The SBR examining team have commented that many student responses do not demonstrate a good technical FR knowledge. However, a good understanding of FR is vital to pass your SBR exam and you need to be able to demonstrate it. Before you begin your studies for SBR, be sure that you have revised all FR topics.

Helping you with your revision

BPP Learning Media – ACCA Approved Content Provider

As an ACCA **Approved Content Provider**, BPP Learning Media gives you the **opportunity** to use revision materials reviewed by the ACCA examining team. By incorporating the ACCA examining team's comments and suggestions regarding the depth and breadth of syllabus coverage, the BPP Learning Media Practice & Revision Kit provides excellent, **ACCA-approved** support for your revision.

These materials are reviewed by the ACCA examining team. The objective of the review is to ensure that the material properly covers the syllabus and study guide outcomes, used by the examining team in setting the exams, in the appropriate breadth and depth. The review does not ensure that every eventuality, combination or application of examinable topics is addressed by the ACCA Approved Content. Nor does the review comprise a detailed technical check of the content as the Approved Content Provider has its own quality assurance processes in place in this respect.

BPP Learning Media do everything possible to ensure the material is accurate and up to date when sending to print. In the event that any errors are found after the print date, they are uploaded to the following website: www.bpp.com/learningmedia/Errata.

The structure of this Practice & Revision Kit

This Practice & Revision Kit is divided into three sections. The questions in Section 1 are preparation questions to help develop your knowledge. Section 2 contains exam-standard questions which are of appropriate complexity and format to mimic the style of the final exam. Section 3 contains four mock exams. You should attempt all four mock exams, preferably under exam conditions, as this will provide excellent preparation before you take the real exam.

Question practice

Question practice under timed conditions is absolutely vital. We strongly advise you to create a revision study plan which focuses on question practice. This is so that you can get used to the pressures of answering exam questions in limited time, and develop proficiency in the skills required. Ideally, you should aim to cover all questions in this Kit, and very importantly, all four mock exams.

Selecting questions

To help you plan your revision, we have provided a full **topic index** which maps the questions to topics in the syllabus (see page viii).

Making the most of question practice

At BPP Learning Media we realise that you need more than just questions and model answers to get the most from your question practice.

- Our **Top tips**, included for certain questions, provide essential advice on tackling questions, presenting answers and the key points that answers need to include.
- We include **marking guides** to show you what the examining team rewards.
- We include **comments from the examining team** to show you where students struggled or performed well in the actual exam

Attempting mock exams

This Kit has four mock exams, including ACCA's two Specimen Exams and the December 2018 real exam, all of which have been updated for applicable changes in examinable documents. We strongly recommend that you attempt the mock exams under exam conditions.

Topics to revise

ACCA's examining team consistently warn very strongly against question-spotting and trying to predict the topics that will be included in the exam. Students should not be surprised if the same topic area is examined in two successive sittings. ACCA's examining team regards few areas as off-limits for questions, and all of the syllabus can be tested.

That said, the following areas of the syllabus are very important, and your revision therefore needs to cover them particularly well.

- **Group accounts**: Group accounts will always be examined as part of Section A but may also feature in Section B. You are unlikely to be asked to prepare full consolidated financial statements in SBR but do need to be able to prepare extracts from them or key calculations within. You must also be able to explain the accounting treatment, as the marks for numerical aspects will be limited.
- **Ethical issues**: Ethical issues will feature in Section A of every exam and may also be examined in Section B. It is important that you can analyse ethical issues with regards to the fundamental principles of ACCA's *Code of Ethics and Conduct.*
- **Analysis and appraisal of information** will be tested in Section B. You should not focus only on 'traditional' financial analysis such as ratios. You will need to appraise companies using a range of financial and non-financial information, and from the perspective of different stakeholders.
- An in-depth **knowledge of the *Conceptual Framework*** is required. You are expected to be able discuss the consistency of each examinable IFRS with the *Conceptual Framework*.
- **Developments in Financial Reporting**: You need to be able to discuss the effect of a change or proposed change in accounting standards and other developments, such as the IFRS Practice Statement 2 *Making Materiality Judgements*, including the effect it may have on how stakeholders will analyse the financial statements. You need to read widely to develop your knowledge of current issues, including reading articles published on ACCA's website and looking at real published annual reports.
- More complex IFRSs such as IFRS 15 *Revenue from Contracts with Customers* and IFRS 16 *Leases,* as there is significant scope for discussion and justification in more complex standards.

Essential skill areas

There are three areas you should develop in order to achieve exam success in Strategic Business Reporting (SBR). These are:

(1) Knowledge application
(2) Specific Strategic Business Reporting skills
(3) Exam success skills

At the revision and final exam preparation phases **these should be developed together as part of a comprehensive study plan of focused question practice**.

Take some time to revisit the **Specific Strategic Business Reporting skills** and **Exam success skills**. These are shown in the diagram below and followed by tutorial guidance of how to apply them.

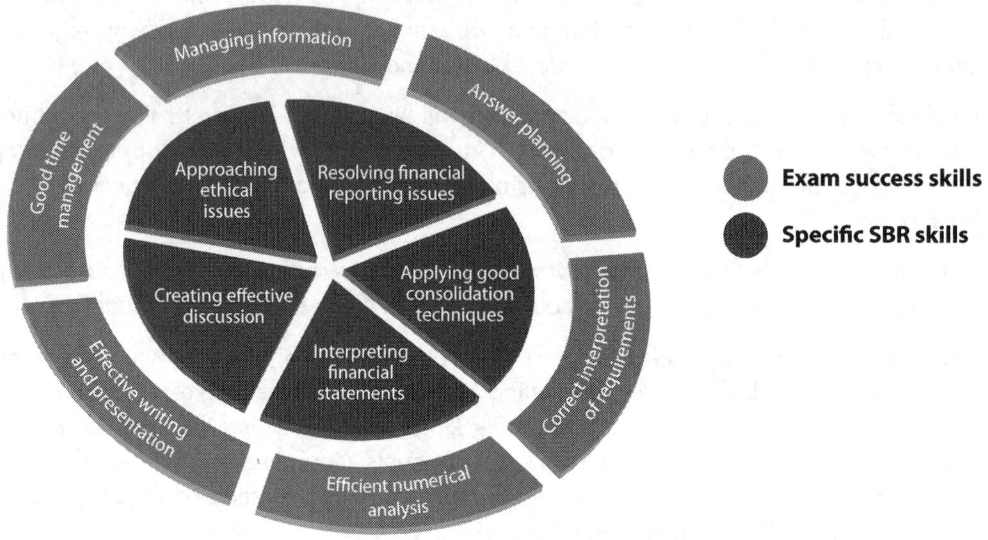

Specific SBR skills

These are the skills specific to SBR that we think you need to develop in order to pass the exam.

In the BPP Strategic Business Reporting Workbook, there are five **Skills Checkpoints** which define each skill and show how it is applied in answering a question. A brief summary of each skill is given below.

Skill 1: Approaching ethical issues

Question 2 in Section A of the exam will require you to consider the **reporting implications** and the **ethical implications** of specific events in a given scenario. The two Section B questions could deal with any aspect of the syllabus. Therefore, ethics could feature in this part of the exam too.

Given that ethics will feature in every exam, it is essential that you master the appropriate technique for approaching ethical issues in order to maximise your mark.

BPP recommends a step-by-step technique for approaching questions on ethical issues:

STEP 1 Work out how many minutes you have to answer the question.

STEP 2 Read the requirement and analyse it.

STEP 3 Read the scenario, identify which IAS or IFRS may be relevant, whether the proposed accounting treatment complies with that IAS or IFRS and whether there are any threats to the fundamental ethical principles.

STEP 4 Prepare an answer plan using key words from the requirements as headings.

STEP 5 Write up your answer using key words from the requirements as headings.

Skills Checkpoint 1 in the BPP Workbook for Strategic Business Reporting covers this technique in detail through application to an exam-standard question. Consider revisiting Skills Checkpoint 1 and completing the scenario-based question to specifically improve this skill.

Skill 2: Resolving financial reporting issues

Financial reporting issues are highly likely to be tested in both sections of your Strategic Business Reporting exam, so it is essential that you master the skill for resolving financial reporting issues in order to maximise your chance of passing the exam.

The basic approach BPP recommends for resolving financial reporting issues is very similar to the one for ethical issues. This consistency is important because in Question 2 of the exam, both will be tested together.

STEP 1 Work out how many minutes you have to answer the question.

STEP 2 Read the requirement and analyse it, identifying sub-requirements.

STEP 3 Read the scenario, identifying relevant IASs or IFRSs and their application to the scenario.

STEP 4 Prepare an answer plan ensuring that you cover each of the issues raised in the scenario.

STEP 5 Write up your answer, using separate headings for each item in the scenario.

Skills Checkpoint 2 in the BPP Workbook for Strategic Business Reporting covers this technique in detail through application to an exam-standard question. Consider revisiting Skills Checkpoint 2 and completing the scenario based question to specifically improve this skill.

Skill 3: Applying good consolidation techniques

Question 1 of Section A of the exam will be based on the financial statements of group entities, or extracts thereof. Section B of the exam could deal with any aspect of the syllabus so it is also possible that groups feature in Question 3 or 4.

Good consolidation techniques are therefore essential when answering both written and numerical aspects of group questions.

Skills Checkpoint 3 focuses on the more challenging technique for correcting errors in group financial statements that have already been prepared.

A step-by-step technique for applying good consolidation techniques is outlined below.

STEP 1 Work out how many minutes you have to answer the question.

STEP 2 Read the requirement for each part of the question and analyse it, identifying sub-requirements.

STEP 3 Read the scenario, identify exactly what information has been provided and what you need to do with this information. Identify which consolidation workings/adjustments may be required.

STEP 4 Draw up a group structure. Make notes in the margins of the question as to which consolidation working, adjustment or correction to error is required. Do not perform any detailed calculations at this stage.

STEP 5 Write up your answer using key words from the requirements as headings (if preparing narrative). Perform calculations first, then explain. Remember that marks will be available for a discussion of the principles underpinning any calculations.

Skills Checkpoint 3 in the BPP Workbook for Strategic Business Reporting covers this technique in detail through application to an exam-standard question. Consider revisiting Skills Checkpoint 3 and completing the scenario based question to specifically improve this skill.

Skill 4: Interpreting financial statements

Section B of the SBR exam will contain two questions, which may be scenario or case-study or essay based and will contain both discursive and computational elements. Section B could deal with any aspect of the syllabus but will always include either a full question, or part of a question that requires appraisal of financial or non-financial information from either the preparer's and/or another stakeholder's perspective. Two professional marks will be awarded to the question in Section B that requires analysis.

Given that appraisal of financial and/or non-financial information will feature in Section B of every exam, it is essential that you have mastered the appropriate technique in order to maximise your chance of passing the SBR exam.

A step-by-step technique for performing financial analysis is outlined below.

STEP 1 Work out how many minutes you have to answer the question

STEP 2 Read and analyse the requirement

STEP 3 Read and analyse the scenario

STEP 4 Prepare an answer plan

STEP 5 Write up your answer

Skills Checkpoint 4 in the BPP Workbook for Strategic Business Reporting covers this technique in detail through application to an exam-standard question. Consider revisiting Skills Checkpoint 4 and completing the scenario based question to specifically improve this skill.

Skill 5: Creating effective discussion

Significantly more marks in the Strategic Business Reporting exam will relate to written answers than numerical answers. It is very tempting to only practise numerical questions as they are easy to mark because the answer is right or wrong, whereas written questions are more subjective and a range of different answers will be given credit. Even when attempting written questions, it is tempting to write a brief answer plan and then look at the answer rather than writing a full answer to plan. Unless you practise written questions in full to time, you will never acquire the necessary skills to tackle discussion questions.

The basic five steps adopted in Skills Checkpoint 4 should also be used in discussion questions.

Steps 2 and 4 are particularly important for discussion questions. You will definitely need to spend a third of your time reading and planning. Generating ideas at the planning stage to create a comprehensive answer plan will be the key to success in this style of question. Consideration of the *Conceptual Framework*, ethical principles and the perspective of stakeholders will often help with discursive questions in SBR.

Skills Checkpoint 5 in the BPP Workbook for Strategic Business Reporting covers this technique in detail through application to an exam-standard question. Consider revisiting Skills Checkpoint 5 and completing the scenario based question to specifically improve this skill.

Exam success skills

Passing the SBR exam requires more than applying syllabus knowledge and demonstrating the Specific SBR skills; it also requires the development of excellent exam technique through question practice.

We consider the following six skills, or exam techniques, to be vital for exam success. These skills were introduced in the BPP Workbook and you can revisit the five Skills Checkpoints in the BPP Workbook for tutorial guidance of how to apply each of the six Exam success skills in your question practice and in the exam.

Aim to consider your performance in all six Exam success skills during your revision stage question practice and reflect on your particular strengths and weaker areas which you can then work on.

Exam success skill 1

Managing information

Questions in the exam will present you with a lot of information. The skill is how you handle this information to make the best use of your time. The key is determining how you will approach the exam and then actively reading the questions.

Advice on Managing information

Approach

The exam is 3 hours 15 minutes long. There is no designated 'reading' time at the start of the exam, however, one approach that can work well is to start the exam by spending 10–15 minutes carefully reading through all of the questions to familiarise yourself with the exam.

Once you feel familiar with the exam, consider the order in which you will attempt the questions; always attempt them in your order of preference – for example, you may want to leave to last the question you consider to be the most difficult.

If you do take this approach, remember to adjust the time available for each question appropriately – see Exam success skill 6: Good time management.

If you find that this approach doesn't work for you, don't worry – you can develop your own technique.

Active reading

You must take an active approach to reading each question. Focus on the requirement first, underlining key verbs, for example, prepare, comment, explain or discuss, to ensure you answer the question properly. Then read the rest of the question, underlining and annotating important and relevant information, and making notes of any relevant technical information you think you will need.

Exam success skill 2

Correct interpretation of the requirements

The active verb used often dictates the approach that written answers should take (eg 'explain', 'discuss', 'evaluate'). It is important you identify and use the verb to define your approach. The **Correct interpretation of the requirements** skill is correctly producing only what is being asked for by a requirement. Anything not required will not earn marks.

Advice on Correct interpretation of the requirements

This skill can be developed by analysing question requirements and applying this process:

Step 1 **Read the requirement**

Firstly, read the requirement a couple of times slowly and carefully and highlight the active verbs. Use the active verbs to define what you plan to do. Make sure you identify any sub-requirements.

Step 2 **Read the rest of the question**

By reading the requirement first, you will have an idea of what you are looking out for as you read through the case overview and exhibits. This is a great time saver and means you don't end up having to read the whole question in full twice. You should do this in an active way – see Exam success skill 1: Managing information.

Step 3 **Read the requirement again**

Read the requirement again to remind yourself of the exact wording before starting your written answer. This will capture any misinterpretation of the requirements or any requirements missed entirely. This should become a habit in your approach and, with repeated practice, you will find the focus, relevance and depth of your answer plan will improve.

Exam success skill 3

Answer planning: Priorities, structure and logic

This skill requires the planning of the key aspects of an answer which accurately and completely responds to the requirement.

Advice on Answer planning: Priorities, structure and logic

Everyone will have a preferred style for an answer plan. For example, it may be a mind map, bullet-pointed lists or simply annotating the question. Choose the approach that you feel most comfortable with or if you are not sure, try out different approaches for different questions until you have found your preferred style.

For a discussion question, annotating the question is likely to be insufficient. It would be better to draw up a separate answer plan in the format of your choosing (eg a mind map or bullet-pointed lists). For a groups question, you will typically spend less time planning than for a discussion type question. You should aim to draw up the group structure. Then, rather than drawing up a formal plan, the best use of your time is to annotate the question margins noting which group working, adjustment or correction of error will be required.

Exam success skill 4

Efficient numerical analysis

This skill aims to maximise the marks awarded by making clear to the marker the process of arriving at your answer. This is achieved by laying out an answer such that, even if you make a few errors, you can still score subsequent marks for follow-on calculations. It is vital that you do not lose marks purely because the marker cannot follow what you have done.

Advice on Efficient numerical analysis

This skill can be developed by applying the following process:

Step 1 **Use a standard proforma working where relevant**

If answers can be laid out in a standard proforma then always plan to do so. This will help the marker to understand your working and allocate the marks easily. It will also help you to work through the figures in a methodical and time-efficient way.

Step 2 **Show your workings**

Keep your workings as clear and simple as possible and ensure they are cross-referenced to the main part of your answer. Where it helps, provide brief narrative explanations to help the marker understand the steps in the calculation. This means that if a mistake is made then you do not lose any subsequent marks for follow-on calculations.

Step 3 **Keep moving!**

It is important to remember that, in an exam situation, it is difficult to get every number 100% correct. The key is therefore ensuring you do not spend too long on any single calculation. If you are struggling with a solution then make a sensible assumption, state it and move on.

Exam success skill 5

Effective writing and presentation

Written answers should be presented so that the marker can clearly see the points you are making, presented in the format specified in the question. The skill is to provide efficient written answers with sufficient breadth of points that answer the question, in the right depth, in the time available.

Advice on Effective writing and presentation

Step 1 **Use headings**

Using the headings and sub-headings from your answer plan will give your answer structure, order and logic. This will ensure your answer links back to the requirement and is clearly signposted, making it easier for the marker to understand the different points you are making. Underlining your headings will also help the marker.

Step 2 **Write your answer in short, but full, sentences**

Use short, punchy sentences with the aim that every sentence should say something different and generate marks. Write in full sentences, ensuring your style is professional.

Step 3 **Do your calculations first, explanation second**

Questions often ask for an explanation with suitable calculations, the best approach is to prepare the calculation first but present it on the bottom half of the page of /next page to your answer. Then add the explanation before the calculation. Performing the calculation first should enable you to explain what you have done.

Exam success skill 6

Good time management

This skill means planning your time across all the requirements so that all tasks have been attempted at the end of the 3 hours 15 minutes available and actively checking on time during your exam. This is so that you can flex your approach and prioritise requirements which, in your judgement, will generate the maximum marks in the available time remaining.

Advice on Good time management

The exam is 3 hours 15 minutes long, which translates to 1.95 minutes per mark. Therefore a 10-mark requirement should be allocated a maximum of 20 minutes to complete your answer before you move on to the next task. At the beginning of a question, work out the amount of time you should be spending on each requirement and write the finishing time next to each requirement on your exam. If you take the approach of spending 10–15 minutes reading and planning at the start of the exam, adjust the time allocated to each question accordingly, eg if you allocate 15 minutes to reading, then you will have 3 hours remaining which is 1.8 minutes per mark.

Keep an eye on the clock

Aim to attempt all requirements, but be ready to be ruthless and move on if your answer is not going as planned. The challenge for many is sticking to planned timings. Be aware this is difficult to achieve in the early stages of your studies and be ready to let this skill develop over time.

If you find yourself running short on time and know that a full answer is not possible in the time you have, consider recreating your plan in overview form and then add key terms and details as time allows. Remember, some marks may be available, for example, simply stating a conclusion which you don't have time to justify in full.

Question Bank

Section 1 – Preparation questions

Tutorial note.

The Section 1 questions are designed to help you prepare for the SBR examination. They are not of a full exam standard but are still very helpful in testing your understanding of key areas of the syllabus. The number of marks and time allocated to each question in this section is for indicative purposes only.

1 Financial instruments **12 mins**

(a) Graben Co purchases a bond for $441,014 on 1 January 20X1. It will be redeemed on 31 December 20X4 for $600,000. The bond is held at amortised cost and carries no coupon.

Required

Calculate the valuation of the bond for the statement of financial position as at 31 December 20X1 and the finance income for 20X1 shown in profit or loss. **(3 marks)**

Compound sum of $1: $(1 + r)^n$

Year	*2%*	*4%*	*6%*	*8%*	*10%*	*12%*	*14%*
1	1.0200	1.0400	1.0600	1.0800	1.1000	1.1200	1.1400
2	1.0404	1.0816	1.1236	1.1664	1.2100	1.2544	1.2996
3	1.0612	1.1249	1.1910	1.2597	1.3310	1.4049	1.4815
4	1.0824	1.1699	1.2625	1.3605	1.4641	1.5735	1.6890
5	1.1041	1.2167	1.3382	1.4693	1.6105	1.7623	1.9254

(b) Baldie Co issues 4,000 convertible bonds on 1 January 20X2 at par. The bonds are redeemable three years later at a par value of $500 per bond, which is the nominal value.

The bonds pay interest annually in arrears at an interest rate (based on nominal value) of 5%. Each bond can be converted at the maturity date into 30 $1 shares.

The prevailing market interest rate for three year bonds that have no right of conversion is 9%.

Required

Show how the convertible bond would be presented in the statement of financial position at 1 January 20X2. **(3 marks)**

Cumulative three year annuity factors:

5% 2.723
9% 2.531

(Total = 6 marks)

2 Leases **20 mins**

Sugar Co leased a machine from Spice Co. The terms of the lease are as follows:

Inception of lease	1 January 20X1
Lease term	4 years at $78,864 per annum payable in arrears
Present value of future lease payments	$250,000
Useful life of asset	4 years

Required

(a) Calculate the interest rate implicit in the lease, using the table below. **(3 marks)**

This table shows the cumulative present value of $1 per annum, receivable or payable at the end of each year for n years.

Years		*Interest rates*	
(n)	*6%*	*8%*	*10%*
1	0.943	0.926	0.909
2	1.833	1.783	1.736
3	2.673	2.577	2.487
4	3.465	3.312	3.170
5	4.212	3.993	3.791

(b) Explain, with suitable workings and extracts from the financial statements, how Sugar Co should account for the lease for the year ended 31 December 20X1. Notes to the accounts are not required. **(7 marks)**

(Total = 10 marks)

3 Defined benefit plan **20 mins**

BPP note. In this question, proforma are given to you to help you get used to setting out your answer. You may wish to transfer them to a separate sheet, or alternatively to use a separate sheet for your workings.

Brutus operates a defined benefit pension plan for its employees. The present value of the future benefit obligations and the fair value of its plan assets on 1 January 20X1 were $110 million and $150 million respectively.

The pension plan received contributions of $7 million and paid pensions to former employees of $10 million during the year.

Extracts from the most recent actuarial report shows the following:

Present value of pension plan obligation at 31 December 20X1	$116m
Fair value of plan assets at 31 December 20X1	$140m
Present cost of pensions earned in the period	$11m
Yield on high quality corporate bonds at 1 January 20X1	10%

On 1 January 20X1, the rules of the pension plan were changed to improve benefits for plan members. The actuary has advised that this will cost $10 million.

Required

Prepare extracts from the notes to Brutus' financial statements for the year ended 31 December 20X1 which show how the pension plan should be accounted for. **(10 marks)**

Note. Assume contributions and benefits were paid on 31 December.

NOTES TO THE STATEMENT OF PROFIT OR LOSS AND OTHER COMPREHENSIVE INCOME

Defined benefit expense recognised in profit or loss

	$m
Current service cost	
Past service cost	
Net interest on the net defined benefit asset	

Other comprehensive income (items that will not be reclassified to profit or loss)
Remeasurement of defined benefit plans

	$m
Remeasurement gain on defined benefit obligation	
Remeasurement loss on plan assets	

NOTES TO THE STATEMENT OF FINANCIAL POSITION

Net defined benefit asset recognised in the statement of financial position

	31 December 20X1 $m	*31 December 20X0* $m
Present value of pension obligation		
Fair value of plan assets		
Net asset		

Changes in the present value of the defined benefit obligation

	$m
Opening defined benefit obligation	
Interest on obligation	
Current service cost	
Past service cost	
Benefits paid	
Gain on remeasurement of obligation (balancing figure)	
Closing defined benefit obligation	

Changes in the fair value of plan assets

	$m
Opening fair value of plan assets	
Interest on plan assets	
Contributions	
Benefits paid	
Loss on remeasurement of assets (balancing figure)	
Closing fair value of plan assets	

4 Sundry standards **59 mins**

(a) Penn has a defined benefit pension plan.

Required

Using the information below, prepare extracts from the statement of financial position and the statement of profit or loss and other comprehensive income for the year ended 31 January 20X8. Ignore taxation. **(10 marks)**

(i) The opening plan assets were $3.6 million on 1 February 20X7 and plan liabilities at this date were $4.3 million.

(ii) Company contributions to the plan during the year amounted to $550,000. The contributions were paid at the start of the year.

(iii) Pensions paid to former employees amounted to $330,000. These were paid at the start of the year.

(iv) The yield on high quality corporate bonds was 8% at 1 February 20X7.

(v) On 31 January 20X8, five staff were made redundant, and an extra $58,000 in total was added to the value of their pensions.

(vi) Current service costs as provided by the actuary are $275,000.

(vii) At 31 January 20X8, the actuary valued the plan liabilities at $4.64 million and the plan assets at $4.215 million.

(b) Sion operates a defined benefit pension plan for its employees. Sion has a 31 December year end. The following details relate to the plan.

	$'000
Present value of obligation at 1 January 20X8	40,000
Market value of plan assets at 1 January 20X8	40,000

	20X8	*20X9*
	$'000	$'000
Current service cost	2,500	2,860
Benefits paid out	1,974	2,200
Contributions paid by entity	2,000	2,200
Present value of obligation at end of the year	46,000	40,800
Market value of plan assets at end of the year	43,000	35,680
Yield on corporate bonds at start of the year	8%	9%

During 20X8, the benefits available under the plan were improved. The resulting increase in the present value of the defined benefit obligation was $2 million as at 31 December 20X8.

Contributions were paid into the plan and benefits were paid out of the plan on the final day of each accounting period.

On 31 December 20X9, Sion divested of part of its business, and as part of the sale agreement, transferred the relevant part of its pension fund to the buyer. The present value of the defined benefit obligation transferred was $11.4 million and the fair value of plan assets transferred was $10.8 million. Sion also made a cash payment of $400,000 to the buyer in respect of the plan.

Required

(i) Calculate the net defined benefit liability as at the start and end of 20X8 and 20X9 showing clearly any remeasurement gain or loss on the plan each year.

(ii) Show amounts to be recognised in the financial statements in each of the years 20X8 and 20X9 in respect of the plan. **(15 marks)**

(c) Bed Investment Co entered into a contract on 1 July 20X7 with Em Bank. The contract consisted of a deposit of a principal amount of $10 million, carrying an interest rate of 2.5% per annum and with a maturity date of 30 June 20X9. Interest will be receivable at maturity together with the principal. In addition, a further 3% interest per annum will be payable by Em Bank if the exchange rate of the dollar against the Ruritanian kroner (RKR) exceeds or is equal to $1.15 to RKR 1.

Bed's functional currency is the dollar.

Required

Explain how Bed should account for the above investment in the financial statements for the year ended 31 December 20X7 (no calculations are required). **(5 marks)**

(Total = 30 marks)

5 Control — 23 mins

(a) IFRS 10 *Consolidated Financial Statements* focuses on control as the key concept underlying the parent/subsidiary relationship.

Required

Explain the circumstances in which an investor controls an investee according to IFRS 10.

(3 marks)

(b) Twist holds 40% of the voting rights of Oliver and 12 other investors each hold 5% of the voting rights of Oliver. A shareholder agreement grants Twist the right to appoint, remove and set the remuneration of management responsible for directing the relevant activities. To change the agreement, a two-thirds majority vote of the shareholders is required. To date, Twist has not exercised its rights with regard to the management or activities of Oliver.

Required

Explain whether Twist should consolidate Oliver in accordance with IFRS 10. **(3 marks)**

(c) Copperfield holds 45% of the voting rights of Spenlow. Murdstone and Steerforth each hold 26% of the voting rights of Spenlow. The remaining voting rights are held by three other shareholders, each holding 1%. There are no other arrangements that affect decision-making.

Required

Explain whether Copperfield should consolidate Spenlow in accordance with IFRS 10.

(3 marks)

(d) Scrooge holds 70% of the voting rights of Cratchett. Marley has 30% of the voting rights of Cratchett. Marley also has an option to acquire half of Scrooge's voting rights, which is exercisable for the next two years, but at a fixed price that is deeply out of the money (and is expected to remain so for that two-year period).

Required

Explain whether either of Scrooge or Marley should consolidate Cratchett in accordance with IFRS 10. **(3 marks)**

(Total = 12 marks)

6 Associate **39 mins**

The statements of financial position of J Co and its investee companies, P Co and S Co, at 31 December 20X5 are shown below.

STATEMENTS OF FINANCIAL POSITION AS AT 31 DECEMBER 20X5

	J Co	*P Co*	*S Co*
	$'000	$'000	$'000
Assets			
Non-current assets			
Freehold property	1,950	1,250	500
Plant and equipment	795	375	285
Investments	1,500	–	–
	4,245	1,625	785
Current assets			
Inventories	575	300	265
Trade receivables	330	290	370
Cash	50	120	20
	955	710	655
	5,200	2,335	1,440
Equity and liabilities			
Equity			
Share capital ($1 ordinary shares)	2,000	1,000	750
Retained earnings	1,460	885	390
	3,460	1,885	1,140
Non-current liabilities			
12% debentures	500	100	–
Current liabilities			
Bank overdraft	560		
Trade payables	680	350	300
	1,240	350	300
	5,200	2,335	1,440

Additional information

(a) J Co acquired 600,000 ordinary shares in P Co on 1 January 20X0 for $1,000,000 when the accumulated retained earnings of P Co were $200,000.

(b) At the date of acquisition of P Co, the fair value of its freehold property was considered to be $400,000 greater than its value in P Co's statement of financial position. P Co had acquired the property ten years earlier and the buildings element (comprising 50% of the total value) is depreciated on cost over 50 years.

(c) J Co acquired 225,000 ordinary shares in S Co on 1 January 20X4 for $500,000 when the retained profits of S Co were $150,000.

(d) P Co sells goods to J Co at cost plus 25%. J Co held $100,000 of these goods in inventories at 31 December 20X5.

(e) It is the policy of J Co to review goodwill for impairment annually. The goodwill in P Co was written off in full some years ago. An impairment test conducted at the year end revealed impairment losses on the investment in S Co of $92,000.

(f) It is the group's policy to value the non-controlling interest at acquisition at fair value. The market price of the shares of the non-controlling shareholders just before the acquisition was $1.65.

Required

Prepare, in a format suitable for inclusion in the annual report of the J Group, the consolidated statement of financial position at 31 December 20X5. **(20 marks)**

7 Part disposal 49 mins

BPP note. In this question, proforma are given to you to help you get used to setting out your answer. You may wish to transfer them to a separate sheet or to use a separate sheet for your workings.

Angel Co bought 70% of the share capital of Shane Co for $120,000 on 1 January 20X6. At that date Shane Co's retained earnings stood at $10,000.

The statements of financial position at 31 December 20X8, summarised statements of profit or loss and other comprehensive income to that date and movement on retained earnings are given below.

	Angel Co	*Shane Co*
	$'000	$'000
STATEMENTS OF FINANCIAL POSITION		
Non-current assets		
Property, plant and equipment	200	80
Investment in Shane Co	120	–
	320	80
Current assets	890	140
	1,210	220
Equity		
Share capital – $1 ordinary shares	500	100
Retained reserves	400	90
	900	190
Current liabilities	310	30
	1,210	220

SUMMARISED STATEMENTS OF PROFIT OR LOSS AND OTHER COMPREHENSIVE INCOME

	$'000	$'000
Profit before interest and tax	100	20
Income tax expense	(40)	(8)
Profit for the year	60	12
Other comprehensive income (not reclassified to P/L), net of tax	10	6
Total comprehensive income for the year	70	18

MOVEMENT IN RETAINED RESERVES

Balance at 31 December 20X7	330	72
Total comprehensive income for the year	70	18
Balance at 31 December 20X8	400	90

Angel Co sells one half of its holding in Shane Co for $120,000 on 30 June 20X8. At that date, the fair value of the 35% holding in Shane was slightly more at $130,000 due to a share price rise. The remaining holding is to be dealt with as an associate. This does not represent a discontinued operation.

No entries have been made in the accounts for the above transaction.

Assume that profits accrue evenly throughout the year.

It is the group's policy to value the non-controlling interest at acquisition fair value. The fair value of the non-controlling interest on 1 January 20X6 was $51.4 million.

Required

(a) Prepare the consolidated statement of financial position, statement of profit or loss and other comprehensive income and a reconciliation of movement in retained reserves for the year ended 31 December 20X8. **(20 marks)**

Ignore income taxes on the disposal. No impairment losses have been necessary to date.

PART DISPOSAL PROFORMA

ANGEL GROUP
CONSOLIDATED STATEMENT OF FINANCIAL POSITION
AS AT 31 DECEMBER 20X8

	$'000
Non-current assets	
Property, plant and equipment	
Investment in Shane	
Current assets	
Equity attributable to owners of the parent	
Share capital	
Retained earnings	
Current liabilities	

CONSOLIDATED STATEMENT OF PROFIT OR LOSS AND OTHER COMPREHENSIVE INCOME FOR THE YEAR ENDED 31 DECEMBER 20X8

	$'000
Profit before interest and tax	
Profit on disposal of shares in subsidiary	
Share of profit of associate	
Profit before tax	
Income tax expense	
Profit for the year	
Other comprehensive income (not reclassified to P/L) net of tax:	
Share of other comprehensive income of associate	
Other comprehensive income for the year	
Total comprehensive income for the year	
Profit attributable to:	
Owners of the parent	
Non-controlling interests	
Total comprehensive income attributable to:	
Owners of the parent	
Non-controlling interests	

CONSOLIDATED RECONCILIATION OF MOVEMENT IN RETAINED RESERVES

	$'000
Balance at 31 December 20X7	
Total comprehensive income for the year	
Balance at 31 December 20X8	

(b) Explain the accounting treatment that would be required if Angel had disposed of 10% of its holding in Shane. **(5 marks)**

(Total = 25 marks)

8 Step acquisition — 29 mins

SD acquired 60% of the 1 million $1 ordinary shares of KL on 1 July 20X0 for $3,250,000 when KL's retained earnings were $2,760,000. The group policy is to measure non-controlling interests at fair value at the date of acquisition. The fair value of non-controlling interests at 1 July 20X0 was $1,960,000. There has been no impairment of goodwill since the date of acquisition.

SD acquired a further 20% of KL's share capital on 1 March 20X1 for $1,000,000.

The retained earnings reported in the financial statements of SD and KL as at 30 June 20X1 are $9,400,000 and $3,400,000 respectively.

KL sold goods for resale to SD with a sales value of $750,000 during the period from 1 March 20X1 to 30 June 20X1. 40% of these goods remain in SD's inventories at the year-end. KL applies a mark-up of 25% on all goods sold.

Profits of both entities can be assumed to accrue evenly throughout the year.

Required

(a) Explain the impact of the additional 20% purchase of KL's ordinary share capital by SD on the consolidated financial statements of the SD Group for the year ended 30 June 20X1. **(5 marks)**

(b) Calculate the amounts that will appear in the consolidated statement of financial position of the SD Group as at 30 June 20X1 for:

(i) Goodwill;
(ii) Consolidated retained earnings; and
(iii) Non-controlling interests. **(10 marks)**

(Total = 15 marks)

9 Foreign operation — 49 mins

BPP note. In this question, proformas for the translation workings are given to assist you with the approach. You will need to also need to draw up proformas for the consolidated financial statements and the remaining group workings.

Standard acquired 80% of Odense SA for $520,000 on 1 January 20X5 when the retained reserves of Odense were 2,500,000 Danish krone.

The financial statements of Standard and Odense for the year ended 31 December 20X6 are as follows:

STATEMENTS OF FINANCIAL POSITION AT 31 DECEMBER 20X6

	Standard	*Odense*
	$'000	Kr'000
Property, plant and equipment	1,285	4,400
Investment in Odense	520	–
	1,805	4,400
Current assets	410	2,000
	2,215	6,400
Share capital	500	1,000
Retained earnings	1,115	4,300
	1,615	5,300
Loans	200	300
Current liabilities	400	800
	600	1,100
	2,215	6,400

STATEMENT OF PROFIT OR LOSS AND OTHER COMPREHENSIVE INCOME
FOR YEAR ENDED 31 DECEMBER 20X6

	Standard	*Odense*
	$'000	Kr'000
Revenue	1,125	5,200
Cost of sales	(410)	(2,300)
Gross profit	715	2,900
Other expenses	(180)	(910)
Dividend from Odense	40	–
Profit before tax	575	1,990
Income tax expense	(180)	(640)
Profit/Total comprehensive income for the year	395	1,350

STATEMENTS OF CHANGES IN EQUITY FOR THE YEAR 31 DECEMBER 20X6 (EXTRACT FOR RETAINED EARNINGS)

	Standard	*Odense*
	$'000	Kr'000
Balance at 1 January 20X6	915	3,355
Dividends paid on 31 December 20X6	(195)	(405)
Total comprehensive income for the year	395	1,350
Balance at 31 December 20X6	1,115	4,300

In the year ended 31 December 20X5, Odense's total comprehensive income was 1,200,000 Danish krone. On 31 December 20X5, Odense paid dividends of 345,000 Danish krone.

An impairment test conducted at 31 December 20X6 revealed impairment losses of 148,000 Danish krone relating to Odense's goodwill. No impairment losses had previously been recognised. It is group policy to translate impairment losses at the closing rate.

At the date of acquisition, Standard chose to measure the non-controlling interest in Odense at the proportionate share of the fair value of net assets.

Exchange rates were as follows:

	Kr to $1
1 January 20X5	9.4
31 December 20X5	8.8
Average 20X5	9.1
31 December 20X6	8.1
Average 20X6	8.4

Required

Prepare the consolidated statement of financial position and consolidated statement of profit or loss and other comprehensive income of the Standard Group for the year ended 31 December 20X6 (round your answer to the nearest $'000). **(25 marks)**

TRANSLATION OF ODENSE – STATEMENT OF FINANCIAL POSITION

	Kr'000	Rate	$'000
Property, plant and equipment		X6 CR	
Current assets		X6 CR	
Share capital		HR	
Pre-acquisition retained earnings		HR	
Post-acquisition retained earnings:			
20X5 profit		X5 AR	
20X5 dividend		X5 Actual	
20X6 profit		X6 AR	
20X6 dividend		X6 Actual	
Exchange difference on net assets		Bal. fig.	
Loans		X6 CR	
Current liabilities		X6 CR	

TRANSLATION OF ODENSE – STATEMENT OF PROFIT OR LOSS AND OTHER COMPREHENSIVE INCOME

	Odense Kr'000	*Rate* (AR)	*Odense* $'000
Revenue			
Cost of sales			
Gross profit			
Other expenses			
Profit before tax			
Income tax expense			
Profit/Total comprehensive income for the year			

10 Consolidated statement of cash flows — 39 mins

> **BPP note.** In this question, proformas are given to you to help you get used to setting out your answer. You may wish to transfer them to a separate sheet, or alternatively to use a separate sheet for your workings.

On 1 September 20X5 Swing Co acquired 70% of Slide Co for $5,000,000 comprising $1,000,000 cash and 1,500,000 $1 shares.

The statement of financial position of Slide Co at acquisition was as follows:

	$'000
Property, plant and equipment	2,700
Inventories	1,600
Trade receivables	600
Cash	400
Trade payables	(300)
Income tax payable	(200)
	4,800

The consolidated statement of financial position of Swing Co as at 31 December 20X5 was as follows:

	20X5	*20X4*
Non-current assets	$'000	$'000
Property, plant and equipment	35,500	25,000
Goodwill	1,400	–
	36,900	25,000
Current assets		
Inventories	16,000	10,000
Trade receivables	9,800	7,500
Cash	2,400	1,500
	28,200	19,000
	65,100	44,000
Equity attributable to owners of the parent		
Share capital	12,300	10,000
Share premium	5,800	2,000
Revaluation surplus	350	–
Retained earnings	32,100	21,900
	50,550	33,900
Non-controlling interest	1,750	–
	52,300	33,900
Current liabilities		
Trade payables	7,600	6,100
Income tax payable	5,200	4,000
	12,800	10,100
	65,100	44,000

The consolidated statement of profit or loss and other comprehensive income of Swing Co for the year ended 31 December 20X5 was as follows:

	20X5
	$'000
Profit before tax	16,500
Income tax expense	(5,200)
Profit for the year	11,300
Other comprehensive income (not reclassified to P/L)	
Revaluation surplus	500
Total comprehensive income for the year	11,800
Profit attributable to:	
Owners of the parent	11,100
Non-controlling interest	200
	11,300
Total comprehensive income for the year attributable to:	
Owners of the parent	11,450
Non-controlling interest 200 + (500 × 30%)	350
	11,800

Notes

1 Depreciation charged for the year was $5,800,000. The group made no disposals of property, plant and equipment.

2 Dividends paid by Swing Co amounted to $900,000.

It is the group's policy to value the non-controlling interest at its proportionate share of the fair value of the subsidiary's identifiable net assets.

Required

Prepare the consolidated statement of cash flows of Swing Co for the year ended 31 December 20X5. No notes are required. **(20 marks)**

CONSOLIDATED STATEMENT OF CASH FLOWS PROFORMA
STATEMENT OF CASH FLOWS FOR THE YEAR ENDED 31 DECEMBER 20X5

	$'000	$'000
Cash flows from operating activities		
Profit before tax		
Adjustments for:		
Depreciation		
Impairment losses		
Increase in trade receivables (W4)		
Increase in inventories (W4)		
Increase in trade payables (W4)		
Cash generated from operations		
Income taxes paid (W3)		
Net cash from operating activities		
Cash flows from investing activities		
Acquisition of subsidiary, net of cash acquired (W5)		
Purchase of property, plant & equipment (W1)		
Net cash used in investing activities		

	$'000	$'000
Cash flows from financing activities		
Proceeds from issue of share capital		
Dividends paid		
Dividends paid to non-controlling interest (W2)		
Net cash used in financing activities		
Net increase in cash and cash equivalents		
Cash and cash equivalents at the beginning of the period		
Cash and cash equivalents at the end of the period		

Workings

1 *Assets*

	Property, plant and equipment $'000	*Goodwill* $'000
b/d		–
OCI (revaluation)		
Depreciation/Impairment		β
Acquisition of sub/associate		
Cash paid/(rec'd) β		–
c/d		

2 *Equity*

	Share capital $'000	*Share premium* $'000	*Retained earnings* $'000	*Non-controlling interest* $'000
b/d				–
P/L				
Acquisition of subsidiary				
Cash (paid)/rec'd β			*	
c/d				

*Dividend paid is given in question but working shown for clarity.

3 *Liabilities*

	Tax payable $'000
b/d	
P/L	
Acquisition of subsidiary	
Cash (paid)/rec'd	β
c/d	

4 *Working capital changes*

	Inventories $'000	*Receivables* $'000	*Payables* $'000
Balance b/d			
Acquisition of subsidiary			
Increase/(decrease) (balancing figure)			
Balance c/d			

5 *Purchase of subsidiary*

	$'000
Cash received on acquisition of subsidiary	
Less cash consideration	
Cash outflow	

Note. Only the **cash** consideration is included in the figure reported in the statement of cash flows. The **shares** issued as part of the consideration are reflected in the share capital working (W2) above.

Goodwill on acquisition (to show no impairment):

	$'000
Consideration	
Non-controlling interest	
Net assets acquired	
Goodwill	

11 Robby 59 mins

Adapted from P2 June 2012

You work in the finance department of Robby, an entity which has two subsidiaries, Hail and Zinc. Robby has recently appointed two new directors, with limited finance experience, to its board. You have received the following email from the finance director.

To: **An accountant**
From: **Finance director**
Subject: **New directors – help required**

Hi, our two new directors are keen to understand the group financial statements. In particular, they want to understand the effect of acquisitions and joint operations on the consolidated accounts.

I am putting together a briefing document for them and would like you to prepare sections for inclusion in the document on goodwill and on joint operations. Please use the acquisitions of Hail and Zinc (**Attachment 1**) to explain the how the goodwill on acquisition of subsidiaries is accounted for in the group financial statements at 31 May 20X3. Use the gas station joint operation (**Attachment 2**) to explain what a joint operation is and how we account for it in the group financial statements. Make sure you explain the financial reporting principles that underlie both of these.

Attachment 1 – details of acquisitions of Hail and Zinc

Accounting policy: measure non-controlling interests at acquisition at fair value.

(1) **Hail acquisition.** On 1 June 20X2, acquisition of 80% of the equity interests of Hail. The purchase consideration comprised cash of $50 million payable on 1 June 20X2 and $24.2 million payable on 31 May 20X4. A further amount is payable on 31 August 20X6 if the cumulative profits of Hail for the four-year period from 1 June 20X2 to 31 May 20X6 exceed $150 million. On 1 June 20X2, the fair value of the contingent consideration was measured at $40 million. On 31 May 20X3, this fair value was remeasured at $42 million.

On the acquisition date, the fair value of the identifiable net assets of Hail was $130 million.

The notes to the financial statements of Hail at acquisition disclosed a contingent liability. On 1 June 20X2, the fair value of this contingent liability was reliably measured at $2 million. The non-controlling interest at fair value was $30 million on 1 June 20X2. An appropriate discount rate to use is 10% per annum.

(2) **Zinc acquisition.** On 1 June 20X0, acquisition of 5% of the ordinary shares of Zinc. Robby had treated this investment at fair value through profit or loss.

On 1 December 20X2, acquisition of a further 55% of the ordinary shares of Zinc, obtaining control.

Consideration:

	Shareholding	*Consideration*
	%	$m
1 June 20X0	5	2
1 December 20X2	55	16
	60	18

At 1 December 20X2, the fair value of the equity interest in Zinc before the business combination was $5 million.

The non-controlling interest at fair value was $9 million on 1 December 20X2.

The fair value of the identifiable net assets at 1 December 20X2 of Zinc was $26 million, and the retained earnings were $15 million. The excess of the fair value of the net assets was due to an increase in the value of property, plant and equipment (PPE), which was provisional pending receipt of the final valuations. These valuations were received on 1 March 20X3 and resulted in an additional increase of $3 million in the fair value of PPE at the date of acquisition. This increase does not affect the fair value of the non-controlling interest at acquisition.

At 31 May 20X2 the carrying amount of the investment in Zinc in Robby's separate financial statements was $3 million.

Attachment 2 – details of joint operation

Joint operation – 40% share of a natural gas station. No separate entity was set up under the joint operation. Assets, liabilities, revenue and costs are apportioned on the basis of shareholding.

(i) The natural gas station cost $15 million to construct, was completed on 1 June 20X2 and is to be dismantled at the end of its life of ten years. The present value of this dismantling cost to the joint operation at 1 June 20X2, using a discount rate of 5%, was $2 million.

(ii) In the year, gas with a direct cost of $16 million was sold for $20 million. Additionally, the joint operation incurred operating costs of $0.5 million during the year.

The revenue and costs are receivable and payable by the other joint operator who settles amounts outstanding with Robby after the year end.

Required

(a) Prepare for inclusion in the briefing note to the new directors:

(i) An explanation, with suitable calculations, of how the goodwill on acquisition of Hail and Zinc should be accounted for in the consolidated financial statements at 31 May 20X3. **(16 marks)**

(ii) An explanation as to the nature of a joint operation and, showing suitable calculations, of how the joint operation should be accounted for in Robby's separate and consolidated statements of financial position at 31 May 20X3. (Ignore retained earnings in your answer.) **(7 marks)**

Note. Marks will be allocated in (a) for a suitable discussion of the principles involved as well as the accounting treatment.

(b) Robby held a portfolio of trade receivables with a carrying amount of $4 million at 31 May 20X3. At that date, the entity entered into a factoring agreement with a bank, whereby it transferred the receivables in exchange for $3.6 million in cash. Robby has agreed to reimburse the bank for any shortfall between the amount collected and $3.6 million. Once the receivables have been collected, any amounts above $3.6 million, less interest on this amount, will be repaid to Robby. The directors of Robby believe that these trade receivables should be derecognised.

Required

Explain the appropriate accounting treatment of this transaction in the financial statements for the year ended 31 May 20X3, and evaluate this treatment in the context of the *Conceptual Framework for Financial Reporting*. **(7 marks)**

(Total = 30 marks)

12 Diamond 59 mins

Adapted from P2 March/June 2017

The following information relates to Diamond, a group listed on a stock exchange, which has a reporting date of 31 March 20X7.

1 On 1 April 20X6, Diamond acquired 70% of the equity interests of Spade and obtained control.

In accounting for the acquisition of Spade, the finance director did not take account of the non-controlling interest, calculating and recording a negative goodwill figure of $460 million on the acquisition, being the purchase consideration of $1,140 million cash less the fair value of the identifiable net assets of Spade at 1 April 20X6 of $1,600 million. However, it is group policy to value non-controlling interests at fair value, which at the date of acquisition was $485 million.

2 On 1 April 20X5, Diamond acquired 40% of the equity interests of Club for cash consideration of $420 million. At this date the carrying amount and fair value of the identifiable net assets of Club was $1,032 million. Diamond correctly treated Club as an associate and equity accounted for Club up to 31 March 20X6. On 1 April 20X6, Diamond took control of Club, acquiring a further 45% interest. On 1 April 20X6, the retained earnings and other components of equity of Club were $293 million and $59 million respectively. The finance director has recorded a negative goodwill figure of $562 million on acquisition, being the cash consideration of $500 million less the fair value of the identifiable net assets of $1,062 million. The share prices of Diamond and Club were $5.00 and $1.60 respectively on 1 April 20X6. The fair value of the original 40% holding and the fair value of the non-controlling interest should both be measured using the market value of the shares. Diamond had 1,650,000 $1 shares in issue and Club had 700,000 $1 shares in issue at 1 April 20X6.

3 Diamond owned a 25% equity interest in Heart for a number of years. Heart had profits for the year ended 31 March 20X7 of $20 million which can be assumed to have accrued evenly. Heart does not have any other comprehensive income. On 30 September 20X6, Diamond sold a 10% equity interest in Heart for cash of $42 million. The finance director of Diamond was unsure how to treat the disposal in the consolidated financial statements. The only accounting undertaken in respect of Heart in the year to 31 March 20X7 was to deduct the proceeds from the carrying amount of the investment at 1 April 20X6 which was $110 million (calculated using the equity accounting method). The fair value of the remaining 15% shareholding was estimated to be $65 million at 30 September 20X6 and $67 million at 31 March 20X7. Diamond no longer exercises significant influence over Heart and has designated the remaining investment as a financial asset at fair value through other comprehensive income.

4 Diamond operates a defined benefit pension scheme. On 31 March 20X7, the company announced that it was to close down a business division and agreed to pay each of its 150 staff a cash payment of $50,000 to compensate them for loss of pension as a result of the closure. It is estimated that the closure will reduce the present value of the pension obligation by $5.8 million. The finance director of Diamond is unsure of how to deal with the settlement and curtailment and has not yet recorded anything within its financial statements.

5 On 1 April 20X6, Diamond acquired a manufacturing unit under an eight-year lease agreement. The lease asset and obligation have been accounted for correctly in the financial statements of Diamond. However, Diamond could not operate from the unit until it had made structural alterations at a cost of $6.6 million. The manufacturing unit was ready for use on 31 March 20X7. The alteration costs of $6.6 million were charged to administration expenses. The lease agreement requires Diamond to restore the unit to its original condition at the end of the lease term. Diamond estimates that this will cost a further $5 million. Market interest rates are currently 6%.

Note. The following discount factors may be relevant:

Years	*6%*
7	0.665
8	0.627

Required

(a) (i) Explain to the finance director of Diamond, with appropriate workings, how goodwill should have been calculated on the acquisitions of Spade and Club. Explain any adjustments needed to correct any errors made by the finance director. **(10 marks)**

(ii) Explain to the finance director of Diamond, with supporting calculations, how to record the disposal of Heart in the consolidated financial statements for the year ended 31 March 20X7. Explain any adjustments needed to correct any errors made by the finance director. **(5 marks)**

(iii) Discuss, with suitable workings, how the settlement and curtailment of Diamond's defined benefit pension scheme should be reflected in the consolidated financial statements for the year ended 31 March 20X7. **(3 marks)**

(iv) Advise the finance director how the manufacturing unit alteration costs should have been dealt with in the consolidated financial statements for the year ended 31 March 20X7. **(3 marks)**

(b) Diamond is looking at ways to improve its liquidity. One option is to sell some of its trade receivables to a debt factor. The directors are considering two possible alternative agreements as described below:

(i) Diamond could sell $40 million receivables to a factor with the factor advancing 80% of the funds in full and final settlement. The factoring is non-recourse except that Diamond would guarantee that it will pay the factor a further 9% of each receivable which is not recovered within six months. Diamond believes that its customers represent a low credit risk and so the probability of default is very low. The fair value of the guarantee is estimated to be $50,000.

(ii) Alternatively, the factor would advance 20% of the $40 million receivables sold. Further amounts will become payable to Diamond as the receivables are collected, but are subject to an imputed interest charge so that Diamond receives progressively less of the remaining balance the longer it takes the factor to recover the funds. The factor has full recourse to Diamond for a six-month period after which Diamond has no further obligations and has no rights to receive any further payments from the factor.

Required

Explain the financial reporting principles involved in debt factoring and advise how each of the above arrangements would impact upon the financial statements of future years.

(9 marks)

(Total = 30 marks)

13 Banana — 59 mins

SBR September 2018 (amended)

Background

Banana is the parent of a listed group of companies which have a year end of 30 June 20X7. Banana has made a number of acquisitions and disposals of investments during the current financial year and the directors require advice as to the correct accounting treatment of these acquisitions and disposals.

The acquisition of Grape

On 1 January 20X7, Banana acquired an 80% equity interest in Grape. The following is a summary of Grape's equity at the acquisition date.

	$m
Equity share capital ($1 each)	20
Retained earnings	42
Other components of equity	8
Total	70

The purchase consideration comprised 10 million of Banana's shares which had a nominal value of $1 each and a market price of $6.80 each. Additionally, cash of $18 million was due to be paid on 1 January 20X9 if the net profit after tax of Grape grew by 5% in each of the two years following acquisition. The present value of the total contingent consideration at 1 January 20X7 was $16 million. It was felt that there was a 25% chance of the profit target being met. At acquisition, the only adjustment required to the identifiable net assets of Grape was for land which had a fair value $5 million higher than its carrying amount. This is not included within the $70 million equity of Grape at 1 January 20X7.

Goodwill for the consolidated financial statements has been incorrectly calculated as follows:

	$m
Share consideration	68
Add NCI at acquisition (20% × $70 million)	14
Less net assets at acquisition	(70)
Goodwill at acquisition	12

The financial director did not take into account the contingent cash since it was not probable that it would be paid. Additionally, he measured the non-controlling interest using the proportional method of net assets despite the group having a published policy to measure non-controlling interest at fair value. The share price of Grape at acquisition was $4.25 and should be used to value the non-controlling interest.

The acquisition and subsequent disposal of Strawberry

Banana had purchased a 40% equity interest in Strawberry for $18 million a number of years ago when the fair value of the identifiable net assets was $44 million. Since acquisition, Banana had the right to appoint one of the five directors on the board of Strawberry. The investment has always been equity accounted for in the consolidated financial statements of Banana. Banana disposed of 75% of its 40% investment on 1 October 20X6 for $19 million when the fair values of the identifiable net assets of Strawberry were $50 million. At that date, Banana lost its right to appoint one director to the board. The fair value of the remaining 10% equity interest was $4.5 million at disposal but only $4 million at 30 June 20X7. Banana has recorded a loss in reserves of $14 million calculated as the difference between the price paid of $18 million and the fair value of $4 million at the reporting date. Banana has stated that they have no intention to sell their remaining shares in Strawberry and wish to classify the remaining 10% interest as fair value through other comprehensive income in accordance with IFRS 9 *Financial Instruments*.

The acquisition of Melon

On 30 June 20X7, Banana acquired all of the shares of Melon, an entity which operates in the biotechnology industry. Melon was only recently formed and its only asset consists of a licence to carry out research activities. Melon has no employees as research activities were outsourced to other companies. The activities are still at a very early stage and it is not clear that any definitive product would result from the activities. A management company provides personnel for Melon to supply supervisory activities and administrative functions. Banana believes that Melon does not constitute a business in accordance with IFRS 3 *Business Combinations* since it does not have employees nor carries out any of its own processes. Banana intends to employ its own staff to operate Melon rather than to continue to use the services of the management company. The directors of Banana therefore believe that Melon should be treated as an asset acquisition.

The acquisition of bonds

On 1 July 20X5, Banana acquired $10 million 5% bonds at par with interest being due at 30 June each year. The bonds are repayable at a substantial premium so that the effective rate of interest was 7%. Banana intended to hold the bonds to collect the contractual cash flows arising from the bonds and measured them at amortised cost.

On 1 July 20X6, Banana sold the bonds to a third party for $8 million. The fair value of the bonds was $10.5 million at that date. Banana has the right to repurchase the bonds on 1 July 20X8 for $8.8 million and it is likely that this option will be exercised. The third party is obliged to return the coupon interest to Banana and to pay additional cash to Banana should bond values rise. Banana will also compensate the third party for any devaluation of the bonds.

Pension advice

Banana intends to divest of part of its business in the next reporting period. If the divestment goes ahead, Banana will also transfer the relevant part of its defined benefit pension fund to the buyer. Banana is unsure how the transfer of part of the pension plan should be accounted for and has asked for your advice. To facilitate their understanding of the accounting treatment, Banana has provided the following estimated figures:

Defined benefit obligation transferred	$5.7 million
Fair value of plan assets transferred	$5.4 million
Cash payment to buyer in respect of the plan	$200,000

Banana is aware that IAS 19 *Employee Benefits* was amended in 2018 and that the amendments related to plan amendments, curtailments and settlements but is unsure how these amendments would impact their financial statements.

Required

(a) Draft an explanatory note to the directors of Banana, discussing the following:

(i) How goodwill should have been calculated on the acquisition of Grape and show the accounting entry which is required to amend the financial director's error **(8 marks)**

(ii) Why equity accounting was the appropriate treatment for Strawberry in the consolidated financial statements up to the date of its disposal showing the carrying amount of the investment in Strawberry just prior to disposal **(4 marks)**

(iii) How the gain or loss on disposal of Strawberry should have been recorded in the consolidated financial statements and how the investment in Strawberry should be accounted for after the part disposal **(4 marks)**

(iv) The impact on the financial statements of the potential transfer of part of the pension plan (using the estimated figures to illustrate your explanation) and advise Banana of any impact of the 2018 amendments to IAS 19 regarding plan amendments, curtailments and settlements **(3 marks)**

Note. Any workings can either be shown in the main body of the explanatory note or in an appendix to the explanatory note.

(b) Discuss whether the directors are correct to treat Melon as a financial asset acquisition. **(4 marks)**

(c) Discuss how the derecognition requirements of IFRS 9 *Financial Instruments* should be applied to the sale of the bond including calculations to show the impact on the consolidated financial statements for the year ended 30 June 20X7. **(7 marks)**

(Total = 30 marks)

14 Hill **68 mins**

SBR Specimen exam 2

Background

Hill is a public limited company which has investments in a number of other entities. All of these entities prepare their financial statements in accordance with International Financial Reporting Standards. Extracts from the draft individual statements of profit or loss for Hill, Chandler and Doyle for the year ended 30 September 20X6 are presented below.

	Hill	*Chandler*	*Doyle*
	$m	$m	$m
Profit/(loss) before taxation	(45)	67	154
Taxation	9	(15)	(31)
Profit/(loss) for the period	(36)	52	123

Acquisition of 80% of Chandler

Hill purchased 80% of the ordinary shares of Chandler on 1 October 20X5. Cash consideration of $150 million has been included when calculating goodwill in the consolidated financial statements. The purchase agreement specified that a further cash payment of $32 million becomes payable on 1 October 20X7 but no entries have been posted in the consolidated financial statements in respect of this. A discount rate of 5% should be used.

In the goodwill calculation, the fair value of Chandler's identifiable net assets was deemed to be $170 million. Of this, $30 million related to Chandler's non-depreciable land. However, on 31 December 20X5, a survey was received which revealed that the fair value of this land was actually only $20 million as at the acquisition date. No adjustments have been made to the goodwill calculation in respect of the results of the survey. The non-controlling interest at acquisition was measured using the proportionate method as $34 million ($170m × 20%).

As at 30 September 20X6, the recoverable amount of Chandler was calculated as $250 million. No impairment has been calculated or accounted for in the consolidated financial statements.

Disposal of 20% holding in Doyle

On 1 October 20X4, Hill purchased 60% of the ordinary shares of Doyle. At this date, the fair value of Doyle's identifiable net assets was $510 million. The non-controlling interest at acquisition was measured at its fair value of $215 million. Goodwill arising on the acquisition of Doyle was $50 million and had not been impaired prior to the disposal date. On 1 April 20X6, Hill disposed of a 20% holding in the shares of Doyle for cash consideration of $140 million. At this date, the net assets of Doyle, excluding goodwill, were carried in the consolidated financial statements at $590 million.

From 1 April 20X6, Hill has the ability to appoint two of the six members of Doyle's board of directors. The fair value of Hill's 40% shareholding was $300 million at that date.

Issue of convertible bond

On 1 October 20X5, Hill issued a convertible bond at par value of $20 million and has recorded it as a non-current liability. The bond is redeemable for cash on 30 September 20X7 at par. Bondholders can instead opt for conversion in the form of a fixed number of shares. Interest on the bond is payable at a rate of 4% a year in arrears. The interest paid in the year has been presented in finance costs. The interest rate on similar debt without a conversion option is 10%.

Discount factors

Year	*Discount rate 5%*	*Discount rate 10%*
1	0.952	0.909
2	0.907	0.826

Required

(a) (i) In respect of the investment in Chandler, explain, with suitable calculations, how goodwill should have been calculated, and show the adjustments which need to be made to the consolidated financial statements for this as well as any implications of the recoverable amount calculated at 30 September 20X6. **(13 marks)**

(ii) Discuss, with suitable calculations, how the investment in Doyle should be dealt with in the consolidated financial statements for the year ended 30 September 20X6.

(7 marks)

(iii) Discuss, with suitable calculations, how the convertible bond should be dealt with in the consolidated financial statements for the year ended 30 September 20X6, showing any adjustments required. **(6 marks)**

(b) Hill has made a loss in the year ended 30 September 20X6, as well as in the previous two financial years.

In the consolidated statement of financial position it has recognised a material deferred tax asset in respect of the carry-forward of unused tax losses. These losses cannot be surrendered to other group companies. On 30 September 20X6, Hill breached a covenant attached to a bank loan which is due for repayment in 20X9. The loan is presented in non-current liabilities on the statement of financial position. The loan agreement terms state that a breach in loan covenants entitles the bank to demand immediate repayment of the loan. Hill and its subsidiaries do not have sufficient liquid assets to repay the loan in full. However, on 1 November 20X6 the bank confirmed that repayment of the loan would not be required until the original due date. Hill has produced a business plan which forecasts significant improvement in its financial situation over the next three years as a result of the launch of new products which are currently being developed.

Required

Discuss the proposed treatment of Hill's deferred tax asset and the financial reporting issues raised by its loan covenant breach. **(9 marks)**

(Total = 35 marks)

15 Angel — 59 mins

Adapted from P2 December 2013

The following draft consolidated financial statements relate to Angel, a public limited company. Angel is a furniture manufacturer which sells its mass-produced goods wholesale to a number of large building contractors with whom it has well established relationships.

Angel's new finance director has explained that he is used to preparing cash flow statements using the direct method and requires some advice on the indirect method as used by his predecessor for the Angel Group.

ANGEL GROUP: EXTRACTS FROM STATEMENT OF FINANCIAL POSITION
AS AT 30 NOVEMBER 20X3

	30 Nov 20X3	*30 Nov 20X2*
	$m	$m
Assets		
Non-current assets		
Property, plant and equipment	475	465
Investment in associate	80	–
Financial assets	215	180
Current assets		
Inventories	155	190
Trade receivables	125	180
Cash and cash equivalents	465	355
	745	725
Current liabilities:		
Trade payables	155	361
Current tax payable	49	138
Total current liabilities	204	499

ANGEL GROUP: EXTRACT FROM STATEMENT OF PROFIT OR LOSS AND OTHER COMPREHENSIVE INCOME FOR THE YEAR ENDED 30 NOVEMBER 20X3

	$m
Revenue	1,238
Cost of sales	(986)
Gross profit	252
Other income	30
Administrative expenses	(45)
Other expenses	(54)
Operating profit	183
Finance costs	(11)
Share of profit of associates	12
Profit before tax	184

The following information relates to the financial statements of the Angel Group:

(i) Angel decided to renovate a building which had a carrying amount of $nil at 1 December 20X2. As a result, $3 million was spent during the year on its renovation. On 30 November 20X3, Angel received a cash grant of $2 million from the government to cover some of the renovation cost and the creation of new jobs which had resulted from the use of the building. The grant related equally to both job creation and renovation. The only elements recorded in the financial statements were a charge to revenue for the renovation of the building and the receipt of the cash grant, which has been credited to additions of property, plant and equipment (PPE).

Angel treats grant income on capital-based projects as deferred income.

(ii) On 1 December 20X2, Angel acquired all of the share capital of Sweety, a manufacturer of bespoke furniture, for cash of $30 million. The fair values of the identifiable assets and liabilities of Sweety at the date of acquisition are set out below. There were no other acquisitions in the period. The fair values in the table below have been reflected in the year end balances of the Angel Group.

	Fair values
	$m
Property, plant and equipment	14
Inventories	6
Trade receivables	3
Cash and cash equivalents	2
Total assets	25
Trade payables	(5)
Net assets at acquisition	20

(iii) Angel's property, plant and equipment (PPE) comprises the following.

	$m
Carrying amount at 1 December 20X2	465
Additions at cost including assets acquired on the purchase of subsidiary	80
Gains on property revaluation	8
Disposals	(49)
Depreciation	(29)
Carrying amount at 30 November 20X3	475

Angel has constructed a machine which is a qualifying asset under IAS 23 *Borrowing Costs* and has paid construction costs of $4 million, which has been charged to other expenses. Angel Group paid $11 million in interest in the year, recorded as a finance cost, which includes $1 million of interest which Angel wishes to capitalise under IAS 23. There was no deferred tax implication regarding this transaction.

The proceeds on disposal of PPE were $63 million. The gain on disposal is included in administrative expenses.

Note. Ignore the effects of any depreciation required on the construction costs.

(iv) Angel purchased a 30% interest in an associate, Digitool, for cash on 1 December 20X2. The associate reported a profit for the year of $40 million and paid a dividend of $10 million out of these profits in the year ended 30 November 20X3.

(v) An impairment test carried out at 30 November 20X3 showed that goodwill and other intangible assets were impaired by $26.5 million and $90 million, respectively. The impairment of goodwill relates to 100% owned subsidiaries.

(vi) The finance costs were all paid in cash in the period.

Required

(a) (i) Explain to the finance director why the building renovation has been incorrectly recorded, setting out the correcting entries. **(4 marks)**

(ii) Explain, showing supporting calculations, the adjustments that need to be made to calculate the correct profit before tax figure for inclusion in a consolidated statement of cash flows for the Angel Group for the year ended 30 November 20X3, prepared using the indirect method. **(4 marks)**

(iii) Prepare the cash generated from operations figure for inclusion in a consolidated statement of cash flows for the Angel Group for the year ended 30 November 20X3, using the indirect method, in accordance with the requirements of IAS 7 *Statement of Cash Flows*. For each line item, explain to the finance director of Angel Group the reason for its inclusion in the reconciliation. **(14 marks)**

(b) The financial statements of Digitool, the associate (note (iv)) that Angel invested in during the year, were presented to the directors at a recent board meeting, along with non-financial disclosures.

Digitool is a data mining and analysis company that earns revenues by providing business insights such as emerging trends and forecasts to other companies. It has a large number of contracts with new customers that it is building relationships with, and it operates from a single data centre employing 100 high-performing people.

Included within Digitool's annual report is information relating to relationships with customers, emissions levels and the company's investment in human capital. Angel does not make similar disclosures. The directors of Angel have asked its finance director to help them manage their expectations in terms of the financial statements of Digitool and to understand why the non-financial disclosures provided might be important to a digital company. As a wholesale manufacturing company, the directors of Angel review its gross profit margin, return on capital employed, inventory holding period and receivables collection period.

Required

(i) Identify the key differences that might be expected between the financial statements of Angel and Digitool with references to the key ratios noted by the directors. You do not need to calculate any ratios. **(5 marks)**

(ii) Discuss why the non-financial disclosures made by Digitool might be important to a digital company. **(3 marks)**

(Total = 30 marks)

16 Moyes — 59 mins

SBR December 2018 (amended)

The following are extracts from the consolidated financial statements of the Moyes group.

GROUP STATEMENT OF PROFIT OR LOSS FOR THE YEAR ENDED 30 SEPTEMBER 20X8

	$m
Revenue	612
Cost of sales	(347)
Gross profit	265
Operating expenses	(123)
Share of profit of associate	67
Profit before tax	209

GROUP STATEMENT OF FINANCIAL POSITION

	30 September 20X8	*30 September 20X7*
	$m	$m
Inventories	126	165
Trade receivables	156	149
Trade payables	215	197

The following information is also relevant to the year ended 30 September 20X8:

Pension scheme

Moyes operates a defined benefit scheme. A service cost component of $24 million has been included within operating expenses. The remeasurement component for the year was a gain of $3 million. Benefits paid out of the scheme were $31 million. Contributions into the scheme by Moyes were $15 million.

Goodwill

Goodwill was reviewed for impairments at the reporting date. Impairments arose of $10 million in the current year.

Property, plant and equipment

Property, plant and equipment (PPE) at 30 September 20X8 included cash additions of $134 million. Depreciation charged during the year was $99 million and an impairment loss of $43 million was recognised. Prior to the impairment, the group had a balance on the revaluation surplus of $50 million of which $20 million related to PPE impaired in the current year.

Inventory

Goods were purchased for Dinar 80 million cash when the exchange rate was $1:Dinar 5. Moyes had not managed to sell the goods at 30 September 20X8 and the net realisable value at that date was estimated to be Dinar 60 million. The exchange rate at this date was $1:Dinar 6. The inventory has been correctly valued at 30 September 20X8 with the loss resulting from both the exchange difference and impairment correctly included within cost of sales.

Changes to group structure

During the year ended 30 September 20X8, Moyes acquired a 60% subsidiary, Davenport, and also sold all of its equity interests in Barham for cash. The consideration for Davenport consisted of a share for share exchange together with some cash payable in two years. 80% of the equity shares of Barham had been acquired several years ago but Moyes had decided to sell as the performance of Barham had been poor for a number of years. Consequently, Barham had a substantial overdraft at the disposal date. Barham was unable to pay any dividends during the financial year but Davenport did pay an interim dividend on 30 September 20X8.

Discontinued operations

The directors of Moyes wish for advice as to whether the disposal of Barham should be treated as a discontinued operation and separately disclosed within the consolidated statement of profit or loss. There are several other subsidiaries which all produce similar products to Barham and operate in a similar geographical area. Additionally, Moyes holds a 52% equity interest in Watson. Watson has previously issued share options to other entities which are exercisable in the year ending 30 September 20X9. It is highly likely that these options would be exercised which would reduce Moyes' interest to 35%. The directors of Moyes require advice as to whether this loss of control would require Watson to be classified as held for sale and reclassified as discontinued.

Required

(a) Draft an explanatory note to the directors of Moyes which should include:

(i) A calculation of cash generated from operations using the indirect method; and

(ii) An explanation of the specific adjustments required to the group profit before tax to calculate the cash generated from operations.

Note. Any workings can either be shown in the main body of the explanatory note or in an appendix to the explanatory note. **(12 marks)**

(b) Explain how the changes to the group structure and dividend would impact upon the consolidated statement of cash flows at 30 September 20X8 for the Moyes group. You should not attempt to alter your answer to Part (a). **(6 marks)**

(c) Advise the directors as to whether Watson should be classified as held for sale and whether both it and Barham should be classified as discontinued operations. **(6 marks)**

(d) Captive is a subsidiary of Moyes. Captive sold goods to Moyes during the year at a 60% mark-up. Similar goods are usually sold to other parties at a mark-up of 20%. The directors of Moyes believe that no ethical issues arise as such transactions will be eliminated within the consolidated financial statements. On 31 October 20X8, Moyes announced its intention to sell its shareholding in Captive to the highest bidder.

Required

Identify the accounting principles which should be considered when accounting for intra-group transactions in the consolidated financial statements and identify any ethical issues which may arise from the scenario. **(6 marks)**

(Total = 30 marks)

17 Weston — 59 mins

Adapted from P2 Mar/Jun 2016

Weston Group, a public limited company, operates a chain of pizza restaurants and has a factory which supplies its restaurants with pizza bases. It has grown by acquiring and rebranding a number of competitor businesses, operating in different regions. The following information relates to the financial statements of the Weston Group.

WESTON GROUP
EXTRACT FROM STATEMENT OF FINANCIAL POSITION AS AT 31 JANUARY

	20X6	*20X5*
	$m	$m
Assets		
Non-current assets		
Other non-current assets	393	432
Investment in associate	102	–
Total non-current assets	495	432
Total current assets	253	312
Total assets	748	744
Equity and liabilities		
Total equity	565	476
Total non-current liabilities	100	135
Total current liabilities	83	133
Total liabilities	183	268
Total equity and liabilities	748	744

WESTON GROUP
EXTRACT FROM STATEMENT OF PROFIT OR LOSS AND OTHER COMPREHENSIVE INCOME
FOR THE YEAR ENDED 31 JANUARY 20X6

	$m
Operating profit	190
Finance costs	(23)
Share of profit of associate	16
Profit before tax	183
Income tax expense	(40)
Profit for the year from continuing operations	143
Discontinued operations	
Loss for the year from discontinued operations (Note (i))	(25)
Profit for the year	118

The following information relates to the financial statements of Weston:

(i) On 31 July 20X5, Weston disposed of its entire 80% equity holding in Northern for cash. The shares had been acquired on 31 July 20X1 for a consideration of $132 million when the fair value of the net assets was $124 million. This included an increase of $16 million in the fair value of land which had a remaining useful life of eight years. Deferred tax at 25% on the fair value adjustment was also correctly provided for in the consolidated accounts and is included within the fair value of net assets. The fair value of the non-controlling interest at acquisition was $28 million. Goodwill, calculated under the full fair value method, was impaired by 75% at 31 January 20X5. There has been no further impairment of Northern in the current year.

The carrying amounts of assets and liabilities in the individual accounts of Northern at disposal are listed below.

	Carrying amount
	$m
Property, plant and equipment	80
Inventory	38
Trade receivables	23
Trade and other payables	(10)
Deferred tax liability	(6)
Bank overdraft	(2)

(ii) The loss for the period from discontinued operations in the consolidated statement of profit or loss and other comprehensive income relates to Northern and can be analysed as follows:

	$m
Profit before tax	6
Income tax expense	(2)
Loss on disposal	(29)
	(25)

The directors have stated that they expect the loss on disposal to be disclosed in the statement of cash flows as a non-cash adjustment to cash generated from operations. They are optimistic that this will display the results of the continuing group in a more positive light, increasing the cash generated from operations.

(iii) Weston purchased a 40% interest in an associate, Southland, for cash on 1 February 20X5. Southland paid a dividend of $10 million in the year ended 31 January 20X6. Weston does not have an interest in any other associates.

(iv) Weston Group prepares its statement of cash flows using the indirect method.

Required

(a) (i) Explain to the directors the effect of the disposal of Northern on the consolidated statement of cash flows for the Weston Group for the year ended 31 January 20X6. You should prepare the relevant extracts and workings to support your explanation. **(16 marks)**

(ii) Explain to the directors the effect of the acquisition of Southland on the consolidated statement of cash flows for the Weston Group for the year ended 31 January 20X6. You should prepare the relevant extracts and workings to support your explanation. **(8 marks)**

Note. Marks will be allocated in (a) for a suitable discussion of the principles involved as well as the accounting treatment.

(b) Weston's directors are planning to dispose of some surplus machinery and small investments (not subsidiaries) that are no longer considered core to the business. They want to include proceeds of the sale of property, plant and equipment and the sale of investments in equity instruments in 'cash generated from operations'. The directors are concerned about the importance of meeting targets in order to ensure job security and feel that this treatment for the proceeds would enhance the 'cash health' of the business.

Required

Discuss the ethical responsibility of Weston's company accountant in ensuring that manipulation of the statement of cash flows, such as that suggested by the directors, does not occur. **(6 marks)**

(Total = 30 marks)

18 Bubble **59 mins**

Adapted from P2 Sep/Dec 2015

The following draft financial statements relate to Bubble Group, a public limited company and two other companies in which it owns investments.

DRAFT STATEMENTS OF FINANCIAL POSITION AS AT 31 OCTOBER 20X5

	Bubble	*Salt*	*Tyslar*
	$m	$m	Dinars m
Assets			
Non-current assets:			
Property, plant and equipment	280	105	390
Investment in Salt	110	–	–
Investment in Tyslar	46	–	–
Financial assets	12	9	98
	448	114	488
Current assets			
Inventories	20	12	16
Trade and other receivables	30	25	36
Cash and cash equivalents	14	11	90
	64	48	142
Total assets	512	162	630

	Bubble	Salt	Tyslar
	$m	$m	Dinars m
Equity			
Ordinary share capital	80	50	210
Retained earnings	230	74	292
Other components of equity	40	12	–
Total equity	350	136	502
Non-current liabilities	95	7	110
Current liabilities	67	19	18
	162	26	128
Total equity and liabilities	512	162	630

The following information is relevant to the Bubble Group.

(a) Bubble acquired 80% of the equity shares of Salt on 1 November 20X3 when Salt's retained earnings were $56 million and other components of equity were $8 million. The fair value of the net assets of Salt were $120 million at the date of acquisition. This does not include a contingent liability which was disclosed in Salt's financial statements as a possible obligation of $5 million. The fair value of the obligation was assessed as $1 million at the date of acquisition and remained unsettled as at 31 October 20X5. Any remaining difference in the fair value of the net assets at acquisition relates to non-depreciable land. The fair value of the non-controlling interest at acquisition was estimated as $25 million. Bubble always adopts the full goodwill method under IFRS 3 *Business Combinations.*

(b) Bubble owns 60% of the equity shares of Tyslar, a company located overseas,which uses the dinar as its functional currency. The shares in Tyslar were acquired on 1 November 20X4 at a cost of 368 million dinars. At the date of acquisition, retained earnings were 258 million dinars and Tyslar had no other components of equity. No fair value adjustments were deemed necessary in relation to the acquisition of Tyslar. The fair value of the non-controlling interest was estimated as 220 million dinars at acquisition. No dividend was paid by Tyslar in the year ended 31 October 20X5.

(c) An impairment review of goodwill was undertaken as at 31 October 20X5. No impairment was necessary in relation to Salt, but the goodwill of Tyslar is to be impaired by 20%. Neither Bubble, Salt nor Tyslar has issued any equity shares since acquisition.

(d) On 1 February 20X5, Bubble gave an interest-free loan to Tyslar for $10 million. Tyslar recorded this correctly in its financial statements using the spot rate of exchange. Tyslar repaid $5 million on 1 July 20X5 when the spot exchange rate was $1 to 10 dinars. Tyslar therefore reduced its non-current liabilities by 50 million dinars. No further entries were made in Tyslar's financial statements. The outstanding balance remains within the financial assets of Bubble and the non-current liabilities of Tyslar.

(e) The following exchange rates are relevant to the preparation of the group financial statements:

	Dinars to $
1 November 20X4	8.0
1 February 20X5	9.0
31 October 20X5	9.5
Average for year to 31 October 20X5	8.5

Required

(a) (i) Explain, with supporting calculations, the entries Tyslar needs to make in its individual financial statements as at 31 October 20X5 in order to correctly reflect the loan from Bubble. **(5 marks)**

(ii) Translate Tyslar's statement of financial position at 31 October 20X5 into dollars for inclusion in the consolidated statement of financial position and explain your calculations to the directors, including how to incorporate the translated figures into Bubble's consolidated financial statements. **(8 marks)**

(iii) Explain, including suitable calculations, and reference to the principles of relevant IFRSs how goodwill should have been calculated on the acquisitions of Salt and Tyslar and subsequently recorded in the consolidated financial statements of Bubble as at 31 October 20X5. **(8 marks)**

(b) The directors of Bubble are not fully aware of the requirements of IAS 21 *The Effects of Changes in Foreign Exchange Rates* in relation to exchange rate differences. They would like advice on how exchange differences should be recorded on both monetary and non-monetary assets in the individual financial statements and how these differ from the requirements for the translation of an overseas entity. The directors also wish to be advised on what would happen to the exchange differences if Bubble were to sell all of its equity shares in Tyslar, and any practical issues which would arise on monitoring exchange differences if the remaining balance on the loan from Bubble to Tyslar was not intended to be repaid.

Required

Provide a brief memo for the directors of Bubble which identifies the correct accounting treatment for the various issues raised. **(9 marks)**

(Total = 30 marks)

19 Elevator — 39 mins

(a) The directors of Elevator, a public limited company, which operates in the UK technology sector, are paid a bonus based on the profit that they achieve in a year. Employees have historically been paid a discretionary bonus based on their individual performance in the year. Elevator's year to date results indicate that it may not achieve the required level of profit to secure a bonus for the directors. Elevator's Chief Executive Officer (CEO) has suggested that one way of managing this is not to pay the employees a bonus in the current year which will keep the wages and salaries expense at a minimum. Elevator reports employee satisfaction scores, staff turnover, gender equality and employee absentee rates as non-financial performance measures in its annual report. The CEO has told the directors in an email that 'no one ever reads the non-financial information anyway' and is therefore not concerned about the impact of his suggestion.

Required

(i) Comment on the ethical consequences of the proposals made by the CEO and the potential implications for the information given in the annual report. **(7 marks)**

(ii) Explain, from the perspective of investors and potential investors, the benefits and potential drawbacks of reporting non-financial performance measures. **(4 marks)**

(b) Immediately prior to the 31 May 20X3 year end, Elevator sold land located adjacent to its UK head offices to a third party at a price of $16 million with an option to purchase the land back on 1 July 20X3 for $16 million plus a premium of 3%. On 31 May 20X3 the market value of the land was $25 million and the carrying amount was $12 million. The cash received from this transaction eliminated Elevator's bank overdraft at 31 May 20X3. As instructed by the CEO of Elevator, the finance director has accounted for the transaction as a sale, and has included a profit on disposal in the statement of profit or loss for the year ended 31 May 20X3.

Required

Discuss the financial reporting and ethical implications of the above scenario. **(7 marks)**

Professional marks will be awarded for the application of ethical principles. **(2 marks)**

(Total = 20 marks)

20 Star **39 mins**

Part (a) adapted from P2 Mar/Jun 2017

(a) Star, a public limited company supplying oil products globally, has debt covenants attached to some of the loan balances included within liabilities on its statement of financial position. The covenants create a legal obligation to repay the debt in full if Star fails to maintain a liquidity ratio and operating profit margin above a specified minimum. The directors are considering entering into a new five-year leasing arrangement but are concerned about the negative impact which any potential lease obligations may have on these covenants. If they proceed, they are proposing to construct the lease agreement in such a way that it is a series of six ten-month leases rather than a single five-year lease in order to utilise the short-term term lease exemption under IFRS 16 *Leases*. It would then account for the leases in accordance with their legal form. The directors believe that this will meet the requirements of the debt covenant, though they are aware that the proposed treatment may be contrary to accounting standards.

Required

Discuss the ethical issues which arise from the proposal by Star. **(6 marks)**

(b) Star is currently suffering a degree of stagnation in its business development. Its domestic and international markets are being maintained but it is not attracting new customers. Its share price has not increased whilst that of its competitors has seen a rise of between 10% and 20%. Additionally, it has recently received a significant amount of adverse publicity because of its poor environmental record and is to be investigated by regulators in several countries. Although Star is a leading supplier of oil products, it has never felt the need to promote socially responsible policies and practices or make positive contributions to society because it has always maintained its market share. It is renowned for poor customer support, bearing little regard for the customs and cultures in the communities where it does business. It had recently made a decision not to pay the amounts owing to certain small and medium entities (SMEs) as the directors feel that SMEs do not have sufficient resources to challenge the non-payment in a court of law. The management of the company is quite authoritarian and tends not to value employees' ideas and contributions.

Required

Discuss the ethical and social responsibilities of Star and whether a change in the ethical and social attitudes of the management could improve business performance. **(9 marks)**

(c) In many organisations, bonus payments related to annual profits form a significant part of the total remuneration of all senior managers, not just the top few managers. The directors of Star feel that the chief internal auditor makes a significant contribution to the company's profitability, and should therefore receive a bonus based on profit.

Required

Advise Star's directors as to whether this is appropriate. **(3 marks)**

Professional marks will be awarded in this question for the application of ethical principles.

(2 marks)

(Total = 20 marks)

21 Farham

39 mins

SBR September 2018

Background

Farham manufactures white goods such as washing machines, tumble dryers and dishwashers. The industry is highly competitive with a large number of products on the market. Brand loyalty is consequently an important feature in the industry. Farham operates a profit-related bonus scheme for its managers based upon the consolidated financial statements but recent results have been poor and bonus targets have rarely been achieved. As a consequence, the company is looking to restructure and sell its 80% owned subsidiary Newall which has been making substantial losses. The current year end is 30 June 20X8.

Factory subsidence

Farham has a production facility which started to show signs of subsidence since January 20X8. It is probable that Farham will have to undertake a major repair sometime during 20X9 to correct the problem. Farham does have an insurance policy but it is unlikely to cover subsidence. The chief operating officer (COO) refuses to disclose the issue at 30 June 20X8 since no repair costs have yet been undertaken although she is aware that this is contrary to international accounting standards. The COO does not think that the subsidence is an indicator of impairment. She argues that no provision for the repair to the factory should be made because there is no legal or constructive obligation to repair the factory.

Farham has a revaluation policy for property, plant and equipment and there is a balance on the revaluation surplus of $10 million in the financial statements for the year ended 30 June 20X8. None of this balance relates to the production facility but the COO is of the opinion that this surplus can be used for any future loss arising from the subsidence of the production facility. **(5 marks)**

Sale of Newall

At 30 June 20X8 Farham had a plan to sell its 80% subsidiary Newall. This plan has been approved by the board and reported in the media. It is expected that Oldcastle, an entity which currently owns the other 20% of Newall, will acquire the 80% equity interest. The sale is expected to be complete by December 20X8. Newall is expected to have substantial trading losses in the period up to the sale. The accountant of Farham wishes to show Newall as held for sale in the consolidated financial statements and to create a restructuring provision to include the expected costs of disposal and future trading losses. The COO does not wish Newall to be disclosed as held for sale nor to provide for the expected losses. The COO is concerned as to how this may affect the sales price and would almost certainly mean bonus targets would not be met. The COO has argued that they have a duty to secure a high sales price to maximise the return for shareholders of Farham. She has also implied that the accountant may lose his job if he were to put such a provision in the financial statements. The expected costs from the sale are as follows:

Future trading losses	$30 million
Various legal costs of sale	$2 million
Redundancy costs for Newall employees	$5 million
Impairment losses on owned assets	$8 million

Included within the future trading losses is an early payment penalty of $6 million for a leased asset which is deemed surplus to requirements. **(6 marks)**

Required

(a) Discuss the accounting treatment which Farham should adopt to address each of the issues above for the consolidated financial statements.

Note. The mark allocation is shown against each of the two issues above.

(b) Discuss the ethical issues arising from the scenario, including any actions which Farham and the accountant should undertake. **(7 marks)**

Professional marks will be awarded in this question for the quality of the discussion. **(2 marks)**

(Total = 20 marks)

22 Ethical issues **39 mins**

Part (a) adapted from P2 June 2014

Part (b) adapted from P2 December 2014

(a) **Columbus**

Columbus plans to update its production process and the directors feel that technology-led production is the only feasible way in which the company can remain competitive. On 1 May 20X3, Columbus entered into a lease for a property and the leasing arrangement was established in order to maximise taxation benefits. However, the financial statements have not shown a lease asset or liability to date.

A new financial controller joined Columbus shortly before the financial year end of 30 April 20X4 and is presently reviewing the financial statements to prepare for the upcoming audit and to begin making a loan application to finance the new technology. The financial controller feels that the lease relating to both the property should be recognised in the statement of financial position, but the managing director, who did a brief accountancy course ten years ago, strongly disagrees. The managing director wishes to charge the rental payments to profit or loss. The managing director feels that the arrangement does not meet the criteria for recognition in the statement of financial position, and has made it clear that showing the lease in the statement of financial position could jeopardise both the company's upcoming loan application and the financial controller's future prospects at Columbus.

Required

Discuss the ethical and accounting issues which face the financial controller in the above situation and advise on the appropriate accounting treatment for the lease. **(9 marks)**

Note. In your answer, assume that IFRS 16 *Leases* is effective.

(b) **Casino**

Casino's directors feel that they need a significant injection of capital in order to modernise plant and equipment as the company has been promised new orders if it can produce goods to an international quality. The bank's current lending policies require borrowers to demonstrate good projected cash flow, as well as a level of profitability which would indicate that repayments would be made. However, the current projected statement of cash flows would not satisfy the bank's criteria for lending. The directors have told the bank that the company is in an excellent financial position, the financial results and cash flow projections will meet the criteria and the chief accountant will forward a report to this effect shortly. The chief accountant has only recently joined Casino and has openly stated that he cannot afford to lose his job because of his financial commitments.

Required

Discuss the potential ethical conflicts which may arise in the above scenario and the ethical principles which would guide how the chief accountant should respond in this situation. **(9 marks)**

Professional marks will be awarded in this question for the application of ethical principles. **(2 marks)**

(Total = 20 marks)

23 Chippin

29 mins

Adapted from P2 December 2010

Chippin, a public limited company, operates in the energy industry and undertakes complex natural gas trading arrangements, which involve exchanges in resources with other companies in the industry. Chippin is entering into a long-term contract for the supply of gas and is raising a loan on the strength of this contract. The proceeds of the loan are to be received over the year to 30 November 20X3 and are to be repaid over four years to 30 November 20X7. Chippin wishes to report the loan proceeds as operating cash inflow because it is related to a long-term purchase contract. The directors of Chippin receive a bonus if the operating cash flow exceeds a predetermined target for the year and feel that the indirect method is more useful and informative to users of financial statements than the direct method.

Required

(a) Comment on the directors' view that the indirect method of preparing statements of cash flows is more useful and informative to users than the direct method. **(7 marks)**

(b) Discuss the reasons why the directors may wish to report the loan proceeds as an operating cash flow rather than a financing cash flow and whether there are any ethical implications of adopting this treatment. **(6 marks)**

Professional marks will be awarded for the application of ethical principles. **(2 marks)**

(Total = 15 marks)

24 Gustoso

29 mins

SBR Specimen exam 2

Gustoso is a public limited company which produces a range of luxury Italian food products which are sold to restaurants, shops and supermarkets. It prepares its financial statements in accordance with International Financial Reporting Standards. The directors of Gustoso receive a cash bonus each year if reported profits for the period exceed a pre-determined target. Gustoso has performed in excess of targets in the year ended 31 December 20X7. Forecasts for 20X8 are, however, pessimistic due to economic uncertainty and stagnant nationwide wage growth.

Provisions

A new accountant has recently started work at Gustoso. She noticed that the provisions balance as at 31 December 20X7 is significantly higher than in the prior year. She made enquiries of the finance director, who explained that the increase was due to substantial changes in food safety and hygiene laws which become effective during 20X8. As a result, Gustoso must retrain a large proportion of its workforce. This retraining has yet to occur, so a provision has been recognised for the estimated cost of $2 million. The finance director then told the accountant that such enquiries were a waste of time and would not be looked at favourably when deciding on her future pay rises and bonuses.

Wheat contract

Gustoso purchases significant quantities of wheat for use in its bread and pasta products. These are high-value products on which Gustoso records significant profit margins. Nonetheless, the price of wheat is volatile and so, on 1 November 20X7, Gustoso entered into a contract with a supplier to purchase 500,000 bushels of wheat in June 20X8 for $5 a bushel. The contract can be settled net in cash. Gustoso has entered into similar contracts in the past and has always taken delivery of the wheat. By 31 December 20X7 the price of wheat had fallen. The finance director recorded a derivative liability of $0.5 million on the statement of financial position and a loss of $0.5 million in the statement of profit or loss. Wheat prices may rise again before June 20X8. The accountant is unsure if the current accounting treatment is correct but feels uncomfortable approaching the finance director again.

Required

Discuss the ethical and accounting implications of the above situations from the perspective of the accountant. **(13 marks)**

Professional marks will be awarded in question 2 for the application of ethical principles.

(2 marks)

(Total = 15 marks)

25 Fiskerton **39 mins**

SBR December 2018

The following is an extract from the statement of financial position of Fiskerton, a public limited entity as at 30 September 20X8.

	$'000
Non-current assets	160,901
Current assets	110,318
Equity share capital ($1 each)	10,000
Other components of equity	20,151
Retained earnings	70,253
Non-current liabilities (bank loan)	50,000
Current liabilities	120,815

The bank loan has a covenant attached whereby it will become immediately repayable should the gearing ratio (long-term debt to equity) of Fiskerton exceed 50%. Fiskerton has a negative cash balance as at 30 September 20X8.

Halam property

Included within the non-current assets of Fiskerton is a property in Halam which has been leased to Edingley under a 40-year lease. The property was acquired for $20 million on 1 October 20X7 and was immediately leased to Edingley.

The asset was expected to have a useful life of 40 years at the date of acquisition and have a minimal residual value. Fiskerton has classified the building as an investment property and has adopted the fair value model.

The property was initially revalued to $22 million on 31 March 20X8. Interim financial statements had indicated that gearing was 51% prior to this revaluation. The managing director was made aware of this breach of covenant and so instructed that the property should be revalued. The property is now carried at a value of $28 million which was determined by the sale of a similar sized property on 30 September 20X8. This property was located in a much more prosperous area and built with a higher grade of material. An independent professional valuer has estimated the value to be no more than $22 million. The managing director has argued that fair values should be referenced to an active market and is refusing to adjust the financial statements, even though he knows it is contrary to international accounting standards.

Sales contract

Fiskerton has entered into a sales contract for the construction of an asset with a customer whereby the customer pays an initial deposit. The deposit is refundable only if Fiskerton fails to complete the construction of the asset. The remainder is payable on delivery of the asset. If the customer defaults on the contract prior to completion, Fiskerton has the right to retain the deposit. The managing director believes that, as completion of the asset is performed over time, revenue should be recognised accordingly. He has persuaded the accountant to include the deposit and a percentage of the remaining balance for construction work in revenue to date.

Required

(a) Discuss how the Halam property should have been accounted for and explain the implications for the financial statements and the debt covenant of Fiskerton. **(7 marks)**

(b) In accordance with IFRS 15 *Revenue from Contracts with Customers*, discuss whether revenue arising from the sales contract should be recognised on a stage of completion basis. **(4 marks)**

(c) Explain any ethical issues which may arise for the managing director and the accountant from each of the scenarios. **(7 marks)**

Professional marks will be awarded in question 2(c) for the quality of the discussion. **(2 marks)**

(Total = 20 marks)

26 Janne — 49 mins

Part (a) adapted from P2 June 2013

Janne is a listed real estate company which specialises mainly in industrial property. Investment properties constitute more than 60% of its total assets.

(a) Janne measures its industrial investment property using the fair value method, which is measured using the 'new-build value less obsolescence'. Valuations are conducted by a member of the board of directors. In order to determine the obsolescence, the board member takes account of the age of the property and the nature of its use. According to the board, this method of calculation is complex but gives a very precise result, which is accepted by the industry. There are sales values for similar properties in similar locations available as well as market rent data per square metre for similar industrial buildings.

Required

(i) Discuss whether the above valuation technique is appropriate, making reference to the principles of relevant IFRSs. **(5 marks)**

(ii) Discuss Janne's selection of fair value as a measurement basis with reference to the *Conceptual Framework for Financial Reporting.* **(4 marks)**

(b) Janne has received criticism that its annual report is too detailed, and therefore it is difficult to understand and analyse. In response to the criticism, the managing director has proposed a reduction in disclosures provided in the annual report. This includes, but is not limited to, reducing the accounting policies note, and removing the related party transactions note, which he does not consider important as all transactions are at arm's length. The managing director has recommended that all disclosures that appear irrelevant should be removed.

The finance director has vigorously defended the annual report, stating that all disclosures made are required by IFRSs, even if some of them appear irrelevant. He has confirmed this by using a 'disclosure checklist' provided by a reputable accountancy firm. He is extremely nervous that the changes proposed risk non-compliance with standards and would not improve the relevance or usefulness of the report for investors.

Required

Discuss the implications of the above in relation to Janne's annual report and its usefulness to investors, with reference to IFRS Practice Statement 2 *Making Materiality Judgements*. **(8 marks)**

(c) The managing director has also proposed to report a new performance measure 'adjusted net asset value per share', which is defined as net assets calculated in accordance with IFRS, adjusted for various items and then divided by the total number of shares. This would be presented instead of earnings per share as the managing director believes it is more relevant to investors. This performance measure is disclosed by several companies in the same industry as Janne.

Required

Discuss the benefits and drawbacks to investors of Janne's plan to disclose 'adjusted net asset value per share' instead of earnings per share. **(8 marks)**

(Total = 25 marks)

27 SunChem 49 mins

P2 September/December 2015 (amended)

(a) SunChem trades in the chemical industry. The entity operates one large development and production facility. It has entered into an agreement with a separate entity, Jomaster, under which SunChem will acquire a licence to use Jomaster's technology to manufacture a chemical compound, Volut. The technology has a fair value of $4 million. SunChem cannot use the technology for manufacturing any other compound than Volut. SunChem has not concluded the amount of economic benefits that are likely to flow from Volut, but will use Jomaster's technology for a period of three years. SunChem will have to keep updating the technology in accordance with Jomaster's requirements. The agreement stipulates that SunChem will make a non-refundable payment of $4 million to Jomaster to acquire the licence to use Jomaster's technology.

SunChem is also interested in another compound, Yacton, which is being developed by Jomaster. The compound is in the second phase of development. The intellectual property of compound Yacton has been transferred to a newly formed shell company, Conew, which has no employees. The compound is the only asset of Conew. SunChem is intending to acquire a 65% interest in Conew, which will give it control over the entity and the compound. SunChem will provide the necessary resources to develop Yacton. **(10 marks)**

Required

Discuss how the above should be dealt with in the financial statements of SunChem under IFRS Standards.

(b) At 30 November 20X6, three people own the shares of SunChem. The finance director owns 60%, and the operations director owns 30%. The third owner is a passive investor who does not help manage the entity. All ordinary shares carry equal voting rights. The husband of the finance director is the sales director of SunChem. Their son is currently undertaking an internship with SunChem and receives a salary of $30,000 per annum, which is normal compensation for the role. Recently, SunChem sold an almost fully depreciated laptop computer to the finance director's son at the going market rate for a laptop of similar make and age.

The finance director and sales director have together set up an investment company, Baleel. They jointly own Baleel and their shares in Baleel will eventually be transferred to their son when he has finished his internship with SunChem.

In addition, on 1 June 20X6 SunChem entered into a five-year maintenance contract with Ocean. Ocean is a new company which is owned and managed by the wife of the operations director. Although the contract with Ocean was more expensive than similar contracts, the board considered that Ocean would provide better service than other companies.

The finance director is of the opinion that none of the above should be disclosed in the financial statements. She believes that it is not relevant to the passive investor, and as she and the operations director are the other two shareholders, they already have all the information they need.

The finance director has heard that that the IASB has issued a new practice statement on materiality. She has not read the practice statement as she doesn't understand what value it can add given that materiality is not a new issue in financial reporting. However, she is concerned that she has missed something mandatory in the practice statement.

Required

(i) Explain to the finance director the reason the IASB has issued IFRS Practice Statement 2 *Making Materiality Judgements*, a brief summary of the key points contained within it and whether it will give rise to any mandatory requirements. **(4 marks)**

(ii) Advise the finance director on the identification of related parties for the year ending 30 November 20X6. You should refer to IFRS Standards where relevant. **(5 marks)**

(iii) Explain to the finance director why the company's passive investor may be interested in related party disclosures and comment on the finance director's opinion that the information should not be disclosed. You should refer to IFRS Practice Statement 2 *Making Materiality Judgements* where relevant. **(6 marks)**

(Total = 25 marks)

28 Egin group 49 mins

Part (b) adapted from ACR June 2006

The International Accounting Standards Board (IASB) issued the revised *Conceptual Framework for Financial Reporting* in March 2018.

Required

(a) Discuss why it is beneficial to develop an agreed conceptual framework and the extent to which an agreed conceptual framework can be used to resolve practical accounting issues. **(10 marks)**

(b) On 1 June 20X5, Egin, a public limited company, was formed out of the reorganisation of a group of companies which undertake transactions with each other at normal market prices. Egin's directors are reluctant to disclose related party information as they feel that such transactions are a normal feature of business and need not be disclosed.

Under the new group structure, Egin owns 80% of Briars, 60% of Doye, and 30% of Eye. Egin has control over Briars and Doye and exercises significant influence over Eye. The directors of Egin are also directors of Briars and Doye but only one director of Egin sits on the management board of Eye. The management board of Eye comprises six directors. Originally the group comprised five companies but the fifth company, Tang, which was a 70% subsidiary of Egin, was sold on 31 January 20X6. There were no transactions between Tang and the Egin Group during the year to 31 May 20X6. 30% of the shares of Egin are owned by another company, Atomic, which exerts significant influence over Egin. The remaining 40% of the shares of Doye are owned by Spade, which exerts significant influence over Doye.

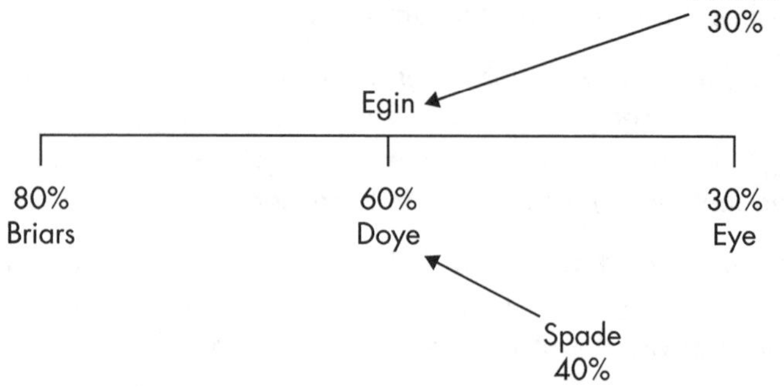

During the current financial year to 31 May 20X6, Doye has sold a significant amount of plant and equipment to Spade at the normal selling price for such items. The directors of Egin have proposed that where related party relationships are determined and sales are at normal selling price, any disclosures will state that prices charged to related parties are made on an arm's length basis.

One of the directors of Briars, who is not on the management board of Egin, owns the whole of the share capital of a company, Blue, that sells goods at market price to Briars. The director is in charge of the production at Briars and also acts as a consultant to the management board of the group.

Required

(i) Discuss why it is important to disclose related party transactions, making reference to the principles in IFRS Practice Statement 2 *Making Materiality Judgements* in your answer. **(6 marks)**

(ii) Describe the nature of any related party relationships and transactions which exist for the Egin Group, commenting on whether transactions should be described as being at 'arm's length'. **(9 marks)**

(Total = 25 marks)

29 Lockfine — 49 mins

P2 June 2011 (amended)

Lockfine, a public limited company, operates in the fishing industry and has recently made the transition to IFRS. Lockfine's reporting date is 30 April 20X9.

(a) In the IFRS opening statement of financial position at 1 May 20X7, Lockfine elected to measure its fishing fleet at fair value and use that fair value as deemed cost in accordance with IFRS 1 *First-Time Adoption of International Financial Reporting Standards*. The fair value was an estimate based on valuations provided by two independent selling agents, both of whom provided a range of values within which the valuation might be considered acceptable. Lockfine calculated fair value at the average of the highest amounts in the two ranges provided. One of the agents' valuations was not supported by any description of the method adopted or the assumptions underlying the calculation. Valuations were principally based on discussions with various potential buyers. Lockfine wished to know the principles behind the use of deemed cost and whether agents' estimates were a reliable form of evidence on which to base the fair value calculation of tangible assets to be then adopted as deemed cost. **(6 marks)**

(b) Lockfine was unsure as to whether it could elect to apply IFRS 3 *Business Combinations* retrospectively to past business combinations on a selective basis, because there was no purchase price allocation available for certain business combinations in its opening IFRS statement of financial position.

As a result of a major business combination, fishing rights of that combination were included as part of goodwill. The rights could not be recognised as a separately identifiable intangible asset at acquisition under the local GAAP because a reliable value was unobtainable for the rights. The fishing rights operated for a specified period of time.

On transition from local GAAP to IFRS, the fishing rights were included in goodwill and not separately identified because they did not meet the qualifying criteria set out in IFRS 1, even though it was known that the fishing rights had a finite life and would be fully impaired or amortised over the period specified by the rights. Lockfine wished to amortise the fishing rights over their useful life and calculate any impairment of goodwill as two separate calculations. **(6 marks)**

(c) Lockfine has internally developed intangible assets comprising the capitalised expenses of the acquisition and production of electronic map data which indicates the main fishing grounds in the world. The intangible assets generate revenue for the company in their use by the fishing fleet and are a material asset in the statement of financial position. Lockfine had constructed a database of the electronic maps. The costs incurred in bringing the information about a certain region of the world to a higher standard of performance are capitalised. The costs related to maintaining the information about a certain region at. that same standard of performance are expensed. Lockfine's accounting policy states that intangible assets are valued at historical cost. The company considers the database to have an indefinite useful life which is reconsidered annually when it is tested for impairment. The reasons supporting the assessment of an indefinite useful life were not disclosed in the financial statements and neither did the company disclose how it satisfied the criteria for recognising an intangible asset arising from development. **(7 marks)**

(d) The Lockfine board has agreed two restructuring projects during the year to 30 April 20X9:

Plan A involves selling 50% of its off-shore fleet in one year's time. Additionally, the plan is to make 40% of its seamen redundant. Lockfine will carry out further analysis before deciding which of its fleets and related employees will be affected. In previous announcements to the public, Lockfine has suggested that it may restructure the off-shore fleet in the future.

Plan B involves the reorganisation of the headquarters in 18 months' time, and includes the redundancy of 20% of the headquarters' workforce. The company has made announcements before the year end but there was a three month consultation period which ended just after the year end, whereby Lockfine was negotiating with employee representatives. Thus individual employees had not been notified by the year end.

Lockfine proposes recognising a provision in respect of Plan A but not Plan B. **(6 marks)**

Required

Discuss the principles and practices to be used by Lockfine in accounting for the above valuation and recognition issues.

Note. The mark allocation is shown against each of the four items above.

(Total = 25 marks)

30 Alexandra **49 mins**

Adapted from P2 June 2012

Alexandra, a public limited company, designs and manages business solutions and infrastructures.

(a) In November 20X0, Alexandra defaulted on an interest payment on an issued bond loan of $100 million repayable in 20X5. The loan agreement stipulates that such default leads to an obligation to repay the whole of the loan immediately, including accrued interest and expenses. The bondholders, however, issued a waiver postponing the interest payment until 31 May 20X1. On 17 May 20X1, Alexandra requested a meeting of the bondholders and agreed a further waiver of the interest payment to 5 July 20X1, when Alexandra was confident it could make the payments. Alexandra classified the loan as long-term debt in its statement of financial position at 30 April 20X1 on the basis that the loan was not in default at the end of the reporting period as the bondholders had issued waivers and had not sought redemption.

Required

(i) Explain, with reference to the principles of relevant IFRSs, the appropriate accounting treatment for the above issue in Alexandra's financial statements for the year ended 30 April 20X1. **(6 marks)**

(ii) Discuss, in respect of the above issue, any ethical implications and any potential impact on the analysis of Alexandra's financial statements by its investors. **(5 marks)**

(b) Alexandra has a two-tier board structure consisting of a management and a supervisory board. Alexandra remunerates its board members as follows:

- Annual base salary
- Variable annual compensation (bonus)
- Share options

In the consolidated financial statements, within the related parties note under IAS 24 *Related Party Disclosures*, Alexandra disclosed the total remuneration paid to directors and a total for each of these boards. No further breakdown of the remuneration was provided.

The management board comprises both the executive and non-executive directors. The remuneration of the non-executive directors, however, was not included in the key management disclosures as the board believed the amounts involved to be immaterial. Some members of the supervisory and management boards are of a particular nationality. Alexandra was of the opinion that in that jurisdiction, it is not acceptable to provide information about remuneration that could be traced back to individuals. Consequently, the finance director of Alexandra explained that the board had instructed her to provide the related party information in the annual report in an ambiguous way to prevent users of the financial statements from tracing remuneration information back to specific individuals.

The finance director believes that the new practice statement on materiality supports the idea that not all the disclosures required in IAS 24 need to be made, and therefore that this treatment is acceptable.

Required

(i) Explain how the transactions above should be dealt with in Alexandra's financial statements, discussing the application of IFRS Practice Statement 2 *Making Materiality Judgements* and the reasons why this treatment is important to investors. **(11 marks)**

(ii) Discuss any ethical issues arising in relation to this scenario. **(3 marks)**

(Total = 25 marks)

31 Verge

49 mins

Parts (a) – (c) adapted from P2 June 2013

(a) Verge entered into a contract with a government body on 1 April 20X1 to undertake maintenance services on a new railway line. The total revenue from the contract is $5 million over a three-year period. The contract states that $1 million will be paid at the commencement of the contract but although invoices will be subsequently sent at the end of each year, the government authority will only settle the subsequent amounts owing when the contract is completed. The invoices sent by Verge to date (including $1 million above) were as follows:

Year ended 31 March 20X2	$2.8 million
Year ended 31 March 20X3	$1.2 million

The balance will be invoiced on 31 March 20X4. Verge has only accounted for the initial payment in the financial statements to 31 March 20X2 as no subsequent amounts are to be paid until 31 March 20X4. The amounts of the invoices reflect the work undertaken in the period. Verge wishes to know how to account for the revenue on the contract in the financial statements to date.

The interest rate that would be used in a separate financing transaction between Verge and the government agency is 6%. This reflects the credit characteristics of the government agency.

(6 marks)

(b) In February 20X2, an inter-city train caused what appeared to be superficial damage to a storage facility of a local company. The directors of the company expressed an intention to sue Verge but in the absence of legal proceedings, Verge had not recognised a provision in its financial statements to 31 March 20X2. In July 20X2, Verge received notification for damages of $1.2 million, which was based upon the estimated cost to repair the building. The local company claimed the building was much more than a storage facility as it was a valuable piece of architecture which had been damaged to a greater extent than was originally thought. The head of legal services advised Verge that the company was clearly negligent but the view obtained from an expert was that the value of the building was $800,000. Verge had an insurance policy that would cover the first $200,000 of such claims. After the financial statements for the year ended 31 March 20X3 were authorised, the case came to court and the judge determined that the storage facility actually was a valuable piece of architecture. The court ruled that Verge was negligent and awarded $300,000 for the damage to the fabric of the facility. **(6 marks)**

(c) Verge was given a building by a private individual in February 20X2. The benefactor included a condition that it must be brought into use as a train museum in the interests of the local community or the asset (or a sum equivalent to the fair value of the asset) must be returned. The fair value of the asset was $1.5 million in February 20X2. Verge took possession of the building in May 20X2. However, it could not utilise the building in accordance with the condition until February 20X3 as the building needed some refurbishment and adaptation and in order to fulfil the condition. Verge spent $1 million on refurbishment and adaptation.

On 1 July 20X2, Verge obtained a cash grant of $250,000 from the government. Part of the grant related to the creation of 20 jobs at the train museum by providing a subsidy of $5,000 per job created. The remainder of the grant related to capital expenditure on the project. At 31 March 20X3, all of the new jobs had been created. **(7 marks)**

Required

Advise Verge on how the above accounting issues should be dealt with in its financial statements for the years ending 31 March 20X2 (where applicable) and 31 March 20X3.

Note. The mark allocation is shown against each of the three issues above.

(d) The finance director at Verge is aware that the IASB has issued an exposure draft relating to accounting policy changes. She hasn't yet looked at the details of the exposure draft but has asked whether this will mean it will be easier to change Verge's accounting policies, particularly those that seem outdated.

Required

Explain the proposals in ED 2018/1 *Accounting Policy Changes* and respond to the director's question regarding Verge's accounting policies, discussing any ethical issues which may arise.

(6 marks)

(Total = 25 marks)

32 Avco 49 mins

Part (a) adapted from P2 June 2014

(a) The directors of Avco, a public limited company, are reviewing the financial statements of two entities which are acquisition targets, Cavor and Lidan. They have asked for clarification on the treatment of the following financial instruments within the financial statements of the entities.

Cavor has two classes of shares: A and B shares. A shares are Cavor's ordinary shares and are correctly classed as equity. B shares are not mandatorily redeemable shares but contain a call option allowing Cavor to repurchase them. Dividends are payable on the B shares if, and only if, dividends have been paid on the A ordinary shares. The terms of the B shares are such that dividends are payable at a rate equal to that of the A ordinary shares.

Lidan has in issue two classes of shares: A shares and B shares. A shares are correctly classified as equity. Two million B shares of nominal value of $1 each are in issue. The B shares are redeemable in two years' time. Lidan has a choice as to the method of redemption of the B shares. It may either redeem the B shares for cash at their nominal value or it may issue one million A shares in settlement. A shares are currently valued at $10 per share. The lowest price for Lidan's A shares since its formation has been $5 per share.

Required

Discuss whether the above arrangements regarding the B shares of each of Cavor and Lidan should be treated as liabilities or equity in the financial statements of the respective issuing companies. Your answer should refer to relevant IFRSs and the *Conceptual Framework*.

(8 marks)

(b) At its recent general meeting, a shareholder asked the board to explain how it decides whether certain financial instruments are classified as equity whereas other seemingly similar financial instruments are classified as debt. The shareholder suggested that the directors do not understand the impact of the classification on investors and their analysis of the financial statements.

Required

(i) Explain the key classification differences between debt and equity under IFRSs.

(8 marks)

(ii) Explain why it is important for entities to understand the impact of the classification of a financial instrument as debt or equity in the financial statements. **(4 marks)**

(c) The finance director of Avco has suggested that it invests in cryptocurrencies as part of its investment strategy. The board understands what cryptocurrencies are, but has asked the finance director to explain how they would be presented in the financial statements. The finance director has stated that they should be accounted for as financial assets but is unsure if this is consistent with IFRSs and the *Conceptual Framework*.

Required

Explain to the directors whether the cryptocurrencies should be accounted for as financial assets with reference to relevant IFRSs and the *Conceptual Framework*.

(5 marks)

(Total = 25 marks)

33 Pensions 49 mins

Part (a) adapted from P2 December 2007

(a) **Joydan**

Joydan, a public limited company, is a leading support services company which focuses on the building industry. The company would like advice on how to treat certain items under IAS 19 *Employee Benefits*. The company operates the Joydan Pension Plan B which commenced on 1 November 20X6 and the Joydan Pension Plan A, which was closed to new entrants from 31 October 20X6, but which was open to future service accrual for the employees already in the scheme. The assets of the schemes are held separately from those of the company in funds under the control of trustees. The following information relates to the two schemes.

Joydan Pension Plan A

The terms of the plan are as follows.

(i) Employees contribute 6% of their salaries to the plan.

(ii) Joydan contributes, currently, the same amount to the plan for the benefit of the employees.

(iii) On retirement, employees are guaranteed a pension which is based upon the number of years' service with the company and their final salary.

The following details relate to the plan in the year to 31 October 20X7:

	$m
Present value of obligation at 1 November 20X6	200
Present value of obligation at 31 October 20X7	240
Fair value of plan assets at 1 November 20X6	190
Fair value of plan assets at 31 October 20X7	225
Current service cost	20
Pension benefits paid	19
Total contributions paid to the scheme for year to 31 October 20X7	17

Remeasurement gains and losses are recognised in accordance with IAS 19.

Assume that contributions are paid into the plan and pension benefits are withdrawn from the plan on 31 October 20X7.

Joydan Pension Plan B

Under the terms of the plan, Joydan does not guarantee any return on the contributions paid into the fund. The company's legal and constructive obligation is limited to the amount that is contributed to the fund. The following details relate to this scheme:

	$m
Fair value of plan assets at 31 October 20X7	21
Contributions paid by company for year to 31 October 20X7	10
Contributions paid by employees for year to 31 October 20X7	10

The interest rate on high quality corporate bonds for the two plans are:

1 November 20X6	*31 October 20X7*
5%	6%

The company would like advice on how to treat the two pension plans, for the year ended 31 October 20X7, together with an explanation of the differences between a defined contribution plan and a defined benefit plan.

Required

Prepare a briefing note for the directors of Joydan which includes:

(i) An explanation of the nature of and differences between a defined contribution plan and a defined benefit plan with specific reference to the company's two schemes. **(8 marks)**

(ii) The accounting treatment for the two Joydan pension plans for the year ended 31 October 20X7 under IAS 19 *Employee Benefits*. **(8 marks)**

(b) **Wallace**

Wallace, a listed entity with a reporting date of 31 October, operates a defined benefit pension plan for its employees. During September 20X7, Wallace decided to relocate a division from one country to another, where labour and raw material costs are cheaper. The relocation is due to take place in May 20X8. On 30 September 20X7, a detailed formal plan for the relocation was approved and the affected employees were informed. Half of the affected division's employees will be made redundant in December 20X7, and will accrue no further benefits under Wallace's defined benefit pension plan. The resulting reduction in the net pension liability due to the relocation is estimated to have a present value of $15 million as at 31 October 20X7.

The directors of Wallace have correctly recognised a restructuring provision relating to the relocation in the financial statements for the year ended 31 October 20X7, but would like advice on how to account for the reduction in the net pension liability.

The directors are aware that the IASB has recently amended IAS 19 but are unsure of the detail of the amendments or whether they will have any effect on Wallace's financial statements for the year ended 31 October 20X7.

Required

Prepare a briefing note for the directors of Wallace which includes:

(i) An explanation of how to account for the reduction in the net pension liability for the year ended 31 October 20X7 in accordance with IAS 19 *Employee Benefits*. **(5 marks)**

(ii) An explanation of the amendments to IAS 19 issued in 2018 (Plan Amendment, Curtailment or Settlement *(Amendments to IAS 19)*) and of any effect of these amendments, giving consideration to materiality, on Wallace's financial statements for the year ended 31 October 20X7. You should assume that the amendments are effective for Wallace for the year ended 31 October 20X7. **(4 marks)**

(Total = 25 marks)

34 Calendar — 49 mins

SBR Specimen exam 2

Calendar has a reporting date of 31 December 20X7. It prepares its financial statements in accordance with International Financial Reporting Standards. Calendar develops biotech products for pharmaceutical companies. These pharmaceutical companies then manufacture and sell the products. Calendar receives stage payments during product development and a share of royalties when the final product is sold to consumers. A new accountant has recently joined Calendar's finance department and has raised a number of queries.

(a) (i) During 20X6 Calendar acquired a development project through a business combination and recognised it as an intangible asset. The commercial director decided that the return made from the completion of this specific development project would be sub-optimal. As such, in October 20X7, the project was sold to a competitor. The gain arising on derecognition of the intangible asset was presented as revenue in the financial statements for the year ended 31 December 20X7 on the grounds that development of new products is one of Calendar's ordinary activities. Calendar has made two similar sales of development projects in the past, but none since 20X0.

The accountant requires advice about whether the accounting treatment of this sale is correct. **(6 marks)**

(ii) While searching for some invoices, the accountant found a contract which Calendar had entered into on 1 January 20X7 with Diary, another entity. The contract allows Calendar to use a specific aircraft owned by Diary for a period of three years. Calendar is required to make annual payments.

On 1 January 20X7, costs were incurred negotiating the contract. The first annual payment was made on 31 December 20X7. Both of these amounts have been expensed to the statement of profit or loss.

There are contractual restrictions concerning where the aircraft can fly. Subject to those restrictions, Calendar determines where and when the aircraft will fly, and the cargo and passengers which will be transported.

Diary is permitted to substitute the aircraft at any time during the three-year period for an alternative model and must replace the aircraft if it is not working. Any substitute aircraft must meet strict interior and exterior specifications outlined in the contract. There are significant costs involved in outfitting an aircraft to meet Calendar's specifications.

The accountant requires advice as to the correct accounting treatment of this contract. **(9 marks)**

Required

Advise the accountant on the matters set out above with reference to International Financial Reporting Standards.

Note. The split of the mark allocation is shown against each of the two issues above.

(b) The new accountant has been reviewing Calendar's financial reporting processes. She has recommended the following:

- All purchases of property, plant and equipment below $500 should be written off to profit or loss. The accountant believes that this will significantly reduce the time and cost involved in maintaining detailed financial records and producing the annual financial statements.
- A checklist should be used when finalising the annual financial statements to ensure that all disclosure notes required by specific IFRSs and IASs are included.

Required

With reference to the concept of materiality, discuss the acceptability of the above two proposals.

Note. Your answer should refer to IFRS Practice Statement 2: *Making Materiality Judgements.* **(10 marks)**

(Total = 25 marks)

35 Lupin 49 mins

Part (a) adapted from ACR December 2005

(a) The directors of Lupin, a public limited company, want advice on how the provision for deferred taxation should be calculated for the year ended 31 October 20X5 in the following situations under IAS 12 *Income Taxes*:

(i) On 1 November 20X3, the company had granted ten million share options worth $40 million subject to a two-year vesting period. Local tax law allows a tax deduction at the exercise date of the intrinsic value of the options. The intrinsic value of the ten million share options at 31 October 20X4 was $16 million and at 31 October 20X5 was $46 million. The increase in the share price in the year to 31 October 20X5 could not be foreseen at 31 October 20X4. The options were exercised at 31 October 20X5. The directors are unsure how to account for deferred taxation on this transaction for the years ended 31 October 20X4 and 31 October 20X5.

(ii) Lupin is leasing plant over a five-year period. A right-of-use asset was recorded at the present value of the lease payments of $12 million at the inception of the lease which was 1 November 20X4. The right-of-use asset is depreciated on a straight-line basis over the five years. The annual lease payments are $3 million payable in arrears on 31 October and the effective interest rate is 8% per annum. The directors have not leased an asset before and are unsure as to the treatment of leases for deferred taxation. The company can claim a tax deduction for the annual lease payments. (You should assume that the IAS 12 recognition exemption for assets and liabilities does not apply in this situation.)

(iii) A wholly owned overseas subsidiary, Dahlia, a limited liability company, sold goods costing $7 million to Lupin on 1 September 20X5, and these goods had not been sold by Lupin before the year end. Lupin had paid $9 million for these goods. The directors do not understand how this transaction should be dealt with in the financial statements of the subsidiary and the group for taxation purposes. Dahlia pays tax locally at 30%.

Assume a tax rate of 30%.

Required

Discuss, with suitable computations, how the situations (i) to (iii) above will impact on the accounting for deferred tax under IAS 12 in the consolidated financial statements of Lupin.

Note. The situations in (i) to (iii) above carry equal marks. **(12 marks)**

(b) At the last annual meeting, one of Lupin's shareholders raised a question regarding deferred tax to the company's executives. The shareholder stated that he did not understand the concept of deferred tax and did not understand why the accounting standards make adjustments for tax that do not reflect the actual amount of tax paid. He questioned the benefit of the tax reconciliation that is included within the disclosure note as it is too complicated to understand.

The finance director has since suggested that the tax reconciliation could be removed on the grounds that it is difficult to prepare and does not serve its purpose if the users cannot understand it anyway.

Required

(i) In response to the shareholder's statement regarding the concept of deferred tax, discuss the conceptual basis for the recognition of deferred taxation using the temporary difference approach to deferred taxation. **(5 marks)**

(ii) Discuss the view of the finance director and the shareholder that the tax reconciliation is difficult to understand and comment on the finance director's suggestion that it should not be disclosed. You should refer to the requirements of IFRS, the *Conceptual Framework* and IFRS Practice Statement 2, *Making Materiality Judgements* where relevant. **(4 marks)**

(c) The finance director would like advice on how the IASB's recent exposure draft on deferred tax will affect Lupin's deferred tax calculation.

Required

Explain to the finance director the main principles contained in ED 2019/5 *Deferred Tax Related to Assets and Liabilities Arising from a Single Transaction* and its potential effect on Lupin's deferred tax calculation.

(4 marks)

(Total = 25 marks)

36 Lizzer — 49 mins

Adapted from P2 June 2013

(a) The directors of Lizzer have decided not to disclose any information concerning the two matters below.

(i) Lizzer is a debt issuer whose business is the securitisation of a portfolio of underlying investments and financing their purchase through the issuing of listed, limited recourse debt. The repayment of the debt is dependent upon the performance of the underlying investments. Debt-holders bear the ultimate risks and rewards of ownership of the underlying investments. Given the debt specific nature of the underlying investments, the risk profile of individual debt may differ.

Lizzer does not consider its debt-holders as being amongst the primary users of its financial statements and, accordingly, does not wish to disclose the debt-holders' exposure to risks in the financial statements (as distinct from the risks faced by the company's shareholders) in accordance with IFRS 7 *Financial Instruments: Disclosures.*

Required

Discuss the reasons why the debt-holders of Lizzer may be interested in its financial statements and advise the directors whether their decision not to disclose the debt-holders' exposure to risks is consistent with the principles of IFRS 7. **(6 marks)**

(ii) At the date of the financial statements, 31 January 20X3, Lizzer's liquidity position was quite poor, such that the directors described it as 'unsatisfactory' in the management report. During the first quarter of 20X3, the situation worsened with the result that Lizzer was in breach of certain loan covenants at 31 March 20X3. The financial statements were authorised for issue at the end of April 20X3. The directors' and auditor's reports both emphasised the considerable risk of not being able to continue as a going concern.

The notes to the financial statements indicated that there was 'ample' compliance with all loan covenants as at the date of the financial statements. No additional information about the loan covenants was included in the financial statements. Lizzer had been close to breaching the loan covenants in respect of free cash flows and equity ratio requirements at 31 January 20X3.

The directors of Lizzer felt that, given the existing information in the financial statements, any further disclosure would be excessive and confusing to users.

Required

Discuss, from the perspective of the investors and potential investors of Lizzer, the decision of the directors not to include further disclosure about the breach of loan covenants. **(6 marks)**

(b) The directors of Lizzer have read various reports about excessive disclosure in annual reports. Some reports suggested that excessive disclosure is burdensome and can overwhelm users. However, other reports argued that there is no such thing as too much 'useful' information for users.

Required

(i) Discuss why it is important to ensure the optimal level of disclosure in annual reports, describing the reasons why users of annual reports may have found disclosure to be excessive in recent years and the actions taken by the IASB to address this issue. **(9 marks)**

(ii) Describe the barriers which may exist to reducing excessive disclosure in annual reports. **(4 marks)**

(Total = 25 marks)

37 Jogger — 49 mins

Part (a) adapted from P2 June 2010

Jogger is a public limited company operating in the retail sector. It has recently appointed a new managing director who is reviewing the draft financial statements for the year ended 30 September 20X9.

(a) The managing director is intrigued by why the annual report and financial statements contains 'more than just numbers' and questions you as to why it is beneficial to Jogger to produce so much information.

Required

Explain the factors which provide encouragement to companies to disclose social and environmental information in their financial statements, briefly discussing whether the content of such disclosure should be at the company's discretion. **(8 marks)**

(b) The managing director is keen to present the financial results from his first period of leadership in the best possible light. He considers EBITDA to be the most important measure of performance and has suggested that the reported profits under IFRS and alternative measures such as EDITBA can be managed to ensure Jogger reports strong performance. He wants to know whether the finance team have taken advantage of all of the options available to enable this and has reminded the financial controller that he will receive a substantial bonus if earnings targets are met.

Required

Discuss, from the perspective of investors and potential investors, the benefits and shortfalls of reporting EBITDA and comment on the nature of, and incentives for, 'management of earnings' and whether such a process can be deemed to be ethically acceptable. **(15 marks)**

Professional marks will be awarded in Part (b) of this question for clarity and quality of discussion. **(2 marks)**

(Total = 25 marks)

38 Moorland **49 mins**

(a) Management commentary is a narrative report that relates to financial statements and is published voluntarily by companies in their annual report.

Required

Describe the principles and objectives of management commentary with reference to IFRS Practice Statement 1 *Management Commentary* and discuss whether the commentary should be made mandatory or whether directors should be free to use their judgement as to what should be included in such a commentary. **(11 marks)**

(b) Moorland is a listed entity with several subsidiaries. Tybull is Moorland's only overseas subsidiary and Moorland has always disclosed Tybull as an operating segment within the consolidated financial statements. The directors of Moorland are considering how the company identifies its operating segments and the rationale for disclosing segmental information. In particular, they are interested in whether it is possible to reclassify their operating segments and whether this may impact on the usefulness of segmental reporting for the business. There have been no internal organisational changes at Moorland for the past five years.

The CEO of Moorland has proposed to report 'underlying earnings per share' in its annual report, calculated by adjusting earnings for various items that are considered to be non-recurring, divided by the weighted average number of ordinary shares outstanding during the period. A similar performance measure is disclosed by several companies in the same industry as Moorland. The CEO believes that presenting underlying earnings per share will aid investors in their analysis of Moorland's performance, and therefore it should be presented prominently. In calculating underlying earnings per share, one item the CEO wishes to exclude from earnings is a large impairment loss relating to the goodwill of a subsidiary. He believes that this cost can be excluded as it is unlikely to reoccur.

Required

(i) Advise the directors as to how operating segments are identified and whether they can be reclassified. Include in your discussion whether Tybull should be treated as a separate segment and how it may impact on the usefulness of the information if its results were not separately disclosed in accordance with IFRS 8 *Operating Segments*. **(8 marks)**

(ii) Discuss the usefulness to investors of Moorland's plan to report underlying earnings per share, and suggest ways in which the directors could improve its usefulness to investors. **(6 marks)**

(Total = 25 marks)

39 Calcula **49 mins**

Calcula is a listed company that operates through several subsidiaries. The company develops specialist software for use by accountancy professionals.

(a) In its annual financial statements for both 20X2 and 20X3, Calcula classified a subsidiary as held for sale and presented it as a discontinued operation. On 1 January 20X2, the shareholders had, at a general meeting of the company, authorised management to sell all of its holding of shares in the subsidiary within the year. In the year to 31 May 20X2, management made the decision public but did not actively try to sell the subsidiary as it was still operational within the group.

Calcula had made certain organisational changes during the year to 31 May 20X3, which resulted in additional activities being transferred to the subsidiary. Also during the year to 31 May 20X3, there had been draft agreements and some correspondence with investment bankers, which showed in principle only that the subsidiary was still for sale.

Required

Discuss whether the classification of the subsidiary as held for sale and its presentation as a discontinued operation is appropriate, making reference to the principles of relevant IFRSs and evaluating the treatment in the context of the *Conceptual Framework for Financial Reporting.*

(9 marks)

(b) Asha Alexander has recently been appointed as the chief executive officer (CEO) of Calcula. During the last three years, there have been significant senior management changes and organisational restructuring which resulted in confusion among shareholders and employees as to the strategic direction of the company. One investor complained that the annual report made it hard to know where the company was headed.

The specialist software market in which Calcula operates is particularly dynamic and fast changing. It is common for competitors to drop out of the market place. The most successful companies have been particularly focused on enhancing their offering to customers through creating innovative products and investing heavily in training and development for their employees.

The last CEO introduced an aggressive cost-cutting programme aimed at improving profitability. At the beginning of the financial year there were redundancies and the employee training and development budget was significantly reduced and has not been reviewed since the change in management.

In response to the confusion surrounding the company's strategic direction, Asha and the board published a new mission, which centres on making Calcula the market leader of specialist accountancy software. In her previous role Asha oversaw the introduction of an integrated approach to reporting performance. This is something she is particularly keen to introduce at Calcula.

During the company's last board meeting, Asha was dismayed by the finance director's reaction when she proposed introducing integrated reporting at Calcula. The finance director made it clear that he was not convinced of the need for such a change, arguing that 'all this talk of integrated reporting in the business press is just a fad, requiring a lot more work, simply to report on things people do not care about. Shareholders are only interested in the bottom line'.

Required

(i) Discuss how integrated reporting may help Calcula to communicate its strategy to investors and other stakeholders, and improve the company's strategic performance. Your answer should briefly discuss the principles of integrated reporting and make reference to the concerns raised by the finance director. **(12 marks)**

(ii) Briefly discuss why the previous CEO's aggressive cost-cutting programme might have led to ethical challenges for Calcula's management team. **(2 marks)**

Professional marks will be awarded in Part (b)(i) for clarity and quality of discussion. **(2 marks)**

(Total = 25 marks)

40 Toobasco 49 mins

SBR September 2018

(a) Toobasco is in the retail industry. In the reporting of financial information, the directors have disclosed several alternative performance measures (APMs), other than those defined or specified under IFRS. The directors have disclosed the following APMs:

(i) 'Operating profit before extraordinary items' is often used as the headline measure of the Group's performance, and is based on operating profit before the impact of extraordinary items. Extraordinary items relate to certain costs or incomes which are excluded by virtue of their size and are deemed to be non-recurring. Toobasco has included restructuring costs and impairment losses in extraordinary items. Both items had appeared at similar amounts in the financial statements of the two previous years and were likely to occur in future years.

(ii) 'Operating free cash flow' is calculated as cash generated from operations less purchase of property, plant and equipment, purchase of own shares, and the purchase of intangible assets. The directors have described this figure as representing the residual cash flow in the business but have given no detail of its calculation. They have emphasised its importance to the success of the business. They have also shown free cash flow per share in bold next to earnings per share in order to emphasise the entity's ability to turn its earnings into cash.

(iii) 'EBITDAR' is defined as earnings before interest, tax, depreciation, amortisation and rent. EBITDAR uses operating profit as the underlying earnings. In an earnings release, just prior to the financial year end, the directors disclosed that EBITDAR had improved by $180 million because of cost savings associated with the acquisition of an entity six months earlier. The directors discussed EBITDAR at length describing it as 'record performance' but did not disclose any comparable information under IFRS and there was no reconciliation to any measure under IFRSs. In previous years, rent had been deducted from the earnings figure to arrive at this APM.

(iv) The directors have not taken any tax effects into account in calculating the remaining APMs.

Required

Advise the directors whether the above APMs would achieve fair presentation in the financial statements. **(10 marks)**

(b) Daveed is a car retailer who leases vehicles to customers under operating leases and often sells the cars to third parties when the lease ends.

Net cash generated from operating activities for the year ended 31 August 20X8 for the Daveed Group is as follows:

Year ended 31 August 20X8	$m
Cash generated from operating activities	345
Income taxes paid	(21)
Pension deficit payments	(33)
Interest paid	(25)
Associate share of profits	12
Net cash generated from operating activities	278

Net cash flows generated from investing activities included interest received of $10 million and net capital expenditure of $46 million excluding the business acquisition at (iii) below.

There were also some errors in the presentation of the statement of cash flows which could have an impact on the calculation of net cash generated from operating activities.

The directors have provided the following information as regards any potential errors:

(i) Cars are treated as property, plant and equipment when held under operating leases and when they become available for sale, they are transferred to inventory at their carrying amount. In its statement of cash flows for the year ended 31 August 20X8, cash flows from investing activities included cash inflows relating to the disposal of cars ($30 million).

(ii) On 1 September 20X7, Daveed purchased a 25% interest in an associate for cash. The associate reported a profit after tax of $16 million and paid a dividend of $4 million out of these profits in the year ended 31 August 20X8. The directors had incorrectly included a figure of $12 million in cash generated from operating activities as the cash generated from the investment in the associate. The associate was correctly recorded at $23 million in the statement of financial position at 31 August 20X8 and profit for the year of $4 million was included in the statement of profit or loss.

(iii) Daveed also acquired a digital mapping business during the year ended 31 August 20X8. The statement of cash flows showed a loss of $28 million in net cash inflow generated from operating activities as the effect of changes in foreign exchange rates arising on the retranslation of this overseas subsidiary. The assets and liabilities of the acquired subsidiary had been correctly included in the calculation of the cash movement during the year.

(iv) During the year to 31 August 20X8, Daveed made exceptional contributions to the pension plan assets of $33 million but the statement of cash flows had not recorded the cash tax benefit of $6 million.

(v) Additionally, Daveed had capitalised the interest paid of $25 million into property, plant and equipment ($18 million) and inventory ($7 million).

(vi) Daveed has defined operating free cash flow as net cash generated by operating activities as adjusted for net capital expenditure, purchase of associate and dividends received, interest received and paid. Any exceptional items should also be excluded from the calculation of free cash flow.

Required

Prepare:

(i) An adjusted statement of net cash generated from operating activities to correct any errors above; **(4 marks)**

(ii) A reconciliation from net cash generated by operating activities to operating free cash flow (as described in note (vi) above); and **(4 marks)**

(iii) An explanation of the adjustments made in parts (i) and (ii) above. **(5 marks)**

Professional marks will be awarded in Part (b) for clarity and quality of discussion.

(2 marks)

(Total = 25 marks)

41 Tufnell **49 mins**

Tufnell, a public limited company, operates in the fashion sector and has undertaken a group re-organisation during the current financial year to 30 September 20X7. As a result, the following events occurred.

(a) (i) Tufnell identified two manufacturing units, North and South, which it had decided to dispose of in a single transaction. These units comprised non-current assets only. One of the units, North, had been impaired prior to 30 September 20X7 and it had been written down to its recoverable amount of $35 million. The criteria in IFRS 5 *Non-current Assets Held for Sale and Discontinued Operations*, for classification as held for sale had been met for North and South at 30 September 20X7. The following information related to the assets of the cash-generating units at 30 September 20X7:

	Depreciated historical cost	*Fair value less costs of disposal and recoverable amount*	*Carrying amount under IFRS 5*
	$m	$m	$m
North	50	35	35
South	70	90	70
	120	125	105

The fair value less costs of disposal had risen at the year end to $40 million for North and $95 million for South. The increase in the fair value less costs of disposal had not been taken into account by Tufnell. **(7 marks)**

(ii) As a consequence of the re-organisation, and a change in government legislation, the tax authorities have allowed a revaluation of the non-current assets of the holding company for tax purposes to market value at 30 September 20X7. There has been no change in the carrying amounts of the non-current assets in the financial statements. The tax base and the carrying amounts after the revaluation are as follows:

	Carrying amount at 30 September 20X7	*Tax base at 30 September 20X7 after revaluation*	*Tax base at 30 September 20X7 before revaluation*
	$m	$m	$m
Property	50	65	48
Vehicles	30	35	28

Other taxable temporary differences amounted to $5 million at 30 September 20X7. Assume income tax is paid at 30%. The deferred tax provision at 30 September 20X7 had been calculated using the tax values before revaluation. **(6 marks)**

(iii) A subsidiary company had purchased computerised equipment for $4 million on 30 September 20X6 to improve the manufacturing process. Whilst re-organising the group, Tufnell had discovered that the manufacturer of the computerised equipment was now selling the same system for $2.5 million. The projected cash flows from the equipment are:

	Cash flows
	$
Year ended 30 September 20X8	1.3
20X9	2.2
20Y0	2.3

The residual value of the equipment is assumed to be zero. The company uses a discount rate of 10%. The directors think that the fair value less costs of disposal of the equipment is $2 million. The directors of Tufnell propose to write down the non-current asset to the new selling price of $2.5 million. The company's policy is to depreciate its computer equipment by 25% per annum on the straight line basis. **(5 marks)**

(iv) The directors are worried about the impact that the above changes will have on the value of its non-current assets and its key performance indicator which is 'Return on Capital Employed' (ROCE). ROCE is defined as net profit before interest and tax divided by share capital, other reserves and retained earnings. The directors have calculated ROCE as $30 million divided by $220 million, ie 13.6% before any adjustments required by the above. **(2 marks)**

Required

Discuss the accounting treatment of the above transactions and the impact that the resulting adjustments to the financial statements would have on ROCE.

Note. Your answer should include appropriate calculations where necessary and a discussion of the accounting principles involved.

(b) The directors are considering alternative methods for measuring the performance of its subsidiaries, including residual income.

Required

Explain what is meant by alternative performance measures and how residual income could be used to measure the relative performance of each subsidiary from the point of view of the shareholders. **(3 marks)**

Professional marks will be awarded in this question for clarity and quality of the discussion.

(2 marks)

(Total = 25 marks)

42 Amster 49 mins

P2 December 2017 (amended)

When an entity issues a financial instrument, it has to determine its classification either as debt or as equity. The result of the classification can have a significant effect on the entity's reported results and financial position. An understanding of what an entity views as capital and its strategy for capital management is important to all companies and not just banks and insurance companies. There is diversity in practice as to what different companies see as capital and how it is managed.

Required

(a) (i) Discuss why the information about the capital of a company is important to investors, setting out the nature of the published information available to investors about a company's capital.

Note. Your answer should briefly set out the nature of financial capital in integrated reports. **(8 marks)**

(ii) Discuss the importance of the classification of equity and liabilities under IFRS and how this classification has an impact on the information disclosed to users in the statement of profit or loss and other comprehensive income and the statement of financial position. **(6 marks)**

(b) Amster has issued two classes of preference shares. The first class was issued at a fair value of $50 million on 30 November 20X7. These shares give the holder the right to a fixed cumulative cash dividend of 8% per annum of the issue price of each preferred share. The company may pay all, part or none of the dividend in respect of each preference share. If the company does not pay the dividend after six months from the due date, then the unpaid amount carries interest at twice the prescribed rate subject to approval of the management committee. The preference shares can be redeemed but only on the approval of the management committee.

The second class of preference shares was issued at a fair value of $25 million and is a non-redeemable preference share. The share has a discretionary annual dividend which is capped at a maximum amount. If the dividend is not paid, then no dividend is payable to the ordinary shareholders. Amster is currently showing both classes of preference shares as liabilities.

On 1 December 20X6, Amster granted 250 cash-settled share awards to each of its 1,500 employees on the condition that the employees remain in its employment for the next three years. Cash is payable at the end of three years based on the share price of the entity's shares on that date. During the year to 30 November 20X7, 65 employees left and, at that date, Amster estimates that an additional 115 employees will leave during the following two years. The share price at 30 November 20X7 is $35 per share and it is anticipated that it will rise to $46 per share by 30 November 20X9. Amster has charged the expense to profit or loss and credited equity with the same amount.

The capitalisation table of Amster is set out below:

Amster Group – capitalisation table

	30 November 20X7
	$m
Long-term liabilities	81
Pension plan deficit	30
Cumulative preference shares	75
Total long-term liabilities	186
Non-controlling interest	10
Shareholders' equity	150
Total group equity	160
Total capitalisation	346

Required

Discuss whether the accounting treatment of the above transactions is acceptable under International Financial Reporting Standards including any adjustment which is required to the capitalisation table and the effect on the gearing and the return on capital employed ratios.

(9 marks)

Professional marks will be awarded in this question for clarity and quality of presentation.

(2 marks)

(Total = 25 marks)

43 Havanna — 49 mins

Adapted from P2 December 2013

Havanna is seeking advice on transactions it has entered into in the year ended 30 November 20X3.

(a) Havanna owns a chain of health clubs and has entered into binding contracts with sports organisations, which earn income over given periods. The services rendered in return for such income include access to Havanna's database of members and admission to health clubs, including the provision of coaching and other benefits. These contracts are for periods of between 9 and 18 months. Havanna's accounting policy for revenue recognition is to recognise the contract income in full at the date when the contract is signed. The rationale is that the contracts are binding and at the point of signing the contract, the customer gains access to Havanna's services. The directors are reluctant to change their accounting policy.

Required

Advise the directors, with reference to the underlying principles of IFRS 15 *Revenue from Contracts with Customers*, how the revenue in relation to the contracts should be recognised. **(5 marks)**

(b) In May 20X3, Havanna decided to sell one of its regional business divisions through a mixed asset and share deal. The decision to sell the division at a price of $40 million was made public in November 20X3 and gained shareholder approval in December 20X3. It was decided that the payment of any agreed sale price could be deferred until 30 November 20X5. It is estimated that the cost of allowing the deferred payment is $0.5 million and that legal and other professional fees associated with the disposal will be around $1 million. The business division was identified correctly as 'held for sale' and was presented as a disposal group in the statement of financial position as at 30 November 20X3. At the initial classification of the division as held for sale, its net carrying amount was $90 million. In writing down the disposal group's carrying amount, Havanna accounted for an impairment loss of $30 million which represented the difference between the carrying amount and value of the assets measured in accordance with applicable IFRS .

Required

Advise the directors how to account for the disposal group in the financial statements for the year ended 30 November 20X3. **(5 marks)**

(c) Havanna has decided to sell its main office building to a third party for $5 million and lease it back on a ten-year lease. The current fair value of the property is $5 million and the carrying amount of the asset is $4.2 million. The present value of the lease payments has been calculated as $3.85 million. The remaining useful life of the building is 15 years. The transaction constitutes a sale in accordance with IFRS 15 *Revenue from Contracts with Customers*.

Havanna's CEO believes this represents a very good deal for Havanna and has told you that the profit on disposal of $0.8 million will help to ensure that the company meets the covenants imposed by the bank in respect of Havanna's interest cover ratio.

Havanna's board of directors would like information about the effect of the introduction of IFRS 16 *Leases*, particularly for its own bank covenants, but also for investors more generally. They have been told that IFRS 16 should be helpful for investors in their analysis of financial statements but are unsure as to why this is the case.

Required

Prepare a briefing note for the directors which:

(i) Discusses the key changes to financial statements which investors will see when companies apply the lessee accounting requirements in IFRS 16 *Leases*. **(6 marks)**

(ii) Explains to the directors how to account for the sale of the main office building at the start of the lease, including any gain on the sale. **(5 marks)**

(iii) Comments on the effect of this transaction Havanna's interest cover ratio. **(2 marks)**

Professional marks will be awarded in part (c) of this question for clarity and quality of presentation. **(2 marks)**

(Total = 25 marks)

44 Operating segments 49 mins

Adapted from P2 December 2011

(a) **Accell**

Accell has three distinct business segments. Management has calculated the net assets, revenue and profit before common costs, which are to be allocated to these segments. However, they are unsure as to how they should allocate certain common costs and whether they can exercise judgement in the allocation process. They wish to allocate head office management expenses; pension expense; the cost of managing properties and interest and related interest-bearing assets. They also are uncertain as to whether the allocation of costs has to conform to the accounting policies used in the financial statements.

Required

Advise the management of Accell on the issues raised in the above paragraph. **(7 marks)**

(b) **Velocity**

For the year ended 31 March 20X3, the directors of Velocity, a public limited company operating in the transport sector, identified the following operating segments.

(i) Segment 1 local train operations
(ii) Segment 2 inter-city train operations
(iii) Segment 3 railway constructions

The finance director has determined that segments 1 and 2 should be aggregated into a single reportable operating segment on the basis of their similar business characteristics, and the nature of their products and services.

The characteristics of each market are as follows:

- Local train market: the local transport authority awards the contract and pays Velocity for its services; contracts are awarded following a competitive tender process; the ticket prices paid by passengers are set by and paid to the transport authority.
- Inter-city train market: ticket prices are set by Velocity and the passengers pay Velocity for the service provided.

The managing director is pleased about this as segment 1 has seen a sharp decline in profits during the year, whereas segment 2 has shown improved margins. The managing director doesn't believe that segment information is relevant to investors, he believes that investors simply provide funds and aren't interested in how management derives a return from them.

Required

(i) Discuss whether it is appropriate to aggregate segments 1 and 2 with reference to IFRS 8 *Operating Segments*. **(4 marks)**

(ii) Discuss, with reference to Velocity, whether the disclosure of segment information is relevant to an investor's appraisal of the financial statements and comment on the managing director's opinion that investors are not interested in how management derives a return from their investment. **(4 marks)**

(c) Segmental information reported externally is more useful if it conforms to information used by management in making decisions. The information can differ from that reported in the financial statements. Although reconciliations are required, these can be complex and difficult for the user to understand. Additionally, there are other standards where subjectivity is involved and often the profit motive determines which accounting practice to follow. The directors have a responsibility to shareholders in disclosing information to enhance corporate value but this may conflict with their corporate social responsibility.

Required

Discuss how the ethics of corporate social responsibility disclosure are difficult to reconcile with shareholder expectations. **(8 marks)**

Professional marks will be awarded in this question. **(2 marks)**

(Total = 25 marks)

45 Skizer **49 mins**

SBR September 2018 (amended)

(a) Skizer is a pharmaceutical company which develops new products with other pharmaceutical companies that have the appropriate production facilities.

Stakes in development projects

When Skizer acquires a stake in a development project, it makes an initial payment to the other pharmaceutical company. It then makes a series of further stage payments until the product development is complete and it has been approved by the authorities. In the financial statements for the year ended 31 August 20X7, Skizer has treated the different stakes in the development projects as separate intangible assets because of the anticipated future economic benefits related to Skizer's ownership of the product rights. However, in the year to 31 August 20X8, the directors of Skizer decided that all such intangible assets were to be expensed as research and development costs as they were unsure as to whether the payments should have been initially recognised as intangible assets. This write off was to be treated as a change in an accounting estimate.

Sale of development project

On 1 September 20X6, Skizer acquired a development project as part of a business combination and correctly recognised the project as an intangible asset. However, in the financial statements to 31 August 20X7, Skizer recognised an impairment loss for the full amount of the intangible asset because of the uncertainties surrounding the completion of the project. During the year ended 31 August 20X8, the directors of Skizer judged that it could not complete the project on its own and could not find a suitable entity to jointly develop it. Thus, Skizer decided to sell the project, including all rights to future development. Skizer succeeded in selling the project and, as the project had a nil carrying value, it treated the sale proceeds as revenue in the financial statements. The directors of Skizer argued that IFRS 15 *Revenue from Contracts with Customers* states that revenue should be recognised when control is passed at a point in time. The directors of Skizer argued that the sale of the rights was part of their business model and that control of the project had passed to the purchaser.

Required

(i) Explain the criteria in the *Conceptual Framework for Financial Reporting* for the recognition of an asset and discuss whether there are inconsistencies with the criteria in IAS 38 *Intangible Assets*. **(6 marks)**

(ii) Discuss the implications for Skizer's financial statements for both the years ended 31 August 20X7 and 20X8 if the recognition criteria in IAS 38 for an intangible asset were met as regards the stakes in the development projects above. Your answer should also briefly consider the implications if the recognition criteria were not met. **(5 marks)**

(iii) Discuss whether the proceeds of the sale of the development project above should be treated as revenue in the financial statements for the year ended 31 August 20X8. **(4 marks)**

(b) External disclosure of information on intangibles is useful only insofar as it is understood and is relevant to investors. It appears that investors are increasingly interested in and understand disclosures relating to intangibles. A concern is that, due to the nature of disclosure requirements of IFRSs, investors may feel that the information disclosed has limited usefulness, thereby making comparisons between companies difficult. Many companies spend a huge amount of capital on intangible investment, which is mainly developed within the company and thus may not be reported. Often, it is not obvious that intangibles can be valued or even separately identified for accounting purposes.

The *Integrated Reporting Framework* may be one way to solve this problem.

Required

(i) Discuss the potential issues which investors may have with:

- Accounting for the different types of intangible asset acquired in a business combination;
- The choice of accounting policy of cost or revaluation models, allowed under IAS 38 *Intangible Assets* for intangible assets; and
- The capitalisation of development expenditure. **(7 marks)**

(ii) Discuss whether integrated reporting can enhance the current reporting requirements for intangible assets. **(3 marks)**

(Total = 25 marks)

46 Cloud **49 mins**

P2 December 2015 (amended)

(a) IAS 1 *Presentation of Financial Statements* defines profit or loss and other comprehensive income. The purpose of the statement of profit or loss and other comprehensive income (OCI) is to show an entity's financial performance in a way which is useful to a wide range of users so that they may attempt to assess the future net cash inflows of an entity. The statement should be classified and aggregated in a manner which makes it understandable and comparable. However, the International Integrated Reporting Council (IIRC) is calling for a shift in thinking more to the long term, to think beyond what can be measured in quantitative terms and to think about how the entity creates value for its owners. Historical financial statements are essential in corporate reporting, particularly for compliance purposes, but it can be argued that they do not provide meaningful information. Preparers of financial statements seem to be unclear about the interaction between profit or loss and OCI especially regarding the notion of reclassification, but are equally uncertain about whether the IIRC's *International Integrated Reporting Framework* (<IR> Framework) constitutes suitable criteria for report preparation.

Required

(i) Describe the current presentation requirements relating to the statement of profit or loss and OCI and discuss the issues surrounding the conceptual basis for the distinction between profit and loss and OCI. Your answer should refer to the requirements of IAS 1 and to the *Conceptual Framework*. **(6 marks)**

(ii) Discuss, with examples, the nature of a reclassification adjustment, any issues surrounding the conceptual basis for reclassification and the arguments for and against allowing reclassification of items from OCI to profit or loss. Your answer should refer to the *Conceptual Framework*. **(5 marks)**

(iii) Discuss the principles and key components of the IIRC's *International Integrated Reporting Framework,* and any concerns which could question the <IR> Framework's suitability for assessing the prospects of an entity. **(8 marks)**

(b) Cloud, a public limited company, regularly purchases steel from a foreign supplier and designates a future purchase of steel as a hedged item in a cash flow hedge. The steel was purchased on 1 May 20X4 and at that date, a cumulative gain on the hedging instrument of $3 million had been credited to other comprehensive income. At the year end of 30 April 20X5, the carrying amount of the steel was $8 million and its net realisable value was $6 million. The steel was finally sold on 3 June 20X5 for $6.2 million. On a separate issue, Cloud purchased an item of property, plant and equipment for $10 million on 1 May 20X3. The asset is depreciated over five years on the straight-line basis with no residual value. At 30 April 20X4, the asset was revalued to $12 million. At 30 April 20X5, the asset's value has fallen to $4 million. The entity makes a transfer from revaluation surplus to retained earnings for excess depreciation, as the asset is used.

Required

Show how the above transactions would be dealt with in the financial statements of Cloud from the date of the purchase of the assets.

Note. Ignore any deferred taxation effects. **(6 marks)**

(Total = 25 marks)

47 Allsop — 49 mins

Part (a) adapted from P2 June 2014 and P2 Sep/Dec 2015

Part (b) adapted from P2 Mar/Jun 2016

Allsop, a public limited company which reports under IFRS, has some overseas operations. Allsop's functional currency is the dollar and it has an accounting year end of 30 November 20X5.

Allsop has a foreign branch which also has the dollar as its functional currency. The foreign branch's taxable profits are determined in dinars. On 1 December 20X4, the foreign branch acquired a property for 6 million dinars. The property had an expected useful life of 12 years with zero residual value. The asset is written off for tax purposes over eight years. The tax rate in Allsop's jurisdiction is 30% and in the foreign branch's jurisdiction is 20%. The foreign branch uses the cost model for valuing its property and measures its tax base at the exchange rate at the reporting date.

EXCHANGE RATES

	$1 = dinars
1 December 20X4	5.0
30 November 20X5	6.0
Average exchange rate for year ended 30 November 20X5	5.6

(8 marks)

Allsop entered into a contract on 1 December 20X4 to construct a machine on a customer's premises for a promised consideration of $1,500,000 with a bonus of $100,000 if the construction is completed within 24 months of the contract commencement. At the inception of the contract, Allsop correctly accounted for the promised bundle of goods and services as a single performance obligation in accordance with IFRS 15. At that date, Allsop expected to incur costs associated with the contract of $800,000 and concluded that it was highly probable that a significant reversal in the amount of cumulative revenue recognised would occur. Completion of the machine was highly susceptible to factors outside of Allsop's influence, mainly issues with the supply of components.

At 30 November 20X5, Allsop had satisfied 65% of its performance obligation on the basis of costs incurred to date and concluded that the variable consideration was still constrained in accordance with IFRS 15. However, on 4 December 20X5, the contract was modified with the result that the fixed consideration and expected costs increased by $110,000 and $60,000 respectively. The time allowed for achieving the bonus was extended by six months. As a result, Allsop concluded it was highly probable the bonus would be achieved and that it would not result in a significant reversal of the revenue recognised. The contract remained a single performance obligation after the modification. **(7 marks)**

Required

(a) Explain to the directors of Allsop:

(i) Why a deferred tax charge relating to the foreign branch's property arises in the group financial statements for the year ended 30 November 20X5 and the impact on the financial statements if the tax base had been translated at the historical rate. Your explanation should include calculations.

(ii) How the contract for the construction of the machine should be accounted for. Your advice should include the accounting treatment up to 4 December 20X5.

Note. The mark allocation is shown against each of the items above.

(b) The directors of Allsop have been reviewing the International Integrated Reporting Council's *Framework for Integrated Reporting*. The directors believe that IFRS are already extensive and provide stakeholders with a comprehensive understanding of an entity's financial position and performance for the year. In particular, statements of cash flows enable stakeholders to assess the liquidity, solvency and financial adaptability of a business. They are concerned that any additional disclosures could be excessive and obscure the most useful information within the financial statements. They are therefore unsure as to the rationale for the implementation of a separate, or combined, integrated report.

Required

Discuss the extent to which statements of cash flows provide stakeholders with useful information about an entity and whether this information would be improved by the entity introducing an Integrated Report. **(8 marks)**

Professional marks will be awarded in part (b) for the quality of the discussion.

(2 marks)

(Total = 25 marks)

48 Kiki — 49 mins

SBR Specimen exam 2

(a) Kiki is a public limited entity. It designs and manufactures children's toys. It has a reporting date of 31 December 20X7 and prepares its financial statements in accordance with International Financial Reporting Standards. The directors require advice about the following situations.

(i) Kiki sells $50 gift cards. These can be used when purchasing any of Kiki's products through its website. The gift cards expire after 12 months. Based on significant past experience, Kiki estimates that its customers will redeem 70% of the value of the gift card and that 30% of the value will expire unused. Kiki has no requirement to remit any unused funds to the customer when the gift card expires unused. The directors are unsure about how the gift cards should be accounted for. **(6 marks)**

(ii) Kiki's best-selling range of toys is called Scarimon. In 20X6 Colour, another listed company, entered into a contract with Kiki for the rights to use Scarimon characters and imagery in a monthly comic book. The contract terms state that Colour must pay Kiki a royalty fee for every issue of the comic book which is sold. Before signing the contract, Kiki determined that Colour had a strong credit rating. Throughout 20X6, Colour provided Kiki with monthly sales figures and paid all amounts due in the agreed-upon period. At the beginning of 20X7, Colour experienced cash flow problems. These were expected to be short term. Colour made nominal payments to Kiki in relation to comic sales for the first half of the year. At the beginning of July 20X7, Colour lost access to credit facilities and several major customers. Colour continued to sell Scarimon comics online and through specialist retailers but made no further payments to Kiki.

The directors are unsure how to deal with the above issues in the financial statements for the year ended 31 December 20X7. **(6 marks)**

Required

Advise the accountant on the matters set out above with reference to International Financial Reporting Standards.

Note. The split of the mark allocation is shown against each of the two issues above.

(b) As a result of rising property prices, Kiki purchased five buildings during the current period in order to benefit from further capital appreciation. Kiki has never owned an investment property before. In accordance with IAS 40 *Investment Property*, the directors are aware that they can measure the buildings using either the fair value model or the cost model. However, they are concerned about the impact that this choice will have on the analysis of Kiki's financial performance, position and cash flows by current and potential investors.

Required

Discuss the potential impact which this choice in accounting policy will have on investors' analysis of Kiki's financial statements. Your answer should refer to key financial performance ratios. **(11 marks)**

Professional marks will be awarded in Part (b) for clarity and quality of presentation.

(2 marks)

(Total = 25 marks)

49 Holls — 49 mins

SBR December 2018

(a) IFRS Practice Statement 1 *Management Commentary* provides a broad, non-binding framework for the presentation of management commentary which relates to financial statements which have been prepared in accordance with IFRSs. The management commentary is within the scope of the *Conceptual Framework* and, therefore, the qualitative characteristics will be applied to both the financial statements and the management commentary.

Required

(i) Discuss briefly the arguments for and against issuing IFRS Practice Statement 1 *Management Commentary* as a non-binding framework or as an IFRS.

(4 marks)

(ii) Discuss how the qualitative characteristics of understandability, relevance and comparability should be applied to the preparation of the management commentary. **(5 marks)**

(b) Holls Group is preparing its financial statements for the year ended 30 November 20X7. The directors of Holls have been asked by an investor to explain the accounting for taxation in the financial statements.

The Group operates in several tax jurisdictions and is subject to annual tax audits which can result in amendments to the amount of tax to be paid.

The profit from continuing operations was $300 million in the year to 30 November 20X7 and the reported tax charge was $87 million. The investor was confused as to why the tax charge was not the tax rate multiplied by the profit from continuing operations. The directors have prepared a reconciliation of the notional tax charge on profits as compared with the actual tax charge for the period.

	$m
Profit from continuing operations before taxation	300
Notional charge at local corporation tax rate of 22%	66
Differences in overseas tax rates	10
Tax relating to non-taxable gains on disposals of businesses	(12)
Tax relating to the impairment of brands	9
Other tax adjustments	14
Tax charge for the year	87

The amount of income taxes paid as shown in the statement of cash flows is $95 million but there is no current explanation of the tax effects of the above items in the financial statements.

The tax rate applicable to Holls for the year ended 30 November 20X7 is 22%. There is a proposal in the local tax legislation that a new tax rate of 25% will apply from 1 January 20X8. In the country where Holls is domiciled, tax laws and rate changes are enacted when the government approves the legislation. The government approved the legislation on 12 November 20X7. The current weighted average tax rate for the Group is 27%. Holls does not currently disclose its opinion of how the tax rate may alter in the future but the government is likely to change with the result that a new government will almost certainly increase the corporate tax rate.

At 30 November 20X7, Holls has deductible temporary differences of $4.5 million which are expected to reverse in the next year. In addition, Holls also has taxable temporary differences of $5 million which relate to the same taxable company and the tax authority. Holls expects $3 million of those taxable temporary differences to reverse in 20X8 and the remaining $2 million to reverse in 20X9. Prior to the current year, Holls had made significant losses.

Required

With reference to the above information, explain to the investor the nature of accounting for taxation in financial statements.

Note. Your answer should explain the tax reconciliation, discuss the implications of current and future tax rates, and provide an explanation of accounting for deferred taxation in accordance with relevant IFRSs. **(14 marks)**

Professional marks will be awarded in part (b) for clarity and quality of discussion. **(2 marks)**

(Total = 25 marks)

50 Kayte — 49 mins

Part (a) SBR December 2018 (amended)

Part (b) adapted from P2 December 2014

(a) The 2010 *Conceptual Framework for Financial Reporting* included a probability criterion which specified that in order for an asset or liability to qualify for recognition, it must be probable that any future economic benefit associated with an asset or liability will flow to or from an entity.

Some current accounting standards, which were developed under the 2010 *Conceptual Framework*, have been criticised for not necessarily applying the probability criterion relating to future economic benefits on a consistent basis.

The IASB issued a significantly revised *Conceptual Framework* in 2018. The recognition criteria in the 2018 *Conceptual Framework* no longer include a probability criterion.

Required

Explain how the probability criterion in the 2010 *Conceptual Framework* has not been applied consistently across accounting standards, illustrating your answer with reference to any inconsistencies with the measurement of assets held for sale, provisions and contingent consideration, and discuss how the revised 2018 *Conceptual Framework* may address this issue. **(6 marks)**

(b) (i) Kayte has a year end of 31 May. It operates in the shipping industry and owns vessels for transportation. Kayte's vessels constitute a material part of its total assets. The economic life of the vessels is estimated to be 30 years, but the useful life of some of the vessels is only 10 years because Kayte's policy is to sell these vessels when they are 10 years old. Kayte estimated the residual value of these vessels at sale to be half of acquisition cost and this value was assumed to be constant during their useful life. Kayte argued that the estimates of residual value used were conservative in view of an immature market with a high degree of uncertainty and presented documentation which indicated some vessels were being sold for a price considerably above carrying amount. Broker valuations of the residual value were considerably higher than those used by Kayte. Kayte argued against broker valuations on the grounds that it would result in greater volatility in reporting.

Kayte keeps some of the vessels for the whole 30 years and these vessels are required to undergo an engine overhaul in dry dock every 10 years to restore their service potential, hence the reason why some of the vessels are sold. The residual value of the vessels kept for 30 years is based upon the steel value of the vessel at the end of its economic life. At the time of purchase, the service potential which will be required to be restored by the engine overhaul is measured based on the cost as if it had been performed at the time of the purchase of the vessel. Normally, engines last for the 30-year total life if overhauled every 10 years. Additionally, one type of vessel was having its funnels replaced after 15 years, but the funnels had not been depreciated separately. **(12 marks)**

(ii) On 1 June 20X1, Kayte acquired a property for $5 million and annual depreciation of $500,000 is charged on the straight-line basis with no residual value. At 31 May 20X3, when accumulated depreciation was $1 million, an impairment loss of $350,000 was recognised, which resulted in the property being valued at its estimated value in use. On 1 October 20X3, as a consequence of a proposed move to new premises, the property was classified as held for sale. At the time of classification as held for sale, the fair value less costs to sell was $3.4 million. At the date of the published interim financial statements, 30 November 20X3, the property market had improved and the fair value less costs to sell was reassessed at $3.52 million and at the year end on 31 May 20X4 it had improved even further, so that the fair value less costs to sell was $3.95 million. The property was sold on 5 June 20X4 for $4 million. **(7 marks)**

Required

Discuss the accounting treatment of the above transactions in the financial statements of Kayte.

Note. The mark allocation is shown against each of the issues above.

(Total = 25 marks)

51 Fill **49 mins**

SBR December 2018

(a) Fill is a coal mining company that sells its coal on the spot and futures markets. On the spot market, the commodity is traded for immediate delivery and, on the forward market, the commodity is traded for future delivery. The inventory is divided into different grades of coal. One of the categories included in inventories at 30 November 20X6 is coal with a low carbon content that is of a low quality. Fill will not process this low quality coal until all of the other coal has been extracted from the mine, which is likely to be in three years' time. Based on market information, Fill has calculated that the three-year forecast price of coal will be 20% lower than the current spot price.

The directors of Fill would like advice on two matters:

(i) Whether the *Conceptual Framework* affects the valuation of inventories

(ii) How to calculate the net realisable value of the coal inventory, including the low quality coal **(7 marks)**

(b) At 30 November 20X6, the directors of Fill estimate that a piece of mining equipment needs to be reconditioned every two years. They estimate that these costs will amount to $2 million for parts and $1 million for the labour cost of their own employees. The directors are proposing to create a provision for the next reconditioning which is due in two years' time in 20X8, along with essential maintenance costs. There is no legal obligation to maintain the mining equipment.

As explained above, it is expected that there will be future reductions in the selling prices of coal which will affect the forward contracts being signed over the next two years by Fill.

The directors of Fill require advice on how to treat the reconditioning costs and whether the decline in the price of coal is an impairment indicator. **(8 marks)**

(c) Fill also jointly controls coal mines with other entities. The Theta mine is owned by four participants. Fill owns 28%, and the other three participants each own 24% of the mine. The operating agreement requires any major decisions to be approved by parties representing 72% of the interest in the mine. Fill is considering purchasing one of the participant's interests of 24%.

The directors of Fill wish advice on whether the revised *Conceptual Framework* will affect the decision as to whether Fill controls the mine.

The directors are also wondering whether the acquisition of the interest would be considered a business combination under IFRSs. **(10 marks)**

Required

Advise the directors of Fill on how the above transactions should be dealt with in its financial statements with reference to relevant IFRSs and the *Conceptual Framework* where indicated.

Note. The split of the mark allocation is shown against each of the three issues above.

(Total = 25 marks)

52 Zedtech **49 mins**

SBR Mar/Jun 2019 (amended)

(a) In the revised 2018 *Conceptual Framework for Financial Reporting* (the *Conceptual Framework*), the accounting model is built on the definitions and principles for the recognition of assets and liabilities.

The 2010 *Conceptual Framework* specified three recognition criteria which apply to all assets and liabilities:

(a) the item meets the definition of an asset or a liability;

(b) it is probable that any future economic benefit associated with the asset or liability will flow to or from the entity; and

(c) the asset or liability has a cost or value which can be measured reliably.

However, these definitions were not always consistently applied by the standard setters. The result is that many existing IFRS are inconsistent with the 2010 *Conceptual Framework*.

Required

(i) Discuss and contrast the criteria for the recognition of assets and liabilities as set out in the 2018 *Conceptual Framework* and its predecessor, the 2010 *Conceptual Framework* (given above). **(7 marks)**

(ii) Discuss how the recognition of assets and liabilities under IAS 12 *Income Taxes* and IAS 37 *Provisions, Contingent Liabilities and Contingent Assets* are both inconsistent with the definitions in the 2010 *Conceptual Framework* and how certain items recognised in a business combination may not be recognised in the individual financial statements of the group companies. **(6 marks)**

(b) Zedtech is a software development company which provides data hosting and other professional services. As part of these services, Zedtech also securely hosts a range of inventory management software online which allows businesses to manage inventory from anywhere in the world. It also sells hardware in certain circumstances.

Zedtech sells two distinct software packages. The first package, named 0inventory, gives the customer the option to buy the hardware, professional services and hosting services as separate and distinct contracts. Each element of the package can be purchased without affecting the performance of any other element. Zedtech regularly sells each service separately and generally does not integrate the goods and services into a single contract.

With the second package, InventoryX, the hardware is always sold along with the professional and hosting services and the customer cannot use the hardware on its own. The hardware is integral to the delivery of the hosted software. Zedtech delivers the hardware first, followed by professional services and finally, the hosting services. However, the professional services can be sold on a stand-alone basis as this is a distinct service which Zedtech can offer any customer.

Zedtech has decided to sell its services in a new region of the world which is suffering an economic downturn. The entity expects the economy to recover and feels that there is scope for significant growth in future years. Zedtech has entered into an arrangement with a customer in this region for promised consideration of $3 million. At contract inception, Zedtech feels that it may not be able to collect the full amount from the customer and estimates that it may collect 80% of the consideration.

Required

(i) Discuss the principles in IFRS 15 *Revenue from Contracts with Customers* which should be used by Zedtech to determine the recognition of the above contracts. **(5 marks)**

(ii) Discuss how the above contracts should be recognised in the financial statements of Zedtech under IFRS 15. **(7 marks)**

(Total = 25 marks)

53 Royan **49 mins**

(a) Explain the guidance in IAS 37 *Provisions, Contingent Liabilities and Contingent Assets* as regards the recognition and measurement of provisions and discuss any shortcomings of the Standard and any inconsistencies with the *Conceptual Framework* **(12 marks)**

(b) Royan, a public limited company, extracts oil and has a present obligation to dismantle an oil platform at the end of the platform's life, which is ten years. Royan cannot cancel this obligation or transfer it. Royan intends to carry out the dismantling work itself and estimates the cost of the work to be $150 million in ten years' time. The present value of the work is $105 million.

A market exists for the dismantling of an oil platform and Royan could hire a third-party contractor to carry out the work. The entity feels that if no risk or probability adjustment were needed then the cost of the external contractor would be $180 million in ten years' time. The present value of this cost is $129 million. If risk and probability are taken into account, then there is a probability of 40% that the present value will be $129 million and 60% probability that it would be $140 million, and there is a risk that the costs may increase by $5 million.

The directors of Royan are aware of the requirements of IAS 37. However, they propose that the costs to dismantle the oil platform described above are expensed as incurred, at the end of the platform's life, with no entries or disclosures being made in the latest financial statements. They argue that application of IFRS involves judgement, and although prudence is mentioned in the *Conceptual Framework*, it is only one among several ways of achieving faithful representation.

Required

(i) Describe the accounting treatment in respect of the oil platform under IAS 37. **(3 marks)**

(ii) Discuss whether the directors are acting unethically in the above circumstance and what the group accountant's proposed course of action should be. **(5 marks)**

(c) Royan acquired another entity, Chrissy, on 1 May 20X3. At the time of the acquisition, Chrissy was being sued due to an alleged mis-selling case potentially implicating the entity. The claimants are suing for damages of $10 million. Royan estimates that the fair value of any contingent liability is $4 million but feels that it is more likely than not that no payment will be required.

Royan wishes to know how to account for this potential liability in Chrissy's entity financial statements and whether the treatment would be the same in the consolidated financial statements. **(5 marks)**

(Total = 25 marks)

54 Formatt — 49 mins

Part (a) adapted from P2 Sep/Dec 2017

Part (b) adapted from P2 December 2009

(a) On 30 November 20X4, Formatt loaned $8 million to a third party at an agreed interest rate. At the same time, it sold the third-party loan to Window whereby, in exchange for an immediate cash payment of $7 million, Formatt agreed to pay to Window the first $7 million plus interest collected from the third party loan. Formatt retained the right to $1 million plus interest. The 12-month expected credit losses are $300,000 and Formatt has agreed to suffer all credit losses. A receivable of $1 million has been recognised in the financial statements at 30 November 20X4. As a result of the agreement with Window, the directors of Formatt are unsure as to whether they should recognise any part of the interest-bearing loan of $8 million in the statement of financial position at 30 November 20X4. They understand that the *Conceptual Framework* mentions 'control' as part of the definition of an asset but do not understand the interaction between the *Conceptual Framework* and IFRS 9 *Financial Instruments* as regards the recognition of a financial asset.

Required

Advise the directors of Formatt on how the above arrangement should be dealt with in its financial statements with reference to relevant IFRSs and the *Conceptual Framework* (2018).

(8 marks)

(b) Formatt has a subsidiary, Key, which has a significant amount of non-current assets. There are specific assets on which the directors of Key wish to seek advice.

(i) Key holds non-current assets which cost $3 million on 1 June 20X3 and are depreciated on the straight-line basis over their useful life of five years. An impairment review was carried out on 31 May 20X4 and the projected cash flows relating to these assets were as follows:

Year to	*31 May 20X5*	*31 May 20X6*	*31 May 20X7*	*31 May 20X8*
Cash flows ($'000)	280	450	500	550

The company used a discount rate of 5%. At 30 November 20X4, the directors used the same cash flow projections and noticed that the resultant value in use was above the carrying amount of the assets and wished to reverse any impairment loss calculated at 31 May 20X4. The government has indicated that it may compensate the company for any loss in value of the assets up to 20% of the impairment loss.

(ii) Key holds a non-current asset, which was purchased for $10 million on 1 December 20X1 with an expected useful life of ten years. On 1 December 20X3, it was revalued to $8.8 million. At 30 November 20X4, the asset was reviewed for impairment and written down to its recoverable amount of $5.5 million.

(iii) Key committed itself at the beginning of the financial year to selling a property that is being under-utilised following the economic downturn. As a result of the economic downturn, the property was not sold by the end of the year. The asset was actively marketed but there were no reasonable offers to purchase the asset. Key is hoping that the economic downturn will change in the future and therefore has not reduced the price of the asset.

Required

Discuss, with suitable computations and reference to the principles of relevant IFRSs, how to account for any potential impairment of the above non-current assets in Key's individual financial statements for the year ended 30 November 20X4.

(17 marks)

Note. The following 5% discount factors may be relevant.

Year 1	0.9524
Year 2	0.9070
Year 3	0.8638
Year 4	0.8227

(Total = 25 marks)

55 Emcee 49 mins

P2 Mar/Jun 2016 (amended)

Emcee, a public limited company, is a sports organisation which owns several football and basketball teams. It has a financial year end of 31 May 20X6.

(a) Emcee needs a new stadium to host sporting events which will be included as part of Emcee's property, plant and equipment. Emcee commenced construction of a new stadium on 1 February 20X6, and this continued until its completion which was after the year end of 31 May 20X6. The direct costs were $20 million in February 20X6 and then $50 million in each month until the year end. Emcee has not taken out any specific borrowings to finance the construction of the stadium, but it has incurred finance costs on its general borrowings during the period, which could have been avoided if the stadium had not been constructed. Emcee has calculated that the weighted average cost of borrowings for the period 1 February to 31 May 20X6 on an annualised basis amounted to 9% per annum. Emcee needs advice on how to treat the borrowing costs in its financial statements for the year ended 31 May 20X6. **(6 marks)**

(b) Emcee purchases and sells players' registrations on a regular basis. Emcee must purchase registrations for that player to play for the club. Player registrations are contractual obligations between the player and Emcee. The costs of acquiring player registrations include transfer fees, league levy fees, and player agents' fees incurred by the club. Often players' former clubs are paid amounts which are contingent upon the performance of the player whilst they play for Emcee. For example, if a contracted basketball player scores an average of more than 20 points per game in a season, then an additional $5 million may become payable to his former club. Also, players' contracts can be extended and this incurs additional costs for Emcee.

At the end of every season, which also is the financial year end of Emcee, the club reviews its playing staff and makes decisions as to whether they wish to sell any players' registrations. These registrations are actively marketed by circulating other clubs with a list of players' registrations and their estimated selling price. Players' registrations are also sold during the season, often with performance conditions attached. Occasionally, it becomes clear that a player will not play for the club again because of, for example, a player sustaining a career threatening injury or being permanently removed from the playing squad for another reason. The playing registrations of certain players were sold after the year end, for total proceeds, net of associated costs, of $25 million. These registrations had a net book value of $7 million.

Emcee would like to know the financial reporting treatment of the acquisition, extension, review and sale of players' registrations in the circumstances outlined above. **(11 marks)**

(c) Emcee uses the revaluation model to measure its stadiums. The directors have been offered $100 million from an airline for the property naming rights of all the stadiums for three years. There are two directors who are on the management boards of Emcee and the airline. Additionally, there are regulations in place by both the football and basketball leagues which regulate the financing of the clubs. These regulations prevent capital contributions from a related party which 'increases equity without repayment in return'. The aim of these regulations is to promote sustainable business models. Sanctions imposed by the regulator include fines and withholding of prize monies. Emcee wishes to know how to take account of the naming rights in the valuation of the stadium and the potential implications of the financial regulations imposed by the leagues. **(8 marks)**

Required

Discuss how the above events would be shown in the financial statements of Emcee under International Financial Reporting Standards.

Note. The mark allocation is shown against each of the three issues above.

(Total = 25 marks)

56 Scramble 49 mins

P2 December 2011 (amended)

Scramble, a public limited company, is a developer of online computer games.

(a) At 30 November 20X1, 65% of Scramble's total assets were mainly represented by internally developed intangible assets comprising the capitalised costs of the development and production of online computer games. These games generate all of Scramble's revenue. The costs incurred in relation to maintaining the games at the same standard of performance are expensed to profit or loss for the year. The accounting policy note states that intangible assets are valued at historical cost. Scramble considers the games to have an indefinite useful life, which is reconsidered annually when the intangible assets are tested for impairment. Scramble determines value in use using the estimated future cash flows which include maintenance expenses, capital expenses incurred in developing different versions of the games and the expected increase in revenue resulting from the cash outflows mentioned above. Scramble does not conduct an analysis or investigation of differences between expected and actual cash flows. Tax effects were also taken into account. **(7 marks)**

(b) Scramble has two cash-generating units (CGU) which hold 90% of the internally developed intangible assets. Scramble reported a consolidated net loss for the period and an impairment charge in respect of the two CGUs representing 63% of the consolidated profit before tax and 29% of the total costs in the period. The recoverable amount of the CGUs is defined, in this case, as value in use. Specific discount rates are not directly available from the market, and Scramble estimates the discount rates, using its weighted average cost of capital. In calculating the cost of debt as an input to the determination of the discount rate, Scramble used the risk-free rate adjusted by the company specific average credit spread of its outstanding debt, which had been raised two years previously. As Scramble did not have any need for additional financing and did not need to repay any of the existing loans before 20X4, Scramble did not see any reason for using a different discount rate. Scramble did not disclose either the events or circumstances that led to the recognition of the impairment loss or the amount of the loss recognised in respect of each cash-generating unit. Scramble felt that the events and circumstances that led to the recognition of a loss in respect of the first CGU were common knowledge in the market and the events and the circumstances that led to the recognition loss of the second CGU were not needed to be disclosed. **(8 marks)**

(c) Scramble wished to diversify its operations and purchased a professional football club, Rashing. In Rashing's financial statements for the year ended 30 November 20X1, it was proposed to include significant intangible assets which related to acquired players' registration rights comprising registration and agents' fees. The agents' fees were paid by the club to players' agents either when a player is transferred to the club or when the contract of a player is extended. Scramble believes that the registration rights of the players are intangible assets but that the agent's fees do not meet the criteria to be recognised as intangible assets as they are not directly attributable to the costs of players' contracts. Additionally, Rashing has purchased the rights to 25% of the revenue from ticket sales generated by another football club, Santash, in a different league. Rashing does not sell these tickets nor has any discretion over the pricing of the tickets. Rashing wishes to show these rights as intangible assets in its financial statements. **(10 marks)**

Required

Discuss the validity of the accounting treatments proposed by Scramble in its financial statements for the year ended 30 November 20X1.

Note. The mark allocation is shown against each of the three accounting treatments above.

(Total = 25 marks)

57 Estoil — 49 mins

P2 December 2014 (amended)

(a) An assessment of accounting practices for asset impairments is especially important in the context of financial reporting quality in that it requires the exercise of considerable management judgement and reporting discretion. The importance of this issue is heightened during periods of ongoing economic uncertainty as a result of the need for companies to reflect the loss of economic value in a timely fashion through the mechanism of asset write-downs. There are many factors which can affect the quality of impairment accounting and disclosures. These factors include changes in circumstance in the reporting period, the market capitalisation of the entity, the allocation of goodwill to cash-generating units, valuation issues and the nature of the disclosures.

Required

Discuss the importance and significance of the above factors when conducting an impairment test under IAS 36 *Impairment of Assets.* **(15 marks)**

(b) (i) Estoil is an international company providing parts for the automotive industry. It operates in many different jurisdictions with different currencies. During 20X4, Estoil experienced financial difficulties marked by a decline in revenue, a reorganisation and restructuring of the business and it reported a loss for the year. An impairment test of goodwill was performed but no impairment was recognised. Estoil applied one discount rate to all cash flows for all cash-generating units (CGUs), irrespective of the currency in which the cash flows would be generated. The discount rate used was the weighted average cost of capital (WACC) and Estoil used the ten-year government bond rate for its jurisdiction as the risk-free rate in this calculation. Additionally, Estoil built its model using a forecast denominated in the functional currency of the parent company. Estoil felt that any other approach would require a level of detail which was unrealistic and impracticable. Estoil argued that the different CGUs represented different risk profiles in the short term, but over a longer business cycle, there was no basis for claiming that their risk profiles were different.

(ii) Fariole specialises in the communications sector with three main CGUs. Goodwill was a significant component of total assets. Fariole performed an impairment test of the CGUs. The cash flow projections were based on the most recent financial budgets approved by management. The realised cash flows for the CGUs were negative in 20X4 and far below budgeted cash flows for that period. The directors had significantly raised cash flow forecasts for 20X5 with little justification. The projected cash flows were calculated by adding back depreciation charges to the budgeted result for the period with expected changes in working capital and capital expenditure not taken into account.

Required

Discuss the acceptability of the above accounting practices under IAS 36 *Impairment of Assets.* **(10 marks)**

(Total = 25 marks)

58 Evolve 49 mins

P2 Sep/Dec 2016 (amended)

(a) Evolve is a real estate company, which is listed on the stock exchange and has a year end of 31 August. On 21 August 20X6, Evolve undertook a scrip (bonus) issue where the shareholders of Evolve received certain rights. The shareholders are able to choose between:

(i) Receiving newly issued shares of Evolve, which could be traded on 30 September 20X6; or

(ii) Transferring their rights back to Evolve by 10 September 20X6 for a fixed cash price which would be paid on 20 September 20X6.

In the financial statements at 31 August 20X6, Evolve believed that the criteria for the recognition of a financial liability as regards the second option were not met at 31 August 20X6 because it was impossible to reliably determine the full amount to be paid, until 10 September 20X6. Evolve felt that the transferring of the rights back to Evolve was a put option on its own equity, which would lead to recording changes in fair value in profit or loss in the next financial year. Evolve disclosed the transaction as a non-adjusting event after the reporting period. **(9 marks)**

(b) At 31 August 20X6, Evolve controlled a wholly owned subsidiary, Resource, whose only assets were land and buildings, which were all measured in accordance with International Financial Reporting Standards. On 1 August 20X6, Evolve published a statement stating that a binding offer for the sale of Resource had been made and accepted and, at that date, the sale was expected to be completed by 31 August 20X6. The non-current assets of Resource were measured at the lower of their carrying amount or fair value less costs to sell at 31 August 20X6, based on the selling price in the binding offer. This measurement was in accordance with IFRS 5 *Non-Current Assets Held for Sale and Discontinued Operations*. However, Evolve did not classify the non-current assets of Resource as held for sale in the financial statements at 31 August 20X6 because there were uncertainties regarding the negotiations with the buyer and a risk that the agreement would not be finalised. There was no disclosure of these uncertainties and the original agreement was finalised on 20 September 20X6. **(10 marks)**

(c) Evolve operates in a jurisdiction with a specific tax regime for listed real estate companies. Upon adoption of this tax regime, the entity has to pay a single tax payment based on the unrealised gains of its investment properties. Evolve purchased Monk whose only asset was an investment property for $10 million. The purchase price of Monk was below the market value of the investment property, which was $14 million, and Evolve chose to account for the investment property under the cost model. However, Evolve considered that the transaction constituted a 'bargain purchase' under IFRS 3 *Business Combinations*. As a result, Evolve accounted for the potential gain of $4 million in profit or loss and increased the 'cost' of the investment property to $14 million. At the same time, Evolve opted for the specific tax regime for the newly acquired investment property and agreed to pay the corresponding tax of $1 million. Evolve considered that the tax payment qualifies as an expenditure necessary to bring the property to the condition necessary for its operations, and therefore was directly attributable to the acquisition of the property. Hence, the tax payment was capitalised and the value of the investment property was stated at $15 million. **(6 marks)**

Required

Advise Evolve on how the above transactions should be correctly dealt with in its financial statements with reference to relevant International Financial Reporting Standards.

Note. The mark allocation is shown against each of the three issues above.

(Total = 25 marks)

59 Gasnature **49 mins**

P2 Sep/Dec 2015 (amended)

(a) Gasnature is a publicly traded entity involved in the production and trading of natural gas and oil. Gasnature jointly owns an underground storage facility with another entity, Gogas. Both parties extract gas from offshore gas fields, which they own and operate independently from each other. Gasnature owns 55% of the underground facility and Gogas owns 45%. They have agreed to share services and costs accordingly, with decisions regarding the storage facility requiring unanimous agreement of the parties. The underground facility is pressurised so that the gas is pushed out when extracted. When the gas pressure is reduced to a certain level, the remaining gas is irrecoverable and remains in the underground storage facility until it is decommissioned. Local legislation requires the decommissioning of the storage facility at the end of its useful life. Gasnature wishes to know how to treat the agreement with Gogas including any obligation or possible obligation arising on the underground storage facility and the accounting for the irrecoverable gas. **(9 marks)**

(b) Gasnature has entered into a ten-year contract with Agas for the purchase of natural gas. Gasnature has made an advance payment to Agas for an amount equal to the total quantity of gas contracted for ten years which has been calculated using the forecasted price of gas. The advance carries interest of 6% per annum, which is settled by way of the supply of extra gas. Fixed quantities of gas have to be supplied each month and there is a price adjustment mechanism in the contract whereby the difference between the forecasted price of gas and the prevailing market price is settled in cash monthly. If Agas does not deliver gas as agreed, Gasnature has the right to claim compensation at the current market price of gas. Gasnature wishes to know whether the contract with Agas should be accounted for under IFRS 9 *Financial Instruments*. **(6 marks)**

(c) Additionally, Gasnature is finalising its financial statements for the year ended 31 August 20X5 and has the following issues.

(i) Gasnature purchased a major refinery on 1 January 20X5 and the directors estimate that a major overhaul is required every two years. The costs of the overhaul are approximately $5 million which comprises $3 million for parts and equipment and $2 million for labour. The directors proposed to accrue the cost of the overhaul over the two years of operations up to that date and create a provision for the expenditure. **(5 marks)**

(ii) From October 20X4, Gasnature had undertaken exploratory drilling to find gas and up to 31 August 20X5 costs of $5 million had been incurred. At 31 August 20X5, the results to date indicated that it was probable that there were sufficient economic benefits to carry on drilling and there were no indicators of impairment. During September 20X5, additional drilling costs of $2 million were incurred and there was significant evidence that no commercial deposits existed and the drilling was abandoned. **(5 marks)**

Required

Discuss, with reference to International Financial Reporting Standards, how Gasnature should account for the above agreement and contract, and the issues raised by the directors

Note. The mark allocation is shown against each of the items above.

(Total = 25 marks)

60 Complexity 49 mins

Part (a) adapted from P2 December 2009

(a) Complexity borrowed $47 million on 1 December 20X4 when the market and effective interest rate was 5%. On 30 November 20X5, the company borrowed an additional $45 million when the current market and effective interest rate was 7.4%. Both financial liabilities are repayable on 30 November 20X9 and are single payment notes, whereby interest and capital are repaid on that date.

Complexity's creditworthiness has been worsening. It has entered into an interest rate swap agreement which acts as a hedge against a $2 million 2% bond issue which matures on 31 May 20X6. The directors of Complexity wish to know in which circumstances it can use hedge accounting. In particular, they need advice on hedge effectiveness and whether this can be calculated.

Required

(i) Discuss the accounting for the financial liabilities under IFRS 9 under the amortised cost method, and additionally using fair value method as at 30 November 20X5. **(6 marks)**

(ii) Advise Complexity's directors as to the circumstances in which it can use hedge accounting and whether it can calculate hedge effectiveness. **(9 marks)**

(b) The type and value of financial instruments that Complexity holds has increased in recent years which has resulted in increased disclosures regarding financial instruments in the financial statements. Complexity's reporting accountant is concerned that the users of the financial statements find financial instruments complicated and has argued that there is no point in providing detailed information in this area as the users will not understand the disclosures.

Required

(i) Discuss, from the perspective of the users of financial statements, how the measurement of financial instruments under IFRSs can create confusion. **(6 marks)**

(ii) Discuss the reporting accountant's view that detailed disclosures in respect of financial instruments do not provide useful information to the users of financial statements. **(4 marks)**

(Total = 25 marks)

61 Blackcutt 49 mins

P2 December 2012 (amended)

Blackcutt is a local government organisation whose financial statements are prepared using International Financial Reporting Standards.

(a) Blackcutt wishes to create a credible investment property portfolio with a view to determining if any property may be considered surplus to the functional objectives and requirements of the local government organisation. The following portfolio of property is owned by Blackcutt.

Blackcutt owns several plots of land. Some of the land is owned by Blackcutt for capital appreciation and this may be sold at any time in the future. Other plots of land have no current purpose as Blackcutt has not determined whether it will use the land to provide services such as those provided by national parks or for short-term sale in the ordinary course of operations.

The local government organisation supplements its income by buying and selling property. The housing department regularly sells part of its housing inventory in the ordinary course of its operations as a result of changing demographics. Part of the inventory, which is not held for sale, is to provide housing to low-income employees at below market rental. The rent paid by employees covers the cost of maintenance of the property. **(8 marks)**

(b) Blackcutt has outsourced its waste collection to a private sector provider called Waste and Co and pays an annual amount to Waste and Co for its services. Waste and Co purchases the vehicles and uses them exclusively for Blackcutt's waste collection. The vehicles are painted with the Blackcutt local government organisation name and colours. Blackcutt can use the vehicles and the vehicles are used for waste collection for nearly all of the asset's life. If a vehicle breaks down or no longer functions, Waste and Co must provide replacement vehicles fitted with the same waste disposal containers and equipment and painted with the local government organisations name and colours. **(6 marks)**

(c) Blackcutt owns a warehouse. Chemco has leased the warehouse from Blackcutt and is using it as a storage facility for chemicals. The national government has announced its intention to enact environmental legislation requiring property owners to accept liability for environmental pollution. As a result, Blackcutt has introduced a hazardous chemical policy and has begun to apply the policy to its properties. Blackcutt has had a report that the chemicals have contaminated the land surrounding the warehouse. Blackcutt has no recourse against Chemco or its insurance company for the clean-up costs of the pollution. At 30 November 20X6, it is virtually certain that draft legislation requiring a clean-up of land already contaminated will be enacted shortly after the year end. **(4 marks)**

(d) On 1 December 20X0, Blackcutt opened a school at a cost of $5 million. The estimated useful life of the school was 25 years. On 30 November 20X6, the school was closed because numbers using the school declined unexpectedly. The school is to be converted for use as a library, and there is no expectation that the building will be reopened for use as a school. The current replacement cost for a library of equivalent size to the school is $2.1 million. Because of the nature of the non-current asset, value-in-use and net selling price are unrealistic estimates of the value of the school. The change in use would have no effect on the estimated life of the building. **(7 marks)**

Required

Discuss how the above events should be accounted for in the financial statements of Blackcutt.

Note. The mark allocation is shown against each of the four events above.

(Total = 25 marks)

62 Carsoon 49 mins

P2 Mar/Jun 2017 (amended)

Carsoon Co is a company which manufactures and retails motor vehicles. It also constructs premises for third parties. It has a year end of 28 February 20X7.

(a) The entity enters into lease agreements with the public for its motor vehicles. The agreements are normally for a three-year period. The customer decides how to use the vehicle within certain contractual limitations. The maximum mileage per annum is specified at 10,000 miles without penalty. Carsoon is responsible for the maintenance of the vehicle and insists that the vehicle cannot be modified in any way. At the end of the three-year contract, the customer can purchase the vehicle at a price which will be above the market value, or alternatively hand it back to Carsoon. If the vehicle is returned, Carsoon will then sell the vehicle on to the public through one of its retail outlets. These sales of vehicles are treated as investing activities in the statement of cash flows.

The directors of Carsoon wish to know how the leased vehicles should be accounted for, from the commencement of the lease to the final sale of the vehicle, in the financial statements including the statement of cash flows. **(9 marks)**

(b) On 1 March 20X6, Carsoon invested in a debt instrument with a fair value of $6 million and has assessed that the financial asset is aligned with the fair value through other comprehensive income business model. The instrument has an interest rate of 4% over a period of six years. The effective interest rate is also 4%. On 1 March 20X6, the debt instrument is not impaired in any way. During the year to 28 February 20X7, there was a change in interest rates and the fair value of the instrument seemed to be affected. The instrument was quoted in an active market at $5.3 million but the price based upon an in-house model showed that the fair value of the instrument was $5.5 million. This valuation was based upon the average change in value of a range of instruments across a number of jurisdictions.

The directors of Carsoon felt that the instrument should be valued at $5.5 million and that this should be shown as a Level 1 measurement under IFRS 13 *Fair Value Measurement.* There has not been a significant increase in credit risk since 1 March 20X6, and expected credit losses should be measured at an amount equal to 12-month expected credit losses of $400,000. Carsoon sold the debt instrument on 1 March 20X7 for $5.3 million.

The directors of Carsoon wish to know how to account for the debt instrument until its sale on 1 March 20X7. **(8 marks)**

(c) Carsoon constructs retail vehicle outlets and enters into contracts with customers to construct buildings on their land. The contracts have standard terms, which include penalties payable by Carsoon if the contract is delayed, or payable by the customer, if Carsoon cannot gain access to the construction site.

Due to poor weather, one of the projects was delayed. As a result, Carsoon faced additional costs and contractual penalties. As Carsoon could not gain access to the construction site, the directors decided to make a counter-claim against the customer for the penalties and additional costs which Carsoon faced. Carsoon felt that because a counter claim had been made against the customer, the additional costs and penalties should not be included in contract costs but shown as a contingent liability. Carsoon has assessed the legal basis of the claim and feels it has enforceable rights.

In the year ended 28 February 20X7, Carsoon incurred general and administrative costs of $10 million, and costs relating to wasted materials of $5 million.

Additionally, during the year, Carsoon agreed to construct a storage facility on the same customer's land for $7 million at a cost of $5 million. The parties agreed to modify the contract to include the construction of the storage facility, which was completed during the current financial year. All of the additional costs relating to the above were capitalised as assets in the financial statements.

The directors of Carsoon wish to know how to account for the penalties, counter claim and additional costs in accordance with IFRS 15 *Revenue from Contracts with Customers.*

(8 marks)

Required

Advise Carsoon on how the above transactions should be dealt with in its financial statements with reference to relevant International Financial Reporting Standards.

Note. The mark allocation is shown against each of the three issues above.

(Total = 25 marks)

63 Leigh 49 mins

ACR June 2007 (amended)

(a) Leigh, a public limited company, purchased the whole of the share capital of Hash, a limited company, on 1 June 20X6. The whole of the share capital of Hash was formerly owned by the five directors of Hash and under the terms of the purchase agreement, the five directors were to receive a total of three million ordinary shares of $1 of Leigh on 1 June 20X6 (market value $6 million) and a further 5,000 shares per director on 31 May 20X7, if they were still employed by Leigh on that date. All of the directors were still employed by Leigh at 31 May 20X7.

Leigh granted and issued fully paid shares to its own employees on 31 May 20X7. Normally share options issued to employees would vest over a three-year period, but these shares were given as a bonus because of the company's exceptional performance over the period. The shares in Leigh had a market value of $3 million (one million ordinary shares of $1 at $3 per share) on 31 May 20X7 and an average fair value of $2.5 million (one million ordinary shares of $1 at $2.50 per share) for the year ended 31 May 20X7. It is expected that Leigh's share price will rise to $6 per share over the next three years. **(10 marks)**

(b) On 31 May 20X7, Leigh purchased property, plant and equipment for $4 million. The supplier has agreed to accept payment for the property, plant and equipment either in cash or in shares. The supplier can either choose 1.5 million shares of Leigh to be issued in six months' time or to receive a cash payment in three months' time equivalent to the market value of 1.3 million shares. It is estimated that the share price will be $3.50 in three months' time and $4 in six months' time.

Additionally, at 31 May 20X7, one of the directors recently appointed to the board has been granted the right to choose either 50,000 shares of Leigh or receive a cash payment equal to the current value of 40,000 shares at the settlement date. This right has been granted because of the performance of the director during the year and is unconditional at 31 May 20X7. The settlement date is 1 July 20X8 and the company estimates the fair value of the share alternative is $2.50 per share at 31 May 20X7. The share price of Leigh at 31 May 20X7 is $3 per share, and if the director chooses the share alternative, they must be kept for a period of four years. **(9 marks)**

(c) Leigh acquired 30% of the ordinary share capital of Handy, a public limited company, on 1 April 20X6. The purchase consideration was one million ordinary shares of Leigh which had a market value of $2.50 per share at that date and the fair value of the net assets of Handy was $9 million. The retained earnings of Handy were $4 million and other reserves of Handy were $3 million at that date. Leigh appointed two directors to the Board of Handy, and it intends to hold the investment for a significant period of time. Leigh exerts significant influence over Handy. The summarised statement of financial position of Handy at 31 May 20X7 is as follows.

	$m
Share capital of $1	2
Other reserves	3
Retained earnings	5
	10
Net assets	10

There had been no new issues of shares by Handy since the acquisition by Leigh and the estimated recoverable amount of the net assets of Handy at 31 May 20X7 was $11 million. **(6 marks)**

Required

Discuss with suitable computations how the above share-based transactions should be accounted for in the financial statements of Leigh for the year ended 31 May 20X7.

(Total = 25 marks)

64 Yanong **49 mins**

P2 June 2015 (amended)

The directors of Yanong, a public limited company, would like advice, with reference to IFRS 13 *Fair Value Measurement*, on several transactions.

(a) Yanong owns several farms and also owns a division which sells agricultural vehicles. It is considering selling this agricultural retail division and wishes to measure the fair value of the inventory of vehicles for the purpose of the sale. Three markets currently exist for the vehicles. Yanong has transacted regularly in all three markets. At 30 April 20X5, Yanong wishes to find the fair value of 150 new vehicles, which are identical. The current volume and prices in the three markets are as follows:

Market	*Sales price – per vehicle*	*Historical volume – vehicles sold by Yanong*	*Total volume of vehicles sold in market*	*Transaction costs – per vehicle*	*Transport costs to the market – per vehicle*
	$			$	$
Europe	40,000	6,000	150,000	500	400
Asia	38,000	2,500	750,000	400	700
Africa	34,000	1,500	100,000	300	600

Yanong wishes to value the vehicles at $39,100 per vehicle as these are the highest net proceeds per vehicle, and Europe is the largest market for Yanong's product. Yanong would like advice as to whether this valuation would be acceptable under IFRS 13 *Fair Value Measurement.* **(6 marks)**

(b) The company uses quarterly reporting for its farms as they grow short-lived crops such as maize. Yanong planted the maize fields during the quarter to 31 October 20X4 at an operating cost of $10 million. The fields originally cost $20 million. There is no active market for partly grown fields of maize and therefore Yanong proposes to use a discounted cash flow method to value the maize fields. As at 31 October 20X4, the following were the cash flow projections relating to the maize fields:

	3 months to 31 January 20X5	*3 months to 30 April 20X5*	*Total*
	$m	$m	$m
Cash inflows		80	80
Cash outflows	(8)	(19)	(27)
Notional rental charge for land usage	(1)	(1)	(2)
Net cash flows	(9)	60	51

In the three months to 31 January 20X5, the actual operating costs amounted to $8 million and at that date Yanong revised its future projections for the cash inflows to $76 million for the three months to April 20X5. At the point of harvest at 31 March 20X5, the maize was worth $82 million and it was sold for $84 million (net of costs to sell) on 15 April 20X5. In the measurement of fair value of the maize, Yanong includes a notional cash flow expense for the 'rent' of the land where it is self-owned.

The directors of Yanong wish to know how they should have accounted for the above biological asset at 31 October 20X4, 31 January 20X5, 31 March 20X5 and when the produce was sold. Assume a discount rate of 2% per quarter as follows:

	Factor
Period 1	0.980
Period 2	0.961

(7 marks)

(c) On 1 May 20X2, Yanong granted 500 share appreciation rights (SARs) to its 300 managers. All of the rights vested on 30 April 20X4 but they can be exercised from 1 May 20X4 up to 30 April 20X6. At the grant date, the value of each SAR was $10 and it was estimated that 5% of the managers would leave during the vesting period. The fair value of the SARs is as follows:

	Fair value of SAR
	$
30 April 20X3	9
30 April 20X4	11
30 April 20X5	12

All of the managers who were expected to leave employment did leave the company as expected before 30 April 20X4. On 30 April 20X5, 60 managers exercised their options when the intrinsic value of the right was $10.50 and were paid in cash.

Yanong is confused as to whether to account for the SARs under IFRS 2 *Share-based Payment* or IFRS 13 *Fair Value Measurement,* and would like advice as to how the SARs should have been accounted for from the grant date to 30 April 20X5. **(7 marks)**

(d) Yanong uses the revaluation model for its non-current assets. Yanong has several plots of farmland which are unproductive. The company feels that the land would have more value if it were used for residential purposes. There are several potential purchasers for the land but planning permission has not yet been granted for use of the land for residential purposes. However, preliminary enquiries with the regulatory authorities seem to indicate that planning permission may be granted. Additionally, the government has recently indicated that more agricultural land should be used for residential purposes.

Yanong has also been approached to sell the land for commercial development at a higher price than that for residential purposes.

Yanong would like advice on how to measure the fair value of the land in its financial statements. **(5 marks)**

Required

Advise Yanong on how the above transactions should be dealt with in its financial statements with reference to relevant International Financial Reporting Standards.

Notes

1 The mark allocation is shown against each of the four issues above.
2 Ignore any deferred tax implications of the transactions above.

(Total = 25 marks)

65 Mehran — 49 mins

P2 Mar/Jun 2016 (amended)

The directors of Mehran, a public limited company, have seen many different ways of dealing with the measurement and disclosure of the fair value of assets, liabilities and equity instruments. They feel that this reduces comparability among different entities' financial statements. They would like advice on how IFRS 13 *Fair Value Measurement* should be applied to several transactions.

(a) Mehran has just acquired a company, which comprises a farming and mining business. Mehran wishes advice on how to place a fair value on some of the assets acquired.

One such asset is a piece of land, which is currently used for farming. The fair value of the land if used for farming is $5 million. If the land is used for farming purposes, a tax credit arises annually, which is based upon the lower of 15% of the fair market value of land or $500,000 at the current tax rate. The current tax rate in the jurisdiction is 20%.

Mehran has determined that market participants would consider that the land could have an alternative use for residential purposes. The fair value of the land for residential purposes before associated costs is thought to be $7.4 million. In order to transform the land from farming to residential use, there would be legal costs of $200,000, a viability analysis cost of $300,000 and costs of demolition of the farm buildings of $100,000. Additionally, permission for residential use has not been formally given by the legal authority and because of this, market participants have indicated that the fair value of the land, after the above costs, would be discounted by 20% because of the risk of not obtaining planning permission.

In addition, Mehran has acquired the brand name associated with the produce from the farm. Mehran has decided to discontinue the brand on the assumption that it will gain increased revenues from its own brands. Mehran has determined that if it ceases to use the brand, then the indirect benefits will be $20 million. If it continues to use the brand, then the direct benefit will be $17 million. **(7 marks)**

(b) Mehran wishes to place a fair value on the inventory of the entity acquired. There are three different markets for the produce, which are mainly vegetables. The first is the local domestic market where Mehran can sell direct to retailers of the produce. The second domestic market is one where Mehran sells directly to manufacturers of canned vegetables. There are no restrictions on the sale of produce in either of the domestic markets other than the demand of the retailers and manufacturers. The final market is the export market but the government limits the amount of produce which can be exported. Mehran needs a licence from the government to export its produce. Farmers tend to sell all of the produce that they can in the export market and, when they do not have any further authorisation to export, they sell the remaining produce in the two domestic markets.

It is difficult to obtain information on the volume of trade in the domestic market where the produce is sold locally direct to retailers but Mehran feels that the market is at least as large as the domestic market – direct to manufacturers. The volumes of sales quoted below have been taken from trade journals.

	Domestic market – direct to retailers	*Domestic market – direct to manufacturers*	*Export market*
Volume – annual	Unknown	20,000 tonnes	10,000 tonnes
Volume – sales per month	10 tonnes	4 tonnes	60 tonnes
Price per tonne	$1,000	$800	$1,200
Transport costs per tonne	$50	$70	$100
Selling agents' fees per tonne	–	$4	$6

(10 marks)

(c) Mehran owns a non-controlling equity interest in Erham, a private company, and wishes to measure the interest at its fair value at its financial year end of 31 March 20X6. Mehran acquired the ordinary share interest in Erham on 1 April 20X4. During the current financial year, Erham has issued further equity capital through the issue of preferred shares to a venture capital fund.

As a result of the preferred share issue, the venture capital fund now holds a controlling interest in Erham. The terms of the preferred shares, including the voting rights, are similar to those of the ordinary shares, except that the preferred shares have a cumulative fixed dividend entitlement for a period of four years and the preferred shares rank ahead of the ordinary shares upon the liquidation of Erham. The transaction price for the preferred shares was $15 per share.

Mehran wishes to know the factors which should be taken into account in measuring the fair value of their holding in the ordinary shares of Erham at 31 March 20X6 using a market-based approach. **(8 marks)**

Required

Discuss the way in which Mehran should measure the fair value the above assets with reference to the principles of IFRS 13 *Fair Value Measurement.*

Note. The mark allocation is shown against each of the three issues above.

(Total = 25 marks)

66 Canto — 49 mins

P2 Mar/Jun 2017 (amended)

Canto Co is a company which manufactures industrial machinery and has a year end of 28 February 20X7. The directors of Canto require advice on the following issues:

(a) On 1 March 20X4, Canto acquired a property for $15 million, which was used as an office building. Canto measured the property on the cost basis in property, plant and equipment. The useful life of the building was estimated at 30 years from 1 March 20X4 with no residual value. Depreciation is charged on the straight-line basis over its useful life. At acquisition, the value of the land content of the property was thought to be immaterial.

During the financial year to 28 February 20X7, the planning authorities approved the land to build industrial units and retail outlets on the site. During 20X7, Canto ceased using the property as an office and converted the property to an industrial unit. Canto also built retail units on the land during the year to 28 February 20X7. At 28 February 20X7, Canto wishes to transfer the property at fair value to investment property at $20 million. This valuation was based upon other similar properties owned by Canto. However, if the whole site were sold including the retail outlets, it is estimated that the value of the industrial units would be $25 million because of synergies and complementary cash flows.

The directors of Canto wish to know whether the fair valuation of the investment property is in line with International Financial Reporting Standards and how to account for the change in use of the property in the financial statements at 28 February 20X7. **(9 marks)**

(b) On 28 February 20X7, Canto acquired all of the share capital of Binlory, a company which manufactures and supplies industrial vehicles. At the acquisition date, Binlory has an order backlog, which relates to a contract between itself and a customer for ten industrial vehicles to be delivered in the next two years.

In addition, Binlory requires the extensive use of water in the manufacturing process and can take a pre-determined quantity of water from a water source for industrial use. Binlory cannot manufacture vehicles without the use of the water rights. Binlory was the first entity to use water from this source and acquired this legal right at no cost several years ago. Binlory has the right to continue to use the quantity of water for manufacturing purposes but any unused water cannot be sold separately. These rights can be lost over time if non-use of the water source is demonstrated or if the water has not been used for a certain number of years. Binlory feels that the valuation of these rights is quite subjective and difficult to achieve.

The directors of Canto wish to know how to account for the above intangible assets on the acquisition of Binlory. **(8 marks)**

(c) Canto acquired a cash-generating unit (CGU) several years ago but, at 28 February 20X7, the directors of Canto were concerned that the value of the CGU had declined because of a reduction in sales due to new competitors entering the market. At 28 February 20X7, the carrying amounts of the assets in the CGU before any impairment testing were:

	$m
Goodwill	3
Property, plant and equipment	10
Other assets	19
Total	32

The fair values of the property, plant and equipment and the other assets at 28 February 20X7 were $10 million and $17 million respectively and their costs to sell were $100,000 and $300,000 respectively.

The CGU's cash flow forecasts for the next five years are as follows:

Date year ended	*Pre-tax cash flow*	*Post-tax cash flow*
	$m	$m
28 February 20X8	8	5
28 February 20X9	7	5
28 February 20Y0	5	3
28 February 20Y1	3	1.5
28 February 20Y2	13	10

The pre-tax discount rate for the CGU is 8% and the post-tax discount rate is 6%. Canto has no plans to expand the capacity of the CGU and believes that a reorganisation would bring cost savings but, as yet, no plan has been approved.

The directors of Canto need advice as to whether the CGU's value is impaired. The following extract from a table of present value factors has been provided.

Year	*Discount rate 6%*	*Discount rate 8%*
1	0.9434	0.9259
2	0.8900	0.8573
3	0.8396	0.7938
4	0.7921	0.7350
5	0.7473	0.6806

(8 marks)

Required

Advise the directors of Canto on how the above transactions should be dealt with in its financial statements with reference to relevant International Financial Reporting Standards.

Note. The mark allocation is shown against each of the three issues above.

(Total = 25 marks)

67 Ethan — 49 mins

P2 December 2012 (amended)

Ethan, a public limited company, develops, operates and sells investment properties.

(a) Ethan focuses mainly on acquiring properties where it foresees growth potential, through rental income as well as value appreciation. The acquisition of an investment property is usually realised through the acquisition of the entity, which holds the property.

In Ethan's consolidated financial statements, investment properties acquired through business combinations are recognised at fair value, using a discounted cash flow model as approximation to fair value. There is currently an active market for this type of property. The difference between the fair value of the investment property as determined under the accounting policy, and the value of the investment property for tax purposes results in a deferred tax liability.

Goodwill arising on business combinations is determined using the measurement principles for the investment properties as outlined above. Goodwill is only considered impaired if and when the deferred tax liability is reduced below the amount at which it was first recognised. This reduction can be caused both by a reduction in the value of the real estate or a change in local tax regulations. As long as the deferred tax liability is equal to, or larger than, the prior year, no impairment is charged to goodwill. Ethan explained its accounting treatment by confirming that almost all of its goodwill is due to the deferred tax liability and that it is normal in the industry to account for goodwill in this way.

Since 20X0, Ethan has incurred substantial annual losses except for the year ended 31 May 20X3, when it made a small profit before tax. In year ended 31 May 20X3, most of the profit consisted of income recognised on revaluation of investment properties. Ethan had announced early in its financial year ended 31 May 20X4 that it anticipated substantial growth and profit. Later in the year, however, Ethan announced that the expected profit would not be achieved and that, instead, a substantial loss would be incurred. Ethan had a history of reporting considerable negative variances from its budgeted results. Ethan's recognised deferred tax assets have been increasing year-on-year despite the deferred tax liabilities recognised on business combinations. Ethan's deferred tax assets consist primarily of unused tax losses that can be carried forward which are unlikely to be offset against anticipated future taxable profits. **(13 marks)**

(b) Ethan wishes to apply the fair value option rules of IFRS 9 *Financial Instruments* to debt issued to finance its investment properties. Ethan's argument for applying the fair value option is based upon the fact that the recognition of gains and losses on its investment properties and the related debt would otherwise be inconsistent. Ethan argued that there is a specific financial correlation between the factors, such as interest rates, that form the basis for determining the fair value of both Ethan's investment properties and the related debt. **(7 marks)**

(c) Ethan has an operating subsidiary, which has in issue A and B shares, both of which have voting rights. Ethan holds 70% of the A and B shares and the remainder are held by shareholders external to the group. The subsidiary is obliged to pay an annual dividend of 5% on the B shares. The dividend payment is cumulative even if the subsidiary does not have sufficient legally distributable profit at the time the payment is due.

In Ethan's consolidated statement of financial position, the B shares of the subsidiary were accounted for in the same way as equity instruments would be, with the B shares owned by external parties reported as a non-controlling interest. **(5 marks)**

Required

Discuss how the above transactions and events should be recorded in the consolidated financial statements of Ethan.

Note. The mark allocation is shown against each of the three transactions above.

(Total = 25 marks)

68 Whitebirk — 43 mins

P2 December 2010 (amended)

(a) The main argument for separate accounting standards for small and medium-sized entities is the undue cost burden of reporting, which is proportionately heavier for smaller firms.

Required

Discuss the main differences and modifications to IFRS which the IASB made when it published the *IFRS for Small and Medium-Sized Entities* (IFRS for SMEs), giving specific examples where possible and include in your discussion how the Board has dealt with the problem of defining an SME. **(11 marks)**

(b) Whitebirk has met the definition of a SME in its jurisdiction and wishes to comply with the IFRS for SMEs. The entity wishes to seek advice on how it will deal with the following accounting issues in its financial statements for the year ended 30 November 20X2. The entity already prepares its financial statements under full IFRS.

(i) Whitebirk purchased 90% of Close, an SME, on 1 December 20X1. The purchase consideration was $5.7 million and the value of Close's identifiable assets was $6 million. The value of the non-controlling interest at 1 December 20X1 was measured at $0.7 million. Whitebirk has used the full goodwill method to account for business combinations and the life of goodwill cannot be estimated with any accuracy. Whitebirk wishes to know how to account for goodwill under the IFRS for SMEs.

(ii) Whitebirk has incurred $1 million of research expenditure to develop a new product in the year to 30 November 20X2. Additionally, it incurred $500,000 of development expenditure to bring another product to a stage where it is ready to be marketed and sold.

(iii) Whitebirk purchased some properties for $1.7 million on 1 December 20X1 and designated them as investment properties under the cost model. No depreciation was charged as a real estate agent valued the properties at $1.9 million at the year end.

(iv) Whitebirk has an intangible asset valued at $1 million on 1 December 20X1. The asset has an indefinite useful life, and in previous years had been reviewed for impairment. As at 30 November 20X2, there are no indications that the asset is impaired.

Required

Discuss how the above transactions should be dealt with in the financial statements of Whitebirk, with reference to the IFRS for SMEs. **(11 marks)**

(Total = 22 marks)

69 Lucky Dairy — 49 mins

ACR June 2002 (amended)

The Lucky Dairy, a public limited company, produces milk for supply to various customers. It is responsible for producing 25% of the country's milk consumption. The company owns 150 farms and has 70,000 cows and 35,000 heifers which are being raised to produce milk in the future. The farms produce 2.5 million kilograms of milk per annum and normally hold an inventory of 50,000 kilograms of milk (Extracts from the draft accounts to 31 May 20X2).

The herds comprise at 31 May 20X2:

70,000 – 3-year old cows (all purchased on or before 1 June 20X1)
25,000 – heifers (average age 1½ years old – purchased 1 December 20X1)
10,000 – heifers (average age 2 years – purchased 1 June 20X1)

There were no animals born or sold in the year. The per unit values less estimated point of sale costs were as follows.

	$
2-year old animal at 1 June 20X1	50
1-year old animal at 1 June 20X1 and 1 December 20X1	40
3-year old animal at 31 May 20X2	60
1½-year old animal at 31 May 20X2	46
2-year old animal at 31 May 20X2	55
1-year old animal at 31 May 20X2	42

The company has had a difficult year in financial and operating terms. The cows had contracted a disease at the beginning of the financial year which had been passed on in the food chain to a small number of consumers. The publicity surrounding this event had caused a drop in the consumption of milk and as a result the dairy was holding 500,000 kilograms of milk in storage.

The government had stated, on 1 April 20X2, that it was prepared to compensate farmers for the drop in the price and consumption of milk. An official government letter was received on 6 June

20X2, stating that $1.5 million will be paid to Lucky on 1 August 20X2. Additionally on 1 May 20X2, Lucky had received a letter from its lawyer saying that legal proceedings had been started against the company by the persons affected by the disease. The company's lawyers have advised them that they feel that it is probable that they will be found liable and that the costs involved may reach $2 million. The lawyers, however, feel that the company may receive additional compensation from a government fund if certain quality control procedures had been carried out by the company. However, the lawyers will only state that the compensation payment is 'possible'.

The company's activities are controlled in three geographical locations, Dale, Shire and Ham. The only region affected by the disease was Dale and the government has decided that it is to restrict the milk production of that region significantly. Lucky estimates that the discounted future cash income from the present herds of cattle in the region amounts to $1.2 million, taking into account the government restriction order. Lucky was not sure that the fair value of the cows in the region could be measured reliably at the date of purchase because of the problems with the diseased cattle. The cows in this region amounted to 20,000 in number and the heifers 10,000 in number. All of the animals were purchased on 1 June 20X1. Lucky has had an offer of $1 million for all of the animals in the Dale region (net of point of sale costs) and $2 million for the sale of the farms in the region. However, there was a minority of directors who opposed the planned sale and it was decided to defer the public announcement of sale pending the outcome of the possible receipt of the government compensation. The board had decided that the potential sale plan was highly confidential but a national newspaper had published an article saying that the sale may occur and that there would be many people who would lose their employment. The board approved the planned sale of Dale farms on 31 May 20X2.

The directors of Lucky have approached your firm for professional advice on the above matters.

Required

Advise the directors on how the biological assets and produce of Lucky should be accounted for under IAS 41 *Agriculture* and discuss the implications for the published financial statements of the above events.

Note. Candidates should produce a table which shows the changes in value of the cattle for the year to 31 May 20X2 due to price change and physical change excluding the Dale region, and the value of the herd of the Dale region as at 31 May 20X2. Ignore the effects of taxation. Heifers are young female cows, whilst 'cattle' refers to both cows and heifers. **(25 marks)**

Answer Bank

Section 1 – Preparation questions

1 Financial instruments

(a) STATEMENT OF PROFIT OR LOSS AND OTHER COMPREHENSIVE INCOME

	$
Finance income	
(441,014 × (W1) 8%)	35,281

STATEMENT OF FINANCIAL POSITION

Non-current assets	
Financial asset (441,014 + 35,281)	476,295

Working: Effective interest rate

$\frac{600,000}{441,014} = 1.3605$ ∴ from tables interest rate is 8%

(b) **Compound instrument**

	$
Presentation	
Non-current liabilities	
Financial liability component of convertible bond (Working)	1,797,467
Equity	
Equity component of convertible bond (2,000,000 – (Working) 1,797,467)	202,533

Working: Fair value of equivalent non-convertible debt

	$
Present value of principal payable at end of 3 years	1,544,367
$(4,000 \times \$500 = \$2m \times \frac{1}{(1.09)^3})$	
Present value of interest annuity payable annually in arrears for 3 years [(5% × $2m) × 2.531]	253,100
	1,797,467

2 Leases

(a) **Interest rate implicit in the lease**

PV = annuity × cumulative discount factor (CDF)

250,000 = 78,864 × CDF

∴ CDF $= \frac{250,000}{78,864}$

= 3.170

∴ Interest rate is 10%

(b) At the inception of the lease, Sugar Co recognises a right-of-use asset and a lease liability. The right-of-use asset is measured at the amount of the lease liability, which is the present value of the future lease payments discounted at the rate of interest implicit in the lease, here \$250,000. At 31 December, the right-of-use asset is measured at cost less accumulated depreciation: \$250,000 – \$(250,000/4) = \$187,500. The lease liability is measured by increasing the carrying amount to reflect interest on the lease liability and reducing the carrying amount to reflect the lease payments made.

STATEMENT OF FINANCIAL POSITION AS AT 31 DECEMBER 20X1 (EXTRACT)

Property, plant and equipment	$
Right-of-use asset	187,500
Non-current liabilities	
Lease liabilities (W)	136,886
Current liabilities	
Lease liabilities (W) (196,136 – 136,886)	59,250

STATEMENT OF PROFIT OR LOSS AND OTHER COMPREHENSIVE INCOME
FOR THE YEAR ENDED 31 DECEMBER 20X1 (EXTRACT) (PROFIT OR LOSS SECTION)

Depreciation on right-of-use asset	62,500
Finance charges	25,000

Working: Lease liability

		$
Year ended 31 December 20X1:		
1.1.X1	Liability b/d	250,000
1.1.X1 – 31.12.X1	Interest at 10%	25,000
31.12.X1	Instalment in arrears	(78,864)
31.12.X1	Liability c/d	196,136
Year ended 31 December 20X2:		
1.1.X2 – 31.12.X2	Interest at 10%	19,614
31.12.X2	Instalment in arrears	(78,864)
31.12.X2	Liability c/d	136,886

3 Defined benefit plan

NOTES TO THE STATEMENT OF PROFIT OR LOSS AND OTHER COMPREHENSIVE INCOME

Defined benefit expense recognised in profit or loss

	$m
Current service cost	11
Past service cost	10
Net interest on the net defined benefit asset (10% × (110 + 10)) – (10% × 150)	(3)
	18

Other comprehensive income (items that will not be reclassified to profit or loss)
Remeasurement of defined benefit plans

	$m
Remeasurement gain on defined benefit obligation	17
Remeasurement loss on plan assets	(22)
	(5)

NOTES TO THE STATEMENT OF FINANCIAL POSITION

Net defined benefit asset recognised in the statement of financial position

	31 December 20X1	*31 December 20X0*
	$m	$m
Present value of pension obligation	116	110
Fair value of plan assets	(140)	(150)
Net asset	(24)	(40)

Changes in the present value of the defined benefit obligation

	$m
Opening defined benefit obligation	110
Interest on obligation (10% × (110 + 10))	12
Current service cost	11
Past service cost	10
Benefits paid	(10)
Gain on remeasurement through OCI (balancing figure)	(17)
Closing defined benefit obligation	116

Changes in the fair value of plan assets

	$m
Opening fair value of plan assets	150
Interest on plan assets (10% × 150)	15
Contributions	7
Benefits paid	(10)
Loss on remeasurement through OCI (balancing figure)	(22)
Closing fair value of plan assets	140

Tutorial note.

The interest on the defined benefit obligation is calculated on the balance at the start of the year ($110 million) plus the increase in obligation of $10 million due to past service costs. Interest is charged on the increase in obligation due to past service costs because the $10 million given in the question is the present value at the start of the year (if it were the present value at the end of the year, no interest would be required).

4 Sundry standards

Workbook reference. Employee benefits are covered in Chapter 5 of the SBR Workbook, embedded derivatives in covered in Chapter 8.

(a) NOTES TO THE STATEMENT OF PROFIT OR LOSS AND OTHER COMPREHENSIVE INCOME

Defined benefit expense recognised in profit or loss

	$'000
Current service cost	275
Net interest on the net defined benefit liability (318 – 306)	12
Curtailment cost	58
	345

Other comprehensive income (items that will not be reclassified to profit or loss)
Remeasurement of defined benefit plans

	$'000
Remeasurement loss on defined benefit obligation	(19)
Remeasurement gain on plan assets	89
	70

NOTES TO THE STATEMENT OF FINANCIAL POSITION

Net defined benefit liability recognised in the statement of financial position

	31 January 20X8	*31 January 20X7*
	$m	$'000
Present value of pension obligation	4,640	4,300
Fair value of plan assets	(4,215)	(3,600)
Net liability	425	700

Changes in the present value of the defined benefit obligation

	$'000
Opening defined benefit obligation	4,300
Benefits paid	(330)
Interest on obligation (4,300 – 330) × 8%	318
Curtailment	58
Current service cost	275
Loss on remeasurement through OCI (balancing figure)	19
Closing defined benefit obligation	4,640

Changes in the fair value of plan assets

	$'000
Opening fair value of plan assets	3,600
Contributions	550
Benefits paid	(330)
Interest on plan assets ((3,600 + 550 – 330) × 8%)	306
Gain on remeasurement through OCI (balancing figure)	89
Closing fair value of plan assets	4,215

(b) **Settlement**

(i) *Calculation of net defined benefit liability*

Changes in the present value of the defined benefit obligation

20X8

	$'000
Opening defined benefit obligation (1.1.X8)	40,000
Interest on obligation (40,000 × 8%)	3,200
Current service cost	2,500
Past service cost	2,000
Benefits paid	(1,974)
	45,726
Loss on remeasurement through OCI (bal. fig.)	274
Closing defined benefit obligation (31.12.X8)	46,000

20X9

	$'000
Opening defined benefit obligation (1.1.X9)	46,000
Interest on obligation (46,000 × 9%)	4,140
Current service cost	2,860
Settlement	(11,400)
Benefits paid	(2,200)
	39,400
Loss on remeasurement through OCI (bal. fig.)	1,400
Closing defined benefit obligation (31.12.X9)	40,800

Changes in the fair value of plan assets

20X8

	$'000
Opening fair value of plan assets (1.1.X8)	40,000
Interest on plan assets (40,000 × 8%)	3,200
Benefits paid	(1,974)
Contributions paid	2,000
	43,226
Loss on remeasurement through OCI (bal. fig.)	(226)
Closing fair value of plan assets (31.12.X8)	43,000

	$'000
Opening fair value of plant assets (1.1.X9)	43,000
Interest on plan assets (43,000 × 9%)	3,870
Settlement	(10,800)
Benefits paid	(2,200)
Contributions paid in	2,200
	36,070
Loss on remeasurement through OCI (bal. fig.)	(390)
Closing fair value of plan assets (31.12.X9)	35,680

- During 20X8, there is an improvement in the future benefits available under the plan and as a result there is a past service cost of $2 million, being the increase in the present value of the obligation as a result of the change.
- During 20X9, Sion sells part of its operations and transfers the relevant part of the pension plan to the purchaser. This is a settlement. The overall gain on settlement is calculated as:

	$'000
Present value of obligation settled	11,400
Fair value of plan assets transferred on settlement	(10,800)
Cash transferred on settlement	(400)
Gain	200

(ii) *Financial statements extracts*

STATEMENT OF FINANCIAL POSITION

	20X8	*20X9*
	$'000	$'000
Net defined benefit liability:		
(46,000 – 43,000)/(40,800 – 35,680)	3,000	5,120

STATEMENT OF PROFIT OR LOSS AND OTHER COMPREHENSIVE INCOME

	20X8	*20X9*
	$'000	$'000
Profit or loss		
Current service cost	2,500	2,860
Past service cost	2,000	–
Gain on settlement	–	(200)
Net interest: (3,200 – 3,200)/(4,140 – 3,870)	–	270
Other comprehensive income		
Remeasurement loss on defined benefit pension plan:		
(274 + 226)/(1,400 + 390)	500	1,790

(c) **Classification of financial assets**

Bed's deposit is a **financial asset**. According to IFRS 9 *Financial Instruments*, financial assets are classified as measured at either **amortised cost or fair value**.

A financial asset is measured at **amortised cost** where:

(i) The asset is held within a **business model** where the objective is to hold financial assets in order to **collect contractual cash flows**; and

(ii) The contractual terms of the financial asset give rise on specified dates to **cash flows that are solely payments of principal and interest** on the principal amount outstanding.

All other financial assets are measured at fair value.

Deposit with Em Bank

At first glance, it appears that this deposit **may meet the criteria to be measured at amortised cost** because Bed will receive cash flows comprising the principal amount ($10 million) and interest (2.5%). However, IFRS 9 requires the **cash flows to be consistent with a basic lending arrangement**, where the **time value of money and credit risk** are typically the most significant elements of interest. **Contractual terms** that **introduce exposure to risk or volatility in the contractual cash flows** that is

unrelated to a basic lending arrangement, such as exposure to changes in exchange rates, **do not give rise to contractual cash flows that are solely payments of principal and interest**.

The **additional 3% interest** Bed will receive if the exchange rate target is reached, exposes Bed to **risk in cash flows** that are **unrelated to a basic lending arrangement** (movement in exchange rates). Therefore, the contract with Em Bank does not give rise to contractual cash flows that are purely payments of principal and interest and as a result, it should not be measured at amortised cost. This type of contract is referred to as a 'hybrid contract'.

This **additional 3%** dependent on exchange rates is an **embedded derivative**. Derivatives embedded within a **host** which is a **financial asset** within the scope of IFRS 9 are **not separated out** for accounting purposes. Instead the **usual IFRS 9 measurement** requirements should be applied to the entire hybrid contract.

Since the **contract with Em Bank** does **not** meet the criteria to be measured at **amortised cost**, the **entire contract** (including the term entitling Bed to an additional 3% if the exchange rate target is met) should be **measured at fair value through profit or loss**.

5 Control

(a) IFRS 10 states that an investor **controls** an investee if and only if it has all of the following.

(1) **Power** over the investee;

(2) Exposure, or rights, to **variable returns** from its involvement with the investee; and

(3) The **ability to use its power** over the investee to affect the amount of the investor's returns.

Power is defined as **existing rights that give the current ability to direct the relevant activities of the investee**. There is no requirement for that power to have been exercised.

Relevant activities may include:

- Selling and purchasing goods or services
- Managing financial assets
- Selecting, acquiring and disposing of assets
- Researching and developing new products and processes
- Determining a funding structure or obtaining funding

In some cases assessing power is straightforward, for example, where power is obtained directly and solely from having the majority of voting rights or potential voting rights, and as a result the ability to direct relevant activities.

(b)

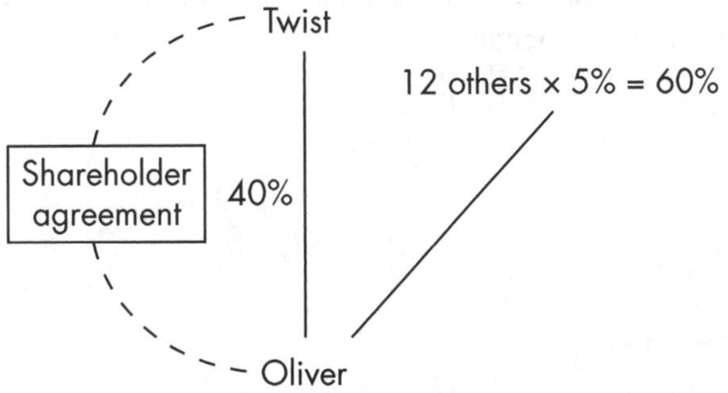

The absolute size of Twist's holding and the relative size of the other shareholdings alone are not conclusive in determining whether the investor has rights sufficient to give it power. However, the fact that Twist has **a contractual right to appoint, remove and set the remuneration of management** is sufficient to conclude that it **has power over Oliver**. The fact that Twist has not exercised this right is not a determining factor when assessing whether Twist has power. In conclusion, Twist does control Oliver, and should consolidate it.

(c)

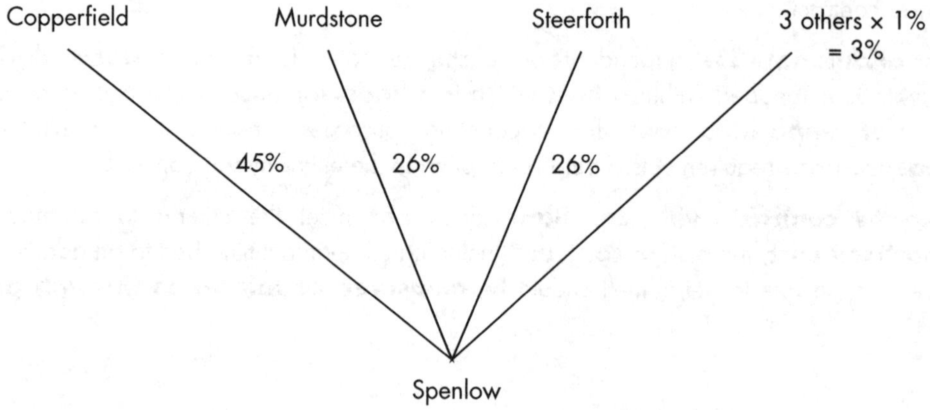

In this case, the size of Copperfield's voting interest and its size relative to the other shareholdings are sufficient to conclude that Copperfield **does not have power**. Only two other investors, Murdstone and Steerforth, would need to co-operate to be able to prevent Copperfield from directing the relevant activities of Spenlow.

(d)

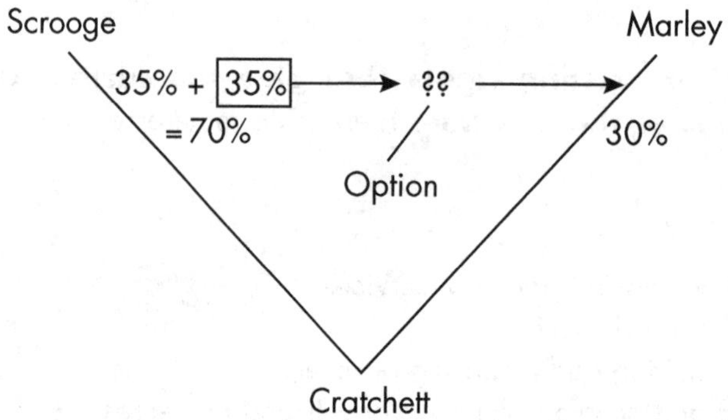

Scrooge holds a majority of the current voting rights of Cratchett, so is likely to meet the power criterion because it appears to have the current ability to direct the relevant activities. Although Marley has currently exercisable options to purchase additional voting rights (that, if exercised, would give it a majority of the voting rights in Cratchett), the terms and conditions associated with those options are such that the options are not considered substantive.

Thus voting rights, even combined with potential voting rights, may not be the deciding factor. Scrooge should consolidate Cratchett.

6 Associate

J GROUP CONSOLIDATED STATEMENT OF FINANCIAL POSITION AS AT 31 DECEMBER 20X5

Assets	$'000
Non-current assets	
Freehold property (1,950 + 1,250 + 370 (W7))	3,570
Plant and equipment (795 + 375)	1,170
Investment in associate (W3)	480
	5,220
Current assets	
Inventories (575 + 300 – 20 (W6))	855
Trade receivables (330 + 290))	620
Cash at bank and in hand (50 + 120)	170
	1,645
	6,865
Equity and liabilities	
Equity attributable to owners of the parent	
Issued share capital	2,000
Retained earnings	1,785
	3,785
Non-controlling interests (W5)	890
Total equity	4,675
Non-current liabilities	
12% debentures (500 + 100)	600
Current liabilities	
Bank overdraft	560
Trade payables (680 + 350)	1,030
	1,590
Total liabilities	2,190
	6,865

Workings

1 *Group structure*

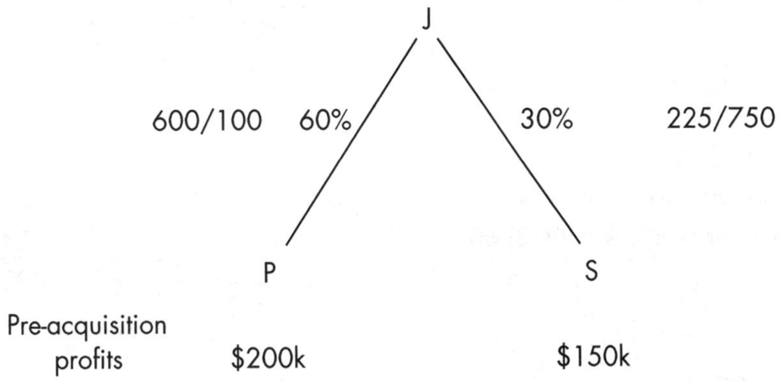

2 *Goodwill*

	$'000	$'000
Consideration transferred		1,000
NCI (at 'full' FV: 400 × $1.65)		660
Net assets acquired:		
Share capital	1,000	
Retained earnings at acquisition	200	
Fair value adjustment (W7)	400	
		(1,600)
		60
Impairments to date		(60)
Year-end value		–

3 *Investment in associate*

	$'000
Cost of associate	500.0
Share of post-acquisition retained reserves (W4)	72.0
Less impairment of investment in associate	(92.0)
	480.0

4 *Retained earnings*

	J Co $'000	*P Co* $'000	*S Co* $'000
Retained earnings per question	1,460	885	390
Unrealised profit (W6)		(20)	
Fair value adjustment movement (W6)		(30)	
Retained earnings at acquisition		(200)	(150)
		635	240
P Co: share of post-acquisition retained earnings 60% × 635	381		
S Co: share of post-acquisition retained earnings 30% × 240	72		
Goodwill impairments to date			
P Co: 60 (W2) × 60%	(36)		
S Co	(92)		
	1,785		

5 *Non-controlling interests*

	$'000
NCI at acquisition (W2)	660
NCI share of post-acquisition retained earnings ((W4) 635 × 40%)	254
NCI share of impairment losses ((W2) 60 × 40%)	(24)
	890

6 *Unrealised profit on inventories*

P Co ⟶ J Co $100k × 25/125 = $20,000

7 Fair value adjustment table

	At acquisition $'000	Movement $'000	At reporting date $'000
Land	200		200
Buildings	200	(30)	170 (200 × 34/40)
	400	(30)	370

7 Part disposal

(a) ANGEL GROUP
CONSOLIDATED STATEMENT OF FINANCIAL POSITION AS AT 31 DECEMBER 20X8

	$'000
Non-current assets	
Property, plant and equipment	200.00
Investment in Shane (W3)	133.15
	333.15
Current assets (890 + 120 (cash on sale))	1,010.00
	1,343.15
Equity attributable to owners of the parent	
Share capital	500.00
Retained reserves (W4)	533.15
	1,033.15
Current liabilities	310.00
	1,343.15

ANGEL GROUP
CONSOLIDATED STATEMENT OF PROFIT OR LOSS AND OTHER COMPREHENSIVE INCOME
FOR THE YEAR ENDED 31 DECEMBER 20X8

	$'000
Profit before interest and tax [100 + (20 × 6/12)]	110.00
Profit on disposal of shares in subsidiary (W6)	80.30
Share of profit of associate (12 × 35% × 6/12)	2.10
Profit before tax	192.40
Income tax expense [40 + (8 × 6/12)]	(44.00)
Profit for the year	148.40
Other comprehensive income (not reclassified to P/L) net of tax [10 + (6 × 6/12)]	13.00
Share of other comprehensive income of associate (6 × 35% × 6/12)	1.05
Other comprehensive income for the year	14.05
Total comprehensive income for the year	162.45

	$'000
Profit attributable to:	
Owners of the parent	146.60
Non-controlling interests (12 × 6/12 × 30%)	1.80
	148.40
Total comprehensive income attributable to:	
Owners of the parents	159.75
Non-controlling interests (18 × 6/12 × 30%)	2.70
	162.45

ANGEL GROUP
CONSOLIDATED RECONCILIATION OF MOVEMENT IN RETAINED RESERVES

	$'000
Balance at 31 December 20X7 (W5)	373.40
Total comprehensive income for the year	159.75
Balance at 31 December 20X8 (W4)	533.15

Workings

1 *Timeline*

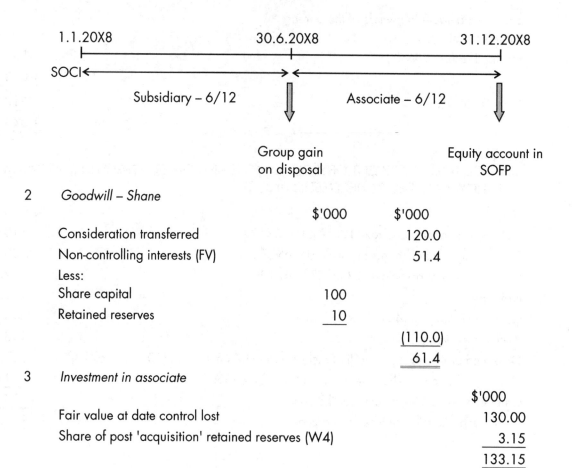

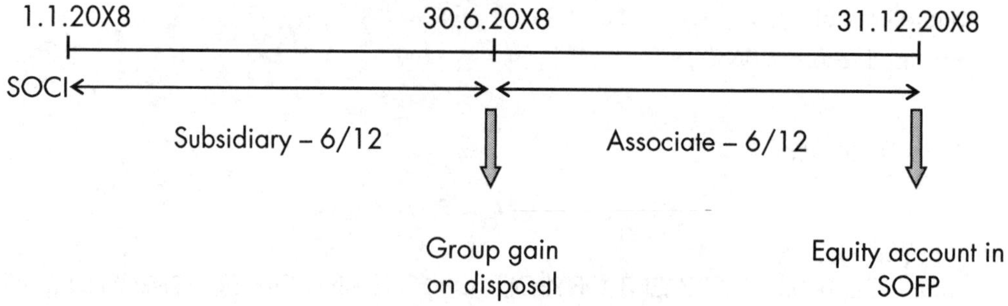

2 *Goodwill – Shane*

	$'000	$'000
Consideration transferred		120.0
Non-controlling interests (FV)		51.4
Less:		
Share capital	100	
Retained reserves	10	
		(110.0)
		61.4

3 *Investment in associate*

	$'000
Fair value at date control lost	130.00
Share of post 'acquisition' retained reserves (W4)	3.15
	133.15

4 *Group retained reserves*

	Angel	Shane	Shane
	$'000	$'000	$'000
		70%	35% retained
Per question/date of disposal (90 – (18 × 6/12))	400.00	81	90
Group profit on disposal (W4)	80.30		
Less retained reserves at acquisition/date of disposal		(10)	(81)
		71	9
Shane: 70% × 71	49.70		
Shane: 35% × 9	3.15		
	533.15		

5 *Retained reserves b/f*

	Angel	Shane
	$'000	$'000
Per question	330.0	72
Less pre-acquisition retained reserves		(10)
	330.0	62
Shane – Share of post-acquisition ret'd reserves (62 × 70%)	43.4	
	373.4	

6 *Group profit on disposal of Shane*

	$'000	$'000
Fair value of consideration received		120.0
Fair value of 35% investment retained		130.0
Less share of carrying amount when control lost		
Net assets 190 – (18 × 6/12)	181.0	
Goodwill (W2)	61.4	
Less non-controlling interests (W7)	(72.7)	
		(169.7)
		80.3

7 *Non-controlling interests at date of disposal*

	$'000
Non-controlling interest at acquisition (FV)	51.4
NCI share of post-acq'n retained earnings (30% × 71(W4))	21.3
	72.7

(b) **Angel disposes of 10% of its holding**

If Angel disposes of 10% of its holding in Shane, Shane goes from being a 70% subsidiary to a 60% subsidiary. In other words **control is retained**. No accounting boundary has been crossed, and the event is treated as a transaction between owners.

The accounting treatment is as follows:

Statement of profit or loss and other comprehensive income

(i) The subsidiary is **consolidated in full** for the whole period.

(ii) The **non-controlling interest in the statement of profit or loss and other comprehensive income** will be based on percentage before and after disposal, ie time apportion.

(iii) There is **no profit or loss on disposal**.

Statement of financial position

(i) The **change (increase) in non-controlling interests** is shown as an **adjustment to the parent's equity**.

(ii) **Goodwill** on acquisition **is unchanged** in the consolidated statement of financial position.

In the case of Angel and Shane you would time apportion the non-controlling interest in the statement of profit or loss and other comprehensive income, giving 30% for the first half the year and 40% for the second half. You would also calculate the adjustment to the parent's equity as follows:

	$'000
Fair value of consideration received	X
Increase in NCI in net assets and goodwill at disposal	(X)
Adjustment to parent's equity	X

8 Step acquisition

(a) Prior to the acquisition of 20% on 1 March 20X1, **SD already controls KL** with its 60% investment, so **KL is already a subsidiary** and would be fully consolidated. In substance, this is **not an acquisition**. Instead, it is treated in the group accounts as a **transaction between the group shareholders** ie the parent has purchased a 20% shareholding from the non-controlling interests (NCI). No goodwill is calculated on the additional investment.

The value of the NCI needs to be worked out at the date of the additional investment (1 March 20X1), and the **proportion purchased by the parent needs to be removed from NCI**. The difference between the consideration transferred and the amount of the reduction in the NCI is included as an **adjustment to equity**.

KL must be **consolidated** in the group **statement of profit or loss and other comprehensive income** for the **full year** but **NCI will be pro-rated** with 40% for the first eight months and 20% for the following four months. In the **consolidated statement of financial position**, KL will be **consolidated with a 20% NCI**.

(b) (i) Goodwill $1,450,000 (W2)
(ii) Group retained earnings $9,843,999 (W3)
(iii) Non-controlling interests $1,096,001 (W4)

Workings

1 *Group structure*

SD

	1.7.X0	60%
	1.3.X1	20%
		80%

KL Pre-acquisition retained earnings $2,760,000

Timeline

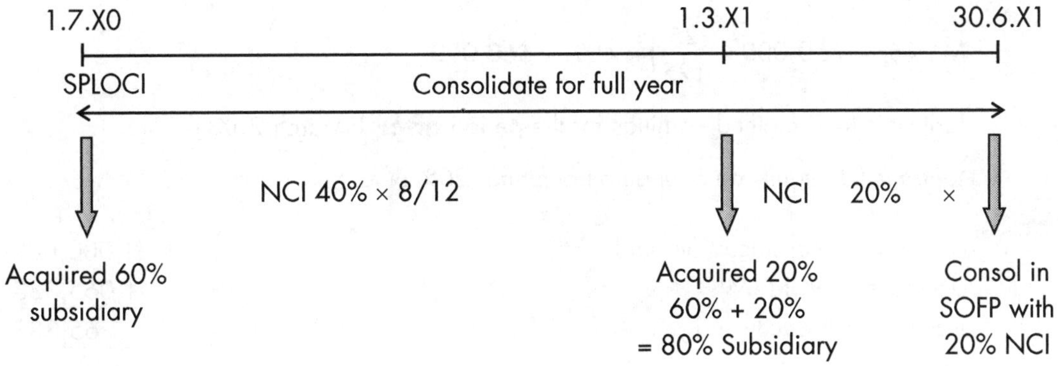

2 *Goodwill (calculated at date when control was originally obtained)*

	$	$
Consideration transferred		3,250,000
NCI at fair value		1,960,000
Less net assets at acquisition:		
Share capital	1,000,000	
Pre-acquisition retained earnings (W1)	2,760,000	
		(3,760,000)
Goodwill		1,450,000

3 *Consolidated retained earnings*

	SD	*KL* 60%	*KL* 80%
	$	$	$
At year end/step acquisition	9,400,000	3,186,667	3,400,000
Unrealised profit (W5)			(60,000)
At acquisition/step acquisition		(2,760,000)	(3,186,667)
		426,667	153,333
Group share (60% × 426,667)	256,000		
(80% × 153,333)	122,666		
Adjustment to parent's equity W6)	65,333		
	9,843,999		

KL's retained earnings for the year to 30 June 20X1 (3,400,000 – 2,760,000) = $640,000
KL's retained earnings for the 8 months to 28 February 20X1 (640,000 × 8/12) = $426,667
KL's retained earnings as at 28 February 20X1 (2,760,000 + 426,667) = $3,186,667

4 *Non-controlling interest*

	$
NCI at acquisition	1,960,000
NCI share of post-acquisition retained earnings to 28.2.X1 (40% × 426,667 (W3))	170,667
	2,130,667
Decrease in NCI on further acquisition (20%/40% × 2,130,667)	(1,065,333)
NCI share of post-acquisition retained earnings to 30.6.X1 (20% × 153,333 (W3))	30,667
	1,096,001

5 *Provision for unrealised profit*

Intragroup sales by KL $750,000

Mark-up ($750,000 × $\frac{25}{125}$) × 40% = $60,000

(adjust in KL's retained earnings for the period **after** 1 March 20X1)

6 *Adjustment to equity on acquisition of further 20% of KL*

	$
Fair value of consideration paid	(1,000,000)
Decrease in NCI (W4)	1,065,333
Adjustment to equity	65,333

Adjustment would be:

	$	$
DEBIT (↓) Non-controlling interest	1,065,333	
CREDIT (↑) Group equity		65,333
CREDIT (↓) Cash (consideration)		1,000,000

9 Foreign operation

CONSOLIDATED STATEMENT OF FINANCIAL POSITION

	$'000
Property, plant and equipment (1,285 + 543 (W2))	1,828
Goodwill (W4)	240
	2,068
Current assets (410 + 247 (W2))	657
	2,725
Share capital	500
Retained earnings (W5)	1,260
Other components of equity – translation reserve (W8)	98
	1,858
Non-controlling interest (W6)	131
	1,989
Loans (200 + 37 (W2))	237
Current liabilities (400 + 99 (W2))	499
	736
	2,725

CONSOLIDATED STATEMENT OF PROFIT OR LOSS AND OTHER COMPREHENSIVE INCOME

	$'000
Revenue (1,125 + 619 (W3))	1,744
Cost of sales (410 + 274 (W3))	(684)
Gross profit	1,060
Other expenses (180 + 108 (W3))	(288)
Goodwill impairment loss (W4)	(18)
Profit before tax	754
Income tax expense (180 + 76 (W3))	(256)
Profit for the year	498
Other comprehensive income	
Items that may subsequently be reclassified to profit or loss	
Exchange difference on translating foreign operations (W9)	69
Total comprehensive income for the year	567
Profit attributable to:	
Owners of the parent (balancing figure)	466
Non-controlling interests (W7)	32
	498
Total comprehensive income attributable to:	
Owners of the parent	525
Non-controlling interests (W7)	42
	567

Workings

1 *Group structure*

Standard

1.1.20X5 | 80%

Odense — Pre-acquisition retained earnings = 2,500,000 krone

2 *Translation of Odense – Statement of financial position*

	Kr'000	Rate	$'000	
Property, plant and equipment	4,400	8.1	543	
Current assets	2,000	8.1	247	
	6,400		790	
Share capital	1,000	9.4	106	
Pre-acquisition retained earnings	2,500	9.4	266	
Post-acquisition retained earnings:				
– 20X5 profit	1,200	9.1	132	
– 20X5 dividend	(345)	8.8	(39)	470
– 20X6 profit	1,350	8.4	161	
– 20X6 dividend	(405)	8.1	(50)	
Exchange difference on net assets		Bal fig	78	
	5,300		654	
Loans	300	8.1	37	
Current liabilities	800	8.1	99	
	1,100		136	
	6,400		790	

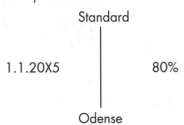

3 *Translation of Odense – statement of profit or loss and other comprehensive income*

	Odense Kr'000	Rate	Odense $'000
Revenue	5,200	8.4	619
Cost of sales	(2,300)	8.4	(274)
Gross profit	2,900		345
Other expenses	(910)	8.4	(108)
Profit before tax	1,990		237
Income tax expense	(640)	8.4	(76)
Profit/Total comprehensive income for the year	1,350		161

4 *Goodwill*

	Kr'000	Kr'000	Rate	$'000
Consideration transferred (520 × 9.4)		4,888		520
Non-controlling interests (3,500 × 20%)		700		74
Share capital	1,000		9.4	
Retained earnings	2,500			
		(3,500)		(372)
		2,088		222
Exchange differences 20X5		–	β	15
At 31.12.X5		2,088	8.8	237
Impairment losses 20X6		(148)	8.1	(18)
Exchange differences 20X6		–	β	21
At 31.12.X6		1,940	8.1	240

5 *Consolidated retained earnings*

	Standard $'000	Odense $'000
At year end	1,115	470
At acquisition		(266)
		204
Group share of post-acquisition retained earnings (204 × 80%)	163	
Less: impairment losses to date (W4)	(18)	
	1,260	

6 *Non-controlling interests (statement of financial position)*

	$'000
NCI at acquisition (W4)	74
NCI share of post-acquisition retained earnings of Odense (204 (W5) × 20%)	41
NCI share of exchange differences on net assets (78 (W2) × 20%)	16
	131

7 *Non-controlling interests (statement of profit or loss and other comprehensive income)*

	PFY $'000	TCI $'000
Profit/Total comprehensive income for the year (W3)	161	161
Other comprehensive income: exchange differences on net assets (W9)	–	48
	161	209
NCI share	× 20%	× 20%
	= 32	= 42

8 *Consolidated translation reserve*

	$'000
Exchange differences on net assets (78 (W2) × 80%)	62
Exchange differences on goodwill (15 + 21 (W4))	36
	98

9 *Exchange differences*

	$'000
On translation of net assets:	
Closing NA @ CR (W2)	654
Opening NA @ OR (1,000 + 3,355 = 4,355* @ 8.8)	(495)
Less retained profit as translated (PFY – dividends)(161 (W3) – 405 @ 8.1)	(111)
	48
On goodwill (W4)	21
	69

* The opening net assets have been calculated as share capital (from Odense's statement of financial position) plus opening retained earnings (from Odense's statement of changes in equity extract). Alternatively, they could have been calculated as closing net assets less total comprehensive income for the year plus dividends: Kr(5,300,000 – 1,350,000 + 405,000).

Tutorial note.

As Standard chose to measure the non-controlling interest in Odense at the proportionate share of net assets at acquisition, the partial goodwill method has been adopted. This means that only group goodwill is recognised in the consolidated statement of financial position and therefore, no goodwill is recognised for the non-controlling interests (NCI). Therefore, there are no exchange differences on goodwill relating to NCI. This is why only the exchange differences on net assets (and not the exchange differences on goodwill) are included in the NCI workings ((W6) and (W7)). Since all the recognised goodwill relates to the group, in the consolidated translation reserve working (W8), the exchange differences on goodwill are not multiplied by the group share.

If Standard had measured NCI at fair value at acquisition (the full goodwill method), both group goodwill and goodwill relating to the NCI would have been recognised. Therefore, in the NCI workings, the exchange differences on goodwill would be included. In the consolidated translation reserve working, the exchange differences on goodwill would be multiplied by the group share (in the same way as the exchange differences on net assets have been treated).

It might help if you think about the treatment of exchange differences on goodwill as being the same as the treatment for impairment losses on goodwill. So under the partial goodwill method, as all of the recognised goodwill relates to the group, all of the impairment losses and exchange differences on goodwill belong to the group so they should be recognised in full in the consolidated retained earnings and translation reserve workings respectively and neither would be included in NCI workings. Whereas for the full goodwill method, impairment losses and exchange differences on goodwill are apportioned between the group (in the retained earnings and translation reserve workings) and the NCI (in the NCI workings).

10 Consolidated statement of cash flows

STATEMENT OF CASH FLOWS FOR THE YEAR ENDED 31 DECEMBER 20X5

	$'000	$'000
Cash flows from operating activities		
Profit before tax	16,500	
Adjustments for:		
Depreciation	5,800	
Impairment losses (W1)	240	
	22,540	
Increase in trade receivables (W4)	(1,700)	
Increase in inventories (W4)	(4,400)	
Increase in trade payables (W4)	1,200	
Cash generated from operations	17,640	
Income taxes paid (W3)	(4,200)	
Net cash from operating activities		13,440
Cash flows from investing activities		
Acquisition of subsidiary net of cash acquired	(600)	
Purchase of property, plant and equipment (W1)	(13,100)	
Net cash used in investing activities		(13,700)
Cash flows from financing activities		
Proceeds from issue of share capital (W2)	2,100	
Dividends paid (W2)	(900)	
Dividends paid to non-controlling interest (W2)	(40)	
Net cash from financing activities		1,160
Net increase in cash and cash equivalents		900
Cash and cash equivalents at the beginning of the period		1,500
Cash and cash equivalents at the end of the period		2,400

Workings

1 *Assets*

	Property, plant and equipment $'000	*Goodwill* $'000
b/d	25,000	–
OCI (revaluation)	500	
Depreciation/Impairment	(5,800)	**(240)** β
Acquisition of sub/associate	2,700	1,640 (W5)
Cash paid/(rec'd) β	**13,100**	–
c/d	35,500	1,400

2 *Equity*

	Share capital $'000	*Share premium* $'000	*Retained earnings* $'000	*Non-controlling interest* $'000
b/d	10,000	2,000	21,900	–
SPLOCI			11,100	350
Acquisition of subsidiary	1,500	2,500		1,440 (W5)
Cash (paid)/rec'd β	**800**	**1,300**	**(900)***	**(40)**
c/d	12,300	5,800	32,100	1,750

*Dividend paid is given in question but working shown for clarity.

3 *Liabilities*

	Tax payable
	$'000
b/d	4,000
P/L	5,200
Acquisition of subsidiary	200
Cash (paid)/rec'd	**(4,200)** β
c/d	5,200

4 *Working capital changes*

	Inventories	*Receivables*	*Payables*
	$'000	$'000	$'000
Balance b/d	10,000	7,500	6,100
Acquisition of subsidiary	1,600	600	300
	11,600	8,100	6,400
Increase/(decrease) (balancing figure)	**4,400**	**1,700**	**1,200**
Balance c/d	16,000	9,800	7,600

5 *Purchase of subsidiary*

	$'000
Cash received on acquisition of subsidiary	400
Less cash consideration	(1,000)
Cash outflow	(600)

Note. Only the **cash** consideration is included in the figure reported in the statement of cash flows. The **shares** issued as part of the consideration are reflected in the share capital working (W2) above.

Goodwill on acquisition (before impairment):

	$'000
Consideration: 55 + 695 (W3) + 120 (W2) + 216	5,000
Non-controlling interest: 4,800 × 30%	1,440
Net assets acquired	(4,800)
Goodwill	1,640

11 Robby

Workbook references. The underlying principles of IFRS 3 are covered in Chapter 11. Business combinations achieved in stages are covered in Chapter 12. Joint operations are covered in Chapter 15 and financial instruments in Chapter 8. The *Conceptual Framework* is covered in Chapter 1.

Top tips. You must make sure that you explain the principles underlying the accounting for goodwill as the marks available for calculations are limited. The examining team is looking for an understanding of the accounting involved and not rote learning of consolidation workings.

In Part (b), you need to evaluate whether the requirements of IFRS 9 relating to the factoring arrangement are in agreement with the *Conceptual Framework*. This kind of evaluation in light of the *Conceptual Framework* is likely to be a feature of questions in the SBR examination, so you need to make sure you are familiar enough with the *Conceptual Framework* to be able to answer questions in this way.

Marking scheme

			Marks
(a)	(i)	Goodwill	
		Explanation of IFRS 3 principles	10
		Hail – calculation	3
		Zinc – calculation	3
			16
	(ii)	Joint operation	
		SOFP	3
		Explanation – 1 mark per point up to a maximum	4
			7
(b)	Discussion – 1 mark per point up to a maximum		7
			30

(a) **Sections for inclusion in the finance director's report**

(i) **Goodwill**

IFRS 3 *Business Combinations* requires goodwill to be recognised in a business combination. A business combination takes place when one entity, the acquirer, obtains control of another entity, the acquiree. IFRS 3 requires goodwill to be calculated and recorded as a non-current asset at the acquisition date.

Goodwill is calculated at the acquisition date as the fair value of the consideration transferred by the acquirer plus the amount of any non-controlling interest less the fair value of the net assets of the acquiree. When the business combination is achieved in stages, as is the case for Zinc, the consideration transferred by the acquirer will include any previously held interest in the new subsidiary which must be remeasured to its fair value at the date control is obtained.

Goodwill is not amortised, but instead is tested for impairment at each year end.

Applying these principles, the goodwill on the acquisition of Hail and Zinc for inclusion in the consolidated financial statements at 31 May 20X3 is calculated as follows.

Goodwill related to the acquisition of Hail

Goodwill at acquisition:	$m	$m
Consideration transferred for 80% interest		
Cash payable on 1 June 20X1	50	
Deferred cash consideration ($24.2 million/$(1.10)^2$)	20	
Contingent consideration	40	
Fair value of non-controlling interest	30	
		140
Fair value of identifiable net assets acquired	130	
Contingent liability	(2)	
		(128)
		12

The immediate, deferred and contingent consideration transferred should be measured at their fair values at the acquisition date.

Deferred consideration

The fair value of the deferred consideration is the amount payable on 31 May 20X4 discounted to its present value at the acquisition date. The requirement to discount to present value is consistent with other standards. The present value should be unwound in the period to 31 May 20X3 which will increase the carrying amount of the obligation and result in a finance cost in profit or loss. The unwinding of the discount does not affect the goodwill calculation as it is based on the amount payable at the date of acquisition.

Contingent consideration

The fair value of the contingent consideration payable should take into account the various milestones set under the acquisition agreement. At the acquisition date the fair value of the contingent consideration is $40 million.

As the contingent consideration will be paid in cash, the amount payable should be remeasured at 31 May 20X3 to its fair value of $42 million. This remeasurement does not affect the goodwill calculation, but the increase in the fair value of the obligation of $2 million should be taken to profit or loss. If the contingent consideration was to be settled in equity, no remeasurement would be required.

Contingent liability

The contingent liability disclosed in Hail's financial statements is recognised as a liability on acquisition in accordance with IFRS 3, provided that its fair value can be reliably measured and it is a present obligation. This is contrary to the normal rules in IAS 37 *Provisions, Contingent Liabilities and Contingent Assets* where contingent liabilities are not recognised but only disclosed.

Conclusion

There is no indication that the goodwill balance is impaired at 31 May 20X3. Thus goodwill of $12 million on acquisition of Hail should be included in the group financial statements at 31 May 20X3.

Goodwill related to the acquisition of Zinc

Substance over form drives the accounting treatment for a subsidiary acquired in stages. The legal form is that shares have been acquired, however, in substance:

(1) The 5% investment has been 'sold'. Per IFRS 3, the investment previously held is remeasured to fair value at the date control is obtained and a gain or loss reported in profit or loss:

	$m
Fair value of 5% at date control achieved (1 December 20X2)	5
Fair value of carrying amount of 5% per SOFP at 31 May 20X2	(3)
Remeasurement gain (1 June 20X2 to 1 December 20X2)	2

(2) A subsidiary has been 'purchased'. The previously held 5% investment is effectively re-acquired at fair value, and so goodwill is calculated including the fair value of the previously held 5% investment.

Goodwill	$m	$m
Consideration transferred – for 55%	16	
Fair value of non-controlling interest	9	
Fair value of previously held interest (for 5% at 1 December 20X2)	5	
		30
Fair value of identifiable net assets at acquisition:		
Provisional measurement	26	
Adjustment to fair value of PPE (within measurement period)	3	
		(29)
		1

Fair value of PPE

The fair value of PPE was provisional at the date of acquisition, with an increase of $3 million subsequently identified when the figures were finalised in March 20X3. IFRS 3 permits adjustments to goodwill for adjustments to the fair value of assets and liabilities acquired, provided this adjustment is made within one year of the date of acquisition (the measurement period).

Conclusion

There is no indication that the goodwill balance is impaired at 31 May 20X3. Thus goodwill related to the acquisition of Zinc to be included in the group financial statements at 31 May 20X3 is $1 million.

(ii) **Joint operation**

Robby has a joint arrangement with another party in respect of the natural gas station. Under IFRS 11 *Joint Arrangements*, a joint arrangement is one in which two or more parties are bound by a contractual arrangement which gives them joint control over the arrangement.

Joint arrangements can either be joint ventures or joint operations. The classification as a joint venture or joint operation depends on the rights and obligations of the parties to the arrangement. It is important to correctly classify the arrangement as the accounting requirements for joint ventures are different to those for joint operations.

IFRS 11 states that a joint arrangement that is not structured through a separate vehicle is a joint operation. In Robby's case, no separate entity has been set up for the joint arrangement, therefore it is a joint operation. Robby has joint rights to the assets and revenue, and joint obligations for the liabilities and costs of the joint arrangement.

Therefore, Robby, in its capacity as a joint operator, must recognise on a line-by-line basis its own assets, liabilities, revenues and expenses plus its share (40%) of the joint assets, liabilities, revenue and expenses of the joint operation as prescribed by IFRS 11. This treatment is applicable to both the consolidated and separate financial statements of Robby.

The figures are calculated as follows:

Statement of financial position

	$m
Property, plant and equipment:	
1 June 20X2 cost: gas station (15 × 40%)	6.00
dismantling provision (2 × 40%)	0.80
	6.80
Accumulated depreciation: 6.8/10 years	(0.68)
31 May 20X3 carrying amount	6.12
Trade receivables (from other joint operator): 20 (revenue) × 40%	8.00
Trade payables (to other joint operator): (16 + 0.5) (costs) × 40%	6.60
Dismantling provision:	
At 1 June 20X2	0.80
Finance cost (unwinding of discount): 0.8 × 5%	0.04
At 31 May 20X3	0.84

(b) **Accounting treatment**

Trade receivables are financial assets and therefore the requirements of IFRS 9 *Financial Instruments* need to be applied. The main question here is whether the factoring arrangement means that Robby should derecognise the trade receivables from the financial statements.

Per IFRS 9, an entity should derecognise a **financial asset** when:

(1) The **contractual rights** to the cash flows from the financial asset **expire**; or

(2) The entity **transfers the financial asset or substantially all the risks and rewards of ownership** of the financial asset to another party.

In the case of Robby, the contractual rights to the cash flows have not expired as the receivables balances are still outstanding and expected to be collected.

In respect of the risks and rewards of ownership, the substance of the factoring arrangement needs to be considered rather than its legal form. Robby has transferred the receivables to the bank in exchange for $3.6 million cash, but remains liable for any shortfall between $3.6 million and the amount collected. In principle, Robby is liable for the whole $3.6 million, although it is unlikely that the default would be as much as this. **Robby therefore retains the credit risk**.

In addition, Robby is entitled to receive the benefit (less interest) of repayments in excess of $3.6 million once the $3.6 million has been collected and therefore retains the potential rewards of full settlement.

Substantially all the risks and rewards of the financial asset **therefore remain with Robby**, and the receivables should **continue to be recognised**. In addition, a **financial liability** should be recognised in respect of the consideration received from the bank.

Conceptual Framework

According to the *Conceptual Framework* derecognition normally occurs when **control** of all or part of an asset is lost.

The requirements for derecognition should aim to **faithfully represent** both:

(a) Any assets and liabilities retained after derecognition; and
(b) The change in the entity's assets and liabilities as a result of derecognition.

Meeting both of these aims becomes difficult if the entity disposes of only part of an asset or retains some exposure to that asset. It can be difficult to faithfully represent the legal form (which in this case is the decrease in assets under the factoring arrangement) with the substance of retaining the corresponding risks and rewards.

Because of the difficulties in practice in meeting these two aims, the *Conceptual Framework* does not advocate using a control approach or the risks-and-rewards approach to derecognition in every circumstance. Instead, it describes the options available and discusses what factors the IASB would need to consider when developing Standards.

As such, there appears to be no conflict in principles between the *Conceptual Framework* and the requirements of IFRS 9 for derecognition.

12 Diamond

Workbook references. Group accounting is covered in Chapters 11–15. Employee benefits are covered in Chapter 5, non-current assets in Chapter 4, leasing in Chapter 9 and debt factoring in Chapter 8.

Top tips. This question focuses on the calculation of goodwill and a disposal in which significant influence is lost. It is important that you focus on the requirements and ensure that you give advice as well as preparing relevant calculations. Providing the calculations alone will not be sufficient to meet the requirements of the question.

Easy marks. Both the pensions and lease parts of the question contain easy marks if you are familiar with these areas of the syllabus.

Marking scheme

			Marks
(a)	(i)	Goodwill on acquisition of – Spade	5
		– Club	5
			10
	(ii)	Disposal of Heart	5
	(iii)	Pension adjustment	3
	(iv)	Leased manufacturing unit	3
			21
(b)		Debt factoring	9
			30

(a) Diamond Group

(i) **Goodwill on acquisition of Spade**

Diamond obtained control of Spade on 1 April 20X6. On acquisition, IFRS 3 requires that goodwill is calculated as the excess of:

The sum of:

- The fair value of the **consideration transferred** which is the cash paid at 1 April 20X6; plus

- The 30% **non-controlling interest**, measured at its fair value (per Diamond's accounting policy) of $485 million at 1 April 20X6

Less the **fair value of Spade's net assets** of $1,600 million 1 April 20X6.

The finance director has not taken into account the fair value of the non-controlling interest in calculation. As the finance director had calculated negative goodwill, the gain on a bargain purchase will have been recognised in profit and loss under IFRS 3.

Goodwill on the acquisition of **Spade** should have been calculated as follows:

	$m
Cash consideration	1,140
Non-controlling interest – fair value	485
	1,625
Fair value of identifiable net assets acquired	(1,600)
Goodwill	25

The adjustment required to the consolidated financial statements is:

DEBIT (increase) Goodwill	$25 million	
DEBIT (decrease) Profit or loss	$460 million	
CREDIT (increase) NCI		$485 million

Goodwill on the acquisition of Club

From 1 April 20X5 to 31 March 20X6, Club is an **associate of Diamond** and equity accounting is applied. On acquisition of the additional 45% investment on 1 April 20X6, Diamond obtained **control** of Club, making it a **subsidiary**.

This is a step acquisition where control has been achieved in stages. In **substance**, on 1 April 20X6, on obtaining control, Diamond **'sold' a 40% associate** and **'purchased' an 85% subsidiary**. Therefore, **goodwill** is calculated using the **same principles** that would be applied **if Diamond had purchased the full 85%** shareholding at fair value on 1 April 20X6.

IFRS 3 requires that goodwill is calculated as the excess of:

The sum of:

- The fair value of the **consideration transferred** for the additional 45% holding, which is the cash paid at 1 April 20X6; plus
- The 15% **non-controlling interest**, measured at its fair value at 1 April 20X6 of (15% × $700m × $1.60) = $168 million; plus
- The fair value at 1 April 20X6 of the **original 40% investment 'sold'** of (40% × $700m × $1.60) = $448 million.

Less the **fair value of Club's net assets** of $1,062 million at 1 April 20X6.

Goodwill is calculated as follows:

	$m
Cash consideration	500
Fair value of original 40% interest	448
Non-controlling interest	168
	1,116
Fair value of identifiable net assets acquired	(1,062)
Goodwill	54

The finance director has incorrectly recorded a negative goodwill balance of $562 million and so will have recognised a gain on a bargain purchase of $562 million in consolidated profit or loss.

The adjustments required to the consolidated financial statements are:

DEBIT (increase) Goodwill	$54 million	
DEBIT (decrease) Profit or loss	$562 million	
CREDIT (increase) NCI		$168 million
CREDIT (decrease) Investment in Club		$448 million

Tutorial note.

In a step-acquisition, the investment in associate balance in the consolidated financial statements is first remeasured to fair value (for inclusion in the goodwill calculation) and a gain recognised in consolidated profit or loss. This calculation is not asked for in the question, but for tutorial purposes it would be as follows.

Gain on remeasurement of the 40% investment

	$m	$m
Fair value of original investment (40%)		448
Less carrying amount of associate:		
Cost of associate	420	
Share of post-acquisition reserves (40% × [700 + 293 + 59] – 1,032])	8	
		(428)
Gain on remeasurement		20

The double entry to record the remeasurement is:

DEBIT investment in associate	$20m	
CREDIT profit or loss		$20m

(ii) **Disposal of Heart**

Up to 30 September 20X6, Heart is an associate of Diamond. The finance director of Diamond has equity accounted for Heart up to 31 March 20X6, however he should have equity accounted up to 30 September 20X6, at which point significant influence is lost. A further $2.5 million (25% × $20m × 6/12) should have been added to the investment in associate balance and included within retained earnings. The total investment in associate balance at 30 September 20X6 should therefore have been $112.5 million ($110m + $2.5m)

On losing significant influence, a profit or loss on disposal should be calculated:

	$m
Proceeds	42.0
Fair value of remaining interest at 30 September 20X6	65.0
	107.0
Investment in associate at 30 September 20X6	(112.5)
Loss on disposal	(5.5)

The remaining 15% holding is an equity investment under IFRS 9 *Financial Instruments* which Diamond has elected to classify as an equity investment measured at fair value through other comprehensive income. The investment should be remeasured to fair value of $67 million at 31 March 20X7, resulting in a gain of $2 million ($67m – $65m) which should be recognised in other comprehensive income.

The adjustments required to correct the finance director's errors and correctly record the disposal are as follows:

(1) To record Diamond's share of Heart's results from 1 April to 30 September 20X6

DEBIT (increase) Investment in Heart	$2.5 million	
CREDIT (increase) Retained earnings		$2.5 million

(2) To record the loss on disposal of 10% interest in Heart

DEBIT (decrease) Profit or loss	$5.5 million	
DEBIT (increase) Cash	$42.0 million	
CREDIT (decrease) Investment in Heart		$47.5 million

(3) To record the gain on remeasurement of the equity investment to fair value

DEBIT (increase) Investment in Heart	$2 million	
CREDIT (increase) Other comprehensive income		$2 million

(iii) **Pension adjustment**

Here a curtailment and settlement are happening together, as Diamond is limiting the future benefits from its defined benefit plan for this group of employees due to the restructuring (curtailment) and compensating them by settling part of the existing expected future obligation with a one-off lump sum payment as part of their termination benefits (settlement). The estimated settlement on the pension liability is $7.5 million (150 × $50,000) and should be included within current liabilities, as it appears to be immediately due to Diamond's employees. As this is $1.7 million more than the estimated curtailment gain of $5.8 million, a loss of $1.7 million should be taken to profit or loss. Non-current liabilities are reduced by the reduction in pension obligations of $5.8 million.

The adjustments to incorporate the transaction into Diamond's financial statements would be as follows:

DEBIT (decrease) Profit or loss – settlement loss	$1.7 million	
DEBIT (decrease) Retirement benefit obligation	$5.8 million	
CREDIT (increase) Current liabilities		$7.5 million

Being entries to reflect pension settlement and curtailment on closure of division, unrecorded by Diamond

(iv) **Leased manufacturing unit**

The fact that this is a leased asset does not change how the subsequent expenditure on the asset should be treated. Because the structural alterations represent access to future economic benefits, the alteration costs of $6.6 million should not have been expensed but should be capitalised and depreciated over the remaining lease term.

Diamond has a present obligation (to restore the manufacturing unit to its original condition) to incur expenditure as a result of a past event (the structural alterations it has made to the manufacturing unit). Under IAS 37 *Provisions, Contingent Liabilities and Contingent Assets* a provision should be recognised for the present value of the restoration costs of $3.3 million ($5m × 0.665). This amount should also be capitalised as part of the carrying amount of the asset and depreciated over the remaining lease term.

The adjustments required to correct the finance director's error, capitalise the alteration costs and record the restoration provision are as follows:

DEBIT (increase) Property, plant and equipment	$9.9 million	
CREDIT (increase) Profit or loss		$6.6 million
CREDIT (increase) Non-current liabilities – restoration cost provision		$3.3 million

The additional property, plant and equipment costs of $9.9 million should be depreciated over the remaining 7 years of the lease ($1.4 million per year).

(b) IFRS 9 *Financial Instruments* requires Diamond to consider the commercial substance rather than the legal form of the debt factoring arrangements. IFRS 9 suggests that the trade receivables should be derecognised from the financial statements of Diamond when the following conditions are met:

(i) When Diamond has no further rights to receive cash from the factor

(ii) When the risks and rewards of ownership relating to the receivables have substantially been transferred to the factor

(iii) When Diamond has no further control over the trade receivables

Agreement one

With agreement one there is a sharing of the risks and rewards of ownership as the factoring is non-recourse except that Diamond retains an obligation to refund the factor 9% of irrecoverable debts. It can be seen, however, that substantially all the risks and rewards of ownership have passed to the factor. The probability of an individual default is low given that there is low credit risk and the factor would suffer the vast majority of the loss arising from any default. Diamond also has no further access to the rewards of ownership as the initial $32 million (80% × $40 million) is in full and final settlement. Furthermore, the factor has assumed full control over the collectability of the receivables. The trade receivables should be derecognised from the financial statements of Diamond and $8 million, being the difference between the value of the receivables sold and the cash received, should be charged as an irrecoverable debt expense against the profits of Diamond.

The guarantee should be treated as a separate financial liability in accordance with IFRS 9. This would initially be measured at its fair value of $50,000.

Agreement two

The risks and rewards of ownership do not initially pass to the factor in relation to agreement two. The factor has full recourse to Diamond for a six-month period so the irrecoverable debt risk is still with Diamond. Furthermore, Diamond still has the right to receive further cash payments from the factor, the amounts to be received being dependent on when and if the customers pay the factor. Diamond therefore still has the risks associated with slow payment by their customers. The receivables must not initially be derecognised from the financial statements with the $8 million (20% x $40m) proceeds being treated as a short-term liability due to the factor. The receivables and liability balances would gradually be reduced as the factor recovered the cash from Diamond's customers which would be adjusted for the imputed interest and expensed in profit or loss. Should there be any indication of impairment during the six-month period, the receivables should be credited with a corresponding charge to profit or loss.

Following six months the risks and rewards of ownership have passed to the factor and the balances on the loan and the receivables would be offset. The remaining balance following offset within the receivables of Diamond should be expensed in profit or loss as an irrecoverable debt.

13 Banana

Marking scheme

				Marks
(a)	(i)	Application of the following discussion to the scenario:		
		Goodwill and contingent consideration	3	
		Why the existing goodwill valuation is incorrect	4	
		Correcting entry	1	8
	(ii)	Application of the following discussion to the scenario:		
		Nature of significant influence	2	
		The equity method of accounting for an associate	1	
		Calculation of the carrying amount of the investment	1	4
	(iii)	Calculation of the gain on disposal of Strawberry	2	
		Application of the following discussion to the scenario:		
		Rationale for the calculation of gain on disposal	1	
		Correct treatment of Strawberry after disposal	1	4
	(iv)	Explanation of treatment of settlement	2	
		Explanation of 2018 amendments to IAS 19	1	
				3
(b)		Application of the following discussion to the scenario:		
		Rationale for inclusion as business combination		4
(c)		Application of the following discussion to the scenario:		
		Consideration of IFRS 9 principles	4	
		Transfer of rights/conclusion	1	
		Carrying amount of bonds	2	7
				30

(a) **Explanatory note to: Directors of Banana**
Subject: Consolidation of Grape and Strawberry

(i) Goodwill should be calculated by comparing the fair value of the consideration with the fair value of the identifiable net assets at acquisition. The shares have been correctly valued using the market price of Banana at acquisition. Contingent consideration should be included at its fair value which should be assessed taking into account the probability of the targets being achieved as well as being discounted to present value. It would appear reasonable to measure the consideration at a value of $4 million ($16 million × 25%). A corresponding liability should be included within the consolidated financial statements with subsequent remeasurement. This would be adjusted prospectively to profit or loss rather than adjusting the consideration and goodwill.

The finance director has erroneously measured non-controlling interest using the proportional method rather than at fair value. Although either method is permitted on an acquisition by acquisition basis, the accounting policy of the Banana group is to measure non-controlling interest at fair value. The fair value of the non-controlling interest at acquisition is (20% × $20 million × $4.25) = $17 million.

Net assets at acquisition were incorrectly included at their carrying amount of $70 million. This should be adjusted to fair value of $75 million with a corresponding $5 million increase to land in the consolidated statement of financial position. Goodwill should have been calculated as follows:

	$m
Fair value of share exchange	68
Contingent consideration	4
Non-controlling interest at acquisition	17
Fair value of identifiable net assets acquired	(75)
Goodwill	14

The correcting entry required to the consolidated financial statements is:

DEBIT Goodwill	$2 million	
DEBIT Land	$5 million	
CREDIT Non-controlling interest		$3 million
CREDIT Liabilities		$4 million

(ii) If an entity holds 20% or more of the voting power of the investee, it is presumed that the entity has significant influence unless it can be clearly demonstrated that this is not the case. The existence of significant influence by an entity is usually evidenced by representation on the board of directors or participation in key policy making processes. Banana has 40% of the equity of Strawberry and can appoint one director to the board. It would appear that Banana has significant influence but not control. Strawberry should be classified as an associate and be equity accounted for within the consolidated financial statements.

The equity method is a method of accounting whereby the investment is initially recognised at cost and adjusted thereafter for the post-acquisition change in the investor's share of the investee's net assets. The investor's profit or loss includes its share of the investee's profit or loss and the investor's other comprehensive income includes its share of the investee's other comprehensive income. At 1 October 20X7, Strawberry should have been included in the consolidated financial statements at a value of $20.4 million ($18 million + 40% × $50 million – $44 million).

(iii) On disposal of 75% of the shares, Banana no longer exercises significant influence over Strawberry and a profit on disposal of $3.1 million should have been calculated.

	$m
Proceeds	19.0
Fair value of retained interest	4.5
Carrying amount of investment in associate (see part (ii))	(20.4)
Gain on disposal	3.1

Banana is incorrect to have recorded a loss in reserves of $14 million and this should be reversed. Instead, a gain of $3.1 million should have been included within the consolidated statement of profit or loss. The investment is initially restated to fair value of $4.5 million. Banana does not intend to sell their remaining interest and providing that they make an irrecoverable election, they can treat the remaining interest at fair value through other comprehensive income. The investment will be restated to $4 million at the reporting date with a corresponding loss of $0.5 million reported in other comprehensive income.

(iv) The potential transfer of part of Banana's defined benefit pension plan is a **settlement** under IAS 19. A gain or loss on a settlement is recognised in profit or loss when the settlement occurs. At the date of settlement, the fair value of the plan assets and the present value of the obligation should be remeasured. Using the estimated figures for illustration purposes, a gain of $100,000 should be recognised:

	$m
Present value of obligation settled	5.7
Fair value of plan assets transferred on settlement	(5.4)
Cash transferred on settlement	(0.2)
Gain	0.1

The accounting entries that would be required are:

DEBIT (decrease) Obligation	$5.7 million	
CREDIT (decrease) Plan assets		$5.4 million
CREDIT (decrease) Cash		$0.2 million
CREDIT (increase) Profit or loss		$0.1 million

The 2018 amendments to IAS 19 require that, when a plan amendment, curtailment or settlement takes place, the updated actuarial assumptions used to remeasure the net defined benefit/asset should also be used to determine current service cost and net interest for the remainder of the reporting period. Prior to the amendments, the current service cost and net interest would have been calculated using the assumptions in place at the beginning of the reporting period.

(b) Melon should only be treated as an asset acquisition where the acquisition fails the definition of a business combination. In accordance with IFRS 3 *Business Combinations*, an entity should determine whether a transaction is a business combination by applying the definition of a business in IFRS 3. A business is an integrated set of activities and assets which are capable of being conducted and managed for the purpose of providing a return in the form of dividends, lower costs or other economic benefits directly to investors or other owners, members or participants. A business will typically have inputs and processes applied to the ability to create outputs. Outputs are the result of inputs and processes and are usually present within a business but are not a necessary requirement for a set of integrated activities and assets to be defined as a business at acquisition.

It is clear that Melon has both inputs and processes. The licence is an input as it is an economic resource within the control of Melon which is capable of providing outputs once one or more processes are applied to it. Additionally, the seller does not have to be operating the activities as a business for the acquisition to be classified as a business. It is not relevant therefore that Melon does not have staff and outsources its activities. The definition of a business requires just that the activities could have been operated as a business. Processes are in place through the research activities, integration with the management company and supervisory and administrative functions performed. The research activities are still at an early stage, so no output is yet obtainable but, as identified, this is not a necessary prerequisite for the acquisition to be treated as a business. It can be concluded that Melon is a business and it is incorrect to treat Melon as an asset acquisition.

(c) IFRS 9 *Financial Instruments* requires that a financial asset only qualifies for derecognition once the entity has transferred the contractual rights to receive the cash flows from the asset or where the entity has retained the contractual rights but has an unavoidable obligation to pass on the cash flows to a third party. The substance of the disposal of the bonds needs to be assessed by a consideration of the risks and rewards of ownership.

Banana has not transferred the contractual rights to receive the cash flows from the bonds. The third party is obliged to return the coupon interest to Banana and to pay additional amounts should the fair values of the bonds increase. Consequently, Banana still has the rights associated with the interest and will also benefit from any appreciation in the value of the bonds. Banana still retains the risks of ownership as it has to compensate the third party should the fair value of the bonds depreciate in value.

It would be expected that, if the sale were a genuine transfer of risks and rewards of ownership, then the sales price would be approximate to the fair value of the bonds. It would only be in unusual circumstances such as a forced sale of Banana's assets arising from severe financial difficulties that this would not be the case. The sales price of $8 million is well below the current fair value of the bonds of $10.5 million. Additionally, Banana is likely to exercise their option to repurchase the bonds.

It can be concluded that no transfer of rights has taken place and therefore the asset should not be derecognised. To measure the asset at amortised cost, the entity must have a business model where they intend to collect the contractual cash flows over the life of the asset. Banana maintains these rights and therefore the sale does not contradict their business model. The bonds should continue to be measured at amortised cost in the consolidated financial statements of Banana. The value of the bonds at 30 June 20X6 would have been $10.2 million ($10 million + 7% × $10 million – 5% × $10 million). Amortised cost prohibits a restatement to fair value. The value of the bonds at 30 June 20X7 should be $10.414 million ($10.2 million + 7% × $10.2 million – 5% × $10 million). The proceeds of $8 million should be treated as a financial liability and would also be measured at amortised cost. An interest charge of $0.8 million would accrue between 1 July 20X6 and 1 July 20X8, being the difference between the sale and repurchase price of the bonds.

14 Hill

Marking scheme

			Marks
(a)	(i)	Discussion 1 mark per point to a maximum	8
		Calculation	5
			13
	(ii)	Discussion 1 mark per point to a maximum	3
		Calculation	4
			7
	(iii)	1 mark for each point to a maximum	6
(b)	1 mark for each point to a maximum		9
			35

(a) (i) **Deferred consideration**

When calculating goodwill, IFRS 3 *Business Combinations* states that purchase consideration should be measured at fair value. For deferred cash consideration, this will be the present value of the cash flows. This amounts to $29 million ($32m × 0.907). Goodwill arising on acquisition should be increased by $29 million and a corresponding liability should be recognised:

DEBIT Goodwill	$29 million	
CREDIT Liability		$29 million

Interest of $1.5 million ($29m × 5%) should be recorded. This is charged to the statement of profit or loss and increases the carrying amount of the liability:

DEBIT Finance costs	$1.5 million	
CREDIT Liability		$1.5 million

Property, plant and equipment (PPE)

During the measurement period IFRS 3 states that adjustments should be made retrospectively if new information is determined about the value of consideration transferred, the subsidiary's identifiable net assets, or the non-controlling interest. The measurement period ends no later than 12 months after the acquisition date.

The survey detailed that Chandler's PPE was overvalued by $10 million as at the acquisition date. It was received four months after the acquisition date and so this revised valuation was received during the measurement period. As such, goodwill at acquisition should be recalculated. As at the acquisition date, the carrying amount of PPE should be reduced by $10 million and the carrying amount of goodwill increased by $10 million:

DEBIT Goodwill	$10 million	
CREDIT PPE		$10 million

NCI

The NCI at acquisition was valued at $34 million but it should have been valued at $32 million (($170m – $10m PPE adjustment) × 20%). Both NCI at acquisition and goodwill at acquisition should be reduced by $2 million:

DEBIT NCI	$2 million	
CREDIT Goodwill		$2 million

Goodwill

Goodwill arising on the acquisition of Chandler should have been calculated as follows:

	$m
Fair value of consideration ($150m + $29m)	179
NCI at acquisition	32
Fair value of identifiable net assets acquired	(160)
Goodwill at acquisition	51

Goodwill impairment

According to IAS 36 *Impairment of Assets*, a cash-generating unit to which goodwill is allocated should be tested for impairment annually by comparing its carrying amount to its recoverable amount. As goodwill has been calculated using the proportionate method, then this must be grossed up to include the goodwill attributable to the NCI.

	$m	$m
Goodwill	51.0	
Notional NCI ($51m × 20/80)	12.8	
Total notional goodwill		63.8
Net assets at reporting date:		
Fair value at start of period	160.0	
Profit for period	52.0	
		212.0
Total carrying amount of assets		275.8
Recoverable amount		(250.0)
Impairment		25.8

The impairment is allocated against the total notional goodwill. The NCI share of the goodwill has not been recognised in the consolidated financial statements and so the NCI share of the impairment is also not recognised. The impairment charged to profit or loss is therefore $20.6 million ($25.8m × 80%) and this expense is all attributable to the equity holders of the parent company.

DEBIT Operating expenses	$20.6 million	
CREDIT Goodwill		$20.6 million

The carrying amount of the goodwill relating to Chandler at the reporting date will be $30.4 million ($51m acquisition – $20.6m impairment).

(ii) **Doyle**

The share sale results in Hill losing control over Doyle. The goodwill, net assets and NCI of Doyle must be derecognised from the consolidated statement of financial position. The difference between the proceeds from the disposal (including the fair value of the shares retained) and these amounts will give rise to a $47 million profit on disposal. This is calculated as follows:

	$m	$m
Proceeds	140	
Fair value of remaining interest	300	
		440
Goodwill at disposal		(50)
Net assets at disposal		(590)
NCI:		
At acquisition	215	
NCI % of post acquisition profit (40% × ($590m – $510m))	32	
NCI at disposal		247
Profit on disposal		47

After the share sale, Hill owns 40% of Doyle's shares and has the ability to appoint two of the six members of Doyle's board of directors. IAS 28 *Investments in Associates and Joint Ventures* states that an associate is an entity over which an investor has significant influence. Significant influence is presumed when the investor has a shareholding of between 20 and 50%. Representation on the board of directors provides further evidence that significant influence exists.

Therefore, the remaining 40% shareholding in Doyle should be accounted for as an associate. It will be initially recognised at its fair value of $300 million and accounted for using the equity method. This means that the group recognises its share of the associate's profit after tax, which equates to $24.6 million ($123m × 6/12 × 40%). As at the reporting date, the associate will be carried at $324.6 million ($300m + $24.6m) in the consolidated statement of financial position.

(iii) **Convertible bond**

Hill has issued a compound instrument because the bond has characteristics of both a financial liability (an obligation to repay cash) and equity (an obligation to issue a fixed number of Hill's own shares). IAS 32 *Financial Instruments: Presentation* specifies that compound instruments must be split into:

- A liability component (the obligation to repay cash); and
- An equity component (the obligation to issue a fixed number of shares).

The split of the liability component and the equity component at the issue date is calculated as follows:

- The liability component is the present value of the cash repayments, discounted using the market rate on non-convertible bonds;
- The equity component is the difference between the cash received and the liability component at the issue date.

The initial carrying amount of the liability should have been measured at $17.9 million, calculated as follows:

Date	*Cash flow* $m	*Discount rate*	*Present value* $m
30 September 20X6	0.8	0.909	0.73
30 September 20X7	20.8	0.826	17.18
			17.91

The equity component should have been initially measured at $2.1 million ($20m – $17.9m). The adjustment required is:

DEBIT Non-current liabilities	$2.1m	
CREDIT Equity		$2.1m

The equity component remains unchanged. After initial recognition, the liability is measured at amortised cost, as follows:

1 October 20X5	*Finance charge (10%)*	*Cash paid*	*30 September 20X6*
$m	$m	$m	$m
17.9	1.8	(0.8)	18.9

The finance cost recorded for the year was $0.8 million and so must be increased by $1.0 million ($1.8m – $0.8m).

DEBIT Finance costs	$1.0m	
CREDIT Non-current liabilities		$1.0m

The liability has a carrying amount of $18.9 million as at the reporting date.

(b) **Deferred tax**

According to IAS 12 *Income Taxes*, an entity should recognise a deferred tax asset in respect of the carry-forward of unused tax losses to the extent that it is probable that future taxable profit will be available against which the losses can be utilised. IAS 12 stresses that the existence of unused losses is strong evidence that future taxable profit may not be available. For this reason, convincing evidence is required about the existence of future taxable profits.

IAS 12 says that entities should consider whether the tax losses result from identifiable causes which are unlikely to recur. Hill has now made losses in three consecutive financial years, and therefore significant doubt exists about the likelihood of future profits being generated.

Although Hill is forecasting an improvement in its trading performance, this is a result of new products which are currently under development. It will be difficult to reliably forecast the performance of these products. More emphasis should be placed on the performance of existing products and existing customers when assessing the likelihood of future trading profits.

Finally, Hill breached a bank loan covenant and some uncertainty exists about its ability to continue as a going concern. This, again, places doubts on the likelihood of future profits and suggests that recognition of a deferred tax asset for unused tax losses would be inappropriate.

Based on the above, it would seem that Hill is incorrect to recognise a deferred tax asset in respect of its unused tax losses.

Covenant breach

Hill is currently presenting the loan as a non-current liability. IAS 1 *Presentation of Financial Statements* states that a liability should be presented as current if the entity:

- Settles it as part of its operating cycle;
- Is due to settle the liability within 12 months of the reporting date; or
- Does not have an unconditional right to defer settlement for at least 12 months after the reporting date.

Hill breached the loan covenants before the reporting date but only received confirmation after the reporting date that the loan was not immediately repayable. As per IAS 10 *Events after the Reporting Period*, the bank confirmation is a non-adjusting event because, as at the reporting date, Hill did not have an unconditional right to defer settlement of the loan for at least 12 months. In the statement of financial position as at 30 September 20X6 the loan should be reclassified as a current liability.

Going concern

Although positive forecasts of future performance exist, management must consider whether the breach of the loan covenant and the recent trading losses place doubt on Hill's ability to continue as a going concern. If material uncertainties exist, then disclosures should be made in accordance with IAS 1.

15 Angel

Workbook reference. Group statements of cash flow are covered in Chapter 17. Interpretation of financial statements of different companies is included in Chapter 18.

Top tips. There are many straightforward, non-group aspects to this extracts from consolidated statement of cash flows question, so make sure you don't get bogged down in the information provided at the expense of these. We have set up workings for working capital reconciliations even though the movements are straightforward.

Make sure you allocate enough time to Part (b) – it has eight marks available for fairly straightforward knowledge that is not technically challenging.

Easy marks. These are available for the workings in Part (a)(iii) as well as explanations for the adjustments in Part (a), all of which are straightforward, along with valid points made in Part (b) on the differences between manufacturing and digital companies. The key point with cash flows is to ensure your understanding of the signage of each adjustment is clear, this will be important not only for your workings but also your explanation to the directors.

Marking scheme

			Marks
(a)	(i)	Building renovation	4
	(ii)	Profit before taxation	4
	(iii)	Cash generated from operations – up to 2 marks per item	14
(b)	(i)	Discussion 1 mark per point to a maximum	5
	(ii)	Discussion 1 mark per point for each non-financial disclosure to a maximum	3
			30

(a) (i) **Building renovation**

The building renovation has been incorrectly accounted for because Angel has debited the cash spent to revenue and this needs to be corrected in order to capitalise the correct amount for the enhancement of the asset. The correcting entries are:

DEBIT	Property, plant and equipment (PPE)	$3m	
CREDIT	Revenue		$3m

Being capitalisation of renovation of building and correction of charge to revenue

Angel treats grant income on capital-based projects as deferred income so it should not have credited the cash received from the grant to PPE and it needs to be reclassified to deferred income on the statement of financial position. The grant will then be released in line with future depreciation charges so as to recognise the benefit over the same period as the related costs it is intended to compensate. However, the grant of $2 million needs to be split equally between renovation (capital) and job creation (revenue). There do not appear to be any future performance conditions relating to the job creation portion of the grant, so that part may be released immediately to profit and loss at the time the cash has become receivable. The correcting entries for this are:

DEBIT	Property, plant and equipment (PPE)	$2m	
CREDIT	Retained earnings – profit or loss		$1m
CREDIT	Deferred income		$1m

Being correction of treatment of grant income

(ii) *Adjustments to profit before tax*

Profit before tax needs to be adjusted to take account of:

(1) The correcting entries for the building refurbishment and grant in Part (a)(i).

(2) The $4 million construction costs for the machine have been incorrectly charged to other expenses and need to be capitalised as part of property, plant and equipment (information point (iii)).

(3) The related interest of $1 million which is allowable as part of the cost of the asset under IAS 23 *Borrowing Costs* needs to be capitalised (information point (iii)):

Correcting entries for points (2) and (3) are:

DEBIT	Property, plant and equipment	$5m	
CREDIT	Profit or loss		$5m

Being correction of construction costs charged to operating expenses and capitalisation of interest under IAS 23.

Therefore, profit before tax may be adjusted as follows to arrive at a correct figure for inclusion in the cash flow statement:

	$m
Per question	184
Correction of renovation costs and grant (a)(i)	4
Correction of construction costs and interest (a)(ii)	5
	193

(iii) ANGEL GROUP

EXTRACT FROM STATEMENT OF CASH FLOWS
FOR THE YEAR ENDED 30 NOVEMBER 20X3

	$m
Operating activities	
Profit before tax (Part (a)(ii))	193.0
Adjustments for:	
Profit on sale of property, plant and equipment: (W1)	(14.0)
Depreciation (per question/W2)	29.0
Impairment of goodwill and intangible assets (per question/W3): $26.5m + $90m	116.5
Share of profit of associate (per question/W4)	(12.0)
Interest expense: $11m per question less $1m capitalised ((a)(ii) (W5)	10.0
	322.5
Decrease in trade receivables (W6)	58.0
Decrease in inventories (W6)	41.0
Decrease in trade payables (W6)	(211.0)
Cash generated from operations	210.5

Workings

1 *Profit on sale of property, plant and equipment (PPE)*

	$m
Proceeds from sale of PPE	63
Less carrying amount of PPE disposed	(49)
Profit on sale of property, plant and equipment	14

This amount needs to be deducted from profit before tax because the profit of $14 million is a non-cash credit currently included within profit before tax. The cash proceeds figure of $63 million will be included in the investing activities section.

2 *Depreciation*

The depreciation charge of $29 million which has been deducted in arriving at the profit before tax figure. It is non-cash and must be added back.

3 *Impairment of goodwill and intangible assets*

The impairment charge of $116.5 million, which has been deducted in arriving at the profit before tax figure, is a non-cash movement and, as with depreciation, it must be added back.

4 *Share of profit of associate*

The profit share of $12 million recorded in Angel's profit or loss is again a non-cash figure and should therefore be deducted to arrive at a cash figure related to operations. Any dividend received by Angel from its associate during the year will be included as a cash receipt in the investing activities section of Angel's cash flow statement.

5 *Interest expense*

The interest charge of $10 million (being the $11m paid less the $1m capitalised) is a cash payment. It is reclassified and shown in the cash flow statement below cash generated from operations as a charge to this figure, along with tax, to arrive at a net cash from operating activities figure.

6 *Working capital changes*

	Inventories	*Trade receivables*	*Trade payables*
	$m	$m	$m
b/d	190	180	361
Acquisition of subsidiary	6	3	5
∴ **Increase/(decrease)**	**(41)** β	**(58)** β	**(211)** β
c/d	155	125	155

Movements in working capital are brought into the cash generated from operations figure. If the inventories balance has fallen, there is less cash tied up in inventory held and the cash position benefits. The key point here is that Angel acquired a subsidiary, Sweety, during the financial year and gained inventory and trade receivable and payable balances without a related operational movement in cash. Therefore, these amounts must be adjusted when calculating the correct cash flow. The cash payment to acquire Sweety (net of the cash acquired) will be included in the investing activities section of the cash flow statement.

(b) (i) **Financial statement differences**

Angel is a wholesale manufacturer and has made an investment gaining significant influence in a digital company. It is important that the stakeholders of Angel, which includes is directors, manage their expectations in terms of the information presented in the financial statements of Digitool. At a high level, as a wholesale manufacturer, Angel will have a significant level of property, plant and equipment (a factory, a distribution warehouse and manufacturing machinery) and it will hold inventories either in the form of finished goods or work in progress. As a result of its long established relationships with large customers, it would be expected to have a relatively high level of trade receivables. Contrast this with Digitool. Its non-current assets will comprise its data centre and related equipment. Digital companies also frequently invest in research and development relating to new techniques and processes and may therefore have significant capitalised development costs. It would not be expected to have inventory, other than some work in progress relating to any ongoing contracts,

In terms of the ratios commonly reviewed, it is important that ratios are reviewed in the context of the specific entity. It is unlikely that the directors will be able to compare the ratios they regularly review for Angel with equivalent ratios for Digitool. The gross profit margin will not be comparable between the companies. The cost of sales of Digitool will mainly comprise employee costs and therefore its gross profit margin is likely to be higher than that for Angel. Digitool will, however, have additional operating costs relating to research, and advertising and promotion expenditure incurred in generating new customers that Angel is unlikely to have, thus net profit margins may be more comparable. The return on capital employed is likely to be lower for Angel as it has been established for a number of years, has goodwill from its investments in other entities and is heavily capitalised. The inventory holding period is a very important ratio for a manufacturing company but is not relevant for a digital company as it does not hold a physical inventories and any work in progress would be expected to convert to revenue quickly. It is not clear what the credit terms offered to customers are, but given

Angel has long-standing contracts with regular customers, it is likely to have a longer receivables collection period than Digitool which has a number of new contracts.

(ii) **Non-financial performance measures**

The non-financial performance measures reported by Digitool are in keeping with expectations for a digital company:

- Relationships with customers – it is essential for companies that do not sell a physical product and instead sell 'business solutions' to their customers to communicate well with their customers to understand their needs and be able to tailor solutions to them. Digitool may report factors such as customer satisfaction scores, the number of individual engagements with their customers in a period or the average number of repeat customers. Although traditional manufacturers must also have a customer focus to keep their products relevant, because Angel produces mass-produced furniture, it is less likely to interact with the final customer.
- Emissions levels – perhaps surprisingly, data centres produce large levels of emissions and digital companies come under the same social and political pressures to reduce emissions as heavy manufacturing companies.
- Investment in human capital – digital companies rely on their staff to be at the cutting edge of technological developments in order to keep them ahead of competitors. Companies compete to attract the best talent and are renowned for having creative working spaces, flexible working conditions and good salaries to ensure they are seen as good places to work. Traditional companies have requirements to pay staff fair rates and must comply with strict health and safety requirements, particularly when operating machinery, but will generally have a more traditional work environment.

16 Moyes

Marking scheme

				Marks
(a)	(i)	Calculation of cash flow generated from operations	6	
	(ii)	Explanation of the adjustments and use of the scenario	6	
				12
(b)		Application of the following discussion to the scenario:		
	•	Purchase consideration (shares and deferred cash)	1	
	•	Impact on consolidated statement of cash flows of:		
		– Subsidiary acquisition (including dividend)	3	
		– Subsidiary disposal	2	
				6
(c)		IFRS 5 definition of discontinued operation and application to the scenario	3	
		Consideration of held for sale and application to the scenario	1	
		Consideration of loss of control and application to the scenario	2	
				6
(d)		Intra-group transactions and ethics		6
				30

(a) **Explanatory note to: The directors of Moyes**
Subject: Cash generated from operations

(i)

	$
Profit before tax	209
Share of profit of associate	(67)
Service cost component	24
Contributions into the pension scheme	(15)
Impairment of goodwill	10
Depreciation	99
Impairment of property, plant and equipment ($43m – $20m)	23
Movement on inventory ($165m – $126m – $6m)	33
Loss on inventory	6
Increase in receivables	(7)
Increase in current liabilities	18
Cash generated from operations	333

(ii) Cash flows from operating activities are principally derived from the key trading activities of the entity. This would include cash receipts from the sale of goods, cash payments to suppliers and cash payments on behalf of employees. The indirect method adjusts profit or loss for the effects of transactions of a non-cash nature, any deferrals or accruals from past or future operating cash receipts or payments and any items of income or expense associated with investing or financing cash flows.

The share of profit of associate is an item of income associated with investing activities and so has been deducted. Likewise cash paid to acquire property, plant and equipment is an investing cash flow rather than an operating one. Non-cash flows which have reduced profit and must subsequently be added back include the service cost component, depreciation, exchange losses and impairments. With the impairment of property, plant and equipment, the first $20 million of impairment will be allocated to the revaluation surplus so only $23 million would have reduced operating profits and should be added back. In relation to the pension scheme, the remeasurement component can be ignored as it is neither a cash flow nor an expense to operating profits. Cash contributions should be deducted, though, as these represent an operating cash payment ultimately to be received by Moyes' employees. Benefits paid are a cash outflow for the pension scheme rather than Moyes and so should be ignored.

The movements on receivables, payables and inventory are adjusted so that the timing differences between when cash is paid or received and when the items are accrued in the financial statements are accounted for. Inventory is measured at the lower of cost and net realisable value. The inventory has suffered an overall loss of $6 million (Dinar 80 million/5 – Dinar 60 million/6). Of this, $2.7 million is an exchange loss (Dinar 80 million/5 – Dinar 80 million/6) and $3.3 million is an impairment (Dinar (80 – 60) million/6). Neither of these are cash flows and would be added back to profits in the reconciliation. However, the loss of $6 million should also be adjusted in the movement of the inventory as a non-cash flow. The net effect on the statement of cash flows will be nil.

(b) When the parent company acquires or sells a subsidiary during the financial year, cash flows arising from the acquisition or disposal are presented within investing activities. In relation to Davenport, no cash consideration has been paid during the current year since the consideration consisted of a share for share exchange and some deferred cash. The deferred cash would be presented as a negative cash flow within investing activities but only when paid in two years' time.

This does not mean that there would be no impact on the current year's statement of cash flows. On gaining control, Moyes would consolidate 100% of the assets and liabilities of Davenport which would presumably include some cash or cash equivalents at the date of acquisition. These would be presented as a cash inflow at the date of acquisition net of any overdrafts held at acquisition. Adjustments would also need to be made to the opening balances of assets and liabilities by adding the fair values of the identifiable net assets at acquisition to the respective balances. This would be necessary to ensure that only the cash flow effects are reported in the consolidated statement of cash flows. Fair value adjustments to assets and liabilities could also have deferred tax effects which would need adjusting so that only cash payments for tax are included within the statement of cash flows. Dividends received by Moyes from Davenport are not included in the consolidated statement of cash flows since cash has in effect been transferred from one group member to another. The non-controlling interest's share of the dividend would be presented as a cash outflow in financing activities.

On the disposal of Barham, the net assets at disposal, including goodwill, are removed from the consolidated financial statements. Since Barham is overdrawn, this will have a positive cash flow effect for the group. The overdraft will be added to the proceeds (less any cash and cash equivalents at disposal) to give an overall inflow presented in investing activities. Care would once again be necessary to ensure that all balances at the disposal date are removed from the corresponding assets and liabilities so that only cash flows are recorded within the consolidated statement of cash flows.

(c) IFRS 5 *Non-current Assets Held for Sale and Discontinued Operations* defines a discontinued operation as a component of an entity which either has been disposed of or is classified as held for sale, and:

(i) Represents a separate major line of business or geographical area of operations;

(ii) Is a single co-ordinated plan to dispose of a separate major line or area of operations; and

(iii) Is a subsidiary acquired exclusively for resale.

Both entities would be components of the Moyes group since their operations and cash flows are clearly distinguishable for reporting purposes. Barham has been sold during the year but there appears to be other subsidiaries which operate in similar geographical regions and produce similar products. Little guidance is given as to what would constitute a separate major line of business or geographical area of operations. The definition is subjective and the directors should consider factors such as materiality and relevance before determining whether Barham should be presented as discontinued or not.

To be classified as held for sale, a sale has to be highly probable and the entity should be available for sale in its present condition. At face value, Watson would not appear to meet this definition as no sales transaction is to take place.

IFRS 5 does not explicitly extend the requirements for held for sale to situations where control is lost. However, the International Accounting Standards Board (IASB) have confirmed that in instances where control is lost, the subsidiaries' assets and liabilities should be derecognised. Loss of control is a significant economic event and fundamentally changes the investor – investee relationship. Therefore situations where the parent is committed to lose control should trigger a reclassification as held for sale. Whether this should be extended to situations where control is lost to other causes would be judgemental. It is possible therefore that Watson should be classified as held for sale but to be classified as a discontinued operation, Watson would need to represent a separate major line of business or geographical area of operation.

(d) The purpose of consolidated financial statements is to show the transactions of the group as if it is a single economic entity. Moyes has control over the economic resources of its subsidiaries and therefore a clear picture of the group's position and performance can only be ascertained by combining the financial statements of the parent and all subsidiaries.

Transactions between a parent and its subsidiaries are a normal aspect of business relationships. There are no specific rules as to what level of mark-up should be applied to such transactions. Entities are therefore free to determine the sales price that they wish on intra-group transactions and it need not be at arm's length. Intra-group transactions and unrealised profits are eliminated so that the consolidated financial statements best reflect substance and faithfully represent the transactions which pertain to the group. The mark-up will therefore not alter the profits of the group, however, the impact upon the individual financial statements should still be considered.

A clear self-interest threat arises from the intention to sell the shares in Captive. The directors of Moyes have an incentive to increase the profits of Captive in order to secure as high a price as possible for the sale of the shares.

When assessing whether an ethical issue has arisen from the mark-up applied, consideration of IAS 24 *Related Party Disclosures* is relevant. Moyes and Captive are related parties and the transfer of goods is a related party transaction. Information must be disclosed, in the individual financial statements of Moyes and Captive, on the related party transactions and balances necessary for users to understand the potential effect of the relationship on the financial statements. This is required since related party transactions are often not carried out on an arm's length basis. Indeed, related party transactions include transfers of resources, services or obligations regardless of whether a price is charged. Provided that the full effects of the transaction were properly disclosed, no ethical issue would arise from selling the goods at an unusually high mark-up.

17 Weston

Workbook reference. Group statements of cash flow are covered in Chapter 17. Ethics is covered in Chapter 2.

Top tips. In Part (a), the proceeds of disposal calculation is a little tricky, but the best way to approach it is to set out the working as for a profit/loss on disposal and find the proceeds as a balancing figure. It is also important to distinguish between cash flows and non-cash flows as well as being clear on signage. In Part (b) you should refer to the principles of ACCA's *Code of Ethics and Conduct.*

Easy marks. There are many straightforward cash flows included in this question; the key is to think each transaction through and ensure you include all of the areas of the statement of cash flows affected in your answer. It is usually more than one.

Marking scheme

			Marks
(a)	(i)	Discussion of director's expectation	3
		IAS 7 requirements	2
		IAS 7 extracts	2
		Loss on disposal working	2
		Net assets at disposal working	3
		Goodwill working	2
		NCI at disposal working	2
			16

		Marks
(ii)	Discussion of impact of Southland acquisition	4
	IAS 7 extract and workings	4
		8
(b)	Ethical discussion	6
		30

(a) (i) **Effect of Northern disposal on Weston's consolidated statement of cash flow**

The directors' expectation that the loss on disposal of Northern will be added back to the profit before tax figure in the operating cash flows section of the cash flow to arrive at net cash flow from operating activities is incorrect. The profit before tax figure of $183 million excludes the results from the discontinued operation, which is presented separately in accordance with IFRS 5 *Non-current Assets Held for Sale and Discontinued Operations.* The overall discontinued result of $25 million must be analysed between the element relating to the trading activities of Northern, which will cease on disposal, and that relating to the disposal transaction, which is a one-off benefit (in the case of disposal proceeds) to the ongoing group.

The 'trading' cash flows of Northern will be included in Weston's consolidated statement of cash flow until the date of disposal. In preparation, the profit before tax from discontinued operations of $6 million is initially combined with the Weston Group's other profits for the year, as are the other line items in the financial statements of Northern, to arrive at a consolidated position.

Subsequently, whether on the face of the cash flow or in the notes, the net cash flows attributable to the operating, investing and financing activities of the Northern discontinued operation must be disclosed, in accordance with IFRS 5, so that a picture of the continuing group can be derived by the user.

In accordance with IAS 7 *Statement of Cash Flows,* the net cash flows arising from losing control of a subsidiary, that is the proceeds on disposal less any cash held in the subsidiary, must be presented separately and classified as investing activities.

In accordance with IAS 7, Weston must disclose each of the following:

(i) The total consideration received $85.4m (W1);

(ii) The portion of the consideration consisting of cash and cash equivalents $85.4m;

(iii) The amount of cash and cash equivalents held by Northern when control is lost ($2m); and

(iv) The amount of the assets and liabilities other than cash or cash equivalents in Northern when control is lost, summarised by each major category (see W2 below).

EXTRACT FROM WESTON GROUP STATEMENT OF CASH FLOWS
FOR THE YEAR ENDED 31 JANUARY 20X6:

Proceeds on disposal of Northern

Cash flows from investing activities	$m	$m
Proceeds on disposal of Northern: 85.4 (W1) + 2	87.4	
Net cash from investing activities		87.4

The bank overdraft of $2 million is added back to the fair value of consideration received of $85.4 million, in order to show proceeds net of cash and cash equivalents disposed of as part of the transaction.

Workings

1 *Loss on disposal of Northern*

	$'000	$'000
Fair value of consideration received **β**		85.4
Less share of carrying amount when control lost:		
Net assets (W2)	129.0	
Goodwill (W3)	9.0	
Less non-controlling interests (W4)	(23.6)	
		(114.4)
Loss on disposal per question		(29.0)

2 *Net assets at date of disposal*

The fair value of the property, plant and equipment at disposal will be $80m as per the question plus the remaining balance of the $16m fair value uplift ($16m less 4/8 years depreciation = $88m). A deferred tax liability on the fair value adjustment would arise of (25% x $16m) = $4m which would be released in line with the extra depreciation, so the carrying amount at disposal will be only $2m ($4m – ($4m x 4/8)). The carrying amount of the entire deferred tax liability at disposal is therefore $8m ($6m per question + $2m).

	$'000
Property, plant and equipment (see Note above)	88
Inventories	38
Trade and other receivables	23
Trade and other payables	(10)
Deferred tax (see Note above)	(8)
Bank overdraft	(2)
	129

3 *Goodwill on acquisition of Northern*

	$m
Consideration transferred	132
Fair value of non-controlling interest	28
	160
Fair value of net assets at acquisition	(124)
Goodwill at acquisition	36
Impairment (75%)	(27)
Carrying amount of goodwill at disposal	9

4 *Non-controlling interests at date of disposal*

	$'000
Non-controlling interest at acquisition (FV)	28.0
NCI share of post-acquisition retained earnings:	
20% × (129 (W2) – 124 (W3))	1.0
NCI share of goodwill impairment (20% × 27 (W3))	(5.4)
	23.6

(ii) **Impact of acquisition of Southland on Weston's consolidated statement of cash flows**

In accordance with IAS 7 *Statement of Cash Flows,* when accounting for an investment in an associate, the statement of cash flows should show the cash flows between the investor and associate, for example, dividends and advances. So, Weston includes in its statement of cash flows the cash flows in respect of its investments in Southland, and distributions and other payments or receipts between it and the associate.

Therefore, the net cash flow from operating activities of the Weston group is determined by adjusting the consolidated profit or loss for the share of profits of the associate, Southland, because it is a non-cash contribution to group profits.

The investing section of the statement of cash flows incorporates:

(i) The cash outflow on the purchase of the 40% interest in Southland on 1 February 20X5.

(ii) The cash inflow received by the Weston Group, being its 40% share of the dividend paid out by Southland during the financial year, received in Weston's capacity as an equity shareholder.

EXTRACTS FROM WESTON GROUP STATEMENT OF CASH FLOWS: FOR THE YEAR ENDED 31 JANUARY 20X6: Impact of Southland associate

Cash flow from operating activities		
Profit for the year:		X
Share of profit of associate		(16)
		X
Cash flows from investing activities		
Dividends received from associate ($10m × 40%)	4	
Purchase of associate (W1)	(90)	
Net cash used in investing activities		(86)

Workings

1

	Associate
	$m
b/d (per question)	0
P/L	16
Acquisition of associate	**90** β
Cash rec'd (div. from associate)	10 × 40%
	(4)
c/d (per question)	102

(b) **Ethical responsibility of accountant**

Directors may in order to meet targets, wish to **present a company's results in a favourable light**. This may involve manipulation by creative accounting techniques such as window dressing, or, as is proposed by the directors of Weston, an **inaccurate classification**.

If the proceeds of the sale of investments in equity instruments and property, plant and equipment are presented in Weston's cash flow statement as part of 'cash generated from operations', the picture is **misleading**. Operating cash flow is crucial, in the long-term, for the survival of the company, because it derives from trading activities, which is what the company is there to do. Operating cash flows are seen as recurring whereas investing and financing cash flows tend to be more one-off. Weston's operations would not normally see it selling surplus machinery and equity investments as part of its trading operations. **Sales of**

assets generate short-term cash flow, and cannot be repeated year-on-year, unless there are to be no assets left to generate trading profits with. This misclassification could be regarded as a deliberate attempt to mislead stakeholders about the performance of Weston, and its potential future performance, which is unethical.

As **a professional, the accountant has a duty**, not only to the **company** they work for, but also to their **professional body**, and to the **stakeholders** in the company. Classification of proceeds from selling machinery and investments should be classified as 'cash flows from **investing activities**' (rather than 'operating activities') according to IAS 7 *Statement of Cash Flows*. Also, IAS 1 *Presentation of Financial Statements* requires fair presentation. Under ACCA's *Code of Ethics and Conduct*, the accountant should adhere to the fundamental principle of **professional competence** and **due care** which includes preparing financial statements that comply with IFRS. Should the accountant permit the directors to proceed with their proposed accounting treatment, they would be in breach of this principle of professional competence and due care. There is a danger that the accountant feels pressured to follow the directors' proposed incorrect accounting treatment in order to protect their job security. Therefore, there is a **self-interest threat** in relation to the directors and an **advocacy threat** in relation to the accountant feeling pressured to act in the directors' best interests.

It is essential that the accountant **tries to persuade the directors not to proceed with the adjustments**, which they must know violate IAS 7, and may well go against the requirements of local legislation. If, despite their protests, the directors insist on the misleading presentation, then the accountant has a duty to **bring this to the attention of the auditors**. If unsure of what to do, the accountant should seek professional advice from ACCA.

18 Bubble

Workbook reference. Foreign exchange is covered in Chapter 16.

Top tips. In Part (a), you are asked to set out and explain various extracts from the preparation of a consolidated statement of financial position for a simple group structure involving an overseas subsidiary with an adjustment for an intra-group loan. It is important to grab the easy marks for basic consolidation workings and not get bogged down in any adjustments you find challenging. Part (a)(ii) requests the translation of Tyslar's statement of financial position, which is very straightforward. It is necessary to provide a brief explanation of the adjustments, in case the figures are wrong.

Part (b) consists mainly in describing the principles of IAS 21. Do not worry too much if you did not know the answer to the last part of the question, relating to the potential disposal of shares in Tyslar – you can score a pass on this part of the question without getting it all right.

Easy marks. These are available in Part (a)(ii) for simply translating the statement of financial position at the correct rate. The Salt goodwill calculation is also a straightforward one. Clear workings, referenced logically, are always important.

In Part (b), make sure you read the question properly and discuss the treatment of monetary and non-monetary items as well as the elements of the question related to the translation and possible disposal of an overseas entity, with the retention of a loan.

Marking scheme

				Marks
(a)	(i)	Intragroup loan		5
	(ii)	Translation of Tyslar SOFP		
		Discussion	4	
		Calculation	4	
				8
	(iii)	Goodwill – Salt	3	
		Goodwill – Tyslar	5	
				8
(b)		1 mark per point up to a maximum		9
			Maximum	30

(a) (i) **Intragroup loan**

The loan is a foreign currency **monetary item** in Tyslar's financial statements which means it needs to be retranslated at the **closing rate** of exchange. The **exchange differences** should have been recorded through Tyslar's **profit or loss** and will therefore affect **retained earnings**.

	$m	*Exchange rate*	Dinars m
1 February 20X5	10	9 dinars:$1	90.0
Cash paid 1 July 20X5	(5)	10 dinars:$1	(50.0)
			40.0
Exchange rate loss – balancing figure	–		7.5
31 October 20X5	5	9.5 dinars:$1	47.5

As Tyslar has not retranslated the loan outstanding at year end, a correction is needed to increase Tyslar's **non-current liabilities by 7.5 million dinars** and **reduce retained earnings** by a corresponding amount.

DEBIT	Profit or loss (retained earnings)	7.5 dinars (to (a) (ii))	
CREDIT	Non-current liabilities		7.5 dinars (to (a) (ii))

In addition, after retranslation, **$5 million will be cancelled** from both financial assets and non-current liabilities to **eliminate intragroup balances** on consolidation.

The intragroup loan will be eliminated from the consolidated SOFP.

DEBIT	Non-current liabilities	$5m	
CREDIT	Financial assets		$5m

(ii) **Translation of Tyslar's SOFP**

In order to covert Tyslar's statement of financial position appropriately in preparation for consolidation into Bubble's financial statements, the **assets and liabilities** shown in the foreign operation's statement of financial position are **translated at the closing rate** at the year end, being 9.5 dinars to the dollar as at 31 October 20X5, regardless of the date on which those items originated. For consolidation purposes, a subsidiary's **share capital and any reserves balances at acquisition** are translated at the **historic rate at the date of acquisition** (being 8 dinars to the dollar on 1 November 20X4 when Bubble acquired its interest).

The **post-acquisition** movements in **retained earnings** are broken down into the profit and dividend for each year post-acquisition (here just one year – the year ended 31 October 20X5). The **profit** for each post-acquisition year is translated at actual rate or **average rate** for that year if it is a close approximation. **Dividends** are translated at the **actual rate**. Tyslar did not pay a dividend in the current year.

The **balancing figure** on translating the statement of financial position represents the **exchange difference** on translating the foreign subsidiary's **net assets**. A further **exchange difference** arises on **goodwill** because it is treated as an asset of the subsidiary and is therefore retranslated at the **closing rate** each year end. The **exchange difference** for the year is reported in **other comprehensive income** in the consolidated statement of profit or loss and other comprehensive income. The group share of **cumulative exchange differences** are recorded in the **translation reserve** and the non-controlling interests' (NCI) share is recorded in the **NCI working**.

The **translated assets and liabilities** must then be **aggregated** with Tyslar's assets and liabilities in the consolidated statement of financial position on a line by line basis.

The **loan correction** calculated in (a)(i) must be **incorporated** into Tyslar's statement of financial position stated in dinars **before the translation** into dollars of the corrected position is performed.

Translation of SOFP of Tyslar at 31 October 20X5

	Dinars (m)	*Dinars (m) loan adj (a)(i)*	*Rate*	$m
Property, plant and equipment	390		9.5	41.1
Financial assets	98		9.5	10.3
Inventories	16		9.5	1.7
Trade and other receivables	36		9.5	3.8
Cash and cash equivalents	90		9.5	9.5
	630			66.4
Share capital	210		8	26.3
Retained earnings				
Pre-acquisition	258		8	32.3
Post-acquisition:				
– Profit: y/e 31 October 20X5 (292 – 258)*	34	(7.5) ((a)(i)) = 26.5	8.5	3.1
Exchange difference (bal.fig)				(9.6)
				52.1
Non-current liabilities	110	7.5((a)(i))	9.5	12.4
Current liabilities	18		9.5	1.9
	630			66.4

* As Bubble has only owned its controlling shareholding in Tyslar for one year and no dividends have been paid in the current year, profit for the year can be calculated as the year end retained earnings less retained earnings at acquisition.

(iii) **Goodwill**

Goodwill: Salt acquired 1 November 20X3

	$m	$m
Consideration transferred (for 80%)		110
Non-controlling interests at fair value		25
Fair value of identifiable assets acquired and liabilities assumed (per Q $120m – $1m)		
Share capital	50	
Retained earnings	56	
Other components of equity	8	
Fair value adjustment re non-depreciable land (120 – (50 (SC) + 56 (RE) + 8 (OCE)))	6	
Contingent liability at fair value	(1)	
		(119)
		16

In accordance with IFRS 3 *Business Combinations,* contingent liabilities should be recognised in the goodwill calculation where they are a present obligation arising as the result of a past event and their fair value can be measured reliably even if their settlement is not probable, as in Salt's case where a possible obligation has been disclosed and the fair value has been measured at the acquisition date.

Goodwill: Tyslar acquired 1 November 20X4

	Dinars (m)	*Rate*	$m
Consideration transferred	368		46.0
Non-controlling interests	220		27.5
	588	8	
Less fair value of net assets at acq'n: $210m + $258m	(468)		(58.5)
At 1 November 20X4	120		15.0
Impairment loss (20% × $120m)	(24)	8.5	(2.8)
			12.2
Exchange loss (bal.fig.)	–		(2.1)
At 31 October 20X5	96	9.5	10.1

Any goodwill arising on the acquisition of Tyslar is treated as an asset of the foreign operation and expressed in its functional currency, here dinars, and is retranslated at the closing rate, here 9.5 as at 31 October 20X5. Since goodwill is under the 'full goodwill' fair value method, both the impairment and the exchange loss will be apportioned 60:40 between the shareholders of the parent and the non-controlling interest respectively.

In summary:

Goodwill for consolidated SOFP will be ($16m + $10.1m) = $26.1m.

The impairment loss is $2.8m of which 60% ($1.7m) will be charged against group retained earnings and 40% ($1.1m) will be charged to the NCI.

Tutorial note.

Here impairment of Tyslar's goodwill has been translated at the average rate of 8.5 but IAS 21 also permits translation at the closing rate rate (9.5 here). Therefore, your answer would also have been marked correct if you had used the closing rate – this would have resulted in an impairment of $2.5 million and an exchange loss of $2.4 million as shown below:

Goodwill: Tyslar acquired 1 November 20X4

	Dinars (m)	*Rate*	$m
Consideration transferred	368		46.0
Non-controlling interests	220		27.5
	588	8	
Less fair value of net assets at acq'n:			
(210m share capital + 258m retained earnings)	(468)		(58.5)
At 1 November 20X4	120		15.0
Impairment loss (20% × $120m)	(24)	9.5	(2.5)
			12.5
Exchange loss (bal.fig.)	–		(2.4)
At 31 October 20X5	96	9.5	10.1

(b) **IAS 21 issues**

Monetary items are units of currency held and assets and liabilities to be received or paid in a **fixed or determinable number of units of currency**. This would include foreign bank accounts, receivables, payables and loans. **Non-monetary** items are **other items** which are in the statement of financial position. For example, non-current assets, inventories and investments.

Monetary items are **retranslated** using the **closing exchange rate** (the year end rate). The exchange differences on retranslation of monetary assets must be recorded in profit or loss. IAS 21 *The Effects of Changes in Foreign Exchange Rates*, is not specific under which heading the exchange gains and losses should be classified.

Non-monetary items which are measured in terms of **historical cost** in a foreign currency are translated using the **exchange rate at the date of the transaction**; and **non-monetary** items which are measured at **fair value** in a foreign currency are translated using the **exchange rates at the date when the fair value was measured**. **Exchange differences** on such items are **recorded consistently** with the recognition of the **movement in fair values**. For example, exchange differences on an investment property, a fair value through profit and loss financial asset, or arising on an impairment, will be recorded in profit or loss. Exchange differences on property, plant and equipment arising from a revaluation gain would be recorded in other comprehensive income.

When translating a **foreign subsidiary**, the **exchange differences on all the net assets**, including goodwill, are recorded within **other comprehensive income**. The proportion belonging to the shareholders of the parent will usually be held in a **separate translation reserve**. The **proportion belonging to the non-controlling interest** is not shown separately but **subsumed within the non-controlling interest figure** in the consolidated financial statements. If Bubble were to **sell all of its equity shares in Tyslar**, the translation reserve will be **reclassified** from equity to profit or loss. In addition, the cumulative exchange differences attributable to the non-controlling interest would be derecognised but would not be reclassified to profit or loss.

When a **monetary item** relating to a **foreign operation** is **not intended to be settled**, the item is treated as **part of the entity's net investment in its subsidiary**. There will be no difference in the accounting treatment in the **individual accounts of Tyslar** and hence exchange differences on the loan would **remain in profit or loss**. However, in the **consolidated financial statements** such differences should initially be recorded in **other comprehensive income**. These will be **reclassified** from equity to profit or loss on subsequent **disposal** of the subsidiary. This can cause practical issues in terms of monitoring all of the individual exchange differences to ensure that they are all correctly classified in the consolidated financial statements.

19 Elevator

Workbook reference. Ethical issues are specifically covered in Chapter 2 of the Workbook but feature throughout all chapters. Non-financial reporting is covered in Chapter 18.

Top tips. Part (a)(i) on the ethical implications of the suggestion combines knowledge of non-financial reporting and ethics. There are marks available for comment on each. Part (a)(ii) discusses the benefits and drawbacks of reporting non-financial information from an investor's perspective, focusing on the employee information given in the question. Part (b) requires discussion of the ethics surrounding the dubious land transaction.

Easy marks. In Parts (a) and (b), there are plenty of marks available for sensible discussion of ethics as well as marks available in Part (b) for straightforward knowledge of ratios and repurchase agreements. Link your answer to the scenario.

Marking scheme

				Marks
(a)	(i)	Ethical considerations	3	
		Implications for reported information	4	
	(ii)	Comment on non-financial performance measures	4	
				11
(b)		Financial reporting – 1 mark per point up to maximum	4	
		Ethical issues – 1 mark per point up to maximum	3	
				7
Professional marks				2
				20

(a) (i) **Ethical considerations**

Ethical behaviour in the fair treatment of employees is important to the long term success of a company, and how it is perceived by stakeholders. The directors of Elevator are considering not paying employees a discretionary bonus in order to achieve profit targets. This will enable the directors to collect their bonus. It is worth noting that there is nothing illegal about the proposal – the bonus paid to employees is discretionary rather than contractual and therefore the company has no legal obligation to pay the bonus. It is the reason behind the non-payment that gives rise to ethical considerations. The suggestion by the CEO would work in reducing expenses and improving profit.

Morally, the suggestion is likely to have negative consequences for the company. The employees will be unhappy that their bonus has been withdrawn, particularly if there has been a past policy of paying annual bonuses. This may have a negative impact on productivity and staff morale, and therefore on employee satisfaction scores and possibly on employee retention rates that are reported as non-financial information within the annual report. It is not clear what the gender composition of the company is to understand whether there would also be implications for the information reported on gender equality, which is a matter being widely reported in the media. Companies are also under increasing pressure to reduce the wage gap between management and employees. Not paying staff a bonus will have a negative impact on this metric.

The comments of the CEO imply that he does not think the negative impact on non-financial reporting will have an impact on the company as the information is not widely read. This type of information is becoming increasingly important to the users of financial statements as they care about companies' treatment of their employees and see it as being important in the long term success of the company. If Elevator did not report employee matters, it may have been able to 'hide' the proposal to not pay the employee bonus from the users of the financial statements, however this additional reporting will bring the issue more to their attention.

(ii) **Implications for reported information**

Financial performance measures are often criticised for being backward-looking as they report historical information, too focused on short-termism as there are often incentives for achieving, for example, profit or revenue targets and for failing to provide enough relevant information on the factors that drive the success of the business. Whilst some speculative investors may only be interested in short term performance, others will base investment decisions on how a business performs over time and how well the business is expected to perform in the future. Information that can help investors to evaluate this will be valuable. Reporting non-financial performance information such as the staff information reported by Elevator has the benefit of disclosing to the investors the factors that management considers important in ensuring the longer term viability and success of the business. Staff are seen as important assets to businesses and employee satisfaction is an important consideration for companies. Reporting non-financial information can help companies to attract and retain the appropriate level of staff.

There are drawbacks of reporting non-financial information. It is generally more difficult for investors to verify than quantitative information which can lead to concerns about its reliability. As companies decide what information to report, it can be difficult for investors to compare between companies and across different periods. Non-financial information is also more open to manipulation than IFRS-based information as there are no underlying standards or principles which companies must apply. The IASB's Disclosure Initiative project is also concerned as to the volume of information being reported by companies and whether extensive disclosures are clouding the information that is relevant to investors within the financial statements.

(b) **Sale of land**

Accounting treatment

The sale of land is a repurchase agreement under IFRS 15 *Revenue from Contracts with Customers* as Elevator has an option to buy the land back from the third party and, therefore, control has not transferred as the purchaser's ability to use and gain benefit from the land is limited. Elevator must treat the transaction as a financing arrangement and record both an asset (the land) and a financial liability (the cash amount received which is repayable to the third party).

Elevator should not have derecognised the land from the financial statements because the risks and rewards of ownership have not been transferred. The substance of the transaction is a loan of $16 million, and the 3% 'premium' on repurchase is effectively an interest payment.

Recording the transaction as a sale is an attempt to manipulate the financial statements in order to show an improved profit figure and more favourable cash position. The sale must be reversed and the land reinstated at its carrying amount before the transaction. The repurchase, ie the repayment of the loan, takes place one month after the year end, and so this is a current liability:

DEBIT	Property, plant and equipment	$12m	
DEBIT	Retained earnings (to reverse profit on disposal (16 – 12))	$4m	
CREDIT	Current liabilities		$16m

Ethical issues

ACCA qualified accountants are required to comply with the fundamental principles of ACCA's *Code of Ethics and Conduct*. This includes acting with integrity. The integrity of the finance director appears to be compromised in this situation. The effect of the sale just before the year end was to improve profits and to eliminate the bank overdraft, making the cash position look better. However, this is effectively 'window dressing', and is not honest as it does not represent the actual position and performance of Elevator.

Accountants must also act with objectivity, which means that they must not allow bias, conflict of interest or undue influence of others to override professional or business judgements. Therefore, the directors must put the interests of the company and its shareholders before their own interests. The pressure to meet profit targets and achieve a bonus is in the self-interest of the directors and seems to have at least partly driven the transaction and the subsequent accounting, which is clearly a conflict of interest.

Accountants must also comply with the principle of professional behaviour, which requires compliance with relevant laws and regulations. In this case the accounting treatment does not conform to IFRS. It is not clear from the scenario whether the finance director is aware of this or not. If he is aware, but he has applied an incorrect treatment anyway, he has not complied with the principle of professional behavior. It may be that he was under undue pressure from the CEO to record the transaction in this manner, if so there is potentially an intimidation threat. If however, he is not aware that the treatment is incorrect, then he has not complied with the principle of professional competence as his knowledge and skill are not up to date.

20 Star

Workbook references. Ethics are covered in Chapter 2. Leasing is covered in Chapter 9.

Top tips. There are generous marks available for this three-part ethics question. Ensure you split your time appropriately across the parts. Do not waffle. Remember to link your answer to the scenario, the information is given for you to use it. In both parts (a) and (b) you must ensure that your answer demonstrates a good understanding of ethical principles rather than simply the ability to reiterate the ethical codes.

Easy marks. Parts (b) and (c) are more generic so there is scope to gain marks for sensible discussion.

Marking scheme

		Marks
(a)	Lease agreement	6
(b)	Ethical and social responsibilities	9
(c)	Internal auditor profit-related bonus	3
Professional marks		2
		20

(a) **Lease agreement substance presentation**

It is of crucial importance that stakeholders of a company can rely on the financial statements in order to make informed and accurate decisions. The directors of Star have an ethical responsibility to produce financial statements which comply with accounting standards, are transparent and free from material error. Lenders will often attach covenants to the terms of an agreement in order to protect their interests in an entity. They would also be of crucial importance to potential debt and equity investors when assessing the risks and returns from any future investment in the entity.

The proposals by Star appear to be a deliberate attempt to circumvent the terms of the covenants. The legal form would be to treat the lease as a series of short-term leases. This would be accounted for as expenses in profit or loss and not recognise the right-of-use asset and the associated lease obligation that the substance of the transaction and IFRS 16 *Leases* requires. This would be a form of 'off-balance sheet finance' and would not report the true assets and obligations of Star. It is likely that liquidity ratios would be adversely misrepresented from the proposed accounting treatment. The operating profit margins are likely to be adversely affected by the attempt to use the short-term exemption, as the expenses associated with the lease are likely to be higher than the depreciation charge if a leased asset was recognised, hence the proposal may actually be detrimental to the operating profit covenant.

Star is aware that the proposed accounting treatment may be contrary to accounting standards. Such manipulation would be a clear breach of the fundamental principles of objectivity and integrity as outlined in the ACCA *Code of Ethics.* It is important that accountants are seen to exercise professional behaviour and due care at all times. The proposals by Star are likely to mislead stakeholders in the entity. This could discredit the profession creating a lack of confidence within the profession. The directors of Star must be reminded of their ethical responsibilities and persuaded that the accounting treatment must fully comply with accounting standards and principles outlined within the framework should they proceed with the debt factoring agreements.

(b) **Ethical and social responsibilities**

Ethics and corporate social responsibility are important in themselves, but also because they can improve business performance. At present the company is stagnating, because it has focused on maintaining market share and on its own shareholders at the expense of other stakeholders. Corporate social responsibility is concerned with a company's accountability to a wide range of stakeholders, not just shareholders. For Star, the most significant of these include:

(i) Regulators
(ii) Customers
(iii) Creditors
(iv) Employees

Regulators

The relationship with regulators is not good, mainly because of a poor reputation on environmental matters. Star just does the bare minimum, for example cleaning up contamination only when legally obliged to do so.

Adopting environmentally friendly policies and reporting in detail on these in an environmental report will go some way towards mending the relationship. Litigation costs, which have a direct impact on profit, can be avoided.

Customers

Currently, Star provides poor customer support and makes no effort to understand the customs and cultures of the countries in which it operates. Moreover, it makes no positive contributions and does not promote socially responsible policies. This attitude could easily alienate its present customers and deter new ones. A competitor who does make positive contributions to the community, for example in sponsoring education or environmental programmes, will be seen as having the edge and could take customers away from Star. Corporate social responsibility involves thinking long-term about the community rather than about short-term profits, but in the long-term, profits could suffer if socially responsible attitudes are not adopted.

Creditors

Suppliers are key stakeholders who must be handled responsibly if a reputation in the wider business community is not to suffer. Star's policy of not paying small and medium-sized companies is very shortsighted. While such companies may not be in a position to sue for payment, the effect on goodwill and reputation will be very damaging in the long-term. Suppliers may be put off doing business with Star. Perhaps a key component can only be sourced from a small supplier, who will not sell to Star if word gets around that it does not pay. This unethical and damaging policy must be discontinued and relationships with all suppliers fostered.

Employees

Employees are very important stakeholders. Star's authoritarian approach to management and its refusal to value employees or listen to their ideas, is potentially damaging to business performance. High staff turnover is costly as new staff must be recruited and trained. Employees who do not feel valued will not work as hard as those who do. In addition, employees may have some good ideas to contribute that would benefit performance; at the moment Star is missing out on these ideas. Acting responsibly and ethically is not just right; it should also lead to the company being more profitable in the long term.

(c) **Internal auditor bonus**

For

The chief internal auditor is an employee of Star, which pays a salary to them. As part of the internal control function, they are helping to keep down costs and increase profitability. It could therefore be argued that the chief internal auditor should have a reward for adding to the profit of the business.

Against

Conversely, the problem remains that, if the chief internal auditor receives a bonus based on results, they may be tempted to allow certain actions, practices or transactions which should be stopped, but which are increasing the profit of the business, and therefore the bonus.

Conclusion

On balance, it is not advisable for the chief internal auditor to receive a bonus based on the company's profit.

21 Farham

Marking scheme

			Marks
(a)	Application of the following discussion to the scenario:		
	Factory subsidence as an indication of impairment	2	
	Fair value	2	
	Allocation of impairment loss	1	
	Sale of Newall – HFS criteria, valuation and impairment	4	
	Required accounting treatment of the expected costs of sale	2	11
(b)	Discussion of ethical principles	2	
	Application of ethical principles to the scenario	5	7
Professional marks			2
			20

(a) **Factory subsidence**

The subsidence is an **indication of impairment** in relation to the production facility. Consideration would be required to choose a suitable cash-generating unit as presumably the factory would not independently generate cash flows for Farham as a standalone asset. The facility is likely to consist of both the factory and various items of plant and machinery and so it would not be possible to independently measure the cash flows from each of the assets. The recoverable amount of the unit would need to be assessed as the higher of fair value less costs to sell and value in use. Reference to IFRS 13 *Fair Value Measurement* would be required in estimating the fair value of the facility. For example, by considering whether similar facilities have been on the market or recently sold. Value in use would be calculated by estimating the present value of the cash flows generated from the production facility discounted at a suitable rate of interest to reflect the risks to the business. Where the carrying amount exceeds the recoverable amount, an impairment has occurred. Any **impairment loss** is allocated to reduce the carrying amount of the assets of the unit. This will be expensed in profit or loss and cannot be netted off the revaluation surplus as the surplus does not specifically relate to the facility impaired. **No provision for the repair to the factory** should be made because there is no legal or constructive obligation to repair the factory.

Sale of Newall

The disposal of Newall appears to meet the **held for sale criteria**. Management has shown commitment to the sale by approving the plan and reporting it to the media. A probable acquirer has been found in Oldcastle, the sale is highly probable and expected to be completed six months after the year end, well within the 12-month criteria. Newall would be treated as a disposal group since a single equity transaction is the most likely form of disposal. Should Newall be deemed to be a separate major component of business or geographical area of the group, the losses of the group should be presented separately as a discontinued operation within the consolidated financial statements of Farham.

Assets held for sale are valued at the **lower of carrying amount and fair value less costs to sell**. The carrying amount consists of the net assets and goodwill relating to Newall less the non-controlling interest's share. Assets within the disposal group which are not within the scope of IFRS 5 *Assets Held for Sale and Discontinued Operations* are adjusted for in accordance with the relevant standard first. This includes leased assets and it is highly likely that the leased asset deemed surplus to requirements should be written off with a corresponding expense to profit or loss. Any further impairment loss recognised to reduce Newall to fair value less costs to sell would be allocated first to goodwill and then on a pro rata basis across the other non-current assets of the group.

The chief operating officer is wrong to exclude any form of restructuring provision from the consolidated financial statements. The disposal has been communicated to the media and a constructive obligation exists. However, only **directly attributable costs of the restructuring** should be included and not ongoing costs of the business. **Future operating losses** should be excluded as no obligating event has arisen and no provision is required for the impairments of the owned assets as they would have been accounted for on remeasurement to fair value less costs to sell. The legal fees and redundancy costs should be provided for. The early payment fee should also be provided for despite being a future operating loss. This is because the contract is onerous and the losses are consequently unavoidable. A provision is required for $13 million ($2 million + $5 million + $6 million). The $6 million will be offset against the corresponding lease liability with only a net figure being recorded in profit or loss.

(b) **Ethics**

Accountants have a duty to ensure that the financial statements are **fair, transparent and comply with accounting standards**. The accountant appears to have made a couple of mistakes which would be unexpected from a professionally qualified accountant. In particular, the accountant appears unaware of which costs should be included within a restructuring provision and has failed to recognise that there is no obligating event in relation to future operating losses. Accountants must carry out their work with **due care and attention** for the financial statements to have credibility. They must therefore ensure that their knowledge is kept up to date and that they do carry out their work in accordance with the relevant ethical and professional standards. Failure to do so would be a breach of **professional competence**. The accountant must make sure that they address this issue through, for example, attending regular training and professional development courses.

There are a number of instances which suggest that the chief operating officer is happy to **manipulate** the financial statements for their own benefit. She is not willing to account for an impairment loss for the subsidence despite knowing that this is contrary to IFRSs. She is also unwilling to reduce the profits of the group by properly applying the assets held for sale criteria in relation to Newall nor to create a restructuring provision. All of the adjustments required to ensure the financial statements comply with IFRS will reduce profitability. It is true that the directors do have a responsibility to run the group on behalf of their shareholders and to try to maximise their return. This must not be to the detriment, though, of producing financial statements which are **objective** and **faithfully represent** the performance of the group. It is likely that the chief operating officer is motivated by bonus targets and is therefore unfairly trying to misrepresent the results of the group. The chief operating officer must make sure that she is not unduly influenced by this **self-interest threat**.

The chief operating officer is also acting unethically by threatening to dismiss the accountant should they try to correct the financial statements. It is not clear whether the chief operating officer is a qualified accountant but the ethical principles should extend to all employees and not just qualified accountants. **Threatening and intimidating behaviour** is unacceptable and against all ethical principles. The accountant faces an **ethical dilemma**. They have a duty to produce financial statements which are objective and fair but to do so could mean that they lose their job. The accountant should approach the chief operating officer and remind them of the basic ethical principles and try to persuade them of the need to put the adjustments through the consolidated accounts so that they are fair and objective. Should the chief operating officer remain unmoved, the accountant may wish to contact the ACCA ethical helpline and take legal advice before undertaking any further action.

22 Ethical issues

Workbook references. Ethics are covered in Chapter 2 and leases in Chapter 9.

Top tips. Part (a) concerned the tension between judgement and conflict of interest, in the context of recognising a lease in the statement of financial position. It is important to tailor your answer to the requirements in discussion parts of questions – the ACCA examining team has criticised candidates in the past for failure to **apply** their knowledge.

Marking scheme

			Marks
(a)	**Columbus**		
	Ethical and accounting issues – discussion 1 mark per point to a maximum of 9 marks. Points may include:		
	Accounting issues		
	Recognition in statement of financial position	1	
	IFRS 16 definition of a lease	1	
	Initial recognition and measurement	2	
	Ethical issues		
	Threats to fundamental principles	2	
	Professional competence	1	
	Appropriate action	2	
			9
(b)	**Casino**		
	Ethical conflicts and ethical principles – discussion 1 mark per point to a maximum of 9 marks. Points may include:		
	Ethical conflicts		
	Pressure to obtain finance	1	
	Personal circumstances	1	
	Duty to shareholders, employees and bank	2	
	Ethical principles		
	Self-interest threat	1	
	Advocacy threat	1	
	Potential breach of objectivity, integrity, professional competence	2	
	Appropriate action	1	
			9
	Professional marks		2
	Total		20

(a) **Columbus**

Accounting issues

The arrangement meets the IFRS 16 criteria for a lease in that there is an identifiable asset and the contract conveys the right to control the use of that asset for a period of time in exchange for consideration.

Columbus must recognise a right-of-use asset representing its right to use the property and a lease liability representing its obligation to make lease payments. At the commencement date, Columbus should recognise the right-of-use asset at cost. This will include:

(a) The amount of the initial measurement of the lease liability;

(b) Any lease payments made or incentives received before the start date;

(c) Any initial direct costs; and

(d) Any costs to be incurred for dismantling or removing the underlying asset or restoring the site at the end of the lease term.

Columbus must initially recognise the liability at the present value of the future lease payments including any payments expected at the end of the lease discounted using the rate implicit in the lease.

Ethical issues

If the managing director is trying to compel the financial controller to change what would be the appropriate treatment because of business pressures, then this presents the financial controller with an ethical dilemma. The pressure will be greater because the financial controller is new.

Threats to fundamental principles

As the financial controller's future position at Columbus has been threatened if the managing director's proposed accounting treatment is not adopted, there has been an **intimidation threat** to the fundamental principles of **objectivity and integrity** from the ACCA *Code of Ethics and Conduct.*

Furthermore, as the managing director has flagged the risk that Columbus may not secure its future loan finance if the lease is recorded is the statement of financial position, there is an **advocacy threat** because the financial controller may feel compelled to follow an incorrect accounting treatment to maximise the changes of obtaining the loan. The pressure will be greater because the financial controller is new

Professional competence

When preparing the financial statements, the financial controller should adhere to the fundamental principle of **professional competence** which requires preparing accounts that **comply with IFRS**.

Thus, if the arrangement meets the IFRS 16 criteria for a lease, which it appears to, the lease should not be kept out of the statement of financial position in order to understate the liabilities of the entity for the purposes of raising a loan and future job security of the financial controller. If the financial controller were to **accept the managing director's proposed treatment**, this would contravene IFRS 16 and **breach the fundamental principle of professional competence**.

Appropriate action

The ACCA *Code of Ethics and Conduct* will be an essential point of reference in this situation, since it sets out boundaries outside which accountants should not stray. If the managing director refuses to allow the financial controller to apply the IFRS 16 treatment, then the financial controller **should disclose this to the appropriate internal governance authority**, and thus feel confident that their actions were ethical.

The difference of opinion that has arisen between the financial controller and the managing director best resolved by the **financial controller seeking** professional advice from the ACCA and legal advice if required.

(b) **Casino**

In this scenario, there is a **twofold conflict of interest:**

(i) *Pressure to obtain finance and chief accountant's personal circumstances*

The chief accountant is under pressure to provide the bank with a projected cash flow statement that will meet the bank's criteria when in fact the actual projections do not meet the criteria. The chief accountant's financial commitments mean that that he cannot afford to lose his job. **The ethical and professional standards required of the accountant are at odds with the pressures of his personal circumstances.**

(ii) *Duty to shareholders, employees and bank*

The **directors have a duty to act in the best interests of the company's shareholders and employees, and a duty to present fairly any information the bank may rely on**. Although the injection of capital to modernise plant and equipment might appear in the shareholders' and employees' best interests through generation of future profits, if the new finance is obtained on the basis of misleading information, it could actually be detrimental to the survival of the company.

It could be argued that there is a **conflict between the short-term and medium term interests of the company** (the need to modernise) **and its long-term interests** (the detriment to the company's reputation if its directors do not act ethically).

Ethical principles guiding the accountant's response

Specifically here, there is a **self-interest threat** in the form of the risk of the chief accountant losing his job and an **advocacy threat** in the form of disclosing favourable information in order to obtain the loan finance.

The chief accountant's financial circumstances and pressure from the directors could result in him knowingly disclosing incorrect information to the bank which means that the fundamental principles of **objectivity, integrity and professional competence** from ACCA's *Code of Ethics and Conduct* may be compromised.

In the case of **objectivity**, the chief accountant is likely to be **biased** due to the **risk of losing his job** if he does not report a favourable cash flow forecast to the bank. **Disclosing the incorrect information knowingly** would compromise his **integrity** as he would not be acting in a straightforward and honest manner is his professional and business relationships. Although forecasts, unlike financial statements, do not typically specify that they have been prepared in accordance with IFRS, the principle of **professional competence** requires the accountant to prepare cash flow projections to the **best of his professional judgement** which would not be the case if the projections showed a more positive position than is actually anticipated.

Appropriate action

The **chief accountant is faced with an immediate ethical dilemma** and must apply his moral and ethical judgement. As a professional, he has a responsibility to present the truth fairly, and not to indulge in 'creative accounting' in response to pressure.

The chief accountant should therefore put the interests of the company and professional ethics first, and insist that the report to the bank is an honest reflection of the current financial position. As an advisor to the directors he must not allow a deliberate misrepresentation to be made to the bank, no matter what the consequences are to him personally. The accountant must not allow any undue influence from the directors to override his professional judgement or undermine his integrity. This is in the long-term interests of the company and its survival.

The chief accountant should try to persuade the directors to accept the submission of the correct projected statement of cash flows to the bank. If they refuse, he should consider consulting ACCA for professional advice and if necessary, seek legal counsel.

23 Chippin

Workbook references. Statements of cash flows are covered in Chapter 17. Ethical issues are covered in Chapter 2.

Top tips. Make sure you allow adequate time for both Parts (a) and (b). You cannot expect to do well if you do not answer the whole question. There are 15 marks for this question.

Easy marks. In part (a), easy marks are available for a brief explanation of the direct and indirect methods. However, do not be tempted to write all you know about the two methods. The requirement is very specific and requires you to focus on the usefulness to users so this should form the main focus of your answer. Part (b) follows on from Part (a) because one of the key problems with the indirect method is manipulation, and this has ethical implications. Easy marks are available in Part (b) for applying your knowledge of IAS 7 *Statements of Cash Flows* and linking the proposed accounting treatment to the threats and fundamental principles of ACCA's *Code of Ethics and Conduct.*

Marking scheme

		Marks
(a)	Indirect versus direct method – discussion 1 mark per point to a maximum of 7 marks. Points may include:	
	Direct method	
	Explanation	1
	Advantages to users	1
	Disadvantages to users	1
	Indirect method	
	Explanation	1
	Advantages	1
	Disadvantages	1
	Apply to context of Chippin	1
		7
(b)	Reporting loan proceeds as an operating cash flow – discussion 1 mark per point to a maximum of 6 marks. Points may include:	
	Incentive to increase operating cash flow to receive extra income	1
	Motivation for using indirect method – reduce clarity for users	1
	Objective for IAS 7's flexibility in cash flow classification is fair presentation	1

	Marks
Ethical behaviour important in financial statements preparation	1
Directors must put company's and stakeholder's interests first	1
Classify as 'financing' not 'operating'	1
	6
Professional marks	2
	15

(a) **Preparing statements of cash flows: indirect method versus direct method**

Direct method

The **direct method** of preparing cash flow statements reports cash flows from operating activities as **major classes of gross cash receipts and gross cash payments**. It shows the items that affected cash flow and the size of those cash flows. Cash received from, and cash paid to, specific sources such as customers, suppliers and employees are presented separately. This contrasts with the indirect method, where accruals-basis net profit/(loss) before tax is converted to cash flow information by means of add-backs and deductions.

An important **advantage** of the direct method is that it is easier for the users to understand as they can see and understand the actual **cash flows**, and how they relate to items of income or expense. For example, payments of expenses are shown as cash disbursements and are deducted from cash receipts. In this way, the **user is able to recognise the cash receipts and payments** for the period.

From the point of view of the **user, the direct method is preferable** because it discloses information not available elsewhere in the financial statements, which could be of use in estimating future cash flow.

However, where the user is an investor, the direct method may reduce shareholder returns because preparation of **the direct method is typically more time-consuming and expensive** than the indirect method due to the extra workings required to ascertain gross cash receipts and payments relating to operating activities.

Indirect method

The **indirect method** involves **adjusting the net profit or loss** for the period for:

(1) Changes during the period in inventories, operating receivables and payables

(2) Non-cash items, eg depreciation, movements in provisions, deferred taxes and unrealised foreign currency gains and losses

(3) Other items, the cash flows from which should be classified under investing or financing activities, eg profits or losses on sales of assets, investment income

From the point of view of the **preparer of accounts, the indirect method is easier to use,** and **nearly all companies use it in practice**. The main argument companies have for using the indirect method is that the **direct method is too costly**. The **indirect method** is cheaper for the company to prepare and will result in **higher shareholder returns**.

The **disadvantage** of the indirect method is that **users find it difficult to understand** and it is therefore more **open to manipulation**. This is particularly true with regard to classification of cash flows. Companies may wish to classify cash inflows as operating cash flows and cash outflows as non-operating cash flows.

The directors' proposal to report the loan proceeds as operating cash flow may be an example of such manipulation. For Chippin, the indirect method would **not**, as is claimed, **be more useful and informative to users** than the direct method. IAS 7 *Statement of Cash Flows* allows both methods, however, so the indirect method would still be permissible. Because users find the indirect method less easy to understand, it can be more open to manipulation by misclassifying cash flows.

(b) **Reporting the loan proceeds as operating cash flow**

The directors of Chippin have an **incentive to enhance operating cash flow**, because they receive a bonus if operating cash flow exceeds a predetermined target. This represents a **self-interest threat** under ACCA's *Code of Ethics and Conduct*. Accordingly, their proposal to classify the loan proceeds as operating cash flow should come under scrutiny.

Their proposal should first of all be considered in the light of their claim that the indirect method is more useful to users than the direct method. The opposite is the case, so while both methods are allowed, the directors' **motivation for wishing to use the method that is less clear to users** should be questioned.

IAS 7 allows some flexibility in classification of cash flows under the indirect method. For example, dividends paid by the entity can be shown as financing cash flows (showing the cost of obtaining financial resources) or operating cash flows (so that users can assess the entity's ability to pay dividends out of operating cash flows). However, the **purpose of such flexibility is to present the position as fairly as possible**. Classifying loan proceeds as operating cash flow does not do this.

Ethical behaviour in the preparation of financial statements, and in other areas, is of **paramount importance**. Directors act unethically if they use 'creative' accounting in accounts preparation to make the figures look better, in particular if their presentation is determined not by finding the best way to apply International Financial Reporting Standards in order to report the cash flow position fairly to stakeholders, but, as here, by **self-interest**.

To act ethically, the directors must put the interests of the company and its shareholders first, and must also have regard to other stakeholders such as the loan provider. Accordingly, the **loan proceeds should be reported as cash inflows from financing activities**, not operating activities.

24 Gustoso

Marking scheme

	Marks
Accounting issues – 1 mark per point up to maximum	6
Ethical issues – 1 mark per point up to maximum	7
	13
Professional	2
	15

Provision

IAS 37 *Provisions, Contingent Liabilities and Contingent Assets* states that a provision should only be recognised if:

- There is a present obligation from a past event;
- An outflow of economic resources is probable; and
- The obligation can be measured reliably.

No provision should be recognised because Gustoso does not have an obligation to incur the training costs. The expenditure could be avoided by changing the nature of Gustoso's operations and so it has no present obligation for the future expenditure.

The provision should be derecognised. This will reduce liabilities by $2 million and increase profits by the same amount.

Contract

IFRS 9 *Financial Instruments* applies to contracts to buy or sell a non-financial item which are settled net in cash. Such contracts are usually accounted for as derivatives. However, contracts which are for an entity's 'own use' of a non-financial asset are exempt from the requirements of IFRS 9. The contract will qualify as 'own use' because Gustoso always takes delivery of the wheat. This means that it falls outside IFRS 9 and so the recognition of a derivative is incorrect.

The contract is an executory contract. Executory contracts are not initially recognised in the financial statements unless they are onerous, in which case a provision is required. This particular contract is unlikely to be onerous because wheat prices may rise again. Moreover, the finished goods which the wheat forms a part of will be sold at a profit. As such, no provision is required. The contract will therefore remain unrecognised until Gustoso takes delivery of the wheat.

The derivative liability should be derecognised, meaning that profits will increase by $0.5 million.

Ethical implications

The users of Gustoso's financial statements, such as banks and shareholders, trust accountants and rely on them to faithfully represent the effects of a company's transactions. IAS 1 *Presentation of Financial Statements* makes it clear that this will be obtained when accounting standards are correctly applied.

Both of the errors made by Gustoso overstate liabilities and understate profits. It is possible that these are unintentional errors. However, incentives exist to depart from particular IFRS and IAS standards: most notably the bonus scheme. The bonus target in 20X7 has been exceeded, and so the finance director may be attempting to shift 'excess' profits into the next year in order to increase the chance of meeting 20X8's bonus target. In this respect, the finance director has a clear self-interest threat to objectivity and may be in breach of ACCA's *Code of Ethics and Conduct.*

The accountant is correct to challenge the finance director and has an ethical responsibility to do so. Despite the fact that the finance director is acting in an intimidating manner, the accountant should explain the technical issues to the director. If the director refuses to comply with accounting standards, then it would be appropriate to discuss the matter with other directors and to seek professional advice from ACCA. Legal advice should be considered if necessary. The accountant should keep a record of conversations and actions. Resignation should be considered if the matters cannot be satisfactorily resolved.

25 Fiskerton

Marking scheme

			Marks
(a)	Application of the following discussion to the scenario:		
	• Correct accounting treatment of the lease	3	
	• Implications for the financial statements	2	
	• Implications for the debt covenant	2	
			7
(b)	Consideration of whether it is performance satisfied over time or at a point in time and application to the scenario	3	
	Conclusion and implications for revenue	1	
			4
(c)	Application of the following discussion of ethical issues to the scenario:		
	• Classification of property as investment property	2	
	• Revaluation and manipulation of the debt covenant	3	
	Consideration of the ethical implications and their resolution	2	
			7
Professional			2
			20

(a) The Halam property should not have been classified as an investment property because it is a finance lease as the lease term is equal to the useful life and its residual value is deemed to be minimal. Edingley should record a right to use asset and Fiskerton should derecognise the property. Fiskerton should instead record a lease receivable equal to the net investment in the lease. The property needs to be removed from investment properties and the fair value gains of $8 million reversed. In any case, the fair value gains were incorrectly calculated since adjustments should have been made for the differences between the Halam building and the one sold due to the different location and quality of the materials between the two buildings. It would appear that $22 million would have been a more accurate reflection of fair value.

The incorrect treatment has enabled Fiskerton to remain within its debt covenant limits. Gearing per the financial extracts is currently around 49.8% (50,000/(10,000 + 20,151 + 70,253)). Fair value gains on investment properties are reported within profit or loss. Retained earnings would consequently be restated to $64.53 million ($70.253m – $8m). Gearing would subsequently become 52.8% (50,000/10,000 + 20,151 + 64,530). Furthermore, retained earnings would be further reduced by correcting for rental receipts. These presumably have been included in profit or loss rather than deducted from the net investment in the lease. This would in part be offset by interest income which should be recorded in profit or loss at the effective rate of interest. After correcting for these errors, Fiskerton would be in breach of their debt covenants. They have a negative cash balance and would appear unlikely to be able to repay the loan. Serious consideration should therefore be given as to whether Fiskerton is a going concern. It is likely that non-current assets and non-current liabilities should be reclassified to current and recorded at their realisable values. As an absolute minimum, should Fiskerton be able to renegotiate with the bank, the uncertainties surrounding their ability to continue to trade would need to be disclosed.

(b) At the inception of the contract, Fiskerton must determine whether its promise to construct the asset is a performance obligation satisfied over time. Fiskerton only has rights during the production of the asset over the initial deposit paid. They have no enforceable rights to the remaining balance as construction takes place. Therefore they would not be able to receive payment for work performed to date. Additionally, Fiskerton has to repay the deposit should they fail to complete the construction of the asset in accordance with the contract. There is a single performance obligation which is only met on delivery of the asset to the customer. Revenue should not be recognised on a stage of completion basis but must be deferred and recognised at a point of time. That is, on delivery of the asset to the customer.

(c) It is concerning that the property has been incorrectly classified as an investment property. Accountants have an ethical duty to be professionally competent and act with due care and attention. It is fundamental that the financial statements comply with the accounting standards and principles which underpin them. This may be a genuine mistake but even so would not be one expected from a professionally qualified accountant. The financial statements must comply with the fair presentation principles embedded within IAS 1 *Presentation of Financial Statements*.

The managing director appears to be happy to manipulate the financial statements. A self-interest threat arises from the issue over the debt covenants. It is likely that the managing director is concerned about his job security should the bank recall the debt and deem Fiskerton to no longer be a going concern. It appears highly likely that the revaluation was implemented in the interim financial statements to try to maintain a satisfactory gearing ratio. Even more concerning is that the managing director has deliberately overstated the valuation for the year-end financial statements, even though he is aware that it breaches accounting standards. Such deliberate manipulation is contrary to the ethical principles of integrity, professional behaviour and objectivity. It appears that the managing director is trying to defraud the bank by misrepresenting the liquidity of the business to avoid repayment of the loan. This would be in breach of anti-money laundering regulations.

The sales contract is further evidence that the managing director may be attempting to manipulate the financial statements. The proposed treatment will overstate both revenue and assets which would improve the gearing ratio. A governance issue arises from the behaviour of the managing director. It is important that no one individual is too powerful and domineering in running an entity's affairs. An intimidation threat arises from the managing director pressurising the accountant to overstate revenue from the contract. It was also the managing director who implemented the excessive revaluations on the property. It would appear that the managing director is exercising too much power over the financial statements. The accountant must not be influenced by the behaviour of the managing director and should produce financial statements which are transparent and free from bias. Instead, the managing director should be reminded of their ethical responsibilities. The accountant may need to consider professional advice should the managing director refuse to correct the financial statements.

26 Janne

Workbook references. Investment property and fair value measurement are covered in Chapter 4. IFRS Practice Statement 2 *Making Materiality Judgements* is covered in Chapter 20. Alternative performance measures are covered in Chapter 18.

Top tips. For Part (a)(i) ensure that you relate your answer to the relevant accounting standards, IAS 40 and IFRS 13. The key message is that there is guidance on the measurement of fair value which Janne should have been applying. In Part (a)(ii) requires a discussion of the measurement principles in the *Conceptual Framework* in relation to Janne.

In Part (b) you need to make sure you answer the requirement: relate your answer to Janne's investors and reference the key applicable points of the practice statement. Part (c) covers alternative performance measures which is a key topic for SBR. Again you need to consider Janne's investors in your answer. Wider reading of articles, particularly those on the ACCA website, will be extremely helpful in being able to answer questions such as those seen here in Parts (b) and (c). The ESMA (European Securities and Markets Authority) Guidelines on Alternative Performance Measures, which are available online, provide another perspective and will be beneficial to read.

Marking scheme

		Marks
(a)	Investment properties discussion – 1 mark per valid point up to	9
(b)	Annual report discussion – 1 mark per valid point up to	8
(c)	Alternative performance measure discussion – 1 mark per valid point up to	8
		25

(a) (i) **Investment properties**

IAS 40 *Investment Property* allows two methods for valuing investment property: the fair value model and the cost model. If the fair value method is adopted, **then the investment property must be valued in accordance with IFRS 13** *Fair Value Measurement.* Fair value is the price that would be received to sell an asset or paid to transfer a liability in an orderly transaction between market participants at the measurement date.

Fair value is a **market-based measurement** rather than specific to the entity, so a company is not allowed to choose its own way of measuring fair value. Valuation techniques must be those which are appropriate and for which sufficient data are available. Entities should maximise the use of relevant **observable inputs** and minimise the use of **unobservable inputs**. The standard establishes a hierarchy for the inputs that valuation techniques use to measure fair value.

Level 1 Quoted prices (unadjusted) in active markets for identical assets or liabilities

Level 2 Inputs other than quoted prices included within Level 1 that are observable for the asset or liability, either directly or indirectly

Level 3 Unobservable inputs for the asset or liability

Although the directors claim that 'new-build value less obsolescence' is accepted by the industry, it **may not be in accordance with IFRS 13**. As investment property is often unique and not traded on a regular basis, fair value measurements are likely to be categorised as Level 2 or Level 3 valuations.

IFRS 13 mentions three valuation techniques: the market approach, the income approach and the cost approach. A market or income approach would usually be more appropriate for an investment property than a cost approach. The 'new-build value less obsolescence' (cost approach) does not take account of the Level 2 inputs such as sales value (market approach) and market rent (income approach). Nor does it take account of reliable estimates of future discounted cash flows, or values of similar properties.

In conclusion, Janne must apply IFRS 13 to the valuation of its investment property, taking account of Level 2 inputs.

(ii) **Selection of measurement basis**

Janne should ensure that it has given adequate consideration to its particular facts and circumstances in deciding to use fair value as the measurement basis for its investment property.

Applying the principles in the *Conceptual Framework*, Janne should choose a measurement basis should that provides information that is **useful** to the primary users of its financial statements. To be useful, the information must be **relevant** and provide a **faithful representation**.

The relevance of a measurement basis is affected by:

- The characteristics of the asset – eg if information about changes in the value of investment property is important to Janne's primary users, using a cost basis may not provide relevant information.
- How the asset contributes to future cash flows – which in part depends on Janne's business activities.

As investment property makes up 60% of Janne's total assets and assuming that Janne is holding investment property both to obtain rental income and to benefit from increases in value, it would be reasonable to assume that primary users would be very interested in changes in value, suggesting cost may not provide the most relevant information.

However, sometimes the level of **measurement uncertainty** associated with a measurement basis is so high that the information would not be a faithful representation. If significant measurement uncertainty exists through the use of fair value, Janne should consider using cost instead. This principle is also included in IAS 40 as it specifies that if, at recognition, fair value is not expected to be reliably measurable on a continuing basis, cost should be used instead.

(b) **Annual report**

Too much information in annual reports can be problematic as it can **obscure relevant information** and prevent investors from identifying the key issues that are likely to affect their decisions.

Removing unnecessary information from the annual report is therefore a good idea. However, it must be done carefully to ensure that financial reports still meet their primary objective of providing financial information that is useful to existing and potential investors, lenders and other creditors in making decisions about providing resources to the entity.

Disclosures are prescribed by IFRS and therefore are **not optional**. Management cannot just determine which disclosures appear irrelevant.

However, **materiality** needs to be taken into account when making disclosures. Practice Statement 2 *Making Materiality Judgements* confirms that **disclosure does not need to be made, even when prescribed by an IFRS, if the resulting information presented is not material**.

Although the finance director has used a disclosure checklist and determined that all disclosures made were 'necessary', it is not clear whether an assessment has been made as to whether the disclosures provide information that is material. If not, there is the potential to reduce disclosure in Janne's annual report.

If the information provided by a disclosure could not reasonably be expected to influence the decisions primary users make on the basis of Janne's financial statements, then it is not material and does not need to be disclosed.

Reducing the size of the accounting policy note is a distinct possibility. Only significant accounting policies are required to be disclosed by IAS 1. Determining what constitutes a significant accounting policy requires judgement.

Janne could consider removing the accounting policies which would not affect a user's understanding of the financial statements if they were not disclosed. Accounting policies that require management judgement are likely to be material and if so, should be clearly presented. This is so that investors can see where management judgement has been applied and can assess management's stewardship.

Disclosures required by IAS 24 in relation to related parties are necessary to draw attention to the possibility that an entity's financial position and profit or loss may have been affected by the transactions with related parties. So the managing director is not correct in his assertion that because the transactions are undertaken on terms equivalent to 'arm's length', they are not important to investors.

However, as with other disclosures, they only need to be made if the information provided is material. Related party transactions may be of a relatively small size and therefore considered not material from a **quantitative perspective**. However, Practice Statement 2 considers the fact that the transaction is with a related party to be a **qualitative factor**. A qualitative factor reduces the threshold for assessing whether something is material from a quantitative perspective.

Without considering the transactions more carefully, Janne cannot say that related party transactions are immaterial and need not be disclosed. Conversely, Janne should not assume that just because the transaction is with a related party that it must definitely be disclosed. Janne should apply the guidance provided in Practice Statement 2 in order to make a judgement about what information about related party transactions would be useful to investors and other primary users.

(c) **Alternative performance measure**

'Adjusted net asset value per share' (adjusted NAV per share) is an alternative performance measure (APM). Entities are increasingly reporting APMs in addition to IFRS performance measures, such as earnings per share, in order to enhance a user's understanding of the financial statements. It is possible for Janne to present this APM, however, it cannot present this measure instead of earnings per share (EPS). EPS is required by IAS 33 which must be applied by listed entities. Therefore, in order to comply with IFRS, EPS and diluted EPS must be presented.

APMs should be provided to enhance the understanding of users of the accounts. Investment properties are likely to form the majority of Janne's assets. Therefore management will be interested in the increase in the value of those properties and related finance (eg loans), both of which are taken into account in adjusted NAV per share. Disclosing adjusted NAV per share should therefore enhance the understanding of investors as it will allow them to evaluate Janne through the eyes of management. Additionally, as adjusted NAV per share is used by other companies in the same industry, disclosing it should allow investors to more effectively compare the performance of Janne with other companies in the same industry.

However, APMs can also be misleading. Unlike EPS, there is no official definition of adjusted NAV per share, so management can choose what items to include in the 'adjustment'. Therefore it is open to bias in its calculation as management could decide to only adjust for items that improve the measure. In order to counter the criticisms, management should provide a description of what is included when arriving at adjusted NAV per share and ideally reconcile the information back to the IFRS information included within the financial statements. Similarly, in order to be useful, the basis of the calculation needs to be consistent from year to year, otherwise comparison between years will be inaccurate. Furthermore, different companies may define the same measure in different ways, which reduces the comparability between entities.

Ultimately adjusted NAV per share will only provide useful information to Janne's investors if it is fairly presented. The European Securities and Markets Authority (ESMA) has developed guidelines that address the issues surrounding the use of APMs. The guidelines require appropriate description of APMs, consistency in how the APM is calculated and presented from year to year as well as guidance for presentation, including that APMs should not be presented with more prominence, emphasis or authority than the equivalent IFRS measures, nor should they distract from IFRS disclosures.

It is advisable for Janne's directors to consider this guidance in determining whether to present adjusted NAV per share and how it should be presented. They should also consider whether providing further information in the form of APMs will result in more information being reported in the annual report which they are otherwise attempting to reduce.

27 SunChem

Workbook references. IAS 24 is covered in Chapter 2, IAS 38 in Chapter 4, IFRS 3 in Chapter 11 and IFRS Practice Statement 2 in Chapter 20.

Top tips. Part (a) deals with standards that should be familiar to you, but the issues require in-depth consideration. In particular, you need to consider how IAS 38 and IFRS 3 interact, focusing on the implications of acquiring technology, outlining the fact that the probability recognition criterion is always considered to be satisfied for intangible assets that are acquired separately or in a business combination. You were also expected to discuss that a shell company without employees (and hence without processes required to make it a 'business') is an asset acquisition as opposed to a business combination. Part (b) is on materiality and related parties – identifying the related parties and discussing how such disclosures are useful to investors. You are advised to jot down a plan or diagram of the relationships before launching into your answer.

Easy marks. There are marks for knowing the basics of the standards tested, but those marks will not get you a pass on this question.

Marking scheme

		Marks
(a)	1 mark per point up to maximum	10
(b)	(i) 1 mark per point up to maximum	4
	(ii) 1 mark per point up to maximum	5
	(iii) 1 mark per point up to maximum	6
		25

(a) *Intangible asset*

SunChem has purchased a license which gives it the **right** to use Jomaster's technology for a specified period of time in order to manufacture a specific compound. The acquired license meets the definition of an intangible asset as it is:

- **Identifiable** (it arises from the contractual right to use Jomaster's technology for three years)
- non-monetary, and

- has no physical substance (SunChem has not acquired a physical item of machinery, but instead has acquired the right to use the technology to perform a particular process).

Under IAS 38, an intangible asset should be recognised when

(i) it is probable that the future economic benefits which are attributable to the asset will flow to the entity; and

(ii) the cost of the asset can be measured reliably.

IAS 38 states that the probability recognition criterion is **always considered to be satisfied for intangible assets that are acquired separately** or in a business combination. This is because the price an entity pays to separately acquire an intangible asset will reflect the entity's expectations about the probability of economic benefits flowing to the entity. Put simply, by purchasing the intangible asset, SunChem expects economic benefits to flow from it, even if it is not certain about the timing or amount of those benefits.

Therefore SunChem should recognise the license as an intangible asset measured at its cost of $4 million. As it has a finite useful life, the license should be **amortised** from the date it is available for use, ie when the manufacturing of the compound begins. The amortisation should be included as an expense in the statement of profit or loss.

At the end of each reporting period, SunChem should assess whether there is any indication that the asset may be **impaired**, and if so, the carrying amount of the asset should be reduced and the impairment loss should be recognised as an expense in profit or loss.

Due to the nature of intangible assets, **subsequent expenditure** will only rarely meet the criteria for being recognised in the carrying amount of an asset. Thus, SunChem should expense its own internal development expenditure, incurred in updating the technology in accordance with Jomaster's requirements, until the criteria for capitalisation in IAS 38 are met and economic benefits are expected to flow to the entity from the capitalised asset.

Acquisition of interest in Conew

SunChem wishes to acquire 65% of the equity of Conew. SunChem must assess whether this acquisition qualifies as a business combination under IFRS 3 *Business Combinations*. A business combination is a transaction in which an entity **obtains control of a business**.

Under IFRS 3, a business consists of **inputs** and **processes applied to those inputs** which have the ability to contribute to the **creation of outputs**.

Conew has an 'input' in that it has an intangible asset. However, Conew does not have any employees, and therefore does not have any processes which could be applied to the intangible asset. Therefore, Conew **does not meet the definition of a business.**

The acquisition of an interest in Conew is therefore an **asset acquisition**, not a business combination, and should be accounted for under IAS 38.

(b) (i) **Materiality**

Practice Statement 2 was developed in response to concerns that some companies are unsure how to make judgements concerning materiality. This can result in excessive disclosure of immaterial information while important information can be obscured or even missed out of the financial statements.

This is particularly true for information disclosed in the notes where it appears that some companies use IFRS disclosure requirements as a 'checklist' and therefore provide all disclosures required by a Standard, whether material or not.

Practice Statement 2 is not an IFRS and is therefore **not mandatory** in order to state compliance with IFRS in a financial report.

Key points

- Financial statements are not intended to satisfy the information needs of **all users**, but should provide financial information that is useful to **primary users** (potential and existing investors, lenders and other creditors) in making decisions about providing resources to the entity.
- If the information provided by a disclosure is **not material**, the **entity does not need to make that disclosure**.
- Materiality should be assessed from a **qualitative perspective** as well as a **quantitative perspective**. Practice Statement 2 recommends starting from the quantitative perspective and then applying qualitative factors to further assess immaterial items. The presence of a qualitative factor lowers the quantitative threshold for assessing materiality.

Practice Statement 2 contains a four-step process to help entities make materiality judgements: identify, assess, organise and review.

(ii) **Related parties**

A person or a close member of that person's family is a **related party** of a reporting entity if that person:

(i) has control or joint control over the reporting entity;

(ii) has significant influence over the reporting entity; or

(iii) is a member of the key management personnel of the reporting entity or of a parent of the reporting entity.

> **Tutorial note.**
>
> You will get very few, if any, marks for writing up the requirements of Standards. The vast majority of marks are available for the application of those requirements to the scenario given. The definition of a related party has been given in this solution for completeness, but you do not need to include this definition in an exam answer.

In SunChem:

- The finance director is a related party, as she owns more than half of the voting power (60%). In the absence of evidence to the contrary, she controls SunChem and is a member of the key management personnel.
- The sales director is also a related party of SunChem as he is a member of the key management personnel and is a close member (spouse) of the family of the finance director.
- Their son is a related party of SunChem as he is a close member (son) of their family.
- The operations director is also a related party as he owns more than 20% of the voting power in SunChem. In the absence of evidence to the contrary, the operations director has significant influence over SunChem and is a member of the key management personnel.

An entity is related to a reporting entity if the entity is controlled or jointly controlled by a person identified as a related party:

- Baleel is a related party because it is controlled by related parties, the finance and sales directors, for the benefit of a close member of their family, ie their son.
- Ocean is a related party because it is controlled by a close family member (spouse) of the operations director (a related party).

In the absence of evidence to the contrary, the third owner of the shares is not a related party. The person is a passive investor who does not appear to exert significant influence over SunChem.

(iii) IAS 24 requires related party disclosures in order to draw attention to the possibility that an entity's financial position and profit or loss may have been affected by the existence of related parties and by transactions and outstanding balances with such parties.

In this case, there is a single investor owning 10% of the shares whose investment may be affected by the related party transactions undertaken.

It is not just investors that are interested in such information. The *Conceptual Framework* states that the objective of financial reports is to provide information that is useful to existing and potential investors, lenders and other creditors of an entity. So it is not just the passive investor that must be considered when determining what to disclose.

Practice Statement 2 clarifies that if information provided by a disclosure could not reasonably be expected to influence the decisions primary users make based on the financial statements, then that disclosure need not be made.

The involvement of related parties is a qualitative factor when assessing materiality. This factor reduces the quantitative threshold and the entity should then go back and re-assess whether the information is material.

In the case of the laptop sold to the son, it is unlikely that this transaction would be material from a quantitative perspective. However, because the transaction is with a related party, the quantitative threshold should be lowered. SunChem should give consideration as to whether disclosing information about this transaction would be useful to its primary users. Given that the transaction is so small and has not reoccurred, it is probably not material.

In the case of the maintenance contract, it may be that the contract is below the quantitative threshold even when this threshold is lowered for the fact that the transaction is with a related party. However, given that the contract is ongoing and that it was awarded to a related party despite being more expensive, suggests that disclosing this information would be useful to primary users.

28 Egin Group

Workbook reference. The IASB's *Conceptual Framework for Financial Reporting* is covered in Chapter 1. Related parties are covered in Chapter 2. Practice Statement 2 is covered in Chapter 20.

Top tips. The best way to approach Part (b) is to prepare a plan on your exam by adding to the group structure provided any entities or individuals who are not shown as well as any transactions between the entities and individuals involved. Then you need to apply the IAS 24 related party definitions.

Easy marks. As Part (a) is fairly open ended, it gives scope for different approaches and credit will be given for valid points well expressed. This does not mean you can waffle. You should think about the practical use of a conceptual framework and consider the reasons for differences in accounting.

Marking scheme

				Marks
(a)	Discussion 1 mark per point to a maximum of 10 marks. Points may include:			
	Need for a conceptual framework			
	Useful for decision making		1	
	Theoretical in nature but practical aims		1	
	No framework results in haphazard approach		1	
	Needed for consistency in accounting standards		1	
	Rules-based approach open to manipulation		1	
	Resolve practical accounting issues			
	Framework cannot provide all the answers		1	
	Variety of users of accounts		1	
	Focus on some users at expense of other users		1	
	Provides definitions for use in accounting standards		1	
	Provides guidance in absence of a relevant IAS/IFRS		1	
				10
(b)	(i)	Reasons	4	
		Materiality	2	
	(ii)	Egin Group	5	
		Spade	3	
		Atomic	1	
				15
				25

(a) **The need for a conceptual framework**

The financial reporting process is concerned with providing information that is **useful in the business and economic decision-making process**. Therefore, a conceptual framework will form the theoretical basis for determining which transactions should be accounted for, how they should be measured and how they should be communicated to the user.

Although it is theoretical in nature, a conceptual framework for financial reporting has **highly practical final aims**.

The **danger of not having a conceptual framework** is demonstrated in the way some countries' standards have developed over recent years; standards tend to be produced in a **haphazard and fire-fighting approach**. Where an agreed framework exists, the standard-setting body builds the accounting rules on the foundation of sound, agreed basic principles.

The lack of a conceptual framework also means that **fundamental principles are tackled more than once in different standards**, which can produce **contradictions and inconsistencies** in accounting standards. This leads to ambiguity and it affects the true and fair concept of financial reporting.

Without a conceptual framework, there is a **risk** that a financial reporting environment becomes governed by specific rules rather than general principles. A **rules-based approach** is much **more open to manipulation** than a principles-based one. For example, a rule requiring an accounting treatment based on a transaction reaching a percentage threshold, might encourage unscrupulous directors to set up a transaction in such a way to deliberately to achieve a certain accounting effect (eg keep finance off the statement of financial position).

A conceptual framework can also **bolster standard setters against political pressure** from various 'lobby groups' and interested parties. Such pressure would only prevail if it was acceptable under the conceptual framework.

Can it resolve practical accounting issues?

A framework cannot provide all the answers for standard setters. It can provide **principles** which can be used when deciding between alternatives, and can narrow the range of alternatives that can be considered. The IASB intends to use the principles laid out in the *Conceptual Framework* as the basis for all future IFRSs, which should help to eliminate inconsistences between standards going forward.

However, a conceptual framework is **unlikely**, on past form, to **provide all** the **answers to practical accounting problems**. There are a number of reasons for this:

(i) Financial statements are intended for a variety of users, and it is not certain that a single conceptual framework can be devised which will suit all users.

(ii) Given the diversity of user requirements, there may be a need for a variety of accounting standards, each produced for a different purpose (and with different concepts as a basis).

(iii) It is not clear that a conceptual framework makes the task of preparing and then implementing standards any easier than without a framework.

(b) (i) **Why it is important to disclose related party transactions**

The directors of Egin are correct to say that related party transactions are a normal feature of business. However, where entities are members of the same group, for example parent and subsidiary, the **financial performance and position of both entities can be affected** by these transactions. An obvious instance of this is where one group company sells goods to another at artificially low prices which can have a detrimental impact on the stakeholders of the selling company.

In the absence of other information, users of the financial statements **assume that a company pursues its interests independently** and undertakes transactions on an **arm's length basis** on terms that could have been obtained in a transaction with a third party.

Knowledge of related party relationships and transactions affects the way in which users assess a company's operations and the risks and opportunities that it faces. Therefore, **details of an entity's controlling party and transactions with related parties should be disclosed.**

It is essential to the **stakeholders' positive view of a company's moral and ethical behaviour** that **controls** are in place to **capture related party disclosures** that are accurate and complete. This serves to **minimise the risk of unethical** or fraudulent **behaviour**.

Materiality judgement

Disclosure of related party transactions, like all other disclosure in financial statements, is subject to the over-arching characteristic of materiality, as is confirmed by IFRS Practice Statement 2: *Making Materiality Judgements*.

The size, nature and context of the related party transaction should be taken into account. A transaction may be small, such that it would be immaterial if it were not with a related party. However, the fact that it is with a related party, which is a qualitative factor, lowers the quantitative threshold for determining if it is material. Ultimately, the entity needs to determine whether disclosing the information could reasonably be expected to influence primary users' decisions. If not, then it is not material and disclosure of that information is not required.

(ii) **Nature of related party relationships**

Within the Egin Group

Briars and Doye are related parties of Egin because they are **members of the same group** (both subsidiaries of Egin). For the same reason, as fellow subsidiaries, **Briars and Doye** are also **related parties of each other**. **Eye is also a related party of Egin** because it is an **associate of Egin**. (Egin has **significant influence** over Eye.)

Briars and Doye are also related parties of Eye. There is only one director in common and IAS 24 states that entities are not necessarily related simply because they have a director (or other member of key management personnel) in common, or because a member of key management personnel of one entity has significant influence over the other entity. However, as **Eye is a member of the same group** that Briars and Doye are members of, they are related.

Although Tang was sold several months before the year end it was a **related party** of the Egin Group until then. Therefore, the related party relationship between Tang and the Egin Group **should be disclosed** even though there were no transactions between them during the period.

Blue is a related party of Briars as a **director of Briars controls it.** Because the director is not on the management board of Egin it is **not clear whether Blue is also a related party of Egin group**. This would depend on whether the director is considered key management personnel at a group level. The director's services as a consultant to the group may mean that a related party relationship exists. The issue would depend on whether this role meant that this person was directing or controlling a major part of the group's activities and resources.

Between Spade and the Egin Group

Spade is a related party of Doye because it exerts **significant influence** over Doye. This means that the **sale** of plant and equipment **to Spade must be disclosed. Egin is not necessarily a related party of Spade** simply because both have an investment in Doye. A related party relationship will only exist if one party **exercises influence** over another **in practice**.

The directors have proposed that disclosures should state that prices charged to related parties are set on an **arm's length basis**. Because the transaction took place **between related parties** by definition it **cannot have taken place on an arm's length basis** and this description cannot be substantiated and would be **misleading**. Doye sold plant and equipment to Spade at **normal selling prices** and this is the information that should be disclosed, provided the terms can be substantiated.

Between Atomic and the Egin Group

Atomic is a related party of Egin because it can exercise **significant influence** over it. Atomic's significant influence over Egin gives it **significant influence over Briars and Doye** as they are controlled by Egin. **Eye is not a related party of Atomic** as Atomic has no ability to exercise control or significant influence over Eye.

29 Lockfine

Workbook references. IFRS 1 *First-time Adoption of International Financial Reporting Standards* is covered in Chapter 20, IFRS 13 *Fair Value Measurement* in Chapter 4, and IFRS 3 *Business Combinations* is covered in Chapter 11.

Top tips. This was a scenario question, set in the fishing industry. The question was broken down into four almost equal parts. Parts (a) and (b) covered IFRS 1 *First-time Adoption of International Financial Reporting Standards* in respect of fair value measurement and transition to IFRS 3 *Business Combinations.* The key point here is that the decision to apply IFRS 3 retrospectively cannot be made selectively.

Easy marks. There are some relatively easy marks in Part (d) for listing out the IAS 37 criteria for a constructive obligation to restructure.

Marking scheme

		Marks
(a)	1 mark per question up to maximum	6
(b)	1 mark per question up to maximum	6
(c)	1 mark per question up to maximum	7
(d)	1 mark per question up to maximum	6
Maximum		25

(a) **IFRS 1 and deemed cost**

IFRS 1 *First-time Adoption of International Financial Reporting Standards* states that an entity may elect to measure an item of property, plant and equipment at the **date of transition to IFRS** at fair value and **use that fair value as its deemed cost at that date**. Fair value is defined in IFRS 1 as amended by IFRS 13 *Fair Value Measurement* as:

'The price that would be received to sell an asset or paid to transfer a liability in an orderly transaction between market participants at the measurement date.' (IFRS 13; para 9)

An entity adopting IFRS for the first time may, under IFRS 1 as amended by IFRS 13, elect **to use a previous GAAP revaluation** of an item of property, plant and equipment at or before the date of transition to IFRS as deemed cost at the date of the revaluation under the following conditions.

(i) The revaluation was broadly comparable to fair value.

(ii) The revaluation was broadly comparable to cost or depreciated cost in accordance with IFRS, adjusted to reflect, for example, changes in a general or specific price index.

In addition, IFRS 1 does not give detailed rules about determining fair value, and first-time adopters who use fair value as deemed cost **must only provide limited disclosures**, not a full description of the methods and assumptions used.

In the case of Lockfine, the question to be decided is whether the selling agents' estimates can be used as the fair value to be used, in turn, as deemed cost under IFRS 1.

The selling agents' estimates provide only limited information about the valuation methods and assumptions, and it is doubtful that they can be relied upon for determining fair value in accordance with IAS 16 *Property, Plant and Equipment* and IFRS 13 *Fair Value Measurement.* Under IAS 16 measurement of fair value must be **reliable**. While it is correct to use independent valuers, IAS 16 requires that the reporting entity know the **assumptions** that have been made in assessing reliability. In addition, using the average of the highest amounts may not be prudent.

IFRS 1 allows more latitude than IAS 16. Lockfine is **not in breach of IFRS 1 which does not specify detailed rules for this particular case**, and allows fair value as determined on the basis of selling agents' estimates. This is a cost effective approach for entities that do not perform a full retrospective application of the requirements of IAS 16.

(b) **Fishing rights**

IFRS 1 requires that if an entity which is in the process of adopting IFRS decides to apply IFRS 3 retrospectively to a business combination, it **cannot do so selectively**, but must apply IFRS 3 **consistently to all business combinations** that occur between the date on which it decides to adopt IFRS 3 and the date of transition. An entity must have regard to **similar transactions in the period**. When allocating values to the assets and liabilities of the acquired company, the entity needs to have documentation to support its purchase price allocation. Without this, use of other methods of price allocation is not permitted unless the methods are strictly in accordance with IFRS.

Lockfine was **unable to recognise** the fishing rights of the business combination as separately identifiable because it **could not obtain a reliable value** for the rights, so it included the rights within goodwill.

IAS 38 has two criteria, both of which must be met for an entity to recognise an intangible asset, whether purchased or internally generated:

(i) It is probably that the future economic benefits attributable to the asset will flow to the entity.

(ii) The cost of the asset can be measured reliably.

The fishing rights **satisfy the first, but not the second of these criteria**. Accordingly the fishing rights were **correctly subsumed within goodwill**. As long as the goodwill presented under the first IFRS financial statements did not require a write down for impairment, it should be the net carrying amount at the date of transition.

Although the fishing rights have a finite life, **they will not be amortised over the period** specified by the rights, because they are included within goodwill. Instead, **the goodwill is reviewed annually for impairment** in accordance with IAS 36 *Impairment of Assets*.

(c) **Electronic map data**

The standard that applies here is IAS 38 *Intangible Assets*. Under IAS 38, an intangible asset is an asset with the following characteristics.

(i) It meets the standard's **identifiability criteria**. This means it must be separable or must arise from contractual or other legal rights.

(ii) It is probable that **future economic benefits** attributable to the asset will flow to the entity. These could be in the form of increased revenues or cost savings.

(iii) The entity has **control**, that is, the power to obtain benefits from the asset.

(iv) Its cost can be **measured reliably**.

It appears that the capitalised expenses of the acquisition and production of the electronic map data **meet these criteria**.

(i) The electronic maps are identifiable because they are capable of being separated from the entity as a whole and sold (or transferred or licensed), regardless of whether the entity intends to do this.

(ii) They are controlled by Lockfine.

(iii) It is probable that benefits attributable to the maps will flow to the entity because the electronic maps will generate revenue when used by the fishing fleet.

(iv) Their value can be measured reliably – Lockfine has a record of the costs.

The **electronic maps** will therefore be **recognised as an intangible asset at cost**. Generally they will subsequently be carried at cost less any amortisation and impairment losses.

Regarding the **database**, Lockfine believes that this has an indefinite useful life and, by implication, should not be amortised but should be tested annually for impairment. IAS 38 regards an intangible asset as having an indefinite useful life when, based on analysis of all the relevant factors, there is no foreseeable limit to the period over which the asset is expected to generate net cash inflows for the entity.

Indefinite does not mean the same as infinite and in the context of IAS 38 has specific implications. In particular, the indefinite useful life should not depend on future planned expenditure in excess of that required to maintain the asset. In this respect, **Lockfine complies with IAS 38**.

In addition, IAS 38 identifies certain factors that may affect the useful life, changing it in this instance from indefinite to finite. These include technological or commercial obsolescence and actions by competitors.

There is no specific requirement for an entity to disclose the IAS 38 criteria for recognition of an intangible asset arising from development, although it does require disclosure of assets which have an indefinite useful life (the carrying amount and reasons for assessing the useful life as indefinite). However, under IAS 1 *Presentation of Financial Statements,* entities **must disclose accounting policies that are relevant for an understanding of their financial statements**. The electronic maps and the data base constitute a material amount of total assets, so the accounting policies, including the IAS 38 criteria for development expenditure, need to be disclosed.

(d) **Restructuring plans**

IAS 37 criteria

IAS 37 *Provisions, Contingent Liabilities and Contingent Assets* **contains specific requirements** relating to **restructuring provisions**. The general recognition criteria apply and IAS 37 also states that **a provision should be recognised** if an entity has a **constructive obligation** to carry out a restructuring. A constructive obligation exists where **management has a detailed formal plan** for the restructuring, identifying **as a minimum:**

(i) The business or part of the business being restructured

(ii) The principal locations affected by the restructuring

(iii) The location, function and approximate number of employees who will be compensated for the termination of their employment

(iv) The date of implementation of the plan

(v) The expenditure that will be undertaken

In addition, the plan must have raised a **valid expectation** in those affected that the entity will carry out the restructuring. To give rise to such an expectation and, therefore, a constructive obligation, the **implementation must be planned to take place as soon as possible**, and the timeframe must be such as to make changes to the plan unlikely.

Plan A

Lockfine proposes recognising a provision in respect of the plan to sell 50% of its off-shore fleet in a year's time and to make 40% of the seamen redundant. However, although the plan has been communicated to the public, the above criteria are not met. **The plan is insufficiently detailed**, and various aspects are not finalised. The figure of 40% is tentative as yet, the **fleets and employees affected have not been identified**, and a decision has not been made on whether the off-shore fleet will be restructured in the future. Some of these issues await further analysis.

The proposal does not, therefore, meet the IAS 37 criteria for a detailed formal plan and an announcement of the plan to those affected by it. Lockfine cannot be said to be committed to this restructuring and so **a provision should not be recognised**.

Plan B

Lockfine has not proposed recognising a provision for the plan to reorganise its headquarters and make 20% of the headquarters' workforce redundant. However, it is likely that this treatment is incorrect, because the plan appears to meet the IAS 37 criteria above:

(i) The locations and employees affected have been **identified**.

(ii) An **announcement** has been made and employee representatives notified – it is not necessary to notify individual employees as their representatives have been told.

(iii) The conclusion of the three month consultation period indicates that the above announcement is sufficiently detailed to give rise to a **valid expectation** that the restructuring will take place, particularly if the discussions have been about the terms of the redundancy.

It will be necessary to **consider the above negotiations** – provided these are about details such as the terms of redundancy rather than about changing the plan, then the IAS 37 criteria have been met. Accordingly, a provision needs to be recognised.

30 Alexandra

Workbook references. IAS 1 *Presentation of Financial Statements* is covered in Chapter 1 and IFRS 15 *Revenue from Contracts with Customers* in Chapter 3. Related parties and ethics are covered in Chapter 2. Practice Statement 2 is covered in Chapter 20.

Top tips. Part (a) was on reclassification of long-term debt as current – make sure you are familiar with IAS 1 as it is not a difficult standard but is often overlooked by students – IAS 1 requires a liability to be classified as current if it is due to be settled within 12 months after the date of the statement of financial position. Part (b) was on related party disclosures for key management personnel and the effect of Practice Statement 2.

For learning purposes, this question included some discussion of ethical issues in the context of the scenario given. However, please note that ethics will not feature in Section B questions in the real exam. Ethics will be examined only in Question 2 of the exam.

Easy marks. Part (b) has some easy marks for applying the definitions from IAS 24 to the scenario.

Marking scheme

				Marks
(a)	(i)	Loan – accounting treatment – 1 mark per point up to		6
	(ii)	Ethical implications	2	
		Impact on investors' analysis	3	
				5
(b)	(i)	Directors remuneration accounting treatment – 1 mark per point up to	4	
		Materiality discussion - 1 mark per point up to	5	
		Importance of disclosure to investors – 1 mark per point up to	2	
				11
	(ii)	Ethical implications – 1 mark point up to		3
				25

(a) (i) **Default on loan**

Under IAS 1 *Presentation of Financial Statements,* a **long-term financial liability** due to be **settled within 12 months** of the year end date should be classified as a **current liability**. Furthermore, a **long-term financial liability** that is payable on **demand** because the entity **breached** a **condition** of its loan agreement should be classified as **current** at the year end even if the **lender** has agreed **after the year end**, and **before** the financial statements are **authorised for issue**, **not** to **demand payment** as a consequence of the breach.

November 20X0	*30 April 20X1*	*17 May 20X1*	Date financial statements approved for issue
Condition of loan agreement breached. Long-term liability becomes payable on demand	Year end	Lender agrees not to enforce payment resulting from breach	

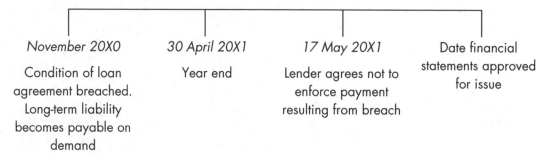

However, if the **lender** has **agreed** by the **year end** to provide a **period of grace** ending **at least 12 months after the year end** within which the entity can rectify the breach and during that time the lender cannot demand immediate repayment, the liability is classified as **non-current**.

In the case of Alexandra, the waiver was given before the year end, but only for the loan to be repaid a month after the year end, then a further waiver was agreed, but again only for a few weeks. It would **not therefore be appropriate for Alexandra to classify the bond as long-term debt** in the statement of financial position as at 30 April 20X1.

The fact that Alexandra has defaulted and sought two loan waivers may cast doubt on its ability to continue as a going concern, especially as the loan waivers may not be renewed. If there is uncertainty regarding Alexandra's going concern status, IAS 1 requires Alexandra to disclose these uncertainties. If Alexandra ceases to be a going concern, then the financial statements would need to be prepared on a break-up basis.

(ii) *Ethical implications*

Presentation of the loan as non-current is unethical as it does not faithfully represent the financial position of Alexandra at the year end.

The motivation of the directors in presenting the loan as non-current should be questioned. It may be that they have presented the loan as such to deliberately mislead their investors, lenders and other creditors as to the precarious financial position they find themselves in. This represents a threat to ACCA's *Code of Ethics and Conduct* fundamental principle of integrity, which requires professional accountants to be honest.

Impact on investors' analysis

Alexandra's incorrect presentation of this loan could have a serious impact on investors as they seek to analyse the financial statements. Investors need information to help them assess the prospects for future net cash inflows to an entity. Given that the bond obligation may become repayable immediately in this case, Alexandra's ability to continue as a going concern and be able to generate any future cash flows is clearly at risk.

According to the *Conceptual Framework*, the objective of financial reporting is to provide financial information about the entity that is useful to primary users of the financial statements when making decisions about providing resources to the entity. In Alexandra's case, reporting the loan as non-current is not useful to primary users, it is misleading. In fact, it is materially misleading as it could quite feasibly influence the economic decisions the primary users of Alexandra's financial statements make on the basis of those financial statements.

(b) **Directors' remuneration**

IAS 24 *Related Party Disclosures* requires that entities should **disclose** key management personnel compensation **not only in total** but also **for each of the** following **categories:**

- Short-term employee benefits
- Post-employment benefits
- Other long-term benefits
- Termination benefits
- Share-based payment

The remuneration for the directors of Alexandra fits into the categories of 'short-term benefits' (ie salary and bonus) and 'share-based payment' (ie share options).

Only totals for each category need to be disclosed, not the earnings of individual board members, so no cultural protocol will be breached by these disclosures. However, Alexandra is a public limited company, and so local legislation and corporate governance rules may require more detailed disclosure.

Non-executive directors

IAS 24 defines **key management personnel** as those persons having authority and responsibility for planning, directing and controlling the activities of the entity, directly or indirectly, including any director (**whether executive or otherwise**) of that entity. Therefore Alexandra's non-executive directors are members of Alexandra's key management personnel. The requirements of IAS 24 therefore also apply to the non-executive directors' pay.

Effect of materiality

Practice Statement 2 reaffirms that if information provided by a disclosure is not material, ie that it could not reasonably be expected to influence the decisions primary users make based on the financial statements, then that disclosure need not be made.

This applies equally to related party disclosures as to any other disclosures required by IFRSs, even if they are required under the Standard as 'minimum disclosures'. So in a sense, the finance director is correct – **but** only if the information provided by those related party disclosures is not material.

How the board assesses whether the information is material is important. The boards' assertion that the 'amounts involved are not material' suggests that perhaps they have only considered materiality from a **quantitative perspective**.

Practice Statement 2 suggests it may be efficient to first assess materiality from a quantitative perspective. If an item is considered immaterial from a quantitative perspective, the entity can then consider the presence of any **qualitative factors** and assess materiality from that perspective.

The involvement of related parties is a qualitative factor. The fact that these transactions are with related parties of Alexandra reduces the quantitative threshold that Alexandra should use to determine if the transactions are material.

Sometimes the effect of a qualitative factor can reduce the quantitative threshold to zero – thus the transaction is material despite how small it might be. This is likely to be the case when considering directors' remuneration given that it is such a contentious area.

As such, Alexandra should make the disclosures required under IAS 24, unless they can provide a well-supported argument as to why the information is not material.

Importance of disclosure to investors

Disclosures about related parties are necessary to draw attention to the possibility that the entity's financial position and profit or loss may have been affected by the existence of related parties and by transactions and outstanding balances with such parties.

Director's remuneration disclosures are particularly contentious. Public concern about excessive director remuneration has existed for some time. Investors want to know how much of an entity's income is being spent on its directors and whether this represents good value for money. Given the default on the bond and waivers to postpone interest payments, it is likely that the company would come under criticism if payments to directors were considered particularly high.

The disclosure of individual components of remuneration is important because it could influence the performance of a director – eg a high early termination payment may be seen to be rewarding poor performance.

Ethical issues

A fundamental principle of ACCA's *Code of Ethics and Conduct* is that of professional behaviour, which includes compliance with relevant regulation. It would therefore be unethical not to disclose all the information required by IAS 24 if those disclosures are material.

The finance director should be fully aware of the requirements of IAS 24 and whether information is material. If he is not aware of these requirements, then this is a serious threat to the fundamental principle of professional competence and due care, as the knowledge and skill of the finance director is questionable.

If the finance director is aware of these requirements, his motivation as to why adequate disclosure was not provided should be investigated further. It may be that his objectivity has been compromised by pressure from the other board members to report the directors' remuneration in this way.

31 Verge

Workbook references. IAS 1 *Presentation of Financial Statements* is covered in Chapter 1 and revenue recognition in Chapter 3. Provisions and contingencies are covered in Chapter 6 and government grants in Chapter 4. Amendments to IAS 8 are covered in Chapter 2.

Top tips. Part (a) needs some thought as possible confusion may arise about the $1m payment in advance, which is also included in an invoice. However, even if you missed this, you could still get good marks for seeing that the payments needed to be discounted in order that revenue should be recognised at fair value, and for seeing that the incorrect accounting treatment applied needed to be corrected retrospectively following IAS 8. You have met provisions (Part (b)) in your earlier studies, but in SBR, questions are likely to go into more depth and may ask you to critique the standard against the *Conceptual Framework*. The information you require is in the scenario, but you need to think about applying the standard. Part (c) asks you to consider the interaction of two property-related standards you have met before in your previous studies, but again in a less straightforward context.

In this type of question, as well as providing a written explanation of the correct accounting treatment, you should also show the accounting entries where this is possible (Parts (b) and (c) in this question).

Part (d) covers a current issue – the amendments proposed to IAS 8.

Easy marks. These are available for identifying which standards apply and outlining the principles applicable, and you will gain these marks whether or not you come to the correct conclusion about the accounting treatment. There are also some easy marks for definitions in Part (b).

Marking scheme

		Marks
(a)	IFRS 15/IAS 8 explanation and calculation	6
(b)	IAS 37 explanation and calculation	6
(c)	IAS 1/16/20 explanation and calculation	7
(d)	Amendments to IAS 8	6
		25

(a) **Maintenance contract**

Recognition of revenue from the maintenance contract

Under IFRS 15, an entity must **adjust the promised amount of consideration for the effects of the time value of money** if the contract contains a **significant financing component**. A significant financing component exists even if the financing is only implied by the payment terms.

In effect Verge is providing interest-free credit to the government body. IFRS 15 requires the use of the **discount rate** which would be reflected in a **separate financing transaction** between the Verge and its customer (the government agency), here 6%. This 6% must be used to calculate the discounted amount of the revenue, and the difference between this and the cash eventually received recognised as **interest income**.

The government agency simultaneously receives and consumes the benefits as the performance takes place so this contract contains a performance obligation satisfied over time. Verge must therefore **recognise revenue from the contract as the services are provided**, that is **as work is performed** throughout the contract's life, and not as the cash is received. The invoices sent by Verge reflect the work performed in each year, but the amounts must be **discounted in order to report the revenue at fair value**. The exception is the $1 million paid at the beginning of the contract. This is paid in advance and therefore not discounted, but it is invoiced and recognised in the year ended 31 March 20X2. The remainder of the amount invoiced in the year ended 31 March 20X2 ($2.8m – $1m = $1.8m) is discounted at 6% for two years.

In the year ended 31 March 20X3, the invoiced amount of $1.2 million will be discounted at 6% for only one year. There will also be interest income of $96,000, which is the **unwinding of the discount** in 20X2.

Recognised in y/e 31 March 20X2

	$m
Initial payment (not discounted)	1.0
Remainder invoiced at 31 March 20X2: $1.8 \times \frac{1}{1.06^2}$	1.6
Revenue recognised	2.6

Recognised in y/e 31 March 20X3

Revenue: $\$1.2\text{m} \times \frac{1}{1.06} = \$1.13\text{m}$

Unwinding of the discount on revenue recognised in 20X2 $1.6m × 6% = $96,000

Correction of prior period error

The accounting treatment previously used by Verge was incorrect because it did not comply with IFRS 15. Consequently, the change to the new, correct policy is **the correction of an error** under IAS 8 *Accounting Policies, Changes in Accounting Estimates and Errors.*

Only including $1 million of revenue in the financial statements for the year ended 31 March 20X2 is clearly a mistake on the part of Verge. As a prior period error, it **must be corrected retrospectively**. This involves **restating the comparative figures** in the financial statements for 20X3 (ie the 20X2 figures) and **restating the opening balances** for 20X3 so that the financial statements are presented as if the error had never occurred.

(b) **Legal claim**

A **provision** is defined by IAS 37 *Provisions, Contingent Liabilities and Contingent Assets* as **a liability of uncertain timing or amount**. IAS 37 states that a provision should only be recognised if:

- There is a **present obligation** as the result of a **past event**;
- An **outflow of resources embodying economic benefits is probable**; and
- A **reliable estimate** of the amount can be made.

If these conditions apply, a provision must be recognised.

The past event that gives rise, under IAS 37, to a present obligation, is known as the **obligating event**. The obligation may be legal, or it may be constructive (as when past practice creates a valid expectation on the part of a third party). The entity must have **no realistic alternative but to settle** the obligation.

Year ended 31 March 20X2

In this case, the obligating event is the damage to the building, and it took place in the year ended 31 March 20X2. As at that date, no legal proceedings had been started, and the damage appeared to be superficial. While Verge should recognise an obligation to pay damages, at 31 March 20X2 **the amount of any provision would be immaterial**. It would a best estimate of the amount required to settle the obligation at that date, taking into account all relevant risks and uncertainties, and at the year end the amount does not look as if it will be substantial.

Year ended 31 March 20X3

IAS 37 requires that **provisions should be reviewed at the end of each accounting period for any material changes** to the best estimate previously made. The legal action will cause such a material change, and Verge will be required to reassess the estimate of likely damages. While the local company is claiming damages of $1.2 million, Verge is not obliged to make a provision for this amount, but rather should **base its estimate on the legal advice** it has received and the opinion of the expert, both of which put the value of the building at $800,000. This amount should be provided for as follows.

DEBIT	Profit or loss for the year	$800,000	
CREDIT	Provision for damages		$800,000

Some or all of the expenditure needed to settle a provision may be expected to be recovered form a third party, in this case the insurance company. If so, the **reimbursement should be recognised only when it is virtually certain that reimbursement will be received if the entity settles the obligation**.

- The reimbursement should be treated as a **separate asset,** and the amount recognised should **not be greater than the provision itself**.
- The provision and the amount recognised for reimbursement **may be netted off in profit or loss** for the year.

There is no reason to believe that the insurance company will not settle the claim for the first $200,000 of damages, and so the company **should accrue for the reimbursement** as follows.

DEBIT	Receivables	$200,000	
CREDIT	Profit or loss for the year		$200,000

Verge lost the court case and is required to pay $300,000. This was after the financial statements were authorised, however, and so it is **not an adjusting event** per IAS 10 *Events After the Reporting Period*. Accordingly the amount of the provision as at 31 March 20X3 does not need to be adjusted.

(c) **Gift of building**

The applicable standards here are IAS 16 *Property, Plant and Equipment,* and IAS 20 *Accounting for Government Grants and Disclosure of Government Assistance,* within the framework of IAS 1 *Presentation of Financial Statements*. IAS 1 requires that all items of income and expense recognised in a period should be included in profit or loss for the period unless a standard or interpretation requires or permits a different treatment.

IAS 16: recognition of building

IAS 16 states that the **cost** of an item of property, plant and equipment should be **recognised when two conditions** have been fulfilled:

- It is probable that future economic benefits associated with the item will flow to the entity.
- The cost of the item can be measured reliably.

These conditions are normally fulfilled when the risks and rewards have transferred to the entity, and they may be assumed to transfer **when the contract is unconditional and irrevocable**. As at 31 March 20X2, the condition of use has **not been complied** with and Verge has not taken possession of the building.

The building may, however, be recognised in the year ended 31 March 20X3, as the conditions of donation were met in February 20X3. The **fair value** of the building of $1.5 million must be recognised as income in **profit or loss** for the year, as it was a gift. The **refurbishment and adaptation cost must also be included** as part of the cost of the asset in the statement of financial position, because, according to IAS 16, the cost includes **directly attributable costs of bringing the asset to the location and condition necessary** for it to be capable of operating in a manner intended by management. The transactions should be recorded as follows.

DEBIT	Property, plant and equipment	$2.5m	
CREDIT	Profit or loss for the year		$1.5m
CREDIT	Cash/payables		$1m

In addition, the building would be depreciated in accordance with the entity's accounting policy, which could (depending on the policy) involve time-apportioning over one or two months (February and March 20X3), depending on when in February the building came into use as a museum.

IAS 20: Government grant

The principle behind IAS 20 is that of accruals or matching: the **grant received must be matched with the related costs** on a systematic basis. Grants receivable as compensation for costs already incurred, or for immediate financial support with no future related costs, should be recognised as income in the period in which they are receivable.

Government grants are assistance by government in the form of transfers of resources to an entity in return for past or future compliance with certain conditions relating to the operating activities of the entity.

There are two main types of grants:

(i) **Grants related to assets**: grants whose primary condition is that an entity qualifying for them should purchase, construct or otherwise acquire long-term assets.

(ii) **Grants related to income**: These are government grants other than grants related to assets.

It is not always easy to match costs and revenues, but in this case the terms of the grant are explicit about the expense to which the grant is meant to contribute. **Part of the grant** relates to the **creation of jobs** and this amount (20 × $5,000 = $100,000) should be **taken to income**.

The **rest of the grant** ($250,000 – $100,000 = $150,000) should be recognised as **capital-based grant** (grant relating to assets). IAS 20 would **two possible approaches** for the capital-based portion of the grant.

(i) Match against the depreciation of the building using a deferred income approach.

(ii) Deduct from the carrying amount of the building, resulting in a reduced depreciation charge.

The double entry would be:

DEBIT	Cash	$250,000	
CREDIT	Profit or loss		$100,000
CREDIT	Deferred income/PPE (depending on the accounting policy)		$150,000

If a deferred income approach is adopted, the **deferred income would be released over the life of the building and matched against depreciation**. Depending on the policy, both may be time-apportioned because conditions were only met in February 20X3.

(d) (i) The amendments proposed in ED 2018/1 are intended to **facilitate voluntary changes in accounting policies** that result from **agenda decisions** published by the IFRS Interpretations Committee. The IASB believes this will improve consistency in application of IFRSs.

Agenda decisions are **not authoritative** so entities are **not required** to change their accounting policies in response, but can do so voluntarily. To encourage this, the IASB proposes to amend IAS 8 so that these changes can be applied **prospectively**, rather than retrospectively as currently required by IAS 8, subject to a cost-benefit analysis.

Verge's accounting policies

At present, this is an exposure draft and not an IFRS, so Verge cannot apply these provisions now. In fact, there has generally been a negative response to the ED as many stakeholders believe that this does not address the fundamental issue – which is that agenda decisions are not mandatory and have no effective date, yet are treated as such by securities regulators. So it is doubtful whether the amendments will go ahead.

If the amendments did go ahead, then only changes in accounting policy resulting from agenda decisions will be affected. All other changes in accounting policy will still need to be applied retrospectively.

It is concerning that the finance director thinks some of Verge's accounting policies are 'outdated'. If she means the policies do not comply with IFRSs, then this should be addressed and corrected as soon as possible. The professional competence of the finance director would be under question if this was the case.

If by outdated, the finance director means that a different policy would provide more useful information for primary users of the financial statements, then the question needs to be asked as to why the change has not been made when IAS 8 permits a change in accounting policy if the change results in reliable and more relevant information. Further investigation is required.

32 Avco

Workbook reference. The distinction between debt and equity is covered in Chapter 8. Cryptocurrencies are covered in Chapter 1 and Chapter 18.

Top tips. The majority of the question covers the distinction between debt and equity, which is quite narrow in focus. The topic has featured in an article by the examining team which is available on ACCA's website. The distinction between debt and equity is fundamental to any set of financial statements, and it is essential that you can explain it with reference to IFRSs and the *Conceptual Framework*. In Part (c), accounting for cryptocurrencies is an emerging issue that the IASB has not yet issued any guidance on. You should critically assess the finance director's suggestion that these are financial assets by reference to relevant Standards and the *Conceptual Framework*.

Easy marks. This is a challenging question overall but you should understand and be able to discuss the basic principles of debt v equity.

Marking scheme

			Marks
(a)	1 mark per point up to maximum		8
(b)	(i)	1 mark per point up to maximum	8
	(ii)	Effects	4
(c)	1 mark per point up to maximum		5
			25

(a) (i) **Cavor**

B shares

The classification of Cavor's B shares will be made by applying **the principles-based definitions of equity and liability in IAS 32** *Financial Instruments: Presentation*, and considering the **substance,** rather than the legal form of the instrument. 'Substance' here relates only to consideration of the contractual terms of the instrument. Factors outside the contractual terms are not relevant to the classification. The following factors demonstrate that Cavor's B shares are **equity instruments**.

(1) **Dividends are discretionary** in that they need only be paid if paid on the A shares, on which there is no obligation to pay dividends. Dividends on the B shares will be paid at the same rate as on the A shares, which will be variable.

(2) Cavor has **no obligation to redeem** the B shares.

(ii) **Lidan**

A financial liability under IAS 32 is **a contractual obligation to deliver cash or another financial asset to another entity**. The contractual obligation may arise from a requirement to make payments of principal, interest or dividends. The contractual obligation may be explicit, but it may be implied indirectly in the terms of the contract.

In the case of Lidan, the **contractual obligation is not explicit**. At first glance it looks as if Lidan has a choice as to how much it pays to redeem the B shares. However, the conditions of the financial instrument are such that the value of the **settlement in own shares is considerably greater than the cash settlement obligation**. The effect of this is that **Lidan is implicitly obliged to redeem the B shares at for a cash amount of $1 per share**. The own-share settlement alternative is uneconomic in comparison to the cash settlement alternative, and cannot therefore serve as a means of avoiding classification as a liability.

IAS 32 states further that where a derivative contract has settlement options, **all of the settlement alternatives must result in it being classified as an equity instrument**, otherwise it is a financial asset or liability.

In conclusion, **Lidan's B shares must be classified as a liability**

(b) (i) **Classification differences between debt and equity**

The distinction between debt and equity in an entity's statement of financial position is not easily distinguishable for preparers of financial statements. Some financial instruments may have features of debt and of equity, which can lead to inconsistency of reporting which can be confusing for the users of financial statements.

IAS 32 requires the **classification to be based on principles** rather than driven by perceptions of users.

IAS 32 defines an **equity instrument** as: 'any contract that evidences a residual interest in the assets of an entity after deducting all of its liabilities' (para. 11). It must first be **established that an instrument is not a financial liability,** before it can be classified as equity.

A key feature of the **IAS 32 definition of a financial liability** is that it **is a contractual obligation to deliver cash or another financial asset to another entity**. The contractual obligation may arise from a requirement to make payments of principal, interest or dividends. The contractual obligation may be explicit, but it may be implied indirectly in the terms of the contract. An example of a debt instrument is a bond which requires the issuer to make interest payments and redeem the bond for cash.

A financial instrument is an **equity instrument** only if there is no obligation to deliver cash or other financial assets to another entity and if the instrument will or may be settled in the issuer's own equity instruments. An example of an equity instrument is **ordinary shares, on which dividends are payable at the discretion of the issuer**. A less obvious example is preference shares required to be converted into a fixed number of ordinary shares on a fixed date or on the occurrence of an event which is certain to occur.

An instrument may be classified as an equity instrument if it contains a **contingent settlement provision** requiring settlement in cash or a variable number of the entity's own shares **only on the occurrence of an event which is very unlikely to occur** – such a provision is **not considered to be genuine**. If the **contingent payment condition** is **beyond the control of** both the entity and the holder of the instrument, then the instrument is classified as a **financial liability**.

A **contract resulting in the receipt or delivery of an entity's own shares is not automatically an equity instrument.** The classification depends on the so-called **'fixed test'** in IAS 32. A contract which will be settled by the entity receiving or delivering a **fixed number of its own equity instruments in exchange for a fixed amount of cash is an equity instrument**. In contrast, if the **amount of cash or own equity shares to be delivered or received is variable**, then the contract is a **financial liability or asset.**

There are **other factors** which might result in an instrument being **classified as debt**.

(1) Dividends are non-discretionary.

(2) Redemption is at the option of the instrument holder.

(3) The instrument has a limited life.

(4) Redemption is triggered by a future uncertain event which is beyond the control of both the issuer and the holder of the instrument.

Other factors which might result in an instrument being **classified as equity** include the following.

(1) Dividends are discretionary.
(2) The shares are non-redeemable.
(3) There is no liquidation date.

Although IAS 32 establishes principles for presenting financial instruments as liabilities or equity, it is not always easy to apply these principles in practice. The IASB acknowledges this difficulty and has issued a discussion paper DP 2018/1 *Financial Instruments with Characteristics of Equity* to investigate the issues further.

(ii) **Significance of debt/equity classification for the financial statements**

The distinction between debt and equity is very important for users who analyse the financial statements. The classification **can have a significant impact on the entity's reported earnings and gearing ratio**, which in turn can affect investment decisions. Companies may wish to classify a financial instrument as **equity**, in order to give a **favourable impression of gearing,** but this may in turn have a **negative effect** on the perceptions of existing shareholders if it is seen **as diluting existing equity interests**.

The distinction is also relevant in the context of a **business combination** where an entity **issues financial instruments as part consideration, or to raise funds to settle a business combination in cash**. Management is often called upon to **evaluate different financing options**, and in order to do so must **understand the classification rules and their potential effects**. For example, **classification as a liability** generally means that **payments are treated as interest** and charged to profit or loss, and this may, in turn**, affect the entity's ability to pay dividends** on equity shares.

(c) The finance director has suggested that the investment in cryptocurrencies should be recorded as a financial asset. Under IAS 32, a financial asset is 'cash, an equity instrument of another entity or a contractual right to receive cash, an equity instrument or exchange financial instruments on favourable terms' (para. 11). Cryptocurrencies do not meet the definition of cash as they are not generally accepted as legal tender and also do not give a contractual right to receive cash or other instruments. As such, it is not appropriate for Avco to classify the investment as a financial asset.

In the absence of an IFRS covering investments in cryptocurrencies, the directors of Avco should use judgement to develop an appropriate accounting policy in accordance with IAS 8 *Accounting Policies, Changes in Accounting Estimates and Errors*. The directors should consider:

- IFRSs dealing with similar issues. As we have discussed, the cryptocurrencies do not meet the definition of financial assets and they do not have physical substance and therefore cannot be accounted for as property, plant and equipment or inventories. As the cryptocurrencies do not have physical substance, it is likely that IAS 38 *Intangible Assets* is the most appropriate accounting standard to refer to. They also meet the other criteria of IAS 38 as they are identifiable and they are non-monetary (as they do not result in fixed or determinable amounts of money).

- The *Conceptual Framework*. The investment appears to meet the definition of an asset: a present economic resource controlled by the entity as a result of past events. Consideration should be given to the recognition criteria and to other issues such as the measurement basis to apply and how measurement uncertainty may affect that choice given the volatility of cryptocurrencies.

- The most recent pronouncements of other national GAAPs based on a similar conceptual framework and accepted industry practice. There is not a significant amount of guidance in this area from any of the national bodies at present.

The directors of Avco need to account for the investment in a way which provides **useful** information to the primary users of its financial statements. This means the information provided by the accounting treatment should be **relevant** and should **faithfully represent** the investment.

33 Pensions

Workbook reference. Pensions are covered in Chapter 5.

Top tips. Part (a)(i) is very straightforward, but make sure you relate your answer to the pension schemes of Joydan. In Part (a)(ii) it is important that you have an in-depth knowledge of the differences between the two schemes rather than just a general view of the differences.

Part (b): for both of the elements in Part (b) you must ensure that you are identifying the rules which surround the issues ad explain them, in order to gain full marks you will need to make sure that you have applied the rules to the scenario in the question.

Easy marks. There are marks for straightforward bookwork that you can get even if you don't get all the calculations right.

Marking scheme

				Marks
(a)	Joydan	(i)	Explanation	8
		(ii)	A scheme	7
			B scheme	1
(b)	Wallace	(i)	Explanation	5
		(ii)	Explanation	4
				25

(a) **Briefing note for the directors of Joydan**

(i) **Defined contribution plans and defined benefit plans**

With **defined contribution** plans, the employer (and possibly, as here, current employees too) pay regular contributions into the plan of a given or 'defined' amount each year. The contributions are invested, and the size of the post-employment benefits paid to former employees depends on how well or how badly the plan's investments perform. If the investments perform well, the plan will be able to afford higher benefits than if the investments performed less well.

The B scheme is a defined contribution plan. The employer's liability is limited to the contributions paid.

With **defined benefit** plans, the size of the post-employment benefits is determined in advance, ie the benefits are 'defined'. The employer (and possibly, as here, current employees too) pay contributions into the plan, and the contributions are invested. The size of the contributions is set at an amount that is expected to earn enough investment returns to meet the obligation to pay the post-employment benefits. If, however, it becomes apparent that the assets in the fund are insufficient, the employer will be required to make additional contributions into the plan to make up the expected shortfall. On the other hand, if the fund's assets appear to be larger than they need to be, and in excess of what is required to pay the post-employment benefits, the employer may be allowed to take a 'contribution holiday' (ie stop paying in contributions for a while).

The **main difference** between the two types of plans lies in **who bears the risk**: if the employer bears the risk, even in a small way by guaranteeing or specifying the return, the plan is a defined benefit plan. A defined contribution scheme must give a benefit formula based solely on the amount of the contributions.

A defined benefit scheme may be created even if there is no legal obligation, if an employer has a practice of guaranteeing the benefits payable.

The A scheme is a defined benefit scheme. Joydan, the employer, guarantees a pension based on the service lives of the employees in the scheme. The company's liability is not limited to the amount of the contributions. This means that the employer bears the investment risk: if the return on the investment is not sufficient to meet the liabilities, the company will need to make good the difference.

(ii) **Accounting treatment: B scheme**

No assets or liabilities will be recognised for this defined contribution scheme, other than current liabilities to reflect amounts due to be paid to the pension scheme at year end. The **contributions** paid by the company of $10 million will be **charged to profit or loss**. The contributions paid by the employees will not be a cost to the company but will be adjusted in calculating employee's net salary.

Accounting treatment: A scheme

The accounting treatment is as follows:

STATEMENT OF PROFIT OR LOSS AND OTHER COMPREHENSIVE INCOME NOTES

Expense recognised in profit or loss for the year ended 31 October 20X7

	$m
Current service cost	20.0
Net interest on the net defined benefit liability (10 – 9.5)	0.5
Net expense	20.5

Other comprehensive income: remeasurement of defined benefit plans (for the year ended 31 October 20X7)

	$m
Remeasurement gains or losses on defined benefit obligation	(29.0)
Remeasurement gains or losses on plan assets (excluding amounts in net interest)	27.5
	(1.5)

STATEMENT OF FINANCIAL POSITION NOTES

Amounts recognised in statement of financial position

	31 October 20X7	*1 November 20X6*
	$m	$m
Present value of defined benefit obligation	240	200
Fair value of plan assets	(225)	(190)
Net liability	15	10

Change in the present value of the defined benefit obligation

	$m
Present value of obligation at 1 November 20X6	200
Interest on obligation: 5% × 200	10
Current service cost	20
Benefits paid	(19)
Loss on remeasurement through OCI (balancing figure)	29
Present value of obligation at 31 October 20X7	240

Change in the fair value of plan assets

	$m
Fair value of plan assets at 1 November 20X6	190.0
Interest on plan assets: 5% × 190	9.5
Contributions	17.0
Benefits paid	(19.0)
Gain on remeasurement through OCI (balancing figure)	27.5
Fair value of plan assets at 31 October 20X7	225.0

(b) **Briefing note for directors of Wallace**

(i) **Reduction to net pension liability**

The reduction in the net pension liability as a result of the employees being made redundant and no longer accruing pension benefits is a **curtailment** under IAS 19 *Employee Benefits.*

IAS 19 defines a curtailment as occurring when an entity significantly reduces the number of employees covered by a plan. It is **treated as a type of past service costs**. The past service cost may be negative (as is the case here) when the benefits are withdrawn so that the present value of the defined benefit obligation decreases. IAS 19 requires the past service cost to be **recognised in profit or loss** at the earlier of:

- When the plan curtailment occurs; and
- When the entity recognises the related restructuring costs.

Here the restructuring costs (and corresponding provision) are recognised in the year ended 31 October 20X7 and the plan curtailment will not take place until after the year end in December 20X7 when the employees are made redundant. Therefore, the reduction in the net pension liability and corresponding income in profit or loss should be recognised at the earlier of these two dates, ie when the restructuring costs are recognised in the year ended 31 October 20X7.

The accounting entry for the reduction in the net pension liability required at 31 October 20X7 is:

DEBIT present value of defined benefit obligation	$15m	
CREDIT profit or loss		$15m

(ii) **Amendments**

IAS 19 was amended in 2018 to clarify that when a net defined benefit liability is remeasured as a result of a curtailment (or plan amendment or settlement), updated actuarial assumptions should be used to determine current service cost and net interest for the remainder of the reporting period.

Prior to the amendment, the accounting was not clear as IAS 19 implied that entities should not update the actuarial assumptions for the calculation of current service cost and net interest during the period, even if a plan amendment, curtailment or settlement had resulted in remeasurement of the net defined benefit liability.

The IASB believes that by amending IAS 19 to require updated assumptions to be used, the resulting information will be more useful to users of accounts.

Effect on Wallace

The amendments require updated assumptions to be used for the calculations of current service cost and net interest for the **remainder** of the reporting period. As the curtailment was accounted for on 30 September 20X7, the calculation of current service cost and net interest for the remaining one month of the reporting period should be based on the updated actuarial assumptions used to remeasure the net defined benefit liability.

However, as the updated assumptions will only need to be applied for one month, it may be that the applying the updated assumptions will not give a materially different result. As clarified by IFRS Practice Statement 2 *Making Materiality Judgements*, requirements in IFRSs only need to be applied when their effect is material. It may well be that the use of updated assumptions to calculate current service cost and net interest for one month will not produce a materially different result, given that the curtailment is recorded so close to the reporting date. If so, then this requirement need not be applied.

34 Calendar

Marking scheme

			Marks
(a)	(i)	1 mark per point up to maximum	6
	(ii)	1 mark per point up to maximum	9
(b)	1 mark per point up to maximum		10
			25

(a) (i) **Sale of intangible**

IFRS 15 *Revenue from Contracts with Customers* defines revenue as income arising from an entity's ordinary activities. Calendar's ordinary activities do not involve selling development projects. In fact, Calendar has made no such sales since 20X0. It would seem that Calendar's business model instead involves developing products for its customers, who then take over its production, marketing and sale. Stage payments and royalties are the incomes which arise from Calendar's ordinary activities and should be treated as revenue.

Based on the above, Calendar is incorrect to recognise the gain as revenue. In fact, IAS 38 *Intangible Assets* explicitly prohibits the classification of a gain on derecognition of an intangible asset as revenue.

IAS 38 defines an intangible asset as an identifiable non-monetary asset without physical substance. Intangible assets held for sale in the ordinary course of business are outside the scope of IAS 38 and are instead accounted for in accordance with IAS 2 *Inventories*. The fact that the development project was classified as an intangible asset upon initial recognition further suggests that it was not held for sale in the ordinary course of business.

If the development was incorrectly categorised in the prior year financial statements as an intangible asset, then, as per IAS 8 *Accounting Policies, Changes in Accounting Estimates and Errors,* this should be corrected retrospectively. However, based on the infrequency of such sales, it seems unlikely that the development was misclassified.

(ii) **Contract**

IFRS 16 *Leases* says that a contract contains a lease if it conveys the right to control the use of an identified asset for a period of time in exchange for consideration. When deciding if a contract involves the right to control an asset, the customer must assess whether they have:

- The right to substantially all of the identified asset's economic benefits;
- The right to direct the asset's use.

Calendar has the right to use a specified aircraft for three years in exchange for annual payments. Although Diary can substitute the aircraft for an alternative, the costs of doing so would be prohibitive because of the strict specifications outlined in the contract.

Calendar appears to have control over the aircraft during the three-year period because no other parties can use the aircraft during this time, and Calendar makes key decisions about the aircraft's destinations and the cargo and passengers which it transports. There are some legal and contractual restrictions which limit the aircraft's use. These protective rights define the scope of Calendar's right of use but do not prevent it from having the right to direct the use of the aircraft.

Based on the above, the contract contains a lease. IFRS 16 permits exemptions for leases of less than 12 months or leases of low value. However, this lease contract is for three years, so is not short term, and is for a high value asset so a lease liability should have been recognised at contract inception. The lease liability should equal the present value of the payments yet to be made, using the discount rate implicit in the lease. A finance cost accrues over the year, which is charged to profit or loss and added to the carrying amount of the lease liability. The year-end cash payment should be removed from profit or loss and deducted from the carrying amount of the liability.

A right-of-use asset should have been recognised at the contract inception at an amount equal to the initial value of the lease liability plus the initial costs to Calendar of negotiating the lease. The right-of-use asset should be depreciated over the lease term of three years and so one year's depreciation should be charged to profit or loss.

(b) **Materiality**

Calendar's financial statements should help investors, lenders and other creditors to make economic decisions about providing it with resources. An item is material if its omission or misstatement might influence the economic decisions of the users of the financial statements. Materiality is not a purely quantitative consideration; an item can be material if it triggers non-compliance with laws and regulations, or bank covenants. Calendar should consider materiality throughout the process of preparing its financial statements to ensure that relevant information is not omitted, misstated or obscured.

Property, plant and equipment (PPE)

IAS 16 *Property, Plant and Equipment* states that expenditure on PPE should be recognised as an asset and initially measured at the cost of purchase. Writing off such expenditure to profit or loss is therefore not in accordance with IAS 16.

According to IAS 8 *Accounting Policies, Changes in Accounting Estimates and Errors,* financial statements do not comply with International Financial Reporting Standards if they contain material errors, or errors made intentionally in order to present the entity's financial performance and position in a particular way. However, assuming that the aggregate impact of writing off small PPE purchases to profit or loss is not material, then the financial statements would still comply with International Financial Reporting Standards. Moreover, this decision seems to be a practical expedient which will reduce the time and cost involved in producing financial statements, rather than a decision made to achieve a particular financial statement presentation.

If implemented, this policy must be regularly reassessed to ensure that PPE and the statement of profit or loss are not materially misstated.

Disclosure notes

IAS 1 *Presentation of Financial Statements* states that application of IFRSs in an entity's financial statements will result in a fair presentation. As such, the use of a checklist may help to ensure that all disclosure requirements within IFRSs are fulfilled. However, IAS 1 and IFRS Practice Statement 2 *Making Materiality Judgements* both specify that the disclosures required by IFRSs are only required if the information presented is material.

The aim of disclosure notes is to further explain items included in the primary financial statements as well as unrecognised items (such as contingent liabilities) and other events which might influence the decisions of financial statement users (such as events after the reporting period). As such, Calendar should exercise judgement about the disclosures which it prepares, taking into account the information needs of its specific stakeholders. This is because the disclosure of immaterial information clutters the financial statements and makes relevant information harder to find.

Calendar may also need to disclose information in addition to that specified in IFRS if relevant to helping users understand its financial statements.

35 Lupin

Workbook references. Current and deferred tax is covered in Chapter 7. IFRS 2 is covered in Chapter 10 and IFRS 16 in Chapter 9.

Top tips. Part (a) is asking you to apply the requirements to three different items including share options, a leasing transaction and an intra company sale. Part (b)(i) can be broken down into its component parts of discussion of the conceptual framework and temporary differences, and credit is available for fairly general discussion of both. In (b)(ii). The tax reconciliation is intended to be useful in helping stakeholders to understand the income tax expense in the statement of profit or loss and cannot be omitted just because it is complex to prepare. Part (c) was straightforward if you could remember what the exposure draft was about.

Easy marks. Part (a)(iii) is easier than (i) and (ii), though they carry the same number of marks.

Marking scheme

			Marks
(a)	(i)	Share options	4
	(ii)	Leased plant	4
	(iii)	Intra company	4
			12

			Marks
(b)	(i)	*Conceptual Framework*	3
		Temporary difference	2
		Liability	1
			6
	(ii)	Tax reconciliation discussion	1
		Omit from disclosures	2
			3
(c)	Principles of ED 2019/5		2
	Potential effect on Lupin		2
			4
Total			25

(a) (i) **Share options**

Under IFRS 2 *Share-based Payment* the company **recognises an expense** for the employee services received in return for the share options granted over the vesting period. The related tax deduction **does not arise until the share options are exercised**. Therefore, a **deferred tax asset arises**, based on the difference between the intrinsic value of the options and their carrying amount (normally zero).

At 31 October 20X4 the tax benefit is as follows:

	$m
Carrying amount of share based payment	–
Less tax base of share based payment (16/2)	(8)
Temporary difference	(8)

The **deferred tax asset is $2.4 million** (30% × 8). This is recognised at 31 October 20X4 provided that taxable profit is available against which it can be utilised. Because the tax effect of the remuneration expense is greater than the tax benefit, the tax benefit is **recognised in profit or loss**. (The tax effect of the remuneration expense is 30% × $40 million ÷ 2 = $6 million.)

At 31 October 20X5 there is **no longer a deferred tax asset** because the options have been exercised. The **tax benefit receivable is $13.8 million** (30% × $46 million). Therefore, the deferred tax asset of $2.4 million is no longer required.

(ii) **Leased plant**

Under IFRS 16 *Leases*, a **right-of-use asset** and a **lease obligation** are recognised.

The lease liability is measured at the **present value of the lease payments** discounted using, if available, the interest rate implicit in the lease. The obligation to pay lease rentals is **recognised as a liability**. Each instalment payable is allocated partly as interest and partly as repayment of the liability.

The right-of-use asset is measured at the amount of the initial measurement of the lease liability, plus certain other direct costs not incurred in this case, such as legal fees. It is depreciated on a straight-line basis over the five years. The **carrying amount** of the plant for accounting purposes is the **initial amount of the right-of-use asset less depreciation**.

A **temporary difference** effectively arises between the carrying amount of the plant for accounting purposes and the equivalent of the outstanding obligations, as the annual rental payments qualify for the relief. The tax base of the asset is the amount deductible for tax in future, which is zero. The tax base of the liability is the carrying amount less any future tax-deductible amounts, which will give a **tax base of zero**.

Therefore at 31 October 20X5 a **net temporary difference** will be as follows:

	$m	$m
Carrying amount in financial statements:		
Asset:		
Right-of-use asset	12.00	
Less depreciation (12/5)	(2.40)	
		9.60
Less lease liability		
Liability at inception of lease	12.00	
Interest (8% × 12)	0.96	
Lease rental	(3.00)	
		(9.96)
		0.36
Less tax base		(0.00)
Temporary difference		0.36

A **deferred tax asset of $108,000** (30% × 360,000) arises.

(iii) **Intra-group sale**

Dahlia has **made a profit of $2 million** on its sale to Lupin. Tax is **payable on the profits of individual companies**. Dahlia is liable for tax on this profit in the current year and will have provided for the related tax in its individual financial statements. However, **from the viewpoint of the group** the profit **will not be realised until the following year**, when the goods are sold to a third party and must be **eliminated** from the consolidated financial statements. Because the group **pays tax before the profit is realised** there is a **temporary difference of $2 million** and a **deferred tax asset of $600,000** (30% × $2 million).

(b) (i) The conceptual basis for accounting for deferred tax is questionable.

On one hand, deferred tax is focused on the statement of financial position, which is in keeping with the *Conceptual Framework*. However, it can be argued that deferred tax assets and liabilities **do not meet the definition of assets and liabilities** under the *Conceptual Framework*. An asset is defined as a **present economic resource** controlled by an entity as a result of past events and a liability is a **present obligation** to transfer economic benefits, again as a result of past events. It is not clear whether deferred tax assets and obligations can be considered present resources or obligations.

IAS 12 *Income Taxes* is based on the idea that **all changes in assets and liabilities** have **unavoidable tax consequences**. Where the recognition criteria in IFRS are different from those in tax law, **the carrying amount of an asset or liability in the financial statements is different from its tax base** (the amount at which it is stated for tax purposes). These differences are known as **temporary differences**.

The practical effect of these differences is that the recognition of the transaction or event occurs in a different accounting period from its tax consequences. For example, unless the accounting depreciation and tax depreciation (capital allowances in the UK) are calculated on exactly the same basis, the amount of accounting depreciation recognised in the financial statements in an accounting period is different to the amount of tax on the same asset in the same period.

Under IAS 12, the tax effects of transactions are recognised in the same period as the transactions themselves, but in practice, tax is paid in accordance with tax legislation when it becomes a legal liability. This is considered another **conceptual weakness** or inconsistency, in that only one liability, that is tax, is being provided for, and not other costs, such as overhead costs that may be associated with the same transaction.

Conclusion

The shareholder is correct to question the basis for providing for deferred tax as there does appear to be some inconsistency between IAS 12 and the *Conceptual Framework*. Nonetheless, Lupin should apply the requirements of IAS 12.

(ii) The tax reconciliation shows how the tax charge in the statement of profit or loss can be reconciled back to the expectation of some users of financial statements that income tax is simply a company's profit before tax multiplied by the applicable tax rate.

It is true that the tax reconciliation can be complicated. This is particularly the case when the tax affairs of the entity are complex. However, this does not mean that the information should be excluded. The *Conceptual Framework* states that excluding information about complex phenomena from financial statements might make the financial statements easier to understand, but it would also make them incomplete and therefore potentially misleading.

The *Conceptual Framework* expects users of financial statements to have a reasonable knowledge of business and economic activities. Lupin should consider whether this is the case for this particular shareholder. However, if several shareholders are complaining about the tax reconciliation, then Lupin could consider including an explanatory note to the tax reconciliation to enable users of the financial statements to fully understand it. While this is not required by IAS 12, IAS 1 requires entities to consider whether additional information should be presented to enable users to understand the impact of transactions or conditions on the entity's financial position or performance.

The fact that the finance director finds the tax reconciliation difficult to prepare is not a valid reason for omitting it. In fact, the finance director's comment raises ethical concerns – is the finance director competent and aware of the requirements of IFRS? The tax reconciliation is a key disclosure required by IAS 12. That is not to say that all disclosures required by an accounting standard must be given – it depends on whether the disclosure is material.

IFRS Practice Statement 2 *Making Materiality Judgements* requires a preparer to make materiality judgements and clarifies that if information provided by a disclosure could not reasonably be expected to influence the decisions users make based on the financial statements, then that disclosure need not be made.

Given that the finance director finds it difficult to prepare the reconciliation suggests that Lupin's tax affairs may be complex and therefore disclosing information about them is unlikely to be immaterial.

(c) *Principles*

Exposure draft ED 2019/5 proposes amendments to IAS 12 to clarify that the recognition exemption in IAS 12 does not apply to assets and liabilities that arise from a single transaction.

The recognition exemption in IAS 12 is that deferred tax is not recognised on temporary differences that arise from the initial recognition of an asset or a liability, provided that the asset or liability was not acquired in a business combination and provided the transaction that resulted in the recognition of the asset or liability had no effect on accounting profit or taxable profit.

Divergence has arisen in practice over whether deferred tax should be recognised for transactions which, on initial recognition, result in the recognition of an asset **and** a related liability.

For example, when an entity first accounts for a **lease transaction**, it recognises both an asset (a right-of-use asset) and a liability (a lease liability). There is no effect on accounting profit or taxable profit when the lease is first accounted for.

At present, it is not clear in IAS 12 whether the initial recognition exemption applies in this situation. Some entities have therefore recognised deferred tax related to the lease believing the recognition exemption does not apply, while other entities have not recognised any deferred tax, believing that the recognition exemption does apply.

The proposed amendments clarify that the recognition exemption **does not apply** in this situation and therefore, if temporary differences arise on the recognition of the lease, the entity should recognise the related deferred tax.

Effect on Lupin

Assuming that Lupin takes the advice provided in part (a) and recognises deferred tax related to the temporary differences arising on the right-of-use asset and the lease liability, there would be no effect of the amendments on Lupin's deferred tax calculation in relation to leases.

36 Lizzer

Workbook references. Disclosures relating to financial instruments are covered in Chapter 8 and disclosures relating to events after the reporting period in Chapter 6. The user perspective, which features throughout this question, is included in Chapter 18.

Top tips. Part (a)(i) asks for application of the disclosure requirements of IFRS 7, focusing on the information provided to the debt-holders of Lizzer. Part (a)(ii) considers the specific requirements of IAS 10 relating to events after the reporting date from the perspective of Lizzer's investors. Both parts require you to apply your knowledge of the relevant standards in determining whether disclosure should be made in two instances where the directors' view was that no further information should be disclosed in the financial statements. It is important to refer to the user perspectives in your answer. You do not need a detailed knowledge of IFRS 7 to be able to answer Part (a)(i). Marks could be gained for a logical discussion of the scenario involved. Part (b) asks for a discussion about the optimal level of disclosure, and barriers to reducing disclosure. Arguments both for and against extensive disclosure could be made, as well as the case that too much disclosure means that material information is obscured.

Easy marks. There are no obvious easy marks. However, Part (b) is rather open ended, so the trick is to keep on writing, drawing on your own experiences and examples and backing up your arguments.

Marking scheme

			Marks
(a)	(i)	Reasons for debt-holders interest/advise directors – discussion 1 mark per point to a maximum of	6
	(ii)	Critique of directors' decision – discussion 1 mark per point to a maximum of	6
(b)	(i)	Optimal level of disclosure – discussion 1 mark per point to a maximum of	9
	(ii)	Barriers to reducing disclosure – discussion 1 mark per point to a maximum of	4
			25

(a) (i) **Disclosure of debt risk**

Users of financial statements

It is not for Lizzer alone to determine who the primary users of its financial statements are. Primary users are defined by the *Conceptual Framework* as existing and potential investors, lenders and **other creditors**.

The debt-holders of Lizzer are creditors of the entity. They have provided funds to the entity from which they expect to receive a return, based on the performance of the underlying investments. The debt holders ultimately bear the risks and rewards associated with the investments Lizzer has made. They will be interested in the financial statements of Lizzer in order to understand the risks associated with the underlying investments and assess the impact on their own risk and return.

IFRS 7 requirements

The objective of IFRS 7 is to require entities to provide disclosures in their financial statements that enable users to evaluate:

(1) The significance of financial instruments for the entity's financial position and performance

(2) The nature and extent of risks arising from financial instruments to which the entity is exposed during the period and at the reporting date, and how the entity manages those risks

The key requirement of IFRS 7 is to **show the extent to which an entity is exposed to different types of risk**, relating to both recognised and unrecognised financial instruments. The risk disclosures required by IFRS 7 are given from the perspective of management which should allow the users of financial statements to better understand how management perceives, measures and manages the risks associated with financial instruments.

Credit risk is one such risk. Credit risk is the risk of loss to one party to a financial instrument by failure to pay by the other party to the instrument.

Clearly disclosures about credit risk are important to debt-holders. Such disclosures are **qualitative** (exposure to risk and objectives, policies and processes for managing risk)

and **quantitative**, based on the information provided internally to management, enhanced if this is insufficient.

More important in this context is **market risk**. Market risk is the risk of fluctuations in either fair value or cash flows because of changes in market prices. It comprises currency risk, interest rate risk and other price risk. The debt-holders are exposed to the risk of the underlying investments whose value could go up or down depending on market value.

Disclosures required in connection with market risk are:

(1) **Sensitivity analysis**, showing the effects on profit or loss of changes in each market risk

(2) If the sensitivity analysis reflects interdependencies between risk variables, such as interest rates and exchange rates the method, **assumptions and limitations** must be disclosed

(ii) **Potential breach of loan covenants**

The applicable standards here are IFRS 7 and IAS 10 *Events after the Reporting Period.*

The directors of Lizzer are not correct in their decision not to disclosure additional information about the breach of loan covenants after the year end date. According to IFRS 7, Lizzer **should have included additional information** about the loan covenants **sufficient to enable the users of its financial statements to evaluate the nature and extent of risks arising from financial instruments** to which Lizzer is exposed at the end of the reporting period.

This is particularly important in Lizzer's case because there was considerable risk at the year end (31 January 20X3) that the loan covenants would be breached in the near future, as indicated by the directors' and auditors' doubts about the company continuing as a going concern.

The breach of loan covenants does not directly impact the investors as they have not provided borrowings to Lizzer. However there are implications in terms of the ability of Lizzer to continue as a going concern as this will have negative consequences for the returns investors receive. Potential investors are unlikely to invest in a company that is a going concern risk due to the uncertainty around its future.

Information should have been given about the **conditions attached to the loans and how close the entity was at the year end to breaching** the covenants. IFRS 7 requires disclosure of additional information about the covenants relating to each loan or group of loans, including headroom (the difference between the amount of the loan facility and the amount required).

The **actual breach of the loan covenants** at 31 March 20X3 was a **material event after the reporting period**. The breach, after the date of the financial statements but before those statements were authorised, represents a material **non-adjusting event**, which should have given rise to further disclosures under IAS 10.

Although the breach is a non-adjusting event, there appears to be some **inconsistency** between the information in the directors' and auditor's reports (which express going-concern doubts) and the information in the financial statements, which are prepared on a going-concern basis. **If any of the figures** in the statement of financial position are **affected**, these will **need to be adjusted**.

(b) (i) **Optimal level of disclosure**

It is important to ensure the optimal level of disclosure in annual reports because excessive disclosure can **obscure relevant information** and make it harder for users to find the key points about the performance of the business and its prospects for long-term success. It is important that financial statements are **relevant, reliable** and can be **understood**.

However, it is equally important that useful information is **presented in a coherent way** so that users can find what they are looking for and gain an understanding of the company's business and the opportunities, risks and constraints that it faces.

There has been a gradual increase in the length of annual reports over time. This, often, **has not resulted in better information for the users of financial statements, but more confusion** as to the reason for the disclosure.

Causes of excessive disclosure

Requirements of different regulators and standard-setters

A significant cause of excessive disclosure in annual reports is the vast array of requirements imposed by laws, regulations and financial reporting standards. **Regulators and standard setters have a key role to play in reducing excessive disclosure**, both by cutting the requirements that they themselves already impose and by guarding against the imposition of unnecessary new disclosures. A listed company may have to comply with listing rules, company law, international financial reporting standards and the corporate governance codes. Thus **a major source of excessive disclosure is the fact that different parties require differing disclosures for the same matter**.

Furthermore, many disclosure requirements have been introduced in new or revised international financial reporting standards in previous years without any review of their overall impact on the length or usefulness of the resulting financial statements.

Consideration of other stakeholders

Preparers now have to consider many other stakeholders including employees, unions, environmentalists, suppliers, customers, etc. **The disclosures required to meet the needs of this wider audience have contributed to the increased volume of disclosure**. The growth of previous initiatives on going concern, sustainability, risk, the business model and others that have been identified by regulators as 'key' has also expanded the annual report size.

Inappropriate use of 'checklists'

A problem that seems to exist is that **disclosures are being made because a disclosure checklist suggests it may need to be made**, without assessing **whether the information provided by the disclosure is material** in a company's particular circumstances. This requires judgement.

Response of IASB

The IASB launched the Disclosure Initiative in 2013 to try to address the perceived disclosure problem. The Disclosure Initiative includes:

- Materiality projects
  - The IASB believes that uncertainty on behalf of the preparers of financial statements as to how the concept of materiality should be applied has compounded the disclosure issue. In response, the IASB issued **IFRS Practice Statement 2 *Making Materiality Judgements*** in 2017.

The practice statement contains a process to help entities determine whether information is material, as well as guidance on materiality factors, both quantitative and qualitative. Ultimately the entity has to judge whether information can reasonably be expected to influence the decisions of the primary users. If not, the information is immaterial and does not have to be disclosed, irrespective of the requirements of the individual IFRS.

– In 2018 the IASB **amended the definition of materiality** to make it clearer that information is material if omitting, misstating or **obscuring it** could reasonably be expected to influence the decisions of users of the financial statements, addressing the issue that too much information can be just as problematic as the omission of information.

- ED 2019/6 Disclosure of Accounting Policies

  IAS 1 currently requires an entity to disclose in its financial statements its **significant** accounting policies. ED 2019/6 proposes to amend IAS 1 to instead require disclosure of **material** accounting policies. The amendments clarify that accounting policies that relate to immaterial transactions, events or conditions are themselves immaterial and do not need to be disclosed.

(ii) **Barriers to reducing disclosure**

Entities are sometimes reluctant to reduce the level of disclosure. These barriers are behavioural and include the following:

(1) **The perception that disclosing everything will satisfy all interested parties.**

(2) **The threat of criticism or litigation.** Preparers of financial statements err on the side of caution rather than risk falling foul of the law by omitting a required disclosure. Removing disclosures is seen as creating a risk of adverse comment and regulatory challenge.

(3) **Cut and paste mentality.** If items were disclosed in last year's annual report and the issue is still ongoing, there is a tendency to copy the disclosures into this year's report. It is thought that, if such disclosures are removed, stakeholders may wonder whether the financial statements still give a true and fair view. Disclosure is therefore the safest option and the default position.

(4) **Checklist approach.** While materiality should determine what is disclosed, because what is material is what may influence the user, the assessment of what is material can be a matter of judgement. The purpose of checklists is to include all possible disclosures that could be material. Users may not know which of the checklist disclosures is actually material in the context of their specific needs.

37 Jogger

Workbook references. Social and environmental reporting is covered in Chapter 18 of the Workbook. Alternative performance measures such as EBITDA are also covered in Chapter 18. Ethics is covered in Chapter 2.

Top tips. This is a fully written question for both Parts (a) and (b) so don't be tempted to waffle. You are encouraged to read widely while studying for Strategic Business Reporting. For example you could look at the ESMA (European Securities and Markets Authority) Guidelines on Alternative Performance Measures which are available online.

For learning purposes, this question included some discussion of ethical issues in the context of the scenario given. However, please note that ethics will not feature in Section B questions in the real exam. Ethics will be examined only in Question 2 of the exam.

Easy marks. There are lots of easy marks available for straightforward knowledge. Explain your points clearly and in the context of the question.

Marking scheme

		Marks
(a)	Discussion 1 mark per point to a maximum	8
(b)	Reporting EBITDA advantages and disadvantages	5
	Description of management of earnings	5
	Moral/ethical considerations	5
		15
Professional marks		2
		25

(a) **Social and environmental information**

There are a number of factors which encourage companies to disclose social and environmental information in their financial statements. **Public interest** in corporate social responsibility has increased in recent years and in an age where society is increasingly aware of the impact of both individual and business decisions on the climate, environment and sustainability, it remains a key area of focus for reporting accountants.

Although financial statements are intended for present and potential investors, lenders and other creditors, there is recognition that companies have a responsibility to **a number of different stakeholders**. These include **customers, employees and the general public,** all of whom are **potentially interested** in the way in which a company's operations affect the natural environment and the wider community. These stakeholders can have a **considerable effect on a company's performance**. As a result, most companies now take positive steps to build a **reputation for social and environmental responsibility**. Therefore, the disclosure of environmental and social information is essential.

It is also generally accepted that **corporate social responsibility is actually an important part of an entity's overall performance**. Responsible practice in areas such as reduction of damage to the environment and fair recruitment practices **increase shareholder value**. Companies that act responsibly and make social and environmental disclosures are **perceived as better investments** than those that do not.

Another factor is **commitments by governments** to achieve, for example, climate change targets or to meet Sustainable Development Goals by 2030 and the pressure placed on companies to make a positive contribution towards achieving such targets. Although there are **no IFRS** that specifically require environmental and social reporting, it may be required by **company legislation**. There are now a number of **awards for environmental and social reports** and high-quality disclosure in financial statements. These provide further encouragement to disclose information.

At present companies are normally able to disclose **as much or as little information as they wish in whatever manner that they wish**. This causes a number of **problems**. Companies tend to disclose information **selectively** and it is difficult for users of the financial statements to **compare the performance of different companies**. However, there are **good arguments** for continuing to allow companies a certain amount of freedom to determine the information that they disclose. If detailed rules are imposed, **companies are likely to adopt a 'checklist' approach** and will **present information in a very general and standardised way**, so that it is of very little use to stakeholders.

(b) **EBITDA and the management of earnings**

EBITDA is a widely used measure of corporate earnings, but it is also a controversial figure. EBITDA attempts to show earnings before tax, depreciation and amortisation. Depreciation and amortisation are expenses that arise from historical transactions over which the company now has very little control, and are often arbitrary in nature as they involve subjectivity in estimating useful lives and residual values. As they are non-cash, it is argued that they do not have any real impact on a company's operations. Companies also argue that they are not in control of tax and it should therefore not be a component of earnings. Interest is the result of financing decisions which are also often historic and influenced by a company's financing decisions. EBITDA is said to eliminate the effect of financing and accounting decisions and therefore gives investors and potential investors better insight into the performance of management and the impact of management decisions.

There are, however, criticisms of EBITDA. The main criticism is that EBITDA is not defined in IFRS and therefore is open to manipulation as companies can choose which items to include/exclude from its calculation. The fact that EBITDA is not defined can also reduce its usefulness to investors and potential investors as comparisons with previous years or to other companies may not be meaningful.

The managing director is proposing EBITDA is managed to report Jogger in a favourable light. 'Earnings management' involves exercising judgement with regard to financial reporting and structuring transactions so as to give a **misleadingly optimistic picture** of a company's performance. Commonly it involves manipulating earnings in order to meet a target predetermined by management.

Earnings management can take place in respect of reported profit under IAS 1, or in alternative performance measures such as EBITDA is as suggested here. Earnings management is done with the intention, whether consciously or not, of **influencing outcomes that depend on stakeholders' assessments**. It is the **intent** to deceive stakeholders that is unethical even if the earnings management remains within the acceptable boundaries of GAAP. For example, a potential investor may decide to invest in a company or an existing investor may be encouraged to increase their shareholding on the basis of a favourable performance or position. A director may wish to delay a hit to profit or loss for the year in order to ensure a particular year's results are well received by investors, or to secure a bonus that depends on profit. Indeed earnings management, sometimes called 'creative accounting', may be described as manipulation of the financial reporting process for private gain.

The directors may also wish to present the company favourably in order to maintain a **strong position within the market**. The motive is not always private gain – they may be thinking of the company's stakeholders, such as employees, suppliers or customers – but in the long term, earnings management is not a substitute for sound and profitable business, and cannot be sustained. In this case, the financial controller has been reminded that he will receive a substantial bonus if earnings targets are met. This represents a self-interest threat under ACCA's *Code of Ethics and Conduct* as the financial controller will personally benefit from the management of earnings. The 'reminder' from the managing director could also be interpreted as an intimidation threat if the financial controller feels unduly pressured as a result of the statement.

'Aggressive' earnings management is a form of fraud and differs from reporting error. Nevertheless, all forms of earnings management may be **ethically questionable**, even if not illegal.

The flexibility allowed by IFRSs may cause some variability to occur as a result of the accounting treatment options chosen, but the accounting profession has a responsibility to provide a framework that does not encourage earnings management.

A more positive way of looking at earnings management is to consider the **benefits of not manipulating earnings:**

(i) Stakeholders can rely on the data. Word gets around that the company 'tells it like it is' and does not try to bury bad news.

(ii) It encourages management to safeguard the assets and exercise prudence.

(iii) Management set an example to employees to work harder to make genuine profits, not arising from the manipulation of accruals.

(iv) Focus on cash flow rather than accounting profits keeps management anchored in reality.

Earnings management goes against **the principle of corporate social responsibility**. Companies have a duty not to mislead stakeholders, whether their own shareholders, suppliers, employees or the government. Because the temptation to indulge in earnings management may be strong, particularly in times of financial crisis, it is important to have **ethical frameworks** (such as ACCA's *Code of Ethics and Conduct*) **and guidelines** in place. The letter of the law may not be enough.

38 Moorland

Workbook reference. Chapter 18: Interpretation of financial statements for different stakeholders.

Top tips. Part (a) requires knowledge of the purpose of a management commentary and the requirements of IFRS Practice Statement 1. If you struggled with this, go back and revise the content in Chapter 18. Management commentary featured in the December 2018 exam – so it can and will be tested.

Part (b)(ii) covers alternative performance measures which is a key topic for SBR. You need to consider Moorland's investors in your answer. Wider reading of articles, particularly those on the ACCA website, will be extremely helpful in being able to answer questions such as this. The ESMA (European Securities and Markets Authority) Guidelines on Alternative Performance Measures and IOSCO's (International Organisation of Securities Commissions) Statement on Non-GAAP Financial Measures, both available online, provide another perspective and will be beneficial to read.

Easy marks. Some marks are available for the principles of IFRS 8.

(a) The purpose of the management commentary is to provide a context for interpreting a company's **financial position, performance and cash flows**. According to IFRS Practice Statement 1 *Management Commentary*, the principles and objectives of a Management Commentary (MC) are as follows:

(i) To provide **management's view** of the entity's performance, position and progress
(ii) To **supplement and complement** information presented in the financial statements

To align with these principles, an MC should include **forward-looking information**, and all information provided should possess the **qualitative characteristics** described in the *Conceptual Framework*.

Practice Statement 1 says that to meet the objective of management commentary, an entity should include information that is essential to an understanding of:

(i) The **nature of the business**

(ii) Management's **objectives and its strategies** for meeting those objectives

(iii) The entity's most significant **resources, risks and relationships**

(iv) The **results** of operations and **prospects**

(v) The critical **performance measures and indicators** that management uses to evaluate the entity's performance against stated objectives

The arguments for a mandatory MC are largely to do with content and comparability. It is argued that a mandatory MC will make it easier for companies themselves to judge what is required in such a report and the required standard of reporting, thereby making such reports more **robust, transparent and comparable**. If an MC is not mandatory then there may be **uncertainty** as to content and the possibility of **misinformation**. There is also the risk that, without a mandatory MC, directors may take a **minimalist approach** to disclosure which will make the MC less useful and the information to be disclosed will be in hands of senior executives and directors.

However, the **arguments against** a mandatory MC are that it could **stifle the development of the MC as a tool** for communication and may lead to a **checklist approach** to producing it. It is argued that a mandatory MC is not required as market forces and the needs of investors should lead to companies feeling the pressure to provide a useful and reliable report. The IASB decided to issue a Practice Statement rather than an IFRS and to leave it to regulators to decide who would be required to publish a management commentary. This approach avoids the **adoption hurdle**, ie that the perceived cost of applying IFRSs might increase, which could otherwise dissuade jurisdictions/countries not having adopted IFRSs from requiring its adoption, especially where requirements differ significantly from existing national requirements.

(b) (i) **Operating segment**

IFRS 8 *Operating Segments* describes an operating segment as a component of an entity:

(1) Which engages in business activities from which it may earn revenues and incur expenses;

(2) Whose operating results are regularly reviewed by the entity's chief operating decision-maker to make decisions about resources to be allocated to the segment and assess its performance;

(3) For which discrete financial information is available.

There is a considerable amount of subjectivity in how an entity may apply these criteria to its choice of operating segments. Usually an operating segment would have a segment manager who maintains regular contact with the chief operating decision-maker to discuss operating activities, financial results, forecasts or plans for the segment. Therefore segment managers could have overall responsibility for a particular product, service line or geographical area and so there could be considerable overlap in how an entity may apply the criteria. In such situations the directors of Moorland should consider the core principles of the standard. Information should be disclosed to enable users of its financial statements to evaluate the nature and financial effects of the business activities in which it engages and the economic environments in which it operates.

Since Tybull is the only overseas subsidiary, it is likely that separate disclosure is necessary so that users can better assess the performance of Tybull and its significance to the group. The directors should consider whether there are other segments which exhibit similar long-term financial performance and similar economic characteristics to Tybull. In such circumstances it is possible to aggregate the operating segments into a single segment. For example, the segments should have products of a similar nature and similar methods to distribute their products. The segments should also have similar types of customer, production processes and regulatory environment. The directors of Moorland would need to assess whether such aggregation would limit the usefulness of the disclosures for the users of the financial statements. For example, it would no longer be possible to assess the gross margins and return on capital employed for Tybull on an individual basis, without referring to its individual financial statements.

Operating segments can be reclassified where an entity changes its internal organisational structure. As Tybull has not changed its organisational structure, it is unlikely that it would be able to argue for a reclassification of its operating segments. Should the directors of Moorland decide to reclassify the operating segments and combine Tybull with other segments, IAS 8 *Accounting Policies, Changes in Accounting Estimates and Errors* would need to be applied. A retrospective adjustment would be required to the disclosures and the change would need to be justified. An entity should only change its policy if it enhances the reliability and relevance of the financial statements. This would appear unlikely given the circumstances.

(ii) **Underlying earnings per share**

Underlying earnings per share (underling EPS) is an alternative performance measure (APM). APMs should be provided to enhance the understanding of users of the accounts.

However, APMs can be misleading. Unlike earnings per share, which is defined in IAS 33 *Earnings per Share*, there is no official definition of underlying EPS, so management can choose what items to include or exclude in the underlying earnings. Therefore it is open to bias in its calculation as management could decide to only adjust for items that improve the measure. Furthermore, different companies may define the measure in different ways, which reduces the comparability between entities.

The CEO's wish to exclude impairment on goodwill from the calculation of earnings on the basis that it is unlikely to reoccur is also misleading to investors. An impairment loss on goodwill could quite feasibly re-occur in the future as it is at least partly dependent on circumstances outside of Moorland's control, such as the state of the economy. Therefore, it could be argued that excluding the impairment loss would make the measure of underlying earnings per share less useful to investors.

The CEO wishes to present underlying EPS 'prominently'. It is not clear what is meant by this comment, however, Moorland should ensure that it complies with the requirements of IAS 33 regarding the calculation and presentation of this alternative EPS. IOSCO's (International Organisation of Securities Commissions) Statement on Non-GAAP Financial Measures recommends that APMs are not presented more prominently than GAAP measures, or in a way that confuses or obscures GAAP measures.

Ultimately underlying earnings per share will only provide useful information to Moorland's investors if it is fairly presented.

Moorland could improve the usefulness of underlying EPS by:

- Including an appropriate description of how the measure is calculated
- Ensuring that the calculation of underlying EPS is consistent year on year and that comparatives are presented
- Explaining the reasons for presenting the measure, why it is useful for investors and for what purpose management may use it
- Presenting a reconciliation to the most directly reconcilable measure in the financial statements, for example EPS calculated in accordance with IAS 33
- Not excluding items from underlying EPS that could legitimately reoccur in the future, such as impairment losses on goodwill

39 Calcula

Workbook reference. IFRS 5 is covered in Chapter 14. Integrated reporting is covered in Chapter 18.

Top tips. In Part (a) you are required to provide an analysis of whether the classification of the subsidiary as 'held for sale' and presentation as a discontinued operation is correct in accordance with IFRS 5. You need to apply your knowledge to the scenario, and not just write down the requirements of IFRS 5. Relating the treatment to the *Conceptual Framework* was not easy, but is likely to be a feature of questions in the SBR exam. Reading the 'Basis for conclusions' accompanying IFRSs provides insight into the decisions of the IASB in developing a standard and often highlights potential conflicts with the *Conceptual Framework*.

To score well in Part (b) it is critical that your answer is related to Calcula. The scenario is provided to give you the opportunity to show two things. Firstly, that you understand the theory – ie what integrated reporting is – and secondly, for you to show that can apply your knowledge. A good approach to dealing with such questions is to set the scene by identifying what has gone wrong in the scenario. In this case stakeholders (shareholders and employees) are confused as to the strategic direction that Calcula is trying to pursue.

Next, use your knowledge to explain how integrated reporting can help Calcula to communicate its strategy. Integrated reporting places a strong emphasis on relaying what the company stands for through setting out its objectives and strategy to realise these. The introduction of integrated reporting would therefore provide the company with a great opportunity to convey Asha Alexander's new mission.

Marking scheme

			Marks
(a)	IFRS 5 – 1 mark per valid point up to		9
(b)	(i)	Integrated reporting – 1 mark per valid point up to	12
	(ii)	Cost-cutting programme – 1 mark per valid point up to	2
Professional marks			2
			25

(a) **Subsidiary held for sale**

The subsidiary is a **disposal group** under IFRS 5 *Non-current Assets Held for Sale and Discontinued Operations*. A disposal group is a group of assets and associated liabilities which are to be disposed of together in a single transaction.

IFRS 5 classifies a disposal group as **held for sale** when its carrying amount will be recovered principally through sale rather than use. The held for sale criteria in IFRS 5 are very strict, and often the decision to sell an asset or disposal group is made well before the criteria are met.

IFRS 5 requires an asset or disposal group to be classified as held for sale where it is **available for immediate sale** in its **present condition** subject only to **terms that are usual** and customary and the sale is **highly probable**.

For a sale to be **highly probable:**

- Management must be **committed** to the sale.
- An **active programme to locate a buyer** must have been initiated.
- The asset must be **marketed at a price** that is **reasonable in relation to its own fair value**.
- The sale must be **expected to be completed within one year** from the date of classification.
- It is **unlikely** that **significant changes** will be made to the plan **or the plan withdrawn**.

The draft agreements and correspondence with bankers are **not specific enough** to prove that the subsidiary met the IFRS 5 criteria at the date it was classified. More detail would be required to confirm that the subsidiary was available for immediate sale and that it was being actively marketed at an appropriate price in order to satisfy the criteria in the year to 31 May 20X2.

In addition, the **organisational changes** made by Calcula in the year to 31 May 20X3 are a **good indication that the subsidiary was not available for sale in its present condition at the point of classification**. Additional activities have been transferred to the subsidiary, which is not an insignificant change. The shareholders' authorisation was given for a year from 1 January 20X2. There is **no evidence that this authorisation was extended beyond 1 January 20X3**.

Conclusion

From the information provided, it appears that Calcula should **not classify the subsidiary as held for sale** and should report the results of the subsidiary as a **continuing operation** in the financial statements for the year ended 31 May 20X2 and 31 May 20X3.

Evaluation of treatment in the context of the Conceptual Framework

The *Conceptual Framework* states that the users need information to allow them to assess the amount, timing and uncertainty of the prospects for future net cash inflows. Separately highlighting the results of discontinued operations provides users with information that is relevant to this assessment as the discontinued operation will not contribute to cash flows in the future.

If an entity has made a firm decision to sell the subsidiary, it could be argued that the subsidiary should be classified as discontinued, even if the criteria to classify it as 'held for sale' per IFRS 5 have not been met, because this information would be more useful to users. However, the IASB decided against this when developing IFRS 5. This decision could be argued to be in conflict with the *Conceptual Framework*.

(b) (i) **Integrated reporting at Calcula**

Confusion

As a result of the recent management changes at Calcula, the company has struggled to communicate its 'strategic direction' to key stakeholders. The company's annual report has made it hard for shareholders to understand Calcula's strategy which in turn has led to confusion. Uncertainty among shareholders and employees is likely to increase the risk of investors selling their shares and talented IT developers seeking employment with competitors.

Integrated reporting

The introduction of integrated reporting may help Calcula to overcome these issues as it places a strong focus on the organisation's future orientation. Integrated reporting is fundamentally concerned with evaluating value creation, and uses qualitative and quantitative performance measures to help stakeholders assess how well an organisation is creating value. In the context of integrated reporting, an entity's resources are referred to as 'capitals'. The International Integrated Reporting Council have identified six capitals which can be used to assess value creation.

Integrated reporting helps to ensure that a balanced view of performance is presented by requiring organisations to report on both positive and negative movements in capital. When preparing an integrated report, management should also disclose matters which are likely to impact on an entity's ability to create value. Internal weaknesses and external threats regarded as being materially important are evaluated and quantified. This provides users with an indication of how management intends to combat such instances should they materialise.

Communicating strategy

An integrated report should detail the entity's mission and values, the nature of its operations, along with features on how it differentiates itself from its competitors.

Including Calcula's new mission to become the market leader in the specialist accountancy software industry would instantly convey what the organisation stands for.

In line with best practice in integrated reporting, Calcula could supplement its mission with how the board intend to achieve this strategy. Such detail could focus on resource allocations over the short to medium term. For example, plans to improve the company's human capital through hiring innovative software developers working at competing firms would help to support the company's long-term mission. To assist users in appraising the company's performance, Calcula should provide details on how it will measure value creation in each capital. 'Human capital' could be measured by the net movement in new joiners to the organisation compared to the previous year.

A key feature of integrated reporting focuses on the need for organisations to use non-financial customer-orientated performance measures (KPIs) to help communicate the entity's strategy. The most successful companies in Calcula's industry are committed to enhancing their offering to customers through producing innovative products. Calcula could report through the use of KPIs how it is delivering on this objective, measures could be set which for example measure the number of new software programs developed in the last two years or report on the number of customer complaints concerning newly released software programs over the period. When reporting on non-financial measures such as KPIs, it is important for Calcula to be consistent in the measures it reports year on year and it should consider reporting similar measures as its competitors as it gives investors a basis on which to compare similar companies.

Improving long-term performance

The introduction of integrated reporting may also help Calcula to enhance its performance. Historically, the company has not given consideration to how decisions in one area have impacted on other areas. This is clearly indicated by the former CEO's cost cutting programme which served to reduce the staff training budget. Although this move may have enhanced the company's short-term profitability, boosting financial capital, it has damaged long term value creation.

The nature of the software industry requires successful organisations to invest in staff training to ensure that the products they develop remain innovative in order to attract customers. The decision to reduce the training budget will most likely impact on future profitability if Calcula is unable to produce the software customers' demand.

Finance director's comments

As illustrated in the scenario, the finance director's comments indicate a very narrow understanding of how the company's activities and 'capitals' interact with each other in delivering value. To dismiss developments in integrated reporting as simply being a 'fad', suggest that the finance director is unaware of current developments in financial reporting and the commitment of ACCA in promoting its introduction. ACCA's support for integrated reporting may lead to backing from other global accountancy bodies thereby reducing the scope for it be regarded as a passing 'fad'.

However, some critics dispute this and argue that the voluntary nature of integrated reporting increases the likelihood that companies will choose not to pursue its adoption. Such individuals highlight that until companies are legally required to comply with integrated reporting guidelines, many will simply regard it as an unnecessary effort and cost.

The finance director's assertion regarding shareholders is likely to some degree to be correct. Investors looking for short term results from an investment might assess Calcula's performance based on improvements in profitability. However, many shareholders will also be interested in how the board propose to create value in the future. Ultimately, Calcula's aim to appease both groups is its focus on maximising shareholder value, the achievement of which requires the successful implementation of both short and long-term strategies.

Furthermore, unlike traditional annual reports, integrated reports highlight the importance of considering a wider range of users. Key stakeholder groups such as Calcula's customers and suppliers are likely to be interested in assessing how the company has met or not met their needs beyond the 'bottom line'. Integrated reporting encourages companies to report performance measures which are closely aligned to the concepts of sustainability and corporate social responsibility. This is implied by the different capitals used: consideration of social relationships and natural capitals do not focus on financial performance but instead are concerned, for example, with the impact an organisation's activities have on the natural environment.

(ii) **Cost-cutting programme**

The cost-cutting programme may have put his management team in a difficult position because they were being asked to prioritise profit above all else.

Managers have a duty to aim to maximise profit but at the same time they have a duty to guard, preserve and enhance the value of the entity for the good of all affected by it, including employees and the general public. The high management turnover may show evidence of Calcula not treating its employees adequately and them choosing or being made to leave their employment under difficult circumstances.

The cuts to staff training funding may have brought further challenges. Managers have a responsibility to ensure that their own employees are protected from danger. Training cuts may introduce unacceptable risks to health and safety, leading to dangerous working conditions or to inadequate safety standards in products, putting the general public/Calcula's customers at risk.

40 Toobasco

Marking scheme

				Marks
(a)	Discussion of the comparability of APMs		1	
	Application of the following discussion to the scenario:			
	Extraordinary items		2	
	Free cash flow and its description		2	
	EBITDAR		4	
	Tax effects		1	10
(b)	(i)	Adjustment of net cash generated from operating activities		4
	(ii)	Reconciliation to free cash flow		4
	(iii)	Application of the following discussion to the scenario:		
		Purchase and sale of cars	1	
		Purchase of associate	1	
		Foreign exchange losses	1	
		Pension payments	1	
		Interest paid	1	5
Professional marks				2
				25

(a) (i) APMs are not defined by IFRSs and therefore may not be directly comparable with other companies' APMs, including those in the group's industry. Where the same category of material items recurs each year and in similar amounts (in this example, restructuring costs and impairment losses), the entity should consider whether such amounts should be included as part of underlying profit.

Under IFRS, items cannot be presented as 'extraordinary items' in the financial statements or in the notes. Thus it may be confusing to users of the APMs to see this term used. It is not appropriate to state that a charge or gain is non-recurring unless it meets the criteria. Items such as restructuring costs or impairment losses should not be labelled as non-recurring where it is misleading. However, the entity can make an adjustment for a charge or gain which they believe is appropriate, but they cannot describe such adjustments inaccurately.

(ii) The deduction of capital expenditures, purchase of own shares and the purchase of intangible assets from the IAS 7 measure of cash flows from operating activities is acceptable as free cash flow does not have a uniform definition. As a result, a clear description and reconciliation showing how this measure is calculated should be disclosed. Entities should also avoid misleading inferences about its usefulness. Free cash flow does not normally represent the residual cash flow available as many entities have mandatory debt service requirements which are not normally deducted from the measure. It would also be misleading to show free cash flow per share in bold alongside earnings per share as they are not comparable.

(iii) When an entity presents an APM, it should present the most directly comparable measure which has been calculated in accordance with IFRSs with equal or greater prominence. The level of prominence would depend on the facts and circumstances. In this case, the entity has omitted comparable information from an earnings release which includes APMs such as EBITDAR. Additionally, the entity has emphasised the APM measure by describing it as 'record performance' without an equally prominent description of the measure calculated in accordance with IFRSs. Further, the entity has provided a discussion of the APM measure without a similar discussion and analysis of the same information presented from an IFRS perspective.

The entity has presented EBITDAR as a performance measure; such measures should be reconciled to profit for the year as presented in the statement of comprehensive income. Operating profit would not be considered the best starting point as EBITDAR makes adjustments for items which are not included in operating profit such as interest and tax.

The entity has changed the way it calculates the APM because it has treated rent differently. However, if an entity chooses to change an APM, the change and the reason for the change should be explained and any comparatives restated. A change would be appropriate only in exceptional circumstances where the new APM better achieves the same objectives, perhaps if there has been a change in the strategy. The revised APM should be reliable and more relevant.

(iv) The entity should provide income tax effects on its APMs depending on the nature of the measures. The entity should include current and deferred income tax expense commensurate with the APM and the APM should not be presented net of tax as income taxes should be shown as a separate adjustment and explained.

(b) (i) *Adjustment of net cash generated from operating activities for errors in the statement*

	$m
Net cash generated from operating activities per question	278
Add cash inflows relating to the disposal of cars	30
Effect of changes in foreign exchange rates	28
Reclassification of interest paid	18
Tax credit not recorded	6
	360
Less	
Associate's profit – incorrectly included	(12)
Associate's profit – non-cash flow	(4)
Net cash generated from operating activities	344

(ii) *Free cash flow reconciliation*

	$m
Net cash generated from operating activities	344
Net capital expenditure	(46)
Purchase of associate	(20)
Dividend received from associate	1
Interest received	10
Interest paid	(18)
Pension deficit payments	27
Free cash flow	298

(iii) *Purchase and sale of cars*

Daveed's presentation of cash flows from the sale of cars as being from investing activities is incorrect as cash flows from the sale of cars should have been presented as cash flows from operating activities ($30 million). IAS 16 *Property, Plant and Equipment* (PPE) states that an entity which normally sells items of PPE which are held for rental to others should transfer such assets to inventories at their carrying amount when they cease to be rented and become held for sale. Subsequent proceeds from the sale of such assets should be recognised as revenue in accordance with IFRS 15 *Revenue from Contracts with Customers* and thus shown as cash flows from operating activities.

Purchase of associate

	$m
Balance at 31 August 20X8	23
Less profit for period $16m × 25%	(4)
Add dividend received $4m × 25%	1
Cost of acquisition (cash)	20

Therefore, cash paid for the investment is $20 million, and cash received from the dividend is $1 million.

In order to arrive at the correct figure for net cash generated from operating activities, the incorrect treatment of the profit for the year for the associate must be eliminated ($12 million) and the correct adjustment of $4 million shown in net cash generated by operating activities.

Foreign exchange losses

IAS 7 *Statement of Cash Flows* states that unrealised gains and losses arising from changes in foreign exchange rates are not cash flows. The amounts reported in the statement of cash flows included, in error, the effect of changes in foreign exchange rates arising on the retranslation of its overseas operations. As a consequence, cash generated from operating activities should be increased by $28 million. All exchange differences relating to the subsidiary are taken to a separate component of equity, until disposal of the foreign operation when they are recycled to the income statement.

Pension payments

The pension payments are correctly included in operating cash flows. However, they are excluded when calculating free cash flow. As the tax cash benefit has not been included, net cash generated from operating activities will be adjusted for the $6 million and $27 million ($33m – $6m) will be excluded from the free cash flow calculation.

Interest paid

Interest paid which is capitalised into the cost of property, plant, and equipment should be treated as cash flows arising from investing activities whereas interest paid and capitalised into inventory should be classified in the operating section of the statement of cash flows. Thus there should be a reclassification of interest paid of $18 million from the operating section to the investing activities section.

41 Tufnell

Workbook references. IFRS 5 is included in Chapter 14, deferred tax in Chapter 7, impairment in Chapter 4 and ROCE and residual income are included in Chapter 18.

Top tips. This question deals with a group re-organisation, deferred tax and revaluation, impairment and re-classification of a lease. These are all linked in with a calculation of the effect on ROCE. In Part (a)(i) there is no need to spend time giving the IFRS 5 criteria for classification as held for sale, since we are told in the question that these criteria have been met.

Easy marks. None of this question is easy except for the calculation of ROCE. Do the parts you feel sure about, but have a go at all parts as the first few marks are the easiest to pick up. The professional marks would be awarded for analysing the impact of the information, drawing conclusions and considering the implications for ROCE.

Marking scheme

			Marks
(a)	(i)	Discontinuance	7
	(ii)	Deferred tax asset	6
	(iii)	Impairment	5
	(iv)	Formation of opinion of impact on ROCE	2
(b)	APM and residual income		3
Professional marks			2
Maximum			25

(a) (i) The criteria in IFRS 5 have been met for North and South. As the assets are to be disposed of in a single transaction, North and South together are deemed to be a **disposal group** under IFRS 5.

The disposal group as a whole is **measured on the basis required for non-current assets held for sale**. Any impairment loss reduces the carrying amount of the non-current assets in the disposal group, the loss being allocated in the order required by IAS 36 *Impairment of Assets*. Before the manufacturing units are classified as held for sale, impairment is tested for on an individual cash-generating unit basis. Once classified as held for sale, the impairment testing is done on a **disposal group basis**.

A disposal group that is held for sale should be measured at the **lower of** its **carrying amount** and **fair value less costs to sell**. Any impairment loss is generally recognised in profit or loss, but if the asset has been measured at a revalued amount under IAS 16 *Property, Plant and Equipment* or IAS 38 *Intangible Assets,* the impairment will be treated as a revaluation decrease.

A **subsequent increase** in fair value less costs to sell may be **recognised** in profit or loss **only to the extent of any impairment previously recognised**. To summarise:

Step 1 Calculate carrying amount under the individual standard, here given as $105 million.

Step 2 Classified as held for sale. Compare the carrying amount ($105m) with fair value less costs to sell ($125m). Measure at the lower of carrying amount and fair value less costs to sell, here $105 million.

Step 3 Determine fair value less costs to sell at the year end (see below) and compare with carrying amount of $105 million.

Tufnell has not taken account of the increase in fair value less cost to sell, but only part of this increase can be recognised, calculated as follows.

	$m
Fair value less costs to sell: North	40
Fair value less costs to sell: South	95
	135
Carrying value	(105)
Increase	30

Impairment previously recognised in North: $15m ($50m – $35m)

Step 4 The change in fair value less cost to sell is recognised but the gain recognised cannot exceed any impairment losses to date. Here the gain recognised is $50m – $35m = $15m

Therefore **carrying amount can increase** by $15 million to $120 million as loss reversals are limited to impairment losses previously recognised (under IFRS 5 or IAS 36).

These adjustments **will affect ROCE**.

(ii) IAS 12 *Income Taxes* requires that deferred tax liabilities must be recognised for all taxable temporary differences. Deferred tax assets should be recognised for deductible temporary differences but only to the extent that taxable profits will be available against which the deductible temporary differences may be utilised.

The differences between the carrying amounts and the tax base represent temporary differences. These **temporary differences are revised** in the light of the revaluation for tax purposes to market value permitted by the government.

Deferred tax liability before revaluation

	Carrying amount	*Tax base*	*Temporary difference*
	$m	$m	$m
Property	50	48	2
Vehicles	30	28	2
			4
Other temporary differences			5
			9

Provision: 30% × $9m = $2.7m

Deferred tax asset after revaluation

	Carrying amount	*Tax base*	*Temporary difference*
	$m	$m	$m
Property	50	65	15
Vehicles	30	35	5
Other temporary differences			(5)
			15

Deferred tax asset: $1 5m × 30% = $4.5m

This will have a **considerable impact on ROCE**. While the release of the provision of $2.7 million and the creation of the asset of $4.5 million will not affect profit **before** interest and **tax**, it will **significantly affect the capital employed figure**.

(iii) IAS 36 requires that no asset should be carried at more than its recoverable amount. At each reporting date, Tufnell must **review all assets for indications of impairment**, that is, indications that the carrying amount may be higher than the recoverable amount. Such indications include fall in the market value of an asset or adverse changes in the technological, economic or legal environment of the business. (IAS 36 has an extensive list of criteria.) If **impairment is indicated**, then the asset's **recoverable amount** must be calculated. The manufacturer has reduced the selling price, but this does not automatically mean that the asset is impaired.

The **recoverable amount** is defined as the **higher of the asset's fair value less costs of disposal and its value in use**. If the recoverable amount is less than the carrying amount, then the resulting impairment loss should be charged to profit or loss as an expense (unless the asset was previously revalued).

Value in use is the discounted present value of estimated future cash flows expected to arise from the continuing use of an asset and from its disposal at the end of its useful life. The value in use of the equipment is calculated as follows:

Year ended 30 September	*Cash flows*	*Discounted (10%)*
	$m	$m
20X8	1.3	1.2
20X9	2.2	1.8
20Y0	2.3	1.7
		4.7

The directors are proposing to write the asset down to its fair value of $2.5 million. However, its value in use is higher than fair value and also higher than the carrying amount of the asset ($3m). So there has been no impairment and the asset should remain at its carrying amount. Consequently there will be no effect on ROCE.

(iv) **Recalculation of ROCE**

	$m
Profit before interest and tax	30.0
Add increase in value of disposal group	15.0
	45.0
Capital employed	220.0
Add increase in value of disposal group	15.0
Add release of deferred tax provision and deferred tax asset: 4.5 + 2.7	7.2
	242.2

∴ROCE is 45/242.2 = 13.6%

The directors were concerned that the above changes would adversely affect ROCE. In fact, the effect has been favourable, as **ROCE has risen from 13.6% to 18.6%,** so the **directors' fears were misplaced**.

(b) Alternative performance measures (APMs) report information that is not included on the face of the financial statements. Companies often adjust reported financial information in order to provide helpful additional information for the users of financial statements, telling a clearer story of how the business has performed over the period. They allow the directors of a company more freedom and flexibility to report performance measures that are important to them.

Residual income is one type of APM. Residual income is an entity valuation method that accounts for the cost of equity capital. Performance of the subsidiaries should be measured, in the interests of the group's shareholders, in such a way as to indicate what sort of return each subsidiary is making on the shareholder's investment. Shareholders themselves are likely to be interested in the performance of the group as a whole, measured in terms of return on shareholders' capital, earnings per share, dividend yield, and growth in earnings and dividends. These performance ratios cannot be used for subsidiaries in the group, and so an alternative measure has to be selected, which compares the return from the subsidiary with the value of the investment in the subsidiary.

Residual income would provide a suitable indication of performance from the point of view of the group's shareholders. This could be calculated as:

	Profit after debt interest
Minus	A notional interest charge on the value of assets financed by shareholders' capital
Equals	Residual income

Alternatively, residual income might be measured as:

	Profit before interest (controllable by the subsidiary's management)
Minus	A notional interest charge on the controllable investments of the subsidiary
Equals	Residual income

Each subsidiary would be able to increase its residual income if it earned an incremental profit in excess of the notional interest charges on its incremental investments – ie in effect, if it added to the value of the group's equity.

42 Amster

Workbook references. Financial instruments are covered in Chapter 8. The *Conceptual Framework* is covered in Chapter 1.

Top tips. This question might have alarmed you as you might not have seen a capitalisation table before. However, you must be prepared to encounter disclosures such as this, which are a common feature of published financial statements and useful to investors. You should be able to work out that it requires adjusting in the same way as a statement of financial position would be. For (a)(ii), you need to think about the principles around debt and equity classification for financial instruments and try and relate this to the definitions in the *Conceptual Framework.*

Marking scheme

			Marks
(a)	(i)	1 mark per point up to maximum	8
	(ii)	1 mark per point up to maximum	6
(b)		1 mark per point up to maximum	9
Professional marks			2
			25

(a) (i) **Importance of information concerning an entity's capital**

Essentially there are two classes of capital reported in financial statements, namely debt and equity. However, debt and equity instruments can have different levels of right, benefit and risks. Hence, the details underlying a company's capital structure are absolutely essential to assessing the prospects for changes in a company's financial flexibility, and ultimately, its value.

For investors who are assessing the risk profile of an entity, the management and level of an entity's capital is an important consideration. Disclosures about capital are normally in addition to disclosures required by regulators as their reasons for disclosure may differ from those of the International Accounting Standards Board (IASB). The details underlying a company's capital structure are essential to the assessment of any potential change in an entity's financial standing.

Investors have specific but different needs for information about capital depending upon their approach to their investment in an entity. If their approach is income based, then shortage of capital may have an impact upon future dividends. If ROCE is used for comparing the performance of entities, then investors need to know the nature and quantity of the historical capital employed in the business. Some investors will focus on historical invested capital, others on accounting capital and others on market capitalisation.

Published information

As an entity's capital does not relate solely to financial instruments, the IASB has included these disclosures in IAS 1 *Presentation of Financial Statements* rather than IFRS 7 *Financial Instruments: Disclosures*. Although IFRS 7 requires some specific disclosures about financial liabilities, it does not have similar requirements for equity instruments.

As a result, IAS 1 requires an entity to disclose information which enables users to evaluate the entity's objectives, policies and processes for managing capital. This objective is obtained by disclosing qualitative and quantitative data. The former should include narrative information such as what the company manages as capital, whether there are any external capital requirements and how those requirements are incorporated into the management of capital. The IASB decided that there should be disclosure of whether the entity has complied with any external capital requirements and, if not, the consequences of non-compliance.

Besides the requirements of IAS 1, the IFRS *Practice Statement, Management Commentary* suggests that management should include forward-looking information in the commentary when it is aware of trends, uncertainties or other factors which could affect the entity's capital resources. Additionally, some jurisdictions refer to capital disclosures as part of their legal requirements.

In addition to the annual report, an investor may find details of the entity's capital structure where the entity is involved in a transaction, such as a sale of bonds or equities. It can be seen that information regarding an entity's capital structure is spread across several documents including the management commentary, the notes to financial statements, interim financial statements and any document required by securities regulators.

Integrated reporting

The capitals identified by the International Integrated Reporting Council (IIRC) are: financial capital, manufactured capital, intellectual capital, human capital, social and relationship capital, and natural capital. Together, they represent stores of value which are the basis of an organisation's value creation. Financial capital is broadly understood as the pool of funds available to an organisation. This includes both debt and equity finance. This description of financial capital focuses on the source of funds, rather than its application which results in the acquisition of manufactured or other forms of capital. Financial capital is a medium of exchange which releases its value through conversion into other forms of capital. It is the pool of funds which is available to the organisation for use in the production of goods or the provision of services obtained through financing, such as debt, equity or grants, or generated through operations or investments.

(ii) Whether an instrument is classified as either a financial liability or as equity is important as it has a direct effect on an entity's reported results and financial position. The critical feature of a liability is that, under the terms of the instrument, the issuer is or can be required to deliver either cash or another financial asset to the holder and it cannot avoid this obligation. An instrument is classified as equity when it represents a residual interest in the issuer's assets after deducting all its liabilities. If the financial instrument provides the entity an unconditional discretion, the financial instrument is equity.

IAS 32 *Financial Instruments Presentation* sets out the nature of the classification process but the standard is principle based and sometimes the outcomes are surprising to users. IAS 32 focuses on the contractual obligations of the instrument and considers the substance of the contractual rights and obligations. The variety of instruments issued by entities makes this classification difficult with the application of the principles occasionally resulting in instruments which seem like equity being accounted for as liabilities. Recent developments in the types of financial instruments issued have added more complexity to capital structures with the resultant difficulties in interpretation and understanding.

Equity and liabilities are classified separately in the statement of financial position. The *Conceptual Framework* distinguishes the two elements by the obligation of the entity to deliver cash or other economic resources from items which create no such obligation. The statement of profit or loss and other comprehensive income (OCI) includes income and expenses arising from liabilities which is interest and, if applicable, remeasurement and gain or loss on settlement. The statement does not report as income or expense any changes in the carrying amount of the entity's own equity instruments but does include expenses arising from the consumption of services which fall under IFRS 2 *Share-based Payment.* IFRS 2 requires a valuation of the services consumed in exchange for the financial liabilities or equity instruments.

In the statement of financial position, the carrying amount of many financial liabilities changes either with the passage of time or if the liability is remeasured at fair value. However, the amount reported for classes of equity instruments generally does not change after initial recognition except for non-controlling interest.

Liability classification typically results in any payments on the instrument being treated as interest and charged to earnings. This may in turn affect the entity's ability to pay dividends on its equity shares depending upon local legislation.

Equity classification avoids the negative impact which liability classification has on reported earnings, gearing ratios and debt covenants. It also results in the instrument falling outside the scope of IFRS 9 *Financial Instruments*, thereby avoiding the complicated ongoing measurement requirements of that standard.

(b) In the case of the first class of preference shares, even though there are negative consequences of not paying dividends on the preferred shares as agreed contractually, the company can avoid the obligation to deliver cash. The preferred shares do have redemption provisions but these are not mandatory and are at the sole discretion of the management committee and therefore the shares should be classified as equity.

In the case of the second class, the contractual term requires no dividend to be paid to ordinary shareholders if a payment is not made on the preferred shares. In this case, as

Amster can avoid the obligation to settle the annual dividend, the shares are classified as equity. Thus $75 million should be transferred from liabilities to equity.

IFRS 2 *Share-based Payment* states that cash settled share-based payment transactions occur where goods or services are paid for at amounts which are based on the price of the company's equity instruments. The expense for cash settled transactions is the cash paid by the company and any amounts accrued should be shown as liabilities and not equity. Therefore Amster should remove the following amount from equity and show it as a liability.

Expense for year to 30 November 20X7 is:

((1,500 – 180 employees × 250 awards × $35) × ⅓ = $3.85 million

As a result of the adjustments to the financial statements, Amster's gearing ratio will be lowered significantly as the liabilities will drop from 53.8% of total capitalisation to 33.2% of total capitalisation. However, the ROCE may stay the same even though there is an increase in shareholders equity as total capitalisation has not changed. However, this will depend upon the definition used by the entity for capital employed.

Amster Group – capitalisation table

	30 November 20X7	*Adjustment*	*30 November 20X7*
	$m	$m	$m
Long-term liabilities	81	3.85	84.85
Pension plan deficit	30		30.00
Cumulative preference shares	75	(75)	–
Liabilities	186		114.85
Non-controlling interest	10		10.00
Shareholders equity	150	(75 – 3.85)	221.15
Group equity	160		231.15
Total capitalisation	346		346.00

43 Havanna

Workbook references. Revenue recognition is covered in Chapter 3, IFRS 5 *Non-current Assets Held for Sale and Discontinued Operations* in Chapter 14 and sale and leaseback in Chapter 9.

Top tips. Revenue recognition is an area in which preparers of accounts may wish to interpret the standard in such a way as to present the results in a favourable light. In Part (a), you need to explain why the proposed treatment is unacceptable, not just state that it is.

Part (b), which tests IFRS 5, requires clear, logical thinking: there are two potential impairments, the first in calculating the adjusted carrying amount of the disposal group at the time of classification as held for sale, and then again on comparison of this adjusted carrying amount with fair value less costs to sell.

Part (c)(i) requires you to demonstrate wider reading on the impact of IFRS 16. For part (c)(ii), the difficulty with sale and leaseback often lies with identifying whether the transfer of the asset constitutes a sale but here the question actually states that the transaction constitutes a sale so you just need to explain why the directors' understanding is incorrect and advise on the correct accounting treatment in the context of the scenario.

Marking scheme

			Marks
(a)	Revenue recognition – 1 mark per point to a maximum		5
(b)	IFRS 5 explanation – 1 mark per point to a maximum		5
(c)	(i)	Key changes to financial statements from IFRS 16 – 1 mark per point to a maximum	6
	(ii)	Sale and leaseback – 1 mark per point to a maximum	5
	(iii)	Effect on interest cover – 1 mark per point to a maximum	2
Professional marks			2
			25

(a) **Contracts with sports organisations**

Havanna has treated the services provided under the contracts as a single performance obligation satisfied at a point in time, when the customer signs the contract.

However, there are **potentially at least three separate performance obligations** in the form of the different services provided by Havanna to the sports organisations. These are access to Havanna's database of members, admission to health clubs and provision of coaching (and other benefits).

Under IFRS 15, Havanna is providing a **series of distinct services** that are **substantially the same** and have the **same pattern of transfer** to the customer.

This is the case because both of the following criteria are met:

1) Each distinct service in the series **meets the criteria to be a performance obligation satisfied over time** (ie when the customer simultaneously receives and consumes the benefits provided by the entity). This is the case with all three of the services offered by Havanna to the sports organisations.

2) **The same method** would be used to **measure the entity's progress towards complete satisfaction of the performance obligation** to transfer each distinct service in the series to the customer. This is the case for Havanna as the most appropriate measure would be a time-based measure as Havanna has an obligation to provide their services on a continuous basis over the 9 to 18-month contract.

Therefore, Havanna's services qualify as a series of distinct goods and services that are substantially the same which should be grouped together as a **single performance obligation** which is satisfied over time.

For performance obligations satisfied over time, IFRS 15 requires an entity to recognise revenue over time by measuring progress towards complete satisfaction of that performance obligation.

Havanna should recognise revenue on a **straight-line basis over the period of the contract** rather than when the customer signs the contract.

(b) **Sale of division**

The division to be sold meets the criteria in IFRS 5 *Non-current Assets Held for Sale and Discontinued Operations* to be classified as held for sale and has been classified as a **disposal group** under IFRS 5.

A disposal group that is held for sale should be measured at the **lower of** its **carrying amount** and **fair value less costs to sell**. Immediately before classification of a disposal group as held for sale, the entity must recognise impairment in accordance with applicable IFRS. Any impairment loss is generally recognised in profit or loss, but if the asset has been measured at a revalued amount under IAS 16 *Property, Plant and Equipment* or IAS 38 *Intangible Assets,* the impairment will be treated as a revaluation decrease.

Once the disposal group has been **classified as held for sale**, any further **impairment loss** will be based on the **difference between the adjusted carrying amounts and the fair value less cost to sell**. The impairment loss (if any) will be **recognised in profit or loss**. For assets carried at fair value prior to initial classification, the requirement to deduct costs to sell from fair value will result in an immediate charge to profit or loss.

Havanna has calculated the impairment as $30 million, being the difference between the carrying amount at initial classification and the value of the assets measured in accordance with IFRS. However, applying the treatment described above:

Step 1 Calculate carrying amount under applicable IFRS: $90m – $30m = $60m

Step 2 Classified as held for sale. Measure at the **lower** of the adjusted carrying amount under applicable IFRS ($60m) and fair value less costs to sell of $38.5 million ($40m expected sales prices less expected costs of $1.5m). Therefore, an **additional impairment loss of $21.5 million is required** to write down the carrying amount of $60 million to the fair value less costs to sell of $38.5 million.

(c) **Briefing note for directors**

(i) *Key changes investors will see as a result of IFRS 16*

IFRS 16 has brought all lease obligations (with limited exemptions for short-term leases and low value assets) on to the statement of financial position because on lease commencement, a lessee recognises a right-of-use asset and a corresponding lease liability.

Under IAS 17, lessees only recognised an asset and liability in respect of leases that met the definition of a finance lease. Leases that were not classified as finance leases were therefore 'off-balance sheet'. This made investor analysis of financial statements more difficult as investors had to estimate the assets and liabilities resulting from off-balance sheet leases when calculating ratios.

IFRS 16 will reduce complexity in financial statements as it should allow comparisons to be made between those companies who lease assets and those who borrow to buy assets.

The requirement to recognise right-of-use assets and lease liabilities under IFRS 16 will result in more information about leases both on the statement of financial position and in the notes and will provide a more accurate reflection of the impacts of lease arrangements on an entity's financial statements.

The carrying amount of lease assets will typically reduce more quickly than the carrying amount of lease liabilities. This will result in a reduction in reported equity for companies with previous material off-balance sheet leases.

IFRS 16 requires a lessee to disclose lease liabilities separately from other liabilities as a separate line item, or together with other similar liabilities, in a manner which is relevant to understanding the lessee's financial position. A lessee will also split lease liabilities into current and non-current portions, based on the timing of payments.

Investors should bear in mind that some sectors and some companies will be more affected than others. As a result, companies with previous material off-balance sheet leases will report higher assets and financial liabilities.

(ii) *Sale and leaseback*

This is a sale and leaseback transaction which should be accounted for in accordance with IFRS 16 *Leases*. IFRS 16 requires an **initial assessment** to be made regarding **whether** the **transfer constitutes a sale,** here we are told the **IFRS 15 criteria have been met**.

Havanna should **derecognise the carrying amount** of the asset ($4.2m) and **recognise a right-of-use asset** at the proportion of the previous carrying amount that relates to the right-of-use asset retained.

A **gain or loss** should then be recognised in relation to the **rights transferred** to the buyer-lessor. Although there is a gain to be recognised in profit or loss, this will not be the $0.8 million (being sales price of $5m – carrying amount of $4.2m) the CEO has calculated.

Havanna should also recognise a **lease liability** at the present value of lease payments of $3.85 million.

The right-of-use asset at the start of the leaseback should be calculated as:

Carrying amount × present value of lease payments/Fair value
= $4.2m × $3.85m/$5m = $3,234,000.

Havanna should only recognise the amount of gain that relates to the rights transferred. The gain on sale of the building is $800,000 ($5,000,000 – $4,200,000), of which:

($800,000 × $3.85m/$5m) = $616,000 relates to the rights retained.

The balance, $184,000 ($800,000 – $616,000), relates to the rights transferred to the buyer and should be recognised as a gain.

At the start of the lease Havanna should account for the transaction as follows:

	Debit	*Credit*
	$	$
Cash	5,000,000	
Right-of-use asset	3,234,000	
Building		4,200,000
Lease liability		3,850,000
Gain on rights transferred		184,000
	8,234,000	8,234,000

The **right-of-use asset** should be **depreciated over ten years** (being the shorter of the lease term and the remaining useful life of the asset). The **gain will be recognised in profit or loss** and the **lease liability** will be **increased** each year by the **interest charge** and **reduced by the lease payments**.

(iii) *Effect on interest cover*

The interest cover ratio in its most simple form is an entity's earnings before interest and tax divided by its interest expense for the period. In stating that the transaction will help to ensure that the interest cover covenant will be met, the CEO has failed to take into account the additional finance cost that will arise as a result of the lease liability.

Furthermore, earnings will be increased by the gain on the rights transferred of \$0.184 million, but this is far less than the \$0.8 million gain expected by the CEO. More information would be required as to the interest payable on the lease in order to quantify whether the interest cover will indeed improve as a result of the sale and leaseback.

44 Operating segments

Workbook references. The topics in this question are covered in Chapter 18.

Top tips: Parts (a) and (b) require you to apply the criteria in IFRS 8 to two different companies. In (a) you need to consider the allocation of common costs to operating segments and explain how those costs differ to amounts in the financial statements because IFRS 8 is based on internally reported information. In (b) you need to determine whether the company was correct in aggregating two reportable segments (there is plenty of information in the scenario to suggest otherwise) and consider how investors use segmental information in their appraisal of companies. Part (c) considers how CSR and ethics interact and the potential conflict between them.

For learning purposes, this question included some discussion of ethical issues in the context of the scenario given. However, please note that ethics will not feature in Section B questions in the real exam. Ethics will be examined only in Question 2 of the exam.

Easy marks. There are some easy marks for definitions in Part (b).

Marking scheme

				Marks
(a)	Accell – allocation of common costs – discussion 1 mark per point to a maximum of 7 marks. Points may include:			
	Impact on profit/net assets of allocation		1	
	IFRS 8 guidance on allocation		1	
	Suggested basis for allocation for each cost in scenario		3	
	Differing amounts in segment report to financial statements		2	
				7
(b)	(i)	Velocity – application of IFRS 8:		
		Criteria for aggregation	1	
		Customer base/risk	2	
		Conclusion	1	
				4
	(ii)	Velocity – discussion of investor appraisal and segments:		
		Used to determine cash flows	1	
		Aggregation less useful	1	
		Conclusion	1	
		Ethics	1	
				4

		Marks
(c)	Reconciliation of ethics of CSR disclosure to shareholder expectations – discussion 1 mark per point to a maximum of 8 marks. Points may include:	
	Expectation for businesses to be socially and environmentally responsible	1
	Responsibility to all stakeholders, not just shareholders, conflict of interest	2
	Reasons for not wanting to disclose information	1
	Good CSR can result in increased shareholder value	2
	Most companies provide disclosures beyond those required by IFRS	2
		8
Professional marks		2
		25

(a) **Accell – allocation of common costs under IFRS 8**

If operating segment disclosure is to fulfil a useful function, costs need to be appropriately assigned to segments. Centrally incurred expenses and central assets can be significant, and the basis chosen by an entity to allocate such costs **can therefore have a significant impact** on the financial statements. In the case of Accell, head office management expenses, pension expenses, the cost of managing properties and interest and related interest-bearing assets could be material amounts, whose misallocation could mislead users.

IFRS 8 **does not prescribe a basis** on which to allocate common costs, but it does require that that basis should be **reasonable**. For example, it would not be reasonable to allocate the head office management expenses to the most profitable business segment to disguise a potential loss elsewhere. Nor would it be reasonable to allocate the pension expense to a segment with no pensionable employees.

A reasonable basis on which to allocate common costs for Accell might be as follows:

(i) **Head office management costs**. These could be allocated on the basis of revenue or net assets. Any allocation might be criticised as arbitrary – it is not necessarily the case that a segment with a higher revenue requires more administration from head office – but this is a fairer basis than most.

(ii) **Pension expense**. A reasonable allocation might be on the basis of the number of employees or salary expense of each segment.

(iii) **Costs of managing properties**. These could be allocated on the basis of the value of the properties used by each business segment, or the type and age of the properties (older properties requiring more attention than newer ones).

(iv) **Interest and interest-bearing assets**. These need not be allocated to the same segment – the interest receivable could be allocated to the profit or loss of one segment and the related interest-bearing asset to the assets and liabilities of another. IFRS 8 calls this asymmetrical allocation.

The **amounts reported under IFRS 8 may differ from those reported in the financial statements** because IFRS 8 requires the information to be presented on the same basis as it is reported internally, even if the accounting policies are not the same as those of the consolidated financial statements. For example, segment information may be reported on a cash basis rather than an accruals basis or different accounting policies may be adopted in the segment report when allocating centrally incurred costs if necessary for a better understanding of the reported segment information.

IFRS 8 requires **reconciliations** between the segments' reported amounts and those in the consolidated financial statements. Entities must disclose the nature of such differences, and of the basis of accounting for transactions between reportable segments.

(b) (i) **Velocity – operating segments**

IFRS 8 *Operating Segments* requires operating segments to be reported separately if they exceed at least one of certain qualitative thresholds. Two or more operating segments **below** the thresholds may be **aggregated** to produce a reportable segment if the segments have **similar economic characteristics**, and the segments are similar in a **majority** of the following aggregation criteria:

(i) The nature of the products and services
(ii) The nature of the production process
(iii) The type or class of customer for their products or services
(iv) The methods used to distribute their products or provide their services
(v) If applicable, the nature of the regulatory environment

Velocity has aggregated segments 1 and 2, but this aggregation may not be permissible under IFRS 8. While the products and services are similar, the **customers for those products and services are different**. Therefore the third aggregation criteria has not been met.

In the local market, the decision to award the contract is in the hands of the local authority, which also sets prices and pays for the services. The **company is not exposed to passenger revenue risk**, since a contract is awarded by competitive tender.

By contrast, in the inter-city train market, the **customer ultimately determines whether a train route is economically viable** by choosing whether or not to buy tickets. Velocity sets the ticket prices, but will be influenced by customer behaviour or feedback. The **company is exposed to passenger revenue risk**, as it sets prices which customers may or may not choose to pay.

It is possible that the fifth criteria, regulatory environment, is not met, since the local authority is imposing a different set of rules to that which applies in the inter-city market.

In conclusion, the two segments have different economic characteristics and so **should be reported as separate segments** rather than aggregated.

(ii) **Relevance to investor analysis**

Contrary to the managing director's views, IFRS 8 provides information that makes the financial statements more useful to investors. The objective of financial statements is to provide financial information to primary users (not just investors) which enables them to make decisions about providing resources to the entity.

In making those decisions, investors and creditors consider the returns they are likely to make on their investment. This requires assessment of the amount, timing and uncertainty of the future cash flows of Velocity as well as of management's stewardship of Velocity's resources. How management derives profit is therefore relevant information to an investor.

Inappropriately aggregating segments reduces the usefulness of segment disclosures to investors. IFRS 8 requires information to be disclosed that is not readily available elsewhere in the financial statements, therefore it provides additional information which aids an investor's understanding of how the business operates and is managed.

In Velocity's case, if the segments are aggregated, then the increased profits in segment 2 will hide the decreased profits in segment 1. However, the fact profits have sharply declined in segment 1 would be of interest to investors as it may suggest that future cash flows from this segment are at risk.

The fact that the director was pleased at the aggregation of the segments raises concern that perhaps Velocity is trying to conceal facts from investors. The reasons for this should be investigated further to determine if there is any unethical practice taking place.

(c) **Reconciliation of ethics of corporate social responsibility disclosure with shareholder expectations**

There is sustained government and societal pressure on businesses to be **socially and environmentally responsible as well as profitable**. There is a trend towards less focus on short-term profit and increasing awareness that a commitment to sustainable business practises is essential for long-term success.

Strategic decisions by businesses, particularly global businesses nearly always have wider social and environmental consequences. It could be argued that a company produces two outputs: goods and services, and the social and environmental consequences of its activities, such as carbon emissions.

The requirement to be a **good corporate citizen goes beyond the normal duty of ethical behaviour** in the preparation of financial statements. To act ethically, the directors must put the interests of the company and its shareholders first, for example they must not mislead users of financial statements and must exercise competence in their preparation. Corporate citizenship, on the other hand, is concerned with a company's **accountability to a wide range of stakeholders**, not just shareholders. There may well be a **conflict of interest between corporate social responsibility and maximising shareholder wealth**; for example it may be cheaper to source raw materials from an overseas supplier which does not commit to fair employment practices, but doing so will negatively impact on both the delivery miles associated with the product and the reputation of the company.

However, the two goals **need not conflict**. It is possible that being a good corporate citizen can **improve business performance**. **Customers may buy from a company that they perceive as being committed to sustainability**, such as one that avoids using products derived from animals, and **employees may remain loyal** to such a company, and both these factors are likely to increase shareholder wealth in the long term. If a company engages constructively with the country or community in which it is based, it may be seen by shareholders and potential shareholders as being a **good long-term investment** rather than in business for short-term profits.

As regards disclosure, a company that makes **detailed disclosures**, particularly when these go beyond what is required by legislation or accounting standards, will be seen as **responsible and a good potential investment**, provided they are clear, concise, relevant and understandable. For example, many quoted companies now prepare social and environmental disclosures following guidelines such as the International Integrated Reporting <IR> Framework or the Global Reporting Initiative. The IASB have also provided guidance in the form of an IFRS Practice Statement for entities preparing a management commentary.

45 Skizer

Marking scheme

				Marks
(a)	(i)	Discussion of the conceptual framework and IAS 38 recognition criteria		6
	(ii)	Application of the following discussion to the scenario:		
		20X7 initial assessment of recognition criteria (met/not met), IAS 38 derecognition criteria and potential impairment assessment	2	
		20X8 reclassification as R&D is not a change in estimate and impairment assessment	2	
		If recognition criteria not met	1	5
	(iii)	Application of the following discussion to the scenario:		
		Consideration of Skizer's business model	2	
		The application of IFRS 15 to Skizer	2	4
(b)	(i)	Discussion of IFRS 3 recognition of intangible assets and information provided about different intangible assets so that investor adjustments can be made	3	
		Discussion of cost or revaluation under IAS 38 and differences	2	
		Discussion of differences in treatment of R&D and development expenditure	2	7
	(ii)	Discussion of measurement choices made in the financial statements	2	
		Consideration of whether IR can supplement financial statements thereby providing more useful information for investors	1	3
				25

(a) (i) The *Conceptual Framework* defines an asset as a present economic resource **controlled** by the entity as a result of past events. An economic resource is a **right** that has the **potential** to produce economic benefits. Assets should be recognised if they meet the *Conceptual Framework* definition of an asset and such recognition provides users of financial statements with information that is useful (ie it is relevant and results in faithful representation). This is subject to the criteria that the benefits the information provides must be sufficient to justify the costs of providing that information. The wording of the recognition criteria in the *Conceptual Framework* allows for flexibility in how this criteria could be applied by the IASB in amending or developing Standards.

IAS 38 *Intangible Assets* defines an intangible asset as an identifiable non-monetary asset without physical substance. IAS 38 retains the 2010 *Conceptual Framework* definition of an asset which specifies that future economic benefits are **expected** to flow to the entity. Furthermore IAS 38 requires an entity to recognise an intangible asset, if, and only if:

(a) It is **probable** that the expected future economic benefits that are attributable to the asset will flow to the entity; and

(b) The cost of the asset can be measured reliably.

This requirement applies whether an intangible asset is acquired externally or generated internally. The probability of future economic benefits must be based on reasonable and supportable assumptions about conditions which will exist over the life of the asset. The probability recognition criterion is always considered to be satisfied for intangible assets which are acquired separately or in a business combination. If the recognition criteria are not met, IAS 38 requires the expenditure to be expensed when it is incurred.

The *Conceptual Framework* does not prescribe a 'probability criterion', and thus does not prohibit the recognition of assets or liabilities with a low probability of an inflow or outflow of economic benefits. In terms of intangible assets, it is arguable that recognising an intangible asset with a low probability of economic benefits would not be useful to users given that the asset has no physical substance.

The recognition criteria and definition of an asset in IAS 38 are **different** to those in the *Conceptual Framework*. The criteria in IAS 38 are more specific, but arguably do provide information that is relevant and a faithful representation. When viewed in this way, the requirements of IAS 38 in terms of recognition appear to be consistent with the *Conceptual Framework*.

(ii) Skizer should have assessed whether the recognition criteria in IAS 38 were met at the time the entity capitalised the intangible assets. If the recognition criteria were met, then it was not appropriate to derecognise the intangible assets. According to IAS 38, an intangible asset should be derecognised only on disposal or when no future economic benefits are expected from its use or disposal. If there were any doubts regarding the recoverability of the intangible asset, then Skizer should have assessed whether the intangible assets would be impaired. IAS 36 *Impairment of Assets* would be used to determine whether an intangible asset is impaired.

Further, the reclassification of intangible assets to research and development costs does not constitute a change in an accounting estimate. IAS 8 *Accounting Policies, Changes in Accounting Estimates and Errors* states that a change in accounting estimate is an adjustment of the carrying amount of an asset or liability, or related expense, resulting from reassessing the expected future benefits and obligations associated with that asset or liability. However, if Skizer concludes that the intangible assets' carrying amounts exceed their recoverable amounts, an impairment loss should be recognised. The costs of the stakes in the development projects can be determined and will not have been estimated.

If the recognition criteria were not met, then Skizer would have to recognise retrospectively a correction of an error, in accordance with IAS 8.

(iii) Gains arising from derecognition of an intangible asset cannot be presented as revenue as IAS 38 explicitly forbids it. There is no indication that Skizer's business model is to sell development projects but, rather, it undertakes the development of new products in conjunction with third party entities. Skizer's business model is to jointly develop a product, then leave the production to partners. As Skizer has recognised an intangible asset in accordance with IAS 38, and fully impaired the asset, it cannot argue that it has thereafter been held for sale in the ordinary course of business. Therefore, according to IAS 38, the gain from the derecognition of the intangible asset cannot be classified as revenue under IFRS 15 *Revenue from Contracts with Customers* but as a profit on the sale of the intangible asset.

(b) (i) Under IFRS 3 *Business Combinations*, acquired intangible assets must be recognised and measured at fair value if they are separable or arise from other contractual rights, irrespective of whether the acquiree had recognised the assets prior to the business combination occurring. This is because there should always be sufficient information to reliably measure the fair value of these assets. IFRS 3 requires all intangible assets acquired in a business combination to be treated in the same way in line with the requirements of IAS 38. IAS 38 requires intangible assets with finite lives to be amortised over their useful lives and intangible assets with indefinite lives to be subject to an annual impairment review in accordance with IAS 36.

However, it is unlikely that all intangible assets acquired in a business combination will be homogeneous and investors may feel that there are different types of intangible assets which may be acquired. For example, a patent may only last for a finite period of time and may be thought as having an identifiable future revenue stream. In this case, amortisation of the patent would be logical. However, there are other intangible assets which are gradually replaced by the purchasing entity's own intangible assets, for example, customer lists, and it may make sense to account for these assets within goodwill. In such cases, investors may wish to reverse amortisation charges. In order to decide whether an amortisation charge makes sense, investors require greater detail about the nature of the identified intangible assets. IFRSs do not permit a different accounting treatment for this distinction.

IAS 38 requires an entity to choose either the cost model or the revaluation model for each class of intangible asset. Under the cost model, after initial recognition intangible assets should be carried at cost less accumulated amortisation and impairment losses. Under the revaluation model, intangible assets may be carried at a revalued amount, based on fair value, less any subsequent amortisation and impairment losses only if fair value can be determined by reference to an active market. Such active markets are not common for intangible assets. If an intangible asset is reported using the cost model, the reported figures for intangible assets such as trademarks may be understated when compared to their fair values. Based upon the principle above regarding the different types of intangible asset, it would make sense for different accounting treatments subsequent to initial recognition. Some intangible assets should be amortised over their useful lives but other intangible assets should be subject to an annual impairment review, in the same way as goodwill.

IAS 38 requires all research costs to be expensed with development costs being capitalised only after the technical and commercial feasibility of the asset for sale or use has been established. If an entity cannot distinguish the research phase of an internal project to create an intangible asset from the development phase, the entity treats the expenditure for that project as if it were incurred in the research phase only. There is some logic to the capitalisation of development expenditure as internally generated intangible assets but the problem for investors is disclosure in this area as companies do not have a consistent approach to capitalisation. It is often unclear from disclosures how the accounting policy in respect of research and development was applied and especially how research was distinguished from development expenditure. One of the issues is that the disclosure of relevant information is already contained within IFRSs but preparers are failing to comply with these requirements or the disclosure is insufficient.

Intangible asset disclosure can help analysts answer questions about the innovation capacity of companies and investors can use the disclosure to identify companies with intangible assets for development and commercialisation purposes.

(ii) Measuring the contribution of intangible assets to future cash flows is fundamental to integrated reporting and will help explain the gaps between the carrying amount, intrinsic and market equity value of an entity. As set out above, organisations are required to recognise intangible assets acquired in a business combination. Consequently, the intangible assets are only measured once for this purpose. However, organisations are likely to go further in their integrated report and disclose the change in value of an intangible asset as a result of any sustainable growth strategy or a specific initiative. It is therefore very useful to communicate the value of intangible assets in an integrated report. For example, an entity may decide to disclose its assessment of the increase in brand value as a result of a corporate social responsibility initiative.

46 Cloud

Workbook references. Integrated Reporting and other aspects of performance reporting are covered in Chapter 18 of the Workbook. The *Conceptual Framework* is covered in Chapter 1. Hedge accounting is covered in Chapter 8 and transfers from the revaluation surplus are covered in Chapter 4.

Top tips. Part (a) of the question covered two topics: the issue of recognition of income and expenses in profit or loss vs other comprehensive income, reclassification between the two, and integrated reporting. Because the question is fairly open-ended, our answer is longer than would be needed in an exam where only some of the points would need to be made in order to get the marks.

Part (b) required the application of Part (a) in terms of determining which elements of a profit or loss should be reported in OCI and which elements in profit or loss.

Easy marks. Describing the principles and key components of the <IR> Framework is straightforward textbook knowledge. Other than the hedge accounting, Part (b) on the measurement of assets should be relatively easy.

Marking scheme

			Marks
(a)	(i)	1 mark per point up to maximum	6
	(ii)	1 mark per point up to maximum	5
	(iii)	1 mark per point up to maximum	8
(b)		1 mark per point up to maximum	6
			25

(a) (i) **Current presentation requirements**

IAS 1 requires the presentation of either one combined statement of profit or loss and other comprehensive income (SPLOCI) or two separate statements, the statement of profit or loss (SPL) and the statement of comprehensive income.

Separate disclosure is required of those items of other comprehensive income (OCI) which would be reclassified to profit or loss and those items of OCI which would never be reclassified to profit or loss, along with the related tax effects of each category.

Conceptual basis

The conceptual basis for what should be classified as OCI is not clear. This has led to an **inconsistent use of OCI in IFRS**.

Opinions vary but there is a feeling that **OCI has become a home for anything controversial** because of a lack of clear definition of what should be included in the statement.

Many users are thought to ignore OCI, as the changes reported are not caused by the operating flows used for predictive purposes. It is also difficult for users to understand the concept of OCI as opposed to profit or loss which, although subject to accounting standards, is an easier notion to grasp.

The definitions of profit and loss and OCI in IAS 1 are not particularly helpful in understanding the conceptual basis:

- Profit or loss is the total of all items of income and expenses except those items of income or expense which are recognised in OCI
- OCI comprises items of income and expense that are not recognised in profit or loss as required or permitted by other IFRSs

The IASB has been asked to define what financial performance is, clarify the meaning and importance of OCI and how the distinction between profit or loss and OCI should be made in practice. Many stakeholders were hoping that the *Conceptual Framework* as revised in 2018 would answer these questions, but the matter has not been adequately addressed.

The revised *Conceptual Framework* identifies the SPL as the **primary source** of information about an entity's performance and states that in principle, therefore, all income and expenses are included in it.

However, it goes on to say that in developing IFRSs the IASB may include income or expenses **arising from a change in the current value of an asset or liability as OCI** when they determine it provides more relevant information or a more faithful representation.

So although there is more guidance on what constitutes OCI, the conceptual basis for it is still not clear.

(ii) **Reclassification adjustments**

Reclassification adjustments are **amounts reclassified to profit or loss in the current period which were recognised in OCI in the current or previous periods.**

Items which may be reclassified include foreign currency gains on the disposal of a foreign operation and realised gains or losses on cash flow hedges.

Items which may not be reclassified are changes in a revaluation surplus under IAS 16 *Property, Plant and Equipment*, and actuarial gains and losses on a defined benefit plan under IAS 19 *Employee Benefits*.

However, the notion of reclassification and when or which OCI items should be reclassified is not clear. The revised *Conceptual Framework* (2018) states that in principle, OCI is recycled to profit or loss in a future period when doing so results in the provision of more relevant information or a more faithful representation. While providing more guidance than the previous *Conceptual Framework*, the conceptual basis for when OCI should be reclassified is not clear.

Arguments for and against reclassification

It is argued that reclassification protects the integrity of profit or loss and **provides users with relevant information about a transaction which occurred in the period**. Additionally, it can **improve comparability** where IFRSs permits similar items to be recognised in either profit or loss or OCI.

Those against reclassification argue that the **recycled amounts add to the complexity of financial reporting**, may lead to earnings management and the reclassification adjustments may not meet the definitions of income or expense in the period as the change in the asset or liability may have occurred in a previous period.

(iii) **Integrated Reporting**

The <IR> Framework establishes **principles** and **concepts** which govern the overall content of an integrated report. This enables each company to set out its own integrated report rather than adopting a checklist approach.

The integrated report aims to provide an insight into the company's resources and relationships (known as **capitals**) and how the company interacts with the external environment and the capitals to create value. These capitals can be financial, manufactured, intellectual, human, social and relationship, and natural capital but companies need not adopt these classifications.

Integrated reporting is built around the following key components:

(1) Organisational overview and the external environment under which it operates

(2) Governance structure and how this supports its ability to create value

(3) Business model

(4) Risks and opportunities and how they are dealing with them and how they affect the company's ability to create value

(5) Strategy and resource allocation

(6) Performance and achievement of strategic objectives for the period and outcomes

(7) Outlook and challenges facing the company and their implications

(8) The basis of presentation needs to be determined including what matters are to be included in the integrated report and how the elements are quantified or evaluated

An integrated report should provide insight into the **nature and quality of the organisation's relationships** with its **key stakeholders**, including how and to what extent the organisation understands, takes into account and responds to their **needs and interests**. The report should be consistent over time to enable comparison with other entities.

'Value' depends upon the individual company's own perspective. It can be shown through movement of capital and can be defined as **value created for the company or for others**. An integrated report should not attempt to quantify value, as assessments of value are left to those using the report.

An integrated report does not contain a statement from those 'charged with governance' acknowledging their responsibility for the integrated report. This may undermine the reliability and credibility of the integrated report.

There has been discussion about whether the <IR> Framework constitutes suitable criteria for report preparation and for assurance. There is a degree of uncertainty as to measurement standards to be used for the information reported and how a preparer can ascertain the completeness of the report. The IIRC has stated that the prescription of specific measurement methods is beyond the scope of a principles-based framework.

The <IR> Framework contains information on the principles-based approach and indicates that there is a need to include quantitative indicators whenever practicable and possible. Additionally, consistency of measurement methods across different reports is of paramount importance. There is outline guidance on the selection of suitable quantitative indicators.

There are additional concerns over the ability to assess future disclosures, and there may be a need for confidence intervals to be disclosed. The preparation of an integrated report requires judgement but there is a requirement for the report to describe its basis of preparation and presentation, including the significant frameworks and methods used to quantify or evaluate material matters. Also included is the disclosure of a summary of how the company determined the materiality limits and a description of the reporting boundaries.

A company should consider how to describe the disclosures without causing a significant loss of competitive advantage. The entity will consider what advantage a competitor could actually gain from information in the integrated report, and will balance this against the need for disclosure.

(b) At 30 April 20X5, Cloud should write down the steel, in accordance with IAS 2 *Inventories*, to its net realisable value of $6 million, therefore reducing profit by $2 million. Cloud should reclassify an equivalent amount of $2 million from equity to profit or loss. Thus there is no net impact on profit or loss from the write down of inventory. The gain remaining in equity of $1 million will affect profit or loss when the steel is sold. Therefore, on 3 June 20X5, the gain on the sale of $0.2 million with be recognised in profit or loss, and the remaining gain of $1 million will be transferred to profit or loss from equity.

As regards the property, plant and equipment, at 30 April 20X4, there is a revaluation surplus of $4 million being the difference between the carrying amount of $8 million ($10 million – $2 million) and the revalued amount of $12 million. This revaluation surplus is recognised in other comprehensive income.

At 30 April 20X5 the asset's value has fallen to $4 million and the carrying amount of the asset is $9 million ($12 million – $3 million). The entity will have transferred $1 million from revaluation surplus to retained earnings, being the difference between historical cost depreciation of $2 million and depreciation on the revalued amount of $3 million. The revaluation loss of $5 million will be charged first against the revaluation surplus remaining in equity of ($4 million – $1 million), ie $3 million and the balance of $2 million will be charged against profit or loss.

IAS 1 requires an entity to present a separate statement of changes in equity showing amongst other items, total comprehensive income for the period, reconciliations between the carrying amounts at the beginning and the end of the period for each component of equity, and an analysis of other comprehensive income.

47 Allsop

Workbook reference. Revenue recognition is covered in Chapter 3, deferred tax is covered in Chapter 7 and foreign currency transactions are covered in Chapter 16. Integrated Reporting is covered in Chapter 18.

Top tips. Part (a) of this question is difficult and contains two challenging situations. Make sure you do not spend all of your time on this part of the question and miss out on the marks available for the discussion in part (b). You should aim to generate one point per mark in part (b). Remember that you will gain marks for any valid point – not just those shown in the suggested solution below. In a discussion question like part (b), it is helpful to consider both benefits and limitations then come to a conclusion at the end of your answer.

Easy marks. There were easy marks you could pick up in part (b) for presenting the benefits and limitations of an integrated report.

Marking scheme

			Marks	
(a)	(i)	Explanation	3	
		Calculation	4	
		Explanation – historical rate	1	
				8
	(ii)	Bonus is variable consideration	1	
		Exclude bonus from transaction price at contract inception/end of first year	1	
		Satisfy performance obligation over time so recognise revenue over time	1	
		Recognise 65% of fixed consideration as revenue in first year	1	
		4 December 20X5: contract modified – include bonus in transaction price	1	
		Not an adjusting event after reporting period – account for in second year	1	
		Update percentage complete and estimates of revenue and costs	1	
				7
(b)		Usefulness of statement of cash flows and the Integrated Report – Discussion 1 mark per point to a maximum of 8 marks.		8

Points may include:

Usefulness of statement of cash flows
Liquidity, solvency, financial adaptability
Comparison of cash flows and profit
Predictive value
Link to rest of financial statements

Integrated Report
Limitations of financial statements
Aim of integrated reporting
Benefits of integrated reporting
Problems with integrated reporting

Professional marks	2
	25

(a) (i) **Deferred tax charge**

Investments in foreign branches (or subsidiaries, associates or joint arrangements) are affected by **changes in foreign exchange rates**. In this case, the branch's taxable profits are reported in dinars, and changes in the dinar/dollar exchange rate may give rise to temporary differences. These differences can arise where the carrying amounts of the non-monetary assets, such as property, are translated at historical rates and the tax base of those assets are translated at the closing rate. The **closing rate** may be used to translate the tax base because the resulting figure is an **accurate measure of the amount that will be deductible in future periods. The deferred tax is charged or credited to profit or loss**.

The deferred tax arising will be calculated **using the tax rate in the foreign branch's jurisdiction**, that is **20%**.

Property	Dinars ('000)	*Exchange rate*	Dollars ($'000)
Carrying amount:			
Cost	6,000	5	1,200
Depreciation for the year	(500)		(100)
Carrying amount	5,500		1,100
Tax base:			
Cost	6,000		
Tax depreciation	(750)		
Tax base	5,250	6	875
Taxable temporary difference			225
Deferred tax liability at 20%			45

The deferred tax charge in profit or loss will therefore increase by $45,000.

If the tax base had been translated at the historical rate, the tax base would have been $(5.25m ÷ 5m) = $1.05m. This gives a taxable temporary difference of $1.1m – $1.05m = $50,000, and therefore a deferred tax liability of $50,000 × 20% = $10,000. This is considerably lower than when the closing rate is used.

(ii) **Contract to construct machine**

Allsop should account for the promised bundle of goods and services as a single performance obligation satisfied over time in accordance with IFRS 15. At the inception of the contract, Allsop expects the following:

Transaction price	$1,500,000
Expected costs	$800,000
Expected profit (46.7%)	$700,000

The $100,000 **bonus** is **variable consideration** under IFRS 15. At the contract inception, Allsop should **exclude the $100,000 bonus** from the transaction price because it **cannot conclude** that it is **highly probable that a significant reversal in the amount of cumulative revenue recognised will not occur**. Completion of the construction of the machine is highly susceptible to factors outside the entity's influence.

This is a contract in which Allsop **satisfies its performance obligation over time**. Therefore, **revenue** should also be recognised **over time** by measuring the **progress towards complete satisfaction** of that performance obligation. By the end of the first year, Allsop has satisfied 65% of its performance obligation on the basis of costs incurred to date. Costs incurred to date are therefore $520,000 ($800,000 × 65%). Allsop reassessed the **variable consideration of $100,000** and concluded that the amount was still constrained which means that it **may not yet be recognised**. Therefore, at 30 November 20X5, only the **portion of the fixed consideration of $1,500,000** related to **progress to date** may be recognised as revenue. This results in revenue of $975,000 ($1,500,000 × 65%). The following amounts should therefore be included in the statement of profit or loss:

Revenue	$975,000
Costs	$520,000
Gross profit	$455,000

However, on 4 December 20X5, the contract was **modified**. As a result, the fixed consideration and expected costs increased by $110,000 and $60,000, respectively. This increased the fixed consideration to $1,610,000 ($1,500,000 + $110,000) and the expected costs to $860,000 ($800,000 + $60,000).

The total potential consideration after the modification was $1,710,000 ($1,610,000 fixed consideration + $100,000 completion bonus) as Allsop concluded that receipt of the bonus was highly probable and that including the bonus in the transaction price would **not result in a significant reversal in the amount of cumulative revenue recognised in accordance with IFRS 15**. Allsop also concluded that the contract remained a **single performance obligation**. Thus, Allsop should account for the **contract modification as if it were part of the original contract**. Therefore, Allsop should **update its estimates** of costs and revenue as follows:

Allsop has satisfied 60.5% of its performance obligation ($520,000 actual costs incurred compared to $860,000 total expected costs). It should recognise additional revenue of $59,550 [(60.5% of $1,710,000) – $975,000 revenue recognised to date] at the date of the modification as a cumulative catch-up adjustment. As the **contract amendment** took place **after the year end**, the additional revenue would **not** be treated as an **adjusting event** after the reporting period. Therefore, it should be accounted for in the year ended 30 November 20X6 rather than as an adjustment in the year ended 30 November 20X5.

(c) **Usefulness of statements of cash flows**

Liquidity, solvency and financial adaptability

Statements of cash flows provide valuable information to stakeholders on the entity's **liquidity** (its ability to pay its short-term obligations), **solvency** (its ability to meet its long-term financial commitments) and **financial adaptability** (its ability to take effective action to alter the amount and timing of its cash flows to respond to unexpected needs or opportunities). Information about cash flows helps stakeholders to understand the entity's operations and evaluate its investing and financing activities.

Comparison of cash flows and profit

Cash flows are objective and **verifiable** and so are more easily understood than profits. Profits can be manipulated through the use of judgement or by the choice of a particular accounting policy. Operating cash flows are therefore useful for highlighting the differences between cash and profits. The **cash generated from operations** is a useful **indication of the quality of the profits** generated by a business. Good quality profits will generate cash and increase the financial adaptability of an entity.

Predictive value

Cash flow information will also **have some predictive value**. Information about an entity's cash flows during a period can help users to assess the entity's ability to generate future net cash inflows. Therefore, it may assist stakeholders in making judgements on the amount, timing and degree of certainty of future cash flows.

Link to rest of the financial statements

Cash flow information should be **used in conjunction with the rest of the financial statements**. The adjustment of non-cash items within operating activities may not be easily understood. The classification of cash flows can be manipulated between operating, investing and financing activities, often to present the cash flows from operating activities favourably. It is important therefore not to examine the cash flow information in isolation. It is only through an analysis of the statement of financial position, statement of comprehensive income and notes, together with the cash flow, that a more comprehensive picture of the entity's position and performance develops.

Integrated Report

Limitations of financial statements

It is true that IFRS are extensive and their required disclosures very comprehensive. This has led to criticism that the usefulness of financial statements may be limited where the most **relevant information** is **obscured by immaterial disclosures**. The IASB has sought to address this through the issue of IFRS Practice Statement 2 *Making Materiality Judgements*. An entity should apply judgement when preparing its financial statements – disclosure is not required if the information provided by that disclosure is not material.

Aim of integrated reporting

Integrated reporting is designed to convey a **wider message** on organisational performance, covering **all of an entity's resources** and **how it uses these 'capitals' to create value** over the short-, medium- and long-term, not only its financial resources.

Benefits of integrated reporting

Integrated reporting will provide **stakeholders** with **valuable information** which would not be immediately accessible from an entity's financial statements.

Financial statements are based on **historical information** and may **lack predictive value**. They are essential in corporate reporting, particularly for compliance purposes but do not provide meaningful information regarding business value.

The **primary purpose** of an **integrated report** is to **explain** to providers of capital **how the organisation generates value over time**. This is summarised through an examination of the key activities and outputs of the organisation whether they be financial, manufactured, intellectual, human, social or natural.

An integrated report seeks to **examine the external environment** which the entity operates within and to provide an insight into the entity's resources and relationships to generate value. It is **principles based** and should be **driven by materiality**, including how and to what extent the entity understands and responds to the needs of its stakeholders. This would include an analysis of **how the entity has performed within its business environment**, together with a description of **prospects and challenges for the future**. It is this strategic direction which is lacking from a traditional set of financial statements and will be invaluable to stakeholders to make a more informed assessment of the organisation and its prospects.

Problems with integrated reporting

An integrated reporting system would **increase disclosure** as well as imposing **additional time and cost constraints** on the reporting entity. It may require changes to IT systems in order to capture the data, as well as the initial use of an external consultancy to design the report.

Conclusion

Arguably, an Integrated Report may give improved information to stakeholders and therefore provide a coherent story about the business which **goes above and beyond that provided by the statement of cash flows** regarding liquidity, solvency and the financial adaptability of a business. It may help the entity to think holistically about its strategy and manage key risks, as well as make informed decisions and **build investor confidence**.

However, the entity must assess **whether** it believes those **benefits outweigh the potential disadvantages** of the extra cost and administration it may incur as the report remains voluntary.

48 Kiki

Marking scheme

			Marks
(a)	(i)	1 mark per point up to maximum	6
	(ii)	1 mark per point up to maximum	6
(b)		1 mark per point up to maximum	11
		Professional	2
			25

(a) (i) **Gift cards**

IFRS 15 *Revenue from Contracts with Customers* says that revenue should be recognised when or as a performance obligation is satisfied by transferring the promised good or service to the customer. When a customer buys a gift card they are pre-paying for a product. Revenue cannot be recognised because the entity has not yet transferred control over an asset and so has not satisfied a performance obligation. As such, cash received in respect of gift cards should be initially recognised as a contract liability.

IFRS 15 refers to a customer's unexercised rights as breakage. The guidance for variable consideration is followed when estimating breakage. In other words, the expected breakage is included in the transaction price if it is highly probable that a significant reversal in the amount of cumulative revenue recognised will not occur once the uncertainty is subsequently resolved. This means that if the company is unable to reliably estimate the breakage amount, then revenue for the unused portion of the gift card is recognised when the likelihood of the customer exercising their remaining rights becomes remote. However, if an entity is able to reliably estimate the breakage amount, then it recognises the expected breakage amount as revenue in proportion to the pattern of rights exercised by the customer.

In relation to Kiki, it appears that the amount of breakage can be reliably determined and so this should be recognised in revenue as the gift card is redeemed. For every $1 redeemed, Kiki should recognise $1.43 ($1 × 100/70) in revenue.

(ii) **Royalty**

According to IFRS 15, an entity should only account for revenue from a contract with a customer when it meets the following criteria:

- The contract has been approved;
- Rights regarding goods and services can be identified;
- Payment terms can be identified;
- It is probable the seller will collect the consideration it is entitled to.

At inception of the agreement, Kiki and Colour entered an explicit contract which specified payment terms and conditions. Moreover, Colour had a strong credit rating and so payment was probable. As such, it would seem that the above criteria were met. IFRS 15 says that revenue from a usage-based royalty should be recognised as the usage occurs.

Whether a contract with a customer meets the above criteria is only reassessed if there is a significant change in facts and circumstances. In July 20X7, Colour lost major customers and sources of finance. As such, it was no longer probable that Kiki would collect the consideration it was entitled to. From July 20X7, no further revenue from the contract should be recognised.

According to IFRS 9 *Financial Instruments*, non-payment is an indicator that the outstanding receivables are credit impaired. A loss allowance should be recognised equivalent to the difference between the gross carrying amount of the receivables and the present value of the expected future cash flows receivable from Colour. Any increase or decrease in the loss allowance is charged to profit or loss.

(b) **Investment properties**

In accordance with IAS 40 *Investment Property*, the buildings should be initially measured at cost.

If the cost model is applied, then the buildings will be recognised at cost less accumulated depreciation and impairment losses.

If the fair value model is applied, then the buildings will be remeasured to fair value at each reporting date. Gains and losses on remeasurement are recognised in the statement of profit or loss. No depreciation is charged.

Statement of financial position

Assuming that property prices rise, the fair value model will lead to an increase in reported assets on the statement of financial position. In contrast, investment property measured using the cost model is depreciated, which reduces its carrying amount. This means that the fair value model may make Kiki appear more asset-rich. Some stakeholders may place importance on an entity's asset base, as it can be used as security for obtaining new finance. However, reporting higher assets can sometimes be perceived negatively. For example, asset turnover ratios will deteriorate, and so Kiki may appear less efficient.

If assets increase, then equity also increases. As such, the fair value model may lead to Kiki reporting a more optimistic gearing ratio. This may reduce the perception of risk, encouraging further investment.

Statement of profit or loss

In times of rising prices, the use of the fair value model will lead to gains being reported in the statement of profit or loss. This will increase profits for the period. In contrast, the depreciation charged under the cost model will reduce profits for the period. Therefore, earnings per share, a key stock market and investor ratio, is likely to be higher if the fair value model is adopted.

However, it should be noted that fair values are volatile. In some years, fair value gains may be much larger than in other years. If property prices decline, then the fair value model will result in losses. As such, reported profits are subject to more volatility if the fair value model is adopted. This may increase stakeholders' perception of risk. In contrast, the depreciation expense recorded in accordance with the cost model will be much more predictable, meaning that investors will be better able to predict Kiki's future results.

Many entities now present alternative performance measures (APMs), such as EBITDA (earnings before interest, tax, depreciation and amortisation). Other entities present 'underlying profit' indicators, which strip out the impact of non-operating or non-recurring gains or losses (such as the remeasurement of investment properties). Although the use of APMs has been criticised, Kiki may consider them to be useful in helping investors to assess underlying business performance through the eyes of management and to eliminate the impact of certain accounting policy choices.

Statement of cash flows

Accounting policy choices have no impact on the operating, investing or financing cash flows reported in the statement of cash flows.

Disclosure

It should be noted that entities using the cost model for investment properties are required to disclose the fair value. Such disclosures enable better comparisons to be drawn between entities which account for investment property under different models.

49 Holls

Marking scheme

			Marks	
(a)	(i)	Arguments for and against the non-binding framework		4
	(ii)	• A discussion of understandability, relevance and comparability	3	
		• Application of the above characteristics to MC	2	
				5
(b)		An explanation of why taxable profits are different from accounting profit	2	
		Application of the following explanations to the scenario:		
		• Tax reconciliation	4	
		• Tax rates	3	
		• Deferred taxation	5	
				14
				2
				25

(a) (i) The IFRS Practice Statement *Management Commentary* provides a broad, non-binding framework for the presentation of management commentary. The Practice Statement is not an IFRS. Consequently, entities applying IFRSs are not required to comply with the Practice Statement, unless specifically required by their jurisdiction. Furthermore, non-compliance with the Practice Statement will not prevent an entity's financial statements from complying with IFRSs.

It can be argued that the International Accounting Standards Board's objectives of enhancing consistency and comparability may not be achieved if the framework is not mandatory. A standard is more likely to guarantee a consistent application of the principles and practices behind the management commentary (MC).

However, it is difficult to create a standard on the MC which is sufficiently detailed to cover the business models of every entity or be consistent with all IFRSs. Some jurisdictions take little notice of non-mandatory guidance but the Practice Statement provides regulators with a framework to develop more authoritative requirements.

The Practice Statement allows companies to adapt the information provided to particular aspects of their business. This flexible approach could help generate more meaningful disclosures about resources, risks and relationships which can affect an entity's value and how these resources are managed. It provides management with an opportunity to add context to the published financial information, and to explain their future strategy and objectives without being restricted by the constraints of a standard.

If the MC were a full IFRS, the integration of management commentaries and the information produced in accordance with IFRSs could be challenged on technical grounds, as well as its practical merits. In addition, there could be jurisdictional concerns that any form of integration might not be accepted by local regulators.

(ii) The *Framework* states that 'an essential quality of the information provided in financial statements is that it is readily understandable by users'. The MC should be written in plain language and a style appropriate to users' needs. The primary users of management commentary are those identified in the *Conceptual Framework*. The form and content of the MC will vary between entities, reflecting the nature of their business, the strategies adopted and the regulatory environment in which they operate. Users should be able to locate information relevant to their needs.

Information has the quality of relevance when it has the capacity to influence the economic decisions of users by helping them evaluate past, present or future events or confirming, or correcting, their past evaluations. Relevant financial information is capable of making a difference to the decision made by users. In order to make a difference, financial information has predictive value, confirmatory value or both. The onus is on management to determine what information is important enough to be included in the MC to enable users to 'understand' the financial statements and meet the objective of the MC. If the entity provides too much information, it could reduce its relevance and understandability. If material events or uncertainties are not disclosed, then users may have insufficient information to meet their needs.

However, unnecessary detail may obscure important information especially if entities adopt a boiler-plate approach. If management presents too much information about, for example, all the risks facing an organisation, this will conflict with the relevance objective. There is no single optimal number of disclosures but it is useful to convey their relative importance in a meaningful way.

Comparability is the qualitative characteristic which enables users to identify and understand similarities and differences amongst items. It is important for users to be able to compare information over time and between entities. Comparability between entities is problematic as the MC is designed to reflect the perspectives of management and the circumstances of individual entities. Thus, entities in the same industry may have different perceptions of what is important and how they measure and report it. There are some precedents on how to define and calculate non-financial measures and financial measures which are not produced in accordance with IFRSs but there are inconsistencies in the definition and calculation of these measures.

It is sometimes suggested that the effectiveness of the overall report may be enhanced by strengthening the links between financial statements and the MC. However, such suggestions raise concerns about maintaining a clear distinction between the financial statement information and other information.

An entity should ensure consistency in terms of wording, definitions, segment disclosures, etc between the financial statements and the MC to improve the understanding of financial performance.

(b) Current tax is based on taxable profit for the year. Taxable profit is different from accounting profit due to temporary differences between accounting and tax treatments, and due to items which are never taxable or tax deductible. Tax benefits such as tax credits are not recognised unless it is probable that the tax positions are sustainable.

The Group is required to estimate the corporate tax in each of the many jurisdictions in which it operates. The Group is subject to tax audits in many jurisdictions; as a result, the Group may be required to make an adjustment in a subsequent period which could have a material impact on the Group's profit for the year.

Tax reconciliation

The tax rate reconciliation is important for understanding the tax charge reported in the financial statements and why the effective tax rate differs from the statutory rate.

Most companies will reconcile the group's annual tax expense to the statutory rate in the country in which the parent is based. Hence the rate of 22% is used in the tax reconciliation. It is important that the reconciliation explains the reasons for the differences between the effective rate and the statutory rate. There should be minimal use of the 'other' category. In this case, the other category is quite significant ($14 million) and there is no explanation of what 'other' constitutes.

One-off and unusual items can have a significant effect on the effective tax rate, but financial statements and notes often do not include a detailed discussion of them. For example, the brand impairment and disposals of businesses should be explained to investors, as they are probably material items. The explanation should include any potential reversal of the treatment.

Some profits recognised in the financial statements are non-taxable such as the tax relating to non-taxable gains on disposals of businesses and in some jurisdictions, taxation relief on impairment losses will not be allowable for taxation. The reasons for these items not being allowed for taxation should be explained to investors.

Tax rates

As the Group is operating in multiple countries, the actual tax rates applicable to profits in those countries are different from the local tax rate. The overseas tax rates are higher than local rates, hence the increase in the taxation charge of $10 million. The local rate is different from the weighted average tax rate (27%) of the Group based on the different jurisdictions in which it operates. Investors may feel that using the weighted tax rate in the reconciliation gives a more meaningful number because it is a better estimate of the tax rate the Group expects to pay over the long term. Investors will wish to understand the company's expected long-term sustainable tax rate so they can prepare their cash flow or profit forecasts.

Information about the sustainability of the tax rate over the long term is more important than whether the rate is high or low compared to other jurisdictions. An adjustment can be made to an investor's financial model for a long-term sustainable rate, but not for a volatile rate where there is no certainty over future performance. For modelling purposes, an understanding of the actual cash taxes paid is critical and the cash paid of $95 million can be found in the statement of cash flows.

Deferred taxation

Provision for deferred tax is made for temporary differences between the carrying amount of assets and liabilities for financial reporting purposes and their value for tax purposes. The amount of deferred tax reflects the expected recoverable amount and is based on the expected manner of recovery or settlement of the carrying amount of assets and liabilities, using the basis of taxation enacted or substantively enacted by the financial statement date.

Deferred tax assets are not recognised where it is more likely than not that the assets will not be realised in the future and reference to IAS 37 *Provisions, Contingent Liabilities and Contingent Assets* is useful in this regard. The evaluation of deferred tax assets' recoverability requires judgements to be made regarding the availability of future taxable income.

Management assesses the available evidence to estimate if sufficient future taxable income will be generated to use the existing deferred tax assets. A significant piece of objective negative evidence evaluated was the loss incurred in the period prior to the period ended 30 November 20X7. Such objective evidence may limit the ability to consider other subjective evidence such as projections for future growth. Deferred taxes are one of the most difficult areas of the financial statements for investors to understand. Thus there is a need for a clear explanation of the deferred tax balances and an analysis of the expected timing of reversals. This would help investors see the time period over which deferred tax assets arising from losses might reverse. It would be helpful if the company provided a breakdown of which reversals would have a cash tax impact and which would not.

As the proposed tax law was approved, it is considered to be enacted. Therefore, the rate of 25% should be used to calculate the deferred tax liability associated with the relevant items which affect deferred taxation.

At 30 November 20X7, Holls has deductible temporary differences of $4.5 million which are expected to reverse in the next year. In addition, Holls also has taxable temporary differences of $5 million which relate to the same taxable company and the tax authority. Holls expects $3 million of those taxable temporary differences to reverse in 20X8 and the remaining $2 million to reverse in 20X9. Thus a deferred tax liability of $1.25 million ($5 million × 25%) should be recognised and as $3 million of these taxable temporary differences are expected to reverse in the year in which the deductible temporary differences reverse, Holls can also recognise a deferred tax asset for $0.75 million ($3 million × 25%). The recognition of a deferred tax asset for the rest of the deductible temporary differences will depend on whether future taxable profits sufficient to cover the reversal of this deductible temporary difference are expected to arise. Deferred tax assets and liabilities must be recognised gross in the statement of financial position. However, it may be possible to offset the deferred tax assets and the deferred tax liabilities if there is a legally enforceable right to offset the current income tax assets against current income tax liabilities as the amounts relate to income tax levied by the same taxation authority on the same taxable entity.

After the enactment of a new tax law, when material, Holls should consider disclosing the anticipated current and future impact on their results of operations, financial position, liquidity, and capital resources. In addition, Holls should consider disclosures in the critical accounting estimates section of the management commentary to the extent the changes could materially affect existing assumptions used in making estimates of tax-related balances. Changes in tax laws and rates may affect recorded deferred tax assets and liabilities and the effective tax rate in the future.

50 Kayte

Workbook references. The Conceptual Framework and interim financial reporting are covered in chapter 1. IAS 16 is covered in Chapter 4. IFRS 5 is covered in Chapter 13.

Top tips. Part (a) required you to discuss the probability recognition criterion in the 2010 Conceptual Framework. Don't be put off by the fact this is the 2010 Conceptual Framework, as the relevant part of it has been given in the question. The question told you which standards to discuss – make sure you address what it asks for. Part (b)(i) covered the application of IAS 16 and was demanding, indicative of what could be asked in an SBR exam on topics covered in your earlier studies.

Easy marks. There were some easy marks available in part (a) for stating the recognition criteria in the 2018 Conceptual Framework. In part (b)(ii) you should have been able to apply the IFRS 5 accounting treatment for non-current assets held for sale even if you were unfamiliar with IAS 34.

Marking scheme

			Marks
(a)	Inconsistent application of the probability criterion (one per example)	3	
	Changes to the recognition criteria in 2018 *Conceptual Framework*	3	
			6
(b)	(i) Vessels sold after 10 years	5	
	Vessels kept for 30 years	5	
	Funnels	2	
			12
(c)	Interim follow same accounting policies as for annual financial statements	1	
	Measure asset at lower of carrying amount and fair value less costs to sell	1	
	1.10.20X3: recognise impairment loss of $100,000	1	
	1.12.20X4: reverse impairment loss of $120,000 as less than cumulative impairment losses to date of $45,000	1	
	31.5.20X4: can only recognise $330,000 of the $430,000 increase in fair value less costs to sell (up to remaining cumulative impairment losses to date)	1	
	5.6.20X4: recognise gain on disposal	1	
	Gain on disposal is non-adjusting event after the reporting period	1	
			7
			25

(a) **Probability criterion**

Different accounting standards use different levels of probability to discuss when assets and liabilities should be recognised in the financial statements.

For example:

- Economic benefits from property, plant and equipment and intangible assets need to be **probable** to be recognised; but to be classified as held for sale, the sale has to be **highly probable**.
- Under IAS 37 *Provisions, Contingent Liabilities and Contingent Assets,* a provision should be **probable** to be recognised, but uncertain assets on the other hand would have to be **virtually certain** to be disclosed. This could lead to a situation where two sides of the same court case have two different accounting treatments despite the likelihood of payout being identical for both parties.
- Contingent consideration is recognised in the financial statements **regardless of the level of probability**. Rather the fair value is adjusted to reflect the level of uncertainty of the contingent consideration.

The 2018 *Conceptual Framework* requires an item to be recognised in the financial statements if:

(a) The item meets the definition of an **element** (asset, liability, income, expense or equity); and

(b) Recognition of that element provides users of the financial statements with information that is **useful**, ie with:

- **Relevant** information about the element
- A **faithful representation** of the element

While this will not remove the inconsistencies in recognition criteria that currently exist across IFRS Standards, it does provide a basis for the IASB to consider when developing new Standards and revising existing Standards.

Furthermore, the new criteria may mean that more assets and liabilities with a low probability of inflow or outflow of economic resources are likely to be recognised. The criteria also allow for Standards to contain recognition criteria that may be considered inconsistent, but this may be a necessary consequence of providing the most useful information.

(b) (i) **Vessels**

Vessels sold at ten years old

Kayte's estimate of the residual life of these vessels is **based on acquisition cost.** This is **unacceptable** under IAS 16 Property, Plant and Equipment. IAS 16 defines residual value as:

> 'The estimated amount that an entity would currently obtain from disposal of the asset, after deducting the estimated costs of disposal, if the asset were already of the age and in the condition expected at the end of its useful life.' (para. 6)

IAS 16 requires that property, plant and equipment must be depreciated so that its depreciable amount is allocated on a systematic basis over its useful life. Depreciable amount is the cost of an asset less its residual value. IAS 16 stipulates that the **residual value must be reviewed at least each financial year-end** and, if expectations differ from previous estimates, any change is accounted for prospectively as a change in estimate under IAS 8 *Accounting Policies, Changes in Accounting Estimates and Errors.*

Kayte's model implies that the residual value of the vessels remains constant through the vessels' useful life. However, the **residual value should be adjusted,** particularly as the date of sale approaches and the residual value approaches proceeds of disposal less costs of disposal at the end of the asset's useful life.

Following IAS 16, if the residual value is greater than an asset's carrying amount, the depreciation charge is zero until such time as the residual value subsequently decreases to an amount below the asset's carrying amount. The residual value should be the value at the reporting date as if the vessel were already of the age and condition expected at the end of its useful life. Depreciable amount is affected by an increase in the residual value of an asset because of past events, but not by expectation of changes in future events, other than the expected effects of wear and tear.

The **useful life of the vessels (10 years) is shorter than the total life (30 years)** so it is the residual value at the end of the 10-year useful life that must be established.

Vessels kept for 30 years

Kayte **correctly uses a residual value for these vessels based upon the scrap value of steel**. The depreciable amount of the vessels is therefore the cost less the scrap value of steel, and the vessels should be depreciated over the 30-year period.

The engine is a significant part of the asset and should be depreciated separately over its useful life of ten years until the date of the next overhaul. The cost of the overhaul should be capitalised (a necessary overhaul is not considered a day-to-day servicing cost) and any carrying amount relating to the engine before overhaul should be derecognised. Generally however the depreciation of the original amount capitalised in respect of the engine will be **calculated to have a carrying amount of nil when the overhaul is undertaken**.

Funnels

The funnels should be identified as significant parts of the asset and depreciated across their useful lives of 15 years. As this has not occurred, it will be necessary to **determine what the carrying amount would have been had the funnels been initially separately identified**. The initial cost of the funnels can be determined by reference to replacement cost, and the associated depreciation charge determined using the rate for the vessel (over 30 years). There will therefore be a significant carrying amount to be written off at the time the replacement funnels are capitalised.

(ii) **Property**

IAS 34 requirement

In accordance with IAS 34 *Interim Financial Reporting,* an entity must apply the same accounting policies in its interim financial statements as in its annual financial statements. Measurements should be made on a 'year to date' basis. Kayte's interim financial statements are for the six months to 30 November 20X3.

Kayte must apply the provisions of IFRS 5 *Non-Current Assets Held for Sale and Discontinued Operations* to the valuation of the property.

Application of IFRS 5

In accordance with IFRS 5, an asset held for sale should be measured at the **lower of** its **carrying amount** and **fair value less costs to sell**. Immediately before classification of the asset as held for sale, the entity must recognise impairment in accordance with applicable IFRS. Any impairment loss is generally recognised in profit or loss, but if the asset has been measured at a revalued amount under IAS 16 or IAS 38 the impairment will be treated as a revaluation decrease. **Once** the asset has been **classified as held for sale**, any **impairment loss** will be based on the **difference between the adjusted carrying amounts and the fair value less cost to sell**. The impairment loss (if any) will be **recognised in profit or loss**.

A **subsequent increase** in fair value less costs to sell may be **recognised** in profit or loss **only to the extent of any impairment previously recognised**. To summarise:

Step 1 Calculate carrying amount under the applicable accounting standard, here IAS 16:

Depreciation of $500,000 per year implies a useful life of ten years, of which eight years are remaining at 1 June 20X3. Depreciation must then be charged for the four months to 1 October 20X3, the date of classification as held for sale is calculated on the carrying amount net of the impairment loss incurred on 31 May 20X3, over the remaining useful life of eight years:

$$\frac{\$5\text{m cost} - \$1\text{m accumulated depreciation} - \$0.35\text{m impairment}}{8\text{-year remaining useful life}} \times 4/12$$

= $152,083 (rounded to $0.15 million)

So the carrying amount at 1 October 20X3 is $5m – $1m – $0.35m – $0.15m = $3.5 million

Step 2 Classified as held for sale. Compare the carrying amount ($3.5 million) with fair value less costs to sell ($3.4 million). Measure at the lower of carrying amount and fair value less costs to sell, here $3.4 million, giving an initial write-down of $100,000. Cease depreciation.

Step 3 Determine fair value less costs to sell at the date of the interim financial statements, 1 December 20X3, here given as $3.52 million and compare with carrying amount of $3.4 million. This gives a gain of $120,000.

The impairment previously recognised is: $350,000 + $100,000 = $450,000. The gain of $120,000 is less than this, and may therefore be credited to profit or loss, and the property is carried at $3.52 million.

Step 4 On 31 May 20X4, fair value less costs to sell is $3.95 million. The change in fair value less cost to sell is recognised but the gain recognised cannot exceed any impairment losses to date. Impairment losses to date are $350,000 + $100,000 – $120,000 = $330,000, and this is less than the change in fair value less costs to sell of $430,000 ($3.95m – $3.52m). This restricted gain of $330,000 is recognised, and the property is carried at $3.85 million ($3.52m + $330,000).

51 Fill

Marking scheme

			Marks
(a)	A discussion of potential measurement basis, NRV and relevant Standards	3	
	Application of IAS 2 to the scenario	4	
			7
(b)	A discussion of IAS 16 and application to the scenario	4	
	A discussion of IAS 36 and application to the scenario	4	
			8
(c)	A discussion of control in the *Conceptual Framework* and other relevant Standards	4	
	A discussion of a business combination per IFRS 3	2	
	Application of the above discussions to the scenario	4	
			10
			25

(a) (i) Inventories should be valued at the lower of cost and net realisable value. The *Conceptual Framework* acknowledges a variety of measurement bases including historical cost, current cost, value-in-use and fair value. Historical cost is consistent with the cost valuation in IAS 2, however value in use and fair value are not:

- Value-in-use requires the use of the present value of future cash flows.
- Fair value is a market-based measurement, not an entity-specific measurement. When determining fair value, the assumptions used are those that market participants would use when pricing the asset, this would not take into consideration entity-specific factors like the cost needed to complete an asset and sell it.

The *Conceptual Framework* is not a Standard and does not override the requirements of a Standard, therefore in order to determine NRV, the directors would need to refer to IAS 2 *Inventories*.

(ii) IAS 2 defines NRV as the estimated selling price in the ordinary course of business less the costs of completion and costs of sale.

NRV is an entity-specific measure which should be determined on the basis of conditions which existed at the date of the statement of financial position.

To estimate NRV, Fill should take into consideration future price movements if they provide information about the conditions at the reporting date. However, normally these movements would reflect changes in the market conditions after that date and therefore would not affect the calculation of NRV.

The NRV will be based upon the most reliable estimate of the amounts which will be realised for the coal.

Fill should calculate the NRV of the low carbon coal using the forecast market price based upon when the inventory is expected to be processed and realised. The forecast market price should be adjusted for the time value of money (where this is material) and for processing and selling costs to give a reasonable estimate of NRV.

Future changes in the forecast market price or the processing and sale of the low carbon coal may result in adjustments to the NRV. As these adjustments are changes in estimates, IAS 8 *Accounting Policies, Changes in Accounting Estimates and Errors* will apply with the result that such gains and losses will be recognised in the statement of profit or loss in the period in which they arise.

Tutorial note.

The year-end spot price will provide good evidence of the realisable value of the inventories at the year end. The forward contract price may be appropriate if the company has an executory contract to sell coal at a future date. However, if the company does not have an executory contract, but instead a financial instrument under IFRS 9 *Financial Instruments* or an onerous contract recognised as a provision under IAS 37 *Provisions, Contingent Liabilities and Contingent* Assets, the forward contract price is unlikely to be used to calculate NRV.

(b) IAS 16 *Property, Plant and Equipment* (PPE) requires an entity to recognise in the carrying amount of PPE the cost of replacing part of such an item. When each major inspection is performed, its cost is recognised in the carrying amount of the item of PPE as a replacement if the recognition criteria are satisfied. Any remaining carrying amount of the cost of a previous inspection is derecognised. The costs of performing a major reconditioning are capitalised if it gives access to future economic benefits. Such costs will include the labour and materials costs ($3 million) of performing the reconditioning. However, costs which do not relate to the replacement of components or the installation of new assets, such as routine maintenance costs, should be expensed as incurred.

It is not acceptable to accrue the costs of reconditioning equipment as there is no legal or apparent constructive obligation to undertake the reconditioning. As set out above, the cost of the reconditioning should be identified as a separate component of the mine asset at initial recognition and depreciated over a period of two years. This will result in the same amount of expense being recognised as the proposal to create a provision.

IAS 36 *Impairment of Assets* says that at the end of each reporting period, an entity is required to assess whether there is any indication that an asset may be impaired. IAS 36 has a list of external and internal indicators of impairment. If there is an indication that an asset may be impaired, then the asset's recoverable amount must be calculated.

Past and future reductions in selling prices may indicate that the future economic benefits which relate to the asset have been reduced. Mining assets should be tested for impairment whenever indicators of impairment exist. Impairments are recognised if a mine's carrying amount exceeds its recoverable amount. However, the nature of mining assets is that they often have a long useful life. Commodity prices can be volatile but downward price movements are more significant if they are likely to persist for longer periods. In this case, there is evidence of a decline in forward prices. If the decline in prices is for a significant proportion of the remaining expected life of the mine, this is more likely to be an impairment indicator. It appears that forward contract prices for two years out of the three years of the mine's remaining life indicate a reduction in selling prices. Based on market information, Fill has also calculated that the three-year forecast price of coal will be 20% lower than the current spot price (Part (a) of question).

Short-term market fluctuations may not be impairment indicators if prices are expected to return to higher levels. However, despite the difficulty in making such assessments, it would appear that the mining assets should be tested for impairment.

(c) The *Conceptual Framework for Financial Reporting* states that an entity controls an economic resource if it has the present ability to direct the use of the economic resource and obtain the economic benefits that may flow from it. An entity has the ability to direct the use of an economic resource if it has the right to deploy that economic resource in its activities. Although control of an economic resource usually arises from legal rights, it can also arise if an entity has the present ability to prevent all other parties from directing the use of it and obtaining the benefits from the economic resource. For an entity to control a resource, the economic benefits from the resource must flow to the entity instead of another party.

Although the *Conceptual Framework* gives some guidance on the definition of control, existing IFRSs also provide help in determining whether Fill controls the mine and therefore should account for it as a business combination:

- IFRS 10 *Consolidated Financial Statements* states that an investor controls an investee when it is exposed, or has rights, to variable returns from its involvement with the investee and has the ability to affect those returns through its power over the investee.
- IFRS 15 *Revenue from Contracts with Customers* lists indicators of the transfer of control of an asset to a customer. One of the indicators is that the customer has the significant risks and rewards of ownership of the asset which is basically exposure to significant variations in the amount of economic benefits.

A business combination is defined in IFRS 3 *Business Combinations* as a transaction or other event in which an acquirer obtains control of one or more businesses. A business is further defined as 'an integrated set of activities and assets that is capable of being conducted and managed for the purpose of providing a return...' Thus the producing mine represents a business and Fill now owns a majority of the interest in the business.

However, this is not a business combination as Fill does not have the ability to affect decisions unless another participant agrees to vote with Fill. Although Fill will control 52% of the mine, it cannot direct the use of the economic resource unless one of the other participants agrees with an operating decision proposed by Fill and approval is given by 72% of participants. However, Fill can prevent the other parties from directing the use of the mine if the purchase goes ahead, because the other two parties cannot make an operating decision without Fill's consent. Prior to the purchase of the additional investment, the approval of decisions required agreement by 72% of the participating interests. A joint control situation existed between the entities. Following the additional purchase, there is still a joint control situation as Fill's interest does not meet the 72% threshold. Therefore the transaction will be treated as an asset acquisition and no goodwill will arise on the acquisition.

52 Zedtech

Marking scheme

				Marks
(a)	(i)	– discussion of recognition per current *Conceptual Framework*	2	
		– discussion of the ED's approach to recognition	2	
		– comparison and contrast	3	7
	(ii)	– discussion of IAS 12 recognition criteria	2	
		– discussion of IAS 37 recognition criteria	2	
		– discussion of recognition in business combinations	2	6
(b	(i)	– discussion of the collectability of consideration	2	
		– discussion of performance obligations	3	5
	(ii)	– application of the above principles to:		
		0inventory	2	
		InventoryX	3	
		– collectability assessment	2	7
				25

(a) (i) Existing IFRS did not consistently apply the recognition criteria included in the 2010 *Conceptual Framework* and thus the revised 2018 *Conceptual Framework* sets out new principles for the recognition in the financial statements. The revised 2018 *Conceptual Framework* defines recognition as the process of capturing for inclusion in the financial statements an item which meets the definition of an element. Assets and liabilities are both elements of the financial statements, along with equity, income and expenses. This approach requires recognition decisions to be made by reference to the qualitative characteristics of useful financial information.

The revised 2018 *Conceptual Framework* requires that the elements of financial statements should be recognised if it provides users of financial statements with information that is useful, ie with:

- **Relevant** information about the element
- A **faithful representation** of the element

Recognition is subject to **cost constraints**: the benefits of the information provided by recognising an element should justify the costs of recognising that element.

Recognition may not provide relevant information where it is uncertain whether an asset exists, or is separable from goodwill, or whether a liability exists and where there is only a low probability that an inflow or outflow of economic benefits will occur. Additionally, if the level of measurement uncertainty is so high that the resulting information has little relevance, then recognition should not occur. The IASB decided that the revised 2018 *Conceptual Framework* should not contain a 'probability criterion', which means that there may be recognition of assets or liabilities with a low probability of an inflow or outflow of economic benefit.

(ii) According to IAS 12 *Income Taxes*, deferred tax liabilities are recognised for all taxable temporary differences, with three exceptions. However, deferred tax assets are only recognised to the extent that it is **probable** that taxable profit will be available against which the deductible temporary differences can be utilised. Thus the standard applies a probability threshold to deferred tax assets but not to liabilities.

Although the 2010 *Conceptual Framework* gave the same threshold for recognition of assets and liabilities, IAS 37 *Provisions, Contingent Liabilities and Contingent Assets* requires the recognition of assets when they are virtually certain but for liabilities when they are probable, defined as more likely than not. IAS 37 also requires the recognition of liabilities for constructive obligations. Thus, the definition of an obligation under IAS 37 can often be broader than in other standards, for example, IAS 32 *Financial Instruments: Presentation*. IAS 37 includes a probable outflow threshold for the recognition of provisions but the recognition threshold does not apply to obligations which normally fall within the scope of IAS 37 when they are acquired as part of a business combination.

IFRS 3 *Business Combinations* requires recognition of the contingent liabilities of a subsidiary irrespective of their probability. IFRS 10 *Consolidated Financial Statements* requires recognition at fair value of contingent consideration to be received for a business which is disposed of, even if the inflow is not probable. Thus, these items are recognised under IFRS 3/IFRS 10 when they arise from a business combination, whereas they are not recognised in the normal course of business.

(b) (i) IFRS 15 *Revenue from Contracts with Customers* states that an entity must first identify the contract with the customer and as part of that identification, the entity has to determine whether it is probable that the consideration which the entity is entitled to in exchange for the goods or services will be collected. An assessment of collectability is included as one of the criteria for determining whether a contract with a customer exists.

IFRS 15 states that the entity must identify the performance obligations in the contract. Once an entity has identified the contract with a customer, it evaluates the contractual terms and its customary business practices to identify all the promised goods or services within the contract and determine which of those promised goods or services will be treated as separate performance obligations. An entity will have to decide whether the obligations are distinct or part of a series of distinct goods and services which are substantially the same and have the same pattern of transfer to the customer. A good or service is distinct if the customer can benefit from the good or service on its own.

(ii) Technology entities often enter into transactions involving the delivery of multiple goods and services.

As regards 0inventory, it seems that all of the individual goods and services in the contract are distinct because the entity regularly sells each element of the contract separately and is not providing the significant service of integrating the goods and services. Also, as the customer could purchase each good and service without significantly affecting the other goods and services purchased, there is no dependence upon individual elements of the service. Thus hardware, professional services and hosting services should each be accounted for as separate performance obligations.

Regarding InventoryX, the professional services are distinct because Zedtech frequently sells those services on a stand-alone basis.

However, the hardware is always sold in a combined contract with the professional and hosting services and the customer cannot use the hardware on its own. As a result, the hardware is not distinct and because the hardware is integral to the delivery of the hosted software, the hardware and hosting services should be accounted for as one performance obligation while the professional services, which are distinct, would be a separate performance obligation.

When performing the collectability assessment, Zedtech only considers the customer's ability and intention to pay the expected consideration when due. Zedtech has entered into an arrangement and does not expect to collect the full contractual amount such that the contract contains an implied price concession. Therefore, Zedtech needs to assess the collectability of the amount to which it expects to be entitled, rather than the stated contractual amount. Zedtech assesses whether collectability is probable, whether the customer has the ability and intent to pay the estimated transaction price. Zedtech will determine that the amount to which it expects to be entitled is $2.4 million and performs the collectability assessment based on that amount, rather than the contractual price of $3 million.

53 Royan

Workbook references. Provisions and contingent liabilities are covered in Chapter 6 of your Workbook. Ethics are covered in Chapter 2.

Top tips. Part (a) of the question requires discussion and critique of the general requirements of IAS 37. Providing critique is difficult but you could have scored reasonable credit from discussion of the basic guidance. For part (b),it is very important to read the scenario carefully as there are clues in the question which are there to help you. In part (c), you should be aware that contingent liabilities are treated differently in individual and consolidated financial statements.

For learning purposes, this question included some discussion of ethical issues in the context of the scenario given. However, please note that ethics will not feature in Section B questions in the real exam. Ethics will be examined only in Question 2 of the exam.

Easy marks. There were some marks for simply spelling out current guidance, which is rote learning. Part (b)(ii) on ethics allows you to present both sides of the argument, gaining easy marks if you are able to use the information given in the question to discuss the ethical issues.

Marking scheme

			Marks
(a)	Existing guidance and critique		12
(b)	(i)	IAS 37 treatment	3
	(ii)	Ethics	5
(c)	Contingent liability		5
			25

(a) **Guidance in IAS 37**

Under IAS 37 *Provisions, Contingent Liabilities and Contingent Assets,* provisions must be recognised in the following circumstances.

(i) There is a **legal** or **constructive obligation** to transfer benefits as a result of past events.

(ii) It is **probable** that **an outflow of economic resources** will be required to **settle** the **obligation**.

(iii) The obligation can be **measured reliably**.

IAS 37 considers an outflow to be probable if the event is **more likely than not** to occur.

If the company can **avoid expenditure by its future action, no provision** should be recognised. A legal or constructive obligation is one created by an **obligating event**. Constructive obligations arise when an entity is committed to certain expenditures because of a pattern of behaviour which the public would expect to continue.

IAS 37 states that the amount recognised should be the **best estimate of the expenditure required to settle the obligation at the end of the reporting period**. The estimate should **take the various possible outcomes into account** and should be the **amount that an entity would rationally pay** to settle the obligation at the reporting date or to transfer it to a third party. Where there is **a large population of items**, for example in the case of warranties, the provision will be made at **a probability weighted expected value**, taking into account the risks and uncertainties surrounding the underlying events. Where there is a **single obligation**, **the individual most likely outcome** may be the best estimate of the liability.

The amount of the provision should be **discounted to present value** if the time value of money is material using a **risk adjusted rate**. If some or all of the expenditure is expected to be **reimbursed** by a third party, the reimbursement should be **recognised as a separate asset,** but only if it is virtually certain that the reimbursement will be received.

Shortcomings of IAS 37

IAS 37 is generally consistent with the *Conceptual Framework*. However there are some issues with IAS 37 that have led to it being criticised:

(i) IAS 37 requires recognition of a liability only if it is **probable,** that is more than 50% likely, that the obligation will result in an outflow of resources from the entity. This is **inconsistent with other standards,** for example IFRS 3 *Business Combinations* and IFRS 9 *Financial Instruments* which do not apply the probability criterion to liabilities. In addition, probability is not part of the *Conceptual Framework* definition of a liability nor part of the *Conceptual Framework*'s recognition criteria.

(ii) There is **inconsistency with US GAAP** as regards how they treat the **cost of restructuring** a business. US GAAP requires entities to recognise a liability for individual costs of restructuring only when the entity has incurred that particular cost, while IAS 37 requires recognition of the total costs of restructuring when the entity announces or starts to implement a restructuring plan.

(ii) The **measurement rules** in IAS 37 are **vague and unclear**. In particular, 'best estimate' could mean a number of things: the most likely outcome, the weighted average of all possible outcomes or even the minimum/maximum amount in a range of possible outcomes. IAS 37 does not clarify which costs need to be included in the measurement of a liability, and in practice different entities include different costs. It is also unclear if 'settle' means 'cancel', 'transfer' or 'fulfil' the obligation. IAS 37 also requires provisions to be discounted to present value but gives no guidance on non-performance risk that is the entity's own credit risk. Non-performance risk can have a lead to a significant reduction in non-current liabilities.

(b) (i) **Accounting treatment under IAS 37**

The IAS 37 criteria for recognising a **provision** have been met as there is a present obligation to dismantle the oil platform, of which the present value has been measured at **$105 million**. Because Royan cannot operate the oil without incurring an obligation to pay dismantling costs at the end of ten years, the expenditure also enables it to acquire **economic benefits** (income from the oil extracted). Therefore, Royan should **recognise an asset of $105 million** (added to the 'oil platform' in property, plant and equipment) and this should be **depreciated** over the life of the oil platform, which is ten years. In addition, there will be an adjustment charged in profit or loss each year to the present value of the obligation for the **unwinding of the discount.**

(ii) **Ethical behaviour**

The treatment proposed by the directors is not compliant with IAS 37. It could be due to genuine error and a misunderstanding due to a lack of knowledge, with the directors really believing that the standard is not mandatory. There does not appear to be any motivation to maximise profit to benefit the directors in any way; for example, to increase bonuses or profit related pay, though this could be a consideration. However, in this instance it feels like a deliberate intention to contravene IAS 37 and include a misstatement in the financial statements, rather than a genuine mistake. The directors cannot justify their decision not to apply IAS 37.

If the situation is allowed to continue, one of ACCA's *Code of Ethics and Conduct* fundamental principles will be breached: that of **professional behaviour**. Members should comply with relevant laws and regulations and should avoid any action that discredits the profession. In knowingly allowing the directors not to apply the requirements of an accounting standard, the accountant would not be acting diligently and in accordance with applicable guidance and would not be demonstrating professional competence and due care.

Despite the potential conflict and likely strong or undue influence from the directors over a sole and more junior employee, the accountant must act with **integrity** and **remain unbiased**, recommending to the directors that IAS 37, as it is in issue, must be complied with, and processing the appropriate entries in the financial statements for the year ended 31 July 20X6. A possible approach to achieve resolution may be to discuss the matter with the chairman or a non-executive director, setting out the problem and explaining that the directors have a responsibility to ensure the financial statements are fair and accurate and comply with relevant accounting standards.

(c) **Contingent liability**

The legal claim against Chrissy will be treated differently in Chrissy's individual financial statements as compared with the consolidated accounts of the Royan group.

Chrissy's individual financial statements

The legal claim against Chrissy **does not meet the definition of a provision** under IAS 37 *Provisions, Contingent Liabilities and Contingent Assets.* One of IAS 37's requirements for a provision is that an outflow of resources embodying economic benefits should be probable, and Royan believes that it is more likely than not that a payment will not be made and therefore such an **outflow will not occur**.

However, the possible payment does fall within the IAS 37 definition of a **contingent liability,** which is:

- A possible obligation depending on whether some uncertain future event occurs, or
- A present obligation but payment is not probable or the amount cannot be measured reliably.

Therefore, as **a contingent liability** the details of the claim and the $4 million estimated fair value of the contingent liability would be **disclosed** in the notes to the financial statements.

Consolidated financial statements

Under IFRS 3 *Business Combinations*, an acquirer must allocate the cost of a business combination by recognising the acquiree's identifiable assets, liabilities and contingent liabilities that satisfy the recognition criteria at their **fair values** at the date of the acquisition. Contingent liabilities where there is only a possible obligation which, under IAS 37, depend on the occurrence or non-occurrence of some uncertain future event are not recognised under IFRS 3. However, the **IAS 37 probability criterion does not apply under IFRS 3**: a contingent liability is recognised **whether or not it is probable that an outflow** of economic benefits will take place, where there is a present obligation and its fair value can be measured reliably.

Consequently, Royan should **recognise the contingent liability as part of the business combination at its fair value** of $4 million. This will reduce net assets at acquisition, and therefore increase goodwill.

54 Formatt

Workbook references. The *Conceptual Framework* is covered in Chapter 1. Financial instruments are covered in Chapter 8. Impairments are covered in Chapter 4.

Top tips. In Part (a) you are asked to relate your answer to both IFRSs and the *Conceptual Framework*. Being able to relate and/or critique an accounting treatment in the light of the *Conceptual Framework* is a key skill required for SBR. You must ensure your knowledge of the *Conceptual Framework* is up to date. In Part (b), you must make sure that you explain the calculations you provide and the principles of the accounting standard on which they are based. Do not make the mistake of expecting the calculations to speak for themselves. SBR is preparation for the accountant's role as advisor – and explanations will be just as important in this role as computations so ensure the key issues are discussed in sufficient depth.

Easy marks. These are available for the calculation of value in use and recoverable amount in Part (b).

Marking scheme

		Marks
(a)	Financial asset – discussion 1 mark per point up to	8
(b)	Non-current asset at cost	8
	Non-current asset at valuation	6
	Non-current asset held for sale	3
		25

(a) The *Conceptual Framework* defines an asset as a present economic resource controlled by the entity as a result of past events. It goes on to say that control links the economic resource to the entity and that assessing control helps to identify what economic resource the entity should account for. For example, if an entity has a proportionate share in a property without controlling the entire property, the entity's asset is its share in the property, which it controls, not the property itself, which it does not. An entity controls an economic resource if it has the present ability to direct the use of the economic resource and obtain the economic benefits which may flow from it. However, risks and rewards can be a helpful factor to consider when determining the transfer of control.

The entity should consider whether the contractual rights to the cash flows from the asset have expired as, if so, the asset should be derecognised. Secondly, if the contractual rights to the cash flows have not expired, as is the case with Formatt, the entity should consider whether it has transferred the financial asset. When an entity transfers a financial asset, it should evaluate the extent to which it retains the risks and rewards.

IFRS 9 *Financial Instruments* provides three examples of when an entity has transferred substantially all the risks and rewards of ownership, these are: an unconditional sale of a financial asset, sale of a financial asset with an option to repurchase the financial asset at its fair value and sale of a financial asset which is deeply 'out of the money'. Thus in this case, even though most of the cash flows which are derived from the loan are passed on to Window (up to a maximum of $7 million), Formatt is essentially still in 'control' of the asset as the risks and rewards have not been transferred because of the subordinated retained interest. Formatt's residual interest also absorbs the potential credit losses.

If Formatt has neither retained nor transferred substantially all of the risks and rewards of ownership, the assessment of control is important. If control has been retained, the entity would continue to recognise the asset to the extent of its continuing involvement.

However, as Formatt has retained the risks and rewards, it should recognise the financial asset in the statement of financial position and the 12-month expected credit losses.

(b) **Principles of IAS 36 *Impairment of Assets***

The basic principle of IAS 36 is that an asset should be carried at no more than its recoverable amount, that is, the greater of amount to be recovered through use or sale of the asset. If an **asset's carrying amount** is **higher than its recoverable amount**, an **impairment loss** has occurred. The impairment loss should be **written off** against profit or loss for the year.

An asset's **recoverable amount** is **defined** as the **higher** of:

(1) The **asset's fair value less costs of disposal**. This is the price that would be received to sell the asset in an orderly transaction between market participants at the measurement date under current market conditions, net of costs of disposal.

(2) The asset's **value in use**. This is the present value of estimated future cash flows (inflows minus outflows) generated by the asset, including its estimated net disposal value (if any) at the end of its useful life. A number of factors must be reflected in the calculation of value in use (variations, estimates of cash flows, uncertainty), but the most important is the **time value of money** as value in use is based on **present value calculations**.

(i) **Impairment loss at 31 May 20X4**

The carrying amount of the non-current assets of Key at 31 May 20X4 is cost less accumulated depreciation:

$3m – ($3m/5) = $2.4m.

This needs to be compared to value in use at 31 May 20X4, which, using a discount rate of 5%, is calculated as:

Year ended	*31 May 20X5*	*31 May 20X6*	*31 May 20X7*	*31 May 20X8*	*Total*
Cash flows ($'000)	280	450	500	550	
Discount factors	0.9524	0.9070	0.8638	0.8227	
Discounted cash flows ($'000)	267	408	432	452	1,559

The value in use of $1,559,000 is below the carrying amount, so the carrying amount must be written down, giving rise to an **impairment loss**:

$2,400,000 – $1,559,000 = $841,000

Value in use at 30 November 20X4

The directors wish to reverse the impairment loss calculated as at 31 May 20X4, on the grounds that, using the same cash flows, the value in use of the non-current assets is now above the carrying amount. However, while IAS 36 requires an assessment at each reporting date of whether an impairment loss has decreased, this does not apply to the unwinding of the discount (or goodwill). Since the **same cash flows** have been used, the increase in value in use is **due to the unwinding of the discount, and so cannot be reversed**.

Government reimbursement

The treatment of compensation received in the form of reimbursements is governed by IAS 37 *Provisions, Contingent Liabilities and Contingent Assets.* Reimbursements from governmental indemnities are **recorded** as an asset and in profit or loss for the year when, and only when, it is **virtually certain** that reimbursement will be received if the entity settles the obligation. In practice, this will be **when the compensation becomes receivable**, and the receipt is **treated as a separate economic event** from the item it was intended to compensate for. In this particular case, receipt is by no means certain, since the government has merely indicated that it may compensate.

Thus, **no credit can be taken** for compensation of 20% of the impairment loss.

(ii) **Revalued asset**

When an **impairment loss occurs** for a **revalued asset**, the **impairment loss** should be first be charged to other comprehensive income (that is, treated as a **revaluation decrease**). Any **excess** is then charged to **profit or loss**.

The revaluation gain and impairment loss will be accounted for as follows:

	Revalued carrying amount
	$m
1 December 20X1	10.0
Depreciation (10 × 2/10)	(2.0)
Revaluation (bal. fig.)	0.8
1 December 20X3	8.8
Depreciation (1 year) (8.8 × 1/8)	(1.1)
Impairment loss (bal. fig.)	(2.2)
Recoverable amount at 30 November 20X4	5.5

The impairment loss of $2.2 million is charged to **other comprehensive income** until the revaluation surplus has been eliminated, and the rest is charged to profit or loss. Therefore, the impairment **loss charged to other comprehensive income** will be **$0.8 million**. The **remainder**, $2.2m – $0.8m = $1.4m will be **charged to profit or loss**.

It is possible that the company would have transferred an amount from revaluation surplus to retained earnings to cover the excess depreciation of $0.1 million. If so, the impairment loss charged to OCI would be $(0.8 – 0.1m) = $0.7m.

(iii) **Property to be sold**

The fact that management plans to sell the property because it is being under-utilised may be an **indicator** of **impairment**. Such assets (or cash-generating units) must be tested for impairment when the decision to sell is made.

IFRS 5 *Non-current Assets Held for Sale and Discontinued Operations* may apply in such cases, but the decision to sell the asset is generally made well before the IFRS 5 criteria are met. IFRS requires an asset or disposal group to be classified as held for sale where it is **available for immediate sale** in its **present condition** subject only to **terms that are usual** and customary and the sale is **highly probable**. For a sale to be highly probable:

- Management must be **committed** to the sale;
- An **active programme to locate a buyer** must have been initiated;
- The **market price** must be **reasonable** in relation to the asset's current fair value; and
- The sale must be **expected to be completed within one year** from the date of classification.

An asset (or disposal group) that is held for sale should be measured at the **lower of** its **carrying amount** and **fair value less costs to sell**. Immediately before classification of the asset as held for sale, the entity must update any impairment test carried out. **Once** the asset has been **classified as held for sale**, any **impairment loss** will be based on the **difference between the adjusted carrying amounts and the fair value less cost to sell**. The impairment loss (if any) will be **recognised in profit or loss**.

A **subsequent increase** in fair value less costs of disposal may be **recognised** in profit or loss **only to the extent of any impairment previously recognised**.

In the case of the property held by Key, it is likely that **IFRS 5 would not apply** because **not all the criteria for a highly probable sale** have been met. Management is committed to the sale, and there is an active programme to locate a buyer. However, **Key has not reduced the price of the asset**, **which is in excess of its market value** – one of the IFRS 5 criteria is that the market price must be reasonable in relation to the asset's current fair value. In addition, the asset has remained unsold for a year, so it **cannot be assumed that the sale will be completed within one year** of classification.

The property does not meet the IFRS 5 criteria, so it **cannot be classified as held for sale**. However, an **impairment** has taken place and, in the circumstances, the **recoverable amount** would be **fair value less costs to sell**.

55 Emcee

Workbook references. IAS 38 *Intangible Assets*, IAS 23 *Borrowing Costs* and IFRS 13 *Fair Value Measurement* are covered in Chapter 4. IFRS 5 *Non-current Assets Held for Sale and Discontinued Operations* is covered in Chapter 14 and IAS 24 *Related Party Disclosures* in Chapter 2.

Top tips. This is a multi-standard question in which the three parts are independent. You should scan read all parts of the question and attempt the part you feel most comfortable with first. The issues covered are borrowing costs (Part (a)), intangible assets, non-current assets held for sale and impairment of assets (Part (b)) and fair value measurement and related party transactions (Part (c)). The recommended approach is to discuss the general principles of the relevant standards and then apply them to the scenario. Part (b) is broken down into four elements so ensure you provide an answer to each.

Easy marks. No parts of this question are particularly easy – the main way to get the marks is to break down the scenario into its constituent parts and make sure you deal with each relevant standard.

Marking scheme

		Marks
(a)	Discussion of IAS 23 requirements and calculation of capitalised interest – 1 mark per point to a maximum	6
(b)	Discussion of IAS 38 recognition requirements, applicability of IFRS 5 and impairment under IAS 36 – 1 mark per point to a maximum	11
(c)	Discussion of IFRS 13 and IAS 24 – 1 mark per point to a maximum	8
		25

(a) **Borrowing costs**

IAS 23 *Borrowing Costs* requires borrowing costs incurred on acquiring or constructing an asset to be **capitalised** if the asset takes a substantial period of time to be prepared for its intended use or sale. Borrowing costs should be capitalised during construction and include the costs of general borrowings which would have been avoided if the expenditure on the asset had not occurred. The general borrowing costs are determined by applying the weighted average of the borrowing costs applicable to the general pool

The weighted-average carrying amount of the stadium during the period is:

$(20 + 70 + 120 + 170)m/4, that is $95 million.

The capitalisation rate of the borrowings of Emcee during the period of construction is 9% per annum, therefore the total amount of borrowing costs to be capitalised is the weighted-average carrying amount of the stadium multiplied by the capitalisation rate.

That is ($95m × 9% × 4/12) $2.85 million.

(b) **Players' registrations**

Acquisition

IAS 38 *Intangible Assets* states that an entity should recognise an intangible asset where it is probable that future economic benefits will flow to the entity and the cost of the asset can be measured reliably. Therefore, the **costs** associated with the acquisition of players' registrations should be **capitalised at the fair value of the consideration payable**. Costs would include transfer fees, league levy fees, agents' fees incurred by the club and other directly attributable costs. Costs also **include the fair value of any contingent**

consideration, which is primarily payable to the player's former club with associated league levy fees, once payment becomes probable. Subsequent reassessments of the amount of contingent consideration payable would be also included in the cost of the player's registration. The estimate of the fair value of the contingent consideration payable requires management to assess the likelihood of specific performance conditions being met, which would trigger the payment of the contingent consideration. This assessment would be carried out on an individual player basis. The additional amount of contingent consideration potentially payable, in excess of the amounts included in the cost of players' registrations, would be disclosed. Amounts capitalised would be fully amortised over the period covered by the player's contract.

Extension

Where a playing contract is extended, any **costs associated with securing the extension are added to the unamortised carrying amount** at the date of the extension and the revised carrying amount is amortised over the remaining revised contract life.

Sale of registrations

Player registrations would be classified as assets held for sale under IFRS 5 *Non-Current Assets Held for Sale and Discontinued Operations* when their **carrying amount is expected to be recovered principally through a sale** transaction and a sale is considered to be highly probable. Additionally, the registrations should be actively marketed by Emcee, which it appears that they are. It would appear that in these circumstances that management is committed to a plan to sell the registration, that the asset is available for immediate sale, that an active programme to locate a buyer is initiated by circulating clubs. IFRS 5 requires that it is unlikely that the plan to sell the registrations will be significantly changed or withdrawn. In order to fulfil the last criteria of IFRS 5, it may be prudent to only class these registrations as held for sale where unconditional offers have been received prior to a period end.

However, because of the subjectivity involved, in the case of player registrations these assets would be stated at the lower of the carrying amount and fair value less costs to sell, as the carrying amount will already be stated in accordance with IFRSs.

Gains and losses on disposal of players' registrations would be determined by comparing the fair value of the consideration receivable, net of any transaction costs, with the carrying amount and would be recognised in profit or loss within profit on disposal of players' registrations. Where a part of the consideration receivable is contingent on specified performance conditions, this amount is recognised in profit or loss when the conditions are met.

The player registrations disposed of, subsequent to the year end, for $25 million, with an associated net book value of $7 million, would be disclosed as events after the reporting date.

Impairment review

IAS 36 *Impairment of Assets* states that entities should annually **test their assets for impairment**. An asset is impaired if its carrying amount exceeds its recoverable amount which is the higher of the asset's fair value less costs of disposal and its value in use. It is difficult to determine the value in use of an individual player in isolation as that player (unless via a sale or insurance recovery) cannot generate cash flows on his own. Whilst any individual player cannot really be separated from the single cash-generating unit (CGU), being the basketball or football team, there may be certain circumstances where a player is taken out of the CGU, when it becomes clear that they will not play for the club again. If such circumstances arise, the **carrying amount of the player should be assessed against the best estimate of the player's fair value less any costs to sell and an impairment charge made in profit or loss**, which reflects any loss arising.

(c) **Valuation of stadiums**

IFRS 13 *Fair Value Measurement* would value the stadiums at the **price which would be received to sell the asset in an orderly transaction between market participants** at the measurement date. The price would be the one which **maximises the value of the asset** or the group of assets using the principal of the highest and best use. The price would essentially use Level 2 inputs which are inputs other than quoted market prices included within Level 1 which are observable for the asset or liability, either directly or indirectly. Property naming rights present complications when valuing property. The status of the property dictates its suitability for inviting sponsorship attached to its name. It has nothing to do with the property itself but this can be worth a significant amount. Therefore, Emcee could **include the property naming rights in the valuation** of the stadiums and write it off over three years.

IAS 24 *Related Party Disclosures* sets out the criteria for two entities to be treated as related parties. Such criteria include being members of the same group or where a person or a close member of that person's family is related to a reporting entity if that person has control or joint control over the reporting entity. IAS 24 deems that parties are not related simply because they have a director or key manager in common. In this case, there are **two directors in common** and it appears as though the **entities are not related**. However, the regulator will need to establish whether the **sponsorship deal is a related party transaction** (RPT) for the purpose of the financial control provisions. There would need to be demonstrated that the airline may be expected to influence, or be influenced by, the club or a related party of the club. If the deal is deemed to be an RPT, the regulator will consider whether the sponsorship is at fair value.

56 Scramble

Workbook references. Intangible assets and impairment are covered in Chapter 4. IFRS 9 *Financial Instruments* is covered in Chapter 8.

Top tips. Parts (a) and (b) were on impairment testing. You may have found Part (b), requiring determination of the discount rate to be used, rather difficult, and you may have needed to draw on your financial management studies. Part (c) was on intangible assets (agents' fees on transfer of players to the club and extension of players' contracts) and an IFRS 9 financial asset (rights to ticket sales of another football club).

Easy marks. There are no obvious easy marks in this question.

Marking scheme

		Marks
(a)	Intangible assets – subjective assessment	7
(b)	Cash-generating units – subjective assessment	8
(c)	Intangible assets – subjective assessment	10
		25

(a) **Internally developed intangibles**

IAS 38 *Intangible Assets* **allows internally developed intangibles to be capitalised** provided certain criteria (technological feasibility, probable future benefits, intent and ability to use or sell the software, resources to complete the software, and ability to measure cost) are met. It is assumed, in the absence of information to the contrary, that they have; accordingly Scramble's treatment is correct in this respect.

Scramble is also correct in expensing the maintenance costs. These should not be capitalised as they do not enhance the value of the asset over and above the original benefits.

As regards subsequent measurement, IAS 38 requires that **an entity must choose either the cost model or the revaluation** model for each class of intangible asset. Scramble has chosen cost, and this is acceptable as an accounting policy.

Intangible assets **may have a finite or an indefinite useful life**. IAS 38 states that an entity may treat an intangible asset as having an indefinite useful life, when, having regard to all relevant factors there is no foreseeable limit to the period over which the asset is expected to generate net cash inflows for the entity.

'Indefinite' is not the same as 'infinite'. Computer software is mentioned in IAS 38 as an intangible that is prone to technological obsolescence and whose life may therefore be short. Its **useful life should be reviewed each reporting period** to determine whether events and circumstances continue to support an indefinite useful life assessment for that asset. If they do not, the change in the useful life assessment from indefinite to finite should be accounted for as a change in an accounting estimate.

The asset should also be **assessed for impairment in accordance with IAS 36** *Impairment of Assets*. Specifically, the entity must test the intangible asset for impairment annually, and whenever there is an indication that the asset may be impaired. The asset is tested by **comparing its recoverable amount with its carrying amount**.

The **cash flows** used by Scramble to determine value in use for the purposes of impairment testing **do not comply with IAS 36**. Scramble does not analyse or investigate the differences between expected and actual cash flows, but this is an important way of testing the reasonableness of assumptions about expected cash flows, and IAS 36 requires such **assumptions to be reasonable and supported by evidence**.

Scramble is also **incorrect** to include in its estimate of future cash flows those **expected to be incurred in improving the games and the expected increase in revenue** resulting from that expense. IAS 36 requires cash flow projections to relate to the asset in its current condition. Nor should cash flow estimates include tax payments or receipts as here.

(b) **Discount rate for impairment**

While the cash flows used in testing for impairment are specific to the entity, the **discount rate is supposed to appropriately reflect the current market assessment of the time value of money and the risks specific to the asset or cash-generating unit**. When a specific rate for an asset or cash-generating unit is not directly available from the market, which is usually the case, an estimated discount rate may be used instead. An estimate should be made of a **pre-tax rate that reflects the current market assessment of the time value of money and the risks specific to the asset** that **have not been adjusted** for in the estimate of future cash flows. According to IAS 36, this rate is the return that the investors would require if they chose an investment that would generate cash flows of amounts, timing and risk profile equivalent to those that the entity expects to derive from the assets.

Rates that should be considered are the entity's weighted average cost of capital, the entity's incremental borrowing rate or other market rates. The objective must be to obtain a rate which is sensible and justifiable. Scramble should not use the risk-free rate adjusted by the company specific average credit spread of outstanding debt raised two years ago. Instead the credit spread input applied **should reflect the current market assessment of the credit spread at the time of impairment testing**, even though Scramble does not intend raising any more finance.

Disclosures

With regard to the impairment loss recognised in respect of each cash-generating unit, IAS 36 requires disclosure of:

- The amount of the loss
- The events and circumstances that led to the loss
- A description of the impairment loss by class of asset

It is **no defence** to maintain that this information was **common knowledge in the market**. The disclosures are still needed. It should be noted that IAS 1 requires disclosure of material items, so this information needs to be disclosed if the loses are **material**, with materiality determined using a suitable measure such as percentage of profit before tax.

(c) **Recognition of intangible assets**

Registration rights and agents' fees

The relevant standard here is IAS 38 *Intangible Assets*. An **intangible asset may be recognised** if it is controlled by the entity (it gives the entity the power to benefit from the asset), if it meets the identifiability criteria in IAS 38, if it is probable that future economic benefits attributable to the asset will flow to the entity and if its fair value can be measured reliably. For an intangible asset to be identifiable the asset must be separable or it must arise from contractual or other legal rights. It appears that these **criteria have been met**:

(i) The registration rights are contractual.

(ii) Scramble has control, because it may transfer or extend the rights.

(iii) Economic benefits will flow to Scramble in the form of income it can earn when fans come to see the player play.

IAS 38 specifies the items that make up the **cost** of separately acquired assets:

(i) Its purchase price, including import duties and non-refundable purchase taxes, after deducting trade discounts and rebates; and

(ii) Any directly attributable cost of preparing the asset for its intended use.

IAS 38 specifically mentions, as an example of directly attributable costs, 'professional fees arising directly from bringing the asset to its working condition'. In this business**, the players' registration rights meet the definition of intangible assets**. In addition, **Scramble is incorrect** in believing that the **agents' fees** paid on extension of players' contracts do not meet the criteria to be recognised as intangible assets. The fees are incurred to service the player registration rights, and **should therefore be capitalised as intangible assets**.

Rights to revenue from ticket sales

Whether Rashing can show these rights as intangible assets depends on whether the IAS 38 criteria have been met. Since Rashing has no discretion over the pricing of the tickets and cannot sell them, it cannot be said to control the asset. Accordingly, the rights **cannot be treated as an intangible asset**.

The entity is only entitled to cash generated from ticket sales, so the issue is one of a **contractual right to receive cash**. The applicable standard is therefore not IAS 38 but IFRS 9 *Financial Instruments*, under which the rights to ticket revenue represent a **financial asset**.

IFRS 9 has two classifications for financial assets: amortised cost and fair value. Financial assets are classified as being at **amortised cost** if **both** of the following apply.

(i) The asset is held within a business model whose objective is to hold the assets to collect the contractual cash flows.

(ii) The contractual terms of the financial asset give rise, on specified dates, to cash flows that are solely payments of principal and interest on the principal outstanding.

All other financial assets are measured at fair value.

Rashing's receipts are regular cash flows, but they are based on ticket revenues, which are determined by match attendance. Therefore, they are not solely payments of principal and interest, and **do not meet the criteria for classification at amortised cost**. Consequently, the financial asset should be classified as being **at fair value** under IFRS 9.

57 Estoil

Workbook reference. Impairment is covered in Chapter 4 of your Workbook.

Top tips. IAS 36 is brought forward knowledge from earlier studies, however, in SBR the depth of discussion required is greater, and the scenario requires more thought. Part (a) required a discussion of factors to take account of in conducting an impairment test. There are five factors provided in the question and you should use these as headings under which to structure your answer. The discussion required drew on your financial management knowledge (eg WACC).

Easy marks. There are no obvious easy marks in this question.

Marking scheme

		Marks
(a)	Changes in circumstances	3
	Market capitalisation	2
	Allocating goodwill	2
	Valuation issues	6
	Disclosures	2
		15
(b)	Discount rate	5
	Cash flow forecast	5
		10
		25

(a) Entities must determine, **at each reporting date**, whether there are any indications that impairment has occurred. Indicators of impairment may be internal or external. The following factors need to be considered when conducting an impairment test under IAS 36 *Impairment of Assets*.

(i) **Changes in circumstances in the reporting period**

Circumstances may change due to internal factors, for example matters as physical damage, adverse changes to the methods of use of the asset, management restructuring and over-estimation of cash flows, and external factors, such as **adverse changes** in the **markets** or **business** in which the asset is used, or adverse changes to the **technological, economic or legal environment** of the business.

If such indicators come to light between the date of the impairment test and the end of the next reporting period, **more than one impairment test may be required** in the accounting period. In addition, tests for impairment of goodwill and some other intangible assets may be performed at any time during the accounting period, provided it is performed at the same time each year. Not all goodwill is tested at the year end – some entities test it at an interim period. Should impairment indicators arise after the annual impairment test has been performed, it may be necessary to test goodwill for impairment again at the year end.

A possible indicator of impairment is volatility in the market, for example, sharp changes in commodity prices may cause the assets of mining and energy companies to be impaired. In such cases, the assets affected should be tested in the interim period.

(ii) **Market capitalisation**

A strong indicator of impairment is when the **carrying amount** of an entity's assets exceeds the entity's **market capitalisation,** suggesting that the entity is overvalued. However, there **may not be a direct correlation** between the market capitalisation and the impairment loss arising from a lower return generated on the entity's assets –the market may have taken other factors into account. The discrepancy does, however, **highlight the need for the entity to examine its cash-generating units, and possibly to test goodwill for impairment**. The reason for the shortfall must be examined and understood, even though IAS 36 does not require a formal reconciliation between an entity's market capitalisation, its fair value less costs to sell and its value in use.

(iii) **Allocating goodwill to cash-generating units**

Goodwill arising on an acquisition is required to be allocated to each of the acquirer's cash-generating units (CGUs), or to a group of CGUs, that are expected to benefit from the synergies of the combination. **If CGUs are subsequently revised or operations disposed of, IAS 36 requires goodwill to be reallocated, based on relative values, to the units affected.**

The difficulty with this is that IAS 36 **does not give guidance as to what is meant by relative value.** While **fair value less costs to sell** (FVLCS) could be used, this is not mandated by the standard. However, the entity may still need to carry out a valuation process on the part retained. **Value in use** (VIU) is a possibility, but the measure needs to be one that can be applied equally to both the part retained and the part disposed of. VIU has the obvious problem that it will be much the same as FVLCS for the operations disposed of, but there could be significant differences between VIU and FVLCS for the part retained. Alternatively, there could be reasonable ways of estimating relative value by using an **appropriate industry or business surrogate**, for example revenue, profits, industry KPIs.

(iv) **Valuation issues**

The basic principle of IAS 36 is that an asset should be carried at no more than its recoverable amount, that is the amount to be recovered through use or sale of the asset. If an **asset's value** is **higher than its recoverable amount**, an **impairment loss** has occurred. The impairment loss should be **written off** against profit or loss for the year.

The **recoverable amount** is **defined** as the **higher** of the **asset's fair value less costs of disposal** and the asset's **value in use**. Measuring both of these requires the use of **estimates and assumptions,** some of which **may be problematic**.

(1) **Fair value less costs of disposal** is defined as the price that would be received to sell the asset in an orderly transaction between market participants at the measurement date under current market conditions, net of costs of disposal. IAS 36 gives a 'hierarchy of evidence' for this, with 'price in a binding sale agreement' at the top, only likely to be available if the asset is held for sale, and allowing, in the absence of any active market, estimates based on **a discounted cash flow (DCF) model, which may not be reliable**.

(2) Determining the types of **future cash flows which should be included in the measurement of VIU can also be difficult**. Under IAS 36 an asset or CGU must be tested in its current status, not the status that management wishes it was in or hopes to get it into in the near future. Therefore, the standard requires VIU to be measured at the net present value of the future cash flows the entity expects to derive from the asset or CGU in its current condition over its remaining useful life. This means that it is not appropriate to take account of management plans for enhancing the performance of the asset or CGU, even though these may bring about an increase in value.

(3) While the cash flows used in testing for impairment are specific to the entity, the **discount rate is supposed to appropriately reflect the current market assessment of the time value of money and the risks specific to the asset or cash-generating unit**. When a specific rate for an asset or cash-generating unit is not directly available from the market, which is usually the case, the discount rate to be used is a surrogate. An estimate should be made of a **pre-tax rate that reflects the current market assessment of the time value of money and the risks specific to the asset** that have **not been adjusted** for in the estimate of future cash flows. According to IAS 36, this rate is the return that the investors would require if they chose an investment that would generate cash flows of amounts, timing and risk profile equivalent to those that the entity expects to derive from the assets.

Rates that should be considered are the entity's weighted average cost of capital (WACC), the entity's incremental borrowing rate or other market rates. The objective must be to obtain a rate which is sensible and justifiable.

(4) The test is further complicated by the **impact of taxation**. IAS 36 requires that VIU be measured using pre-tax cash flows and a pre-tax discount rate, but WACC is a post-tax rate, as are most observable equity rates used by valuers.

(5) There is a need for **consistency in determining the recoverable amount and carrying amount which are being compared**. For example, in the case of pensions, there can be significant differences between the measurement basis of the pension asset or (more likely) liability and the cash flows that relate to pensions.

(6) IAS 36 requires that **corporate assets** must be allocated to a cash-generating unit on a 'reasonable and consistent basis, but does not expand on this.

(v) **Disclosures**

With regard to the impairment loss recognised in respect of each cash-generating unit, IAS 36 would disclosure of:

(1) The amount of the loss
(2) The events and circumstances that led to the loss
(3) A description of the impairment loss by class of asset

It is **no defence** to maintain that this information was **common knowledge in the market**. The disclosures are still needed.

(b) (i) **Discount rate**

Estoil has **not complied with IAS 36** *Impairment of Assets* in its use of one discount rate for all cash-generating units (CGUs) regardless of the currency of the country in which the cash flows are generated. IAS 36 requires that **future cash flows must be estimated in the currency in which they will be generated** and then discounted using a discount rate appropriate for that currency. The present value thus calculated must be **translated using the spot exchange rate at the date of the value in use calculation**.

The currency in which the estimated cash flows are denominated has an impact on many of the inputs to the weighted average cost of capital (WACC) calculation, including the risk-free interest rate. **Estoil was incorrect in using the ten-year government bond rate for its own jurisdiction** as the risk-free rate because government bond rates differ between countries due to different expectations about future inflation, and so there may be a discrepancy between the expected inflation reflected in the estimated cash flows and the risk-free rate.

IAS 36 requires that the **discount rate should appropriately reflect the current market assessment of the time value of money and the risks specific to the asset or cash-generating unit**. Applying one discount rate for all the CGUs does not achieve this. The WACC of the CGU or of the company of which the CGU is currently part should generally be used to determine the discount rate. The company's WACC may only be used for all CGUs if the risks associated with the individual CGUs do not materially diverge from the remainder of the group, and this is **not evident** in the case of Estoil.

(ii) **Cash flow forecasts**

IAS 36 requires that any cash flow projections are based upon **reasonable and supportable assumptions** over a maximum period of five years unless it can be proven that longer estimates are reliable. The assumptions should **represent management's best estimate of the range of economic conditions expected to obtain over the remaining useful life of the asset**. Management must also assess the reasonableness of the assumptions by examining the reasons for any differences between past forecasted cash flows and actual cash flows. **The assumptions that form the basis for current cash flow projections must be consistent with past actual outcomes.**

Fariole has **failed to comply** with the requirements of IAS 36 in the preparation of its cash flow forecasts. Although the realised cash flow **forecasts for 20X4 were negative** and well below projected cash flows, **the directors significantly increased budgeted cash flows for 20X5**. This increase was **not justified**, and casts doubts on Fariole's ability to budget realistically.

IAS 36 requires estimates of future cash flows to include:

(1) Projections of cash inflows from the continuing use of the asset

(2) Projections of cash outflows which are necessarily incurred to generate the cash inflows from continuing use of the asset

(3) Net cash flows to be received (or paid) for the disposal of the asset at the end of its useful life

Forecast cash outflows must include those relating to the day-to-day servicing of the asset. This will **include future cash outflows needed to maintain the level of economic benefits expected to be generated by the asset in its current condition**. Fariole has not taken into account expected changes in working capital and capital expenditure, but it is very likely that investments in working capital and capital expenditure would be necessary to maintain the assets of the CGUs in their current condition.

In conclusion, the **cash flow forecasts used by Fariole are not in accordance with IAS 36**.

58 Evolve

Workbook references. IAS 32 *Financial Instruments: Presentation* and IFRS 9 *Financial Instruments* are covered in Chapter 8. IFRS 5 *Non-current Assets Held for Sale and Discontinued Operations* is covered in Chapter 14. IAS 16 *Property, Plant and Equipment* and IAS 40 *Investment Property* are covered in Chapter 4 and IAS 12 *Income Taxes* in Chapter 7.

Top tips. Part (a) is tricky. It asks how the potential payment of cash in the future to equity shareholders should be classified. It had to be classified as a financial liability as there was a contractual obligation to deliver cash as a result of a put option to sell the rights back to the company. An event after the reporting period provided additional evidence of the valuation and should therefore be treated as an adjusting event. Part (b) is more mainstream. The directors had not classified the assets of a subsidiary as held for sale, even though the IFRS 5 criteria were met, on the grounds that they did not have a binding agreement to sell. However, this is not required for a sale to be considered 'highly probable' under IFRS 5, and so the assets should have been classified as held for sale. Part (c) required consideration of three issues. First, a gain arising where a subsidiary which was purchased at less than the market value of its sole asset should not be treated as a bargain purchase because this treatment is only available for a business combination, and the substance of the transaction was the purchase of an asset rather than a business combination. Second, the company wishes to use the cost model, the asset should have been recorded at cost, even if this is less than market value, so the potential gain should not have been recorded in profit or loss or added to the cost of the asset. Third, the deferred tax liability arising on the difference from market value should not be capitalised as it is not linked to bringing the asset to the condition necessary for its operations,

Easy marks. There are no easy marks in this question. Marks are not as difficult to earn in Part (b), as opposed to Parts (a) or (c).

Marking scheme

		Marks
(a)	1 mark per point up to maximum	9
(b)	1 mark per point up to maximum	10
(c)	1 mark per point up to maximum	6
		25

(a) **Obligation to purchase own equity instruments**

A financial liability for the present value of the maximum amount payable to shareholders should be recognised in the financial statements as of 31 August 20X6. At 31 August 20X6, the rights are equivalent to a written put option because they represent for Evolve a purchase obligation which gives shareholders the right to sell the entity's own equity instruments for a fixed price. The fundamental principle of IAS 32 *Financial Instruments: Presentation* is that a financial instrument should be classified as either a financial liability or an equity instrument according to the substance of the contract, not its legal form, and the definitions of financial liability and equity instrument. IAS 32 states that a contract which contains an entity's obligation to purchase its own equity instruments gives rise to a financial liability, which should be recognised at the present value of its redemption amount. IAS 32 also states that a contractual obligation for an entity to purchase its own equity instruments gives rise to a financial liability for the present value of the redemption amount even if the obligation is conditional on the counterparty exercising a right to redeem, as is the case with the scrip issue of Evolve.

Evolve had set up the conditions for the share capital increase in August 20X6 and, therefore, the contract gave rise to financial liabilities from that date and Evolve should have recognised a financial liability for the present value of the maximum amount payable to shareholders in its financial statements for the year ended 31 August 20X6. A non-adjusting event under IAS 10 *Events After the Reporting Period* is an event after the reporting period which is indicative of a condition which arose after the end of the reporting period. However, it could be argued that the transferring of the free allocation rights back to Evolve is in fact an adjusting event as it is an event after the reporting period which provides further evidence of conditions which existed at the end of the reporting period.

(b) **Classification as held for sale**

The non-current assets of Resource should have been presented as held for sale in the financial statements, in accordance with IFRS 5 *Non-current Assets Held for Sale and Discontinued Operations*, as at 31 August 20X6. IFRS 5 states that the appropriate level of management must be committed to a plan to sell the asset for the sale to be probable. Evolve's acceptance of a binding offer in August 20X6 and the publication of this information indicated a high probability of sale. Despite the uncertainties surrounding the sale, the transaction remained highly probable at 31 August 20X6. IFRS 5 requires an entity to classify a non-current asset as held for sale if its carrying amount will be recovered principally through sale rather than through continuing use.

IFRS 5 does not require the existence of a binding sales agreement in order to classify a non-current asset as held for sale but only a high probability of its occurrence. The acceptance of an offer by Evolve indicates that the transaction met the criteria to be classified as held for sale at 31 August 20X6. The finalisation of the agreement on 20 September 20X6 only confirmed the situation existing at 31 August 20X6. Further, Evolve cannot apply IFRS 5 measurement criteria without classifying the item as held for sale in its statement of financial position particularly as a profit or impairment may arise when using such criteria. IFRS 5 also states that immediately before the initial classification of the asset as held for sale, the carrying amount of the asset should be measured in accordance with applicable IFRSs. This was already the case as regards the non-current assets of Resource.

Other criteria which indicate that the non-current assets should be shown as held for sale include the fact that a buyer for the non-current assets has been found, the sale occurred within 12 months of classification as held for sale, the asset was actively marketed for sale at a sales price which has been accepted, and despite the uncertainties at 31 August 20X6, events after the reporting period indicate that the contract was not significantly changed or withdrawn. The fact that the information regarding the uncertainties was not publicly disclosed is irrelevant.

Thus as the non-current assets met the criteria to be classified as held for sale, they should have been measured and presented as such in the financial statements. Assets classified as held for sale must be presented separately on the face of the statement of financial position.

(c) **Investment property**

IFRS 3 *Business Combinations* must be applied when accounting for business combinations, but does not apply where the acquisition is not of a business. In this case, the acquisition was essentially that of an asset and therefore the measurement requirements of IFRS 3 would not apply.

IAS 40 *Investment Property* states that the cost of an investment property comprises its purchase price and any directly attributable expenditure, such as professional fees for legal services. IAS 16 *Property, Plant and Equipment* states that the cost of an item of PPE comprises any cost directly attributable to bringing the asset to the condition necessary for it to be capable of operating in the manner intended by management. Hence if Evolve wishes to use the cost basis for accounting for the investment property, the potential gain should not have been recorded in profit or loss or added to the cost of the asset.

Evolve should have recognised the tax payment as an expense in the statement of profit or loss and other comprehensive income. Administrative and other general overhead costs are not costs of an item of PPE according to IAS 16. The specific fiscal treatment and the tax to be paid were not linked to bringing the asset to the condition necessary for its operations, as the asset would have been operational without the tax. As such, the tax is a cost linked to the activity of Evolve and should be accounted for as an expense in accordance with IAS 12 *Income Taxes* and included in the profit or loss for the period, unless that tax arises from a transaction recognised outside profit or loss.

59 Gasnature

Workbook references. IFRS 9 *Financial Instruments* is covered in Chapter 8, IFRS 11 *Joint Arrangements* in Chapter 15 and IAS 10 *Events after the Reporting Period* in Chapter 6.

Top tips. Part (a) is a good example of applying mainstream syllabus topics (IAS 16) to an unusual situation ('irrecoverable gas'). Part (b) on 'own use' contracts has come up before, and the case could be argued either way. There were marks available for dealing with fundamental principles of whether the contract is a financial contract or an executory contract. If the arguments seem complex, the good news is that there are only six marks for this part of the question, and you can make up the marks in Part (c), which is more mainstream.

Easy marks. Part (c) is relatively straightforward, and you should by now be familiar with the IFRS 11 criteria for distinguishing joint ventures from joint operations.

Marking scheme

			Marks
(a)	1 mark per point up to maximum		9
(b)	1 mark per point up to maximum		6
(c)	(i)	1 mark per point up to maximum	5
	(ii)	1 mark per point up to maximum	5
			25

(a) Joint arrangement

The classification of a joint arrangement as a joint operation or a joint venture depends upon the rights and obligations of the parties to the arrangement (IFRS 11 *Joint Arrangements*). A joint arrangement occurs where two or more parties have joint control. The contractually agreed sharing of control of an arrangement exists only when decisions about the relevant activities require the unanimous consent of the parties sharing control. The structure and form of the arrangement determines the nature of the relationship. However, regardless of the purpose, structure or form of the arrangement, the classification of joint arrangements depends upon the parties' rights and obligations arising from the arrangement. A joint arrangement which is not structured through a separate vehicle is a joint operation. In such cases, the contractual arrangement establishes the parties' rights and obligations. A joint operator accounts for the assets, liabilities, revenues and expenses relating to its involvement in a joint operation in accordance with the relevant IFRSs. The arrangement with Gogas is a joint operation as there is no separate vehicle involved and they have agreed to share services and costs with decisions regarding the platform requiring unanimous agreement of the parties. Gasnature should recognise its share of the asset as property, plant and equipment.

Under IAS 16 *Property, Plant and Equipment* (PPE), the cost of an item of property, plant and equipment includes the initial estimate of the present value of dismantling and removing the item and restoring the site on which it is located. IAS 37 *Provisions, Contingent Liabilities and Contingent Assets* contains requirements on how to measure decommissioning, restoration and similar liabilities. Where the effect of the time value of money is material, the amount of a provision should be the present value of the expenditures expected to be required to settle the obligation. Thus costs incurred by an entity in respect of obligations for dismantling, removing and restoring the site on which an item of property, plant and equipment is located are recognised and measured in accordance with IAS 16 and IAS 37. Gasnature should recognise 55% of the cost of decommissioning the underground storage facility. However, because Gasnature is a joint operator, there is also a contingent liability for 45% of the decommissioning costs and there is a possible obligation for the remainder of the costs depending on whether some uncertain future event occurs, that is Gogas goes into liquidation and cannot fund the decommissioning costs. Therefore Gasnature, should also disclose a contingent liability relating to the Gogas's share of the obligation to the extent that it is contingently liable for Gogas's share.

IAS 16 states that property, plant and equipment are tangible items which:

(i) Are held for use in the production or supply of goods or services, for rental to others, or for administrative purposes; and

(ii) Are expected to be used during more than one period.

Thus Gasnature should classify and account for its share of the irrecoverable gas as PPE. The irrecoverable gas is necessary for the storage facility to perform its function. It is therefore part of the storage facility and should be capitalised as a component of the storage facility asset. The irrecoverable gas should be depreciated to its residual value over the life of the storage facility. However, if the gas is recoverable in full when the storage facility is decommissioned, then depreciation will be recorded against the irrecoverable gas component only if the estimated residual value of the gas decreases below cost during the life of the facility. When the storage facility is decommissioned and the cushion gas extracted and sold, the sale of the irrecoverable gas is accounted for as the disposal of an item of PPE in accordance with IAS 16 and the gain or loss recognised in profit or loss. The natural gas in excess of the irrecoverable gas which is injected into the facility should be treated as inventory in accordance with IAS 2 *Inventories*.

(b) **Contract with Agas**

IFRS 9 *Financial Instruments* applies to those contracts to buy or sell a non-financial item which can be settled net in cash with the exception of contracts which are held for the purpose of the receipt or delivery of a non-financial item in accordance with the entity's expected purchase, sale or usage requirements (own use contract). In other words, it will result in physical delivery of the commodity, in this case the extra gas. Contracts which are for an entity's 'own use' are exempt from the requirements of IFRS 9. Such a contract can be irrevocably designated as measured at fair value through profit or loss even if it was entered into for the above purpose. This designation is available only at inception of the contract and only if it eliminates or significantly reduces a recognition inconsistency (sometimes referred to as an 'accounting mismatch') which would otherwise arise from not recognising that contract because it is excluded from the scope of IFRS 9. There are various ways in which a contract to buy or sell a non-financial item can be settled net in cash or another financial instrument or by exchanging financial instruments. These include the following:

(i) When the terms of the contract permit either party to settle it net in cash

(ii) When the ability to settle net in cash is not explicit in the terms of the contract, but the entity has a practice of settling similar contracts net in cash

(iii) When, for similar contracts, the entity has a practice of taking delivery of the underlying and selling it within a short period after delivery, for the purpose of generating a profit

(iv) When the non-financial item which is the subject of the contract is readily convertible to cash

A written option to buy or sell a non-financial item which can be settled net in cash is within the scope of IFRS 9. Such a contract cannot be entered into for the purpose of the receipt or delivery of the non-financial item in accordance with the entities expected purchase, sale or usage requirements. Contracts to buy or sell a non-financial item, such as a commodity, which can be settled net in cash or another financial instrument, or by exchanging financial instruments, are within the scope of IFRS 9. They are accounted for as derivatives. A level of judgement will be required in this area as net settlements caused by unique events beyond management's control may not necessarily prevent the entity from applying the 'own use' exemption to all similar contracts.

The contract entered into by Gasnature with Agas seems to be an own use contract which falls outside IFRS 9 and therefore would be treated as an executory contract. However, it could be argued that the contract is net settled because the penalty mechanism requires Agas to compensate Gasnature at the current prevailing market price. Further, if natural gas is readily convertible into cash in the location where the delivery takes place, the contract could be considered net settled. Additionally, if there is volume flexibility, then the contract could be regarded as a written option, which falls within the scope of IFRS 9.

However, the contract will probably still qualify as 'own use' as long as it has been entered into and continues to be held for the expected counterparties' sales/usage requirements. Additionally, the entity has not irrevocably designated the contract as measured at fair value through profit or loss, thus adding weight to the 'own use' designation.

(c) (i) It is not acceptable to accrue the costs of the overhaul. The entity does not have a constructive obligation to undertake the overhaul. Under IFRS, costs related to major inspection and overhaul are recognised as part of the carrying amount of property, plant and equipment if they meet the asset recognition criteria in IAS 16 *Property, Plant and Equipment*. The major overhaul component will then be depreciated on a straight-line basis over its useful life (ie over the period to the next overhaul) and any remaining carrying amount will be derecognised when the next overhaul is performed. Costs of the day-to-day servicing of the asset (ie routine maintenance) are expensed as incurred. Therefore the cost of the overhaul should have been identified as a separate component of the refinery at initial recognition and depreciated over a period of two years. This will result in the same amount of expense being recognised in profit or loss over the same period as the proposal to create a provision.

(ii) Since there were no indicators of impairment at the period end, all costs incurred up to 31 August 20X5 amounting to $5 million should remain capitalised by the entity in the financial statements for the year ended on that date. However, if material, disclosure should be provided in the financial statements of the additional activity during the subsequent period which determined the exploratory drilling was unsuccessful. This represents a non-adjusting event as defined by IAS 10 *Events After the Reporting Period* as an event which is indicative of a condition which arose after the end of the reporting period. The asset of $5 million and additional drilling costs of $2 million incurred subsequently would be expensed in the following year's financial statements.

60 Complexity

Workbook references. Financial instruments are covered in Chapter 8.

Top tips. This is a largely discursive question relating to financial instruments, focusing on the perceived problems with accounting for financial instruments. It requires understanding of IFRS 9 and IFRS 13, as well as an awareness of current issues around financial instruments.

Easy marks. The calculation is a good source of easy marks as it is straightforward. And there are marks for bookwork – listing the problems of complexity and advantages of fair value.

Marking scheme

			Marks
(a)	(i)	Identical payment	2
		Carrying amount	2
		Fair value	2
			6
	(ii)	Hedging discussion	5
		Effectiveness discussion	4
			9
(b)	(i)	1 mark per point up to maximum	6
	(ii)	1 mark per point up to maximum	4
			10
			25

(a) (i) IFRS 9 *Financial Instruments* requires an entity to value its financial liabilities at **amortised cost** with an option to designate them as measured at **fair value through profit or loss** if it reduces or eliminates an accounting mismatch or because a group of liabilities is managed and its performance evaluated on a fair value basis. The accounting treatment applied will impact on how the initial and new loans are measured and at what carrying amount they are presented within the financial statements.

The carrying amounts under the amortised cost and fair value methods are calculated as follows:

Amortised cost

Using amortised cost, both the initial loan and the new loan result in **single payments that are almost identical** on 30 November 20X9:

Initial loan: $47m × 1.05 for 5 years = $59.98m

New loan: $45m × 1.074 for 4 years = $59.89m

However, the **carrying amounts at 30 November 20X5 will be different:**

Initial loan: $47m + ($47m × 1.05) = $49.35m

New loan: $45m

Fair value

If the two loans were carried at fair value, both **the initial loan and the new loan would have the same carrying amount,** and be carried at $45 million at 30 November 20X5. This is because both loans result in a single repayment of $59 million on 30 November 20X9 and so are effectively worth the same amount. As the second loan was obtained on 30 November 20X5, the fair value of a loan with repayment of $59 million on 30 November 20X9 must be the amount borrowed at the market rate on that date, ie $45 million. There would be a net profit of $2 million, made up of the interest expense of $47m × 5% = $2.35m and the unrealised gain of $49.35m – $45m = $4.35m.

(ii) **Hedge accounting**

IFRS 9 *Financial Instruments* allows hedge accounting but only if **all** of the following **conditions** are met.

(i) The hedging relationship consists **only of eligible hedging instruments and eligible hedged items**.

(ii) There must be **formal documentation** (including identification of the hedged item, the hedging instrument, the nature of the risk that is to be hedged and how the entity will assess the hedging instrument's effectiveness in offsetting the exposure to changes in the hedged item's fair value or cash flows attributable to the hedged risk).

(iii) The hedging relationship meets all of the IFRS 9 hedge effectiveness criteria.

IFRS 9 defines **hedge effectiveness** as the degree to which changes in the fair value or cash flows of the hedged item attributable to a hedged risk are offset by changes in the fair value or cash flows of the hedging instrument. The directors of Complexity have asked whether hedge effectiveness can be calculated. IFRS 9 uses an **objective-based assessment** for hedge effectiveness, under which the following criteria must be met.

(i) There is an **economic relationship** between the hedged item and the hedging instrument, ie the hedging instrument and the hedged item have values that generally move in the opposite direction because of the same risk, which is the hedged risk;

(ii) The **effect of credit risk does not dominate the value** changes that result from that economic relationship, ie the gain or loss from credit risk does not frustrate the effect of changes in the underlying item on the value of the hedging instrument or the hedged item, even if those changes were significant; and

(iii) The **hedge ratio of the hedging relationship** (quantity of hedging instrument vs quantity of hedged item) is the same as that resulting from the quantity of the hedged item that the entity **actually hedges** and the quantity of the hedging instrument that the entity **actually uses** to hedge that quantity of hedged item.

(b) (i) IFRS 9 *Financial Instruments* provides a model for the classification and measurement of financial instruments that is based on principles and the entity's underlying business model. Many users find financial instruments to be complex often due to the nature of the financial instruments themselves and the **many different ways in which they can be measured**. The measurement method depends on:

(1) The **applicable financial reporting standard.** A variety of IFRSs and IASs apply to the measurement of financial instruments. For example, financial assets may be measured using consolidation for subsidiaries (IFRS 10), the equity method for associates and joint ventures (IAS 28 and IFRS 11) or IFRS 9 for most other financial assets.

(2) The **categorisation of the financial instrument**. IFRS 9 classifies financial assets as measured at **amortised cost, fair value through profit or loss or fair value through other comprehensive income** A financial asset may only be classified as measured at amortised cost if the object of the business model in which it is held is to collect contracted cash flows and its contractual terms give rise on specified dates to cash flows that are solely payments of principal and interest. Financial liabilities are generally accounted for at amortised cost but may be accounted for under the fair value model as was shown in (a)(i).

(3) Whether **hedge accounting** has been applied. As was discussed in (a)(ii), hedge accounting is **complex**, for example when cash flow hedge accounting is used, gains and losses may be split between profit or loss for the year and other comprehensive income (items that may subsequently be reclassified to profit or loss). In addition, there may be mismatches when hedge accounting applies reflecting the underlying mismatches under the non-hedging rules.

Some measurement methods use an estimate of **current value, and others use historical cost**. Some include impairment losses, others do not.

The different measurement methods for financial instruments creates a number of **problems for preparers and users** of accounts:

(1) The treatment of a particular instrument **may not be the best**, but may be determined by other factors.

(2) Gains or losses resulting from different measurement methods may be combined in the same line item in the statement of profit or loss and other comprehensive income. **Comparability** is therefore compromised.

(3) Comparability is also affected when it is **not clear** what measurement method has been used.

(4) It is **difficult to apply the criteria** for deciding which instrument is to be measured in which way. As new types of instruments are created, the criteria may be applied in ways that are not consistent.

(ii) The accountant's suggestion that information relating to financial instruments is too complex to disclose is not a good enough reason to avoid making disclosures in the financial statements. IFRS 7 *Financial Instruments: Disclosure* requires extensive disclosures that will enable the users of financial statements to better understand the quantitative effects of financial instruments (the numbers within the financial statements) and to evaluate the nature and extent of risks that arise from financial instruments and how Complexity manages those risks. That is not to say that all information relating to financial instruments needs to be disclosed and it is important that the accountant focuses on making material disclosures only.

Practice Statement 2 clarifies that if information provided by a disclosure could not reasonably be expected to influence the decisions users make based on the financial statements, then that disclosure need not be made. The assessment of materiality needs to be made from a quantitative perspective first and then any qualitative factors should be considered.

The reporting accountant should not view the requirements of IFRS 7 as a prescriptive list of items that must be disclosed. They must apply judgement to assess what requires disclosure and present it in a manner that will be of benefit to the users of the financial statements.

61 Blackcutt

Workbook references. Investment property and impairment are covered in Chapter 4, leases are covered in Chapter 9 and provisions in Chapter 6.

Top tips. The fact that this is a local government organisation affects the use to which the properties are put in Parts (a) and (d). Part (a) requires a basic understanding of IAS 16 and IAS 40 and requires application rather than just knowledge, but the issues are uncontroversial. Part (b) requires knowledge and application of IFRS 16 *Leases,* focusing on whether an arrangement is or contains a lease. Part (c) dealt with a scenario that many accountants face in practice and should have been fairly straightforward. There were three elements to Part (d) of the question.

Knowledge of the standard, application of the standard and completion of the calculations. The application of knowledge with reference to the question is essential.

Easy marks. Part (a) on investment property should be familiar to you from your earlier studies, and Part (c) is a very straightforward test of IAS 37.

Marking scheme

		Marks
(a)	1 mark per point up to maximum	8
(b)	1 mark per point up to maximum	6
(c)	1 mark per point up to maximum	4
(d)	1 mark per point up to maximum	7
		25

(a) **Investment property**

IAS 40 *Investment Property* applies to the accounting for property (land and/or buildings) **held to earn rentals or for capital appreciation or both**. Examples of investment property given in the standard include, but are not limited to:

(i) Land held for **long-term capital appreciation**
(ii) Land held for **undetermined future use**

Assets which IAS 40 states are not investment property, and which are therefore **not covered** by the standard include:

(i) Property held for use in the **production or supply of goods or services** or for administrative purposes

(ii) Property held for **sale in the ordinary course of business** or in the process of construction of development for such sale

Owner-occupied property, property being **constructed on behalf of third parties** and property leased to a third party **under a finance lease** are also specifically **excluded** by the IAS 40 definition. (Note that finance leases still exist for lessors, though not for lessees.)

If the entity provides **ancillary services** to the occupants of a property held by the entity, the appropriateness of classification as investment property is determined by the significance of the services provided. If those services are a relatively insignificant component of the arrangement as a whole (for instance, the building owner supplies security and maintenance services to the lessees), then the entity may treat the property as investment property. **Where the services provided are more significant** (such as in the case of an owner-managed hotel), the property should be classified as **owner-occupied**.

Applying IAS 40 to Blackcutt's properties, **the land owned for capital appreciation** and which may be sold any time in the future **will qualify as investment property**. Likewise, the **land whose use has not yet been determined** is also covered by the IAS 40 definition of investment property: as it has no current purpose it is deemed to be held for capital appreciation.

Investment property should be recognised as an asset where it is probable that the future economic benefits associated with the property will flow to the entity and the value can be measured reliably. IAS 40 permits an entity to choose between the cost model and the fair value model. Where the fair value model applies, the property is valued in accordance with IFRS 13 *Fair Value Measurement.* Gains or losses arising from changes in the fair value of investment property are recognised in profit or loss for the year.

The **houses routinely bought and sold** by Blackcutt in the ordinary course of its operations will **not qualify as investment property**, but will be treated under IAS 2 *Inventories.*

The **part of the housing inventory** not held for sale but **used to provide housing to low-income employees does not qualify as investment property** either. The properties are **not held for capital appreciation**, and because the rent is **below market rate** and only covers the maintenance costs, **they cannot be said to be held for rentals**. The **rental income is incidental** to the purposes for which the property is held, which is to provide housing services. As with the example of the owner-managed hotel above, the services are significant, and the property should be classified as **owner occupied**. Further indication that it is owner occupied is provided by the fact that it is rented out to **employees of the organisation**. It will be accounted for under IAS 16 *Property, Plant and Equipment.*

(b) **Lease**

The issue here is whether the arrangement with the private sector provider Waste and Co is, or contains, a lease, even if it does not take the legal form of a lease. The **substance of the arrangement should be considered** in connection with the IFRS 16 *Leases.* Key factors to consider are as follows.

(i) Is there an **identifiable asset?**

(ii) Does the customer have the right to **obtain substantially all the economic benefits** from use of the asset throughout the period of use?

(iii) Who has the **right to direct how and for what purpose the asset is used**?

(iv) Does the customer **have the right to operate the asset throughout the period of use** without the supplier having the right to change those operating instructions?

The answer in each case is yes.

(i) The vans are an identifiable asset. Although Waste and Co can substitute another vehicle if one of the existing vehicles needs repairing or no longer works, this substitution right is not substantive because of the significant costs involved in fitting out the vehicle for use by Blackcutt.

(ii) Blackcutt can use the vehicles and uses them exclusively for waste collection for nearly all their life. It therefore has a right to obtain substantially all the economic benefits from the use of the asset.

(iii) Blackcutt controls the vehicles, since it stipulates how they are painted, and ostensibly owns them because they must be painted with Blackcutt's name. It therefore has the right to direct how and for what purpose the asset is used.

(iv) As indicated in (ii) above, Blackcutt has the right to operate the asset throughout the period of use, although it has outsourced the driving to Waste and Co.

The arrangement is **a lease**. A **right-of-use asset** should be recorded, and a **lease liability** set up, equal to the present value of the future lease payments. The **service element** relating to the waste collection must be considered as a **separate component** and charged to profit or loss.

(c) **Provision**

Under IAS 37 *Provisions, Contingent Liabilities and Contingent Assets,* provisions must be recognised in the following circumstances, and must not be recognised if they do not apply.

(i) There is a **legal** or **constructive obligation** to transfer benefits as a result of **past events**.

(ii) It is probably that **an outflow of economic resources** will be required to **settle** the **obligation**.

(iii) A **reliable estimate** of the amount required to settle the obligation can be made.

A legal or constructive obligation is one created by an **obligating event**. Here the obligating event is the **contamination of the land**, because of the virtual certainty of legislation requiring the clean-up. As Blackcutt has no recourse against Chemco or its insurance company this past event will certainly give rise to a **transfer of economic benefits from** Blackcutt.

Consequently, Blackcutt **must recognise a provision** for the best estimate of the clean-up costs. It should **not set up a corresponding receivable**, since no reimbursement may be obtained from Chemco or its insurance company.

(d) **Impairment of building**

The basic principle of IAS 36 *Impairment of Assets* is that an asset should be carried at no more than its recoverable amount, that is, the amount to be recovered through use or sale of the asset. If an **asset's value** is **higher than its recoverable amount**, an **impairment loss** has occurred. The impairment loss should be **written off** against profit or loss for the year.

Entities must determine, at each reporting date, whether there are any indications that impairment has occurred. In this case, **impairment is indicated** because the use to which the building is to be put has changed significantly (from a school to a library), a situation which will continue for the foreseeable future.

The **recoverable amount** is **defined** as the **higher** of the **asset's fair value less costs to sell** and the asset's **value in use**. However, these values are unavailable because of the specialised nature of the asset, and the only information available is depreciated replacement cost. Using a **depreciated replacement cost approach**, the impairment loss would be calculated as follows.

Asset	*Cost/replacement cost*	*Accumulated depreciation 6/25*	*Carrying amount/ replacement cost*
	$'000	$'000	$'000
School	5,000	(1,200)	3,800
Library	2,100	(504)	(1,596)
Impairment loss			2,204

Blackcutt should therefore recognise an **impairment loss of $2.204 million** in profit or loss for the year.

62 Carsoon

Workbook references. Leases are covered in Chapter 9, financial instruments in Chapter 8 and revenue in Chapter 3. Fair value is covered in Chapter 4.

Top tips. Allocate your time appropriately across this three-part question. The parts are independent of each other so you should scan read all parts and attempt the one you feel most comfortable with first. The key to Part (a) is to understand that Carsoon is the lessor, not the lessee and therefore the distinction between finance leases and operating leases applies. Part (b) asks you to advise on measurement issues for a financial instrument. The calculation is straightforward if you have understood the principles; if not, you would be advised to briefly state the measurement principles of IFRS 13 as far as you can and move on quickly to another part of the question. Part (c) of the question, on contractual revenue, is challenging as it gets into the specific detail of IFRS 15, but it is a topical area you should be familiar with. Ensure you breakdown your response to cover each element.

Easy marks. Part (a) contains generous marks for using the information in the question to explain how to classify Carsoon's vehicle leases in the context of IFRS 16. Parts (b) and (c) are more challenging but Part (c) contains some easy marks if you know that the general administration costs and the wasted materials costs should be expensed.

Marking scheme

		Marks
(a)	Classification of lease as operating lease not finance lease, accounting requirements for lease payments and assets and cash flow implications – 1 mark per point up to maximum	9
(b)	Type of financial asset, IFRS 13 requirements, account for financial asset – 1 mark per point up to maximum	8
(c)	Discuss each of penalties, counter claim and additional costs 1 mark per point up to maximum	8
		25

(a) Under IFRS 16 *Leases*, **Carsoon is a lessor** and must classify each lease as an operating or finance lease. A lease is classified as a finance lease if it transfers substantially all of the risks and rewards incidental to ownership of the underlying asset. All other leases are classified as operating leases. Classification is made at the inception of the lease. Whether a lease is a finance lease or an operating lease depends on the **substance of the transaction** rather than the form.

In this case, the **leases are operating leases**. The lease is unlikely to transfer ownership of the vehicle to the lessee by the end of the lease term as the option to purchase the vehicle is at a price which is higher than fair value at the end of the lease term. The lease term is not for the major part of the economic life of the asset as vehicles normally have a length of life of more than three years and the maximum unpenalised mileage is 10,000 miles per annum. Additionally, the present value of the minimum lease payments is unlikely to be substantially all of the fair value of the leased asset as the price which the customer can purchase the vehicle is above market value, hence the lessor does not appear to have received an acceptable return by the end of the lease. Carsoon also stipulates the maximum mileage and maintains the vehicles. This would appear to indicate that the risks and rewards remain with Carsoon.

Carsoon should account for the leased vehicles as property, plant and equipment (PPE) under IAS 16 *Property, Plant and Equipment* and depreciate them taking into account the expected residual value. The rental payments should go to profit or loss on a straight-line basis over the lease term. Where an item of PPE ceases to be rented and becomes held for sale, it should be transferred to inventory at its carrying amount. The proceeds from the sale of such assets should be recognised as revenue in accordance with IFRS 15 *Revenue from Contracts with Customers*.

IAS 7 *Statement of Cash Flows* states that payments from operating activities are primarily derived from the principal revenue-producing activities of the entity. Therefore, they generally result from the transactions and other events which enter into the determination of profit or loss. Therefore, cash receipts from the disposal of assets formerly held for rental and subsequently held for sale should be treated as cash flows from operating activities and not investing activities.

(b) For financial assets which are debt instruments measured at fair value through other comprehensive income (FVOCI), both amortised cost and fair value information are relevant because debt instruments in this measurement category are held for both the collection of contractual cash flows and the realisation of fair values. Therefore, debt instruments measured at FVOCI are measured at **fair value** in the **statement of financial position**. In **profit or loss**, interest revenue is calculated using the **effective interest rate method**. The fair value gains and losses on these financial assets are recognised in other comprehensive income (OCI). As a result, the difference between the total change in fair value and the amounts recognised in profit or loss are shown in OCI. When these financial assets are derecognised, the cumulative gains and losses previously recognised in OCI are reclassified from equity to profit or loss. Expected credit losses (ECLs) do not reduce the carrying amount of the financial assets, which remains at fair value. Instead, an amount equal to the ECL allowance which would arise if the asset were measured at amortised cost is recognised in OCI.

The fair value of the debt instrument therefore needs to be ascertained at 28 February 20X7. IFRS 13 *Fair Value Measurement* states that Level 1 inputs are unadjusted quoted prices in active markets for identical assets or liabilities which the entity can access at the measurement date. In-house models are alternative pricing methods which do not rely exclusively on quoted prices. It would seem that a **Level 1 input is available**, based upon activity in the market and further that, because of the active market, there is no reason to use the in-house model to value the debt.

Therefore, the accounting for the instrument should be as follows:

Initial measurement

The bonds will be initially recorded at $6 million and interest of $0.24 million will be received and credited to profit or loss.

Subsequent measurement

At 28 February 20X7, the bonds will be valued at $5.3 million, which recognises 12-month credit losses and other reductions in fair value. The loss of $0.7 million will be charged as an impairment loss of $0.4 million to profit or loss, representing the 12-month expected credit losses and $0.3 million to OCI. When the bond is sold for $5.3 million on 1 March 20X7, the financial asset is derecognised and the loss in OCI ($0.3 million) is reclassified to profit or loss. Also, the fact that the bond is sold for $5.3 million on 1 March 20X7 illustrates that this should have been the fair value on 28 February 20X7.

(c) IFRS 15 *Revenue from Contracts with Customers* specifies how to account for costs incurred in fulfilling a contract which are not in the scope of another standard. Costs to fulfil a contract which is accounted for under IFRS 15 are divided into those which give rise to an asset and those which are expensed as incurred. Entities will recognise an asset when costs incurred to fulfil a contract meet certain criteria, one of which is that the costs are expected to be recovered.

For costs to meet the 'expected to be recovered' criterion, they need to be either explicitly reimbursable under the contract or reflected through the pricing of the contract and recoverable through the margin.

The penalty and additional costs attributable to the contract should be considered when they occur and Carsoon should have included them in the total costs of the contract in the period in which they had been notified.

As regards the counter claim for compensation, Carsoon accounts for the claim as a contract modification in accordance with IFRS 15. The modification does not result in any additional goods and services being provided to the customer. In addition, all of the remaining goods and services after the modification are not distinct and form part of a single performance obligation. Consequently, Carsoon should account for the modification by updating the transaction price and the measure of progress towards complete satisfaction of the performance obligation. However, on the basis of information available, it is possible to consider that the counter claim had not reached an advanced stage, so that claims submitted to the client should not be included in total revenues.

When the contract is modified for the construction of the storage facility, an additional $7 million is added to the consideration which Carsoon will receive. The additional $7 million reflects the stand-alone selling price of the contract modification. The construction of the separate storage facility is a distinct performance obligation and the contract modification for the additional storage facility is accounted for as a new contract which does not affect the accounting for the existing contract. Therefore the contract is a performance obligation which has been satisfied as assets are only recognised in relation to satisfying future performance obligations. General and administrative costs cannot be capitalised unless these costs are specifically chargeable to the customer under the contract. Similarly, wasted material costs are expensed where they are not chargeable to the customer. Therefore a total expense of $15 million will be charged to profit or loss and not shown as assets.

63 Leigh

Workbook reference. Share-based payments are covered in Chapter 10. Associates are covered in Chapter 11.

Top tips. This was a difficult question which dealt with several share-based payment transactions. However, not all such transactions were dealt with by a single accounting standard. Part (a) dealt with the cost of a business combination and the issue of shares as purchase consideration. It also dealt with shares given to employees as remuneration. The events are dealt with under the separate accounting standards IFRS 2 and IFRS 3. Part (b) dealt with the purchase of property, plant and equipment, and the grant of rights to a director when there is a choice of settlement. This part of the question was quite technically demanding. Part (c) dealt with the issue of shares to acquire an associate and the subsequent accounting for the associate.

Easy marks. It is difficult to identify easy marks for this question.

Marking scheme

		Marks
(a)	Hash	7
	Employees	3
(b)	Property, plant and equipment	5
	Director	4
(c)	Handy	6
		25

(a) **Shares issued to the directors**

The 3 million $1 shares issued to the directors **on 1 June 20X6** as part of the **purchase consideration** for Hash are accounted for under **IFRS 3** *Business Combinations* rather than under IFRS 2 *Share-based Payment*. This is because they are not remuneration or compensation, but simply part of the purchase price of the company. The cost of the business combination will be the total of the fair values of the consideration given by Leigh plus any attributable costs. The total fair value here is $6 million, of which $3 million is share capital and $3 million is share premium.

The **contingent consideration** – 5,000 shares per director to be received on 31 May 20X7 if the directors are still employed by Leigh – may, however, be seen as compensation and thus fall to be treated under IFRS 2. The fact that the additional payment of shares is **linked to continuing employment** suggests that it is a compensation arrangement, and therefore **IFRS 2 will apply**.

Under IFRS 2, the fair value used is that at the **grant date,** rather than when the shares vest. The market value of each share at that date is $2. (Three million shares are valued at $6 million.) So the total value of the compensation is 5 × 5,000 × $2 = **$50,000**.

The $50,000 is charged to profit or loss with a corresponding increase in equity.

Shares issued to employees

These shares are remuneration and are **accounted for under IFRS 2**.

The fair value used is that at the **date of issue,** as the grant date and issue date are the same, **that is, $3 per share**. Because the shares are given as a bonus they vest immediately and are presumed to be consideration for past services.

The total of $3 million would be changed to profit or loss and included in equity.

(b) **Purchase of property, plant and equipment**

Under IFRS 2, the purchase of property, plant and equipment would be treated as a share-based payment in which the counterparty has a **choice of settlement**, in shares or in cash. Such transactions are **treated as cash-settled** to the extent that the entity has incurred a **liability**. It is treated as the issue of a compound financial instrument, with a debt and an equity element.

Similar to IAS 32 *Financial Instruments: Presentation,* IFRS 2 requires the **determination of the liability element and the equity element**. The fair value of the equity element is the fair value of the goods or services (in this case the property) less the fair value of the debt element of the instrument. The fair value of the property is $4 million (per question). The share price of $3.50 is the expected share price in three months' time (assuming cash settlement). The fair value of the liability component at 31 May 20X7 is its present value: 1.3 million × $3 = $3.9m.

The journal entries are:

DEBIT	Property, plant and equipment	$4m	
CREDIT	Liability		$3.9m
CREDIT	Equity		$0.1m

In three months' time, the debt component is remeasured to its fair value. Assuming the estimate of the future share price was correct at $3.50, the liability at that date will be 1.3 million × $3.5 = $4.55m. An adjustment must be made as follows:

DEBIT	Expense (4.55 – 3.9)	$0.65m	
CREDIT	Liability		$0.65m

Choice of share or cash settlement

The share-based payment to the new director, which offers a choice of cash or share settlement, is also treated as the issue of a compound instrument. In this case, the **fair value of the services is determined by the fair value of the equity instruments given**. The fair value of the equity alternative is $2.50 × 50,000 = $125,000. The cash alternative is valued at 40,000 × $3 = $120,000. The **difference** between these two values – $5,000 – is deemed to be the **fair value of the equity component**. At the settlement date, the liability element would be measured at fair value and the method of settlement chosen by the director would determine the final accounting treatment.

At 31 May 20X7, the accounting entries would be:

DEBIT	Profit or loss – directors' remuneration	$125,000	
CREDIT	Liability		$120,000
CREDIT	Equity		$5,000

In effect, the director surrenders the right to $120,000 cash in order to obtain equity worth $125,000.

(c) **Investment in Hardy**

The investment in Hardy should be treated as an **associate under** IAS 28 *Investments in Associates and Joint Ventures.* Between 20% and 50% of the share capital has been acquired, and significant influence may be exercised through the right to appoint directors. Associates are accounted for as cost plus post acquisition change in net assets, **generally cost plus share of post-acquisition retained earnings**. The cost is the fair value of the shares in Leigh exchanged for the shares of Handy. However, negative goodwill arises because the fair value of the net assets of Hardy exceeds this. The negative goodwill must be added back to determine the cost to be used for the carrying amount, and, following a reassessment, credited to profit or loss (Dr Cost 0.2, Cr P/L 0.2).

	$m
Cost: 1m × $2.50	2.5
Add back negative goodwill: (2.5 + (9 × 70% 'NCI') – 9)	0.2
	2.7
Post-acquisition profits: (5 – 4) × 30%	0.3
Carrying amount at 31 May 20X7	3.0

Note. The 0.2 is not part of post-acquisition retained earnings. It is adjustment to the original cost to remove the negative goodwill.

Because negative goodwill has arisen, the investment must be **impairment tested**. A comparison must be made with the estimated recoverable amount of Hardy's net assets. The investment must not be carried above the recoverable amount:

Recoverable amount at 31 May 20X7: $11m × 30% = $3.3m

The recoverable amount is above the carrying amount, so the investment at 31 May 20X7 will be shown at $3 million.

64 Yanong

Workbook references. Agriculture is covered in Chapter 4. Fair value measurement is covered in Chapter 4. Share-based payment is covered in Chapter 10.

Top tips. Part (a) required an understanding of the market definitions given in IFRS 13. You are expected to be able to go beyond memorising the valuation inputs. The fair value measurement of the maize (Part (b)) was challenging. However, valuation techniques are used extensively in corporate reporting and therefore you must become accustomed to using such techniques in answering questions. Balancing this, the cash-settled share-based payment (Part (c)) and valuation of a non-financial asset (the farmland, Part (d)) were more straightforward.

Easy marks. These could be gained by focusing on the parts of the question you were more familiar with, which is likely to be Parts (c) and (d).

Marking scheme

		Marks
(a)	1 mark per point up to maximum	6
(b)	1 mark per point up to maximum	7
(c)	1 mark per point up to maximum	7
(d)	1 mark per point up to maximum	5
		25

(a) **Fair value of agricultural vehicles**

IFRS 13 says that fair value is an exit price in the principal market, which is the market with the highest volume and level of activity. It is not determined based on the volume or level of activity of the reporting entity's transactions in a particular market. Once the accessible markets are identified, market-based volume and activity determines the principal market. There is a presumption that the principal market is the one in which the entity would normally enter into a transaction to sell the asset or transfer the liability, unless there is evidence to the contrary. In practice, an entity would first consider the markets it can access. In the absence of a principal market, it is assumed that the transaction would occur in the most advantageous market. This is the market which would maximise the amount which would be received to sell an asset or minimise the amount which would be paid to transfer a liability, taking into consideration transport and transaction costs. In either case, the entity must have access to the market on the measurement date. Although an entity must be able to access the market at the measurement date, IFRS 13 does not require an entity to be able to sell the particular asset or transfer the particular liability on that date. If there is a principal market for the asset or liability, the fair value measurement represents the price in that market at the measurement date regardless of whether that price is directly observable or estimated using another valuation technique and even if the price in a different market is potentially more advantageous.

The principal (or most advantageous) market price for the same asset or liability might be different for different entities and therefore, the principal (or most advantageous) market is considered from the entity's perspective which may result in different prices for the same asset.

In Yanong's case, Asia would be the principal market as this is the market in which the majority of transactions for the vehicles occur. As such, the fair value of the 150 vehicles would be \$5,595,000 (\$38,000 – \$700 = \$37,300 × 150). Actual sales of the vehicles in either Europe or Africa would result in a gain or loss to Yanong when compared with the fair value, ie \$37,300. The most advantageous market would be Europe where a net price of \$39,100 (after all costs) would be gained by selling there and the number of vehicles sold in this market by Yanong is at its highest. Yanong would therefore utilise the fair value calculated by reference to the Asian market as this is the principal market.

IFRS 13 makes it clear that the price used to measure fair value must not be adjusted for transaction costs, but should consider transportation costs. Yanong has currently deducted transaction costs in its valuation of the vehicles. Transaction costs are not deemed to be a characteristic of an asset or a liability but they are specific to a transaction and will differ depending on how an entity enters into a transaction. While not deducted from fair value, an entity considers transaction costs in the context of determining the most advantageous market because the entity is seeking to determine the market which would maximise the net amount which would be received for the asset.

(b) **Accounting treatment of maize**

Where reliable market-based prices or values are not available for a biological asset in its present location and condition, fair value should be measured using a valuation technique. Relevant observable inputs should be maximised whilst unobservable inputs should be minimised. An appropriate valuation technique would be the present value of expected net cash flows from the asset, discounted at a current market-based rate. In the measurement of fair value of growing crops, a notional cash flow expense should be included for the 'rent' of the land where it is owned in order that the value is comparable to an entity which rents its land. The fair value of the biological asset is separate from the value of the land on which it grows.

	3 months to 31 January 20X5	*3 months to 30 April 20X5*	*Total*
\$m	\$m	\$m	\$m
Cash inflows		80	80
Cash outflows	(8)	(19)	(27)
Notional rental charge for land	(1)	(1)	(2)
Net cash flows	(9)	60	51
Discounted at 2%	(8.82)	57.67	48.85

Thus in the quarterly accounts at 31 October 20X4, the maize fields should be recognised at \$68.85 million (\$20 million land plus \$48.85 million maize). A fair value gain of \$48.85 million should be shown in profit or loss less the operating costs of \$10 million.

At 31 January, Yanong has revised its projections for cash inflows to $76 million, which means that the net cash flows at that date were projected to be $(76 – 19 – 1) million, ie $56 million. Discounted at 2%, this amounts to $54.9 million. Thus, a fair value gain of $(54.9 – 48.85) million, ie $6.05 million, should be shown in profit or loss together with the actual operating costs of $8 million.

At the point of harvest, on 31 March 20X5, the maize is valued at $82 million which means that a fair value gain of $(82 – 54.9) million, ie $27.1 million, is recognised in profit or loss and the maize is classified as inventory. The actual operating costs for the quarter would also be shown in profit or loss. When the maize is sold, a further profit of $(84 – 82) million, ie $2 million, is made on sale.

(c) **Share-based payment**

IFRS 13 applies when another IFRS requires or permits fair value measurements or disclosures about fair value measurements (and measurements, such as fair value less costs to sell, based on fair value or disclosures about those measurements). IFRS 13 specifically excludes transactions covered by certain other standards including share-based payment transactions within the scope of IFRS 2 *Share-based Payment.*

For cash settled share-based payment transactions, the fair value of the liability is measured in accordance with IFRS 2 initially, at each reporting date and at the date of settlement using an option pricing model. The measurement reflects all conditions and outcomes on a weighted average basis, unlike equity settled transactions. Any changes in fair value are recognised in profit or loss in the period. Therefore, the SARs would be accounted for as follows:

Year	*Expense* $	*Liability* $	*Calculation*	
30 April 20X3	641,250	641,250	285 × 500 × $9 × ½	Time-apportioned over vesting period. Using the estimated (300 × 95%) 285 managers.
30 April 20X4	926,250	1,567,500	285 × 500 × $11	Expense is difference between liabilities at 30 April 20X4 and 30 April 20X3
30 April 20X5	97,500	1,350,000	225 × 500 × $12	Cash paid is 60 × 500 × $10.50, ie $315,000. The liability has reduced by $217,500 and therefore the expense is the difference of $97,500

The fair value of the liability would be $1,350,000 at 30 April 20X5 and the expense for the year would be $97,500.

(d) **Farmland**

A fair value measurement of a non-financial asset takes into account a market participant's ability to generate economic benefits by using the asset in its highest and best use or by selling it to another market participant who would use the asset in its highest and best use. The maximum value of a non-financial asset may arise from its use in combination with other assets or by itself. IFRS 13 requires the entity to consider uses which are physically possible, legally permissible and financially feasible. The use must not be legally prohibited. For example, if the land is protected in some way by law and a change of law is required, then it cannot be the highest and best use of the land. In this case, Yanong's land for residential development would only require approval from the regulatory authority and that approval seems to be possible, so this alternative use could be deemed to be legally permissible. Market participants would consider the probability, extent and timing of the approval which may be required in assessing whether a change in the legal use of the non-financial asset could be obtained.

Yanong would need to have sufficient evidence to support its assumption about the potential for an alternative use, particularly in light of IFRS 13's presumption that the highest and best use is an asset's current use. Yanong's belief that planning permission was possible is unlikely to be sufficient evidence that the change of use is legally permissible. However, the fact the government has indicated that more agricultural land should be released for residential purposes may provide additional evidence as to the likelihood that the land being measured should be based upon residential value. Yanong would need to prove that market participants would consider residential use of the land to be legally permissible. Provided there is sufficient evidence to support these assertions, alternative uses, for example, commercial development which would enable market participants to maximise value, should be considered, but a search for potential alternative uses need not be exhaustive. In addition, any costs to transform the land, for example, obtaining planning permission or converting the land to its alternative use, and profit expectations from a market participant's perspective should also be considered in the fair value measurement.

If there are multiple types of market participants who would use the asset differently, these alternative scenarios must be considered before concluding on the asset's highest and best use. It appears that Yanong is not certain about what constitutes the highest and best use and therefore IFRS 13's presumption that the highest and best use is an asset's current use appears to be valid at this stage.

65 Mehran

Workbook references. IFRS 13 is covered in Chapter 4. IFRS 9 is covered in Chapter 8.

Top tips. Most of this question is on IFRS 13 *Fair Value Measurement.* As well as the fair value hierarchy, it is important to be familiar the principles behind the standard, particularly the 'highest and best use' principle, and that of the 'principal and most advantageous market'. You are expected to understand the nature of the valuation hierarchy and not just quote the requirements. Although financial instruments can be tricky, you can use a similar thought process to more common items; for examples, if a fair valuation were to be placed on a motor car, the market prices for a similar car would be used and adjusted if the mileage on the car was significantly different. The same principle applies to shares.

Easy marks. Working out the most advantageous market is quite straightforward. The numbers are given to you for a reason!

Marking scheme

		Marks
(a)	1 mark per point up to maximum	7
(b)	1 mark per point up to maximum	10
(c)	1 mark per point up to maximum	8
Maximum		25

(a) **Land and brand name**

IFRS 13 *Fair Value Measurement* requires the fair value of a non-financial asset to be measured based on its highest and best use from a market participant's perspective. This requirement does not apply to financial instruments, liabilities or equity. The highest and best use takes into account the use of the asset which is physically possible, legally permissible and financially feasible. The highest and best use of a non-financial asset is determined by reference to its use and not its classification and is determined from the perspective of market participants. It does not matter whether the entity intends to use the asset differently. IFRS 13 allows management to presume that the current use of an asset is the highest and best use unless market or other factors suggest otherwise.

In this case, the agricultural land appears to have an alternative use as market participants have considered its use for residential purposes. If the land zoned for agricultural use is currently used for farming, the fair value should reflect the cost structure to continue operating the land for farming, including any tax credits which could be realised by market participants. Thus, the fair value of the land if used for farming would be $(5 + (20% of 0.5)) million, ie $5.1 million.

If used for residential purposes, the value should include all costs associated with changing the land to the market participant's intended use. In addition, demolition and other costs associated with preparing the land for a different use should be included in the valuation. These costs would include the uncertainty related to whether the approval needed for changing the usage would be obtained, because market participants would take that into account when pricing value of the land if it had a different use. Thus, the fair value of the land if used for residential purposes would be $(7.4 – 0.2 – 0.3 – 0.1) million × 80%, ie $5.44 million. Therefore the value of the land would be $5.44 million on the highest and best use basis. In this situation, the presumption that the current use is the highest and best use of the land has been overridden by the market factors which indicate that residential development is the highest and best use. A use of an asset need not be legal at the measurement date, but it must not be legally prohibited in the jurisdiction.

In the absence of any evidence to the contrary, Mehran should value the brand on the basis of the highest and best use. The fair value is determined from the perspective of a market participant and is not influenced by the Mehran's decision to discontinue the brand. Therefore the fair value of the brand is $17 million.

(b) **Fair value of inventory**

IFRS 13 sets out the concepts of principal market and most advantageous market. Transactions take place in either the principal market, which is the market with the greatest volume and level of activity for the inventory, or in the absence of a principal market, the most advantageous market. The most advantageous market is the market which maximises the amount which would be received to sell the inventory, after taking into account transaction costs and transportation costs. The price used to measure the inventory's fair value is not adjusted for transaction costs although it is adjusted for transport costs. The principal market is not necessarily the market with the greatest volume of activity for the particular reporting entity. The principle is based upon the importance of the market from the participant's perspective. However, the principal market is presumed to be the market in which the reporting entity transacts, unless there is evidence to the contrary. In evaluating the principal or most advantageous markets, IFRS 13 restricts the eligible markets to only those which can be accessed at the measurement date. If there is a principal market for the asset or liability, IFRS 13 states that fair value should be based on the price in that market, even if the price in a different market is higher. It is only in the absence of the principal market that the most advantageous market should be used. An entity does not have to undertake an exhaustive search of all possible markets in order to identify the principal or most advantageous market. It should take into account all information which is readily available.

There is a presumption in the standard that the market in which the entity normally transacts to sell the asset or transfer the liability is the principal or most advantageous market unless there is evidence to the contrary.

In this case, the greatest volume of transactions is conducted in the domestic market – direct to manufacturers. There is no problem with obtaining data from trade journals but the problem for Mehran is that there is no data to substantiate the volume of activity in the domestic market – direct to retailers even though Mehran feels that it is at least 20,000 tonnes per annum. The most advantageous market is the export market where after transport and transaction costs the price per tonne is $1,094.

	Domestic market – direct to retailers	*Domestic market – direct to manufacturers*	*Export market*
	$	$	$
Price per tonne	1,000	800	1,200
Transport costs per tonne	50	70	100
Selling agents' fees per tonne	–	4	6
Net price per tonne	950	726	1,094

It is difficult to determine a principal market because of the lack of information. It could be argued that the domestic market – direct to manufacturers has the highest volume for the produce, and is therefore the principal market by which Mehran should determine fair value of $730 ($800 – $70). However, because of the lack of information surrounding the domestic market – direct to retailers, the principal or most advantageous market will be presumed to be the market in which Mehran would normally enter into transactions which would be the export market. Therefore the fair value would be $1,100 ($1,200 – $100) per tonne.

(c) **Investment in Erham**

Measuring the fair value of individual unquoted equity instruments which constitute a non-controlling interest in a private company falls within the scope of IFRS 9 *Financial Instruments* in accordance with the principles set out in IFRS 13. There is a range of commonly used valuation techniques for measuring the fair value of unquoted equity instruments and income approaches as well as the adjusted net asset method are acceptable. IFRS 13 states that fair value is a market-based measurement, although it acknowledges that in some cases observable market transactions or other market information might not be available. IFRS 13 does not contain a hierarchy of valuation techniques nor does it prescribe the use of a specific valuation technique for meeting the objective of a fair value measurement. However, IFRS 13 acknowledges that, given specific circumstances, one valuation technique might be more appropriate than another. The market approach takes a transaction price paid for an identical or a similar instrument in an investee and adjusts the resultant valuation. The transaction price paid recently for an investment in an equity instrument in an investee which is similar, but not identical, to an investor's unquoted equity instrument in the same investee would be a reasonable starting point for estimating the fair value of the unquoted equity instrument.

Mehran would take the transaction price for the preferred shares and adjust it to reflect certain differences between the preferred shares and the ordinary shares. There would be an adjustment to reflect the priority of the preferred shares upon liquidation.

Mehran should acknowledge the benefit associated with control. This adjustment relates to the fact that Mehran's individual ordinary shares represent a non-controlling interest whereas the preferred shares issued reflect a controlling interest. There will be an adjustment for the lack of liquidity of the investment which reflects the lesser ability of the ordinary shareholder to initiate a sale of Erham relative to the preferred shareholder. Further, there will be an adjustment for the cumulative dividend entitlement of the preferred shares. This would be calculated as the present value of the expected future dividend receipts on the preferred shares, less the present value of any expected dividend receipts on the ordinary shares. The discount rate used should be consistent with the uncertainties associated with the relevant dividend streams.

Mehran should review the circumstances of the issue of the preferred shares to ensure that its price was a valid benchmark. Mehran must, however, use all information about the performance and operations of Erham which becomes reasonably available to it after the date of initial recognition of the ordinary shares up to the measurement date. Such information can have an effect on the fair value of the unquoted equity instrument at 31 March 20X6. In addition, Mehran should consider the existence of factors such as whether the environment in which Erham operates is dynamic, or whether there have been changes in market conditions between the issue of the preferred shares and the measurement date.

66 Canto

Workbook references. Property, plant and equipment, investment properties, intangible assets and impairment of assets are all covered in Chapter 3. Basic groups are covered in Chapter 10.

Top tips. Split your time fairly over each part of this three-part question to maximise the marks you gain from the time spent. Parts (a) and (b) both require the discussion of multiple standards to gain the most marks. Part (c) focusses on IAS 36 and the impairment of a CGU. It is more involved, with the selection of appropriate discount rates and the allocation of impairment, but it is not a complicated scenario assuming you have revised IAS 36.

Easy marks. Part (a) has generous marks available for a discussion and application of IFRS 13, IAS 16 and IAS 40 knowledge. There also are marks for straightforward calculations in Part (c).

Marking scheme

		Marks
(a)	1 mark per point up to maximum	9
(b)	1 mark per point up to maximum	8
(c)	1 mark per point up to maximum	8
		25

(a) **Fair value**

IFRS 13 *Fair Value Measurement* defines fair value as the price which would be received to sell an asset or paid to transfer a liability in an orderly transaction between market participants at the measurement date. In respect of property:

- The fair value measurement of a non-financial asset such as property takes into account the entity's ability to generate economic benefits by using the asset in its highest and best use or by selling it to another market participant who would use the asset in its highest and best use.
- The highest and best use of property takes into account the use of the asset which is physically possible, legally permissible and financially feasible.
- There are three levels in the IFRS 13 fair value hierarchy, based on the valuation technique used. Due to the lack of an active market for identical assets, it would be rare for property to be classified in Level 1 of the fair value hierarchy. In market conditions where property is actively purchased and sold, the fair value measurement might be classified in Level 2. However, that determination will depend on the facts and circumstances, including the significance of adjustments to observable data. In this regard, IFRS 13 provides a property specific example, stating that a Level 2 input would

be the price derived from observed transactions involving similar property interests in similar locations. Accordingly, in active and transparent markets, property valuations may be classified as Level 2, provided that no significant adjustments have been made to the observable data. If significant adjustments to observable data are required, the fair value measurement may fall into Level 3.

PPE to Investment property

IAS 40 *Investment Property* permits entities to choose between a fair value model and a cost model. One method must be adopted for all of an entity's investment property. A change is permitted only if this results in a more appropriate presentation. IAS 40 notes that this makes it highly unlikely for a change from a fair value model to a cost model to occur. Transfers to or from investment property should only be made when there is a change in use, which is evidenced by the end of owner-occupation, which has occurred in this case. For a transfer from owner-occupied property to investment property carried at fair value, IAS 16 *Property, Plant and Equipment* (PPE) should be applied up to the date of reclassification. Any difference arising between the carrying amount under IAS 16 at that date and the fair value is dealt with as a revaluation under IAS 16.

The aggregate fair value of the site, including the industrial and retail outlets, is higher to market participants than the sum of the fair value of the individual property interests because of synergies and complementary cash flows. Consequently, the fair value of the site as a whole would be maximised as a group of assets. The fair value is determined for the whole site even if the asset is disaggregated when applying IAS 40.

Thus providing that the above criteria have been met, Canto may value the property at $25 million.

Canto will recognise a depreciation expense of $0.5 million in profit or loss in the year to 28 February 20X7 while the property is accounted for using a cost model under IAS 16. At 28 February 20X7, Canto will transfer the property from PPE to investment property. The investment property will be recognised at its fair value of $25 million, the carrying amount of PPE of $13.5 million ($15 million – accumulated depreciation of $1.5 million) will be derecognised and the increase of $11.5 million will be a revaluation surplus.

(b) IFRS 3 *Business Combinations* states that an acquirer should recognise, separately from goodwill, the identifiable intangible assets acquired in a business combination. An asset is identifiable if it meets either the separability or contractual-legal criteria in IAS 38 *Intangible Assets.*

Customer relationship intangible assets may be either contractual or non-contractual:

(i) Contractual customer relationships are normally recognised separately from goodwill as they meet the contractual-legal criterion.

(ii) However, non-contractual customer relationships are recognised separately from goodwill only if they meet the separable criterion.

Consequently, determining whether a relationship is contractual is critical to identifying and measuring both separately recognised customer relationship intangible assets and goodwill, and different conclusions could lead to substantially different accounting outcomes.

Order backlog

The order backlog should be treated as an intangible asset on the acquisition. The fair value of the order backlog is estimated based on the expected revenue to be received, less the costs to deliver the product or service.

Water acquisition rights

The rights are valuable, as Binlory cannot manufacture vehicles without them. The rights were acquired at no cost and renewal is certain at little or no cost. The rights cannot be sold other than as part of the sale of a business as a whole, so there exists no secondary market in the rights. If Binlory does not use the water, then it will lose the rights. In this case, the legal rights cannot be measured separately from the business as a whole and therefore from goodwill. Therefore, the legal rights should not be accounted for as a separate intangible asset acquired in the business combination because the fair value cannot be measured reliably as the legal rights cannot be separated from goodwill.

(c) IAS 36 *Impairment of Assets* requires that assets be carried at no more than their carrying amount. Therefore, entities should test all assets within the scope of the Standard if indicators of impairment exist. If the recoverable amount (which is the higher of fair value less costs of disposal and value in use) is more than carrying amount, the asset is not impaired. It further says that in measuring value in use, the discount rate used should be the pre-tax rate which reflects current market assessments of the time value of money and the risks specific to the asset. The discount rate should not reflect risks for which future cash flows have been adjusted and should equal the rate of return which investors would require if they were to choose an investment which would generate cash flows equivalent to those expected from the asset. Therefore pre-tax cash flows and pre-tax discount rates should be used to calculate value in use.

Date year ended	*Pre-tax cash flow*	*Discounted cash flows (@ 8%)*
	$m	$m
28 February 20X8	8	7.41
28 February 20X9	7	6.00
29 February 20Y0	5	3.97
28 February 20Y1	3	2.21
28 February 20Y2	13	8.85
Total		28.44

The CGU is impaired by the amount by which the carrying amount of the cash-generating unit exceeds its recoverable amount.

Recoverable amount

The fair value less costs to sell ($26.6 million) is lower than the value in use ($28.44 million). The recoverable amount is therefore $28.44 million.

Impairment

The carrying amount is $32 million and therefore the impairment is $3.56 million.

Allocating impairment losses

Canto will allocate the impairment loss first to the goodwill and then to other assets of the unit pro rata on the basis of the carrying amount of each asset in the cash-generating unit. When allocating the impairment loss, the carrying amount of an asset cannot be reduced below its fair value less costs to sell.

Consequently, the entity will allocate $3 million to goodwill and then allocate $0.1 million on a pro rata basis to PPE (to reduce it to its fair value less costs to sell of $9.9 million) and other assets ($0.46 million to the other assets). This would mean that the carrying amounts would be $9.9 million and $18.54 million respectively.

67 Ethan

Workbook references. Deferred tax is covered in Chapter 7. Investment property and impairment are covered in Chapter 4, financial instruments in Chapter 8 and fair value in Chapter 4.

Top tips. In Part (a), you should focus on IFRS 13. Part (b) required application of the fair value option in IFRS 9 *Financial Instruments.* The option is used where such application would eliminate or significantly reduce a measurement or recognition inconsistency between the debt liabilities and the investment properties to which they were related in this question. In Part (c), candidates needed to recognise that, in classifying the B shares as equity rather than as a liability, the entity had not complied with IAS 32 *Financial Instruments: Presentation.* There were pointers to the shares being classified as a liability, in particular the fact that entity was obliged to pay an annual cumulative dividend on the B shares and did not have discretion over the distribution of such dividend.

Easy marks. There are no obviously easy marks in this question.

Marking scheme

		Marks
(a)	Fair value of investment properties	13
(b)	Fair value option – IFRS 9	7
(c)	B shares of subsidiary	5
		25

(a) **Fair value of investment properties**

The **fair value** of an asset is the price that would be received to sell an asset or paid to transfer a liability in an orderly transaction between market participants at the measurement date (IFRS 13 *Fair Value Measurement*). IFRS 13 states that valuation techniques must be those which are appropriate and for which sufficient data are available. Entities should maximise the use of relevant **observable inputs** and minimise the use of **unobservable inputs**. The standard establishes a three-level hierarchy for the inputs that valuation techniques use to measure fair value.

Level 1	Quoted prices (unadjusted) in active markets for identical assets or liabilities that the reporting entity can access at the measurement date
Level 2	Inputs other than quoted prices included within Level 1 that are observable for the asset or liability, either directly or indirectly, eg quoted prices for similar assets in active markets or for identical or similar assets in non-active markets or use of quoted interest rates for valuation purposes
Level 3	Unobservable inputs for the asset or liability, ie using the entity's own assumptions about market exit value

Although an active market exists for Ethan's investment properties, Ethan uses a discounted cash flow model to measure fair value. This is **not in accordance with IFRS 13**. As the fair value hierarchy suggests, IFRS 13 favours Level 1 inputs, that is market-based measures, over unobservable (Level 3) inputs such as discounted cash flows.

Goodwill and deferred tax

If the **fair value** of the investment properties **is not measured correctly** in accordance with IFRS 13, this means that the **deferred tax liability** on investment properties **may also be incorrect**. In addition, as goodwill is calculated as consideration transferred less fair value of net assets, **goodwill may be incorrect**. This is because deferred tax is calculated on the difference between the carrying amount of the asset and its tax base. So if the carrying amount is incorrect, the deferred tax will be incorrect. The goodwill calculation uses the fair value of **all** net assets, not just the investment properties and the related deferred tax liability, so it is **incorrect to use an increase in the deferred tax liability** as the **basis** for assessing whether goodwill is impaired.

The reasoning behind Ethan's approach is that as the deferred tax liability decreases, the fair value of net assets increases, thereby decreasing goodwill. However, this method of determining whether goodwill is impaired **does not accord with IAS 36** *Impairment of Assets*. IAS 36 requires that goodwill should be **reviewed for impairment annually** for any indicators of impairment, which may be internal or external, and are not confined to changes in the deferred tax liability. Where it is not possible to measure impairment for individual assets, the loss should be measured for a **cash-generating unit**.

The **recoverable amount** is **defined** as the **higher** of:

(i) The **asset's fair value less costs to sell**. This is the price that would be received to sell the asset in an orderly transaction between market participants at the measurement date under current market conditions, net of costs of disposal.

(ii) The asset's **value in use**. This is the present value of estimated future cash flows (inflows minus outflows) generated by the asset, including its estimated net disposal value (if any) at the end of its useful life.

If an **asset's carrying amount** is **higher than its recoverable amount**, an **impairment loss** has occurred. The impairment loss should be **written off against profit or loss** for the year, and the corresponding credit (write-off) applied first to goodwill, then to the investment properties, then to other assets pro-rata.

Deferred tax assets on losses

In theory, unused tax losses give rise to a deferred tax asset. However, IAS 12 *Income Taxes* states that **deferred tax assets should only be recognised to the extent that they are regarded as recoverable**. They should be regarded as recoverable to the extent that on the basis of all the evidence available it is **probable that there will be suitable taxable profits against which the losses can be recovered**. It is unlikely that future taxable profits of Ethan will be sufficient to realise all of the tax loss because of:

(i) The announcement that a substantial loss will be incurred this year instead of the expected profit

(ii) Considerable negative variances against budgets in the past

Consequently, **Ethan should not recognise the deferred tax asset**.

(b) **IFRS 9 fair value option**

Generally under IFRS 9 *Financial Instruments*, the debt issued to finance its investment properties would be accounted for using **amortised cost**, while the properties themselves are at fair value. This is an **accounting mismatch**, that is a recognition or measurement inconsistency between the debt liability and the asset to which it relates. The asset and liability, and the gains and losses arising on them, would be measured on different bases.

The IFRS 9 **fair value option** allows an entity to **designate a liability at initial recognition as being at fair value through profit or loss** if using this option would **eliminate or significantly reduce** an accounting mismatch. Ethan has argued that the basis of measurement of the debt and the investment properties is **similar**, particularly as regards **interest rates**. This argument holds good in respect of the interest, and so the **fair value option would be allowed**.

However, IFRS 9 stipulates that if a liability is designated as being at fair value through profit or loss, **changes in the fair value that are due to changes in the liability's credit risk must be recognised directly in other comprehensive income** rather than profit or loss. Such **changes may not be re-classified** to profit or loss in subsequent years, although a **reserves transfer** is permitted from other components of equity to retained earnings. On the other hand**, if changes in the fair value attributable to the credit risk** of the liability **create or enlarge an accounting mismatch in profit or loss,** then all fair value movements are **recognised in profit or loss**.

(c) **B shares of subsidiary**

Ethan's accounting treatment of the B shares (as equity instruments) does not comply with IAS 32 *Financial Instruments: Presentation*. The IAS 32 definition of a financial liability includes any liability that is **a contractual obligation to deliver cash or another financial asset to another entity**. A financial instrument may only be classified as an equity instrument rather than a liability if the instrument does not include an obligation to deliver cash or other financial asset to another entity, or to exchange financial instruments with another entity under conditions that are potentially unfavourable.

In the **subsidiary's books**, the B shares would be treated as a **financial liability**. They contain an **obligation** to deliver cash in the form of a fixed dividend. The dividend is cumulative and must be paid whether or not the subsidiary has sufficient legally distributable profits when it is due, and so **the subsidiary cannot avoid this obligation**.

In the **consolidated financial statements,** the B shares would also be treated as a financial liability, **the intragroup element of this liability (70%) would cancel against the investment in B shares in the parent's (Ethan's) statement of financial position**. The shares **owned by external parties would not cancel**; they would remain **a financial liability**. It **is incorrect to treat them as non-controlling interest** because they are **not equity**.

68 Whitebirk

Workbook reference. Small and medium-sized entities are covered in Chapter 18 of your Workbook.

Top tips. Part (a) on the main differences between the IFRS for SMEs and full IFRS was reasonably straightforward. Part (b) required you to apply the standard to specific areas: goodwill, research and development expenditure, investment property and impairment. Remember not to use full IFRS!

Easy marks. This was a rich source of easy marks for the well-prepared candidate. Make sure your arguments are well-structured in order to earn those two marks for clarity and quality of discussion.

Marking scheme

			Marks
(a)	Subjective assessment including professional		11
(b)	(i)	Business combination	4
	(ii)	Research and development expenditure	3
	(iii)	Investment property	2
	(iv)	Intangible	2
			22

(a) **Modifications to reduce the burden of reporting for SMEs**

The IFRS for SMEs has **simplifications** that reflect the needs of users of SMEs' financial statements and cost-benefit considerations. It is designed to facilitate financial reporting by small and medium-sized entities in a number of ways:

(i) It provides significantly **less guidance** than full IFRS. A great deal of the guidance in full IFRS would not be relevant to the needs of smaller entities.

(ii) Many of the **principles** for recognising and measuring assets, liabilities, income and expenses in full IFRSs are **simplified**. For example, goodwill and intangibles are always amortised over their estimated useful life (or ten years if it cannot be estimated). Research and development costs must be expensed. With defined benefit pension plans, all actuarial gains and losses are to be recognised immediately in other comprehensive income. All past service costs are to be recognised immediately in profit or loss. To measure the defined benefit obligation, the projected unit credit method must be used.

(iii) Where full IFRSs allow accounting policy choices, the IFRS for SMEs **allows only the easier option**. Examples of alternatives not allowed in the IFRS for SMEs include: revaluation model for intangible assets and property, plant and equipment, proportionate consolidation for investments in jointly-controlled entities and choice between cost and fair value models for investment property (measurement depends on the circumstances).

(iv) **Topics not relevant** to SMEs are **omitted**: earnings per share, interim financial reporting, segment reporting, insurance and assets held for sale.

(v) Significantly **fewer disclosures** are required.

(vi) The standard has been written in **clear language** that can easily be translated.

The above represents a considerable reduction in reporting requirements – perhaps as much as 90% – compared with listed entities. Entities will naturally wish to use the IFRS for SMEs if they can, but **its use is restricted**.

The restrictions are **not related to size**. There are several disadvantages of basing the definition on size limits alone. Size limits are **arbitrary** and **different limits are likely to be appropriate in different** countries. Most people believe that SMEs are **not simply smaller versions of listed entities**, but differ from them in more fundamental ways.

The most important way in which SMEs differ from other entities is that they are **not usually publicly accountable**. Accordingly, there are **no quantitative thresholds** for qualification as a SME; instead, the scope of the IFRS is determined by a **test of public accountability**. The IFRS is suitable for all entities except those whose securities are publicly traded and financial institutions such as banks and insurance companies.

Another way in which the use of the IFRS for SMEs is restricted is that **users cannot cherry pick** from this IFRS and full IFRS. If an entity adopts the IFRS for SMEs, it **must adopt it in its entirety**.

(b) (i) **Business combination**

IFRS 3 *Business Combinations* allows an entity to adopt the full or partial goodwill method in its consolidated financial statements. The IFRS for SMEs **only allows the partial goodwill method**. This avoids the need for SMEs to determine the fair value of the non-controlling interests not purchased when undertaking a business combination.

In addition, IFRS 3 requires goodwill to be tested annually for impairment. The IFRS for SMEs **requires goodwill to be amortised instead**. This is a much simpler approach and the IFRS for SMEs specifies that if an entity is unable to make a reliable estimate of the useful life, it is presumed to be ten years, simplifying things even further.

Goodwill on Whitebirk's acquisition of Close will be calculated as:

	$'000
Consideration transferred	5,700
Non-controlling interest: 10% × $6m	600
	6,300
Less fair value of identifiable net assets acquired	(6,000)
Goodwill	300

This goodwill of $0.3 million will be amortised over ten years, that is $30,000 per annum.

(ii) **Research and development expenditure**

The IFRS for SMEs requires all internally generated research and development expenditure to be **expensed through profit or loss**. This is simpler than full IFRS – IAS 38 *Intangible Assets* requires internally generated assets to be capitalised if certain criteria (proving future economic benefits) are met, and it is often difficult to determine whether or not they have been met.

Whitebirk's total expenditure on research ($0.5m) and development ($1m) must be written off to profit or loss for the year, giving a charge of $1.5 million.

(iii) **Investment property**

Investment properties must be held at fair value through profit or loss under the IFRS for SMEs where their fair value can be measured without undue cost or effort, which appears to be the case here, given that an estate agent valuation is available. Consequently a gain of $0.2 million ($1.9m – $1.7m) will be reported in Whitebirk's profit or loss for the year.

(iv) **Intangible asset**

IAS 36 *Impairment of Assets* requires annual impairment tests for indefinite life intangibles, intangibles not yet available for use and goodwill. This is a complex, time-consuming and expensive test.

The IFRS for SMEs only requires impairment tests where there are indicators of impairment. In the case of Whitebirk's intangible, there are no indicators of impairment, and so an impairment test is not required.

In addition, IAS 38 *Intangible Assets* does not require intangible assets with an indefinite useful life to be amortised. In contrast, under the IFRS for SMEs, all intangible assets must be amortised. If the useful life cannot be established reliably, it must not exceed ten years.

69 Lucky Dairy

Workbook references. IAS 41 is covered in Chapter 3 of your workbook. IAS 37 is covered in Chapter 5 and IFRS 5 in Chapter 13.

Top tips. In this question you are required to deal with a scenario that had as its main theme IAS 41 *Agriculture*. You should not, however, make the mistake of thinking that this question is just about IAS 41; it requires a knowledge of several other standards including IAS 37 and IFRS 5.

The dairy herd

The dairy herd is a **biological asset** as defined by IAS 41 *Agriculture*. IAS 41 states that a biological asset should be **measured at fair value less estimated point of sale costs** unless its fair value cannot be measured reliably. **Gains and losses** arising from a change in fair value should be **included in profit or loss** for the period.

In this case, fair value is based on market price and point of sale costs are the costs of transporting the cattle to the market. Cattle in the Ham and Shire regions is valued on this basis.

IAS 41 encourages companies to **analyse the change in fair value** between the movement due to **physical changes** and the movement due to **price changes** (see the table below). It also encourages companies to provide a quantified description of each group of biological assets. Therefore the value of the cows and the value of the heifers should be **disclosed separately** in the statement of financial position.

Valuing the dairy herd for the Dale Region is less straightforward as its **fair value cannot be measured reliably at the date of purchase**. In this situation IAS 41 requires the herd to be valued at **cost less any impairment losses**. The standard also requires companies to provide an **explanation of why** fair value cannot be measured reliably and the **range of estimates** within which fair value is likely to fall.

Valuation of cattle, excluding Dale region

	Cows	*Heifers*	*Total*
	$'000	$'000	$'000
Fair value of herd at 1 June 20X1 (50,000 × 50)	2,500		2,500
Purchase 1 December 20X1 (25,000 × 40)		1,000	1,000
Increase in fair value less estimated point of sale costs due to price change: (50,000 × (55 – 50)/25,000 × (42 – 40))	250	50	300
Increase in fair value less estimated point of sale costs due to physical change: (50,000 × (60 – 55)/25,000 × (46 – 42))	250	100	350
Fair value less estimated point of sale costs at 31 May 20X2 (50,000 × 60/25,000 × 46)	3,000	1,150	4,150

Valuation of cattle in Dale Region

	$'000
Cost at 1 June 20X1	
Cows (20,000 x 50)	1,000
Heifers (10,000 x 40)	400
	1,400
Less impairment loss	(200)
	1,200

Note. The herd is impaired because its recoverable amount is $1.2 million. This is the higher of fair value less costs to sell of $1 million (the amount that the Lucky Dairy has been offered) and value in use of $1.2 million (discounted value of the milk to be produced).

	$'000
Estimated fair value at 31 May 20X2 (for disclosure only):	
Cows (20,000 × 60)	1,200
Heifers (10,000 × 55)	550
	1,750

Milk

The milk is **agricultural produce** as defined by IAS 41 and should normally be measured at **fair value less estimated point of sale costs at the time of milking**. In this case the company is holding ten times the amount of inventory that it would normally hold and it is probable that much of this milk is unfit for consumption. The company should estimate the amount of milk that will not be sold and **write down** the inventory accordingly. The write down should be disclosed separately in the income statement as required by IAS 1 *Presentation of Financial Statements.*

Government grant

Under IAS 41, the government grant should be recognised as income **when it becomes receivable**. As it was only on 6 June 20X2 that the company received official confirmation of the amount to be paid, the income **should not be recognised in the current year**. The amount may be sufficiently material to justify disclosure as a non-adjusting event after the balance sheet date.

Legal proceedings and additional compensation

The lawyers have indicated that the company will probably be found liable for passing on the disease to consumers. There is a **present obligation as the result of a past obligating event** and therefore a **provision for $2 million should be recognised**, as required by IAS 37 *Provisions, Contingent Liabilities and Contingent Assets.*

IAS 37 states that **reimbursement** should only be recognised when it is **virtually certain** to be received. It is **only possible** that the company will receive compensation for the legal costs and therefore this **cannot be recognised**. However, the compensation should be **disclosed** as a contingent asset in the financial statements.

Planned sale of Dale farms

The Board of Directors has **approved the planned closure**, but there has **not yet been a public announcement**. Despite the fact that a local newspaper has published an article on the possible sale, the company **has not created a valid expectation** that the sale will take place and in fact **it is not certain** that the sale will occur. Therefore, there is **no 'constructive obligation'** and under IAS 37 **no provision should be made** for redundancy or any other costs connected with the planned sale.

Under IFRS 5 *Non-current Assets Held for Sale and Discontinued Operations,* Dale must be treated as a **continuing operation** for the year ended 31 May 20X2 as the sale has not taken place. As management are **not yet fully committed** to the sale **neither the operation as a whole nor any of the separate assets of Dale can be classified as 'held for sale'**.

Government grant

Legal proceedings for accidental contamination

Mock Exams

ACCA

Strategic Business Reporting (International)

Mock Examination 1

Time allowed: 3 hours 15 minutes

This exam is divided into two sections:

Section A – BOTH questions are compulsory and MUST be attempted

Section B – BOTH questions are compulsory and MUST be attempted

Do not open this exam until you are ready to start under examination conditions.

Section A – BOTH questions are compulsory and MUST be attempted

1 Joey

(a) Joey, a public limited company, operates in the media sector. Joey has investments in two companies, Margy and Hulty. The draft statements of financial position at 30 November 20X4 are as follows:

	Joey	*Margy*	*Hulty*
	$m	$m	$m
Assets			
Non-current assets			
Property, plant and equipment	3,295	2,000	1,200
Investments in subsidiaries			
Margy	1,675		
Hulty	700		
	5,670	2,000	1,200
Current assets	985	861	150
Total assets	6,655	2,861	1,350
Equity and liabilities			
Share capital	850	1,020	600
Retained earnings	3,340	980	350
Other components of equity	250	80	40
Total equity	4,440	2,080	990
Total liabilities	2,215	781	360
Total equity and liabilities	6,655	2,861	1,350

The following information is relevant to the preparation of the consolidated financial statements:

(1) On 1 December 20X1, Joey acquired 30% of the ordinary shares of Margy for a cash consideration of $600 million when the fair value of Margy's identifiable net assets was $1,840 million. Joey has equity accounted for Margy up to 30 November 20X3. Joey's share of Margy's undistributed profit amounted to $90 million and its share of a revaluation gain amounted to $10 million for the period 1 December 20X1 to 30 November 20X3. On 1 December 20X3, Joey acquired a further 40% of the ordinary shares of Margy for a cash consideration of $975 million and gained control of the company. The cash consideration paid has been added to the equity accounted balance for Margy at 1 December 20X3 to give the carrying amount at 30 November 20X4.

At 1 December 20X3, the fair value of Margy's identifiable net assets was $2,250 million. At 1 December 20X3, the fair value of the equity interest in Margy held by Joey before the business combination was $705 million and the fair value of the non-controlling interest of 30% was assessed as $620 million. The retained earnings and other components of equity of Margy at 1 December 20X3 were $900 million and $70 million respectively. It is group policy to measure the non-controlling interest at fair value.

(2) At the time of the business combination with Margy on 1 December 20X3, Joey included in the fair value of Margy's identifiable net assets, an unrecognised contingent liability with a fair value of $6 million in respect of a warranty claim in progress against Margy, considered to have been measured reliably. In March 20X4, there was a

revision of the estimate of the liability to $5 million. The amount has met the criteria to be recognised as a provision in current liabilities in the financial statements of Margy and the revision of the estimate is deemed to be a measurement period adjustment.

(3) Buildings with a carrying amount of $200 million had been included in the fair value of Margy's identifiable net assets at 1 December 20X3. The buildings have a remaining useful life of 20 years at 1 December 20X3 and are depreciated on the straight-line basis. However, Joey had commissioned an independent valuation of the buildings of Margy which was not complete at 1 December 20X3 and therefore not considered in the fair value of the identifiable net assets at the acquisition date. The valuations were received on 1 April 20X4 and resulted in a decrease of $40 million in the fair value of property, plant and equipment at the date of acquisition. This decrease does not affect the fair value of the non-controlling interest at acquisition and has not been entered into the financial statements of Margy. The excess of the fair value of the net assets over their carrying amount, at 1 December 20X3, is due to an increase in the value of non-depreciable land and the contingent liability.

(4) On 1 December 20X3, Joey acquired 80% of the equity interests of Hulty, a private entity, in exchange for cash of $700 million, gaining control of Hulty from that date. Because the former owners of Hulty needed to dispose of the investment quickly, they did not have sufficient time to market the investment to many potential buyers. The fair value of the identifiable net assets was $960 million. Joey determined that the fair value of the 20% non-controlling interest in Hulty at that date was $250 million. Joey reviewed the procedures used to identify and measure the assets acquired and liabilities assumed and to measure the fair value of both the non-controlling interest and the consideration transferred. After that review, Hulty determined that the procedures and resulting measures were appropriate. The retained earnings and other components of equity of Hulty at 1 December 20X3 were $300 million and $40 million respectively. The excess in fair value is due to an unrecognised franchise right, which Joey had granted to Hulty on 1 December 20X2 for five years. At the time of the acquisition, the franchise right could be sold for its market price. It is group policy to measure the non-controlling interest at fair value.

All goodwill arising on acquisitions has been impairment tested with no impairment being required.

(5) From 30 November 20X3, Joey carried a property in its statement of financial position at its revalued amount of $14 million in accordance with IAS 16 *Property, Plant and Equipment*. Depreciation is charged at $300,000 per year on the straight-line basis. In March 20X4, the management decided to sell the property and it was advertised for sale. On 31 March 20X4, the sale was considered to be highly probable and the criteria for IFRS 5 *Non-current Assets Held for Sale and Discontinued Operations* were met. At that date, the property's fair value was $15.4 million and its value in use was $15.8 million. Costs to sell the property were estimated at $300,000. On 30 November 20X4, the property was sold for $15.6 million. The transactions regarding the property are deemed to be material and no entries have been made in the financial statements regarding this property since 30 November 20X3 as the cash receipts from the sale were not received until December 20X4.

Required

(a) (i) Explain, showing relevant calculations and with reference to IFRS 3 *Business Combinations*, how the goodwill balance in Joey's consolidated financial statements at 30 November 20X4 should be calculated. **(10 marks)**

(ii) Explain how the transaction described in Note 5 above should be accounted for in Joey's consolidated financial statements at 30 November 20X4. **(6 marks)**

(iii) Prepare, showing required calculations, an extract from Joey's consolidated statement of financial position showing the group retained earnings at 30 November 20X4. **(4 marks)**

(b) The Joey Group has granted to the employees of Margy and Hulty, some of whom are considered key management personnel, options over its own shares as at 7 December 20X4. The options vest immediately. Joey is not proposing to make a charge to the subsidiaries for these options.

Joey does not know how to account for this transaction.

Required

Explain to Joey how the above transaction should be dealt with in the subsidiaries' financial statements and Joey's consolidated financial statements, and advise on any disclosures that may be required to ensure external stakeholders are aware of the transaction. **(5 marks)**

(c) Joey took out a foreign currency loan of 5 million dinars at a fixed interest rate of 8% on 1 December 20X3. The interest is paid at the end of each year. The loan will be repaid after two years on 30 November 20X5. The interest rate is the current market rate for similar two-year fixed interest loans.

Joey is unsure how to account for the loan and related interest.

The average currency exchange rate for the year is not materially different from the actual rate.

Exchange rates:	*$1 = dinars*
1 December 20X3	5.0
30 November 20X4	6.0
Average exchange rate for year ended 30 November 20X4	5.6

Required

Explain to Joey how to account for the loan and interest in the financial statements for the year ended 30 November 20X4. **(5 marks)**

(Total = 30 marks)

2 Ramsbury **39 mins**

The directors of Ramsbury, a public limited company which manufactures industrial cleaning products, are preparing the consolidated financial statements for the year ended 30 June 20X7. In your capacity as advisor to the company, you become aware of the following issues.

In the draft consolidated statement of financial position, the directors have included in cash and cash equivalents a loan provided to a director of $1 million. The loan has no specific repayment date on it but is repayable on demand. The directors feel that there is no problem with this presentation as International Financial Reporting Standards (IFRS) allow companies to make accounting policy choices, and that showing the loan as a cash equivalent is their choice of accounting policy.

On 1 July 20X6, there was an amendment to Ramsbury's defined benefit pension scheme whereby the promised pension entitlement was increased from 10% of final salary to 15%. A bonus is paid to the directors each year which is based upon the operating profit margin of Ramsbury. The directors of Ramsbury are unhappy that there is inconsistency on the presentation of gains and losses in relation to pension scheme within the consolidated financial statements. Additionally, they believe that as the pension scheme is not an integral part of the operating activities of Ramsbury, it is misleading to include the gains and losses in profit or loss. They therefore propose to change their accounting policy so that all gains and losses on the pension scheme are recognised in other comprehensive income. They believe that this will make the financial statements more consistent, more understandable and can be justified on the grounds of fair presentation. Ramsbury's pension scheme is currently in deficit.

Required

Discuss the ethical and accounting implications of the above situations, with reference where appropriate, to International Financial Reporting Standards. **(18 marks)**

Professional marks will be awarded in this question for the application of ethical principles.

(2 marks)

(Total = 20 marks)

Section B – BOTH questions are compulsory and MUST be attempted

3 Klancet

Klancet is a public limited company operating in the pharmaceuticals sector. The company is seeking advice on several financial reporting issues.

(a) Klancet produces and sells its range of drugs through three separate divisions. In addition, it has two laboratories which carry out research and development activities.

In the first laboratory, the research and development activity is funded internally and centrally for each of the three divisions. It does not carry out research and development activities for other entities. Each of the three divisions is given a budget allocation which it uses to purchase research and development activities from the laboratory. The laboratory is directly accountable to the division heads for this expenditure.

The second laboratory performs contract investigation activities for other laboratories and pharmaceutical companies. This laboratory earns 75% of its revenues from external customers and these external revenues represent 18% of the organisation's total revenues.

The performance of the second laboratory's activities and of the three separate divisions is regularly reviewed by the chief operating decision maker (CODM). In addition to the heads of divisions, there is a head of the second laboratory. The head of the second laboratory is directly accountable to the CODM and they discuss the operating activities, allocation of resources and financial results of the laboratory.

The managing director does not think IFRS 8 provides information that is useful to investors. He feels it just adds more pages to financial statements that are already very lengthy. The finance director partially agrees with the managing director and believes that the IASB's practice statement on materiality confirms his opinion that not all the disclosure requirements in IFRS 8 are necessary.

Required

(i) Advise the managing director, with reference to IFRS 8 *Operating Segments*, whether the research and development laboratories should be reported as two separate segments. **(6 marks)**

(ii) Discuss the managing director's view that IFRS 8 does not provide useful information to investors. **(5 marks)**

(iii) Discuss whether the finance director is correct in his opinion about IFRS 8, identifying any ethical concerns you may have. You should briefly refer to Practice Statement 2 *Making Materiality Judgements* in your answer. **(4 marks)**

(b) Klancet is collaborating with Retto, a third party, to develop two existing drugs owned by Klancet.

Project 1

In the case of the first drug, Retto is simply developing the drug for Klancet without taking any risks during the development phase and will have no further involvement if regulatory approval is given. Regulatory approval has been refused for this drug in the past. Klancet will retain ownership of patent rights attached to the drug. Retto is not involved in the marketing and production of the drug. Klancet has agreed to make two non-refundable payments to Retto of $4 million on the signing of the agreement and $6 million on successful completion of the development.

Project 2

Klancet and Retto have entered into a second collaboration agreement in which Klancet will pay Retto for developing and manufacturing an existing drug. The existing drug already has regulatory approval. The new drug being developed by Retto for Klancet will not differ substantially from the existing drug. Klancet will have exclusive marketing rights to the drug if the regulatory authorities approve it. Historically, in this jurisdiction, new drugs receive approval if they do not differ substantially from an existing approved drug.

The contract terms require Klancet to pay an upfront payment on signing of the contract, a payment on securing final regulatory approval, and a unit payment of $10 per unit, which equals the estimated cost plus a profit margin, once commercial production begins. The cost-plus profit margin is consistent with Klancet's other recently negotiated supply arrangements for similar drugs.

Required

Prepare notes for a presentation to the managing director of Klancet as to how to account for the above contracts with Retto in accordance with IFRSs. **(8 marks)**

Professional marks will be awarded in Part (a) for clarity and quality of presentation. **(2 marks)**

(Total = 25 marks)

4 Jayach

(a) Jayach, a public limited company, carries an asset that is traded in different markets. The asset has to be valued at fair value under International Financial Reporting Standards. Jayach currently only buys and sells the asset in the Australasian market. The data relating to the asset are set out below.

Year to 30 November 20X2	*Asian market*	*European market*	*Australasian market*
Volume of market – units	4 million	2 million	1 million
Price	$19	$16	$22
Costs of entering the market	$2	$2	$3
Transaction costs	$1	$2	$2

Additionally, Jayach had acquired an entity on 30 November 20X2 and is required to fair value a decommissioning liability. The entity has to decommission a mine at the end of its useful life, which is in three years' time. Jayach has determined that it will use a valuation technique to measure the fair value of the liability. If Jayach were allowed to transfer the liability to another market participant, then the following data would be used.

Input	*Amount*
Labour and material cost	$2 million
Overhead	30% of labour and material cost
Third party mark-up – industry average	20%
Annual inflation rate	5%
Risk adjustment – uncertainty relating to cash flows	6%
Risk-free rate of government bonds	4%
Entity's non-performance risk	2%

Required

Discuss, with relevant computations, how Jayach should measure the fair value of the above asset and liability under IFRS 13. **(11 marks)**

(b) Jayach has recently employed a new managing director. The managing director has convinced the board that an investment in a new cryptocurrency, iCoin, would generate excellent capital gains. Consequently, Jayach purchased 50 units of iCoin for $250,000 on 20 December 20X1. The finance director has expressed concern about how to report this investment in Jayach's 31 December 20X1 financial statements. Given the lack of an accounting standard for such investments, he sees no alternative but to include it as a cash equivalent. As the amount invested is less than the quantitative threshold Jayach has used to assess materiality, he is not planning to provide any further information about the investment in the financial statements.

Required

(i) In the absence of a specific accounting standard on cryptocurrencies, discuss how Jayach should determine how to account for the investment in iCoin under IFRS Standards. **(4 marks)**

(ii) Discuss the finance director's decision not to provide any further disclosures about the investment in the financial statements, making reference to IFRS Practice Statement 2 *Making Materiality Judgements*. **(4 marks)**

(c) The directors of Jayach have received an email from its majority shareholder.

To: Directors of Jayach **From:** A Shareholder **Re:** Measurement I have recently seen an article in the financial press discussing the 'mixed measurement approach' that is used by lots of companies. I hope this isn't the case at Jayach because 'mixed' seems to imply 'inconsistent'? Surely it would be better to measure everything in the same way? I would appreciate it if you could you provide further information at the next annual general meeting on measurement bases, covering what approach is taken at Jayach and why, and the potential effect on investors trying to analyse the financial statements.

Required

Prepare notes for the directors of Jayach which discuss the issues raised in the shareholder's email. You should refer to the *Conceptual Framework* where appropriate in your answer.

(6 marks)

(Total = 25 marks)

Answers

DO NOT TURN THIS PAGE UNTIL YOU HAVE COMPLETED THE MOCK EXAM

Section A

1 Joey

Workbook references. Basic groups and the principles of IFRS 3 are covered in Chapter 11. Step acquisitions are covered in Chapter 12. IFRS 5 is covered in Chapter 14. Share-based payment is covered in Chapter 10. IAS 21 is covered in Chapter 16.

Top tips. For step acquisitions, it is important to understand the transaction – here you have an associate becoming a subsidiary, so the goodwill calculation for Margy needs to include the fair value of the previously held investments. Remember to discuss the principles rather than just working through the calculations. The examiner has stated that a candidate will not be able to pass the SBR exam on numerical elements alone. The other goodwill calculation is very straightforward, the only unusual aspect being that it is a gain on a bargain purchase.

Don't skimp on parts (b) and (c) – there are five marks available.

Easy marks. There are some easy marks available in Part (a) for the standard parts of calculations of goodwill and retained earnings. The calculations in part (c) should also be relatively easy.

Marking scheme

				Marks
(a)	(i)	Goodwill		
		Calculation	4	
		Discussion – 1 mark per point up to maximum	6	
	(ii)	Asset held for sale		
		Calculation	3	
		Discussion – 1 mark per point up to maximum	3	
	(iii)	Retained earnings	4	
				20
(b)		Subjective assessment of discussion – 1 mark per point up to maximum	5	
(c)		Calculation		
		Discussion	3	
			2	
				10
				30

(a) (i) **Goodwill**

IFRS 3 *Business Combinations* requires goodwill to be recognised in a business combination. A business combination takes place when one entity, the acquirer, obtains control of another entity, the acquiree. IFRS 3 requires goodwill to be calculated and recorded at the acquisition date. Goodwill is the difference between the consideration transferred by the acquirer, the amount of any non-controlling interest and the fair value of the net assets of the acquiree at the acquisition date. When the business combination is achieved in stages, as is the case for Margy, the previously held interest in the now subsidiary must be remeasured to its fair value.

Applying these principles, the goodwill on the acquisition of Hulty and Margy should be calculated as follows:

	Hulty		*Margy*	
	$m	$m	$m	$m
Consideration transferred		700		975
Non-controlling interest (at fair value)		250		620
Fair value of previously held equity interest (Note (1))				705
Less fair value of net assets at acquisition				
Share capital	600		1,020	
Retained earnings	300		900	
Other components of equity	40		70	
Fair value adjustments:				
Land (Note (2) and W1)	–		266	
Contingent liability (Note (3))	–		(6)	
Franchise right (W1)	20		–	
		(960)		(2,250)
Gain on bargain purchase (Note (4))		(10)		50
Measurement period adjustments:				
Add decrease in FV of buildings (Note (5))				40
Contingent liability: $6m – $5m (Note (3))				(1)
Goodwill				89

Notes

(1) Margy is a business combination achieved in stages, here moving from a 30% owned associate to a 70% owned subsidiary on 1 December 20X3. Substance over form dictates the accounting treatment as, in substance, an associate has been disposed of and a subsidiary has been purchased. From 1 December 20X3, Margy is accounted for as a subsidiary of Joey and goodwill on acquisition is calculated at this date. IFRS 3 requires that the previously held investment is remeasured to fair value and included in the goodwill calculation as shown above. Any gain or loss on remeasurement to fair value is reported in consolidated profit or loss.

(2) IFRS 3 requires the net assets acquired to be measured at their fair value at the acquisition date. The increase in the fair value of Margy's net assets (that are not the result of specific factors covered in Notes (3) and (5) below) is attributed to non-depreciable land.

(3) In accordance with IFRS 3, contingent liabilities should be recognised on acquisition of a subsidiary where they are a present obligation arising as the result of a past event and their fair value can be measured reliably (as is the case for the warranty claims) even if their settlement is not probable. Contingent liabilities after initial recognition must be measured at the higher of the amount that would be recognised under IAS 37 *Provisions, Contingent Liabilities and Contingent Assets* and the amount initially recognised under IFRS 3.

(4) As the goodwill calculation for the acquisition of Hulty results in a negative value, this is a gain on a bargain purchase and should be recorded in profit or loss for the year attributable to the parent. Before doing so, Joey must review the goodwill calculation to ensure that it has correctly identified all of the assets acquired and all of the liabilities assumed, along with verifying that its measurement of the consideration transferred and the non-controlling interest is

appropriate. Joey has completed this exercise and thus it is appropriate to record the negative goodwill and related profit.

(5) As a result of the independent property valuation becoming available during the measurement period, the carrying amount of property, plant and equipment as at 30 November 20X4 is decreased by $40 million less excess depreciation charged of $2 million ($40m/20 years), ie $38 million. This will increase the carrying amount of goodwill by $40 million as IFRS 3 allows the retrospective adjustment of a provisional figure used in the calculation of goodwill at the acquisition date where new information has become available about the circumstances that existed at the acquisition date. Depreciation expense for 20X4 is decreased by $2 million.

Workings

1 *Hulty: Fair value adjustments*

	At acq'n 1 Dec 20X3	*Movement (over 4 years)*	*At year end 30 Nov 20X4*
	$m	$m	$m
Franchise: 960 – (600 + 300 + 40)	20	(5)	15

2 *Margy: Fair value adjustments*

	At acq'n 1 Dec 20X3	*Movement (reduced dep'n)*	*At year end 30 Nov 20X4*
	$m	$m	$m
Land: 2,250 – (1,020 + 900 + 70) + 6*	266	–	266
Property, plant and equipment	(40)	2	(38)

*Contingent liability

(ii) **Asset held for sale**

At 31 March 20X4, the criteria in IFRS 5 *Non-current Assets Held for Sale and Discontinued Operations* have been met, and the property should be classified as held for sale. In accordance with IFRS 5, an asset held for sale should be measured at the **lower of** its **carrying amount** and **fair value less costs to sell**. Immediately before classification of the asset as held for sale, the entity must recognise any impairment in accordance with the applicable IFRS. Any impairment loss is generally recognised in profit or loss. The steps are as follows:

Step 1 Calculate carrying amount under applicable IFRS, here IAS 16 *Property, Plant and Equipment*:

At 31 March 20X4, the date of classification as held for sale, depreciation to date is calculated as $300,000 × 4/12 = $100,000. The carrying amount of the property is therefore $13.9 million ($14.0 – $0.1m). The journal entries are:

DEBIT	Profit or loss	$0.1m	
CREDIT	Property, plant and equipment (PPE)		$0.1m

The difference between the carrying amount and the fair value at 31 March 20X4 is material, so the property is revalued to its fair value of $15.4 million under IAS 16's revaluation model:

DEBIT	PPE ($15.4m – $13.9m)	$1.5m	
CREDIT	Other comprehensive income		$1.5m

Step 2 Consider whether the property is impaired by comparing its carrying amount, the fair value of $15.4 million, with its recoverable amount. The recoverable amount is the higher of value in use (given as $15.8 million) and fair value less costs to sell ($15.4m – $3m = $15.1m.) The property is not impaired because the recoverable amount (value in use) is higher than the carrying amount (fair value). No impairment loss is recognised.

Step 3 Classify as held for sale and cease depreciation under IFRS 5. Compare the carrying amount ($15.4 million) with fair value less costs to sell ($15.1 million). Measure at the lower of carrying amount and fair value less costs to sell, here $15.1 million, giving an initial write-down of $300,000.

DEBIT	Profit or loss	$0.3m	
CREDIT	PPE		$0.3m

Step 4 On 30 November 20X4, the property is sold for $15.6 million, which, after deducting costs to sell of $0.3 million gives a profit or $0.2 million.

DEBIT	Receivables	$15.3m	
CREDIT	PPE		$15.1m
CREDIT	Profit or loss		$0.2m

(iii) **Retained earnings**

JOEY GROUP

CONSOLIDATED STATEMENT OF FINANCIAL POSITION AS AT 30 NOVEMBER 20X4 (EXTRACT)

	$m
Retained earnings (W1)	3,451.7

Workings

W1: Group retained earnings

	Joey	*Hulty*	*Margy*
	$m	$m	$m
At year end	3,340.0	350	980
FV adjustment: dep'n reduction (part (a)(i) W2)			2
FV adjustment: franchise amortisation (part (a)(i) W1)		(5)	
Liability adjustment (6 – 1)* (part (a)(i))			5
Gain on bargain purchase (part (a)(i))	10.0		
Profit on derecognition of associate (W2)	5.0		
Asset held for sale: (0.2 – 0.1 – 0.3) (part (a)(ii))	(0.2)		
At acquisition		(300)	(900)
		45	87
Group share:			
Hulty: 80% × 45	36.0		
Margy: 70% × 87	60.9		
	3,451.7		

* The warranty claim provision of $5 million in Margy's financial statements must be reversed on consolidation to avoid double counting. This is because the contingent liability for this warranty claim was recognised in the consolidated financial statements on acquisition of Margy.

W2: Profit on derecognition of 30% associate

	$m
Fair value of previously held equity interest at date control obtained (per question/((a) (i))	705
Carrying amount of associate: 600 cost + 90 (post-acq'n RE) + 10 (post acq'n OCE)	(700)
Profit	5

(b) **Share-based payment**

This arrangement will be governed by IFRS 2 *Share-based Payment,* which includes within its scope **transfers of equity instruments of an entity's parent in return for goods or services**. Clear guidance is given in the Standard as to **when to treat group share-based payment transactions as equity settled and when to treat them as cash settled.**

To determine the accounting treatment, the group entity receiving the goods and services must **consider its own rights and obligations as well as the awards granted**. The amount recognised by the group entity receiving the goods and services will not necessarily be consistent with the amount recognised in the consolidated financial statements.

Group share-based payment transactions **must be treated as equity settled** if either of the following apply:

(i) The entity **grants rights to its own equity instruments**.
(ii) The entity has **no obligation to settle** the share-based payment transactions.

Treatment in consolidated financial statements

Because the group receives all of the services in consideration for the group's equity instruments, the transaction is treated as **equity settled**. The fair value of the share-based payment at the grant date is **charged to profit or loss over the vesting period with a corresponding credit to equity**. In this case, the options vest immediately on the grant date, the employees not being required to complete a specified period of service and the services therefore being presumed to have been received. The fair value will be taken by reference to the market value of the shares because it is deemed not normally possible to measure directly the fair value of the employee services received.

Treatment in subsidiaries' financial statements

The subsidiaries do not have an obligation to settle the awards, so the grant is treated as an **equity settled** transaction. The fair value of the share-based payment at the grant date is **charged to profit or loss over the vesting period with a corresponding credit to equity**. The parent, Joey, is compensating the employees of the subsidiaries, Margy and Hulty, with no expense to the subsidiaries, and therefore the **credit in equity is treated as a capital contribution**. Because the shares vest immediately, the expense recognised in Margy and Hulty's statement of profit or loss will be the full cost of the fair value at grant date.

IAS 24 disclosures

Some of the employees are considered **key management personnel** and therefore IAS 24 *Related Party Disclosures* should be applied. IAS 24 requires disclosure of the related party relationship, the transaction and any outstanding balances at the year end date. Such disclosures are required in order to provide sufficient information to the users of the financial statements about the potential impact of related party transactions on an entity's profit or loss and financial position.

IAS 24 requires that an entity discloses key management personnel compensation in total and for several categories, of which share-based payments is one. IFRS Practice Statement 2 *Making Materiality Judgements* confirms that disclosures required in IFRSs need only be made if the information provided by the disclosure is **material**. Some related party transactions may be assessed as immaterial and therefore not disclosed. That said, the remuneration of key management personnel is of great interest to investors and it would be difficult to see how it could be considered immaterial.

(c) **Foreign currency loan**

On 1 December 20X3

On initial recognition (at 1 December 20X3), the loan is measured at the transaction price translated into the functional currency (the dollar), because the interest is at a market rate for a similar two-year loan. The loan is translated at the rate ruling on 1 December 20X3.

DEBIT	Cash 5m ÷ 5	$1m	
CREDIT	Financial liability (loan payable)		$1m

Being recognition of loan

Year ended 30 November 20X4

Because there are no transaction costs, the effective interest rate is 8%. Interest on the loan is translated at the average rate because this is an approximation for the actual rate

DEBIT	Profit or loss (finance cost): 5m × 8% ÷ 5.6	$71,429	
CREDIT	Financial liability (loan payable)		$71,429

Being recognition of finance costs for the year ended 30 November 20X4

On 30 November 20X4

The interest is paid and the following entry is made, using the rate on the date of payment of $1 = 6 dinars

DEBIT	Financial liability (loan payable) 5m × 8% ÷ 6	$66,667	
CREDIT	Cash		$66,667

Being recognition of interest payable for the year ended 30 November 20X4

In addition, as a monetary item, the loan balance at the year-end is translated at the spot rate at the year end: 5m dinars ÷ 6 = $833,333. This gives rise to an exchange gain of £1,000,000 – $833,333 = $166,667.

The exchange gain on the interest paid of $71,429 – $66,667 = $4,762 is added to the exchange gain on retranslation of the loan of $166,667. This gives a total exchange gain of $4,762 + $166,667 = $171,429.

2 Ramsbury

Workbook references. The *Conceptual Framework* is covered in Chapter 1 and ethics is covered in Chapter 2. Employee benefits are covered in Chapter 5.

Top tips. As with all questions, ensure that you apply your knowledge to the scenario provided and that your answer is in context. It is not enough to simply discuss the accounting requirements. You must draw out the ethical issues. Where relevant, you should identify any threats to the fundamental principles in ACCA's *Code of Ethics and Conduct*.

Marking scheme

	Marks
Accounting issues 1 mark per point to a maximum	9
Ethical issues 1 mark per point to a maximum	9
Professional marks	2
	20

Treatment of loan to director

The directors have included the loan made to the director as part of the cash and cash equivalents balance. It may be that the directors have misunderstood the definition of cash and cash equivalents, believing the loan to be a cash equivalent. IAS 7 *Statement of Cash Flows* defines cash equivalents as short-term, highly liquid investments that are readily convertible to known amounts of cash and which are subject to an insignificant risk of changes in value. However, the loan is not in place to enable Ramsbury to manage its short-term cash commitments, it has no fixed repayment date and the likelihood of the director defaulting is not known. The classification as a cash equivalent is therefore inappropriate.

It is likely that the loan should be treated as a financial asset under IFRS 9 *Financial Instruments.* Further information would be needed, for example, is the $1 million the fair value? A case could even be made that, since the loan may never be repaid, it is in fact a part of the director's remuneration, and if so should be treated as an expense and disclosed accordingly. In addition, since the director is likely to fall into the category of key management personnel, related party disclosures under IAS 24 *Related Party Disclosures* are likely to be necessary.

The treatment of the loan as a cash equivalent is in **breach of the two fundamental qualitative characteristics** prescribed in the IASB's *Conceptual Framework for Financial Reporting,* namely:

(i) **Relevance.** The information should be disclosed separately as it is relevant to users.

(ii) **Faithful representation.** Information must be **complete, neutral** and **free from error**. Clearly this is not the case if a loan to a director is shown in cash.

The treatment is also in breach of the *Conceptual Framework's* key **enhancing qualitative characteristics:**

(i) **Understandability.** If the loan is shown in cash, it hides the true nature of the practices of the company, making the financial statements less understandable to users.

(ii) **Verifiability.** Verifiability helps assure users that information faithfully represents the economic phenomena it purports to represent. It means that different knowledgeable and independent observers could reach consensus that a particular depiction is a faithful representation. The treatment does not meet this benchmark as it reflects the subjective bias of the directors.

(iii) **Comparability.** For financial statements to be comparable year-on-year and with other companies, transactions must be correctly classified, which is not the case here. If the cash balance one year includes a loan to a director and the next year it does not, then you are not comparing like with like.

In some countries, loans to directors are **illegal**, with directors being personally liable. Even if this is not the case, there is a potential **conflict of interest** between that of the director and that of the company, which is why separate disclosure is required as a minimum. Directors are responsible for the financial statements required by statute, and thus it is their responsibility to put right any errors that mean that the financial statements do not comply with IFRS. There is generally a legal requirement to maintain proper accounting records, and recording a loan as cash conflicts with this requirement.

In obscuring the nature of the transaction, it is possible that the directors are **motivated by personal interest**, and are thus failing in their duty to act honestly and ethically. There is potentially a self-interest threat to the fundamental principles of the ACCA *Code of Ethics and Conduct*. If one transaction is misleading, it casts doubt on the credibility of the financial statements as a whole.

In conclusion, the treatment is problematic and **should be rectified**.

Ethical implications of change of accounting policy

IAS 8 *Accounting Policies, Changes in Accounting Estimates and Errors* only permits a change in accounting policy if the change is: (i) required by an IFRS or (ii) results in the financial statements providing reliable and more relevant information about the effects of transactions, other events or conditions on the entity's financial position, financial performance or cash flows. A retrospective adjustment is required unless the change arises from a new accounting policy with transitional arrangements to account for the change. It is possible to depart from the requirements of IFRS but only in the extremely rare circumstances where compliance would be so misleading that it would conflict with the overall objectives of the financial statements. Practically this override is rarely, if ever, invoked.

IAS 19 *Employee Benefits* requires all gains and losses on a defined benefit pension scheme to be recognised in profit or loss except for the remeasurement component relating to the assets and liabilities of the plan, which must be recognised in other comprehensive income. So, current service cost, past service cost and the net interest cost on the net defined benefit liability must all be recognised in profit or loss. There is no alternative treatment available to the directors, which, under IAS 8, a change in accounting policy might be applied to move Ramsbury to. The directors' proposals cannot be justified on the grounds of fair presentation. The directors have an ethical responsibility to prepare financial statements which are a true representation of the entity's performance and comply with all accounting standards.

There is a clear self-interest threat arising from the bonus scheme. The directors' change in policy appears to be motivated by an intention to overstate operating profit to maximise their bonus potential. The amendment to the pension scheme is a past service cost which must be expensed to profit or loss during the period the plan amendment has occurred, ie immediately. This would therefore be detrimental to the operating profits of Ramsbury and depress any potential bonus.

Additionally, it appears that the directors wish to manipulate other aspects of the pension scheme such as the current service cost and, since the scheme is in deficit, the net finance cost. The directors are deliberately manipulating the presentation of these items by recording them in equity rather than in profit or loss. The financial statements would not be compliant with IFRS, would not give a reliable picture of the true costs to the company of operating a pension scheme and this treatment would make the financial statements less comparable with other entities correctly applying IAS 19. Such treatment is against ACCA's *Code of Ethics and Conduct* fundamental principles of objectivity, integrity and professional behaviour. The directors should be reminded of their ethical responsibilities and must be dissuaded from implementing the proposed change in policy.

The directors should be encouraged to utilise other tools within the financial statements to explain the company's results such as drawing users attention towards the cash flow where the cash generated from operations measure will exclude the non-cash pension expense and if necessary alternative performance measures such as EBITDA could be disclosed where non-cash items may be consistently stripped out for comparison purposes.

Section B

3 Klancet

Workbook references. Segment reporting is covered in Chapter 18. Intangible assets are covered in Chapter 4. Financial instruments are covered in Chapter 8. IFRS Practice Statement 2 *Making Materiality Judgements* is covered in Chapter 20.

Top tips. In Part (a)(i), on segment reporting, the key was to argue that the second laboratory met the definition of an operating segment, while the first one did not. In Part (a)(ii) you should consider why segmental information is useful to investors – why would they want this information? What makes this information particularly useful to investors? Part (a)(iii) requires an awareness of current issues in financial reporting, in this case IFRS Practice Statement 2 *Making Materiality Judgements*. It is crucial that you read widely while studying SBR as questions on current issues will definitely feature in your exam.

In Part (b) the key issue was whether the costs could be capitalised as development expenditure, which was the case for the latter, but not the former.

Easy marks. These are available for discussing the principles and quantitative thresholds of IFRS 8 in Part (a).

Marking scheme

			Marks
(a)	(i)	Requirements of IFRS 8 – 1 mark per point up to maximum	6
	(ii)	Usefulness of IFRS 8 – 1 mark per point up to maximum	5
	(iii)	Materiality – 1 mark per point up to maximum	4
(b)		Notes for presentation – 1 mark per point up to maximum	8
Professional marks (Part (a))			2
			25

(a) (i) **Segment reporting**

IFRS 8 *Operating Segments* states that an operating segment is a component of an entity which engages in business activities from which it may earn revenues and incur costs. In addition, discrete financial information should be available for the segment and these results should be regularly reviewed by the entity's chief operating decision maker (CODM) when making decisions about resource allocation to the segment and assessing its performance.

Other factors should be taken into account, including the nature of the business activities of each component, the existence of managers responsible for them, and information presented to the board of directors.

According to IFRS 8, an operating segment is one which meets any of the following quantitative thresholds:

(i) Its reported revenue is 10% or more of the combined revenue of all operating segments.

(ii) The absolute amount of its reported profit or loss is 10% or more of the greater, in absolute amount, of (1) the combined reported profit of all operating segments which did not report a loss and (2) the combined reported loss of all operating segments which reported a loss.

(iii) Its assets are 10% or more of the combined assets of all operating segments.

As a result of the application of the above criteria, the first laboratory will not be reported as a separate operating segment. The divisions have heads directly accountable to, and maintaining regular contact with, the CODM to discuss all aspects of their division's performance. The divisions seem to be consistent with the core principle of IFRS 8 and should be reported as separate segments. The laboratory does not have a separate segment manager and the existence of a segment manager is normally an important factor in determining operating segments. Instead, the laboratory is responsible to the divisions themselves, which would seem to indicate that it is simply supporting the existing divisions and not a separate segment. Additionally, there does not seem to be any discrete performance information for the segment, which is reviewed by the CODM.

The second laboratory should be reported as a separate segment. It meets the quantitative threshold for percentage of total revenues and it meets other criteria for an operating segment. It engages in activities which earn revenues and incurs costs, its operating results are reviewed by the CODM and discrete information is available for the laboratory's activities. Finally, it has a separate segment manager.

(ii) Contrary to the managing director's views, IFRS 8 provides information that makes the financial statements more relevant and more useful to investors. IFRS financial statements are highly aggregated and may prevent investors from understanding the many different business areas and activities that an entity is engaged in. IFRS 8 requires information to be disclosed that is not readily available elsewhere in the financial statements, therefore it provides additional information which aids an investor's understanding of how the business operates and is managed.

IFRS 8 uses a 'management approach' to report information on an entity's segments and results from the point of view of the decision makers of the entity. This allows investors to examine an entity 'though the eyes of management' – to see the business in the way in which the managers who run the business on their behalf see it. This provides investors with more discrete information on the business segments allowing them to better assess the return being earned from those business segments, the risks that are associated with those segments and how those risks are managed. The more detailed information provides investors with more insight into an entity's longer term performance.

The requirement to disclose information that is actually used by internal decision makers is an important feature of IFRS 8, but is also one of its main criticisms. The fact that the reporting does not need to be based on IFRS makes it difficult to make comparisons with information that was reported in prior periods and with other companies in the sector. The flexibility in reporting can make it easier to manipulate what is reported. IFRS 8 disclosures are often most useful if used in conjunction with narrative disclosures prepared by the directors of the company, such as the Strategic Review in the UK.

(iii) The finance director's opinion that 'not all the disclosure in IFRS 8 is necessary' could be interpreted to mean that he believes he can pick and choose which disclosure requirements he feels are necessary and which he believes are not.

This is not correct. IAS 1 *Presentation of Financial Statements* requires all standards to be applied if fair presentation is to be achieved. Directors cannot choose which parts of standards they do or do not apply.

However, as confirmed by Practice Statement 2, if the information provided by a disclosure is immaterial and it therefore cannot reasonably be expected to influence the decisions of primary users of the financial statements, then that disclosure does not need to be made.

If the finance director is suggesting that the information provided about Klancet by some of the disclosures required by IFRS 8 are not material, then assuming that the information is indeed immaterial, he would be correct in stating that those disclosures are not necessary.

The directors should apply the principles given in Practice Statement 2 to review how they have made materiality judgements in their financial reporting. It may be that their current financial report is very lengthy because they include information that is not material.

Both directors appear reluctant to give the disclosures required by IFRS 8. This raises concern. If the finance director is not aware that he cannot pick and choose requirements from IFRSs, then his professional competence may be called into question. If he is aware of this, and an assessment of whether the disclosures are material has not been done, or has been done inappropriately, then it may be that the directors are trying to hide an issue. This should be considered in more detail.

(b) **Development of drugs**

Notes for presentation to the managing director

1 **Criteria for recognising as an asset**

IAS 38 *Intangible Assets* requires an entity to recognise an intangible asset, whether purchased or self-created (at cost) if, and only if, it is **probable** that the future economic benefits which are attributable to the asset will flow to the entity and the cost of the asset can be **measured reliably**.

2 **Internally generated intangible assets**

The recognition requirements of IAS 38 apply whether an intangible asset is acquired externally or generated internally. IAS 38 includes additional recognition criteria for internally generated intangible assets.

Development costs are capitalised only after technical and commercial feasibility of the asset for sale or use have been established. This means that the entity must intend and be able to complete the intangible asset and either use it or sell it and be able to demonstrate how the asset will generate future economic benefits, in keeping with the recognition criteria.

If an entity cannot distinguish the research phase from the development phase of an internal project to create an intangible asset, the entity treats the expenditure for that project as if it were incurred in the research phase only.

The price which an entity pays to acquire an intangible asset reflects its expectations about the probability that the expected future economic benefits in the asset will flow to the entity.

3 **Project 1**

Klancet owns the potential new drug, and Retto is carrying out the development of the drug on its behalf. The risks and rewards of ownership remain with Klancet.

By paying the initial fee and the subsequent payment to Retto, Klancet does not acquire a separate intangible asset. The payments represent research and development by a third party, which need to be expensed over the development period provided that the recognition criteria for internally generated intangible assets are not met.

Development costs are capitalised only after technical and commercial feasibility of the asset for sale or use have been established. This means that the entity must intend and be able to complete the intangible asset and either use it or sell it and be able to demonstrate how the asset will generate future economic benefits. At present, this criterion does not appear to have been met as regulatory authority for the use of the drug has not been given and, in fact, approval has been refused in the past.

4 **Project 2**

In the case of the second project, the drug has already been discovered and therefore the costs are for the development and manufacture of the drug and its slight modification. There is no indication that the agreed prices for the various elements are not at fair value. In particular, the terms for product supply at cost plus profit are consistent with Klancet's other supply arrangements.

Therefore, Klancet should capitalise the upfront purchase of the drug and subsequent payments as incurred, and consider impairment at each financial reporting date. Regulatory approval has already been attained for the existing drug and therefore there is no reason to expect that this will not be given for the new drug. Amortisation should begin once regulatory approval has been obtained. Costs for the products have to be accounted for as inventory using IAS 2 *Inventories* and then expensed as costs of goods sold as incurred.

4 Jayach

Workbook references. Fair value measurement under IFRS 13 is covered in Chapter 4. The *Conceptual Framework* is covered in Chapter 1, IAS 8 in Chapter 2 and Practice Statement 2 in Chapter 20.

Top tips. Fair value measurement affects many aspects of financial reporting. Part (a) requires application of IFRS 13 to the valuation of assets and liabilities. Ensure that you provide explanations to support your workings. Part (b) looks at an investment in cryptocurrency for which there is no specific accounting standard. Don't panic if you see such a question in your exam. Sensible points which apply the principles of IAS 8 and the *Conceptual Framework* will gain marks. Part (c) considers the topic of measurement from a wider perspective. Make sure you relate your answer to the email given in the question. Remember that the examiner has recommended that you read widely, including technical articles and real financial reports, to support your learning.

Easy marks. Credit will be given for textbook knowledge in Part (a).

Marking scheme

				Marks
(a)		1 mark per point up to maximum of	6	
		Calculations	5	
				11
(b)	(i)	1 mark per point up to maximum of	4	
	(ii)	1 mark per point up to maximum of	4	
				8
(c)		1 mark per point up to maximum of		6
				25

(a) **Fair value of asset**

YEAR TO 30 NOVEMBER 20X2	Asian market	European market	Australasian market
Volume of market – units	4m	2m	1m
	$	$	$
Price	19	16	22
Costs of entering the market	(2)	(2)	–
Potential fair value	17	14	22
Transaction costs	(1)	(2)	(2)
Net profit	16	12	20

Notes

1 Because Jayach currently buys and sells the asset in the Australasian market, the **costs of entering that market** are not incurred and therefore **not relevant**.

2 Fair value is **not adjusted for transaction costs**. Under IFRS 13, these are not a feature of the asset or liability, but may be taken into account when determining the most advantageous market.

3 The **Asian market is the principal market** for the asset because it is the market with the greatest volume and level of activity for the asset. If information about the Asian market is available and Jayach can access the market, then Jayach should base its fair value on this market. Based on the Asian market, the **fair value of the asset would be $17**, measured as the price that would be received in that market ($19) less costs of entering the market ($2) and ignoring transaction costs.

4 If **information** about the Asian market is **not available**, or if Jayach **cannot access the market**, Jayach must measure the fair value of the asset using the price in the **most advantageous market**. The most advantageous market is the market that maximises the amount that would be received to sell the asset, after taking into account both transaction costs and usually also costs of entry, which is the net amount that would be received in the respective markets. The most advantageous market here is therefore the **Australasian market**. As explained above, costs of entry are not relevant here, and so, based on this market, the **fair value would be $22**.

It is assumed that market participants are independent of each other and knowledgeable, and able and willing to enter into transactions.

Fair value of decommissioning liability

Because this is a business combination, Jayach must measure the liability at fair value in accordance with IFRS 13, rather than using the best estimate measurement required by IAS 37 *Provisions, Contingent Liabilities and Contingent Assets*. In most cases there will be no observable market to provide pricing information. If this is the case here, Jayach will use **the expected present value technique** to measure the fair value of the decommissioning liability. If Jayach were contractually committed to transfer its decommissioning liability to a market participant, it would conclude that a market participant would use the inputs as follows, arriving at a **fair value of $3,215,000**.

Input	*Amount*
	$'000
Labour and material cost	2,000
Overhead: 30% × 2,000	600
Third party mark-up – industry average: 2,600 × 20%	520
	3,120
Inflation adjusted total (5% compounded over three years): $3{,}120 \times 1.05^3$	3,612
Risk adjustment – uncertainty relating to cash flows: 3,612 × 6%	217
	3,829
Discount at risk-free rate plus entity's non-performance risk (4% + 2% = 6%): $3{,}829/1.06^3$	3,215

(b) (i) It isn't appropriate for Jayach to classify the investment as a cash equivalent purely because it is unsure of how else to account for it. In the absence of an IFRS covering investments in cryptocurrencies, the directors of Jayach should use judgement to develop an appropriate accounting policy.

In developing the policy, IAS 8 *Accounting Policies, Accounting Estimates and Errors* requires that the directors consider:

(1) IFRSs dealing with similar issues. For example, the specific facts and circumstances could lead Jayach to conclude that the investment is an intangible asset accounted for under IAS 38 *Intangible Assets.*

(2) The *Conceptual Framework.* The investment appears to meet the definition of an asset: a present economic resource controlled by the entity as a result of past events. Consideration should be given to the recognition criteria and to other issues such as the measurement basis to apply and how measurement uncertainty may affect that choice given the volatility of cryptocurrencies.

(3) The most recent pronouncements of other national GAAPs based on a similar conceptual framework and accepted industry practice. This is sparse. The Australian Accounting Standards Board have concluded that standard setting activity on cryptocurrencies should be undertaken by the IASB.

Fundamentally, the directors need to account for the investment in a way which provides **useful** information to the primary users of its financial statements. This means the information provided by the accounting treatment should be **relevant** and should **faithfully represent** the investment.

(ii) The finance director's decision to not provide any further disclosure about the investment in iCoin is questionable.

The objective of Jayach's financial report is to provide financial information which is useful to its primary users in making decisions about providing resources to Jayach. Practice Statement 2 re-affirms the principle in IFRS that information that is not material does not need to be disclosed in the financial statements. However, whether this information is material should be properly assessed.

Practice Statement 2 recommends that assessment of materiality should be performed with reference to both quantitative factors and qualitative factors. So far, the finance director has only considered quantitative factors, but qualitative factors should be considered. For example, the fact that this investment not the usual type of investment made by Jayach is a qualitative factor. The presence of a qualitative factor lowers the quantitative threshold below what would otherwise be used – so in this case, the investment could be material.

Furthermore, the investment is risky because cryptocurrencies are highly volatile. If it is Jayach's plan to invest in more cryptocurrencies in the future, or even to accept cryptocurrencies as payment, then this investors are likely to consider this important. Depending on their risk appetite, investors may consider the investment too risky and therefore inappropriate, and may be concerned about the potential future impact should Jayach decide to invest more in such currencies.

Part of the decision-making that primary users make on the basis of financial statements involves assessing management's stewardship of Jayach's resources. Some investors may consider this not to be good stewardship, given the risk involved.

(c) A 'mixed measurement' approach means that a company selects a different measurement basis (eg historical cost or current value) for its various assets and liabilities, rather than using a single measurement basis for all items. The measurement basis selected should reflect the type of entity and sector in which it operates and the business model that the entity adopts.

Some investors have criticised the mixed measurement approach because they think that if different measurement bases are used for assets and liabilities, the resulting totals can have little meaning or lack relevance.

However, a single measurement basis may not provide the most relevant information to users. A particular measurement basis may be easier to understand, more verifiable and less costly to implement. Therefore a mixed measurement approach is not 'inconsistent' but can actually provide more relevant information for stakeholders.

The *Conceptual Framework* confirms that the IASB uses a mixed measurement approach in developing standards. The measurement methods included in standards are those which the IASB believes provide the most relevant information and which most faithfully represent the underlying transaction or event. It seems that most investors feel that this approach is consistent with how they analyse financial statements. The problems of mixed measurement appear to be outweighed by the greater relevance achieved.

Jayach prepares its financial statements under IFRSs, and therefore applies the measurement bases permitted in IFRSs. IFRSs adopt a mixed measurement basis, which includes current value (fair value, value in use, fulfilment value and current cost) and historical cost.

When an IFRS allows a choice of measurement basis, the directors of Jayach must exercise judgement as to which basis will provide the most useful information for its primary users. Furthermore when selecting a measurement basis, the directors should consider measurement uncertainty. The *Conceptual Framework* states that for some estimates, a high level of measurement uncertainty may outweigh other factors to such an extent that the resulting information may have little use.

ACCA

Strategic Business Reporting (International)

Mock Examination 2

Time allowed: 3 hours 15 minutes

This exam is divided into two sections:

Section A – BOTH questions are compulsory and MUST be attempted

Section B – BOTH questions are compulsory and MUST be attempted

Do not open this exam until you are ready to start under examination conditions.

Section A – BOTH questions are compulsory and MUST be attempted

1 Kutchen **59 mins**

The following group financial statements relate to the Kutchen Group which comprised Kutchen, House and Mach, all public limited companies.

GROUP STATEMENT OF FINANCIAL POSITION AS AT 31 DECEMBER 20X6

	$m
Assets	
Non-current assets	
Property, plant and equipment	365
Goodwill	–
Intangible assets	23
	388
Current assets	133
Total assets	521
Equity and liabilities	
Share capital of $1 each	63
Retained earnings	56
Other components of equity	26
Non-controlling interest	3
	148
Non-current liabilities	101
Current liabilities	
Trade payables	272
Total liabilities	373
Total equity and liabilities	521

At the time of the internal review of the group financial statements, the following issues were discovered:

(1) On 1 June 20X6, Kutchen acquired 70% of the equity interests of House. The purchase consideration comprised 20 million shares of $1 of Kutchen at the acquisition date and a further 5 million shares on 31 December 20X7 if House's profit for the year was at least $4 million for the year ending on that date.

The market price of Kutchen's shares on 1 June 20X6 was $2 per share and that of House's shares was $4.20 per share. It is felt that there is a 20% chance of the profit target being met.

In accounting for the acquisition of House, the finance director did not take into account the non-controlling interest (NCI) in the goodwill calculation. He determined that a bargain purchase of $8 million arose on the acquisition of House, being the purchase consideration of $40 million less the fair value of the identifiable net assets of House acquired on 1 June 20X6 of $48 million. This valuation was included in the group financial statements above.

After the directors of Kutchen discovered the error, they decided to measure the NCI at fair value at the date of acquisition. The fair value of the NCI in House was to be based upon quoted market prices at acquisition. House had issued share capital of $1 each, totalling $13 million at 1 June 20X6 and there has been no change in this amount since acquisition.

(2) On 1 January 20X6, Kutchen acquired 80% of the equity interests of Mach, a privately owned entity, for a consideration of $57 million. The consideration comprised cash of $52 million and the transfer of non-depreciable land with a fair value of $5 million. The carrying amount of the land at the acquisition date was $3 million and the land has only recently been transferred to the seller of the shares in Mach and is still carried at $3 million in the group financial statements at 31 December 20X6.

At the date of acquisition, the identifiable net assets of Mach had a fair value of $55 million. Mach had made a profit for the year attributable to ordinary shareholders of $3.6 million for the year to 31 December 20X5.

The directors of Kutchen wish to measure the non-controlling interest at fair value at the date of acquisition but had again omitted NCI from the goodwill calculation. The NCI is to be measured at fair value using a public entity market multiple method. The directors of Kutchen have identified two companies who are comparable to Mach and who are trading at an average price to earnings ratio (P/E ratio) of 21. The directors have adjusted the P/E ratio to 19 for differences between the entities and Mach, for the purpose of fair valuing the NCI. The finance director has determined that a bargain purchase of $3 million arose on the acquisition of Mach being the cash consideration of $52 million less the fair value of the net assets of Mach of $55 million. This gain on the bargain purchase had been included in the group financial statements above.

(3) Kutchen had purchased an 80% interest in Niche for $40 million on 1 January 20X6 when the fair value of the identifiable net assets was $44 million. The partial goodwill method had been used to calculate goodwill and an impairment of $2 million had arisen in the year ended 31 December 20X6. The holding in Niche was sold for $50 million on 31 December 20X6. The carrying amount of Niche's identifiable net assets other than goodwill was $60 million at the date of sale. Kutchen had carried the investment in Niche at cost. The finance director calculated that a gain arose of $2 million on the sale of Niche in the group financial statements being the sale proceeds of $50 million less $48 million being their share of the identifiable net assets at the date of sale (80% of $60 million). This was credited to retained earnings.

(4) Kutchen has decided to restructure one of its business segments. The plan was agreed by the board of directors on 1 October 20X6 and affects employees in two locations. In the first location, half of the factory units were closed on 1 December 20X6 and the affected employees' pension benefits have been frozen. Any new employees will not be eligible to join the defined benefit plan. After the restructuring, the present value of the defined benefit obligation in this location is $8 million. The following table relates to location 1.

Value before restructuring	*Location 1*
	$m
Present value of defined benefit obligation	(10)
Fair value of plan assets	7
Net pension liability	(3)

In the second location, all activities have been discontinued. It has been agreed that employees will receive a payment of $4 million in exchange for the pension liability of $2.4 million in the unfunded pension scheme.

Kutchen estimates that the costs of the above restructuring excluding pension costs will be $6 million. Kutchen has not accounted for the effects of the restructuring in its financial statements because it is planning a rights issue and does not wish to depress the share price. Therefore there has been no formal announcement of the restructuring.

Required

(a) (i) Explain to the directors of Kutchen, with suitable workings, how goodwill should have been calculated on the acquisition of House and Mach showing the adjustments which need to be made to the consolidated financial statements to correct any errors by the finance director. **(10 marks)**

(ii) Explain, with suitable calculations, how the gain or loss on the sale of Niche should have been recorded in the group financial statements. **(5 marks)**

(iii) Discuss, with suitable workings, how the pension scheme should be dealt with after the restructuring of the business segment and whether a provision for restructuring should have been made in the financial statements for the year ended 31 December 20X6. **(7 marks)**

Note. Marks will be allocated in (a) for a suitable discussion of the principles involved as well as the accounting treatment.

(b) When Kutchen acquired the majority shareholding in Mach, there was an option on the remaining non-controlling interest (NCI), which could be exercised at any time up to 31 March 20X7. On 31 January 20X7, Kutchen acquired the remaining NCI in Mach. The payment for the NCI was structured so that it contained a fixed initial payment and a series of contingent amounts payable over the following two years.

The contingent payments were to be based on the future profits of Mach up to a maximum amount. Kutchen felt that the fixed initial payment was an equity transaction. Additionally, Kutchen was unsure as to whether the contingent payments were either equity, financial liabilities or contingent liabilities.

After a board discussion which contained disagreement as to the accounting treatment, Kutchen is preparing to disclose the contingent payments in accordance with IAS 37 *Provisions, Contingent Liabilities and Contingent Assets*. The disclosure will include the estimated timing of the payments and the directors' estimate of the amounts to be settled.

Required

Advise Kutchen on the difference between equity and liabilities, and on the proposed accounting treatment of the contingent payments on acquisition of the NCI of Mach.

(8 marks)

(Total = 30 marks)

2 Abby **39 mins**

Abby is a company which conducts business in several parts of the world.

The accountant has discovered that Abby has purchased goods from a company, Arwight, which its finance director jointly owns with his wife. The accountant believes that this purchase should be disclosed. However, the director refuses to disclose the transaction as in his opinion it is an 'arm's length' transaction. He feels that if the transaction is disclosed, it will be harmful to business and feels that the information asymmetry caused by such non-disclosure is irrelevant as most entities undertake related party transactions without disclosing them. Similarly, the director felt that competitive harm would occur if disclosure of operating segment profit or loss was made. As a result, the entity only disclosed a measure of total assets and total liabilities for each reportable segment.

When preparing the financial statements for the recent year end, the accountant noticed that Arwight has not paid an invoice for several million dollars and it is significantly overdue for payment. It appears that the entity has liquidity problems and it is unlikely that Arwight will pay. The accountant believes that a loss allowance for trade receivables is required. The finance director has refused to make such an allowance and has told the accountant that the issue must not be discussed with anyone within the trade because of possible repercussions for the credit worthiness of Arwight.

Additionally, when completing the consolidated financial statements, the finance director has suggested that there should be no positive fair value adjustments for a recently acquired subsidiary and has stated that the accountant's current position is dependent upon following these instructions. The fair value of the subsidiary is $50 million above the carrying amount in the financial records. The reason given for not fair valuing the subsidiary's net assets is that goodwill is an arbitrary calculation which is meaningless in the context of the performance evaluation of an entity.

Finally, when preparing the annual impairment tests of goodwill arising on other subsidiaries, the finance director has suggested that the accountant is flexible in the assumptions used in calculating future expected cash flows, so that no impairment of goodwill arises and that the accountant should use a discount rate which reflects risks for which future cash flows have been adjusted. He has indicated that he will support a salary increase for the accountant if he follows his suggestions.

Required

Discuss the ethical and accounting implications of the above situations from the perspective of the reporting accountant. **(18 marks)**

Professional marks will be awarded in question 2 for the application of ethical principles. **(2 marks)**

(Total = 20 marks)

Section B – BOTH questions are compulsory and MUST be attempted

3 Africant — 49 mins

(a) Africant owns several farms and also owns a division which sells agricultural vehicles. It is considering selling this agricultural retail division and wishes to measure the fair value of the inventory of vehicles for the purpose of the sale. Three markets currently exist for the vehicles. Africant has transacted regularly in all three markets.

At 31 December 20X5, Africant wishes to find the fair value of 150 new vehicles, which are identical. The current volume and prices in the three markets are as follows:

Market	*Sales price per vehicle*	*Historical volume – vehicles sold by Africant*	*Total volume of vehicles sold in the market*	*Transaction costs per vehicle*	*Transport cost to market per vehicle*
	$			$	$
Europe	40,000	6,000	150,000	500	400
Asia	38,000	2,500	750,000	400	700
Africa	34,000	1,500	100,000	300	600

Africant wishes to value the vehicles at $39,100 per vehicle as these are the highest net proceeds per vehicle, and Europe is the largest market for Africant's product.

(i) Africant wishes to understand the principles behind the valuation of the new vehicles and also whether their valuation would be acceptable under IFRS 13 *Fair Value Measurement*. **(8 marks)**

(ii) Africant uses the revaluation model for its non-current assets. Africant has several plots of farmland which are unproductive. The company feels that the land would have more value if it were used for residential purposes. There are several potential purchasers for the land but planning permission has not yet been granted for use of the land for residential purposes. However, preliminary enquiries with the regulatory authorities seem to indicate that planning permission may be granted. Additionally, the government has recently indicated that more agricultural land should be used for residential purposes.

Africant has also been approached to sell the land for commercial development at a higher price than that for residential purposes and understands that fair value measurement of a non-financial asset takes into account a market perspective.

Africant would like an explanation of what is meant by a 'market perspective' and advice on how to measure the fair value of the land in its financial statements. **(7 marks)**

Required

Advise Africant on the matters set out above (in (i) and (ii)) with reference to relevant International Financial Reporting Standards.

Note. The mark allocation is shown against each of the two issues above.

(b) Africant is about to hold its annual general meeting with shareholders and the directors wish to prepare for any potential questions which may be raised at the meeting. There have been discussions in the media over the fact that the most relevant measurement method should be selected for each category of assets and liabilities. This 'mixed measurement approach' is used by many entities when preparing financial statements. There have also been comments in the media about the impact that measurement uncertainty and price volatility can have on the quality of financial information.

Required

Discuss the impact which the above matters may have on the analysis of financial statements by investors in Africant. **(8 marks)**

Professional marks will be awarded in Part (b) for clarity and quality of presentation. **(2 marks)**

(Total = 25 marks)

4 Rationale **49 mins**

The directors of Rationale are reviewing the published financial statements of the group. The following is an extract of information to be found in the financial statements.

Year ended		*31 December 20X6*	*31 December 20X5*
	$m	$m	$m
Net profit/(loss) before taxation and after the items set out below		(5)	38
Net interest expense		10	4
Depreciation		9	8
Amortisation of intangible assets		3	2
Impairment of property	10		
Insurance proceeds	(7)	3	
Debt issue costs		2	
Share-based payment		3	1
Restructuring charges		4	
Impairment of acquired intangible assets		6	8

The directors use 'underlying profit' to comment on its financial performance. Underlying profit is a measure normally based on earnings before interest, tax, depreciation and amortisation (EBITDA). However, the effects of events which are not part of the usual business activity are also excluded when evaluating performance.

The following items were excluded from net profit to arrive at 'underlying profit'. In 20X6, the entity had to write off a property due to subsidence and the insurance proceeds recovered for this property was recorded but not approved until 20X7, when the company's insurer concluded that the claim was valid. In 20X6, the entity considered issuing loan notes to finance an asset purchase, however, the purchase did not go ahead. The entity incurred costs associated with the potential issue and so these costs were expensed as part of net profit before taxation. The entity felt that the share-based payment was not a cash expense and that the value of the options was subjective. Therefore, the directors wished to exclude the item from 'underlying profit'. Similarly, the directors wish to exclude restructuring charges incurred in the year, and impairments of acquired intangible assets.

Required

(a) (i) Discuss the possible concerns where an entity may wish to disclose additional information in its financial statements and whether the *Conceptual Framework* and IFRS Practice Statement 2 *Making Materiality Judgements* help in determining the boundaries for disclosure. **(8 marks)**

(ii) Discuss the use and the limitations of the proposed calculation of 'underlying profit' by Rationale.

Note. Your answer should include a comparative calculation of underlying profit for the years ended 31 December 20X5 and 20X6. **(9 marks)**

(b) The directors of Rationale are confused over the nature of a reclassification adjustment.

Required

Discuss, with examples, the nature of a reclassification adjustment and the arguments for and against allowing reclassification of items to profit or loss.

Note. A brief reference should be made in your answer to the *Conceptual Framework*.

(8 marks)

(Total = 25 marks)

Answers

DO NOT TURN THIS PAGE UNTIL YOU HAVE COMPLETED THE MOCK EXAM

Section A

1 Kutchen

Marking scheme

			Marks
(a)	(i)	Discussion 1 mark per point to a maximum	6
		Calculation	4
	(ii)	Discussion 1 mark per point to a maximum	3
		Calculation	2
	(iii)	1 mark for each point to a maximum	7
(b)		1 mark for each point to a maximum	8
			30

(a) (i) Goodwill on the acquisition of House and Mach should have been calculated as follows:

House

	$m	$m
Fair value of consideration for 70% interest	42.00	
Fair value of non-controlling interest	16.38	58.38
Fair value of identifiable net assets acquired		(48.00)
Goodwill		10.38

Contingent consideration should be valued at fair value and will have to take into account the various milestones set under the agreement. The expected value is (20% × 5 million shares) 1 million shares × $2, ie $2 million. There will be no remeasurement of the fair value in subsequent periods because the amount is settled in equity. If this were a liability, there would be remeasurement. The contingent consideration will be shown in OCE. The fair value of the consideration is therefore 20 million shares at $2 plus $2 million (above), ie $42 million.

The fair value of the NCI is 30% × 13 million × $4.20 = $16.38 million.

The finance director has not taken into account the fair value of the NCI in the valuation of goodwill or the contingent consideration. If the difference between the fair value of the consideration, NCI and the identifiable net assets is negative, the resulting gain is a bargain purchase in profit or loss, which may arise in circumstances such as a forced seller acting under compulsion. However, before any bargain purchase gain is recognised in profit or loss, and hence in retained earnings in the group statement of financial position, the finance director should have undertaken a review to ensure the identification of assets and liabilities is complete, and that measurements appropriately reflect consideration of all available information.

The adjustment to the group financial statements would be as follows:

DEBIT	Goodwill	$10.38 million	
DEBIT	Profit or loss	$8 million	
CREDIT	NCI		$16.38 million
CREDIT	OCE		$2 million

Mach

Net profit of Mach for the year to 31 December 20X5 is \$3.6 million. The P/E ratio (adjusted) is 19. Therefore the fair value of Mach is 19 × \$3.6 million, ie \$68.4 million. The NCI has a 20% holding; therefore the fair value of the NCI is \$13.68 million.

	\$m	\$m
Fair value of consideration for 80% interest (\$52m + \$5m)	57.00	
Fair value of non-controlling interest	13.68	70.68
Fair value of identifiable net assets acquired		(55.00)
Goodwill		15.68

The land transferred as part of the purchase consideration should be valued at its acquisition date fair value of \$5 million and included in the goodwill calculation. Therefore the increase of \$2 million over the carrying amount should be shown in retained earnings.

DEBIT	PPE	\$2 million	
CREDIT	Retained earnings		\$2 million

The adjustment to the group financial statements would be as follows:

DEBIT	Goodwill	\$15.68 million	
DEBIT	Retained earnings	\$3 million	
CREDIT	NCI		\$13.68 million
CREDIT	PPE		\$5 million

Total goodwill is therefore \$(15.68 + 10.38) million, ie \$26.06 million.

(ii) **Niche**

The finance director had calculated that a gain arose of \$2 million on the sale of Niche in the group financial statements being the sale proceeds of \$50 million less \$48 million which is their share of the identifiable net assets at the date of sale (80% of \$60 million). However, the calculation of the gain or loss on sale should have been the difference between the carrying amount of the net assets (including any unimpaired goodwill) disposed of and any proceeds received. The calculation of net assets will include the appropriate portion of cumulative exchange differences and any other amounts recognised in other comprehensive income and accumulated in equity. Additionally, the loss on sale should have been reported as a loss in profit or loss attributable to the parent.

The gain on the sale of Niche should have been recorded as follows:

	\$m
Gain/(Loss) in group financial statements on sale of Niche	
Sale proceeds	50.0
Less	
Share of identifiable net assets at date of disposal (80% × \$60 million)	(48.0)
Goodwill \$(40m – (80% of \$44m) – impairment \$2m)	(2.8)
Loss on sale of Niche recognised in group profit or loss	(0.8)

(iii) After restructuring, the present value of the pension liability in location 1 is reduced to \$8 million. Thus there will be a negative past service cost in this location of \$(10 – 8) million, ie \$2 million. As regards location 2, there is a settlement and a curtailment as all liability will be extinguished by the payment of \$4 million. Therefore there is a loss of \$(2.4 – 4) million, ie \$1.6 million. The changes to the pension scheme in locations 1 and 2 will both affect profit or loss as follows:

Location 1

DEBIT	Pension obligation	$2m	
CREDIT	Retained earnings		$2m

Location 2

DEBIT	Pension obligation	$2.4m	
DEBIT	Retained earnings	$1.6m	
CREDIT	Current liabilities		$4m

The 2018 amendments to IAS 19 require that, when a plan amendment, curtailment or settlement takes place, the updated actuarial assumptions used to remeasure the net defined benefit/asset should also be used to determine current service cost and net interest for the remainder of the reporting period. As such, the updated actuarial assumptions should be applied from 1 December 20X6 when calculating the amounts recognised in profit of loss.

IAS 37 *Provisions, Contingent Liabilities and Contingent Assets* states that a provision for restructuring should be made only when a detailed formal plan is in place and the entity has started to implement the plan, or announced its main features to those affected. A board decision is insufficient. Even though there has been no formal announcement of the restructuring, Kutchen has started implementing it and therefore it must be accounted for under IAS 37.

A provision of $6 million should also be made at the year end.

(b) The *Conceptual Framework* defines a liability as a present obligation to transfer an economic resource as a result of past events. IAS 32 *Financial Instruments: Presentation* establishes principles for presenting financial instruments as liabilities or equity. IAS 32 does not classify a financial instrument as equity or financial liability on the basis of its legal form but on the substance of the transaction. The key feature of a financial liability is that the issuer is obliged to deliver either cash or another financial asset to the holder. An obligation may arise from a requirement to repay principal or interest or dividends.

In contrast, equity has a residual interest in the entity's assets after deducting all of its liabilities. An equity instrument includes no obligation to deliver cash or another financial asset to another entity. A contract which will be settled by the entity receiving or delivering a fixed number of its own equity instruments in exchange for a fixed amount of cash or another financial asset is an equity instrument. However, if there is any variability in the amount of cash or own equity instruments which will be delivered or received, then such a contract is a financial asset or liability as applicable.

The contingent payments should not be treated as contingent liabilities but they should be recognised as financial liabilities and measured at fair value at initial recognition. IAS 37 *Provisions, Contingent Liabilities and Contingent Assets* excludes from its scope contracts which are executory in nature, and therefore prevents the recognition of a liability. Additionally, there is no onerous contract in this scenario.

Contingent consideration for a business must be recognised at the time of acquisition, in accordance with IFRS 3 *Business Combinations*. However, IFRSs do not contain any guidance when accounting for contingent consideration for the acquisition of a NCI in a subsidiary. The contract for contingent payments does meet the definition of a financial liability under IAS 32. Kutchen has an obligation to pay cash to the vendor of the NCI under the terms of a contract. It is not within Kutchen's control to be able to avoid that obligation. The amount of the contingent payments depends on the profitability of Mach, which itself depends on a number of factors which are uncontrollable. IAS 32 states that a contingent obligation to pay cash which is outside the control of both parties to a contract meets the definition of a financial liability which shall be initially measured at fair value. Since the contingent payments relate to the acquisition of the NCI, the offsetting entry would be recognised directly in equity.

2 Abby

Marking scheme

	Marks
Accounting issues – 1 mark per point up to maximum	10
Ethical issues – 1 mark per point up to maximum	8
Professional	2
	20

Related parties

The objective of IAS 24 *Related Party Disclosures* is to ensure that an entity's financial statements contain the disclosures necessary to draw attention to the possibility that its financial position and profit or loss may have been affected by the existence of related parties and by transactions and outstanding balances with such parties.

If there have been transactions between related parties, there should be disclosure of the nature of the related party relationship as well as information about the transactions and outstanding balances necessary for an understanding of the potential effect of the relationship on the financial statements. The finance director is a member of the key management personnel of the reporting entity and the entity from whom the goods were purchased is jointly controlled by that director. Therefore a related party relationship exists.

Abby should assess whether the information provided by disclosure of the transaction is material – ie could be reasonably expected to influence the decisions of primary users of Abby's financial statements. If yes, then the relevant disclosures under IAS 24 should be made.

Operating segments

IFRS 8 *Operating Segments* requires an entity to report financial and descriptive information about its reportable segments. Reportable segments are operating segments or aggregations of operating segments which meet specified criteria.

IFRS 8 does not contain a 'competitive harm' exemption and requires entities to disclose the financial information which is provided by the chief operating decision maker (CODM). The management accounts reviewed by the CODM may contain commercially sensitive information, and IFRS 8 might require that information to be disclosed externally.

Under IFRS 8, firms should provide financial segment disclosures which enable investors to assess the different sources of risk and income as management does. This sensitive information would also be available for competitors. The potential competitive harm may encourage firms to withhold segment information.

However, this is contrary to IFRS 8 which requires information about the profit or loss for each reportable segment, including certain specified revenues and expenses such as revenue from external customers and from transactions with other segments, interest revenue and expense, depreciation and amortisation, income tax expense or income and material non-cash items.

Impairment of financial assets

Areas such as impairments of financial assets often involve the application of professional judgement. The director may have received additional information, which has allowed him to form a different opinion to that of the accountant. The matter should be discussed with the director to ascertain why no provision is required and to ask whether there is additional information available.

However, suspicion is raised by the fact that the accountant has been told not to discuss the matter. Whilst there may be valid reasons for this, it appears again that the related party relationship is affecting the judgement of the director.

Fair value adjustments

Positive fair value adjustments increase the assets of the acquired company and as such reduce the goodwill recognised on consolidation. However, the majority of positive fair value adjustments usually relate to items of property, plant and equipment.

As a result, extra depreciation based on the net fair value adjustment reduces the post-acquisition profits of the subsidiary. This has a negative impact on important financial performance measures such as EPS. Therefore, by reducing fair value adjustments it will improve the apparent performance of new acquisitions and the consolidated financial statements.

Accountants should act ethically and ignore undue pressure to undertake creative accounting in preparing such adjustments. Guidance such as IFRS 3 *Business Combinations* and IFRS 13 *Fair Value Measurement* should be used in preparing adjustments and professional valuers should be engaged where necessary.

Impairment tests

In measuring value in use, the discount rate used should be the pre-tax rate which reflects current market assessments of the time value of money and the risks specific to the asset.

The discount rate should not reflect risks for which future cash flows have been adjusted and should equal the rate of return which investors would require if they were to choose an investment which would generate cash flows equivalent to those expected from the asset.

Reducing the impairment would have a positive impact on the financial statements. The offer of a salary increase is inappropriate and no action should be taken until the situation is clarified. Inappropriate financial reporting raises issues and risks for those involved and others associated with the company. Whilst financial reporting involves judgement, it would appear that this situation is not related to judgement.

Ethical issues

There are several potential breaches of accounting standards and unethical practices being used by the director. The director is trying to coerce the accountant into acting unethically.

IAS 1 *Presentation of Financial Statements* requires all IFRSs to be applied if fair presentation is to be obtained. Directors cannot choose which standards they do or do not apply.

It is important that accountants identify issues of unethical practice and act appropriately in accordance with ACCA's *Code of Ethics*. The accountant should discuss the matters with the director. The technical issues should be explained and the risks of non-compliance explained to the director.

If the director refuses to comply with accounting standards, then it would be appropriate to discuss the matter with others affected such as other directors and seek professional advice from ACCA. Legal advice should be considered if necessary.

An accountant who comes under pressure from senior colleagues to make inappropriate valuations and disclosures should discuss the matter with the person suggesting this. The discussion should try to confirm the facts and the reporting guidance which needs to be followed.

Financial reporting does involve judgement but the cases above seem to be more than just differences in opinion. The accountant should keep a record of conversations and actions and discuss the matters with others affected by the decision, such as directors. Additionally, resignation should be considered if the matters cannot be satisfactorily resolved.

Section B

3 Africant

Marking scheme

		Marks
(a)	1 mark per point up to maximum	15
(b)	1 mark per point up to maximum	8
Professional		2
		25

(a) (i) IFRS *13 Fair Value Measurement* states that fair value is an exit price in the principal market, which is the market with the highest volume and level of activity. It is not determined based on the volume or level of activity of the reporting entity's transactions in a particular market.

Once the accessible markets are identified, market-based volume and activity determines the principal market. There is a presumption that the principal market is the one in which the entity would normally enter into a transaction to sell the asset or transfer the liability, unless there is evidence to the contrary.

In practice, an entity would first consider the markets it can access. In the absence of a principal market, it is assumed that the transaction would occur in the most advantageous market. This is the market which would maximise the amount which would be received to sell an asset or minimise the amount which would be paid to transfer a liability, taking into consideration transport and transaction costs.

In either case, the entity must have access to the market on the measurement date. Although an entity must be able to access the market at the measurement date, IFRS 13 does not require an entity to be able to sell the particular asset or transfer the particular liability on that date.

If there is a principal market for the asset or liability, the fair value measurement represents the price in that market at the measurement date regardless of whether that price is directly observable or estimated using another valuation technique and even if the price in a different market is potentially more advantageous.

The principal (or most advantageous) market price for the same asset or liability might be different for different entities and therefore, the principal (or most advantageous) market is considered from the entity's perspective which may result in different prices for the same asset.

In Africant's case:

- The principal market is Asia as this is the market in which the majority of transactions for the vehicles occur. As such, the fair value of the 150 vehicles would be $5,595,000 ($38,000 – $700 = $37,300 × 150). Actual sales of the vehicles in either Europe or Africa would result in a gain or loss to Africant when compared with the fair value, ie $37,300.
- The most advantageous market would be Europe where a net price of $39,100 (after all costs) would be gained by selling there and the number of vehicles sold in this market is at its highest.

Africant would therefore utilise the fair value calculated by reference to the Asian market as this is the principal market.

The IASB decided to prioritise the price in the most liquid market (ie the principal market) as this market provides the most reliable price to determine fair value and also serves to increase consistency among reporting entities.

IFRS 13 makes it clear that the price used to measure fair value must not be adjusted for transaction costs, but should consider transportation costs.

Africant has currently deducted transaction costs in its valuation of the vehicles. Transaction costs are not deemed to be a characteristic of an asset or a liability but they are specific to a transaction and will differ depending on how an entity enters into a transaction.

While not deducted from fair value, an entity considers transaction costs in the context of determining the most advantageous market because the entity is seeking to determine the market which would maximise the net amount which would be received for the asset.

(ii) A fair value measurement of a non-financial asset takes into account a market participant's ability to generate economic benefits by using the asset in its highest and best use or by selling it to another market participant who would use the asset in its highest and best use.

The maximum value of a non-financial asset may arise from its use in combination with other assets or by itself.

IFRS 13 requires the entity to consider uses which are physically possible, legally permissible and financially feasible. The use must not be legally prohibited. For example, if the land is protected in some way by law and a change of law is required, then it cannot be the highest and best use of the land.

In this case, Africant's land for residential development would only require approval from the regulatory authority and as that approval seems to be possible, then this alternative use could be deemed to be legally permissible. Market participants would consider the probability, extent and timing of the approval which may be required in assessing whether a change in the legal use of the non-financial asset could be obtained.

Africant would need to have sufficient evidence to support its assumption about the potential for an alternative use, particularly in light of IFRS 13's presumption that the highest and best use is an asset's current use.

Africant's belief that planning permission was possible is unlikely to be sufficient evidence that the change of use is legally permissible. However, the fact the government has indicated that more agricultural land should be released for residential purposes may provide additional evidence as to the likelihood that the land being measured should be based upon residential value. Africant would need to prove that market participants would consider residential use of the land to be legally permissible.

Provided there is sufficient evidence to support these assertions, alternative uses, for example, commercial development which would enable market participants to maximise value, should be considered, but a search for potential alternative uses need not be exhaustive.

In addition, any costs to transform the land, for example, obtaining planning permission or converting the land to its alternative use, and profit expectations from a market participant's perspective should also be considered in the fair value measurement.

If there are multiple types of market participants who would use the asset differently, these alternative scenarios must be considered before concluding on the asset's highest and best use.

It appears that Africant is not certain about what constitutes the highest and best use and therefore IFRS 13's presumption that the highest and best use is an asset's current use appears to be valid at this stage.

(b) A measurement basis must be selected for each element recognised in the financial statements. The *Conceptual Framework* describes the characteristics of historical cost and current value (including fair value) measurement bases and when it may be appropriate to use each basis.

Some investors may be in favour of a **single measurement basis** for all recognised assets and liabilities arguing that the resulting totals and subtotals can have little meaning if different measurement methods are used.

Similarly, they may argue that profit or loss may lack relevance if it reflects a combination of flows based on historical cost and of value changes for items measured on a current value basis.

However, the majority of investors would tend to prefer that the most **relevant measurement method** is selected for each category of assets and liabilities. This is known as a **mixed measurement** approach and is consistent with how investors analyse financial statements.

The *Conceptual Framework* requires selection of a measurement basis that provides the most useful information to primary users, subject to the cost constraint. Therefore it supports a mixed measurement basis as consideration of the qualitative characteristics of useful information/cost constraint is likely to result in the selection of different measurement bases for different items.

The problems of mixed measurement are outweighed by the **greater relevance achieved** if the most relevant measurement basis is used for each class of assets and liabilities. The mixed measurement approach is reflected in recently issued standards. For example IFRS 9 *Financial Instruments* requires the use of cost in some cases and fair value in other cases. While IFRS 15 *Revenue from Contracts with Customers* essentially applies cost allocation.

Most accounting measures of assets and liabilities are uncertain and require estimation. While some measures of historical cost are straightforward as it is the amount paid or received, there are many occasions when the measurement of cost can be uncertain. In particular, recoverable cost, for which impairment and depreciation estimates are required.

In a similar vein, while some measures of fair value can be easily observed because of the availability of prices in an actively traded market (a so-called 'Level 1' fair value), others inevitably rely on management estimates and judgements ('Level 2' and 'Level 3').

High measurement uncertainty may mean that the measurement basis selected does not produce a faithful representation of the entity's financial position and financial performance. In such cases, selecting a slightly less relevant measurement basis but with less measurement uncertainty may provide more useful information to investors.

If a relevant measure of an asset or liability value is volatile, this should not be hidden from investors. To conceal its volatility would decrease the usefulness of the financial statements. Of course, such volatile gains and losses do need to be clearly presented and disclosed, because their predictive value may differ from that provided by other components of performance.

4 Rationale

Marking scheme

			Marks
(a)	(i)	1 mark per point up to a maximum	8
	(ii)	1 mark per point up to a maximum	9
(b)		1 mark per point up to a maximum	8
			25

(a) (i) IFRS requires an entity to disclose additional information which is relevant to an understanding of the entity's financial position and financial performance.

A company may disclose additional information where it is felt that an entity's performance may not be apparent from its financial statements prepared under IFRS. Additional information can help users understand management's view of what is important to the entity and the nature of management's decisions.

However, there are concerns relating to the disclosure of additional information:

- Such information may not readily be derived or reconciled back to the financial statements.
- There may be difficulty comparing information across periods and between entities because of the lack of a standardised approach.
- The presentation of additional information may be inconsistent with that defined or specified in IFRS and the entity may present an excessively optimistic picture of an entity's financial performance.
- Non-IFRS information may make it difficult to identify the complete set of financial statements, including whether the information is audited or not.
- Non-IFRS information may be given undue prominence or credibility merely because of its location within the financial statements.

Although disclosure boundaries are not specifically defined in IFRS, guidance can be found in the *Conceptual Framework* and in IFRS Practice Statement 2.

The *Conceptual Framework* states the objective of financial statements is to provide financial information about an entity's assets, liabilities, equity, income and expenses which is useful to users of financial statements in assessing the prospects for future net cash inflows to the entity and in assessing management's stewardship of the entity's economic resources. It acknowledges that it would be impossible to meet the information needs of all users of financial statements and limits the range of addressees to the **primary users** (existing or potential investors, lenders and other creditors).

IFRS Practice Statement 2 further clarifies that that financial statements cannot provide all the information primary users need. Instead the entity should aim to meet the **common information needs** of its primary users. It further states that if information is given that is not required by an IFRS, that information must not obscure information that is material according to IFRS.

(ii) The directors of Rationale are utilising an alternative performance measure for evaluating the company's performance. Depreciation and amortisation are non-cash expenses related to assets which have already been purchased and they are expenses which are subject to judgement or estimates based on experience and projections. The company, by using EBITDA, is attempting to show operating cash flow since the non-cash expenses are added back.

EBITDA can often be misused and manipulated. For example, depreciation schedules can be extended in order to increase profits with the consequential impact on this ratio. It can be argued that because the estimation of depreciation, amortisation and other non-cash items is vulnerable to judgement error, the profit figure can be distorted but by focusing on profits before these elements are deducted, a truer estimation of cash flow can be given. However, the substitution of EBITDA for conventional profit fails to take into account the need for investment in fixed capital items.

There can be an argument for excluding non-recurring items from the net profit figure. Therefore, it is understandable that the deductions for the impairment of property, the insurance recovery and the debt issue costs are made to arrive at 'underlying profit'. However, IAS 1 *Presentation of Financial Statements* states that an entity shall present additional line items, headings and subtotals in the statements presenting profit and loss and other comprehensive income when such presentation is relevant to an understanding of the entity's financial performance (para. 55). This paragraph should not be used to justify presentation of underlying, adjusted and pre-exceptional measures of performance on the face of the statement of profit or loss. The measures proposed are entity specific and could obscure performance and poor management.

Share-based compensation may not represent cash but if an entity chooses to pay equity to an employee that affects the value of equity, no matter what form that payment is in and therefore it should be charged as employee compensation. It is an outlay in the form of equity. There is therefore little justification in excluding this expense from net profit. Restructuring charges are a feature of an entity's business and they can be volatile. They should not be excluded from net profit because they are part of corporate life. In the case of Rationale, they have occurred in consecutive years and certainly could not be considered 'one-off'. Severance costs and legal fees are not non-cash items.

Impairments of acquired intangible assets usually reflect a weaker outlook for an acquired business than was expected at the time of the acquisition, and could be considered to be non-recurring. However, the impairment charges are a useful way of holding management accountable for its acquisitions. In this case, it seems as though Rationale has not purchased wisely in 20X6.

It appears as though Rationale wishes to disguise a weak performance in 20X6 by adding back a series of expense items. EBITDA, although reduced significantly from 20X5, is now a positive figure and there is an underlying profit created as opposed to a loss. However, users will still be faced with a significant decline in profit whichever measure is disclosed by Rationale. The logic for the increase in profit is flawed in many cases but there is a lack of authoritative guidance in the area. Many companies adopt non-financial measures without articulating the relationship between the measures and the financial statements.

Year ended	*31 December 20X6*	*31 December 20X5*
	$m	$m
Net profit/(loss) before taxation and after the items set out below	(5)	38
Net interest expense	10	4
Depreciation	9	8
Amortisation of intangible assets	3	2
EBITDA	17	52
Impairment of property	10	
Insurance recovery	(7)	–
Debt issue costs	2	–
EBITDA after non-recurring items	22	52
Share-based payment	3	1
Restructuring charges	4	
Impairment of acquired intangible assets	6	8
Underlying profit	35	61

(b) Reclassification adjustments are amounts recycled to profit or loss in the current period which were recognised in OCI in the current or previous periods. An example of items recognised in OCI which may be reclassified to profit or loss are foreign currency gains on the disposal of a foreign operation and realised gains or losses on cash flow hedges. Those items which may not be reclassified are changes in a revaluation surplus under IAS 16 *Property, Plant and Equipment*, and actuarial gains and losses on a defined benefit plan under IAS 19 *Employee Benefits*.

There are several arguments for and against reclassification. If reclassification ceased, then there would be no need to define profit or loss, or any other total or subtotal in profit or loss, and any presentation decisions can be left to specific IFRSs. It is argued that reclassification protects the integrity of profit or loss and provides users with relevant information about a transaction which occurred in the period. Additionally, it can improve comparability where IFRS permits similar items to be recognised in either profit or loss or OCI.

Those against reclassification argue that the recycled amounts add to the complexity of financial reporting, may lead to earnings management and the reclassification adjustments may not meet the definitions of income or expense in the period as the change in the asset or liability may have occurred in a previous period.

The lack of a consistent basis for determining how items should be presented has led to an inconsistent use of OCI in IFRS. Opinions vary but there is a feeling that OCI has become a home for anything controversial because of a lack of clear definition of what should be included in the statement. Many users are thought to ignore OCI, as the changes reported are not caused by the operating flows used for predictive purposes.

The revised *Conceptual Framework* (2018) identifies the statement of profit or loss as the primary source of information about an entity's performance and states that in principle, therefore, all income and expenses are included in it.

However, it goes on to say that in developing IFRSs the IASB may include income or expenses arising from a change in the current value of an asset or liability as OCI when they determine it provides more relevant information or a more faithful representation. In principle, OCI is recycled to profit or loss in a future period when doing so results in the provision of more relevant information or a more faithful representation of the entity's financial performance for that future period. So although there is more guidance on what constitutes OCI and when it should be recycled, the conceptual basis for it is still not clear.

ACCA

Strategic Business Reporting (International)

Mock Examination 3

Time allowed: 3 hours 15 minutes

This exam is divided into two sections:

Section A – BOTH questions are compulsory and MUST be attempted

Section B – BOTH questions are compulsory and MUST be attempted

Do not open this exam until you are ready to start under examination conditions.

Section A – BOTH questions are compulsory and MUST be attempted

1 Carbise

Background

Carbise is the parent company of an international group which has a presentation and functional currency of the dollar. The group operates within the manufacturing sector. On 1 January 20X2, Carbise acquired 80% of the equity share capital of Bikelite, an overseas subsidiary. The acquisition enabled Carbise to access new international markets. Carbise transfers surplus work-in-progress to Bikelite which is then completed and sold in various locations. The acquisition was not as successful as anticipated and on 30 September 20X6 Carbise disposed of all of its holding in Bikelite. The current year end is 31 December 20X6.

Bikelite trading information

Bikelite is based overseas where the domestic currency is the dinar. Staff costs and overhead expenses are all paid in dinars. However, Bikelite also has a range of transactions in a number of other currencies. Approximately 40% of its raw material purchases are in dinars and 50% in the yen. The remaining 10% are in dollars of which approximately half were purchases of material from Carbise. This ratio continued even after Carbise disposed of its shares in Bikelite. Revenue is invoiced in equal proportion between dinars, yen and dollars. To protect itself from exchange rate risk, Bikelite retains cash in all three currencies. No dividends have been paid by Bikelite for several years. At the start of 20X6 Bikelite sought additional debt finance. As Carbise was already looking to divest, funds were raised from an issue of bonds in dinars, none of which were acquired by Carbise.

Acquisition of Bikelite

Carbise paid dinar 100 million for 80% of the ordinary share capital of Bikelite on 1 January 20X2. The net assets of Bikelite at this date had a carrying amount of dinar 60 million. The only fair value adjustment deemed necessary was in relation to a building which had a fair value of dinar 20 million above its carrying amount and a remaining useful life of 20 years at the acquisition date. Carbise measures non-controlling interests (NCI) at fair value for all acquisitions, and the fair value of the 20% interest was estimated to be dinar 22 million at acquisition. Due to the relatively poor performance of Bikelite, it was decided to impair goodwill by dinar 6 million during the year ending 31 December 20X5.

Rates of exchange between the $ and dinar are given as follows:

1 January 20X2:	$1:0.5 dinar
Average rate for year ended 31 December 20X5	$1:0.4 dinar
31 December 20X5:	$1:0.38 dinar
30 September 20X6:	$1:0.35 dinar
Average rate for the nine-month period ended 30 September 20X6	$1:0.37 dinar

Disposal of Bikelite

Carbise sold its entire equity shareholding in Bikelite on 30 September 20X6 for $150 million. Further details relating to the disposal are as follows:

Carrying amount of Bikelite's net assets at 1 January 20X6	dinar 48 million
Bikelite loss for the year ended 31 December 20X6	dinar 8 million
Cumulative exchange gains on Bikelite at 1 January 20X6	$74.1 million
Non-controlling interest in Bikelite at 1 January 20X6	$47.8 million

Required

(a) Prepare an explanatory note for the directors of Carbise which addresses the following issues:

(i) What is meant by an entity's presentation and functional currency. Explain your answer with reference to how the presentation and functional currency of Bikelite should be determined. **(7 marks)**

(ii) A calculation of the goodwill on the acquisition of Bikelite and what the balance would be at 30 September 20X6 immediately before the disposal of the shares. Your answer should include a calculation of the exchange difference on goodwill for the period from 1 January 20X6 to 30 September 20X6. **(5 marks)**

(iii) An explanation of your calculation of goodwill and the treatment of exchange differences on goodwill in the consolidated financial statements. You do not need to discuss how the disposal will affect the exchange differences. **(4 marks)**

Note: Any workings can either be shown in the main body of the explanatory note or in an appendix to the explanatory note.

(b) Explain why exchange differences will arise on the net assets and profit or loss of Bikelite each year and how they would be presented within the consolidated financial statements. Your answer should include a calculation of the exchange differences which would arise on the translation of Bikelite (excluding goodwill) in the year ended 31 December 20X6. **(7 marks)**

(c) (i) Calculate the group profit or loss on the disposal of Bikelite. **(3 marks)**

(ii) Briefly explain how Bikelite should be treated and presented in the consolidated financial statements of Carbise for the year ended 31 December 20X6. **(4 marks)**

(Total = 30 marks)

2 Hudson

Background

Hudson has a year end of 31 December 20X2 and operates a defined benefit scheme for all employees. In addition, the directors of Hudson are paid an annual bonus depending upon the earnings before interest, tax, depreciation and amortisation (EBITDA) of Hudson.

Hudson has been experiencing losses for a number of years and its draft financial statements reflect a small loss for the current year of $10 million. On 1 May 20X2, Hudson announced that it was restructuring and that it was going to close down division Wye. A number of redundancies were confirmed as part of this closure with some staff being reallocated to other divisions within Hudson. The directors have approved the restructuring in a formal directors meeting. Hudson is highly geared and much of its debt is secured on covenants which stipulate that a minimum level of net assets should be maintained. The directors are concerned that compliance with International Financial Reporting Standards (IFRS Standards) could have significant implications for their bonus and debt covenants.

Redundancy and settlement costs

Hudson still requires a number of staff to operate division Wye until its final expected closure in early 20X3. As a consequence, Hudson offered its staff two settlement packages in relation to the curtailment of the defined benefit scheme. A basic settlement was offered for all staff who leave before the final closure of division Wye. An additional pension contribution was offered for staff who remained in employment until the final closure of division Wye.

The directors of Hudson have only included an adjustment in the financial statements for those staff who left prior to 31 December 20X2. The directors have included this adjustment within the remeasurement component of the defined benefit scheme. They do not wish to provide for any other settlement contributions until employment is finally terminated, arguing that an obligation would only arise once the staff were made redundant. On final termination, the directors intend to include the remaining basic settlement and the additional pension contribution within the remeasurement component. The directors and accountant are aware that the proposed treatment does not conform to IFRS Standards. The directors believe that the proposed treatment is justified as it will help Hudson maintain its debt covenant obligations and will therefore be in the best interests of their shareholders who are the primary stakeholder. The directors have indicated that, should the accountant not agree with their accounting treatment, then he will be replaced.

Tax losses

The directors of Hudson wish to recognise a material deferred tax asset in relation to $250 million of unused trading losses which have accumulated as at 31 December 20X2. Hudson has budgeted profits for $80 million for the year ended 31 December 20X3. The directors have forecast that profits will grow by 20% each year for the next four years. The market is currently depressed and sales orders are at a lower level for the first quarter of 20X3 than they were for the same period in any of the previous five years. Hudson operates under a tax jurisdiction which allows for trading losses to be only carried forward for a maximum of two years.

Required

(a) Explain why the directors of Hudson are wrong to classify the basic settlement and additional pension contributions as part of the remeasurement component, including an explanation of the correct treatment for each of these items. Also explain how any other restructuring costs should be accounted for. **(8 marks)**

(b) Explain whether a deferred tax asset can be recognised in the financial statements of Hudson in the year ended 31 December 20X2. **(5 marks)**

(c) Identify any ethical issues which arise from the directors' proposed accounting treatments and behaviour. Your answer should also consider the implications for the accountant arising from the directors' behaviour. **(5 marks)**

Professional marks will be awarded in (c) for quality of discussion. **(2 marks)**

(Total = 20 marks)

Section B – BOTH questions are compulsory and MUST be attempted

3 Crypto

(a) (i) Crypto operates in the power industry, and owns 45% of the voting shares in Kurran. Kurran has four other investors which own the remaining 55% of its voting shares and are all technology companies. The largest of these holdings is 18%. Kurran is a property developer and purchases property for its renovation potential and subsequent disposal. Crypto has no expertise in this area and is not involved in the renovation or disposal of the property.

The board of directors of Kurran makes all of the major decisions but Crypto can nominate up to four of the eight board members. Each of the remaining four board members are nominated by each of the other investors. Any major decisions require all board members to vote and for there to be a clear majority. Thus, Crypto has effectively the power of veto on any major decision. There is no shareholder agreement as to how Kurran should be operated or who will make the operating decisions for Kurran. The directors of Crypto believe that Crypto has joint control over Kurran because it is the major shareholder and holds the power of veto over major decisions.

The directors of Crypto would like advice as to whether or not they should account for Kurran under IFRS 11 *Joint Arrangements*. **(6 marks)**

(ii) On 1 April 20X7, Crypto, which has a functional currency of the dollar, entered into a contract to purchase a fixed quantity of electricity at 31 December 20X8 for 20 million euros. At that date, the spot rate was 1.25 dollars to the euro. The electricity will be used in Crypto's production processes.

Crypto has separated out the foreign currency embedded derivative from the electricity contract and measured it at fair value through other comprehensive income (FVTOCI). However, on 31 December 20X7, there was a contractual modification, such that the contract is now an executory contract denominated in dollars. At this date, Crypto calculated that the embedded derivative had a negative fair value of 2 million euros.

The directors of Crypto would like advice as to whether they should have separated out the foreign currency derivative and measured it at FVTOCI, and how to treat the modification in the contract. **(5 marks)**

Required

Advise the directors of Crypto as to how the above issues should be accounted for with reference to relevant IFRS Standards.

Note: The split of the mark allocation is shown against each of the two issues above.

(b) Previous leasing standards have been criticised about the lack of information they required to be disclosed on leasing transactions. These concerns were usually expressed by investors and so IFRS 16 *Leases* was issued in response to these criticisms.

Required

(i) Discuss some of the key changes to financial statements which investors will see when companies apply the lessee accounting requirements in IFRS 16. **(6 marks)**

(ii) For a company with significant off-balance sheet leases, discuss the likely impact that IFRS 16 will have generally on accounting ratios and particularly on:

– Earnings before interest and tax to interest expense (interest cover);

– Earnings before interest and tax to capital employed (return on capital employed);

– Debt to earnings before interest, tax, depreciation and amortisation (EBITDA).

(6 marks)

Professional marks will be awarded in (b) for clarity and quality of discussion. **(2 marks)**

(Total = 25 marks)

4 Willow

The International Accounting Standards Board (IASB) has been undertaking number of projects to explore how disclosures in IFRS financial reporting can be improved. In 2017, the IASB issued IFRS Practice Statement 2: *Making Materiality Judgements* to provide guidance on the application of materiality to financial statements and in 2018 the IASB amended the definition of materiality to include the obscuring of information.

Materiality is a matter which has been debated extensively in the context of many forms of reporting, including the International Integrated Reporting Framework. There are difficulties in applying the concept of materiality in practice when preparing the financial statements and it is thought that these difficulties contribute to a disclosure problem, namely, that there is too much irrelevant information in financial statements which often makes it difficult to focus on the relevant information.

Required

(a) (i) Discuss the definition of materiality, how the application of the concept of materiality has led to concerns regarding the clarity and understandability of financial statements and briefly discuss the guidance issued in *IFRS Practice Statement 2: Making Materiality Judgements* to address these issues. **(7 marks)**

(ii) Outline the proposals in ED 2019/6 *Disclosure of Accounting Policies* and explain how these amendments are expected to help with the disclosure problem. **(4 marks)**

(iii) Discuss how the concept of materiality would be used in applying the International Integrated Reporting Framework. **(4 marks)**

(b) Willow is a public limited company and would like advice in relation to the following transactions.

(i) Willow leased its head office during the current accounting period and the agreement terminates in six years' time.

There is a clause in the lease relating to the internal condition of the property at the termination of the lease. The clause states that the internal condition of the property should be identical to that at the outset of the lease. Willow has improved the building by adding another floor to part of the building during the current accounting period. There is also a clause which enables the landlord to recharge Willow for costs relating to the general disrepair of the building at the end of the lease. In addition, the landlord can recharge any costs of repairing the roof immediately. The landlord intends to replace part of the roof of the building during the current period. **(5 marks)**

(ii) Willow often sponsors professional tennis players in an attempt to promote its brand. At the moment, it has a three-year agreement with a tennis player who is currently ranked in the world's top ten players. The agreement is that the player receives a signing bonus of $20,000 and earns an annual amount of $50,000, paid at the end of each year for three years, provided that the player has competed in all the specified tournaments for each year. If the player wins a major tournament, she receives a bonus of 20% of the prize money won at the tournament. In return, the player is required to wear advertising logos on tennis apparel, play a specified number of tournaments and attend photo/film sessions for advertising purposes. The different payments are not interrelated. **(5 marks)**

Required

Discuss how the above items should be dealt with in the financial statements of Willow.

Note. The mark allocation is shown against each of the issues above.

(Total = 25 marks)

Answers

DO NOT TURN THIS PAGE UNTIL YOU HAVE COMPLETED THE MOCK EXAM

Section A

1 Carbise

Workbook references. The underlying principles of IFRS 3 are covered in Chapter 11. Disposals of interests in investments are covered in Chapter 14. Foreign transactions and foreign entities are covered in Chapter 16.

Top tips. In part (a), you must make sure that you apply your knowledge to the scenario given: the examiner's report stated that weaker answers to this question tended to list the factors determining the functional currency, with little application to the scenario. Remember that there are very few marks available for stating knowledge, you must apply your knowledge to the scenario to gain the majority of the marks available.

In questions, like this, where complex calculations are required, the examiner has advised that you produce your calculation on one sheet of paper and simultaneously explain the calculation on another sheet of paper. This way of producing an answer will help you to explain each part of a calculation as you perform it, enabling you to generate as many marks as possible.

Marking scheme

				Marks
(a)	(i)	– discussion of presentation and functional currency	2	
		– application of the above discussion to the scenario	5	
				7
	(ii)	– calculation of goodwill	2	
		– calculation of the exchange difference on goodwill	3	
				5
	(iii)	– explanation of the goodwill calculation and application to the scenario	2	
		– explanation of the exchange gain and application to the scenario	2	
				4
(b)		– explanation of Bikelite exchange differences	3	
		– calculation of Bikelite exchange differences for y/e 20X6:		
		translation	3	
		split between parent and NCI	1	
				7
(c)	(i)	– calculation of group profit or loss on disposal		3
	(ii)	– explanation of the accounting treatment of Bikelite		4
				30

(a) **Explanatory note to: Directors of Carbise**

Subject: Foreign subsidiary Bikelite

(i) The presentation currency is the currency in which the financial statements are presented. IAS 21 *The Effects of Changes in Foreign Exchange Rates* permits an entity to present its individual financial statements in any currency. It would therefore be up to the directors of Bikelite to choose a presentation currency for its individual financial statements. Factors which could be considered include the currency used by major shareholders and the currency in which debt finance is primarily raised.

The functional currency is the currency of the primary economic environment in which the entity operates. Since transactions are initially recorded in an entity' s functional currency, the results and financial position would need to be retranslated where this differed to the presentation currency.

When determining the presentation and functional currency of Bikelite, consideration should first be given to whether the functional currency of Bikelite should be the same as Carbise, at least whilst under the control of Carbise. It appears that Bikelite has considerable autonomy over its activities. Despite being acquired to make more efficient use of the surplus inventory of Carbise, purchases from Carbise were only 5% of Bikelite' s total purchases. Revenue is invoiced in a range of currencies suggesting a geographically diverse range of customers which, although this allows Carbise access to new international markets, is unlikely to be classified as an extension of the parent' s operations. The volume of the transactions involved between Carbise and Bikelite would seem to be far too low to come to this conclusion. Bikelite also appears free to retain cash in a range of currencies and is not obliged to remit the cash to Carbise in the form of dividends. Nor does Bikelite appear to be dependent on financing from Carbise with other investors taking up the bond issue at the start of 20X6. The functional currency of Bikelite does not need to be the same as Carbise.

In choosing its functional currency, Bikelite should consider the following primary factors: the currency which mainly influences the sales price for their goods, the currency of the country whose competitive forces and regulations determine the sales price and also the currency which influences labour, material and overhead costs. The key determinant here is the currency which the majority of the transactions are settled in. Bikelite invoices and is invoiced in a large range of currencies and so it would not be immediately clear as to the appropriate functional currency. Nor is there detail about whether there is a currency in which competitive forces and regulations could be important. We do not know, for example, what currency Bikelite' s major competitors invoice in.

Secondary factors including the currency in which financing activities are obtained and the currency in which receipts from operating activities are retained can help guide the entity where it is not immediately clear. In relation to Bikelite, a significant volume of their sales are invoiced in dinars and the majority of their expenses too, given that wages and overheads are also paid in dinars. Funds were raised in dinars from the bond issue and so it would appear that the dinar should probably be the functional currency for Bikelite. It is also possible that Bikelite may lose their autonomy on Carbise' s sale of their shares which could have implications for the determination of the functional currency.

(ii) Goodwill in dinars on the acquisition of Bikelite would be dinar 42 million calculated as follows:

	Dinars millions
Consideration	100
FV of NCI	22
Less net assets at acquisition (60 + 20)	(80)
Goodwill at acquisition	42

On acquisition, the goodwill in $ would be (dinar 42m/0.5) $84 million.

Goodwill at 30 September 20X6 would be:

	Dinar millions	*rate*	$m
Goodwill at 1 January 20X2	42	0.5	84
Impairment y/e 31 December 20X5	(6)	0.4	(15)
Exchange gain			25.7 (bal)
Goodwill at 31 December 20X5	36	0.38	94.7
Current year exchange gain			8.2 (bal)
Goodwill at 30 September 20X6	36	0.35	102.9

Workings

Dinar impairment of 6 million is translated at the average rate of $1:0.4 dinar = $15 million.

Goodwill at 31 December 20X5 would be translated at last year' s closing rate of $1:0.38 dinar = $94.7m.

Goodwill at 31 September 20X6 will be translated at $1:0.35 dinar = $102.9m.

(iii) On a business combination, goodwill is calculated by comparing the fair value of the consideration plus non-controlling interests (NCI) at acquisition with the fair value of the identifiable net assets at acquisition. Carbise measures NCI using the fair value method. This means that goodwill attributable to the NCI is included within the overall calculation of goodwill. An adjustment of dinar 20 million is required to the property of Bikelite to ensure the net assets at acquisition are properly included at their fair value.

At each year end, all assets (and liabilities) are retranslated using the closing rate of exchange. Exchange differences arising on the retranslation are recorded within equity. Since the non-controlling interest is measured under the fair value method, the exchange difference would be apportioned 80%/20% between the owners of Carbise and the non-controlling interest. Only the current year' s exchange difference would initially be recorded within other comprehensive income for the year ended 31 December 20X6 whereas cumulative exchange differences on goodwill at 30 September 20X6 would be recorded within equity.

(b) The net assets of Bikelite would have been retranslated each year at the closing rate of exchange. There is therefore an exchange difference arising each year by comparing the opening net assets at the opening rate of exchange with the opening net assets at the closing rate of exchange. An additional exchange difference arises through the profit or loss of Bikelite each year being translated at the average rate of exchange in the consolidated statement of comprehensive income. The profit or loss will increase or decrease the net assets of Bikelite respectively which, as is indicated above, will be translated at the closing rate of exchange within the consolidated statement of financial position. As with goodwill, the exchange differences are included within equity with 80% attributable to the shareholders of Carbise and 20% to the NCI. Cumulative exchange differences will be included within the consolidated statement of financial position with just current year differences recorded within other comprehensive income.

The carrying amount of the net assets of Bikelite on 1 January 20X6 was dinar 48 million. The fair value of their opening net assets therefore would be dinar 64 million (dinar 48 + 16/20 x dinar 20 million). Bikelite would only be consolidated for the first nine months of the year since Carbise loses control on 30 September 20X6. Losses per the individual accounts for the year ended 31 December 20X6 were dinar 8 million, so only dinar 6 million would be consolidated. Additional depreciation of dinar 0.75 million (dinar 20m/20 x 9/12) would be charged for the first nine months of the year. Net assets at disposal in dinars would therefore be dinar 57.25 million (dinar 64 – dinar 6.75). The exchange difference arising in the statement of comprehensive income for the year ended 31 December 20X6 would be $13.4 million calculated as follows:

	$m
Opening net assets at opening rate (dinar 64/0.38)	168.4
Loss for 9 months at average rate (dinar 6.75/0.37)	(18.2)
Current year exchange gain (balance)	13.4
Net assets at 30 September 20X6 (dinar 57.25/0.35)	163.6

$10.7 million of the exchange differences are attributed to the shareholders of Carbide (80% × $13.4) and $2.7 million to the NCI.

(c) (i) **Group profit or loss on disposal on Bikelite**

	$m
Proceeds	150
Net assets at disposal (see (b))	(163.6)
Goodwill at disposal (see (a)(ii))	(102.9)
NCI at disposal	48.5
Exchange gains recycled to profit and loss	76.6
Group profit on disposal	8.6

Workings

Exchange gains at 1 January 20X6 per question are $74.1 million. Current year exchange differences on goodwill are $8.2 million (see (b)(i)) and on the net assets are $13.4 million (see (b)). Cumulative exchange gains at 30 September 20X6 are therefore $95.7 million. On disposal, the parent' s share (80%) = $76.6 million should be recycled to profit or loss.

NCI at disposal is calculated as follows:

	$m
NCI at 1 January 20X6 per question	47.8
NCI share of loss to 30 September 20X6 (20% × dinar 6.75m (see (b))/0.37)	(3.6)
NCI share exchange gains for 9 months to 30 September 20X6 (20% × (13.4 + 8.2))	4.3
NCI at 30 September 20X6	48.5

(ii) For the year ended 31 December 20X6, Carbise will consolidate Bikelite for the first nine months of the year up to the date of disposal of the shares and subsequent loss of control. NCI will be calculated on the first nine months of losses. Exchange differences on the translation of the net assets, profits and goodwill in relation to the nine months to 30 September 20X6 will initially be recognised in other comprehensive income classified as gains which will be reclassified subsequently to profit or loss.

On 30 September 20X6, a consolidated profit or loss on disposal will be calculated in the consolidated financial statements of Carbise. In effect, the proceeds are compared to the net assets and unimpaired goodwill not attributable to the non-controlling interest at the disposal date. The cumulative exchange differences on the translation of Bikelite would be reclassified to profit or loss.

Consideration should be given as to whether the disposal of Bikelite would constitute a discontinued operation. For Bikelite to be classified as a discontinued operation, it would need to represent a separate major line of business or geographical area of operations. Since Bikelite was initially acquired by Carbise to gain easier access to international markets, it is likely that the criterion would be met.

2 Hudson

Workbook references. Ethics are covered in Chapter 2. Employee benefits and pensions are covered in Chapter 5. Deferred tax is covered in Chapter 7.

Top tips. Question 2 of the exam will always feature a discussion of ethical issues and will have two marks available for the application of ethical principles. In this question, parts (a) and (b) related to the accounting treatment of the issues in the scenario given, and part (c) required a discussion of the ethical issues arising, including actions that the accountant should take.

In this type of question, remember that ethical issues are likely to be interwoven throughout the scenario - you need to be able to spot them. Remember also that you must apply ethical principles to the scenario. Listing out ethical requirements is unlikely to gain you many marks.

Marking scheme

			Marks
(a)	– application of the following discussion to the scenario:		
	what should be included in the remeasurement component	2	
	correct treatment of the basic component	2	
	correct treatment of the additional pension contribution	2	
	– discussion of restructuring costs	2	
			8
(b)	– an explanation of temporary differences and asset tax base	3	
	– application of above discussion to the scenario	2	
			5
(c)	– application of the following discussion of accounting issues to the scenario:		
	termination payments	2	
	tax losses	1	
	– consideration of the ethical implications and their resolution	2	
			5
	Professional marks		2
			20

(a) The remeasurement component is taken to other comprehensive income and comprises:

- Actuarial gains and losses, such as the return on plan assets which differs from the expected return on the assets included within the net interest figure;
- Changes in the asset ceiling not included within the net interest calculation.

Actuarial gains and losses are sometimes referred to as experience adjustments and arise due to differences between actuarial assumptions and what actually occurred during the period. These will arise in instances such as unexpected movements on interest rates, unexpectedly high or low rates of employee turnover or unexpected increases or decreases in wage growth. The redundancies will create an unusually high level of staff turnover but this should not be treated as part of the remeasurement component. The redundancy will cause the present value of the obligations arising from the defined benefit to decrease. This is classified as a curtailment rather than an experience adjustment to be included within other comprehensive income.

A distinction needs to be made between the basic settlement and the additional pension contribution. The basic settlement is an obligation which Hudson has to pay as compensation for terminating the employee's services regardless of when the employee leaves the entity. IAS 19 Employee Benefits requires such payments to be recognised at the earlier of when the plan of termination is announced and when the entity recognises the associated restructuring costs associated with the closure of Wye.

Hudson should therefore have provided in full for the cost of the basic settlement regardless of whether the staff have left or not. This should be recognised as part of the past service cost in the profit or loss of Hudson for the year ended 31 December 20X2.

The additional pension contribution is only paid to employees who complete service up to the closure of division Wye. Since this is expected in early 20X3, these should be accounted for as a short-term benefit. In effect, the contributions are in exchange for the period of service until redundancy. Hudson should estimate the number of employees who will remain with Hudson until the closure of Wye. The cost of this payment should then be spread over the period of service. Since this should be included within the current service cost, this will have an adverse effect on the profit or loss in both 20X2 and 20X3.

In line with the criteria to recognise any provision, as set out in IAS 37 *Provisions, Contingent Liabilities and Contingent Assets*, an 'obligating event' must have arisen for a restructuring provision and for the associated restructuring costs to be recognised. Furthermore, specific conditions must exist for such an obligating event to have arisen in relation to a restructuring provision:

– a detailed formal plan for the restructuring is in place identifying certain criteria required by the accounting standard; and

– a valid expectation has been created in those affected that the restructuring will be carried out, either by starting to implement the plan or publicly announcing its main features.

In the case of Hudson, a valid expectation has been created because the restructuring has been announced, the redundancies have been confirmed and the directors have approved the restructuring in a formal directors meeting. IAS 37 specifically sets out that a provision cannot be made where only a management or board decision to restructure has been taken as it is not considered that this in itself gives rise to an obligation to restructure. IAS 37 also specifies that only the direct expenditure which is necessary as a result of restructuring can be included in the restructuring provision. This includes costs of making employees redundant and costs of terminating certain leases and other contracts directly as a result of restructuring. However, it specifically excludes costs of retraining or relocating staff, marketing or investment in new systems and distribution networks, as these costs relate to future operations and so do not fall under the definition of a provision. Thus the costs of ongoing activities such as relocation activities cannot be provided for.

(b) Deferred taxes represent the amounts of income taxes payable or recoverable in future periods in respect of temporary differences.

Temporary differences are differences between the carrying amount of an asset or liability and its tax base. A deferred tax asset arises where the tax base of an asset exceeds the carrying amount. A deferred tax asset can also occur when the tax base of a liability differs from its carrying amount; the eventual settlement of the liability represents a future tax deduction. In relation to unused trading losses, the carrying amount is zero since the losses have not yet been recognised in the financial statements of Hudson. A potential deferred tax asset does arise but the determination of the tax base is more problematic.

The tax base of an asset is the amount which will be deductible against taxable economic benefits from recovering the carrying amount of the asset. Where recovery of an asset will have no tax consequences, the tax base is equal to the carrying amount.

Hudson operates under a tax jurisdiction which only allows losses to be carried forward for two years. The maximum the tax base could be is therefore equal to the amount of unused losses for 20X1 and 20X2 since these only are available to be deducted from future profits. The tax base though needs to be restricted to the extent that there is a probability of sufficient future profits to offset the trading losses.

The directors of Hudson should base their forecast of the future profitability on reasonable and supportable assumptions. There appears to be evidence that this is not the case. Hudson has a recent history of trading losses and there is little evidence that there will be an improvement in trading results within the next couple of years. The market is depressed and sales orders for the first quarter of 20X3 are below levels in any of the previous five years. It is also likely that Hudson will incur various costs in relation to the restructuring which would increase losses into 20X3 and possibly 20X4. Only directly attributable expenses such as redundancies should be included within a provision and expensed in 20X2 which would increase the current year loss. On-going expenses may be incurred such as retraining and relocating costs but these should only be expensed from 20X3. The forecast profitability for 20X3 and subsequent growth rate therefore appear to be unrealistically optimistic. Given that losses can only be carried forward for a maximum of two years, it is unlikely that any deferred tax asset should be recognised.

(c) The directors of Hudson are paid a bonus based upon earnings before interest, tax depreciation and amortisation (EBITDA). It is possible therefore, despite the losses, that once these items are adjusted for the directors may receive a bonus. A self-interest threat will arise. The directors have an incentive to manipulate the financial statements in order to try to minimise the losses and maximise profits. Directors have an ethical responsibility to produce financial statements which are fair, objective and a transparent record of the entity's affairs.

There is evidence that the directors are willing to manipulate the financial statements in a way directly contrary to the ethical principles of integrity and objectivity. It is likely that a net expense should be recognised for the termination payments on the assumption that they would exceed the reduction in present value of the obligation from the curtailment. The directors are wishing to recognise this within other comprehensive income rather than profit or loss despite knowing that it is contrary to international accounting standards. This would improve profitability although it would not impact upon net assets due to a corresponding decrease in equity. The directors also have not recognised a restructuring provision despite the terms being communicated to staff. It is possible that this would be treated as an exceptional cost and therefore would not impact on the bonus. It would therefore be useful to examine the precise terms of the contracts in order to assess the potential impact on the bonus. The treatment does, however, at least in the short term, help Hudson to improve their net assets position.

The deferred tax asset is based upon forecasts for too long a period and is also based on unrealistic assumptions. Earnings before interest, tax, depreciation and amortisation will be overstated as a direct consequence. Net assets will also be overstated, helping Hudson to meet its debt covenant obligations.

The directors' explanation for their proposed treatments are not justified. Directors are appointed to run the business on behalf of the company's shareholders who are the primary stakeholder. It will be in the shareholders' interests for the company to be profitable and to maintain net assets within the debt covenant stipulations. However, this should not be at the expense of the credibility and transparency of the financial statements. Deliberate manipulation of financial statements will reduce stakeholders' confidence in the reliability of the financial statements and the accountancy profession as a whole. The directors are deliberating flouting International Financial Reporting Standards (IFRS Standards) to improve their bonus and maintain debt covenant obligations.

The directors' actions with regard to the accountant are contrary to the ethical principles of professional behaviour. It appears that the directors have put the accountant under undue pressure to falsify the financial statements to meet their own needs. An intimidation threat arises from the directors' implying that the accountant would lose their job should they not comply with the directors' instructions.

The accountant would also be bound by the ACCA *Code of Ethics* and must adhere to the same ethical principles. They must not therefore comply with the directors' instructions. The accountant should remind the directors of their obligations to comply with the *Code of Ethics*. Should the accountant feel unable to approach the directors directly, they could consider talking to those charged with governance and, in particular, non-executive directors to explain the situation. The accountant could also seek help from the ACCA ethical helpline and take legal advice. Ultimately, if the situation cannot be resolved, the accountant could consider resigning and seeking employment elsewhere.

3 Crypto

Workbook references. IFRS 16 *Leases* is covered in Chapter 9. IFRS 10 is covered in Chapter 11, and IFRS 11 is covered in Chapter 15. IFRS 9 *Financial Instruments* is covered in Chapter 8.

Top tips. There are two professional marks available in this question for clarity and quality of the discussion in part (b). This will be the case for one question in section B of every exam - two professional marks will be available in the question that requires analysis from the perspective of a stakeholder.

Part (a)(i) required advice on the treatment of an investment. The examiner's report stated that many answers to this question were weak - with many candidates focusing on only on IFRS 11, rather than first looking at the issue of control under IFRS 10. Part (a)(ii) was extremely challenging and required advice on the treatment of an embedded derivative contract which was then modified into an executory contract.

Part (b)(i) required a discussion on the key changes from an investor perspective of the application of the lessee accounting requirements in IFRS 16. Remember in this part of your answer to consider the investor and not just state the accounting adjustments required. Part (b)(ii) required a discussion on how IFRS 16 would impact on three accounting ratios and more generally from the financial statements now that previously reported "off-balance sheet" leases are now on-balance sheet. Ensure you link the impact on each ratio to the change in accounting treatment required under IFRS 16.

Marking scheme

				Marks
(a)	(i)	Discussion of the following accounting issues and application to the scenario:		
		– the definition of control per IFRS 10 and joint control per IFRS 11	3	
		– power over the investee	3	
				6
	(ii)	Discussion of the following accounting issues and application to the scenario:		
		– FRS 9 requirements for embedded derivatives and hybrid	3	
		– IFRS 9 requirements for contract modifications	2	
				5
(b)	(i)	Discussion of the IFRS 16 requirements	3	
		Implications for investors	3	
				6
	(ii)	Description of the IFRS 16 impact on accounting numbers	2	
		Impact on the following ratios:		
		– Interest cover	2	
		– ROCE	1	
		– Debt to EBITDA	1	
				6
	Professional marks			2
				25

(a) (i) Before assessing whether an entity has joint control over an arrangement, an entity must first assess whether the parties control the arrangement in accordance with the definition of control in IFRS 10 *Consolidated Financial Statements*. If not, an entity must determine whether it has joint control of the arrangement. IFRS 11 *Joint Arrangements* defines joint control as 'the contractually agreed sharing of control of an arrangement, which exists only when decisions about the relevant activities require the unanimous consent of the parties sharing control'. This means an assessment as to whether any party can prevent any of the other parties from making unilateral decisions without its consent. It must be clear which combination of parties is required to agree unanimously to decisions about the relevant activities of the arrangement. In the case of Kurran, there is more than one combination of parties possible to reach the required majority. As a result, Crypto does not have joint control.

In addition to the above, Crypto does not control Kurran because IFRS 10 states that control requires power over the investee which gives the investor the ability to direct the relevant activities. Crypto does not have the ability to direct the relevant activities as it can only block decisions, and cannot make decisions by itself. Also, there is no shareholder agreement which sets out shareholders' voting rights and obligations and thus the other shareholders can act together to prevent Crypto from making decisions in its own interest. Crypto does not have joint control as agreement between itself and other board members has to occur for a decision to be made. Therefore, it appears that Kurran is an associate of Crypto and would apply IAS 28 *Investments in Associates and Joint Ventures.*

(ii) IFRS 9 *Financial Instruments* states that 'any embedded derivative included in a contract for the sale or purchase of a non-financial item that is denominated in a foreign currency shall be separated when its economic characteristics and risks are not closely related to those of the host contract'. Thus, in contrast to the treatment for hybrid contracts with financial asset hosts, derivatives embedded with a financial liability will often be separately accounted for. That is, they must be separated if they are not closely related to the host contract, they meet the definition of a derivative, and the hybrid contract is not measured at fair value through profit or loss (FVTPL).

The contract is a hybrid contract containing a host contract which is an executory contract to purchase electricity at a price of 20 million euros and a non-closely related embedded foreign currency derivative with an initial fair value of zero to buy 20 million euros, sell 25 million dollars. However, the derivative should have been valued at FVTPL and not fair value through other comprehensive income.

At the date of the modification of the contract to the functional currency of Crypto, there is a significant change to the contract which will trigger a reassessment of its position under IFRS 9. As the contract no longer has a non-closely related embedded derivative, the entire arrangement will be accounted for prospectively as an executory contract which is outside the scope of IFRS 9. The embedded derivative will be derecognised and it is likely that Crypto will have to pay the counterparty 2 million euros in compensation.

(b) (i) IFRS 16 *Leases* introduces a single lessee accounting model and should reduce the number of off-balance sheet leases. Upon lease commencement, a lessee recognises a right-of-use asset and a lease liability. After lease commencement, a lessee measures the right-of-use asset using a cost model less accumulated depreciation and accumulated impairment. The lease liability is initially measured at the present value of the lease payments payable over the lease term, discounted at the rate implicit in the lease if that can be readily determined. Lease liabilities include only economically unavoidable payments.

Investors should bear in mind that some sectors and some companies will be more affected than others. As a result, companies with previous material off-balance sheet leases will report higher assets and financial liabilities. The standard will reduce complexity in financial statements as it should allow comparisons to be made between those companies who lease assets and those who borrow to buy assets.

Investors will no longer have to estimate the assets and liabilities resulting from off-balance sheet leases when calculating ratios as there should be fewer off-balance sheet leases. IFRS 16 will result in more information about leases both on the statement of financial position and in the notes and will provide a more accurate reflection of the economics of leases. The carrying amount of lease assets will typically reduce more quickly than the carrying amount of lease liabilities. This will result in a reduction in reported equity for companies with previous material off-balance sheet leases.

IFRS 16 requires a lessee to disclose lease liabilities separately from other liabilities as a separate line item, or together with other similar liabilities, in a manner which is relevant to understanding the lessee's financial position. A lessee will also split lease liabilities into current and non-current portions, based on the timing of payments.

(ii) The recognition of an asset which was previously unrecognised will result in a higher asset base, which will affect ratios such as asset turnover. The recognition of a liability which was previously unrecognised will result in higher financial liabilities, which will affect gearing. The recognition of depreciation and interest instead of operating lease expense will result in higher operating profit because interest is typically excluded from operating expenses and will affect performance ratios. Similarly, profit measures which exclude interest and depreciation but previously included operating lease expense, such as EBITDA, will be higher under IFRS 16.

Interest cover: there will be an increase in the earnings measure (i.e. EBITDA) which will not be proportionate to the increase in interest. The change in the ratio will depend on the characteristics of the lease portfolio.

Return on capital employed: it is likely that ROCE will be lower under IFRS 16 because the increase in operating profit is unlikely to be proportionate to the increase in capital employed.

Debt to EBITDA: ratio of debt to EBITDA is likely to be higher because debt will increase by more than the increase in earnings. Debt will increase because of the fact that lease liabilities will be recognised on the statement of financial position. For companies which have material off-balance sheet leases, IFRS 16 is expected to result in higher profit before interest because a company presents the implicit interest in lease payments for former off-balance sheet leases as part of finance costs. Previously, the entire expense related to off-balance sheet leases was included as part of operating expenses. The size of the increase in operating profit, and finance costs, will depend on the significance of leasing activities to the company.

4 Willow

Workbook references. Materiality, IFRS Practice Statement 2 and ED 2019/6 are covered in chapter 20. Integrated Reporting is covered in Chapter 18. Intangible assets and property, plant and equipment are covered in Chapter 4.

Top tips. This question dealt with materiality as a current issue in part (a) and covered two reporting issues in part (b). The definition of materiality in part (a)(i) is straightforward, but the consideration of how it could lead to a reduction in clarity and understandability needs more thought. Credit will be given for valid arguments. Integrated reporting has been tested in a number of contexts, here in the context of materiality. You needed to consider how materiality is relevant to the objective of the International Integrated Reporting Framework. In part (b) the key is to draw out the relevant rules or principles from the Standard and apply them to the scenario. Without discussion of the principles and application, you will not score enough marks to pass the question.

Easy marks. The definition of materiality (part (a)(i)) was a good way to earn easy marks. You could also pick up some easy marks by knowing the content of IFRS Practice Statement 2 and ED 2019/6 if you had revised these. In part (b)(i) easier marks are available for applying the accruals concept when determining the correct point at which to recognise the expense. The easier marks in part (b)(ii) related to trying to identify whether an obligation existed and whether a provision should be recognised.

Marking scheme

				Marks
(a)	(i)	Materiality and IFRS Practice Statement 2: 1 mark per well-explained point up to 7 marks	7	
	(ii)	ED 2019/6 *Disclosure of Accounting Policies:* 1 mark per well-explained point up to 4 marks	4	
	(iii)	Materiality and integrated reporting: 1 mark per well-explained point up to 4 marks	4	
				15
(b)	(i)	Additional floor	2	
		General disrepair of building	2	
		Roof repair	1	
				5
	(ii)	Signing bonus	2	
		Annual retainer	2	
		Performance bonus	1	
				5
				25

a) (i) *Definition of materiality and application of the concept*

Information is **material** if **omitting, misstating or obscuring it** could reasonably be expected to **influence decisions** that primary users make on the basis of financial information about a specific reporting entity.

Materiality is an **entity-specific** aspect of relevance, based on the **nature and/or magnitude** of the items to which it relates in the context of the entity's financial report.

It is therefore **difficult to specify a uniform quantitative threshold** for materiality or predetermine what could be material in a particular situation.

Materiality should ensure that **relevant information is not omitted or mis-stated.** In 2018, the IASB amended the definition of materiality to clarify that relevant information **should not be obscured** by information which is not useful to primary users of financial statements, addressing the issue that too much information can be just as problematic as the omission of information.

The *Conceptual Framework* describes materiality as an **application** by a particular **entity** of the fundamental **qualitative characteristic of relevance.** When an entity is assessing materiality, it is assessing whether the information is relevant to the primary users of its own financial statements. Information relevant for one entity might not be as relevant for another entity.

Although **preparers** may understand the concept of materiality, they may be **less certain about how it should be applied**. Preparers may be **reluctant to filter** out **information which is not relevant** to users as **auditors and regulators may challenge** their reasons for the omissions, particularly where the disclosure is required by an IFRS.

IFRS Practice Statement 2: Making Materiality Judgements

IFRS Practice Statement 2 is **non-mandatory guidance.**

The guidance confirms the general requirement in IAS 1 that an entity need not provide information which is not material:

- The recognition and measurement criteria in an IFRS Standard only need to be applied when **the effect** of applying them is **material**.
- An entity **does not need to make a certain disclosure**, even if that disclosure is part of a list of 'minimum required disclosures' in an IFRS Standard if the information provided by that disclosure requirement is **not material**.

The guidance includes a suggested 4-step process to making materiality judgements which includes identifying potentially material information and assessing whether that information is material.

To assess whether the information is material, preparers should assess whether the information could reasonably be expected to influence primary users. This requires the consideration of both **quantitative** and **qualitative factors**.

Quantitative factors consider the size of the effect of the transaction. These can be assessed with the help of a threshold – eg 5% of profit.

Qualitative factors are characteristics that make information more likely to influence the decisions of primary users, they can be internal or external.

It is usually **more efficient** to assess items from a **quantitative perspective first**: if an item exceeds the quantitative threshold, it is material and no further assessment is required.

As the final part of the 4-step process, the entity should review a complete set of draft financial statements, considering whether all material information has been identified and whether materiality has been considered from a wide perspective and in aggregate.

(ii) ED 2019/6 *Disclosure of Accounting Policies*

IASB research resulted in feedback from the users of financial statements that accounting policy disclosures given by entities in their financial statements are rarely useful. This is because the disclosure given is often a long list of all accounting policies the entity uses, including those which are prescribed by IFRS and for which no judgement is involved.

This problem may partly arise because the wording in IAS 1 requires 'significant' accounting policies to be disclosed but does not specifically define 'significant'.

To be useful to users, disclosure about accounting policies should provide insight into how an entity has exercised judgement in selecting and applying accounting policies. This means that 'boilerplate' disclosure of accounting policies which just regurgitate the requirements of accounting standards are not useful. In fact, including this information may obscure information that is relevant to users.

To try and improve the usefulness of accounting policy disclosures, the IASB proposes to amend IAS 1 so that an entity must disclose its **material** accounting policies.

The proposed amendments to IAS 1 (para. 117) state that:

- Accounting policies that relate to immaterial transactions/events/conditions are immaterial.
- An accounting policy is material if information about it is required to understand other material information in the financial statements.
- Just because an accounting policy relates to a material transaction/event/condition, does not mean that the accounting policy itself is material.
- Information on accounting polices is more likely to be useful to primary users if it is entity specific, eg it describes how the entity has applied the recognition and measurement requirements of an IFRS to the entity's own circumstances.

ED 2019/6 also proposes additions to IFRS Practice Statement 2 which includes specific guidance and illustrative examples to help an entity determine whether an accounting policy is material.

(iii) **Materiality and the International Integrated Reporting Framework**

Integrated reporting <IR> takes a broader view of business reporting, emphasising the need for entities to provide information to help investors assess the sustainability of their business model. <IR> is a process which results in communication, through the integrated report, about value creation over time.

An integrated report is a concise communication about how an organisation's strategy, governance, performance and prospects lead to the creation of value over the short, medium and long term.

The materiality definition for <IR> purposes would consider that material matters are those which are of such relevance and importance that they could substantively influence the assessments of the intended report users. In the case of IR, relevant matters are those which affect or have the potential to affect the organisation's ability to create value over time.

For financial reporting purposes, the nature or extent of an omission or misstatement in the organisation's financial statements determines relevance. Matters which are considered material for financial reporting purposes, or for other forms of reporting, may also be material for <IR> purposes if they are of such relevance and importance that they could change the assessments of providers of financial capital with regard to the organisation's ability to create value. Another feature of materiality for IR purposes is that the definition emphasises the involvement of senior management and those charged with governance in the materiality determination process in order for the organisation to determine how best to disclose its value creation development in a meaningful and transparent way.

(b) (i) **Head office**

Additional floor

IAS 16 *Property, Plant and Equipment* is the relevant standard here. The standard requires that Willow should capitalise the costs of the extra floor, which is an improvement to the building, and amortise these costs over the six-year lease period.

IAS 16 states that the initial cost of an asset **should include** the initial estimate of the **costs of dismantling and removing the item and restoring the site** where the entity has an obligation to do so. This is the case here: Willow has an obligation to remove the floor at the end of the lease because of the clause in the lease requiring the building's condition to be identical at the end of the lease to its condition at the beginning of the lease. A **present obligation exists**, as defined by *IAS 37 Provisions, Contingent Liabilities and Contingent Assets* and therefore the entity should also **recognise a provision** for that amount. The provision should be **discounted to its present value** and the unwinding of the discount recognised in profit or loss.

This arrangement is, in substance, a decommissioning liability. The **asset** recognised for the cost of removal should be **amortised over the six-year period of the lease**. Willow may recover the cost from the benefits generated by the new floor over the remainder of the lease.

General disrepair of the building

A **present obligation** arises for the repair costs under IAS 37 because the lease agreement states that the landlord can re-charge these costs to Willow. The **obligating event is the wear and tear** to the building, which arises gradually over the period of the lease and which will result in an outflow of economic benefits. The **estimated costs should be spread over the six-year lease** period. A **reliable estimate** of the yearly obligation can be made, although this may not necessarily be one sixth per year, for example if exceptional wear and tear arises in any given year.

Roof repair

The lease states clearly that the landlord can re-charge any costs of repairing the roof immediately. Accordingly, **an obligation exists** and a **provision needs to be made for the whole of the roof repair work** on the date on which the requirement was identified.

(ii) **Promotional expenditure**

There are three types of payment involved in the arrangement with the tennis player. The question states that the payments are not interrelated, so the interactions between them do not need to be examined and the expense recognition pattern may be different for each.

Signing bonus

The contract is for advertising and promotional expenditure to improve Willow's brand image. IAS 38 *Intangible Assets* requires **that these costs must be expensed when the services are received**. The signing bonus is paid in advance of the services being received, those services being wearing Willow's logo, taking part in a specified number of tournaments and attending photo/film sessions for advertising. The signing bonus of $20,000 is paid to the player at the start of the contract, but relates to the full three-year contract term. It must therefore be treated as a **prepayment at the start of the contract and expensed on a straight-line basis** over the three-year contract period.

If the **contract is terminated** before the end of the three-year period, Willow should **expense immediately any amount not recovered** from the player.

It has been assumed in specifying the above treatment that separate services cannot be identified. However, **if the terms of the contract allow separate services to be identified and measured reliably**, then Willow should **recognise the expense once the separate service is rendered**.

Annual retainer

Willow has also contracted to pay the player an annual retainer of $50,000 provided she has competed in all the specified tournaments for that year. IFRS 9 *Financial Instruments* requires this arrangement to be treated as a **financial liability** because Willow has a **contractual obligation to deliver cash** to the player. The financial liability is recognised at the **present value of the expected cash flows**.

Willow incurs this obligation on the date **when the player has competed in all the specified tournaments** and it is at this point that the **liability should be recognised**.

Performance bonus

Willow must also pay a performance bonus to the player whenever she wins a tournament. These payments are **related to specific events**, and therefore they are treated as **executory contracts**. (An executory contract is a contract in which something remains to be done by one or both parties.) They are **accrued and expensed when the player has won** a tournament.

ACCA

Strategic Business Reporting (International)

Mock Examination 4

Time allowed:	3 hours 15 minutes

This exam is divided into two sections:

Section A – BOTH questions are compulsory and MUST be attempted

Section B – BOTH questions are compulsory and MUST be attempted

Do not open this exam until you are ready to start under examination conditions.

Section A – BOTH questions are compulsory and MUST be attempted

1 Lupl oid

Background

Luploid Co is the parent company of a group undergoing rapid expansion through acquisition. Luploid Co has acquired two subsidiaries in recent years, Colyson Co and Hammond Co. The current financial year end is 30 June 20X8.

Acquisition of Colyson Co

Luploid Co acquired 80% of the five million equity shares ($1 each) of Colyson Co on 1 July 20X4 for cash of $90 million. The fair value of the non-controlling interest (NCI) at acquisition was $22 million. The fair value of the identifiable net assets at acquisition was $65 million, excluding the following asset. Colyson Co purchased a factory site several years prior to the date of acquisition. Land and property prices in the area had increased significantly in the years immediately prior to 1 July 20X4. Nearby sites had been acquired and converted into residential use. It is felt that, should the Colyson Co site also be converted into residential use, the factory site would have a market value of $24 million. $1 million of costs are estimated to be required to demolish the factory and to obtain planning permission for the conversion. Colyson Co was not intending to convert the site at the acquisition date and had not sought planning permission at that date. The depreciated replacement cost of the factory at 1 July 20X4 has been correctly calculated as $17.4 million.

Impairment of Colyson Co

Colyson Co incurred losses during the year ended 30 June 20X8 and an impairment review was performed. The recoverable amount of Colyson Co's assets was estimated to be $100 million. Included in this assessment was the only building owned by Colyson Co which had been damaged in a storm and impaired to the extent of $4 million. The carrying amount of the net assets of Colyson Co at 30 June 20X8 (including fair value adjustments on acquisition but excluding goodwill) are as follows:

	$m
Land and buildings	60
Other plant and machinery	15
Intangibles other than goodwill	9
Current assets (recoverable amount)	22
Total	106

None of the assets of Colyson Co including goodwill have been impaired previously. Colyson Co does not have a policy of revaluing its assets.

Acquisition of Hammond Co

Luploid Co acquired 60% of the 10 million equity shares of Hammond Co on 1 July 20X7. Two Luploid Co shares are to be issued for every five shares acquired in Hammond Co. These shares will be issued on 1 July 20X8. The fair value of a Luploid Co share was $30 at 1 July 20X7. Hammond Co had previously granted a share-based payment to its employees with a three-year vesting period. At 1 July 20X7, the employees had completed their service period but had not yet exercised their options. The fair value of the options granted at 1 July 20X7 was $15 million. As part of the acquisition, Luploid Co is obliged to replace the share-based payment scheme of Hammond Co with a scheme of its own which has the following details:

> Luploid Co issued 100 options to each of Hammond Co's 10,000 employees on 1 July 20X7. The shares are conditional on the employees completing a further two years of service. Additionally, the scheme required that the market price of Luploid Co's shares had to increase by 10% from its value of $30 per share at the acquisition date over the vesting period. It was anticipated at 1 July 20X7 that 10% of staff would leave over the vesting period but this was

revised to 4% by 30 June 20X8. The fair value of each option at the grant date was $20. The share price of Luploid Co at 30 June 20X8 was $32 and is anticipated to grow at a similar rate in the year ended 30 June 20X9.

Required

Draft an explanatory note to the directors of Luploid Co, addressing the following:

(a) (i) How the fair value of the factory site should be determined at 1 July 20X4 and why the depreciated replacement cost of $17.4 million is unlikely to be a reasonable estimate of fair value. **(7 marks)**

(ii) A calculation of goodwill arising on the acquisition of Colyson Co measuring the non-controlling interest at:

- fair value;
- proportionate share of the net assets. **(3 marks)**

(b) Discuss the calculation and allocation of Colyson Co's impairment loss at 30 June 20X8 and why the impairment loss of Colyson Co would differ depending on how non-controlling interests are measured. Your answer should include a calculation and an explanation of how the impairments would impact upon the consolidated financial statements of Luploid Co. **(11 marks)**

(c) (i) How the consideration for the acquisition of Hammond Co should be measured on 1 July 20X7. Your answer should include a calculation of the consideration and a discussion of why only some of the cost of the replacement share-based payment scheme should be included within the consideration. **(4 marks)**

(ii) How much of an expense for the share-based payment scheme should be recognised in the consolidated profit or loss of Luploid Co for the year ended 30 June 20X8. Your answer should include a brief discussion of how the vesting conditions impact upon the calculations. **(5 marks)**

Note: Any workings can either be shown in the main body of the explanatory note or in an appendix to the explanatory note.

(Total = 30 marks)

2 Stent

Background

Stent Co is a consumer electronics company which has faced a challenging year due to increased competition. Stent Co has a year end of 30 September 20X9 and the unaudited draft financial statements report an operating loss. In addition to this, debt covenant limits based on gearing are close to being breached and the company is approaching its overdraft limit.

Cash advance from Budster Co

On 27 September 20X9, Stent Co's finance director asked the accountant to record a cash advance of $3 million received from a customer, Budster Co, as a reduction in trade receivables. Budster Co is solely owned by Stent Co's finance director. The accountant has seen an agreement signed by both companies stating that the $3 million will be repaid to Budster Co in four months' time. The finance director argues that the proposed accounting treatment is acceptable because the payment has been made in advance in case Budster Co wishes to order goods in the next four months. However, the accountant has seen no evidence of any intent from Budster Co to place orders with Stent Co. **(4 marks)**

Preference shares

On 1 October 20X8, the CEO and finance director each paid $2 million cash in exchange for preference shares from Stent Co which provide cumulative dividends of 7% per annum. These preference shares can either be converted into a fixed number of ordinary shares in two years' time, or redeemed at par on the same date, at the choice of the holder. The finance director suggests to the accountant that the preference shares should be classified as equity because the conversion is into a fixed number of ordinary shares on a fixed date ('fixed for fixed') and conversion is certain (given the current market value of the ordinary shares). **(4 marks)**

Deferred tax asset

Stent Co includes a deferred tax asset in its statement of financial position, based on losses incurred in the current and the previous two years. The finance director has asked the accountant to include the deferred tax asset in full. He has suggested this on the basis that Stent Co will return to profitability once its funding issues are resolved. **(3 marks)**

Required

(a) Discuss appropriate accounting treatments which Stent Co should adopt for all issues identified above and their impact upon gearing.

Note: The mark allocation is shown against each issue above.

(b) The accountant has been in her position for only a few months and the finance director has recently commented that 'all these accounting treatments must be made exactly as I have suggested to ensure the growth of the business and the security of all our jobs'. Both finance director and accountant are ACCA qualified accountants.

Required

Discuss the ethical issues arising from the scenario, including any actions which the accountant should take to resolve the issues. **(7 marks)**

Professional marks will be awarded in question 2 for the application of ethical principles. **(2 marks)**

(Total = 20 marks)

Section B – BOTH questions are compulsory and MUST be attempted

3 Digiwire

Background

Digiwire Co has developed a new business model whereby it sells music licences to other companies which then deliver digital music to consumers.

Revenue: sale of three-year licence

Digiwire Co has agreed to sell Clamusic Co, an unlisted technology start-up company, a three-year licence to sell Digiwire Co's catalogue of classical music to the public. This catalogue contains a large selection of classical music which Digiwire Co will regularly update over the three-year period.

As revenue for the three-year licence, Clamusic Co has issued shares to Digiwire Co equivalent to a 7% shareholding. Voting rights are attached to these shares. Digiwire Co received the shares in Clamusic Co on 1 January 20X6, which is the first day of the licence term.

Digiwire Co will also receive a royalty of 5% of future revenue sales of Clamusic Co as revenue for the licence.

Clamusic Co valuation and revenue

On 1 January 20X6, Clamusic Co was valued at between $4–$5 million by a professional valuer who used a market-based approach. The valuation was based on the share price of a controlling interest in a comparable listed company.

For the financial year end of 31 December 20X6, sales of the classical music were $1 million. At 31 December 20X6, a further share valuation report had been produced by the same professional valuer which indicated that Clamusic Co was valued in the region of $6–$7 million.

Investment in FourDee Co

Digiwire Co has agreed to work with TechGame Co to develop a new music platform. On 31 December 20X6, the companies created a new entity, FourDee Co, with equal shareholdings and shares in profit. Digiwire Co has contributed its own intellectual property in the form of employee expertise, cryptocurrency with a carrying amount of $3 million (fair value of $4 million) and an office building with a carrying amount of $6 million (fair value of $10 million). The cryptocurrency has been recorded at cost in Digiwire Co's financial statements. TechGame Co has contributed the technology and marketing expertise. The board of FourDee Co will comprise directors appointed equally by Digiwire Co and TechGame Co. Decisions are made by a unanimous vote.

Pension plan

Digiwire Co provides a pension plan for its employees. From 1 September 20X6, Digiwire Co decided to curtail the plan and to limit the number of participants. The employees were paid compensation from the plan assets and some received termination benefits due to redundancy. Due to the curtailment, the current monthly service cost changed from $9 million to $6 million. The relevant financial information relating to the plan is as follows:

Date	*Net defined liability*	*Discount rate*
	$m	%
1 January 20X6	30	3
1 September 20X6	36	3.5
31 December 20X6	39	3.7

Required

(a) Advise the directors of Digiwire Co on the recognition and measurement of the:

(i) Clamusic Co shares received as revenue for the sale of the three-year licence and how they should be accounted for in the financial statements for the year ended 31 December 20X6; and

(ii) royalties which Clamusic Co has agreed to pay as revenue for the sale of the three-year licence in the financial statements for the year ended 31 December 20X6. Your answer to (a)(ii) should demonstrate how it is supported by the revised Conceptual Framework for Financial Reporting (2018).

(9 marks)

(b) Based on International Financial Reporting Standards (IFRS), advise the directors on the following:

(i) the classification of the investment which Digiwire Co has in FourDee Co;

(ii) the derecognition of the assets exchanged for the investment in FourDee Co and any resulting gain/loss on disposal in the financial statements of Digiwire Co at 31 December 20X6; and

(iii) whether the cryptocurrency should be classified as a financial asset or an intangible asset. Your answer should also briefly consider whether fair value movements on the cryptocurrency should be recorded in profit or loss.

(9 marks)

(c) (i) Explain the reasons behind the issue of the amendment to IAS 19 *Plan Amendment, Curtailment or Settlement* and discuss why the changes to the calculation of net interest and current service cost were considered necessary. **(3 marks)**

(ii) Advise the directors of Digiwire Co on the impact of the amendment to IAS 19 on the calculation of net interest and current service cost for the year ended 31 December 20X6. **(4 marks)**

(Total = 25 marks)

4 Guidance

Background

Guidance Co is considering the financial results for the year ended 31 December 20X6. The industry places great reliance on the return on equity (ROE) as an indicator of how well a company uses shareholders' funds to generate a profit.

Return on equity (ROE)

Guidance Co analyses ROE in order to understand the fundamental drivers of value creation in the company. ROE is calculated as:

$$\text{Return on equity} = \frac{\text{Net profit before tax}}{\text{Sales}} \times \frac{\text{Sales}}{\text{Assets}} \times \frac{\text{Assets}}{\text{Equity}}$$

Guidance Co uses year-end equity and assets to calculate ROE.

The following information in table 1 relates to Guidance Co for the last two years:

	20X5	20X6
	$m	$m
Net profit before tax	30	38
Sales	200	220
Assets	250	210
Equity at 31 December	175	100

Special purpose entity (SPE)

During the year ended 31 December 20X6, Guidance Co stated that it had reorganised its assets and set up a SPE. Guidance Co transferred property to the SPE at its carrying amount of $50 million, but had incorrectly charged revaluation reserves with this amount rather than showing the transfer as an investment in the SPE. The property was the SPE's only asset. However, Guidance Co still managed the property, and any profit or loss relating to the assets of the entity was remitted directly to Guidance Co. Guidance Co had no intention of consolidating the SPE.

Miscellaneous transactions

Guidance Co has bought back 25 million shares of $1 for $1.20 per share during the year ended 31 December 20X6 for cash and cancelled the shares. This transaction was deemed to be legal.

Guidance Co also raised loan capital for the first time during the year ended 31 December 20X6 of $20 million in order to help with the buy-back of the company's shares.

Guidance Co had purchased a 25% interest in an associate company on 1 July 20X6 for cash. The investment had cost $15 million and the associate had made profits of $32 million in the year to 31 December 20X6. Guidance Co accounted for the purchase of the associate correctly.

All of these miscellaneous transactions have been accounted for in the financial information for the year ended 31 December 20X6 in table 1.

(a) Management's intent and motivation will often influence accounting information. However, corporate financial statements necessarily depend on estimates and judgement. Financial statements are intended to be comparable but their analysis may not be the most accurate way to judge the performance of any particular company. This lack of comparability may be due to different accounting policy choices or deliberate manipulation.

Required

Discuss the reasons why an entity may choose a particular accounting policy where an International Financial Reporting Standard allows an accounting policy choice and whether faithful representation and comparability are affected by such choices. **(6 marks)**

(b) (i) Discuss the usefulness to investors of the ROE ratio and its component parts provided above and calculate these ratios for the years ended 31 December 20X5 and 20X6. These calculations should be based upon the information provided in table 1.

(5 marks)

(ii) Discuss the impact that the setting up of the SPE and miscellaneous transactions have had on ROE and its component parts. Given these considerations, adjust table 1 and recalculate the ROE for 20X6 thereby making it more comparable to the ROE of 20X5.

(12 marks)

Professional marks will be awarded in question 4(b)(i) for clarity and quality of discussion.

(2 marks)

(Total = 25 marks)

Answers

DO NOT TURN THIS PAGE UNTIL YOU HAVE COMPLETED THE MOCK EXAM

1 Lupoid

Workbook references. Fair value measurement under IFRS 13 and IAS 36 *Impairment of Assets* are both covered in Chapter 4. The underlying principles of acquisition accounting given in IFRS 3 *Business Combinations* are covered in Chapter 11. Share-based payment is covered in Chapter 10.

Top tips. Question 1 of the real exam will always test group accounting as well as other financial reporting issues. In this question, part (a)(i) required an explanation of how the fair value of a factory site is determined as part of the acquisition of a subsidiary. This required knowledge of IFRS 13. Part (a)(ii) required the calculation of goodwill on acquisition measuring the non-controlling interest (NCI) under both fair value and proportionate share of net assets. The examiner commented that no explanation was needed to support these goodwill calculations, but that some candidates provided an explanation anyway. This explanation would have not gained any marks as it was not required by the question – make sure you read the questions requirements carefully and only provide explanations for calculations if specified.

Part (b) required a discussion and calculation of an impairment loss relating to a subsidiary, including an explanation of how the impairment would differ depending upon the measurement of non-controlling interest. The examiner commented that very few candidates explained the need for grossing-up goodwill when NCI is measured at the proportionate share of net assets. Make sure you review the suggested solution below carefully if you are unsure of the need to gross up goodwill in this way.

Part (c)(i) regarding the share-based payment was tricky - but you should have been able to pick up some marks in this part of the question for discussing the share exchange. With questions like this, if you are unsure, you should have a go at this part of the question, but make sure you don't spend more than the allocated time of 1.95 minutes per mark.

Part (c)(ii) asked for the resulting share-based expense and a discussion of the vesting conditions. The examiner commented that this was not well answered. If you are unsure about share-based payments, go back to your Workbook, Chapter 10, to revise.

Marking scheme

				Marks
(a)	(i)	– application of the following discussion to the scenario:		
		how FV should be determined	5	
		why depreciation replacement cost is unsuitable	2	7
	(ii)	– calculation marks for:		
		correct FV of net assets	1	
		correct NCI figures	2	3
(b)		– discussion of what constitutes an impairment and CGUs	2	
		– correct calculation of impairment losses for both methods	2	
		– notional goodwill	1	
		– impairment allocation	3	
		– discussion of how and why methods differ	3	11
(c)	(i)	– calculation FV of deferred shares	1	
		– calculation of FV of options	1	
		– discussion of the above calculations and application to the scenario	2	4

			Marks
(ii)	– calculation share expense	1	
	– application of the following discussion to the scenario:		
	why expense required	2	
	vesting conditions	2	5
			30

(a) (i) IFRS 13 *Fair Value Measurement* permits a range of valuation methods to estimate fair value including market based, income estimates and a cost-based approach. However, the characteristics of each asset should be considered when determining the most appropriate methodology.

Fair value is defined as the price which would be received to sell an asset or paid to transfer a liability in an orderly transaction between market participants at the measurement date. Fair value is therefore not supposed to be entity specific but rather to be market focused. The estimate consequently should consider what the market would be prepared to pay for the asset.

The market would consider all alternative uses for the assessment of the price which they would be willing to pay. Fair value should therefore be measured by consideration of the highest and best use of the asset. There is a presumption that the current use would be the highest and best use.

The highest and best use of the asset would appear to be as residential property and not the current industrial use. The intentions of Colyson Co are not relevant as fair value is not entity specific. The alternative use would need to be based upon fair and reasonable assumptions. In particular, it would be necessary to ensure that planning permission to demolish the factory and convert into residential properties would be likely. Since several nearby sites have been given such permission, this would appear to be the case.

The fair value of the factory site should be valued as if converted into residential use. Since this cannot be determined on a stand-alone basis, the combined value of the land and buildings is calculated. The $1 million demolition and planning costs should be deducted from the market value of $24 million. The fair value of the land and buildings should be $23 million. The fair value of the identifiable net assets at acquisition are $88 million ($65m + $23m).

Depreciated replacement cost should only be considered as a possible method for estimating the fair value of the asset when other more suitable methods are not available. This may be the case when the asset is highly specialised and market data is therefore limited or unavailable. This is not the case with the factory site. In any case, the rise in value of land and properties particularly for residential use would mean that to use depreciated replacement cost would undervalue the asset. The exit value for the asset, whether it was based on the principal or most advantageous market, would need to be the same as the entry price. Depreciation may not also be an accurate reflection of all forms of obsolescence including physical deterioration. The estimate would need to be adjusted for such factors even where industrial use remained the best use of the asset.

(ii) Goodwill should be calculated as follows:

	Fair value method	*Proportional method*
	$m	$m
Consideration	90	90
Non-controlling interest (NCI) at acquisition	22	17.6
Net assets at acquisition	(88)	(88)
Goodwill	24	19.6

NCI at acquisition under proportional method is $17.6 million (20% × $88m).

The fair value of the net assets at acquisition is $88 million as per part a(i) ($65m + $23m).

Tutorial note: Goodwill under the proportional method could also be calculated as:

Consideration	$90m
Less FV of net assets acquired (80% × $88m)	($70.4)m
Goodwill on acquisition	$19.6m

(b) An impairment arises where the carrying amount of the net assets exceeds the recoverable amount. Where there is a clear indication of impairment, this asset should be reduced to the recoverable amount.

Where the cash flows cannot be independently determined for individual assets, they should be assessed as a cash generating unit. That is the smallest group of assets which independently generate cash flows. Impairments of cash generating units are allocated first to goodwill and then pro rata on the other assets. It should be noted that no asset should be reduced below its recoverable amount.

Fair value method

The overall impairment of Colyson Co is $30 million ($106m + goodwill $24m – $100m). The damaged building should be impaired by $4 million with a corresponding charge to profit or loss. Since $4 million has already been allocated to the land and buildings, $26 million remains. The goodwill should therefore be written off and expensed in the consolidated statement of profit or loss.

Of the remaining $2 million, $1.25 million will be allocated to the plant and machinery (15/(15 + 9) × 2m) and $0.75 million will be allocated to the remaining intangibles (9/(9 + 15) × 2m). As no assets have been previously revalued, all the impairments are charged to profit or loss. $24 million (80% × $30m) will be attributable to the owners of Luploid Co and $6 million to the NCI in the consolidated statement of comprehensive income.

The allocation of the impairment is summarised in this table:

	Original value	*Impairment*	*Revised CV*
	$m	$m	$m
Land and buildings	60	4	56
Plant and machinery	15	1.25	13.75
Intangibles other than goodwill	9	0.75	8.25
Goodwill	24	24	0
Current assets (at recoverable amount)	22	0	22
Total	130	30	100

Proportionate method

The basic principles and rule for impairment is the same as the fair value method and so $4 million will again first be written off against the land and buildings. The problems arise when performing the impairment review as a cash generating unit. When NCI is measured using the proportional share of net assets, no goodwill is attributable to the NCI since goodwill is not included within the individual net assets of the subsidiary. This means that the goodwill needs to be grossed up when an impairment review is performed so that it is comparable with the recoverable amount. Under the fair value method, the NCI fully represents any premium the other shareholders would be prepared to pay for the net assets and so goodwill does not need to be grossed up.

The goodwill of $19.6 million is grossed up by 100/80 to a value of $24.5 million. This extra $4.9 million is known as notional goodwill. The overall impairment is now $30.5 million ($106m + $24.5m – $100m) of which $4 million has already been allocated. Since the remaining impairment of $26.5 million exceeds the value of goodwill, the goodwill is written down to zero. However, as only $19.6 million goodwill is recognised within the consolidated accounts, the impairment attributable to the notional goodwill is not recognised. Only $19.6 million is deducted in full from the owners of Luploid Co's share of profits since there is no goodwill attributable to the non-controlling interest. The remaining $2 million impairment is allocated between plant and machinery and intangibles (other than goodwill). NCI will be allocated 20% of $6 million ($4m + $2m), i.e. $1.2 million. Consolidated retained earnings will be charged with 80% of $6 million (i.e. $4.8 million) plus $19.6 million goodwill impairment (i.e. $24.4m in total). The allocation of the impairment is summarised in this table:

Tutorial note: Notional goodwill and impairment of notional goodwill does not impact on the consolidated financial statements.

	Original carrying amount	*Impairment*	*Revised carrying amount*
	$m	$m	$m
Land and buildings	60	4	56
Plant and machinery	15	1.25	13.75
Intangibles other than goodwill	9	0.75	8.25
Goodwill	19.6	19.6	0
(Notional goodwill)	4.9	4.9	0
Current assets (at recoverable amount)	22		22
Total	130.5	30.5	100

(c (i) IFRS 3 *Business Combinations* requires all consideration to be measured at fair value on acquisition of a subsidiary. This will include the deferred shares. Since Luploid Co is obliged to replace the share-based scheme of Hammond Co on acquisition, the replacement scheme should also be included as consideration. There is, however, a post combination service period which means that the portion of the replacement scheme attributable to pre-combination service is the market value of the acquiree award multiplied by the ratio of the portion of the vesting period completed to the greater of the total vesting period or the original vesting period of the acquire award.

The vesting period of the acquiree award had vested and was three years. As there is a two-year post combination vesting period, the total vesting period is five years. Therefore the amount attributable to the pre-combination period (and therefore added to the cost of the investment) should be $15 million × 3/5 = $9 million.

Deferred shares should be measured at the fair value at the acquisition date with subsequent changes in fair value ignored. Luploid Co will issue 2.4 million

(60% × 10m × 2/5) shares as consideration. The market price at the date of acquisition was $30, so the fair value is $72 million. The total consideration should be valued as $81 million (72 + 9).

(ii) The fair value of the replacement scheme at the grant date is $18 million (100 × 10,000 × 90% × $20). Since $9 million has been allocated to the cost of the investment, the remaining $9 million should be treated as part of the post combination remuneration package for the employees and measured in accordance with IFRS 2 *Share-based Payment*. The fair value at the grant date of the share-based scheme should be expensed to profit or loss over the two-year vesting period. Subsequent changes to the fair value of the shares are ignored.

Luploid Co will need to consider the impact of market and non-market based vesting conditions. The condition relating to the share price of Luploid Co is a market based vesting condition. These are adjusted for in the calculation of the fair value at the grant date of the option. An expense is therefore recorded in the consolidated profit or loss of Luploid Co irrespective of whether the market based vesting condition is met or not. A corresponding credit should be included within equity.

2 Stent

Workbook references. The *Conceptual Framework* and IAS 1 are covered in Chapter 1. Ethics and related party transactions are covered in Chapter 2. Financial instruments are covered in Chapter 8.

Top tips. Question 2 of the exam will always feature a discussion of ethical issues and will have two marks available for the application of ethical principles. In this question, part (a) related to the accounting treatment of the issues in the scenario given as well as the impact on gearing of those accounting treatments. The examiner commented that a surprising number of candidates did not discuss the impact on gearing and therefore missed out on some marks. Make sure you answer each part of a requirement to maximise your score in each question.

Part (b) required a discussion of the ethical issues arising in the scenario. In SBR, ethical issues are likely to go beyond basic accounting errors and could involve personal relationships and pressures that those relationships create - as seen in this question. Be sure to read the question carefully in order to spot these kinds of issues.

Marking scheme

			Marks
(a)	– application of the following discussion to the scenario:		
	cash advance from related party	4	
	preference shares: convertible	4	
	deferred tax asset	3	11
(b)	– discussion of ethical principles	2	
	– application of ethical principles to the scenario, and recommended action	5	7
	Professional marks		2
			20

Cash advance from Budster Co

Stent Co's finance director also controls Budster Co, the company which has paid a cash advance to Stent Co. International Accounting Standard (IAS) 24 *Related Party Disclosures* requires an entity's financial statements to contain disclosures necessary to draw attention to the possibility that its financial statements may have been affected by the existence of related parties and by transactions and outstanding balances with such parties. Included in the definition of a related party is a person identified as holding significant influence over the entity, or who is a member of the key management personnel of the entity. The finance director, a key management personnel of Stent Co, is a related party. In this case, Stent Co must disclose the nature of the related party relationship as well as information about all transactions and outstanding balances between Stent Co and Budster Co (owned and controlled by the finance director), necessary for users to understand the potential effect of the relationship on the financial statements.

The advance from Budster Co meets the *Conceptual Framework* definition of a liability: Stent Co has a present obligation (legally enforceable as a consequence of a binding contract), the settlement of which involves Stent Co giving up resources embodying economic benefits in order to satisfy the claim. IAS 1 *Presentation of Financial Statements* states that an entity shall not offset assets and liabilities, unless required or permitted by an International Financial Reporting Standard (IFRS). The finance director wants to include the receipt as a credit balance in trade receivables, netting off any amounts owed by Budster Co from trading, with what appears to be a short-term loan. This would result in a misclassification of a current liability under current assets. Offsetting a financial asset and a financial liability is permitted according to IAS 32 *Financial Instruments: Presentation* when, and only when, an entity has a legally enforceable right to set off the recognised amounts and intends either to settle on a net basis, or to realise the asset and settle the liability simultaneously. No such agreement is evident in this case, so Stent Co should report separately both assets and liabilities.

Except when it reflects the substance of the transaction or other event, offsetting detracts from the ability of users both to understand the transactions, other events and conditions which have occurred and to assess the entity's future cash flows. Stent Co would be showing a lower current asset figure and concealing the liability, which if disclosed as a current liability could be included in the debt element of the gearing calculation. Gearing would therefore increase.

Convertible redeemable preference shares

IAS 32 defines an equity instrument as any contract which evidences a residual interest in the assets of an entity after deducting all of its liabilities. An equity instrument has no contractual obligation to deliver cash or another financial asset, or to exchange financial assets or financial liabilities under potentially unfavourable conditions. If settled by the issuer's own equity instruments, an equity instrument has no contractual obligation to deliver a variable number, or is settled only by exchanging a fixed amount of cash or another financial asset for a fixed number of its own equity instruments.

Preference shares which are required to be converted into a fixed number of ordinary shares on a fixed date should be classified as equity (this is known as the 'fixed for fixed' requirement to which the finance director refers). However, a critical feature in differentiating a financial liability from an equity instrument is the existence of a contractual obligation of the issuer either to deliver cash or another financial asset to the holder, or to exchange financial assets or financial liabilities with the holder, under conditions which are potentially unfavourable to the issuer. In this case, Stent Co has issued convertible redeemable preference shares – which makes little commercial sense from the company's perspective, as they offer the holder the benefit of conversion into ordinary shares if share prices rise, and the security of redemption (at the choice of the holder) if share prices fall.

IAS 32 notes that the substance of a financial instrument, rather than its legal form, governs its classification in the entity's statement of financial position. A preference share which provides for mandatory redemption for a fixed or determinable amount at a fixed or determinable future date or gives the holder the right to require the issuer to redeem the instrument at a particular date for a fixed or determinable amount is a financial liability.

Because the preference shares offer the holder the choice of conversion into ordinary shares as well as redemption in two years' time, the terms of the financial instrument should be evaluated to determine whether it contains both a liability and an equity component. Such components are classified separately as compound financial instruments, recognising separately the components of a financial instrument which creates both a financial liability of the entity (a contractual arrangement to deliver cash or another financial asset) and an equity instrument (a call option granting the holder the right, for a specified period of time, to convert it into a fixed number of ordinary shares of the entity).

In accordance with IFRS 9 *Financial Instruments*, when the initial carrying amount of a compound financial instrument is allocated to its equity and liability components, the equity component is assigned the residual amount after deducting from the fair value of the instrument as a whole the amount separately determined for the liability component. Stent Co would measure the fair value of the consideration in respect of the liability component based on the fair value of a similar liability without any associated equity conversion option. The equity component is assigned the residual amount.

Gearing would increase if the draft financial statements had included the preference shares within equity: the correction would increase non-current debt (the present value of the future obligations) and decrease equity.

Deferred tax asset

In accordance with IAS 12 *Income Taxes*, a deferred tax asset shall be recognised for the carry-forward of unused tax losses to the extent that it is probable that future taxable profit will be available against which the unused tax losses can be utilised.

However, the existence of unused tax losses is strong evidence that future taxable profit may not be available. Therefore, when an entity has a history of recent losses, the entity recognises a deferred tax asset arising from unused tax losses only to the extent that it has convincing evidence that sufficient taxable profit will be available against which the unused tax losses can be utilised. In such circumstances, the amount of the deferred tax asset and the nature of the evidence supporting its recognition must be disclosed. The directors of Stent Co should consider whether it is probable that Stent Co will have taxable profits before the unused tax losses or unused tax credits expire, whether the unused tax losses result from identifiable causes which are unlikely to recur; and whether tax planning opportunities are available to the entity which will create taxable profit in the period in which the unused tax losses or unused tax credits can be utilised. To the extent that it is not probable that taxable profit will be available against which the unused tax losses or unused tax credits can be utilised, the deferred tax asset should not be recognised.

The removal of a deferred tax asset would reduce net assets, and equity. Gearing would therefore increase.

Ethical aspects

The ACCA Rulebook contains the bye-laws, regulations and *Code of Ethics and Conduct*, which every ACCA member should follow. The accountant may feel pressured by the finance director's comments on job security given the accountant has only been in her position for a few months. The accountant should comply with the fundamental ethical principles set out in the ACCA Rulebook: to act with integrity, objectivity, professional competence and due care, confidentiality and professional behaviour. The accountant should be mindful of any threats to these fundamental ethical principles. In doing so, the accountant should consider the relevant facts, the ethical issues involved, the fundamental principles which are threatened, whether internal procedures exist which mitigate the threats, and what alternative courses of action could be taken.

In this case, all fundamental ethical principles with the exception of confidentiality appear under threat. The finance director appears to be allowing bias and undue influence from the pressures imposed by debt covenant gearing and overdraft limits into the choice of accounting treatment, rather than following accounting standards. The company is in a precarious position, reporting losses in the year. The finance director should act professionally, in accordance with applicable technical and professional standards, comply with relevant laws and regulations, and avoid any action which discredits the profession.

The finance director faces an advocacy threat by promoting accounting treatments which compromise objectivity. The accountant faces an intimidation threat given the comments from the finance director, who presumably has an influence over career prospects. Assuming the accountant wishes to keep her job, this intimidation threat is also linked to one of self-interest. Before acting, the accountant should speak with the finance director, try to confirm the facts, and discuss the treatment with the finance director and explain the risks of non-compliance: the safeguards of accounting regulations and the sanctions imposed on those professional accountants who do not comply may resolve the issue. A record of conversations and actions should be kept. Stent Co may also have internal procedures which mitigate the threats. It may be that the finance director is not technically up to date, in which case a safeguard would be to undergo continuing professional development. If the finance director refuses to comply with accounting standards, then it would be appropriate to discuss the matter with other directors or an audit committee (if applicable), to seek a solution, then seek professional advice from ACCA, and consider legal advice if necessary. A final consideration for the accountant, if matters cannot be satisfactorily resolved, would be resignation.

3 Digiwire

Workbook references. IFRS 15 on revenue is covered in Chapter 3. IFRS 13 *Fair Value Measurement* is covered in Chapter 4 and IFRS 9 *Financial Instruments* is covered in chapter 8. Pensions and the amendment to IAS 19 are covered in Chapter 5.

Top tips. This question is set in the context of a digital business, something that the examiner has highlighted could be a feature of questions in SBR. The company in the question, Digiwire, sold music licences to other companies who then provide digital music to customers.

Part (a) concerned revenue recognition. In part (a)(ii), you were asked to show how the accounting treatment was supported by the revised 2018 *Conceptual Framework*. The principles in the *Conceptual Framework* are crucial to SBR and are likely to feature in every exam in some way. Therefore you need to make sure you know the principles in the *Conceptual Framework* and be able to show how those principles support accounting standards, or in some cases, are at odds with accounting standards.

Part (b) included a discussion of whether cryptocurrency can be classified as a financial asset or intangible asset. The examiner report expressed surprise that answers to this question were generally weak given that there is a technical article on Cryptocurrency available on the ACCA website. This highlights the importance of reading the technical articles available - see the exam resources section of the ACCA website.

Part (c) included a discussion of the amendments to IAS 19, a current issue which is specifically listed in the current issues section of the syllabus. There are not very many current issues highlighted on the syllabus, so you must make sure you have taken the time to study each of them as current issues will be examined in every exam. In this case, the examiner commented 'candidates who were unaware of the amendments should at least have been in a position to critically describe the previous method by which each cost was calculated. Appropriate discussion would have been awarded marks'.

Marking scheme

				Marks
(a)	(i)	– application of the following discussion to the scenario: IFRS 15 non-cash consideration and IFRS 13 alternatives to value the shares (including share value calculation at year end)	3	
		IFRS 9 remeasurement gains (including calculation)	2	
	(ii)	– application of the following discussion to the scenario: revenue recognised over time	2	
		revised *Conceptual Framework* (2018)	2	9
(b)	(i)	– discussion and application of the IFRS 11 requirements to the scenario	2	
	(ii)	– discussion of the derecognition of non-monetary assets and application to the scenario	2	
		– calculation of carrying amount of the joint venture	1	
	(iii)	– discussion of the potential ways in which the cryptocurrency could be accounted for at fair value	4	9
(c)	(i)	– discussion of the difference in guidance on termination benefits between FRS 102 and IAS 19		3
	(ii)	– calculation of current service cost net interest, remeasurement component	3	
		– discussion of impact	1	4
				25

(a) (i) **Revenue recognition: Clamusic Co shares**

IFRS 15 *Revenue from Contracts with Customers* requires that non-cash consideration received should be measured at the fair value of the consideration received. If fair value cannot be reasonably estimated, the consideration should be measured by reference to the stand-alone selling price of the good or service promised in the contract. The fair value of non-cash consideration may vary. If the non-cash consideration varies for reasons other than the form of the consideration, entities will apply the guidance in IFRS 15 related to constraining variable consideration. However, if fair value varies only due to the form, the variable constraint guidance in IFRS 15 would not apply. In this case, the fair value varies due to the form of the consideration which is equity shares and therefore the variable constraint guidance in IFRS 15 does not apply.

The fair valuation of shares in an unlisted start-up company is problematic. However, IFRS 13 *Fair Value Measurement* gives advice on how to measure unlisted shares. It sets out three approaches: (i) market approach, such as the transaction price paid for identical or similar instruments of an investee; (ii) the income approach, for example, using discounted cash flow; and (iii) the adjusted net asset approach.

In this case, the market approach has been used and the range of fair values is significant based upon the professional valuation report. The range of fair values for a 7% holding of shares would be \$280,000 to \$350,000 (7% of \$4–\$5 million) at the date of the contract and \$420,000 to \$490,000 (7% of \$6–\$7 million) at the year end. As the fair valuation is based upon a similar listed company and is based upon a controlling interest, a discount on the valuation of the shares should be applied to reflect the lack of liquidity and inability to participate in Digiwire Co's policy decisions. Thus an estimated value of the shares can be made which takes into account the above facts. This could be the mid-point of $315,000 (($280,000 + $350,000)/2) at the date of the contract and $455,000 (($420,000 + $490,000)/2) at the year end. Digiwire Co would therefore recognise revenue of $315,000 for the receipt of shares from Clamusic Co, as the fair value of non-cash consideration is measured at the contract inception date of 1 January 20X6. This revenue would not be recognised at a point in time but would be recognised over the period of the licence which is three years.

Clamusic Co share valuation at 31 December 20X6

The shares will be recognised at $455,000 (($420,000 + $490,000)/2) at 31 December 20X6. All equity investments in scope of IFRS 9 *Financial Instruments* should be measured at fair value in the statement of financial position, with value changes being recognised in profit or loss. If an equity investment is not held for trading, an entity can make an irrevocable election at initial recognition to measure it at fair value through other comprehensive income (FVTOCI) with only dividend income recognised in profit or loss.

If Digiwire Co elects to present the remeasurements through other comprehensive income (OCI), gains are never recycled through profit or loss. This means that, if the investment in Clamusic Co is successful, when the investment is sold, there will be no profit or loss effect since all gains will already have been recognised in OCI. Thus at the year end, a gain of $140,000 ($455,000 – $315,000) will be recorded in profit or loss or OCI dependent upon any election being made.

(ii) **Revenue: royalties**

As Digiwire Co retains an active role in the updating and maintenance of a sold licence to ensure its continuing value to the client, revenue would be recognised over the expected length of the contract or related client relationship. An entity must be expected to undertake activities which significantly affect the licence to conclude that revenue is recognised over time. However, reliable measurement of future royalties is not available (see below). Thus, in this case, the revenue would be recognised over the three-year licence based upon the licence agreement. At the year end, however, revenue from royalties can be calculated based upon the sales for the period and it would be $50,000 (5% of $1 million).

The *Conceptual Framework* support

The International Accounting Standards Board has changed the definitions of income and expenses in the revised *Conceptual Framework* (the *Framework*) to align with the revised definitions of an asset and a liability. The definition of income encompasses both revenue and gains. Revenue arises in the course of the ordinary activities of an entity and is referred to by a variety of different names including sales, fees, interest, dividends, royalties and rent. Gains represent other items which meet the definition of income and may, or may not, arise in the course of the ordinary activities of an entity. Gains represent increases in economic benefits and, as such, are no different in nature from revenue. Hence, they are not regarded as constituting a separate element in the IFRS *Framework*.

The revised *Framework* also states that an item which meets the definition of an element should be recognised if:

(a) it is probable that any future economic benefit associated with the item will flow to or from the entity; and

(b) the item has a cost or value which can be measured with reliability.

Thus, in this case, the royalties cannot be measured with any certainty in the future and should not be recognised until certain. The definitions in the Framework relating to revenue, recognition and gains are therefore consistent with the approach taken by Digiwire Co.

(b) (i) It seems that Digiwire Co and TechGame jointly control FourDee Co and it appears as though the arrangement is a joint venture (IFRS 11 *Joint Arrangements*) as the parties have joint control of the arrangement and have rights to the net assets of the arrangement. Joint control is the contractually agreed sharing of control of an arrangement, which exists only when decisions about the relevant activities require the unanimous consent of the parties sharing control. This is the case with FourDee Co.

A joint venturer recognises its interest in a joint venture as an investment and accounts for that investment using the equity method in accordance with IAS 28 *Investments in Associates and Joint Ventures* unless the entity is exempted.

(ii) Digiwire Co has exchanged non-monetary assets for its investment in FourDee Co, and thus needs to de-recognise the assets it is contributing to FourDee Co. The carrying amount of $6 million of the property is derecognised but the intellectual property of Digiwire Co has been generated internally and does not have a carrying amount. The cryptocurrency is recorded as an asset in the financial statements of Digiwire Co at $3 million but will be valued at $4 million, its fair value in the financial statements of FourDee Co.

Accordingly, when a joint venturer contributes a non-monetary asset to a joint venture in exchange for an equity interest in the joint venture, the joint venturer recognises a portion of the gain or loss on disposal which is attributable to the other parties to the joint venture (except when the contribution lacks commercial substance). Essentially, Digiwire Co is required by IAS 28 to limit the profit on disposal of its non-monetary assets to 50%. Effectively, Digiwire has only disposed of 50% of the asset contributed to the joint venture. Thus the carrying amount of the joint venture in Digwire's financial statements at 31 December 20X6 will be $11.5 million (($6 + $3 carrying amounts derecognised for property and cryptocurrency) + ((4 – 3)/2) + ((10 – 6)/2)). A gain of $2.5 million will be recorded in profit or loss.

(iii) If the cryptocurrency meets the definition of a financial asset, it is possible to measure it at fair value. However, cryptocurrency is not cash or cash equivalents as its value is exposed to significant changes in market value and there is no contractual right to receive either cash or cash equivalents. Therefore, cryptocurrency fails the definition of a financial asset.

If the cryptocurrency is to be recognised as an intangible asset, then the default position would be to measure it at cost. However, there may be an argument to say that there is an active market for the cryptocurrency in which case, it would be possible for it to be measured at fair value. In this case, movements in that fair value would be recognised through other comprehensive income and the gain would not be recycled through profit or loss when the cryptocurrency is realised.

The best way to account for a cryptocurrency would be fair value as that is the value at which the entity will realise their investment or transact in exchange for goods and services. Accounting for cryptocurrency at fair value with movements reflected in profit or loss would provide the most useful information to investors but existing accounting requirements do not appear to permit this.

(c) (i) Before the amendment, IAS 19 *Employee Benefits* did not require entities to revise the assumptions for the calculation of current service cost and net interest during the accounting period, even if an entity remeasured the net defined benefit liability or asset in the event of a plan amendment, curtailment or settlement. The calculations were based on the actuarial assumptions as at the start of the financial year.

However, the International Accounting Standards Board felt that it was inappropriate to ignore any updated assumptions when determining current service cost and net interest for the period.

Therefore, an amendment to IAS 19 states that when a plan amendment, curtailment or settlement occurs during the annual reporting period, an entity must:

- Determine current service cost for the remainder of the period after the plan amendment, curtailment or settlement using the actuarial assumptions used to remeasure the net defined benefit liability/asset reflecting the benefits offered under the plan and the plan assets after that event.
- Determine net interest for the remainder of the period after the plan amendment, curtailment or settlement using: (i) the net defined benefit liability/asset reflecting the benefits offered under the plan and the plan assets after that event; and (ii) the discount rate used to remeasure that net defined benefit liability/asset.

(ii) If Digiwire Co had not applied the revised IAS 19, then the current service cost would have been \$108 million (12 months × \$9 million). On the application of the revised standard, the current service cost would be \$96 million ((8 months × \$9 million) + (4 months × \$6 million)).

Thus there will be a reduction in the current service cost of \$12 million.

Similarly, the net interest component before the amendment would have been \$900,000 (3% × \$30 million).

After the amendment it would be \$1,020,000 ((\$900,000 × 8/12) + (3.5% × \$36m × 4/12)).

Therefore, there will be a change in the net interest element of \$120,000 (\$1,020,000 – \$900,000).

The net effect will be to change the re-measurement component by \$11,880,000.

4 Guidance

Workbook references. The *Conceptual Framework* is covered in Chapter 1. Analysis is covered in Chapter 18. IFRS 10 *Consolidated Financial Statements* is covered in Chapter 11.

Top tips. There are two professional marks available in this question for clarity and quality of the discussion in part (b). This will be the case for one question in section B of every exam - two professional marks will be available in the question that requires analysis from the perspective of a stakeholder.

Part (a) required a discussion of why a reporting entity may choose a particular accounting policy where IFRS allows a choice, and the impact of faithful representation and comparability on the choice. You need to know that faithful representation and comparability are qualitative characteristics of useful information, as described in the *Conceptual Framework*. The *Conceptual Framework* is fundamental to SBR, you must make sure you are familiar with it.

Part (b)(i) required calculation of return on equity ratio (ROE) and discussion on the usefulness to investors of that ratio and its component parts. The examiner commented that some candidates didn't include discussion of the component parts of ROE, despite this being clearly stated in the requirement – make sure you read requirements carefully and ensure you answer each part of each requirement.

Part (b)(ii) asked for a discussion of the impact of the accounting transactions in the scenario on the ROE ratio (and its components), and a recalculation of a more comparable ROE between the two years. The examiner commented 'better answers included a description of the impact on each component as well as the ROE (meeting the question's whole requirement) and provided a table in which the original accounting data is adjusted for each transaction'. Remember that laying out your answers clearly helps the marker to see what you have done, enabling them to award you marks more easily.

Marking scheme

				Marks
(a)		– discussion of the issues relating to accounting choice	3	
		– discussion of whether faithful representation and comparability are affected	3	6
(b)	(i)	– discussion of the meaning of the return on equity (ROE) and its component parts	3	
		– calculation of ROE for the years ended 31 December 20X5 and 20X6	2	5
	(ii)	– application of the following discussion to the scenario:		
		transfer of property to SPE	2	
		buy back of shares	2	
		raising loan capital	2	
		purchase of associate	2	
		calculation of the impact on ROE and its component parts	4	12
	Professional marks			2
				25

(a) Where an IFRS standard allows an entity an accounting choice, then the financial statements will be influenced and affected by that choice. Management's intent and motivation will influence accounting information. The accounting policy chosen can be driven by self-interest, by a wish to maximise the interests of shareholders, or by a wish to provide information. Where there is flexibility when applying the IFRS standard, the financial statements can become less comparable. Entities may use the financial choices to increase earnings, and manipulate accounting figures in order to influence contractual outcomes which depend on the accounting figures reported.

Accounting choices exist to provide companies which operate under different business models with the option of utilising an accounting method which best represents their operations. Any accounting choice in IFRS standards should still result in the financial statements being faithfully represented. A faithful representation means that to the maximum extent possible, the financial statements are complete, neutral and free from error. A faithful representation is affected by the level of measurement uncertainty in the financial statements.

Comparability is one of the four qualitative characteristics which enhances the usefulness of information. Thus accounting information would be more useful if it can be compared with similar information from other entities, or from the same entity.

However, it is extremely difficult for entities to have 'comparable' financial information. Comparability is crucial to improve financial reporting quality but it can be argued that comparability is made more difficult by the fact that the Board allows entities to choose between alternative measurement bases. Environmental, economic, political, cultural, operational differences could be solved with the existence of accounting choices in the standards, but these choices could be at the cost of comparability, especially if there are internal or external factors influencing the reliable disclosure of an item. A faithful representation might lead to comparability, because it should reflect the characteristics of the asset or liability.

(b) (i) The return on equity (ROE) ratio measures the rate of return which the owners of issued shares of a company receive on their shareholdings in terms of profitability. ROE signifies how good the company is in generating profit on the investment it receives from its shareholders. This metric is especially important from an investor's perspective, as it can be used to judge how efficiently the firm will be able to use shareholder's investment to generate additional revenues.

The net profit margin (net profit/sales) tells how much profit a company makes on every dollar of sales. Asset turnover (sales/assets) ratio measures the value of a company's sales or revenues generated relative to the carrying amount of its assets. The asset turnover ratio can often be used as an indicator of the efficiency with which a company is deploying its assets in generating revenue. The equity ratio indicates the relative proportion that equity is used to finance a company's assets. The equity ratio is a good indicator of the level of leverage used by a company by measuring the proportion of the total assets which are financed by shareholders, as opposed to creditors.

	20X5	*20X6*
Net profit margin	15%	17.3%
Asset turnover	0.8	1.05
Equity ratio	1.43	2.1
Return on equity	17%	38%

(ii) **Setting up of special purpose entity (SPE)**

IFRS 10 *Consolidated Financial Statements* states that an investor controls a SPE when it is exposed, or has rights, to variable returns from its involvement with the SPE and has the ability to affect those returns through its power over the SPE. This revised definition of control focuses on the need to have both power and variable returns before control is present. Power is the current ability to direct the activities which significantly influence returns. Guidance Co obtains the rewards from the assets transferred and is exposed to the risks. By transferring their assets to a SPE, the asset turnover ratio will be significantly larger. However, the SPE should be consolidated by Guidance Co in its group financial statements and the property included in assets and the charge eliminated from revaluation reserves in its single entity financial statements. The latter will increase shareholder equity.

Miscellaneous transactions

A major concern about using ROE is when a company buys back its shares, it decreases the equity on the statement of financial position and in the case of Guidance Co, its cash and consequently its total assets. As a result, the performance metrics – asset turnover and ROE – will be affected. The ROE figure could produce a misleading indicator as to how well a company is being managed. As the equity portion of ROE shrinks, the ROE metric gets larger. The ROE calculation can become meaningless if a company regularly buys back its shares and thus as a result there may be better metrics for investors to use such as the P/E ratio.

Guidance Co has raised loan capital of $20 million during the period and this amount will not be included in the ROE calculations because ROE is based on assets as opposed to net assets. One company may have a higher ROE than another company simply because it finances the business through loan capital rather than raising equity capital. It can be argued that ROE is not a meaningful measure of performance, as it takes no account of the amount of debt involved in creating profits.

Therefore, return on capital employed may be a better current measure for Guidance Co.

Guidance Co has included the profit from the purchase of an associate in the current year's figures. If the share of the results of the associate were excluded, this would allow Guidance Co's profitability to result exclusively from Guidance Co's asset base. It could be argued that the full value of the company's reported profit including the associate could distort the analysis of Guidance Co's performance as compared to the last financial year.

There is no need to adjust for the original $15 million investment in the associate because one asset is merely being replaced by another but the total assets remain the same.

Adjusted amounts

		SPE property $m	*Shares cancelled* $m	*Associate* $m	*Total* $m
Net profit before tax	38			(4)	34
Sales	220		220		
Assets	210	50	30	290	
Equity	100	50	30	(4)	176

Adjusted calculations

	20X5	*20X6 (adjusted)*	*20X6 (unadjusted)*
Net profit margin	15%	15.5%	17.3%
Asset turnover	0.8	0.76	1.05
Equity ratio	1.43	1.65	2.1
ROE	17%	19.3%	38%

It can be seen that if the impact of the transactions in the period were eliminated, then there has been a significant reduction in ROE and its component parts. The buy back of shares and the purchase of the associate were legitimate transactions but they were eliminated in order to determine comparative metrics. The raising of the loan capital was also legitimate but was not adjusted for because ROE is based on assets, not net assets. The transfer of assets to a SPE was contrary to IFRS 10 and would have been reversed in any event. Although financial metrics are intended to enable comparisons between companies, the relative performance of any particular company can be affected by transactions both acceptable and unacceptable under accounting standards.

Mathematical tables

Present value table

Present value of 1 = $(1+r)^{-n}$ where r = discount rate, n = number of periods until payment.

This table shows the present value of £1 per annum, receivable or payable at the end of *n* years.

Periods					**Discount rates (r)**					
(n)	**1%**	**2%**	**3%**	**4%**	**5%**	**6%**	**7%**	**8%**	**9%**	**10%**
1	0.990	0.980	0.971	0.962	0.952	0.943	0.935	0.926	0.917	0.909
2	0.980	0.961	0.943	0.925	0.907	0.890	0.873	0.857	0.842	0.826
3	0.971	0.942	0.915	0.889	0.864	0.840	0.816	0.794	0.772	0.751
4	0.961	0.924	0.888	0.855	0.823	0.792	0.763	0.735	0.708	0.683
5	0.951	0.906	0.863	0.822	0.784	0.747	0.713	0.681	0.650	0.621
6	0.942	0.888	0.837	0.790	0.746	0.705	0.666	0.630	0.596	0.564
7	0.933	0.871	0.813	0.760	0.711	0.665	0.623	0.583	0.547	0.513
8	0.923	0.853	0.789	0.731	0.677	0.627	0.582	0.540	0.502	0.467
9	0.914	0.837	0.766	0.703	0.645	0.592	0.544	0.500	0.460	0.424
10	0.905	0.820	0.744	0.676	0.614	0.558	0.508	0.463	0.422	0.386
11	0.896	0.804	0.722	0.650	0.585	0.527	0.475	0.429	0.388	0.350
12	0.887	0.788	0.701	0.625	0.557	0.497	0.444	0.397	0.356	0.319
13	0.879	0.773	0.681	0.601	0.530	0.469	0.415	0.368	0.326	0.290
14	0.870	0.758	0.661	0.577	0.505	0.442	0.388	0.340	0.299	0.263
15	0.861	0.743	0.642	0.555	0.481	0.417	0.362	0.315	0.275	0.239
16	0.853	0.728	0.623	0.534	0.458	0.394	0.339	0.292	0.252	0.218
17	0.844	0.714	0.605	0.513	0.436	0.371	0.317	0.270	0.231	0.198
18	0.836	0.700	0.587	0.494	0.416	0.350	0.296	0.250	0.212	0.180
19	0.828	0.686	0.570	0.475	0.396	0.331	0.277	0.232	0.194	0.164
20	0.820	0.673	0.554	0.456	0.377	0.312	0.258	0.215	0.178	0.149

Periods					**Discount rates (r)**					
(n)	**11%**	**12%**	**13%**	**14%**	**15%**	**16%**	**17%**	**18%**	**19%**	**20%**
1	0.901	0.893	0.885	0.877	0.870	0.862	0.855	0.847	0.840	0.833
2	0.812	0.797	0.783	0.769	0.756	0.743	0.731	0.718	0.706	0.694
3	0.731	0.712	0.693	0.675	0.658	0.641	0.624	0.609	0.593	0.579
4	0.659	0.636	0.613	0.592	0.572	0.552	0.534	0.516	0.499	0.482
5	0.593	0.567	0.543	0.519	0.497	0.476	0.456	0.437	0.419	0.402
6	0.535	0.507	0.480	0.456	0.432	0.410	0.390	0.370	0.352	0.335
7	0.482	0.452	0.425	0.400	0.376	0.354	0.333	0.314	0.296	0.279
8	0.434	0.404	0.376	0.351	0.327	0.305	0.285	0.266	0.249	0.233
9	0.391	0.361	0.333	0.308	0.284	0.263	0.243	0.225	0.209	0.194
10	0.352	0.322	0.295	0.270	0.247	0.227	0.208	0.191	0.176	0.162
11	0.317	0.287	0.261	0.237	0.215	0.195	0.178	0.162	0.148	0.135
12	0.286	0.257	0.231	0.208	0.187	0.168	0.152	0.137	0.124	0.112
13	0.258	0.229	0.204	0.182	0.163	0.145	0.130	0.116	0.104	0.093
14	0.232	0.205	0.181	0.160	0.141	0.125	0.111	0.099	0.088	0.078
15	0.209	0.183	0.160	0.140	0.123	0.108	0.095	0.084	0.074	0.065
16	0.188	0.163	0.141	0.123	0.107	0.093	0.081	0.071	0.062	0.054
17	0.170	0.146	0.125	0.108	0.093	0.080	0.069	0.060	0.052	0.045
18	0.153	0.130	0.111	0.095	0.081	0.069	0.059	0.051	0.044	0.038
19	0.138	0.116	0.098	0.083	0.070	0.060	0.051	0.043	0.037	0.031
20	0.124	0.104	0.087	0.073	0.061	0.051	0.043	0.037	0.031	0.026

Cumulative present value table

This table shows the present value of £1 per annum, receivable or payable at the end of each year for *n* years.

Periods (n)	Discount rates (r)									
	1%	**2%**	**3%**	**4%**	**5%**	**6%**	**7%**	**8%**	**9%**	**10%**
1	0.990	0.980	0.971	0.962	0.952	0.943	0.935	0.926	0.917	0.909
2	1.970	1.942	1.913	1.886	1.859	1.833	1.808	1.783	1.759	1.736
3	2.941	2.884	2.829	2.775	2.723	2.673	2.624	2.577	2.531	2.487
4	3.902	3.808	3.717	3.630	3.546	3.465	3.387	3.312	3.240	3.170
5	4.853	4.713	4.580	4.452	4.329	4.212	4.100	3.993	3.890	3.791
6	5.795	5.601	5.417	5.242	5.076	4.917	4.767	4.623	4.486	4.355
7	6.728	6.472	6.230	6.002	5.786	5.582	5.389	5.206	5.033	4.868
8	7.652	7.325	7.020	6.733	6.463	6.210	5.971	5.747	5.535	5.335
9	8.566	8.162	7.786	7.435	7.108	6.802	6.515	6.247	5.995	5.759
10	9.471	8.983	8.530	8.111	7.722	7.360	7.024	6.710	6.418	6.145
11	10.37	9.787	9.253	8.760	8.306	7.887	7.499	7.139	6.805	6.495
12	11.26	10.58	9.954	9.385	8.863	8.384	7.943	7.536	7.161	6.814
13	12.13	11.35	10.63	9.986	9.394	8.853	8.358	7.904	7.487	7.103
14	13.00	12.11	11.30	10.56	9.899	9.295	8.745	8.244	7.786	7.367
15	13.87	12.85	11.94	11.12	10.38	9.712	9.108	8.559	8.061	7.606
16	14.718	13.578	12.561	11.652	10.838	10.106	9.447	8.851	8.313	7.824
17	15.562	14.292	13.166	12.166	11.274	10.477	9.763	9.122	8.544	8.022
18	16.398	14.992	13.754	12.659	11.690	10.828	10.059	9.372	8.756	8.201
19	17.226	15.678	14.324	13.134	12.085	11.158	10.336	9.604	8.950	8.365
20	18.046	16.351	14.877	13.590	12.462	11.470	10.594	9.818	9.129	8.514

Periods (n)	Discount rates (r)									
	11%	**12%**	**13%**	**14%**	**15%**	**16%**	**17%**	**18%**	**19%**	**20%**
1	0.901	0.893	0.885	0.877	0.870	0.862	0.855	0.847	0.840	0.833
2	1.713	1.690	1.668	1.647	1.626	1.605	1.585	1.566	1.547	1.528
3	2.444	2.402	2.361	2.322	2.283	2.246	2.210	2.174	2.140	2.106
4	3.102	3.037	2.974	2.914	2.855	2.798	2.743	2.690	2.639	2.589
5	3.696	3.605	3.517	3.433	3.352	3.274	3.199	3.127	3.058	2.991
6	4.231	4.111	3.998	3.889	3.784	3.685	3.589	3.498	3.410	3.326
7	4.712	4.564	4.423	4.288	4.160	4.039	3.922	3.812	3.706	3.605
8	5.146	4.968	4.799	4.639	4.487	4.344	4.207	4.078	3.954	3.837
9	5.537	5.328	5.132	4.946	4.772	4.607	4.451	4.303	4.163	4.031
10	5.889	5.650	5.426	5.216	5.019	4.833	4.659	4.494	4.339	4.192
11	6.207	5.938	5.687	5.453	5.234	5.029	4.836	4.656	4.486	4.327
12	6.492	6.194	5.918	5.660	5.421	5.197	4.988	4.793	4.611	4.439
13	6.750	6.424	6.122	5.842	5.583	5.342	5.118	4.910	4.715	4.533
14	6.982	6.628	6.302	6.002	5.724	5.468	5.229	5.008	4.802	4.611
15	7.191	6.811	6.462	6.142	5.847	5.575	5.324	5.092	4.876	4.675
16	7.379	6.974	6.604	6.265	5.954	5.668	5.405	5.162	4.938	4.730
17	7.549	7.120	6.729	6.373	6.047	5.749	5.475	5.222	4.990	4.775
18	7.702	7.250	6.840	6.467	6.128	5.818	5.534	5.273	5.033	4.812
19	7.839	7.366	6.938	6.550	6.198	5.877	5.584	5.316	5.070	4.843
20	7.963	7.469	7.025	6.623	6.259	5.929	5.628	5.353	5.101	4.870

Notes

Notes

Notes

Notes

Notes

Notes

Notes

Review Form – Strategic Business Reporting (International and United Kingdom) (02/20)

Name: ______________________ **Address:** ______________________

____

____

How have you used this Kit?
(Tick one box only)

☐ Home study (book only)

☐ On a course: college ______________

☐ With 'correspondence' package

☐ Other ______________

Why did you decide to purchase this Kit?
(Tick one box only)

☐ Have used the Workbook

☐ Have used other BPP products in the past

☐ Recommendation by friend/colleague

☐ Recommendation by a lecturer at college

☐ Saw advertising

☐ Other ______________

During the past six months do you recall seeing/receiving any of the following?
(Tick as many boxes as are relevant)

☐ Our advertisement in *Student Accountant*

☐ Our advertisement in *Pass*

☐ Our advertisement in *PQ*

☐ Our brochure with a letter through the post

☐ Our website www.bpp.com

Which (if any) aspects of our advertising do you find useful?
(Tick as many boxes as are relevant)

☐ Prices and publication dates of new editions

☐ Information on product content

☐ Facility to order books off-the-page

☐ None of the above

Which BPP products have you used?

Workbook ☐ *Other* ☐

Kit ☑

Your ratings, comments and suggestions would be appreciated on the following areas.

	Very useful	*Useful*	*Not useful*
Passing SBR	☐	☐	☐
Questions	☐	☐	☐
Top Tips etc in answers	☐	☐	☐
Content and structure of answers	☐	☐	☐
Mock exam answers	☐	☐	☐

Overall opinion of this Kit *Excellent* ☐ *Good* ☐ *Adequate* ☐ *Poor* ☐

Do you intend to continue using BPP products? *Yes* ☐ *No* ☐

The BPP author of this edition can be e-mailed at: learningmedia@bpp.com

Review Form (continued)

TELL US WHAT YOU THINK

Please note any further comments and suggestions/errors below.